November 9–12, 2014
Sanibel Island, Florida, USA

I0060903

Association for Computing Machinery

Advancing Computing as a Science & Profession

GROUP'14

Proceedings of the 18th ACM International Conference on

Supporting Group Work

Sponsored by:
ACM SIGCHI

Supporters:
Microsoft Research & NSF

**Association for
Computing Machinery**

Advancing Computing as a Science & Profession

The Association for Computing Machinery
2 Penn Plaza, Suite 701
New York, New York 10121-0701

Notice to Past Authors of ACM-Published Articles

ISBN: 978-1-4503-3043-5 (Digital)

ISBN: 978-1-4503-3386-3 (Print)

Additional copies may be ordered prepaid from:

ACM Order Department
PO Box 30777
New York, NY 10087-0777, USA

Phone: 1-800-342-6626 (USA and Canada)
+1-212-626-0500 (Global)
Fax: +1-212-944-1318
E-mail: acmhelp@acm.org
Hours of Operation: 8:30 am – 4:30 pm ET

Printed in the USA

ACM Group'14 - Chairs' Welcome

ACM GROUP 2014 is the 18th *International Conference on Supporting Group Work. ACM Group* features deep multidisciplinary engagement of scholars across communities including Human Computer Interaction, Computer Supported Cooperative Work, Organization Science, Small Group Research, Computational Social Science, Sociotechnical System Design, Educational Technology and Computer Supported Collaborative Learning.

Group'14 continues the conference series' tradition of being truly international in both organizational structure and participation. This combination of diverse social and cultural research traditions and scholars from a wide range of disciplines undergirds the sustained discourse and continuing vibrancy of ACM Group.

The Group'14 program includes work conducted using a range of research methods. Go to the sessions. Across the full program participants will discuss the latest findings within broad areas such as technology, society, and human interaction across a range of organizational contexts, including work practices, home, healthcare, and leisure. Group'14 especially encourages practitioners, industrial partners and academics to participate.

This year, for the first time, the ACM Group program chairs introduce "working papers" as a discourse format. The aim is to build on the conferences core strength: At Conference Discourse Communities (ACDC's). Working papers are a formalization of ACDC's, focused on helping a set of participants develop journal papers through short presentations and active engagement with participants. Working paper authors will have a 10 minutes time slot to present their work and initiate conversation with attendees. Short talks to ignite deep discussion.

We had 90 submissions and accepted 27 for a 30% acceptance rate. GROUP reviewing is conducted completely by the Program Committee members without external reviewers. In 2014 reviewing was conducted in two rounds. During the first round all committee members served exclusively as "reviewers". The goal of the first round was to understand the strengths and weaknesses of each paper and provided a structured review designed to help authors improve their papers. In the second round, one reviewer on each paper was assigned the "Primary AC" role and asked to lead an online discussion of the paper and write a Meta-Review based on the content of the reviews and the discussion. The goal of the discussion and Meta-Review is to generate a proposed accept/reject decision. The program co-chairs then considered all of the review scores and comments when making their final decisions.

ACM Group is not an ordinary ACM Conference. We are small, and we are sustained by the unusual commitments of accomplished scholars. We theorize that this commitment emerges from the strengths outlined above. Many of our GROUP colleagues have generously contributed their time and effort to organize the conference, review papers, lead the Doctoral Colloquium, convene workshops, working papers, chair sessions, and be student volunteers. The conference would not be possible without their efforts. THANK YOU ALL SO MUCH!

Now, we'd like to be more specific. Organizing GROUP'14 has been a truly international collaborative effort. First of all, we would like to thank our technical program chairs, David McDonald (University of Washington) and Pernille Bjørn (IT-University of Copenhagen). The strength of Group'14 is anchored by their work. David and Pernille did a fantastic job in developing Group'14, creating new formats, organizing the reviews perfectly and engaging a strong program committee. Thanks goes to Stephan Lukosch (Delft University of Technology), Myriam Lewkowicz (Troyes University of Technology) and Michael Muller (IBM Research) for organizing the new format of the working papers. We are also very grateful to Aleksandra Sarcevic (Drexel University) and Michael Prilla for chairing the poster session; Lionel Robert Jr. (University of Michigan) and Hanna Maurin Söderholm (University of Borås) for organizing the workshops; Dan Cosley (Cornell University), Geraldine Fitzpatrick (Vienna University of Technology) and Thomas Herrmann (Ruhr-University Bochum) for chairing the Doctoral Colloquium. We acknowledge the hard work of David Gurzick (Hood College) as webmaster and social media expert; Marcela Borge (The Pennsylvania State University) and John Cook (University of the West of England) as our publicity co-chairs; Morten Esbensen (IT University Copenhagen) and Amirah Majid (University of Washington) for recruiting and coordinating the important team of student volunteers. Several times over last years, and here in Group'14 once again, Stephen Hayne (Colorado State University) was the treasurer, kept a watchful eye on our finances, and Stephanie Teasley (University of Michigan) took care of local arrangements – thank you very much for your great support over the last years! And especially this year! Stephen and Stephanie do the work that sustains ACM Group.

For the first time, Group'14 is guided by a steering committee. We would like to thank Mark Ackermann (University of Michigan), Hilda Tellioglu (Vienna University of Technology), Kori Inkpen (Microsoft Research), Stephanie Teasley (University of Michigan), Stephan Lukosch (Delft University of Technology) and Tom Gross (University of Bamberg). This group is guiding ACM Group's future.

We appreciate the work of Sheridan Printing Company for assembling our proceedings on a tight timetable. We would like to express our gratitude to the around 35-member international program committee and additional external reviewers who expertly critiqued our submissions in order to provide constructive feedback to all authors.

Finally, we would like to thank our sponsors, including ACM SIGCHI and Microsoft for their continued support of ACM Group. Special thanks go to Kori Inkpen and Microsoft Research; every year Kori and Microsoft supported the GROUP conference. Thank you very much!

Sean P. Goggins
Group'14 General Chair
University of Missouri, USA

Isa Jahnke
Group'14 General Chair
Umea University, Sweden

David W. McDonald
Group'14 Program Chair
University of Washington, USA

Pernille Bjørn
Group'14 Program Chair
IT-University Copenhagen, Denmark

Table of Contents

Session 10: Doctoral Colloquium

Session 11: Poster Abstracts

Session 12: Workshop Summaries

GROUP 2014 Conference Organization

General Chairs: Sean Goggins *(University of Missouri)*
Isa Jahnke *(Umeå University)*

Program Chairs: David W. McDonald *(University of Washington)*
Pernille Bjørn *(IT University Copenhagen)*

Working Papers Chairs: Stephan Lukosch *(Delft University of Technology)*
Myriam Lewkowicz *(Troyes University of Technology)*
Michael Muller *(IBM Research)*

Workshops Chairs: Lionel Robert Jr. *(University of Michigan)*
Hanna Söderholm *(University of Borås)*

Posters Chairs: Aleksandra Sarcevic *(Drexel University)*
Michael Prilla *(Ruhr Universität - Bochum)*

Doctorial Colloquium Chairs: Dan Cosley *(University of Michigan, USA)*
Geraldine Fitzpatrick *(Vienna University of Technology, Austria)*
Thomas Herrmann *(Ruhr-University of Bochum, Germany)*

Local Arrangements: Stephanie Teasley *(University of Michigan)*

Student Volunteers Chairs: Morten Esbensen *(IT University Copenhagen)*
Amirah Majid *(University of Washington)*

Treasurer & Registration: Stephen Hayne *(Colorado State University)*

Publicity: John Cook *(University of the West of England, Bristol)*
Marcela Borge *(The Pennsylvania State University)*

Webmaster: David Gurzick *(Hood College)*

GROUP Steering Committee: Mark Ackerman *(University of Michigan)*
Hilda Tellioglu *(Vienna University of Technology)*
Kori Inkpen *(Microsoft Research)*
Stephanie Teasley *(University of Michigan)*
Stephan Lukosch *(Delft University of Technology)*
Tom Gross *(University of Bamberg)*

Turk-Life in India

Neha Gupta
University of Nottingham
School of Computer Science
Jubilee Campus, Wollaton
Road, Nottingham,
NG8 1BB, UK
psxng1@nottingham.ac.uk

David Martin,
Benjamin V. Hanrahan
Xerox Research Centre Europe
6 chemin de Maupertuis, Grenoble,
France
david.martin@xrce.xerox.com
ben.hanrahan@xrce.xerox.com

Jacki O'Neill
Microsoft Research India
"Vigyan", 9, Lavelle Road
Bangalore, 560 001, India
jacki.oneill@microsoft.com

ABSTRACT

Previous studies on Amazon Mechanical Turk (AMT), the most well-known marketplace for microtasks, show that the largest population of workers on AMT is U.S. based, while the second largest is based in India. In this paper, we present insights from an ethnographic study conducted in India to introduce some of these workers or 'Turkers' – who they are, how they work and what turking means to them. We examine the work they do to maintain their reputations and their work-life balance. In doing this, we illustrate how AMT's design practically impacts on turk-work. Understanding the 'lived work' of crowdwork is a valuable first step for technology design.

Categories and Subject Descriptors

H.5.3 Group and Organizational Interfaces – Computer Supported Cooperative Work

General Terms: Human Factors

Keywords: Crowdsourcing, crowdworkers, Amazon Mechanical Turk (AMT), Turkers, requesters, ethnography, relationship-based crowdsourcing

1. INTRODUCTION

Crowdsourcing, the practice of using a potentially large, anonymous and undefined body of workers to carry out tasks, covers a wide set of activities and relationships. An original idea was that crowdsourcing would enable, *"everyday people [to use] their spare cycles to create content, solve problems, even do corporate R&D"* [9].

The most popular crowdsourcing platform is currently Amazon Mechanical Turk (AMT), and it is primarily used for microtasks that typically take a matter of minutes and are paid in cents. AMT is, in effect, a labour marketplace where interactions between requesters (employers) and providers (Turkers) are mediated through the AMT platform. Both researchers and journalists have been intrigued by this new form of work and have endeavoured to understand how AMT functions, what it is used for and by whom.

GROUP'14, November 9–12, 2014, Sanibel Island, Florida, USA.
Copyright © 2014 ACM 978-1-4503-3043-5/14/11…$15.00.
http://dx.doi.org/10.1145/2660398.2660403

Since the marketplace is wholly technologically mediated, the design of the platform impacts the marketplace in numerous ways, including: how tasks are created and managed; what types of tasks are available; how workers find and access tasks; and the relationships between requesters and providers. The circumscribed nature of requester-provider relationships in AMT has been found to be problematic for providers [5,13,32]. AMT is something of a 'black box.' That is, while Amazon does publish their terms and conditions, little information is released about how these policies are specifically realised. Furthermore, the decision making process is not transparent and there are no public processes for dealing with complaints or grievances. One of the themes of this paper is how this lack of information practically impacts the working lives of the Indian Turkers in our study.

AMT has remained relatively unchanged since its initial public launch in November 2005, and as a crowdsourcing platform it raises various concerns [6]. From the requesters' perspective it does not provide adequate functionality for many tasks [25] and from the Turkers' perspective it has multiple disadvantages, even while providing a valued source of income. This is an area ripe for technology design and understanding the lived work of crowdwork can help design better systems [3,4,27].

Turkers themselves are mostly concentrated in the USA and India [12,13,14] primarily because AMT pays in money in these regions, as opposed to Amazon vouchers used elsewhere. Until now there have been few qualitative analyses of Turkers [23,31,32] and to our knowledge no observational studies of the lived work of turking. In this paper, we describe the findings of, what we believe to be, the first ethnographic study of Indian Turkers. We describe how the conditions of working in India (e.g. culture, education, infrastructure, cost of living, and time difference with the US) impact practically on day-to-day turking. This is valuable, since crowdsourcing has the potential to bring more work to emerging markets. While the particulars of these conditions will certainly vary from market to market, it is likely that roughly the same set of features will come into play.

In elaborating this rich picture of turking in India, we reflect on a number of themes in the crowdsourcing literature. One is fundamental to the original idea of crowdsourcing, that is, as a way to fill spare cycles with profitable activity. The second, is Turking as fun as opposed to work [16]. The third is more fundamental to AMT, rather than crowdsourcing in general – information deficit and asymmetry, or the ways in which the AMT marketplace operates as a black box.

2. RELATED WORK

In this section, we describe the body of crowdsourcing research, to which this paper contributes. The majority of which focuses on Amazon Mechanical Turk, partly because this is one of the most widely used platforms and partly because it is easy to access.

By far the greatest body of research on AMT takes the perspective of the requesters [18,20,22]. In contrast, this paper adds to the growing body of research that seeks to understand the crowdworkers themselves. A deep understanding of the work of crowdwork is important ethically and socio-organisationally, since questions have been raised about the ethics of current crowdsourcing practices [1,31,32]. Silberman, Irani and colleagues used various methods (e.g. holding discussions on turk-related forums, interviews on Skype) to create a 'Turker's Bill of Rights' [31]. This bill of rights pointed to some of the issues faced by Turkers, primarily, unfair rejection of work, uncertain or slow payment, low wages, and lack of proper communication with requesters and AMT [31,32]. Understanding crowdwork is also important practically. In the field of HCI and cooperative work it has long been acknowledged that a deep understanding of how work is actually done can help designers and software engineers who are developing tools to support that work [3,4,10,11,33]. An exemplar study on the design of platforms is the study of low-income workers in India, which explored the barriers preventing such workers working on crowdsourcing platforms [17]. Such barriers included understanding the *intent* of the tasks, complex instructions and user interface, issues with navigation and sequencing of tasks, and the difference in cultures. Based on these findings, Khanna et al., designed and tested an interface with improved instructions, video tutorials and language localization; which produced a significant increase in the quality of work of the workers [17].

Survey-based demographic studies [12,13,29] show that Indian workers form the second largest population on AMT (36%) with an average age of around 26-28 years old, mostly male, and with significantly small annual incomes. In terms of education, 41% of the Indian Turkers had Bachelor degrees and 18% had Graduate degrees. Indian Turkers on average earned a pay of $1.58/hour on AMT, as opposed to $2.30/hour on average for US Turkers as of Nov. 2009 [29]. Over 50% of the Indian Turkers reported earning an annual income of less than $10,000 [12,13]. Approximately 27% of Indian Turkers reported that they required AMT sometimes or always 'to make basic ends meet,' compared to around 14% of U.S. Turkers [29].

Martin et. al [23] analysed the publicly displayed posts of Turkers (primarily from the U.S) on the Turker Nation forum to understand their reasoning about work, community, and Turker-requester relationships. The highest earnings reported by the Turkers to each other were ~$15k per year, but this was extremely rare. Turkers used AMT both as a sole source of income, as well as a complementary income. Turkers oriented their expectations of pay around the minimum wage in the US. Turkers' biggest concerns were to find 'good requesters' and keep their approval ratings high. In later sections of this paper, we will examine some of the above-mentioned aspects of turking and the notion of 'invisible work[1]' [33] in relation to the Indian Turkers.

Beyond AMT, some crowdsourcing platforms take a more positive design approach. For example, platforms that provide microwork via mobile phones (e.g. TxtEagle[2] – now Jana), provide training for work (e.g. Samasource[3]), or simply a provide platform with a mission of 'doing meaningful work for a fair wage' (e.g. mobileworks[4]). These platforms try to provide opportunities within developing nations.

In a country like India, infrastructure plays a big role in the ability to do computer-based jobs. Some experiments have tested these waters. Gawade et al. [8] explored whether or not cybercafés could become informal centres of work, by providing employment through microtasks. They recruited cyber cafés in India and Kenya, where they deployed a crowdwork application. After the experiment they found that 99% of the participants wanted to continue working in the cybercafé. Similarly, eight of the nine participant café owners reported willingness to continue hosting such a setup. While the workers were relatively slow, they were skilled enough to earn acceptable wages in the range of $0.50-$1.75 per hour. This study showed that, when provided with decent infrastructure crowdwork can thrive in developing countries [8]. This finding was also validated by the 18-month long Kelsa+ project which showed that even low-income workers with limited literacy in English and computers, have the potential to develop these skills when provided access to resources, peer support and the freedom to learn at their own pace [28]. The research insights in this paper give further depth to this desire to *learn* and *work*.

3. SETTING AND METHOD

As stated our aim is to flesh out the details of crowdwork– what it consists of and how it is accomplished – and what it means to be a crowdworker. In this case, specifically what it is like to be an Indian crowdworker working on AMT. By its nature, crowdwork is highly distributed and the workers are typically anonymous, we therefore used a mixture of methods (observations, interviews and surveys) to access and understand the population.

Through business contacts we had access to an initial pool of 69 Turkers in India who had waived their anonymity by making direct contact with the business about previous crowdwork tasks that they had completed for that company. We emailed them asking if they would be interested in participating in a survey and or interview about their crowdwork experiences. The survey consisted of 25 questions and was designed to collect basic demographic information and details of their crowdworking. It was posted as a HIT on AMT, where participants had to contact the requester (the authors) to receive the survey link. On completing the survey (hosted on Bristol Online Surveys, a university survey tool), participants were given a completion code to enter into AMT to receive payment. Our idea was to use the survey as a means of collecting basic information but also as a route to getting access to doing more substantial qualitative, ethnographic work.

Beyond the surveys, we conducted open-ended semi-structured interviews through Skype, telephone and face-to-face, typically

---

[1] 'Invisible work' is a concept about perspectives on and understanding of work. It relates to the fact that some forms of work are poorly understood because many aspects of them are hidden from society at large and even employers. This can lead to troubles in getting it recognised, respected and remunerated.

[2] www.jana.com/

[3] samasource.org/

[4] www.mobileworks.com/

lasting between 40 – 75 minutes (and longer for in-person interviews). In the interviews, we asked participants about the various activities they undertook during crowdwork, their thoughts and experiences about AMT, requesters and other Turkers. Interviews gave us a more in-depth view of the turker's work life. For instance, we discussed interesting, memorable HITs and what made them so, challenges with turking based on skills, technology, information available, expectations from turking, AMT, requesters, thoughts on AMT as a system, the support network of people who helped them manage and organise their work and so on. Where relevant we asked them to demonstrate using various artefacts (screen captures, emails, AMT itself).

During the observations we visited participants in their respective workplaces (typically their homes, offices or hostels). We requested them to show us how they worked, how they dealt with challenges in the tasks, how they searched through various tasks available on AMT and to articulate what they were doing as they were doing it. We recorded these using audio-video recordings and screen captures where permitted and through extensive note-taking.

The participants were paid $2.50 for completing the survey HIT, $7.00 for an interview and $20.00 for an observation. Whilst we started our recruitment from the initial group of Turkers in India we had received from business contacts, this was expanded through word-of-mouth referrals and through other Turkers who contacted us after having seen the survey HIT on AMT. At the end of the data collection period, we had 78 survey responses, 32 virtual interviews, 3 in-person interviews, and 12 observations at 5 different locations. Participants who were interviewed and observed were subsets of those completing the survey and there was some overlap between them.

The aim of this paper is to provide an in-depth look at the work of crowdwork from the perspective of those doing that work and to make "*observable the social practices in and through which members produce and manage [that] work*" [4] (p8). We therefore focus primarily on the material from the interviews and observations. Our data has been analysed from a broadly ethnomethodological (EM) perspective [7] as this has been shown to be useful for producing a rich picture of the setting and informing the (re-)design of systems [3,10,27]. The findings and themes outlined here were emergent, that is, they came from the data itself. Within this article we focus on some of the key aspects of crowdwork in the everyday lives of the Turkers who made up our participants. We do not say that our population of Turkers is representative of all Turkers, or even of all Indian Turkers. However, the "typicality, general applicability, reliability and trustworthy character of EM findings is furnished in identifying the recurrent social practices in-and-through which members manage the contingent happenings which constitute setting's daily work *as a matter of course*" [4] (p8). We illustrate our findings with vignettes that capture common aspects of how work is managed, giving an idea of what unites and differentiates the activities and practices of our participants.

4. FINDINGS

We start with an introduction to our participants – who they are, where they turk, with whom, and what technologies they use. We then describe what crowdwork looks like from the workers' perspective, which is something that has not, to our knowledge, been given a detailed treatment. We describe how the black box nature of AMT impacts directly on how Turkers organize their

work and how the burden of reputation management falls on individual Turkers. We examine the idea that turking can be fun and take a closer look at crowdwork as a way to make profit from spare cycles.

4.1 Introducing the Turkers

All of our participants used AMT regularly to find work, whether for a few hours a week or as full time job. Many of the Turkers we interviewed were students or recent graduates from privately owned government-affiliated colleges. We also came across housewives, househusbands, retirees, and people with full-time jobs elsewhere (including a dentist, software engineers, ex-call centre employees, and entrepreneurs). Over 50% of the people we surveyed, said they do crowdwork 'whenever I can find time', and around 25% said they do it 'after full-time work/school/college'. Our Turkers came from Tier 1 cities (or the metros Chennai, Bangalore, Delhi, etc.), Tier 2, Tier 3 cities[5] and even some suburban and rural settings. Their place of residence had a clear influence on their work in terms of infrastructure, resources, and exposure to English.

Some Turkers made a full-time living from AMT and others would have liked to have been able to. Nonetheless, many (although not all) of those with professional qualifications or technical expertise, e.g. in computer networking, software engineering, quality assurance, were either actively looking for more conventional jobs or were planning to move to platforms like Odesk where they could make use of their domain expertise. We examine some of the elements that affect turking below.

4.1.1 English and Computer Literacy

Whilst the range of education levels was wide, we found two factors of particular consequence for Turking; literacy in English and computers. The nature of the work on AMT (primarily serving businesses in the US and English speaking world) means that all of our Turkers had at least some level of literacy in English. Computer literacy includes literacy in the use of digital devices like computers, mobile phones and smartphones as well as software applications, web search and other internet applications.

Unsurprisingly, computer literacy typically arises from access to and regular use of computers. For example, the participants that were students or graduates of Computer Science or IT in our sample had a much higher level of computer literacy than students in other disciplines, including engineering disciplines such as aeronautical engineering, who did not have regular access to computers in college. Computer literacy itself impacts turking in various ways, ranging from typing speed and knowledge of keyboard shortcuts, to using scripts and widgets. For instance, plugins such as "Approval Time" (displays auto-approval time) and "Today's Projected Earnings" (calculates and displays expected earnings) save Turkers time and worry. To illustrate, Mansoor, a recent Computer Science graduate from Hyderabad, described how borrowing a friend's laptop while his was being

---

[5] A classification system used by The Government of India for cities/towns 'X, Y and Z', more commonly known as Tier-I, II, III, on the basis of their population. A list of these cities can be found here: http://www.cag.gov.in/html/Allowances.pdf Areas not covered by this structure fall under villages and towns classification as found in Govt. of India's Census 2011's directory of town and villages. http://censusindia.gov.in/2011census/censusdata2k11.aspx

fixed really slowed him down: *"In my own laptop I use Chrome and have installed many scripts [...] I am usually much faster and better on it."*

The level of English literacy of our participants depended, in part, on where they were living, as well as their socio-economic status. Exposure to the English language is much greater in the metros (large cities) compared to tier 3 cities, in both daily life (TV, films, newspapers, etc.) and education. Basic education (in schools) is typically in English in Tier 1, 2 cities and the local language in Tier 3 cities. The level of English literacy impacts on the types of tasks that Turkers can do successfully. Even visual tasks, such as link checking, image tagging and digitisation typically have English instructions [28]. To illustrate the full range of English literacy, and its effects, we describe two participants from different ends of the spectrum. Rahim is a computer science graduate from a private college from Hyderabad in his early 20's and Nagen, a tradesman turned entrepreneur in his 50's who runs an internet café-cum-DTP (desktop publishing) in a small town near Kanyakumari.

Rahim had a high level of English and computer literacy, which enabled him to complete tasks quickly and accurately. When he started turking, he used forums and other resources to learn how to find quality HITs and requesters. Now, however he primarily works for specific favourite requesters that directly contact him when they post HITs. He has installed plugins to help him save time on the various accounting processes. Rahim started turking in the final year of his studies and when, after graduating, the placements from his college didn't impress him he was able to turk full-time, akin to a regular day job. That said, he is not intending to make a career of turking. Even if he can't find work 'in his own field' he hopes to get a government job[6].

Nagen, in comparison, had a Civil Engineering diploma (which can best be described as a vocational qualification which begins at 14 after 10 years of schooling) and little English proficiency. He worked for several companies for 20 years before moving back to his native town. Nagen's internet café was something of a crowdsourcing hub, where 5-6 people worked on AMT when the computers were available or the café owner required help. As he had limited English, he was restricted in the HITs that he was able to complete successfully. When Nagen started a new task, one of his customers or his teenage son would help him learn how to complete it. They would translate and explain the instructions, then help him practice until he was confident enough to do the task on his own. If there was an especially problematic task, they would simply do the tasks for him. The types of tasks he did included link checking, simple digitisation and video transcription (although for this latter task someone else would do the work for him). There were drawbacks to working on tasks with limited mastery of English: sometimes his understanding was not precise enough to do the task correctly or he might incorrectly believe a task to be the same as the one he had trained on, for example, where requesters post variations on a task. Small changes in instructions were problematic and could mean he did tasks incorrectly, without understanding why. This ambiguity had led to the suspension of his account by AMT, but they had lifted the ban

after a heartfelt plea. However, during our period of research he was suspended a second time, ultimately losing his account.

4.1.2 *Technology, Infrastructure and Turking*
Both the hardware that Turkers work on and the infrastructure through which they access the internet impact their turking. Participants accessed the internet from home, work or internet cafes, through data cards or broadband connections. Many of our participants used mobile phones to turk, others used laptops or computers acquired from relatives or bought second hand, whilst still others had ready access to computers at home and at school or work, or they were provided laptops by their universities or companies. There is of course a financial element to access to computers, i.e. those from more well off families were more likely to have computer and internet access at home. Participants who had access to multiple devices and internet connections typically adjusted their activities on AMT according to their current technological constraints and device usage. The interplay between turking, technologies and locations is of course situational. Turkers decide whether they can Turk and what they can do depending on various factors such as what work is available, what skills they have, how much time they have, what technologies they can access and so on. In Vignette 1, we see how multiple devices are used to accommodate Sapna's turking to her current circumstances.

Vignette 1

Sapna, a dentist who works in a dental clinic in an Indian metro city told us how she accepts HITs at work, *"if there is a HIT which has a sufficient amount of time given i.e. 24 hours or 2 days because I can't complete the HIT when I am sitting with somebody. So normally I accept those HITs (on my smartphone) and keep them; and after I come back home I do them. Sometimes when there are no patients at the clinic, or no appointments also I login just to have a check if there is anything or not."* (Transcribed from skype interview)

Sapna either snatches time to select tasks to be done later at home on her laptop, or uses longer periods of free time at work to complete tasks. This would seem to be a classic example of crowdsourcing as making use of spare cycles to make money. In this case multiple devices are needed to realise this flexibility.

In another example, we observed Pandit, a final year engineering student who had recently acquired a second-hand laptop and had bought a smartphone with his AMT earnings. Based out of Nagen's Internet café, Pandit had a faster internet connection through the café's wi-fi on his mobile phone than on his laptop. He also found it simpler to scroll for jobs on his phone. Pandit used the two devices in parallel – accepting jobs on his mobile phone and completing them on his laptop. In both examples, task selection was done on the mobile whilst the task itself was completed on a computer. This is because, while some tasks such as smartphone application testing are best carried out on a mobile, in general the computer is better suited for a wider range of tasks because of screen real-estate and ease of typing.

As well as devices the speed and quality of the internet connection plays an important role in crowdwork.

Vignette 2

Gopal, a Software Engineer lives in shared accommodation in Chennai in the week and spends the weekends with his parents in his native town, *"On weekends I go to my hometown enjoy working in turk and roam around with friends. I work for 5–6*

---

[6] Here a 'Government job' typically means a job with the central or state government public sector e.g. banking, health, transportation, defence services, etc. The selection criteria for such positions includes a Bachelors or engineering degree.

hours only on weekends when I am at parents' house because we have broadband there. Once I worked for 5–6 hrs and earned $200 in a day doing $.50 HITs collecting information about schools (holiday/term time etc.)[..] I work from Chennai if I can get hold of a laptop and I am not tired." (Translated from phone interview in Tamil-English)

During the week, Gopal uses a datacard with limited internet usage and shares a laptop with his friends in his accommodation. But on the weekends when he is in his parents' home he works on his desktop PC with an unlimited broadband connection. Data cards are cheaper, but slower and this limits the types of jobs one can do. Images, buttons and other functionality of tasks that are large in size often fail to load over slow connections, and a lot of time gets wasted just waiting for such tasks to load. For example, in our observations even a simple business card digitization task took around 30 seconds to load at the Internet cafe – greatly increasing the time required to complete the task and making such low paying tasks even less desirable[7].

Connection quality and speed can also cause problems in task completion, as many tasks display a completion code at the end of a task, which must then be entered into AMT for payment. However, this method is not robust enough for dodgy connections and when the code fails to load or display properly, the Turker will not be paid and their time is wasted, even though the requester still gets their data. This arises because the tasks themselves are hosted outside of AMT, with AMT being used for recruitment and payment only. Decisions about which tasks our participants specialized in were therefore partly based on what technology and infrastructure was available to them.

4.1.3 Types of Jobs

Our participants completed a whole range of jobs including image tagging, categorization and filtering, link checking, digitisation, address verification, research (surveys and experiments), writing (articles, blogs, reviews, etc.), testing smartphone apps, usability testing of websites, transcription and some translation (often into regional languages but two participants translated into Spanish). They specialised in particular tasks according to their abilities and preferences, their access to technology and infrastructure, as well as their qualifications on AMT (individual Requesters can set up qualification tests for Turkers to be eligible for particular tasks). Typically our participants had a range of skills/tasks/requesters in their portfolio – completing their preferred ones when available and doing others, such as transcription, which is time consuming, as back-up tasks when needed.

Vignette 3

A 21 year old final year engineering student from Chandigarh, Aman, says, "*Some of the audio transcription tasks, they are very long and with less pay like $0.50 for 20-30 mins [of work]. So often I try to work on them, [thinking that] I can easily work. But when is going.. going.. going..[i.e. it takes too long to load] I didn't understand; it feel its boring so I reject that task – I have the option to return the task, [so] then I returned it [..] I don't want to waste much time for less pay.*" (Transcribed from skype interview)

---

[7] Even watching the video made the researchers twitchy at the slow download, however for the Turker it is business as usual. He occupied himself by flicking between the task and his email.

A common way of selecting preferred jobs was by *requester*; Turkers came to know particular requesters who paid reasonably and offered jobs they could comfortably complete without error. Individual requesters also favoured the most proficient Turkers. That is, requesters would email them when a batch of HITs was uploaded, typically after the Turker had passed some qualification test set by the requesters. We believe that this type of relationship between requesters and specific Turkers, where jobs are unavailable on the open AMT market, is quite common. We also found out that some jobs might have migrated off AMT (i.e. they are exchanged and completed through direct electronic communication). Such specialisation enables the Turkers to become highly skilled in particular types of work and thus more efficient. The relationship can ensure a steady amount of work and minimize the amount of time spent locating work. The established relationship is more reliable and dependable, and appears to be preferred in a number of cases for both sides, as opposed to the fully open, dynamic, anonymous market.

4.1.4 Online, But Not Isolated

Our participants worked from home (whether their family home, a hostel or other accommodation), work, college or cyber cafes. Often they were part of a small networks of Turkers – either with family and friends who also Turked, or as members of online communities. For example, Sapna, the dentist, describes how she is embedded in a mini-network with her daughter and cousin, where they share passwords and help each other out by informing one another of good HITs, even accepting them on one another's behalf.

Vignette 4

"*Normally I share it* [discussions about mturk] *with my daughter and my cousin who also works on mturk. Sometimes she also helps me out... Sometimes if she* [her cousin] *gets a HIT and I am at my workplace and the HIT has a time period of 24 hours, so she calls me or my daughter, you accept this HIT on her behalf. Anybody can accept the HIT on my behalf if they have the password and I come back and do that HIT. Earlier this used to be, but nowadays you get very less HITs where you can do such things... Sometimes it's the other way around [also]. If I get a good HIT or if I learn that a good requester with a generous amount of bonus, so we skype or call each other.*" (transcribed from skype interview)

Similarly, Rafiq, uses his network of family and turking acquaintances to share information about HITs (see Vignette 8). He quit his job in the city and moved in with his family to a suburban area, making a full-time living from AMT. He has a large network of fellow Turkers as he runs teaching and discussion groups about AMT on Facebook and Skype. As he reports in Vignette 8 he snatches sleep when he has run out of good HITs, but stays 'in the loop' by asking his network to call him "*if those HITS have been uploaded please wake me up.*" Communities of Turkers also crop up around physical places, such as the internet cafe we visited. The Turkers who work from there, share information on requesters, HITs, their experiences on AMT and even help each other out with difficult HITs. Such networks provide mutual benefit, and even training and development opportunities for the Turkers. This is important because there is typically little in the way of feedback and training provided by the requesters themselves, yet such feedback and training can significantly improve performance [21].

As well as their colleagues on AMT, our participants were often supported in their work by their families - bringing them tea, coffee and meals - so that they can concentrate on turking. Whilst communities of fellow Turkers offer practical, moral and social support, families often tend to the physical comfort of Turkers. Despite being online and home based, among our participants turking is socially embedded and only one of our interviewees mentioned missing out on the 'social aspect of working with colleagues.' This is in contrast to the studies of homeworkers for a Business Process Outsourcing company [24] in the US who more frequently mentioned isolation as being a downside of homeworking with fewer opportunities to share knowledge, experience or collaborate with fellow workers.

While some families were fully supportive of turking and glad of the income it provided, others were less content and put pressure on the Turkers to find more suitable, regular employment within their domain of expertise. This was a nagging concern, especially for some of our graduates who had completed their degree 1 or 2 years ago[8]. In contrast, those with family circumstances preventing them from easily finding work elsewhere, such as househusbands and wives, were typically glad of the flexibility offered by crowdworking (see Vignette 5).

We have presented a picture of *who* our participants are, we now taking a closer look at crowdworking as a filler of 'spare cycles'.

4.2 Rhythms of Crowdwork

Earlier we mentioned that over 50% of our participants said they do crowdwork *"whenever I can find time"*. On the surface this seems to fit with Howe's idea of converting 'spare cycles' into productive time. However, when we dig a little deeper we see that the picture is not so clear. Firstly, the concept of crowdsourcing as using 'spare cycles' becomes rather fuzzy for our participants who actually spend a considerable amount of their working time on AMT. That is, while some of their turking takes place in *liminal* (transitional) places and moments it is also clear that turking is managed through multi-tasking and finding time and space within their lives. There is prioritization in relation to other activities, whether this is 'down time' (however one defines it), spending time with family or getting some decent sleep. Whilst turking certainly does allow some flexibility in working hours, in that it can be fitted around other activities (to a greater or lesser extent), it is certainly not the case that Turkers can log onto AMT whenever they like and find work (that they are willing or able to do), as the following vignettes illustrate.

Vignette 5

Ketan, a house-husband from Chennai says *"I worked as an assistant to the Principal of a reputed local engineering college for 10 years. I gave up work to care for our kids at home, and tried various "work-from-home" options then found and started working on Turk[..] I have been working on AMT for over a year[..] My wife works in the Police force, you can't expect her to stay at home, her job doesn't permit it, so I do that. I do the chores, drop and pick up kids from the school, get groceries etc during the day. I also try and look for work on MTurk when I have some time, but mostly I work at night because that's when there are some jobs available. I like this freedom, not having to bow in front of anyone and being your own boss, all while I am at home with my kids."* (translated from phone interview in Tamil-English)

Vignette 6

Mansoor, a recent graduate from Hyderabad who is enrolled in a professional short course says *"You cannot find much work on AMT during the day... in the morning I go to institute for BBA for taught and practical classes. Class starts at 11.30 am, I leave home at 10.30am, we have 1 hour theory, 1 hour practical and then we practice for 1 – 2 hrs.. and then I come back at 4 pm and rest. Then do work on AMT. I do the most work at night time after 7.30 sometimes till 1, 2 or 3 am at night... I also have to do house work in the morning [...] but if I got more work in the mornings I am willing to sit and work all day."* (translated from interview in Hindi)

Vignette 7

Navin a network programmer from the state of West Bengal tells us, *"While I brush my teeth in the morning I check on my phone if there are any HITs available that I can do in 20 minutes, if yes, then I'd take them up, otherwise I'll just get ready and go to work"* (translated from skype interview in Hindi-English)

The picture we get from our participants is that their working life on AMT is heavily dictated by the availability of HITs. This manifests itself in two primary ways. There are only occasionally available HITs during what might be called 'spare cycles' throughout the day, with most of the quality hits available at night. This is because the majority of requesters on AMT are US-based, so HITs are available and their working day coincides with India's night and early morning.

Almost all of our participants described the impact of limited work availability in some way or other. As we described above, Turkers have particular types of jobs or requesters they are happy to work for. However, there are more workers than *good*[9] jobs making availability of work a real issue. While, in theory there might always be *some* HITs on AMT that someone *could* do, in practice there are often no HITs that they are willing or able to do – whether because of pay, difficulty or bandwidth. Almost all of our participants would have liked to have access to more work and several said that when there is work available they will sit and do extra hours, or work in long spells until the 'good work' is gone. These Turkers therefore, are by necessity adaptable to the rhythms of work availability and have developed strategies for juggling work and other activities, so that they can find the 'good jobs.'

Vignette 8

Rafiq, an ex-QA engineer from suburban India says, *"(For) a regular Turker in mturk, has no kind of any predetermined schedule because of work in mturk. We work when there is a work, not 'we', I. If I am sleeping also I let others to keep concentrating on some HITs "if those HITS have been uploaded please wake me up." Since 2 years I've never slept for [...] I sleep for 6 hours very few times, continuously. I sleep in partly, like 2 hrs or 4 hrs. [...]When there is work I work, when there is no work I am taking rest. When there is no work I am just concentrating on the sleep."* (transcribed from skype interview)

This example gives the lie to the idea of working when you want, as it would be rather extreme to characterise sleep as a 'spare cycle.' The picture we get is of flexible working, but it is not always clear who gets the most benefit from 'flexible' work hours.

---

[8] Other concerns about the longer term viability of Turking include the continuing availability of enough work and whether AMT will remain open for business (at all or to Indian Turkers).

[9] Of course what is considered a good job varies from individual to individual according to the fit between their circumstances and the jobs characteristics.

Are the requesters benefiting from being able to employ workers according to their needs, or are the Turkers benefiting from being better able to achieve a Turk-life balance? From our analysis we believe that, to a large extent, it is the *Turker* who has to *be* flexible to fit into the rhythms of work on AMT (see [2] for a discussion of the concept of flexibility in relation to self-employed work).

4.3 Turking for fun?

Many of our participants talked about the enjoyment that came from Turking.

Vignette 9

Niveditha, a Masters student: *"these days, for the past 1 month, I am doing it at home, after I return to my room, I find it more comfortable because I have the privacy and all to do better work when I am at my room. […] If it's a survey based job, then I do it at work, but if its writing, then I don't want to do it in a hurry, it's something that I enjoy so I come back to room and then sit at my computer"*

Vignette 10

A retired Education officer says *"I am retired and have loads of time on my hand. I do turking for 'timepass' and to earn some money. […] while working I tend to take it easy – I don't do complicated HITs or HITs whose instructions are too high-end because there are high chances of rejection. I don't want all that tension. While on computer I also listen to old songs and bhajans (prayers) on youtube or downloaded by family. I am very happy with turk."*

Although on first glance such comments might seem to add fuel to the research which argues that Turkers primary motivation is fun [12,16,30], we suggest that the enjoyment and pleasure our turkers talk about might be better cast as *job satisfaction*. For our participants, as for others [23] turking is clearly work, but this does not mean there is no pleasure to be had. Even those Turkers who did zero dollar hits did them because they had a rationale (sadly not necessarily correct) that they would get paid somewhere down the line for them, for example, in the form of a bonus or access to other higher paying HITs. For these Turkers, job satisfaction comes from a variety of aspects of the work, including: taking part in research, working for US companies, flexibility, not having a boss, doing 'easy' jobs which don't require much concentration or conversely doing tasks which exploit particular skill sets. The work itself can also be fun, for example, some of our crowdworkers actively searched out amusing tasks such as taking pictures of the contents of one's fridge, playing games on smartphones, or solving puzzles.

Since the cost of living in India is much lower than in the US, the Indian Turkers can earn comparatively high wages – which is likely to be key in giving greater job satisfaction. In a country where $250-$300/month is a pretty good wage (15-20k rupees)

the earning potential from AMT is a lot higher than in the US, across a wider set of jobs. This also decreases the need to work at such a high pace, meaning the 'working conditions' are more favourable. However, as the Turkers earn in dollars, but are paid in rupees, currency fluctuations can have quite an impact on their earnings for better or worse. The falling rupee at the time of research therefore worked in favour of our participants, as they ended up with more disposable income in rupees. Currency differentials aside however, the majority of our participants do discriminate and care about price, preferring higher paid work. Reducing pay is therefore, just as likely have a negative impact on the quality of workers and work in India as in the US.

4.4 Reputation, Reputation, Reputation

We now turn to one of the Turkers key concerns – reputation. The availability of good, higher paying HITs for any Turker is dependent on their ratings (e.g. rejection rate, approval rate etc.), their reputations and relationships with requesters and fellow Turkers, their AMT qualifications, e.g. Masters, and sometimes qualification tests set by individual requesters. Maintaining a good reputation is therefore one of the foremost concerns of all of the Turkers in our study. However, aspects of their reputation are not completely in their hands, and in this section we will explore the practical methods and concerns of Turkers in relation to reputation given the opaque nature of AMT.

While qualifications are sought after because they are the route to access better jobs and pay, blocking (by requesters) and suspensions (of the account by AMT) were feared and actively avoided. As has been mentioned elsewhere, requesters can reject work or block workers without giving any reason [23,31,32]. A block may be done legitimately, because the worker has made too many errors, or because the requestor is unscrupulous (e.g. don't pay for good work) or has poor quality assurance (QA) methods or bad HIT design. Turkopticon is a plugin designed to help guard against unscrupulous requestors, enabling the Turkers to review and rate requestors [13] but only a few of our participants used it.

An example of poor practice relates to surveys. A common method for requestors to ensure a 'one survey per person' model is to block Turkers on completion of a survey – they are meant to put a note on the block giving the reason, but this does not always happen, meaning these are then treated as 'hard blocks.' Being blocked by requesters can result in the suspension of the worker's AMT account, meaning they can no longer work and their funds (earnings so far) in the account can be forfeited. The problem with blocks and suspensions is there is very little information on why something has happened – it is rarely clear to them why they have been blocked or if it is deserved since there is typically no feedback on their error rate. The only feedback they have is in terms of work accepted and rejected by requestors, but whilst this is likely to bear some relation to error rate, it certainly does not follow that it is closely correlated. In terms of account suspension, the general belief is that AMT operates a 'three strikes and you're

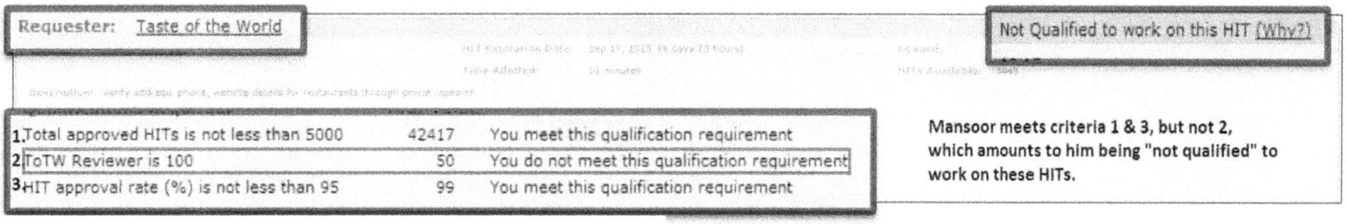

Figure 1. Mansoor's desired HIT (Vignette 11)

out' rule – three blocks equals a suspension. In addition there is no official appeal process and Turkers are left with only the possibility to write an email to Amazon or specific requesters hoping for clemency.

Returning to the topic of qualifications, we look at qualification tasks set by requesters, as these can provide gateways into and access to good HITs.

Vignette 11

Mansoor tells us *"Taste of the World has a score system and he* [a friend and fellow-Turker who has stopped going to a local institute to upgrade his domain expertise] *has scored 100, that's why he still has a lot of work to do, and I don't. 'qualification match' requires that I should have done 5000 HITs, my value is 42000, it says 'I meet this qualification requirement'. The reviewer value required is 100 and mine is 50, basically meaning mine is below 100, so I am not qualified. If I could work on these HITs even I would not go to my institute. Now HITs are available 24X7 for these guys (who have score of a 100) and I see them everyday but can't do them, which hurts a little. I was careless when the Requester was testing Turkers with qualifications, so my score is less. I should have worked hard [...] but I was in a rush."* (translated from interview in Hindi)

In this case, Mansoor did not score well in the qualification test – his requester-specific approval rate is only 50, whereas if he had scored 100 he would be qualified to do higher-paying work. His low score has implications for him in terms of the ability to make a full-time income off AMT, just like it might in a more traditional workplace.

Our Turkers showed an overriding fear of being blocked and many of their turking strategies were devised to protect against this possibility. As mentioned above, it is not exactly clear what causes a Turker to be blocked or to have their account suspended by AMT. Certainly making too many errors on a task will often result in a block, but how about accepting, then returning uncompleted tasks? Does this affect their reputations? Certainly many of our Turkers thought so. Furthermore, Turkers report getting blocked for complaining to requesters[10]. For most of the Turkers in our study, AMT was an important source of income and they frequently chose to implement defensive practices that required extra work, in the name of protecting their reputations. This work is an example of invisible work - the unpaid and unacknowledged "work to make the Turking work" [23]- and is illustrated in the vignette below.

Vignette 12

Pandit tells us *"If in a HIT the survey link is provided I click on the survey, open it and do it before accepting the HIT because sometimes the completion code doesn't load on the last page of the survey, which is bad for my rating [...] It also shows if the requester is genuine… and this also means that I can evaluate if the survey is hard to do or not, whether I can complete it. I have done this many times and 'submitted' HITs successfully but sometimes it doesn't work because by the time I complete the survey the HIT disappears." (translated from interview in Tamil)*

This Turker has developed a strategy to maintain his reputation, which covers a few of the potential problems he might run into

that could negatively impact his rating. Namely, the survey might be too difficult for him to complete, the completion code might not load or the requester might not be genuine. This Turker is well aware that any of these problems, even though they may lie outside of his sphere of control, can negatively impact his reputation and he prefers to risk losing the HIT (as when, for example, it has been completed by the maximum number of other Turkers before he accepts it). This type of defensive practice was common for Turkers, especially when they were unsure of exactly what a task might involve. Another strategy was to accept the HIT first and then return it if it was too hard. This is a safer strategy in terms of safeguarding the HIT for oneself, but our participants had the belief that too many returns would negatively impact their reputation. The problem of HITs disappearing before acceptance was a problem that a number of our participants had experienced and it seemed to occur more commonly with certain types of task.

When participants were more confident with a set of tasks, for instance some batch tasks, they would use the option to auto-accept the next task as the previous one is completed. However, when our participants encountered other task types that may vary considerably (e.g. surveys), or when workers were less confident in their ability, they often checked out each instance before accepting. An example of this was when one of our participants was trying out some new (to him) mapping tasks. This 'try before you buy' tactic is part of the hidden preparatory work of turking.

It is worth taking a moment to examine the issue of HIT difficulty and turkers confidence (or lack thereof) in their ability to complete a HIT, as it was a theme that ran through many of our encounters. The difficulty of a HIT to any turker is of course an individual thing, predicated in part on English language fluency and general comprehension. However, it is often deeper than that, for example, we saw cases where turkers rejected surveys because they did not understand what the questions were actually asking. Answering a question or more generally completing a HIT successfully requires an understanding of the meaning of the question or the 'intention' behind the HIT[11], which goes beyond a simple understanding of the words in English [35]. Deciding whether they understand a task or not necessarily falls under the judgement of the individual turkers. However it is not necessarily a simple decision as the overlap between, what [15] call different 'social worlds' - those of the requester and the turker - may mean the turker thinks they understand the task when in reality they don't. This is similar to how the different 'social worlds' of the participants working on the same task in different countries impact practically on the understanding of and ability to complete tasks correctly [15]. The tendency of many of the turkers we saw was to err on the side of caution, however they did not always do so, with potentially disastrous results e.g. the suspension of Nagen's account.

Such defensive practices evidence the real fear of suspension: nearly all our participants knew someone who had their account suspended by AMT. As with blocks, Turkers have almost no useful information on why they have been suspended. This ambiguity and opaqueness cultivates a climate of concern amongst the communities of Turkers that they too might run into problems. To illustrate the problem of this lack of information, we discuss the Internet café owner's case.

---

[10] The operation of blocks and suspensions is a common topic of discussion in Turk forums and our material, here, is supplemented from our reading of forums.

---

[11] Or at least an understanding of what the instructions are actually asking you to do.

Vignette 13

The Internet café-cum-DTP shop owner, Nagen, explains his way of doing things, *"I only do tasks that I have done before so that I am familiar with the instructions. […] But I think one of past few times, something I did went wrong as I got some warning emails from Amazon and finally got blocked. I was pretty sure I had done the task correctly and had seen the instructions before but perhaps I misunderstood something and now I might get suspended. We keep trying to contact them (AMT) via emails. I still have around $50 in my account. They are an American company, they are pukka (genuine/honest/honourable) in their procedures, I trust they'll be fair to me and give me my money back…"* (translated from interview in Tamil)

Given this Turker's low level of English literacy, it would not be surprising if he had made enough errors to merit a block (from the requester) and even a suspension from Amazon. We would argue however, that the lack of information available to him and Amazon's subsequent treatment of him are problematic. In Figure 2, you can find the response from Amazon to his request to review the suspension, or at the very least to have the funds in his account returned to him. There is little here, or in the original notice of suspension, which indicates which task 'failure' had caused the suspension, or even if it came from doing a task. The only information provided to him was 'for Violation of the Participation Agreement' which could cover a multitude of infractions.

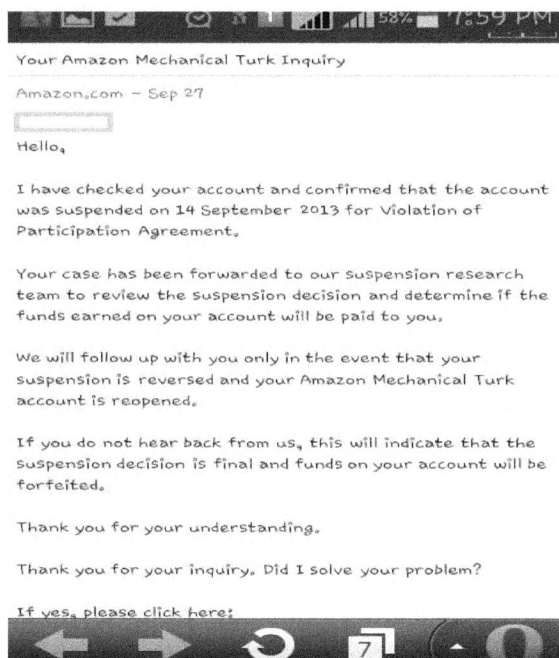

Figure 2. AMT's email to Nagen about his suspended turk account, as viewed on his friend's phone (Vignette 13)

One thing to note is that this *is* a genuine worker, even if his output can be flawed at times. He puts in a lot of effort to try to do tasks well; he is not trying to cheat. However, AMT does not seem to distinguish between scammers – people who are 'gaming' the system, making no attempt at genuine work - and genuine but poor workers. All are treated the same, with a suspension and forfeiting of funds, which genuine workers legitimately earned through crowdwork. By highlighting this case, we hope to speak to both requesters and researchers. There seems to be a tendency to assume that poor work is just scamming or that poor workers

can be treated equivalently to scammers. However, it seems very likely that some proportion (we do not know how large) are genuine workers trying their best but who are not really up to the task at hand. As such, they are mislabelled as scammers. Our internet café owner reveals the human face behind the scammer label. Whilst we would not deny requesters the right to weed out workers who produce bad work, we suggest that some distinction needs to be made, between genuine workers and scammers, even if it is only to ensure they get paid the funds owed when their account is suspended. We hope that this point is an illustration of the need, pointed out by other researchers e.g. [17,19,28,34] for requesters, especially those from global corporations to think how to make their tasks more accessible to wider audiences.

5. DISCUSSION

Turking in India is naturally coloured by the circumstances of life in India, a country of startling diversity. Access to AMT is restricted by the requirement to have a computer or smartphone, internet access, and some amount of English and computer literacy. While these restrictions mean that none of our participants came from populations in India with the lowest levels of income and literacy, the participants in our study were a relatively diverse group.

Infrastructure had a large impact on turking. Clear differences in both speed and reliability were seen between the different configurations of infrastructure, access modes, technologies and places of access, from internet cafes with weak, intermittent Wi-Fi to homes with reliable, fast broadband connections. These impacted the types of jobs our participants could do, the time taken to do those jobs and also the likelihood of failing at the last hurdle and losing money. Whilst some of our participants expressed frustration, for many these features were un-noteworthy - just part of the normal working conditions, and normal, natural troubles [7]. This is not to say that Turkers did not attend to bandwidth and so on, as seen in 1) day-to-day activities when they juggle between devices, or between activities like emailing, or 2) longer term decisions when upgrading their internet connection or acquiring in better devices is judged to be a worthwhile investment. These strategies should come as no surprise since normal troubles have normal, known about solutions both in day-to-day dealings and in the longer term. There were also marked differences in English and techno-literacy amongst our participants, and this clearly impacted their earning potential. In comparison with the US, where the other large population of Turkers reside, there are two additional differences which impact on turking: the time difference – meaning most of the work is available at night for the Indian Turkers - and the cost of living, which is lower in India, making turking a better paid activity.

5.1 Spare Cycles

We have examined the concept of crowdwork as an activity to make 'spare cycles' profitable and found that whilst on the surface it might seem to fit, when we dig deeper it seems less appropriate. Leaving aside for now fundamental questions on the appropriateness of even applying this term to human activity, it is clear that for our participants turking is rarely something to do in snatched minutes. *To turk is to work* and it occupies substantial hours in a week and competes with others activities they would prefer to do. Furthermore, whether turking full-time or just for an hour here or there flexibility of working hours is limited by the availability of good work. It is not so much that turking fills spare cycles, as the turkers have to make 'spare cycles' themselves in which to fit work (cf. [2]). That to turk is to work might seem unsurprising to many, but it is important to reiterate this given the picture that much of the early research created of turking as a leisure activity [13,16,30]. Perhaps, if crowdwork was seen as work from the outset the policies for blocking and suspending would have taken a different form. The fun and enjoyment that turkers speak of would seem to be better respecified as 'job satisfaction.' We hope this also provides a more nuanced perspective on the sometimes overly negative picture of crowdworkers as exploited, which is the counter argument to crowdwork as fun.

5.2 Reputation Management, Feedback and Training

The work of reputation management falls fairly decidedly on the Turkers' shoulders, wherever the challenge to their reputation lies. Whilst the asymmetry in ratings and therefore transparency of reputation *within AMT* [32] has been remarked elsewhere, our paper shows clearly for the first time the hidden work that Turkers do to maintain their ratings and reputations. Reputation management tactics are often defensive and the Turker shoulders the potential cost of the practice. These practices include ensuring they can do the work before accepting it, specialising in known tasks for specific requesters, getting training on tasks from co-workers, ensuring the completion code would load and so on. Our Turkers typically took considerable care over their work to ensure they completed the task correctly so as to not harm their reputations and where they did not they took the consequences (e.g. Vignette 13). It is telling that Turkers would rather lose HITs than damage their reputation. There is of course a simple solution to this, returning work uncompleted should not be counted against workers and certainly should not result in a block. If a Requester has a *genuine reason* for not wanting work to be returned uncompleted they should make it clear in the HIT – whilst at the same time being aware that they are penalising genuine workers who are trying their best, especially those with lower bandwidth connections or lesser skills. One reputation maintenance strategy of many Turkers was to stick with tasks they are really sure they can do. Whilst specialisation can be good – improving speed and quality – this tactic does reduce the opportunity for learning and advancement. It does not offer much of a 'career' or skills development path. We therefore join the voices asking requestors to make training material available and give useful feedback [21]. Even if the training is unpaid, it is likely there would be an uptake among genuine workers, as evidenced by our Turkers' participation in real or virtual learning communities. Turkers specifically talk about devoting time (for no pay) to this learning and the pursuit of qualifications and furthermore some are willing to do zero dollar HITs in the belief they will get some sort of payoff later[12].

---

[12] We would like to say a few words on zero dollar hits: where these HITs are not part of any development or career trajectory, or even where they are so-called small prize HITs (i.e. only the top worker gets paid), they can easily be exploitative. People might do them, however requesters cannot make the assumption workers are doing them with their eyes open. AMT is surrounded by myths, some of them akin to tales of 'golden tickets.' The Turkers who did these HITs honestly believed they would get some benefit or pay out down the line. Even if unknowingly, these HITs play on myth and misunderstanding to exploit the workers.

Feedback and training are interrelated, with feedback on performance being a good aid for learning, however, feedback could also help Turkers handle some of the opaqueness of AMT and the uncertainness that comes with this opacity. Turkers rarely know why work is rejected (their error or some other reason), what would lead to a block/suspension or why they have been blocked/suspended. Whilst AMT normally sends warning emails before suspending someone, they seem to be directed at scammers – people who deliberately do bad work or game the system. They do not give any reasons, which would help genuine workers understand and change their behaviour. Since AMT is an uncertain environment with little clear information, then Turkers' community 'experience' is almost the only source of information about how AMT works. Whilst this can provide a variety of benefits, and help the Turkers work better, it is not necessarily particularly accurate and can contribute to the climate of concern.

Although ours was a self-selecting sample and we do not deny the existence of scammers (wherever there is a system, there will surely be people to game it), our research leads us to ask: Is it fair to treat scammers and workers who produce poor output as the same? It is perhaps convenient for lazy requestors and AMT – however it is a heavy-handed approach to error. We would hope that our paper will give both requestors and researchers pause for thought. There have been strong arguments for relationship-based crowdsourcing and we believe our findings here provide further support for it [1,25,31]. Requesters, your workers are still *your* workers even if they are an anonymous, non-contracted and shifting crowd. You have an obligation to treat them well and you will get benefit from doing so. Indeed, we can see some requesters already engaging in ad-hoc relationship-based crowdsourcing – maintaining a group of known good workers and emailing them when batches of work are ready or moving the relationship wholly off AMT.

6. CONCLUSION

In this article we have presented findings from our qualitative, largely ethnographic studies of Indian Turkers. We have particularly focused on how they organize and schedule their Turking work given their life circumstances, work and family commitments, access to and expertise with technologies and infrastructure, location and learning. This not only serves as a means to better understand these hitherto invisible workers but also to aid in considerations of how best to work with them and utilize their abilities – all of which points to the promise that going forward, relationship-based crowdsourcing can be more fruitful than many current modes of operation.

7. REFERENCES

[1] Bederson, B. B. and Quinn, A. J. 2011. Web workers unite! addressing challenges of online laborers. *In Proceedings of CHI EA '11*. ACM (2011), 97-106.

[2] Bourne, K. A., and Forman, P. J. (2013). Living in a Culture of Overwork: An Ethnographic Study of Flexibility. *Journal of Management Inquiry, 25 March 2013, DOI: 10.1177/1056492613481245*

[3] Crabtree, A. 2003. Designing Collaborative Systems: A Practical Guide to Ethnography, Springer.

[4] Crabtree, A., Nichols, D. M., O'Brien, J., Rouncefield, M., & Twidale, M. B. 2000. Ethnomethodologically informed ethnography and information system design. *Journal of the American Society for Information Science, 51*(7), 666-682.

[5] Felsteiner, A. 2011. Working the crowd: employment and labor law in the crowdsourcing industry. *Berkeley Journal of Employment & Labor Law 32(1)*, 143-204.

[6] Felstiner, A. 2013. The weakness of crowds. Limn, Crowds and Clouds (2), Retrieved from *http://limn.it/the-weakness-ofcrowds/*.

[7] Garfinkel, H., 1967. Studies in ethnomethodology. Englewood Cliffs, N.J.: Prentice-Hall.

[8] Gawade, M., Vaish, R., Waihumbu, M, N., Davis, J., 2012. Exploring Employment Opportunities through Microtasks via Cybercafes. *In Proceedings of IEEE GHTC'12 77-82*.

[9] Howe, J., 2006. The rise of crowdsourcing. *Wired Magazine Issue 14.06*. Available at *http://www.wired.com/wired/archive/14.06/crowds.html*

[10] Hughes: Hughes, J. A., Randall, D., & Shapiro, D. (1992, December). Faltering from ethnography to design. In *Proceedings of the 1992 ACM conference on Computer-supported cooperative work,* 115-122.

[11] Hughes, J., King, V., Rodden, T., Andersen, H. (1994) Moving Out from the Control Room: Ethnography in System Design. *In Proceedings of ACM CSCW'94 Conference on Computer-Supported Cooperative Work ,* 429-439.

[12] Ipeirotis, P. 2010. Analyzing the Amazon Mechanical Turk marketplace. *CeDER Working Papers No. CeDER-10-04. Available at http://hdl.handle.net/2451/29801*

[13] Ipeirotis, P. 2010. Demographics of Mechanical Turk. CeDER Working Papers No. CeDER-10-01. *http://hdl.handle.net/2451/29585*

[14] Irani, L. and Silberman, M. S. 2013. Turkopticon: Interrupting Worker Invisibility in Amazon Mechanical Turk. *In Proceedings of CHI 2013, ACM Press.*

[15] Jensen, R. E., & Bjørn, P. (2012). Divergence and Convergence in Global Software Development: Cultural Complexities as Social Worlds. *From research to practice in the design of cooperative systems.* pp. 123-136

[16] Kaufmann, N., Schulze, T., and Veit, D. 2011. More than fun and money. Worker Motivation in Crowdsourcing – A Study on Mechanical Turk. *In Proceedings of AMCIS 2011.*

[17] Khanna, S., Ratan, A., Davis, J., Thies, W. 2010. Evaluating and Improving the Usability of Mechanical Turk for Low-Income Workers in India. *In Proceedings of ACM DEV 2010.*

[18] Kittur,A., Chi, E. H., and Suh, B. 2008. Crowdsourcing user studies with Mechanical Turk. *In Proceedings of the CHI '08. ACM,* 453-456.

[19] Kittur, A., Nickerson, J. V., Bernstein, M., Gerber, E., Shaw, A., Zimmerman, J., Lease, M. and Horton, J. 2013. The future of crowd work. *In Proceedings of CSCW '13, ACM press,* 1301–1318.

[20] Kochhar, S., Mazzochi, S., Paritosh, P. 2010. The Anatomy of a Large-Scale Human Computation Engine. *HCOMP'10. ACM press.* 10-17.

[21] Le, J., Edmonds, A., Hester, V., Biewald, L. 2010. Ensuring quality in crowdsourced search relevance evaluation: The effects of training question distribution. *SIGIR'10.* 17-20.

[22] Little, G., Chilton, L. B., Goldman, M. and Miller, R. C. 2009. Turkit: tools for iterative tasks on mechanical turk. *In Proceedings of KDD-HCOMP '09, 2009.*

[23] Martin, D., Hanrahan, B. J., O'Neill, J., Gupta, N., 2014. Being a Turker. *In Proceedings of ACM CSCW '14,* 224-235.

[24] O'Neill, J., Roy, S., Grasso, A., Martin, D., 2013. Form Digitization in BPO: From outsourcing to crowdsourcing? *In Proceedings of the SIGCHI Conference on Human Factors in Computing Systems (CHI'13).*

[25] O'Neill J., Martin D. 2013. Relationship-based Business Process Crowdsourcing? *In Proceedings of IFIP Conference on Human-Computer Interaction'13.* 429-446.

[26] Pontin, J., 2007. Artificial Intelligence, With Help From the Humans. The New York Times. *Available at http://www.nytimes.com/2007/03/25/business/yourmoney/25S tream.html*

[27] Randall, D., Harper, R. & Rouncefield, M. (2007). Fieldwork for Design: Theory and Practice. Springer Verlag, New York.

[28] Ratan, A. L., Satpathy, S., Zia, L., Toyama, K., Blagsvedt, S., Pawar, U. S., Subramaniam, T., 2009. Kelsa+: digital literacy for low-income office workers. *Proceedings of the 3rd International Conference on Information and Communication Technologies and Development,* 2009.

[29] Ross, J., Irani, L., Silberman, M. S., Zaldivar, A., and Tomlinson, B. 2010. Who are the crowdworkers?: shifting demographics in mechanical turk. *In Proceedings of CHI EA '10, ACM (2010), 2863–2872.*

[30] Shaw, A., 2010. For love or for money? A list experiment on the motivations behind crowdsourcing work. *Available at https://crowdflower.com/blog/2010/08/for-love-or-for-money-a-list-experiment-on-the-motivations-behind-crowdsourcing-work/*

[31] Silberman, M. S. 2010. What's fair? Rational action and its residuals in an electronic market. *Unpublished manuscript. http://www.scribd.com/doc/86592724/Whats-Fair*

[32] Silberman, M. S., Irani, L., and Ross, J. 2010. Ethics and Tactics of Professional Crowdwork. *ACM XRDS, 17, 2.*

[33] Sommerville, I., Rodden, T., Sawyer, P. & Bentley, R. 1992. Sociologists can be surprisingly useful in interactive systems design. In proceedings of HCI '92, CUP. *People and computers,* 341-341.

[34] Star, S.L. and Strauss, A.L. 1998. Layers of silence, arenas of voice: The ecology of visible and invisible work'. *CSCW Journal, 8: 9-30.*

[35] Tanney, J. (2013) *Rules, Reason and Self-knowledge.* Harvard University Press

[36] Thies, W., Ratan, A., Davis, J.: 2011. Paid crowdsourcing as a vehicle for global development. *In: CHI '11 Workshop on Crowdsourcing and Human Computation*

Routine and Standardization in Global Software Development

Morten Esbensen*
mortenq@itu.dk

*IT University of Copenhagen
Rued Langgaards Vej 7
2300 Copenhagen S, Denmark

Pernille Bjørn*†
pbra@itu.dk

†UCIrvine & Intel Center for Social Computing (ISTC)
Bren Hall, 6th Floor
Irvine, California, USA

ABSTRACT

We present an ethnographic field study of a distributed software development team following the Scrum methodology. During a two-week period, we observed from both sites the collaboration between a Danish software company off-shoring part of their development to an Indian solution provider. Collaboration by its very definition is based on the notion of dependency in work between multiple people. Articulation work is the extra work required to handle these dependencies. In a globally distributed team, managing these dependencies is exacerbated due to the distances of time, space, and culture. To broaden our understanding of dependencies in a global context and how they influence work practices, we made them the focus of our analysis. The main contributions of this paper are (i) an empirical account of the dependencies that are part of the collaborative work in a global software development team, (ii) a discussion of the interlinked properties of dependencies, and (iii) an explanation of how the practices of standardization and routine are developed and used to manage these dependencies.

Categories and Subject Descriptors

K.4.3 [**Organizational Impacts**]: Computer-supported collaborative work

Keywords

Global software development; ethnographic study; dependencies; standardization; routine

1. INTRODUCTION

Work in software development projects is increasingly being carried out by distributed teams. Distributed or global collaboration allows companies to take advantage of a global workforce, execute work at different hours of the day, and keep work close to different target markets. However, this way of working also introduces a number of problems related

GROUP'14, November 9–12, 2014, Sanibel Island, Florida, USA.
Copyright is held by the owner/author(s). Publication rights licensed to ACM.
ACM 978-1-4503-3043-5/14/11 ...$15.00.
http://dx.doi.org/10.1145/2660398.2660413.

to the distances of time, space, and culture by increasing the "reach" [16]. With collaboration spanning multiple countries and time zones, one key challenge concerns the difficulties in handling dependencies as they emerge and become pertinent in the collaboration across geographical sites.

Collaboration by its very definition is based upon the notion of dependency in work between multiple people. People collaborate when *"they are mutually dependent in their work and therefore are required to cooperate in order to get the work done"* [28]. Collaborative actors are interdependent in their work, which requires them to articulate their distributed yet individual activities. Articulation work is the extra work required to handle the dependencies that arise in collaborative work [32], and has in prior research been identified as an important aspect of global software development [4]. However, this extra work tends to be neglected [25]. Strategies such as coordination or knowledge practices have been suggested to solve such issues [3, 29]; however, our interest in this paper is to examine how the articulation work involved in handling dependencies is related to practices of routine and standardization.

Initially we wanted to reveal the basic set of dependencies as they unfold in geographical distributed practices; however, examining our empirical observations it was clear that certain dependencies such as location, people, collaborative activities, and artifacts created particular conditions for how the work and collaboration could unfold in practice. More interestingly, however, it became clear that the key mechanisms software developers enacted when handling the challenges that emerge due to the dependencies in practice concerned standardization and routine. Therefore, the research question investigated in this paper concerns how the mechanisms of routine and standardization were enacted in practice by software developers when overcoming the dependencies that constituted global software development practices.

In this paper we zoom in and explore ethnographically which dependencies are constitutive of the globally distributed work practices within software development. In addition, we investigate how dispersed software developers handle and deal with dependencies in their work and, in particular, the role of standardization and routine. As an empirical case we chose to study global Scrum practices as they emerge between two geographical sites in Denmark and India. What makes this an excellent case to study dependencies is that the project was divided equally between developers at both sites and entailed many diverse types of dependencies, which the participants had to deal with on a daily basis. We had the unique opportunity to follow the work practices between the two sites in detail over a period of 14 days, where one of us observed the work from the site in Denmark while the other observed the work from the Indian location, allowing us access to a global view of the collaborative setup [27]. By exploring these work practices we are able to create a rich understanding of the work as it emerged from the data, while zooming in on the strategies for how the geographical distributed partners succeeded in reducing the effort involved in articulation work through strategies of standardization and routine practices.

The main contributions of this paper are as follows: *(i)* an empirical account of the dependencies that are part of the collaborative work in a global software development team, *(ii)* a discussion of the interlinked properties of dependencies, and *(iii)* an explanation of how the practices of standardization and routine are developed and used to manage these dependencies. Interestingly, we found that standardizing the technology needed for the work seemed much harder than standardizing the processes of work.

The paper is structured as follows. First, we present related work on global software development, dependencies, and standardization and routine. Then we present our empirical case, data material, and analysis method. This is followed by a results section presenting our empirical data structured into subsections, each focusing on particular dependencies that constitute the global software development practices. Then we discuss the empirical findings by enfolding previous literature on standardization and routine.

2. DEPENDENCIES IN GLOBAL SOFTWARE DEVELOPMENT

The term *dependencies* refers to coupling among entities or relations, where change in one area might produce certain changes (sometimes unanticipated) in other areas. When a dependency arises in collaborative work, a certain reliance is created, where individual work becomes interlinked with the work of others, and therefore articulation work is required [32]. Thus, collaborative work by its very definition is based on the notion of dependencies, and articulation work is the work involved in handling these dependencies. Previous research on dependencies in distributed software collaboration projects tends to focus on the software dependencies that affect programming activities [e.g. 7, 11, 19] or documents [8]. Software dependencies occur when one part of a program depends on another, and since most larger IT systems are created by multiple people working together, software dependencies are of crucial importance to understanding the often tight coupling between people.

Although software and document dependencies are important, our interest is to zoom out from the concrete software code and documents, and instead focus on the organizational practices of coordination, which are critical to handling the articulation work in global software development. Dependency in work is part of the definition of collaboration, and much research has thus been conducted in terms of figuring out how practitioners involved in collaboration accommodate the challenges of articulation work [5, 25], for example, in terms coordination [16, 18], knowledge management [3, 22], commitment and transparency [31], or awareness [10]. In this paper, we are particularly interested in coordination as a strategy to handle articulation work. Mal-

lone and Crowston define the very process of coordination as *"the act of managing the interdependencies between activities"* [24, p. 90] and suggest that we may further investigate the processes of managing dependencies by "characterizing different kinds of dependencies and identifying the coordination processes that can be used to manage them" [24, p. 91]. In order for us to unravel the coordination activities in global software work, we will need to look at the dependencies as they manifest themselves in everyday work and what strategies are used for managing these.

Coordination is a strategy to handle articulation work [e.g 16, 21, 28] and in earlier studies it has been investigated in different ways: as coordination mechanisms where a protocol for work is embedded within an artifact [29], as coordination by avoidance [21], or as the difference between segregation and standardization [16]. Segregation or avoidance are both strategies where the aim is to keep work separated and reduce connections within the work, thus reducing the complexity of coordination. As a strategy this has been applied in global software development, where practices of decomposing and recomposing have been identified [18], or in terms of minimizing interaction across sites [20]. In contrast, the strategy of standardization is quite different; instead of trying to divide the work into smaller pieces, thus reducing the relations, standardization seeks to keep the relations within the work but instead create the same (or at least similar) conditions for the collaboration across people. In global software development one of the challenges is to create standardization of practices across multiple heterogeneous sites, since the basic conditions for collaboration are dependent on the geographical site where the people are physically located. The world is not flat [35].

Standardization has often been conceptualized as top-down imposed processes where practitioners are forced or disciplined into working in certain ways guided by the categorization schemes embedded within the technology [1, 33]. However, recent studies on standardizations in practice have shown that standardizations are not stabilized and predetermined entities but instead malleable and negotiated [6], and thus standardization from a practice perspective [15] comprises incomplete and co-constructed practices, where people enact and make the standards work for them in practice [13].

While standardization is a difficult strategy to employ in global work, one of the interesting aspects we found in our data was that this was the preferred strategy of the practitioners, and thus we wanted to investigate why that is and how they manage to deploy the standardization strategy as a general approach to reduce the complexity of articulation work. So our interest is to see how standardization is achieved as a collective and emergent accomplishment [26] where the various dependencies, which affect the collaborative engagement, are coming into place.

3. METHOD

To investigate the enactment of routine and standardization in global software development practice, we examined the empirical observations from our workplace study [23], focusing on the collaborative practices that arose in a global software development team distributed across Denmark and India. What makes this approach particularly applicable for such a study is that we were able to experience the practices as they unfolded rather than forcing a particular theoretical conceptualization on our data. For two weeks we observed the work practices simultaneously from two geographical locations, one observer in Denmark and one in India, collecting data material about their work practices. We also interviewed 12 employees in total.

After the empirical observation, all notes were aligned and the interviews were transcribed. Since the study was designed with one researcher being in India while another was in Denmark, the first part of the analysis was zooming in on the observed practices from each location. To analyze the data, each researcher first went through their own notes, conducted within-case analysis [12], and annotated the dependencies that began to emerge from the data material. We used a grounded-theory-inspired approach [17] where candidates for dependencies emerged from the data rather than applying predefined theoretical categories from the literature. Following the within-case analysis we began to compare the data across the cases by conducting cross-case analysis [12]. This work was done through a shared document within which we identified important actors, activities, and technologies and the relations and associations between them. This approach allowed us to take a broad perspective on the data material, from which we believe we were able to identify many of the dependencies that existed in the work during the observation period.

During our data analysis, we created a dependency graph in which we tried to visualize the connections between observed dependencies. However, we quickly saw, as this graph grew in size, that the dependencies we had observed were all somehow linked in a much larger structure encompassing the whole observation period. Figure 1 shows a small excerpt of our dependency graph.

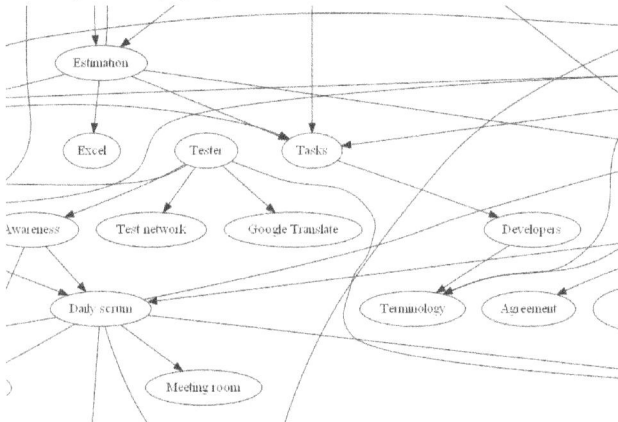

Figure 1: An excerpt of the dependency graph generated from our data material.

Despite our efforts to learn about individual or small clusters of dependencies through a dependency graph visualization, we saw how a myriad of dependencies were linked in much larger structures, and while we could pick and examine one, its meaning and effects were tightly linked to other such dependencies.

While the initial focus concerned the dependencies, as the analysis proceeded and empirical write-ups and thick descriptions were made, it became clear that the important finding of the data was not simply in the descriptions of the dependencies. Instead it became clear that the main interesting findings, which emerged in different ways and places from the data, concerned how mechanisms of standardiza-

tion and routine were enacted. Therefore, in an iterative process of redefining focus and stabilizing the empirical narrative, two main contributions appeared: 1) an empirical account of the dependencies that constitute the global software development practices, 2) the role and practices by which standardization and routine are enacted to handle the complexities of the global work.

3.1 The Case

The organizational setup was an outsourcing setup between a Danish software vendor (DKSoft) working out of Denmark and L&T Infotech, a large Indian outsource specialist working out of India. While two people from L&T Infotech had been temporarily relocated to work in Denmark, most of the collaboration was mediated through technology. The IT system being developed was a financial software system for the Scandinavian market, and it had been worked on for just over a year when we visited. The global work was organized by following the Scrum methodology from the beginning of the project [30]. The decision to apply the Scrum methodology was chosen by the Danish company, as the project was large and targeted the whole Scandinavian market. Given this complexity, the Danish project management estimated that it would be impossible to define requirements up front and opted for an iterative development approach. Additionally, they had prior positive experiences following the Scrum methodology on other projects. The Indian outsourcing company had trained their staff in the execution of Scrum precisely to be able to work with Scandinavian vendors.

The Scrum team we followed was distributed across both Denmark and India. In Denmark, the Scrum master, product owner, and test lead were sitting along two Indian developers that had been temporarily relocated to Denmark. In India, the team consisted of two front-end developers, two back-end developers, and one tester. All but one of the Indian Scrum team members had previously been to Denmark to work for about half a year at the Danish site. The team followed the Scrum process with daily meetings, estimations meetings, sprint planning, demonstration meetings, and sprint retrospective. All meetings with the exception of the demonstration meeting were conducted using videoconferencing with participants from both locations.

The empirical data were collected in the period between Aug 12 2013 and Aug 23 2013 , where one researcher visited L&T Infotech in Mumbai, while another researcher visited DKSoft in Ballerup. In total, 36 hours were spent on observations, where 15 were in DKSoft and 21 in L&T Infotech. Observations included meetings, individuals working, the environment in general, as well as the workspace arrangements, etc. Twelve interviews were conducted with team members in both Denmark and India. Each interview on average lasted about 30 minutes and was later transcribed. In total, we interviewed five team members in India (four developers and one tester) and seven team members in Denmark (the project manager, product owner, test manager, Scrum master, a colleague in charge of the infrastructure, and two temporarily onshore Indian developers).

All the data material was collected and shared across the authors and discussed both during data collection (using Skype) as well as after through the iterative writing process, creating diverse, thick descriptions and cut-down narratives based on the data material.

4. DEPENDENCIES IN A GLOBAL SPRINT

While presenting our empirical data, we will be focusing on the diverse sets of dependencies that we observed during the two-week period of close collaboration between the two sites. We ended up structuring our main findings within four different perspectives, which became evident as our data analysis progressed: the locations, the people, the collaborative activities, and the artifacts. What makes each of these perspectives interesting for our analysis is that they each form a dependency set that is constitutive for the global software development practice. We label these perspectives as "dependencies" as they each, in different ways, interlink the practices while providing certain conditions for how the collaboration could unfold. Dependency concerns a coupling or relation between multiple entities, where change in one entity produces ripple effects in other entities. Coupling and reliance do not appear only in between people; certain other entities, such as the location where one works, create particular conditions for the collaboration, and as such a dependency in the work. It does matter whether the developer who is normally located in Mumbai is temporarily moved to work in Denmark. It creates certain conditions for how the work can be executed in practice. Following this perspective, we identified four different types of dependencies that shaped the work in the empirical case. Furthermore, we experienced instances where exceptions occurred, and finally, we observed how dependencies existed as interlinked entities. Below we zoom in on each of these. For each subsection, we bring the empirical account across the geographical sites we investigated.

4.1 Locations Dependencies

When we first visited the L&T Infotech offices we encountered a large, modern office building, which provided a quite different experience than the outside traffic, noise, and smells of the Mumbai city and its large highways running nearby. The building that housed the L&T Infotech offices was located within a large IT park with several other large, brand-new buildings. In the seven-story building, L&T Infotech occupied two floors. Several departments, some open and some closed off by frosted glass walls, were located side-by-side. They were only accessible after passing through a front gate guarded by three security guards. In all the departments, signs hanging from the ceiling indicated which client they were working for.

The department we were visiting was located at the centre of the floor, closed off by two access-card-operated doors. The security was quite high since DKSoft, the company they work with, develops financial software. The department hosted around 35 people, all working on projects for DKSoft. The people were divided into approximately six teams, supervised by two project managers and one delivery manager. The team we observed consisted of five software developers. Due to the time difference between Denmark and India (3.5 hours), the team usually met in between 10:30 and 11:00 AM to have more overlapping working hours with the Danish team. The department had been decorated to match the Danish company's visual identity; paper flags with the name of the company were scattered throughout the workspace, and the values and mission statement of the Danish company had been printed on large posters that were placed at the entrance to the department. These statements, however, had been modified from the original company's values and missions to fit with the Indian company. On the wall, a Danish and an Indian clock hung next to each other, but both had stopped working.

Around the same time in Denmark, we also entered the DKSoft office building, located in a suburb outside of Copenhagen together with several other IT companies. In front of the parking space of the office were three flagpoles with flags displaying DKSoft's logo. The office sign showed the same logo of DKSoft as well as two smaller logos of subsidiary companies. The three-story office building seemingly hosted many employees – not unexpected for one of the biggest IT solution providers in the banking sector. On the way to the office landscape where the team we observed worked, turnstiles prevented non-employees from passing. In order to enter, each day a temporary pass was handed to the observer at DKSoft. Additionally, any visitor had to be accompanied by one of the local employees while going through the turnstiles. This could not be one of the temporary onshore Indian developers.

The seven members of the project team located in Denmark were seated at two neighbouring islands of desks with a walkway in between, separated only by low dividers. Within the same open office space, about six more of these "desk islands" were located. Two temporarily relocated Indian developers were sitting on one side, while the Danish developers sat together with the product owner and project manager at the other island. The product owner later explained that this setup grew organically as the Indian developers were usually there for shorter periods of time. In contrast to the offices at L&T Infotech, there was no decoration revealing that part of the development team was working at L&T Infotech, except for an Indian gift from one of the Indian developers who temporarily worked onshore. Some stickers on a small cabinet revealed which project the team was working on.

We view the locations and the structure of the locations as forms of dependencies, since each geographical site produces certain conditions for how the work can be executed. For example, when the office in India is located in the heavy traffic in Mumbai, it produces particular conditions for the time it takes to move around in the city, and what time the developers can be at work in the morning and leave in the evening. Travelling in heavy traffic in a large metropolis in India is not an easy task, which means that developers either follow a schedule of company transportation or come in late and thus also stay late to accommodate the traffic. The software developer is dependent on the traffic in terms of making it to work. Turning to the Danish location, it is clear that the traffic is not an issue in the same way. The differences in travelling in traffic at the two different locations thus place particular conditions not only on the people having to make the travel, but also on the collaboration as a whole, as meetings and communication have to be planned around the times at which people can be present in the office. At the Danish offices, however, the office layout creates certain conditions for the work. Being temporarily collocated in the same office, it is possible for the visiting developers to engage with the DKSoft developers. However, a certain distance between the regular and the temporary developers still exists by having them dispersed across different desk islands.

Location dependencies include diverse sets of aspects such as security and office design, and our point here is that it does matter where people's physical bodies are located in terms of what makes the conditions for the global work. Working remotely does not limit the impact of where we are and how this shapes the kind of collaborative engagement we can commit to.

4.2 People Dependencies

The team working on the project we observed was dispersed across two locations, seven members at DKSoft in Denmark and five members at L&T Infotech in India. In Denmark, the seven members took on the role of Scrum master, product owner (one primary and one assistant), team lead, test manager, and developer (one lead and one general). All were permanently located at DKSoft, except the two Indian developers who were temporarily relocated there for six months. In India, the members took on the role of user interface (UI) developer (two members), back-end developer (two members), and one tester. Although the main organizational activities were taken care of in Denmark by the Scrum master and product owner, development on the project occurred from both sites as a collaborative process. This team thus provided an excellent case to study dependencies in closely coupled work across geographical distances.

The whole team relied heavily on the knowledge about the client and the system they were developing, which was organized by the product owner in the team. The product owner represents the client stakeholder – in this case a large Scandinavian financial company – and holds regular meetings with this client. He is thus the close link between the development team and the client. The product owner was responsible for the product backlog, and so the development process depended greatly on his decisions.

The developers also depended on the product owner for the development process. With the product owner being the client stakeholder, he was the person in the team who knew most about these business processes. The developers at L&T Infotech thus needed him for explanation of these different processes.

During the course of the project, DKSoft intended to have all developers from L&T Infotech come to Denmark for a 6-month period. This was handled by having two developers at a time in Denmark. During our observations, these two developers were the lead developer and a UI developer. The motivation for this was clear; if the L&T Infotech developers had been to DKSoft, they would get to know much more about the team in Denmark and how work was organized. When returning to India to work, these developers would not only have a better understanding of how people worked in Denmark, but they would also have developed more personal relationships with the Danish team – giving a more coherent feeling of "team spirit" despite the fact that the team was based in two different companies.

While the relocation of the lead developer from L&T Infotech was temporary, the Scrum master told us that he preferred to keep the lead developer in Denmark as long as possible because they feared that another person could not do the job as well. When asked what they would do when he left for India again, the Scrum master answered, *"We might have to tie him to the table ... "*. With team members from both sites relying heavily on his role as boundary spanner and keeping the collaboration working, they were very dependent on his presence at the Danish site. The

L&T Infotech developers depended on him for their daily development work, while the Danish team relied on him as a boundary spanner between the Indian developers and the Danish team. His role in the project thus had many sides: He was the most experienced programmer from India and thus the natural contact person for questions regarding implementation, he was responsible for hand-picking team members from the Indian outsource company to work on the project, and he maintained continuous communication with the developers in the team.

People dependencies arise in the work practices where different people have diverse sets of knowledge, both in terms of knowledge about the content, process, and the business, as well as knowledge about technologies and the system under construction. What is particularly interesting in this perspective is that part of what makes the global software development team function is dependent upon the practice by which team members are hand-picked across distance, and the special competences of boundary spanners to be able to solve such a task. Also interesting is that people dependencies are not simply one-to-one relations, but instead a multiplicity of relations across people, their roles, and work tasks. Understanding the perspective of people in terms of people dependencies thus points to interlinked practices across diverse subgroups spanning geography, roles, and responsibilities.

4.3 Collaborative Dependencies

While the two preceding sections focus on the location and people dependencies, this subsection zooms in on the collaborative dependencies of the software developers. These dependencies emerged and became observable particularly during the diverse types of meetings (collocated as well as across sites) the team engaged in.

The team we observed used Scrum as their development methodology. Scrum puts forward a number of meetings and processes that should be followed throughout a development process. We observed that some of these processes and meetings were followed in the collaboration and had eventually become routines. These routines also helped integrate new team members into the project. One of the developers from L&T Infotech who had just worked with the team for two sprints explained it as follows:

"We have a daily Scrum meeting every day and we do estimation and we know that in the QC [software requirements management tool] looking at the tasks we know the remaining estimated hours and we have to finish within that time frame. So everything is written within the system, and if you follow the system, you can finish the tasks on time." (Interview, developer, India, 21/08/2013)

During our observations, we observed 10 daily Scrum meetings, two estimation meetings for the estimation of tasks for an upcoming sprint, and the demonstration meeting towards the end of the sprint. These meetings were particularly interesting as they rendered the dependencies between the different sites quite visible.

The daily Scrum meetings were executed as short 15-minute meetings and were attended by the developers and testers from DKSoft and L&T Infotech. In most cases, the product owner also took part in the meeting. In the meetings, each participant took turns explaining the progress of work. Following the same routine, the Danish and Indian team went to their respective videoconferencing rooms at the same time each day – 9:45 AM Danish time / 1:15 PM India time. The same developers at L&T Infotech always prepared the video equipment and made the call to the Danish site.

The meetings proceeded with each present meeting participant taking turns explaining what she had been working on, what she was going to work on, and mentioning any problems that she had experienced. The turn order was not defined and was settled by whoever took initiative to start. The Danish Scrum mater was responsible for deducting hours from the tasks that had been worked on to reflect their new status. At one meeting, for example, an L&T Infotech developer explained that he had been working on the document handling user story and that the Scrum master could deduct 5 hours from that task. The Scrum master then reduced the number of remaining hours on that task from 7 to 2. With the screen shared to the Indian site, this process was visible for the whole team.

The Scrum meetings were usually finished within the 15 allocated minutes. In a few instances, the meetings went over time due to either starting late (as a consequence of change of meeting rooms at the Danish site) or due to discussions about certain issues. In these cases, another team at the Indian site would knock on the door of the meeting room and the meeting was quickly wrapped up. However, in Denmark the room booking system did not allow booking rooms for 15 minutes, so they were always booked for 30 minutes, but only used for 15.

While the daily Scrum meetings were conducted with both the Danish and the Indian parts of the team present, the demonstration meeting at the end of the sprint was deliberately held with the Danish team only. During the demonstration meeting, the developers in the Scrum team demonstrated the features they had implemented in the sprint, and the product owner would then accept or reject the feature. Such a setup, however, would require a different technological setup, as the test environment where the product being developed was running was located on a Danish internal network. Giving access to the Indian team for them to demonstrate what they had implemented would require a virtual private network (VPN) connection from India to Denmark. Instead, the developers at the Danish site handled demonstrating all the features, even those implemented in India. Due to the daily meetings and the lead developer keeping daily contact with the Indian team, the developers in Denmark were quite aware of the features implemented in India and therefore capable of demonstrating them.

One particularly interesting meeting was held each afternoon. By the end of each working day in India, around 3:30 PM Danish time / 6:45 PM India time, the lead developer located in Denmark contacted the development team in India over instant messaging to get feedback on their progress and resolve any issues they might have when meeting for work the next day. These meetings were not a part of the traditional Scrum methodology, however, and they resembled that of the daily meeting in content. The developers at L&T Infotech were given the opportunity to explain their work and discuss any potential issues. One of the Indian developers explained this process as the following:

"We don't have a Scrum board because our team lead is not sitting here... But then, our team lead communicates with us every now and then in the communicator. So we update the daily status before we go – that we have done this, we have done that – even before the daily Scrum meeting." (Interview, developer, India, 21/08/2013)

These meetings were routinely handled and had thus become a natural part of the development process. These procedures had all become routines, and they helped the Danish team gain awareness of the work in India and made sure that the people at L&T Infotech did not have unresolved questions before they went home.

Collaborative dependencies arise in the everyday work when different people are interdependent in the actual work. These dependencies become particularly visible during meetings where distributed actors are brought together. However, they also arise in the arrangement and structure of the work – in this case the iterations of the project in sprints.

4.4 Artifactual Dependencies

We have now discussed the work environment, the team, the task, and the collaborative activities. However, an important part of the closely coupled work also concerns the diverse set of artifacts that the participants use in making their collaboration work. Interestingly, the absence of particular artifacts also places certain constraints on the developers. We will look into how the participants managed to organize their work in particular ways to accommodate limitations of technology.

The team relied heavily on the technical infrastructure for their work. Most common software engineering tools were used to develop the product: integrated development environments for coding, source control management for managing code, and test environments for testing. For project management, an integrated task-tracking tool was used. SAP was used for noting working hours and the team communicated using email, telephone, instant messaging, and videoconferencing.

In order to let daily Scrum meetings take place in a global context, dedicated videoconferencing rooms were used, equipped so that setting up bidirectional communication was as effortless as possible. The conference rooms used on both sides had a meeting table with a central microphone and surrounding chairs. Mounted to the wall were two screens, one to display the video feed of the team on the other side, as well as a smaller video feed of themselves, and another to display a shared screen. The Scrum master was the only one to bring along a laptop, as it was his screen that was shared with the Indian team.

Besides the video conferencing equipment, the Application Lifecycle Management (ALM) tool by HP usually open on the Scrum master's laptop was the central artifact used during global Scrum meetings. It was used to provide an overview of and to update the state of user stories, for example, to reduce the amount of expected hours to work on certain tasks. In order to see the screen shared by the Scrum master in India, one of the Indian developers had to log into the VPN prior to the meeting to set up the screen sharing. Only the Scrum master made changes to the ALM visible on the shared screen as the other developers updated the team on their progress.

The back-end developers used business process modeling notation (BPMN) – a modeling notation used for specifying business processes – to develop the core infrastructure of the product. On an artifact level, the project used BPMN to model their back-end. BPMN is used to model business processes using a graph-like notation. The back-end developers in India modelled the business workflows of the application as graphs, and these graphs, in turn, were used to generate code for the back end.

Arguably, any modelling or programming language is a form of standardization, as it equips programmers with a structured way to construct software and a common way to talk about such implementations. However, we argue, that BPMN adds to this standardization. With the abstraction towards actual business processes that BPMN adds, we observed how it equipped the back-end developers with a language that could be used to talk with the domain knowledge experts. We thus claim that the use of BPMN provided a form of standardization highly suitable for the development of such business-logical applications.

The project followed an agile approach in which the development process was split into four-week iterations during which a fixed workload of features were selected for implementation. Within Scrum these iterations are called "sprints." The sprint we observed lasted 4 weeks and comprised 10 user stories describing certain features that needed to be implemented. Examples of user stories from the project include integrating scanning documents into the business process, providing download links to digital contracts, and implementing "fast track" processes for certain merchants. Depending on the assessed complexity of the user stories, more or less can be taken up into a sprint. The success of a sprint depends on the developers actually finishing them.

Artifactual dependencies concern situations where technology is involved, such as videoconferencing, task-tracking software, communication software, and networks. The division of work into user stories also constitutes an artifactual dependency as these were the objects dictating work in the team.

4.5 Exception Handling

The four previous sections concerning sets of location dependencies, people dependencies, collaborative dependencies, and artifact dependencies all describe situations where work goes as expected. However, there are several situations where exceptions occur, and it is critical to investigate what happens in these situations in terms of dependencies and how these are organized.

Despite the routine manner in which the daily Scrum meetings were executed, we observed different situations were exceptions occurred. The room for the daily meeting was booked for the Indian team for use from 1:15 PM to 1:30 PM each day. The Danes switched rooms according to availability. They used a room booking system to book rooms; however, in several instances, problems with this booking caused a delay in the daily meeting as the Danes had to find an available room. In addition, sometimes some of the Danes showed up on time for the meeting while others were late, as they did not check themselves beforehand which room had been booked for the meeting. Whether people showed up late or not, the meeting always started once the videoconferencing was set up. We observed this on several occasions where the Indian team was on time, as was the Danish Scrum master at the other end, but the rest of the Danish team was still missing. The meeting would be initi-

ated and the rest of the Danish team would show up after a few minutes.

The technology used to facilitate the daily meetings also caused exceptions. Take the following observation, for example, from the preparation of a daily Scrum meeting where a virtual desktop connection needed to be made from a computer in the Indian videoconferencing room to a Danish computer.

"U1 is sick today, so U2 heads for the meeting room to start the video equipment and the projector. He's clearly not as experienced doing that so it is taking longer than when U1 is doing it. He also doesn't have a login to the VPC so he has B1 establish a virtual private network (VPN) connection after which B2 logs in with her account on the VPC." (Observation notes, India, 20/08/2013)

Usually, the same developer from L&T Infotech (U1) would prepare the videoconferencing equipment and make the call to the Danish site. When he was on holiday one day, another person (U2) had to perform this work. Setting up the video and the shared workspace took significantly longer and also forced the person to seek help with login to a virtual PC.

Interestingly, company rules and regulation regarding connectivity and firewalls created particular technical constraints for the development team, forcing them to organize their work in particular ways. As the testing environment was located in Denmark – and the team at L&T Infotech did not have access to this environment over the network – they were forced to run a similar setup on their own computers. This setup consisted of a virtual machine running Linux and the web-server software that the product was developed for. The setup was so heavy on computer power that the team – for this project – had been given new, powerful computers, as opposed to other teams in the company working on other projects. Despite this investment, the developers at L&T Infotech had to reboot this test setup on a daily basis. This process took between 10 and 15 minutes and caused work to halt for that duration. The developers would usually go for a coffee if this happened.

Another example of exception handling became clear when the Scrum master explained the team's testing procedure. Interestingly, the testing and fixing of bugs in the product was done one sprint behind. The Scrum master explained it as follows:

"Yeah, of course optimally we would like to have everything well tested before the end of the sprint so that at least very few defects are found in the next sprint. But we haven't really, that's our goal, but we haven't really succeeded because the implementation just is rarely finished before very close before the end of the sprint. So then there is not enough time to test." (Interview, Scrum master, Denmark, 23/08/2013)

Despite their intention to deliver a working and well-tested version of the product after each sprint, as the implementation was not finished until the very end of the sprint, the testing was left for the next sprint. This process caused some problems, as errors that emerged were to be resolved quickly because the product of the sprint, when it was introduced, had already been marked as done. In one specific case, the two developers at L&T Infotech stayed until midnight to fix an error that was introduced in a previous sprint.

4.6 Sets of Dependencies

We have now presented four sets of dependencies that created certain conditions for how the global software development collaboration was executed and organized. In addition, we looked into the practices by which the developers handled exceptions and unforeseen challenges. The four sets of dependencies were location dependencies, people dependencies, collaborative dependencies, and artifactual dependencies. While this overall categorization of dependencies helps us understand what organizational dependencies in global software development comprise, one important empirical observation remains, namely the interlinked nature of dependencies.

Analyzing our data iteratively, and creating diverse sets of rich descriptions, we realized that even though we were able to label specific dependencies, several categorizations could be applied to a dependency. Therefore, we decided to think in terms of "sets of dependencies" rather than dependencies as singular causal relations. Furthermore, we saw how one set of dependencies (e.g. people dependencies) was tightly linked to others (e.g. collaborative dependencies). This leads us to suggest that dependencies in global software development have an interlinked structure, where it is not easy to pick apart and set boundaries for what is part of and what is outside of the particular dependency, for example, what is technical and what is social. We might, for example, talk about the development process of a particular artifact, such as a user story, and how it has multiple dependencies embedded in the very task: coupling the IT system under development, the technical architecture, the work across developers, and other user stories. But at the same time each user story also has close connections with other artifacts – for example, the range of documents that makes the development project, such as requirement specification or test documents [8]. To handle all these dependencies, a range of tools such as development environments, test setups, and communication tools are being included in the collaborative activities. However, what is more surprising is how participants' hardware and technical infrastructure, which is related to the developer's location dependencies as well as the artifactual dependencies, place particular conditions for how the participants can manage and handle their work, for example, as we saw in the need for powerful computers and the technical setup for demonstration meetings, which placed the participants in a situation where developers located in India could not fully participate. How the technical infrastructure and the hardware devices impact the conditions for collaboration in this particular case was due to the location dependencies in the diverse structure across the different geographical sites. The technical infrastructure locally thus created particular conditions for how the participants could manage to handle and organize their work according to the set of location and artifactual dependencies they need to accommodate.

Similarly, we may find that one particular set of dependencies gives rise other sets of dependencies. As such, the structure across the sets of dependencies resembles that of the documentscape [8]. The documentscape refers to the dynamic interlinked ensemble of project documents in global software development practices between developers located in various locations. It stipulates that while we might zoom in on one single document, the meaning of the document is embedded within the location of the document within the

Category	Features
Location Dependencies	External environment; office design; office security; time zone
People Dependencies	Roles; responsibilities; knowledge
Collaborative Dependencies	Meetings; turn taking; discussions
Artifactual Dependencies	Business process modelling notation; VPN; video conferencing setups; test environment; user stories

Table 1: Categorization of dependencies

documentscape. We may also look at a single dependency; however, its meaning is embedded within the network of dependencies across all sets of dependencies. While we may look at a dependency and label it according to different sets of dependencies, each dependency plays a role in a larger set of interlinked dependencies where the boundaries are not easily defined.

Despite the interlinked nature of dependencies, we may still talk in terms of sets of dependencies. As our analytical cut-downs in the data material demonstrate, we found four important sets of dependencies: location dependencies, people dependencies, collaborative dependencies, and artifactual dependencies. Location dependencies entail the multiplicity of dependencies that are related to the geographical site of the software developers. This includes the external society within which the location is placed, as well as the inner office environment design and the conditions this creates for the collaboration. People dependencies entail the roles, responsibility, and specific knowledge the collaborative actors have and use in the work together. This includes knowledge about competences, knowledge about technologies, as well as knowledge about the business in which the system is being created. Collaborative dependencies in particular become observable in situations where multiple people engage in a common practice – in most cases in meetings, but also outside of meetings. The meetings can take many different forms and shapes and be organized differently. Some meetings involve participants from both locations (e.g. daily stand-up meetings), while others are location specific (e.g. demonstration meeting). Artifactual dependencies are pertinent at all times, since technology is what makes it possible for the dispersed developers to collaborate and interact with the same coding environment, which serves as the main technical infrastructure supporting the work. However, as we have also shown, the artifactual dependencies also comprise other important artifacts such as the user stories, the BPMN notation, the VPN connection, and the video equipment, which all took part in linking and organizing the work and connections between the developers. It is important to notice that in practice these sets of dependencies are not singular entities, but instead function as multiplicities that connect and interrelate across all types of dependencies. Table 1 summarizes the four sets of dependencies and their characteristics.

5. STANDARDIZATION & ROUTINE

Having conceptualized the four main categories of dependencies that emerged in our data, the next question concerns how the developers managed to collaborate despite the diverse set of dependencies and how these each brought about an increasingly complex work arrangement. Looking across the categories of dependencies, we found a repeating pattern in the work regarding the participants' ability to continuously create and apply standardization as a mechanism to reduce complexity. There were standardizations in terms of meeting structure and time for conducting meetings. There were standardizations in terms of the team at L&T Infotech arriving late in the morning to accommodate the time difference between the sites. There were standardizations in terms of people's roles and knowledge, and to some extent there were standardizations in terms of artifacts such as user stories or the use of the BPMN notation form.

What is interesting about how the strategy of standardization was applied by the practitioners in the empirical case was that it did not arrive as a top-down forced structure on the work. Instead, it emerged over time as the practitioners made the methodology of Scrum into a practice fitting their work. It was not that the developers did not follow the methodology; our point here is that they had aligned the methodology with their practices in the global work. In this way, the standardization of when, where, and how to meet supported the developers in organizing their work, taking into account the different sets of dependencies, but at the same time the standardization had a transformative effect on the practice [13], as it was dynamically developed. Engaging with the standardized process of Scrum was not a process by which the developers simply followed Scrum in a scripted manner. Instead, they adjusted and recreated the process, making it fit their practices while still taking into account the conditions for collaboration created by the location and artifactual dependencies. So when the Indian developers could not participate in the demonstration meeting due to the lack of a standardized technical setup across sites – the artifactual dependencies not letting them participate – they adjusted the work accordingly and found other ways to demonstrate the requirements developed at L&T Infotech. In this way, the standardization was a transformative practice where processes and technologies were being accommodated, and thus standardization was incomplete initially. What is also fascinating with this example is that while we expected that standardization across the technical platforms would be easy to create (e.g. having access to the same tools and applications etc.), this turned out to be the most challenging area, where local artifactual dependencies place certain constraining conditions on the collaboration.

We observed how the daily meetings were executed in a routine manner, giving rise to frequent interaction across sites. However, whereas the team at L&T Infotech always had the same meeting room booked for their meetings, the team at DKSoft had a different meeting room with videoconferencing equipment booked on a day-to-day basis. This caused several situations where people from DKSoft arrived a bit late since they first arrived at the wrong meeting room prior to finding out the designated meeting room for that day – in other words, the complexities of relation work increased [2, 9]. This lack of standardization in terms of rooms for daily meetings thus created extra challenges – not only for the developers at the Danish location, but also for the developers at the location in Mumbai, since they had to wait for the videoconferencing to be started from the remote location. In contrast, the room in Mumbai never changed, and as such the location dependencies did create different types of conditions for the work, both locally and in the distributed situation. However, not only did the location constraints affect the daily meetings, we also observed an exception-handling situation where the developer who was normally in charge of setting up the VPN connection was not present. Here it turned out that the developer who wanted to set up the equipment instead did not have a VPN login, and extra work was required to locate a person with a VPN login before the daily meeting could take place. The complexities of managing the dependencies – in this case the amount of relation work needed to establish a connection between the two sites – increased.

What also becomes obvious in the example above is the role of routine [14]. For each activity the developers engage in, both locally and in between the two sites, the more frequent the activity, the more aligned and transformed their common practice becomes. Routine is the practice by which the developers turn standardization strategies into concrete activities that support their practice. It is through the enactment of routine behavior in daily interaction that the developers are able to reduce the effort required for articulation work and to spend more time on the actual project they are developing. We observed routines as repeating patterns of coordination employed to handle the complexities of the diverse set of dependencies. Routines, as opposed to strategies, exist only through the actual enactment and the different activities [14]. Referring to the concepts of plans and situated actions [34], standardization constitutes the plan whereas the routine is embedded within the situated action. In our case it was clear that the routinized behaviors were mostly connected to the various types of meeting activities in the distributed team, as in the example where the developers explain why they have an additional meeting at the Danish location to ensure that the team at the Indian site is kept up to date. They explained how this meeting was a replacement of the Scrum board, and how this practice supported their work.

Other artifactual dependencies gave rise to exception handling. The lack of standardization regarding access to the test network required the developers at L&T Infotech to be equipped with much more powerful computers than the rest of the employees. The restrictions caused by firewalls and the generally slow bandwidth out from India forced the developers to have a local version of the testing environment running, which was only possible on these more powerful computers. While it was not possible to standardize the technical connectivity across the geographical sites due to firewall, bandwidth, and privacy issues, the developers created other routine behaviors in terms of testing practice, making it possible for them to collaborate despite the technical constraints.

Standardization and routine did not solve all issues of dependencies. Our data clearly demonstrated that a repeating pattern across sprints was the testing that was pushed back to the next sprint, often causing the developers at L&T Infotech to work overtime. Here it is important to notice that working late at the Mumbai location means evening and late evening, and since this occurred quite often it clearly impacted the work at L&T Infotech. The reason for the delay was that the developers were implementing source code until the very last minute, not leaving time for the testers to reach their goal within the pre-allocated time of the sprint. The developers depend on the tester to report defects. However, the tester cannot begin until the developers have delivered the source code. The product owner in the end depends on the developers to fix the defects detected by the tester. All of this is organized through the bug report artifact. This made the activity of testing a closely coupled activity requiring closely coupled coordination. No routine or standardization was able to solve this activity, which meant that major defects in the software sometimes occurred in subsequent sprints, forcing the team to work even later, solving tasks from the last sprint while neglecting their tasks for the current sprint.

In summary, in many cases the practitioners applied standardization as a strategy to handle the complexity evolving from heterogeneous locations, people, and artifacts, and in most cases it worked well. However, there were also situations where standardization did not work – and surprisingly this was largely in the technical infrastructure and hardware across the sites. This lack of standardization did increase the complexity of including participants equally in, for example, the demonstration meeting, and also in terms of having enough machine power to execute the work. It was clear that standardization made it possible for the participants to reduce their effort required to organize their collaboration, making it possible to focus on the task ahead. However, at the same time the extra standardization also required work – articulation work – and as such the standardization strategy was not "free". Standardization is a known strategy to handle coordination [16]; however, what was interesting in our study was how the standardization process made it possible for the participants to handle and deal with many complexities that emerged from the diverse set of dependencies. On the other hand, issues of solving the closely coupled task of testing remained. Similar to how specific artifacts reduce the complexities of articulation work [29], knowing the standardization practices in a routine manner made it possible for the participants to reduce time spent on articulation work and instead made them focus on the content of the development project.

6. CONCLUSION

In the very definition of collaboration exists the notion of dependencies in work. However, dependencies as pertinent in collaborative work might take different forms and shapes. In this paper, we reported on an ethnographic study of global software work executed across two sites – Denmark and India – zooming in on what makes the pertinent dependencies in such work. We observed how various types of dependencies constitutive of the collaborative practice across the developers included location dependencies, people dependencies, collaborative dependencies, and artifactual dependencies. In addition, we saw how the strategies of standardization form a repetitive pattern in how the dependencies were managed across sites, and in particular how routine in the work was crucial for making the collaboration function. Based on our observations, this paper puts forward three main contributions: (i) Global software development is based on a multiplicity of dependencies that fall into four broad categories: location, people, collaboration, and artifactual. Using these categories, we can start to examine more carefully how dependencies constitute global work, and in particular point to situations where dependencies are challenging for the collaboration. (ii) Dependencies in global software development are not singular entities, but instead exist as one multiplicity of interlinked practices, which makes it difficult to clearly define and distinguish the borders between the dependencies. (iii) Standardization and routine can be used as specific coordination mechanisms to handle dependencies, thus reducing the complexity of the associated articulation work. However, surprisingly, our data suggest that it is more difficult to standardize the artifactual dependencies (e.g. hardware and software practices) across geographical sites, compared to standardizing the organizational practices such as user stories, roles and responsibility, or daily meetings.

7. ACKNOWLEDGEMENTS

This research was conducted in collaboration with L&T Infotech, both in terms of funding as well as in terms of access to the empirical sites. In particular, we would like to mention the efforts and work of Sarbajit Deb (Vice President, L&T Infotech, the Nordic Region) and Muthuramalingam P. (Deputy Head, Banking & Financial Services, L&T Infotech, Denmark) in making this research possible. Without such strong connections between industry and academia, we would never have been able to conduct such ethnographic research.

Furthermore, we would like to thank the employees at DKSoft for welcoming us into their company, working with us, and allowing us to follow them during their work. Lastly, we thank Steven Jeuris for his participation and help in the study.

This research has been funded by the Danish Agency for Science, Technology and Innovation under the project "Next Generation Technology for Global Software Development", #10-092313.

References

[1] P. Bjørn and E. Balka. Health care categories have politics too: Unpacking the managerial agendas of electronic triage systems. In *ECSCW 2007*, pages 371–390. Springer London, 2007.

[2] P. Bjørn and L. R. Christensen. Relation work: Creating socio-technical connections in global engineering. In *ECSCW 2011: Proceedings of the 12th European Conference on Computer Supported Cooperative Work, 24-28 September 2011, Aarhus Denmark*, pages 133–152. Springer London, 2011.

[3] A. Boden, G. Avram, L. Bannon, and V. Wulf. Knowledge management in distributed software development teams - does culture matter? In *Global Software Engineering, 2009. ICGSE 2009. Fourth IEEE International Conference on*, pages 18–27, July 2009.

[4] A. Boden, B. Nett, and V. Wulf. Articulation work in small-scale offshore software development projects. In *Proceedings of the 2008 International Workshop on Cooperative and Human Aspects of Software Engineering*, CHASE '08, pages 21–24, New York, NY, USA, 2008. ACM.

[5] A. Boden, F. Rosswog, G. Stevens, and V. Wulf. Articulation spaces: Bridging the gap between formal and informal coordination. In *Proceedings of the 17th*

ACM Conference on Computer Supported Cooperative Work & Social Computing, CSCW '14, pages 1120–1130, New York, NY, USA, 2014. ACM.

[6] G. C. Bowker and S. L. Star. *Sorting things out : classification and its consequences.* MIT Press, Cambridge, Mass., 1999.

[7] M. Cataldo, M. Bass, J. Herbsleb, and L. Bass. On coordination mechanisms in global software development. In *Global Software Engineering, 2007. ICGSE 2007. Second IEEE International Conference on*, pages 71–80, Aug 2007.

[8] L. R. Christensen and P. Bjørn. Documentscape: Intertextuality, sequentiality & autonomy at work. In *Proceedings of the SIGCHI Conference on Human Factors in Computing Systems*, CHI '14, New York, NY, USA, 2014. ACM.

[9] L. R. Christensen, R. E. Jensen, and P. Bjørn. Creating relation work: Characteristics for local and gloval collaboration. COOP '14. Springer, 2014.

[10] C. de Souza and D. Redmiles. The awareness network, to whom should i display my actions? and, whose actions should i monitor? *Software Engineering, IEEE Transactions on*, 37(3):325–340, May 2011.

[11] C. R. de Souza, S. Quirk, E. Trainer, and D. F. Redmiles. Supporting collaborative software development through the visualization of socio-technical dependencies. In *Proceedings of the 2007 international ACM conference on Supporting group work*, pages 147–156. ACM, 2007.

[12] K. M. Eisenhardt. Building theories from case study research. *The Academy of Management Review*, 14(4):pp. 532–550, 1989.

[13] G. Ellingsen, E. Monteiro, and G. Munkvold. Standardization of work: Co-constructed practice. *The Information Society*, 23(5):309–326, Oct. 2007.

[14] M. S. Feldman and W. J. Orlikowski. Theorizing practice and practicing theory. *Organization Science*, 22(5):1240–1253, 2011.

[15] M. S. Feldman and A. Rafaeli. Organizational routines as sources of connections and understandings. *Journal of Management Studies*, 39(3):309–331, 2002.

[16] E. Gerson. Reach, bracket, and the limits of rationalized coordination: Some challenges for cscw. In *Resources, Co-Evolution and Artifacts*, Computer Supported Cooperative Work, pages 193–220. Springer London, 2008.

[17] B. G. Glaser and A. L. Strauss. *The Discovery of Grounded Theory: Strategies for Qualitative Research.* Aldine de Gruyter, New York, NY, 1967.

[18] R. Grinter. Recomposition: Coordinating a web of software dependencies. *Computer Supported Cooperative Work (CSCW)*, 12(3):297–327, 2003.

[19] J. D. Herbsleb, A. Mockus, T. A. Finholt, and R. E. Grinter. Distance, dependencies, and delay in a global collaboration. In *Proceedings of the 2000 ACM Conference on Computer Supported Cooperative Work*, CSCW '00, pages 319–328, New York, NY, USA, 2000. ACM.

[20] M. Hertzum and J. Pries-Heje. *Is Minimizing Interaction a Solution to Cultural and Maturity Inequality in Offshore Outsourcing?*, pages 77–97. TAPIR Akademisk Forlag, 2011. 2011; 4.

[21] N. Holten Møller and P. Dourish. Coordination by avoidance: Bringing things together and keeping them apart across hospital departments. In *Proceedings of the 16th ACM International Conference on Supporting Group Work*, GROUP '10, pages 65–74, New York, NY, USA, 2010. ACM.

[22] R. E. Jensen and P. Bjørn. Divergence and convergence in global software development: Cultural complexities as social worlds. In *From Research to Practice in the Design of Cooperative Systems: Results and Open Challenges*, pages 123–136. Springer London, 2012.

[23] P. Luff and e. al. *Workplace Studies: Recovering Work Practices and Informing System Design.* Cambridge University Press, 2000.

[24] T. W. Malone and K. Crowston. The interdisciplinary study of coordination. *ACM Comput. Surv.*, 26(1):87–119, Mar. 1994.

[25] S. Matthiessen, P. Bjørn, and L. M. Petersen. "figuring out how to code with the hands of others": Recognizing cultural blind spots in global software development. In *Proceedings The 17th ACM Conference on Computer Supported Cooperative Work*, CSCW '14, New York, NY, USA, 2014. ACM.

[26] T. Meum, E. Monteiro, and G. Ellingsen. The pendulum of standardization. In *ECSCW 2011: Proceedings of the 12th European Conference on Computer Supported Cooperative Work, 24-28 September 2011, Aarhus Denmark*, pages 101–120. Springer London, 2011.

[27] R. Prikladnicki, A. Boden, G. Avram, C. Souza, and V. Wulf. Data collection in global software engineering research: learning from past experience. *Empirical Software Engineering*, pages 1–35, 2013.

[28] K. Schmidt and L. Bannon. Taking cscw seriously. *Computer Supported Cooperative Work (CSCW)*, 1(1-2):7–40, 1992.

[29] K. Schmidt and C. Simone. Coordination mechanisms: Towards a conceptual foundation of cscw systems design. *Computer Supported Cooperative Work (CSCW)*, 5(2-3):155–200, 1996.

[30] K. Schwaber and J. Sutherland. The scrum guide: The definitive guide to scrum: The rules of the game, 2011.

[31] A.-M. Søderberg, S. Krishna, and P. Bjørn. Global software development: Commitment, trust and cultural sensitivity in strategic partnerships. *Journal of International Management*, 19(4):347 – 361, 2013. Developing Offshoring Capabilities for the Contemporary Offshoring Organization.

[32] A. Strauss. The articulation of project work: An organizational process. *Sociological Quarterly*, 29(2):163–178, 1988.

[33] L. Suchman. Do categories have politics? the language/action perspective reconsidered. In *Proceedings of the Third Conference on European Conference on Computer-Supported Cooperative Work*, ECSCW'93, pages 1–14, Norwell, MA, USA, 1993. Kluwer Academic Publishers.

[34] L. A. Suchman. *Plans and Situated Actions: The Problem of Human-machine Communication*. Cambridge University Press, New York, NY, USA, 1987.

[35] G. Walsham. Icts and global working in a non-flat world. In *Information Technology in the Service Economy: Challenges and Possibilities for the 21st Century*, volume 267, pages 13–25. Springer US, 2008.

Why Closely Coupled Work Matters
in Global Software Development

Rasmus Eskild Jensen
IT-University of Copenhagen
Rued Langgaards vej 7
2300 Copenhagen
raej@itu.dk

ABSTRACT

We report on an ethnographic study of an offshore global software development project between Danish and Philippine developers in a Danish company called GlobalSoft. We investigate why the IT-developers chose to engage in more closely coupled work as the project progressed and argue that closely coupled work supported the collaboration in a very challenging project. Three key findings are presented: 1) Closely coupled work practices established connections across the collaboration ensuring knowledge exchange and improving coordination between project members, 2) Closely coupled work practices diminished the formation of sub-groups locally and established new faultlines across the geographical distance, and 3) Closely coupled work enabled the creation of connections across organizational hierarchies allowing information to travel seamlessly between layers in the organization and consequently the project members could better anticipate issues and act accordingly. The implications of these findings include a reconsideration of the significance of closely coupled work in distributed settings. Also our findings open up discussions of why closely coupled work matters in global software development.

Categories and Subject Descriptors

H.1.2 [**User/machine information**]: Human factors.

H.5.3 [**Group and Organizational Interfaces**]: Computer-supported cooperative work.

General Terms

Human Factors.

Keywords

Closely coupled work; Global Software Development (GSD); Ethnographic study; Computer-Supported Cooperative Work (CSCW).

1. INTRODUCTION

The CSCW community has in the past years added more importance to the collaborative practices of global software development (Jensen and Bjørn 2012, Avram et al. 2009, Boden and Avram 2009). Working in a geographically distributed setting

across cultural differences and time zones influence the work practices of IT-developers (Noll et al. 2010, Matthiessen et al. 2014). Overcoming challenges such as coordination (Christensen and Bjørn 2014, Herbsleb 2007) establishing trust (Boden et al. 2009), and managing culture (Krishna et al. 2004).are critical for the IT-developers to successfully manage global software development projects. Researchers have proposed different strategies to overcome these challenges and some have even proposed that complex and highly interdependent software development tasks are unmanageable in geographically distributed teams (Olson and Olson 2000). Instead IT-developers should focus on reducing connections across the geographical distance and minimizing interaction between the developers (Hertzum and Pries-Heje 2011). Conversely this paper presents a case where the IT-developers were able to create a complex software solution while working in closely coupled collaboration and consequently experiencing the best offshore collaboration to date. We found that key to this outcome was the IT-developers ability to shift their work practices from a loosely coupled to a more closely coupled configuration

In this paper we ask: *Why did the IT-developers choose to engage in more closely coupled work?* Answering this question, we provide empirical data from a software development setup between a large Danish company and a Philippine offshore office. In this case the Philippine office had initially been functioning as an outsource software supplier for three years before it was bought by the Danish company. This paper report from the point in time when the Philippine office became an offshore office and events that followed in the next three years. Financially the company had benefitted from having a outsource supplier in terms of competitive power that thus led to buying the Philippine office. However, the collaboration between the Danish and Filipino IT-developers had not been optimal during the first three years of collaboration. There was a lack of trust between the two groups, little to no social interaction and a general feeling of being them and us. Work practices were loosely coupled, tasks were divided among the IT-developers and the collaboration consisted of relatively strict barriers in the collaborative work in terms of limited travel funding and using the Philippine office as a resource rather than a strategic partner (Søderberg et al. 2013).

We observed over the period of three years how the IT-developers slowly transformed their work practices to overcome the challenges experienced in the collaboration. The transition was not carefully orchestrated by the management group but rather carried out as a non-sequential process that involved a range of different employees in the company. Over time the IT-developers facilitated more closely coupled work, which was essential to solve the task. This paper point to three key factors of how the collaboration improved during the transformation from loosely to closely coupled work. Firstly, closely coupled work practices established many connections across the collaboration ensuring knowledge exchange and improving coordination. Secondly, closely coupled work practices diminished the formation of subgroups locally and established new faultlines across the geographical distance by intensifying travels, collocating people and increasing the frequency of meetings between distributed members. Lastly, closely coupled work created connections across organizational hierarchies and enabled people to take responsibility and share mutual accountability of the project outcome. Connections across organizational hierarchies allowed information to travel seamlessly between layers in the organization and consequently the practitioners could better anticipate issues and act accordingly.

The paper begins with a description of the research method followed by a section on related work. Subsequently the case is described and the empirical results are presented in order to answer the research question. Finally the findings are discussed and the conclusion is presented.

2. METHOD

The company we investigated is called GlobalSoft (a pseudonym). It was incorporated in 1994 and has its origin in Denmark. GlobalSoft employs more than 1700 people in various destinations such as Denmark, China, Switzerland and the Philippines. The Philippine office was originally an independent supplier of programming resources for GlobalSoft. In 2009, the Philippine office was bought by GlobalSoft, which had 85 employees at the time. The Philippine office merged with an existing department in Denmark.

Data collection was undertaken by three researchers and took place from December 2010 to October 2013. The subjects under study were highly professional and worked with expertise within their fields. We conducted on-site observations in Denmark and the Philippines, shadowing employees, participating in video meetings, and observing everyday practices. The data include 28 audio-recorded and transcribed interviews (19 in Denmark, 9 in the Philippines), each about an hour long. We interviewed, observed, and interacted with developers, testers, IT-architects, project leaders, and managers. We spent a total of almost two months in the Philippines during four different visits (December 2010, July 2011, November 2011, and January 2012), and 12 months in Denmark. During data collection, we discussed initial findings with the workers in casual conversation and in official presentations and workshops. Two researchers held four video-recorded workshops were held in the Philippines and Denmark. The data material such as the presentations and workshops was used to interrogate and validate our findings (Eisenhardt 1989). Lastly, we analyzed the video recording and internal company documents. Our methodological approach was an open-ended study design inspired by grounded theory (Strauss and Glaser 1967). The variety of data collection methods helped establish a grounded understanding of the complexities of geographical distributed development practices. The analysis of the data material required several iterations of re-reading, coding, and write-ups to categorize and connect the themes that emerged

3. CLOSELY COUPLED WORK IN DISTRIBUTED TEAMS

To understand why the developers engaged in more closely coupled work practices one has to investigate the notion of a collaborative task. The CSCW research on coupling of work focuses on collaborative work and the nature of the task. Collaborative work is defined by multiple people being mutually engaged within a common field of work, and where individual activities have a direct impact on the collaborative partners (Schmidt and Bannon 1992). Coupling of work has been the subject of CSCW for many years (Neale et al. 2004, Pinelle and Gutwin 2003, Herbsleb et al. 2000). Coupling of work refers to the nature and degree of communication needed to solve a specific task (Olson and Olson 2000). A cooperative arrangement involves a range of more or less interdependent activities that can be described as a set of activities (Schmidt 2011). Some of these activities can be characterized as 'loosely coupled' while others can be characterized as 'tightly coupled'. Teams working individually on distinct contributions can be characterized as loosely coupled whereas teams with sequential or reciprocal interdependence in the cooperative arrangement are tightly coupled (Balakrishnan et al. 2011). According to Olson and Olson (2000) loosely coupled work is composed of simple standardized tasks with few interlinked dependencies whereas tightly coupled work, however, is ambiguous and highly interdependent nature and thus very difficult to divide into smaller segments. Software products with many ambiguities and a high degree of dependency among the software components can be characterized as tightly coupled work. Some research propose that loosely coupled tasks are more suitable for distributed work (Hertzum and Pries-Heje 2011, Olson and Olson 2000) which can easily be divided into smaller sub-tasks. Since loosely coupled tasks have few dependencies they can be reassembled again and requires little coordination and interaction across geographical distance (Mockus and Weiss 2001, Grinter 2003). Tightly coupled work should preferably be used in a collocated setting because collocated people typically share a common ground and are better able to solve the ambiguities of tightly coupled work (Olson and Olson 2000). Contrary to this other researchers have suggested that tightly coupled tasks are actually better suited for distributed work because it requires close connections and thus enables the practitioners to engage with each other on a mutually shared task (Bjørn and Ngwenyama 2009). Thus this line of research points to the necessity of closely coupled work as an incentive for increasing interaction and forming partnerships among distributed members (Bhat et al. 2006). Collocated software development requires a lot of coordination (Grinter 2003) and the added geographical distance only increases the need to coordinate (Boden and Avram 2009, Avram et al. 2009). However, closely coupled work in a geographically distributed setting is difficult to achieve and will require changes in the work practices both locally and remotely (Matthiessen et al. 2014). In global software development projects the IT-developers are often dependent on each other in order to solve the task especially in those situations where the final product is applied into a specific domain area for instance when one group of IT-developers has the necessary domain knowledge, which needs to be communicated across the geographical distance (Jensen and Bjørn 2012). Strategies to minimize the need for coordination are segregation and standardization where tasks are divided into smaller pieces with specific requirements (Gerson 2008, Mockus and Weiss 2001). However, standardization and segregation do not eliminate the need for coordination in software development projects because all the separated parts have to be assembled to a functioning software product. The reassembling of the software requires coordination to ensure that dependencies between the small pieces are correct when the all the pieces are collected (Gerson 2008, Grinter 2003).

The increased need for coordination is further complicated in projects that span cultural differences (Krishna et al. 2004).

Culture defined as a set of values, beliefs or norms (Søderberg and Holden 2002) allows for a deeper understanding of how cultural distance impacts distributed teams unlike a cultural understanding based on national categories (Hofstede and Hofstede 2004). Moving away from national stereotypes recent research have proposed that culture can instead be understood as *"a shared web of meanings that shapes roles and interpretations, and is dynamically (re)negotiated by the actors in the course of their daily work"* (Boden et al. 2012). A lack of a shared web of meanings can lead to misunderstandings and collaboration can be further obscured due to emergent faultlines within groups (Cramton and Hinds 2005). Faultlines increase the likelihood of alignment among group member's demographic attributes, which is the foundation for sub-group formation. Demographic faultlines such as gender, age, cultural background or professional expertise have increased risk of forming in distributed teams. Research has shown that sub-group dynamics can impact negatively on the collaborative work and establish a sense of "us and them" based on ethnocentrism (Cramton and Hinds 2005). Sub-groups within a project can be damaging for the collaboration and result in conflict as other studies of global software development projects have shown (see for example Marrewijk 2010, or Metiu 2006). These studies found that strong internal groupings hindered the collaborative work or even caused the collaboration to end permanently. Negative sub-group dynamics can be mitigated by focusing on creating strong connections across distributed groups that establishes cross-cutting faultlines across the groups located in the different locations. The positive aspects of sub-groups are specifically achieved when faultlines are established between distributed team members that potentially can create cross-cultural learning (Cramton and Hinds 2005).

While the increased need of coordination required for closely coupled work might be challenging in a distributed setting, it may also offset positive aspects in the collaborative work. Research has shown that social translucence, which is key for collaborative work, is a process of negotiation among project participants. Bjørn and Ngwenyama states that: *"Creating translucence and building shared meaning at the work practice level is a negotiation process between the participants where sub-languages are in contact, new languages are formed and meanings are developed."* (2007 p. 20). Thus participants distributed teams need to engage in on-going negotiation to develop new meaning and establish social translucence. Social translucence consists of three principles for social interaction i.e. visibility, availability and accountability (Erickson and Kellogg 2000). Within the field of CSCW studies of a similar concept, namely awareness has shown how collocated employees display and monitor activities in order to act accordingly (Schmidt 2002, Heath and Luff 1992). Social translucence contains elements that are key to coordinating activities between people. Firstly it gives visibility of our surroundings and enables people to act accordingly. Secondly it establishes a mutual visibility where others can see you and you know that they can see you. Finally, shared visibility creates accountability because we adhere to social norms of behavior and act within the rationale of these norms. In a collocated setting social interaction is seamless and achieved without much effort whereas in a distributed setting the social pressure to reinforce norms of behavior is usually weak (Mark 2002). Thus it can be very challenging to create the necessary conditions for social translucence in distributed teams.

In summary working on tightly coupled tasks in a distributed setting requires more effort due to the geographical distance and cultural differences. To overcome the burden of coordination software development teams often choose to use segregation or standardization with few connections across the different locations. So why does closely coupled work matter in global software development projects? Interestingly we observed in our case how the IT-developers chose to engage in more closely coupled work as the project progressed. This would appear to be a counter-intuitive solution seemed to help the IT-developers overcome the challenges they were facing in the collaborative work. However, we saw that the trade-off of loosely coupled work is that no shared meaning is developed, the risk of communication breakdowns increase and sub-group dynamics emerge along demographic faultlines. In the following section we are going to present the findings and show in detail why the closely coupled work is important for global software development projects.

4. FINDINGS

This section consists of four sub-sections that identify the work practices at different stages. The sections illustrate the transformation of going from loosely coupled work to closely coupled work practices in a global software development department. The first section describes the situation prior the project where the initial steps towards offshoring is taken. The second section describes the status of the collaboration in the initial stages and focuses on examples that illustrate the work practices during this period. The third section describes how work practices changed over time as the collaboration transformed to more closely coupled work. The fourth and final section describes the emerging work practices in an offshore collaboration.

4.1 Going from outsourcing to offshore

The focus of this paper is a single department in Globalsoft. The department is the largest of its kind in Denmark and in charge of developing new software systems to primarily Danish clients. The department was able to handle all stages of the development e.g. specification, development, testing and implementation. In 2006 a Philippine outsource supplier was hired to support the Danish department. The main contribution from the Philippine supplier was recognized to be scalability and low costs, but had the potential to contribute with specific developmental expertise. The Philippine supplier was bought by Globalsoft in 2009 and became an official part of the company. The Philippine office merged with the Danish department, so that it consisted of two offices – one in Denmark and one in the Philippines. At the time the Philippine office consisted of 85 employees.

The transition from working in a collocated environment to geographical distributed setting was challenging for the Danish employees. The Philippine office had been working in distributed setting for a longer time and could be characterized as "born global". The employees in the Danish office were used to do everything by themselves and were thus quite skeptical towards this change, which many described as a nuisance enforced upon them by the management group in GlobalSoft. The collaboration with the Philippine office lacked success stories and many remained skeptical. As one Danish developer said *"There has not been a success story yet. If they existed they would have been talked about. I am certain of that."* The managers defended the change to offshore by referring to the market dynamics, stating that the GlobalSoft required an offshore component to remain competitive even though the Danish employees had experienced few clearly successful projects with the Philippine office.

4.1.1 Persistent loosely coupled work practices

Initially the work practices between the Danish and Philippine office were still affected by the setup used when the Philippine office was merely a supplier of services and not fully integrated into the department. The Philippine office was assigned hours according to a fixed-price model meaning that they would estimate the number of hours for a task and give a fixed price for doing the task. This practice carried with it some negative implications for the employees in both Denmark and the Philippines, but to really appreciate this we need to understand the organizational setup between the Philippine office, the Danish office and the clients. The Danish office was responsible for client relations and would typically try to establish a close connection to the clients. In our case we observed that the client came every week to GlobalSoft to spend the day with the project members in the office. The employees in the Philippine office had no contact with the client at any time during the project. It was a deliberate strategy from the company to keep the offshore component hidden from the client and leave the impression that the product was the same regardless of the organizational setup.

The organizational setup with the fixed prices created on-going discussions about change requests and whether they are legitimate changes or an error caused by the department. If the change request could be characterized as legitimate change then the client would have to pay for the extra hours needed to fix the problem whereas errors put cost on the project budget. Since the Danish employees had the client contact they also had to negotiate change requests with client. But with the fixed price setup the Danes were now in a position where they had to negotiate on two front namely with the client and the Philippine office. In the days before outsourcing to the Philippines this issue had been less of a problem, because the Danish office only had to negotiate with client to solve a problem. The fixed price setup consequently required negotiation with both client and the Philippine office when neither of them was willing to pay the extra cost of a change. Moreover some employees in the Danish department would state outright that they did not trust the estimates coming from the Philippine office and several of the Danish employees we interviewed suspected Filipino employees of padding time estimates. Danish employees felt that within this arrangement the Filipino workers did not share full responsibility for outcomes of the projects, and were only concerned with covering their estimated hours. Moreover at the time the employees in the Danish and Philippine office shared little insight into each other's work conditions because intra-organizational travels were limited by relatively strict company rules. Organizational constrains at the time limited the funding for traveling between Denmark and the Philippines since travels were not part of project budgets. Funding for travels had to granted by the vice president in the department and the requests would often be denied. Travel requests were denied because the gain of face-to-face interaction was difficult to determine and weighed against the cost for the project often led to rejection.

4.1.2 Working as "us and them"
The work practices in the collaborative work seemed experimental and haphazardly implemented according to the employees. As a Danish IT-architect told us during an interview:

[...] The projects I have been involved in were more or less like shooting buck shots at the problems when these urgent needs occurred. Like putting out fires – you just do something, right? But we have not yet had the discussion of how the basic premises of this collaboration are going to work.

The past three years of experience with the Philippine office had been dominated by a trial and error approach. The problem was that mistakes were repeated in new projects. One example of this

was a model for global collaboration that was introduced in the department. The employees in the Philippine office received training in this new model that specifically described the roles and responsibilities for global collaboration. However, the Danish employees were more reluctant to accept this new model and kept using the work practices they had used in previous projects. The implication of one group of employees working with one model in mind and the other group working differently caused some frustration for the Philippine employees since they had spent time and effort in order to learn the new global work practices. The Filipino employees were generally well prepared for working in a global context in terms of language skills and their use of CMC-tools such as instant messenger. On several occasions we observed them actively engaged in conversations on instant messenger even with people located right next to them. They were however concerned about the lack of awareness of the "global component" as one Filipino manager said:

Because a lot of it isn't culture specific. It's really problems with time zone, problems with, well not problems, but rather just people having to get used to be more professional and people having to realize that they have a global, there's a global component in the work that we're doing. Not just on the Danish side but also on our side.

Clearly, both the Danish and Filipino developers felt that the collaborative aspects of the work could be improved, but they identified different challenges as the root of the problems. Filipino employees generally felt that the Danes lacked sufficient English skills to master geographically distributed work, which was evident when Danish employees were reluctant to call directly to their Filipino colleagues. Moreover the Filipinos expressed a concern of being excluded in the collaboration and felt a "lack of interest" from the Danish employees. One example of this, which happened on several occasions, was emails written in Danish that was sent to the Filipino employees. For instance a string of forwarded emails where the first email would have a sentence like "Important! See below" and then the rest of the emails would all be written in Danish. The Danes, on the other hand, had little trust in the technical expertise of their Filipino colleagues and often perceived themselves superior in terms of experience. Arguably the Danes largely had more experience because they were typically older and not hired straight from the university. In the Philippines promotions was sometimes used as an incentive structure for the employees to make them stay at the company. Of course this would also be the case in the Danish office to some extent, but the competition over skilled employees was much more present in the booming offshore market in the Philippines. As a result the Philippine developers got promoted faster than their Danish colleagues and typically had less experience. For instance, one who had approximately two years of experience held the role as developer lead in the Philippine office which is very little compared to the Danish developers average experience. Thus the people who held the project roles in the Philippine office often had a lot less practical experience compared to the Danish employees. Consequently the employees in the Danish office sometimes expected more from the Philippine employees based on their position and not their actual experience. The experience gap was sometimes ignored or forgotten in the project planning and thus expectations to the technical expertise of the Filipino developers failed on several occasions.

4.1.3 Still working as an outsourcing company
The situation caused some serious constraints on the relationship between the Danish and Filipino employees, which heightened by

the relatively strict travelling rules at the time. Less travelling meant that employees in the projects rarely met and had little change of building strong social ties with each other. The challenge that was most prominent at this stage was the general feeling of "us and them" in the projects. This feeling was shared in both offices and exemplified in the little social interaction that happened at this stage. Locally people had casual interaction, shared dinner together and attended social activities but globally no shared activities occurred. The work practices were still primarily based on an outsourcing setup with clear distinctions of them and us, both in terms of social relations but also the division of work and the economic setup between the two offices.

4.2 The initial stages of the project

The department won a call for tender for a big project during this period of transforming from outsource to offshore. This project was thus the first major project with the Philippine office as an offshore component and the changes in the project illustrates the general transformation of practices in the department. The project was the largest development project undertaken in the history of the Danish-Philippine department. The contract for this particular project was signed late 2010 and the preliminary preparations took place in spring 2011. In late 2010 the department undertook its biggest task to date when it won the call for tender of a large project for the Danish government. It was going to span more than three years with the largest budget to date and require technical competences that the department did not have at the time. However, no one in the department or the client was fully aware of the scale and complexity of the project at this moment in time.

The fixed price model had been changed meaning that the both offices shared the responsibility in the project. The Philippine office was now integrated into the project budget along similar offices in the company. The discussion of change requests ended because everybody was equally responsible for fixing errors. Travels no longer needed managerial approval and each project had a travel budget allowing the project leader to make flexible decisions regarding travels. This made travels between Denmark and the Philippines possible to a greater scale. The changes that came from the management group were based partly on the feedback received from the employees in the department.

4.2.1 Changing the scope of the project

The work practices at this stage had a great impact on the outcome of the project primarily because the scope of the project was changed. The project contract signed stated that the Philippine office was fully responsible for the development of the product to the Danish municipalities. However, the people who had authored the contract left the company and an experienced IT-architect from the Danish office was assigned to write the requirement specification to the Philippine office. During this task the IT-architect from the Danish office apprehended the complexity of the task both in terms of technical expertise but also the amount of interaction with public institutions located in Denmark. The IT-architect brought his concerns to the management group where he argued for a reorganization of the entire project. The Danish IT-architect argued strongly against having the Philippine department do this task alone. The IT-architect told us that he had learned from previous experience that the Philippine office would not be able to handle this task single-handedly. While asked about the details regarding the contract the IT-architect said:

Actually I had no part in the original contract description. So when I finally get to see the contract together with a couple of colleagues, I realize how severe the situation is. I have at least four or five years of experience working with the Philippine office

and I know fairly well of their strengths and weaknesses. The requirement specification was clearly outside of their competences. Maybe not all of it but some of the components planned to be developed there. Which is why one of the first decisions we took was to withdraw parts of the project. That was not a very popular decision, but we did it.

It should be noted that at this point in time the Danes generally claimed that a successful offshore project in the company was yet to be seen and it was thus unrealistic that the Philippine office would be able to handle such a big project alone primarily because they were not technically equipped for the task or had the necessary experience. The Philippine employees had counter-argued by saying that they had the competences and the main problem was actually not lack of competences but rather how the collaborative work was done. Nevertheless, since this IT-architect was also very experienced and had worked for the company more than ten years his arguments carried much weight and the management group decided to follow his recommendations. His arguments against letting the Philippine office complete the project alone was weighed against the economic setback and the management group was convinced that the project had been scoped wrongly from the beginning. It was decided that Danish developers should develop approximately 50 % of the project. At this stage the organizational practice still largely dictated a practice of reducing links between the Danish and Philippine office thus moving everything offshore does not emphasize closely coupled work but a tendency to insist on the distinction of sites rather than collaboration.

4.2.2 Dividing the tasks across different sites

The decision to withdraw 50 % of the project from the Philippine office would seem to afford more links between the two offices but the initial work practices still focused on reducing links between the Danish and the Philippine employees instead of taking advantage of the diversity of competences across the two sites. The new scope of the project required the involvement of more Danish employees and the Danish IT-architect decided that the project should be divided into 4 separate releases. Release A was to be developed in Denmark because it was deemed to very complex both due to its technical nature and due to the required integrations with a range of systems operated by local Danish municipalities and institutions. Release B and C where estimated to be the least complicated in terms of the technical expertise required, partly because the sensitive personal data was all to be handled in Release A. The sensitive data was subject to legal requirements according to Danish law and was thus easier to handle in Denmark. Thus the Philippine office was assigned to develop Release B and C while the Danish office began development on Release A. The final release, which was called release D was left undecided at the time, but the Danish office, would most likely be in charge of the development. The work practices at this stage focused on limited links with few people "bridging" the two offices. A Danish IT-architect was the primary collaboration partner with Philippine office while the remaining Danish employees focused their effort on release A. The collaborative work consisted of weekly technical meetings with a video link. The Danish IT-architect would be present as well as the Philippine system analyst. Typically there would also be 2- 3 Philippine developers present and sometimes even the Philippine IT-architect. These meetings were used to discuss the finished software components, solve technical issues and discuss the development for the following week. The interaction can be characterized as closely coupled but it only reflected a relatively small group of people in the entire project.

Another example of the loosely coupled work at the time was happening between two groups of Danish employees. One group consisted of the IT-architects and developers who primarily worked with the Philippine office but they also engaged with group of employees from another department in the company, namely the back office. Back office was responsible for the implementation of the technical solutions as well as integrating the software with the new hardware required to handle the sensitive information. The two groups were not collocated to begin with and did not even share the same building and the individual dependencies on each other were poorly communicated. The back office group were not aware of their important role until late into the project and when they finally began working on the task they realized that the hardware was much more complex than anticipated. Although these two groups shared the same cultural background they lacked an understanding of the dependencies between them. Although the geographical distance was much shorter between the two Danish groups they also experienced a feeling of "us and them" in the work practices at this stage.

4.2.3 Few bridges in the collaborative work

Although the organizational practices from the first stage had been removed there was still a prevalent feeling of them and us in the collaboration both between Danes and Philippine employees but also between employees located in Denmark. The strict division of work with few links between the groups replaced the previous constrains of the fixed price model and travelling. Moreover even with the removal of the restrictions on travels still only one person had actually travelled to the Philippines in the first seven months of the project. During the following year another three Danish employees went to the Philippines for a period of one week. No Philippine developers visited the Danish office in the first two years of the project. The project consisted of up to forty people at peak times, which gives an indication of the low travel frequency during the initial stages of the project. The reasons given for this were firstly that few Danish employees were actually interested in leaving Denmark for 2-3 weeks because of their families and although the Filipino developers expressed their willingness to travel this opportunity were not utilized at this stage. Therefore much of the collaborative work was coordinated mainly through the requirement specification or the product descriptions that described the task. While this is a typical way of coordination offshore software development projects the complexity and scope of this particular project created closely coupled dependencies that were not easily communicated in documents. The Danish employees spent a lot of time writing these documents and when the descriptions were misunderstood it led to frustrations on both sides and costly extra hours fixing the errors. An IT-architect described the process like this:

I had hoped that it [the documents] had had a greater effect compared to the energy that I spent producing them. On many occasions I had to remind them [the Philippine developers] to read the documents thoroughly. I feel like they should have gotten the information if they had read the document. [...] It seems to me that everything is going a little bit too fast in the Philippines.

The loosely coupled work practices gave little opportunity for interaction. Employees knew little of each other across the geographical distance and social relations between the two offices were sparse or non-existent. Lack of interaction was not only prevalent across the geographical distance but also between the back office group and the developers located in Denmark. The loosely coupled work practices with the back office group lacked

coordination since the two groups were practically unaware of their individual dependencies and how to solve them. At this stage both the scope and the budget had exceeded the project plan and the situation was slowly becoming critical in the project.

4.3 The state of the project becomes critical

Eight months into the project serious problems began to emerge. The quality of release B did live up to the expected quality. The IT-architects in Denmark were frustrated because they had tried to anticipate these problems by being extra careful with the wording in the requirements specification to ensure that misunderstandings were minimized. Since their hourly rate was high the time was very costly for the project when it had not worked as intended. However few of the Danish employees questioned the method of communication. Instead they emphasized all the work that had gone into detailing the requirements specification – work that seemed useless now that the misunderstandings occurred. The Filipino employees questioned the communication format and argued that there should be a lot more emphasis on domain knowledge, since the software was going to be applied to a Danish context with very specific institutional structures. Critical information was communicated mostly by emails since only few people held video meetings across the two sites.

4.3.1 Changing to daily Scrum meetings

The developers in the Philippines said that the reason behind the poor quality was because they were implementing a new work practices. The Philippine project leader had adopted in the Philippine development team. This meant that the Philippine developers would now have daily sprint meetings and work in 2-weeks cycles instead of the 3-week cycle they used before. Also they changed the name of these cycles from iterations to sprints. The time spent learning the new procedure had caused a lower than expected result on Release B. A newly assigned Filipino project leader described the situation at the time like this:

[...] When I came into the project this was already in Scrum. Although I had my reservations initially because of the fixed project and the fixed timeline project. It seemed strange at the time doing scrum. But on the other side, it did help quite a bit. Maybe not so much in term of the deadlines, but in terms of actually, let's say having better deliveries, better quality. It did help. And we're reaping the fruits of that now for [Release B].

Adapting to the Scrum had been weird in the beginning but the change became rewarding for the developers in Philippines. During the same period the Danish project leader travelled to the Philippines to ensure that they were actually able to finish release C due to the low quality of Release B. At the time the project leader said that it had been close to a termination of the collaboration with the Philippine office after seeing the quality of Release B. However, after going to the Philippines and meeting with the developer team, he was convinced to continue the collaborative work. Once implemented the scrum meetings greatly helped the Philippine employees primarily because the Philippine development team would now meet every morning and discuss their current tasks. This helped them to see the overall picture of the individual tasks and delegate tasks if needed.

4.3.2 Formalizing communication patterns

Collaborative work practices changed slowly towards a more closely coupled practice in various ways after the crisis with Release B. One example of this was that the project members met face-to-face before the development of release C began in the Philippines. Two IT-architects travelled to the Philippines to kick-start the development of Release C. They held presentations for the Philippines developers and one of the IT-architects held 3-hour long meetings with the system analyst to discuss the technical aspects and implications of Release C. Another example of closely coupled work practices that emerged had its course over a year of the project. A Danish IT-architect slowly also began to formalize communication structures between the developers to overcome the misunderstandings. He had been in charge of facilitating the development of Release B and was one of the few who frequently interacted with Filipino developers. The antecedent to formalizing the communication was a more flexible communication strategy that had been used from the beginning of the project. The flexible approach meant that the Philippine developers could direct all their queries and questions to the Danish IT architect. However, this eventually led to a situation where the Danish IT architect was spending most of his time answering questions from Philippine developers leaving him little time to do other tasks. The flexible communication strategy became too time consuming for the IT architect, so the team decided to try another approach:

We actually changed the model so that Tom (a Philippine system analyst) would be the primary contact person, and he would gain the knowledge discussing with me what should be *developed, and then he will distribute the knowledge from there (Obs.: May 24th Denmark).*

Thus, to reestablish a formalized communication pattern and create a less ambiguous process, the Danish IT architect devised a communication model based on his experience with the different communication norms across Denmark and the Philippines. The purpose of the model was to formalize the communication flow between the Danish IT architect and the Philippine developers. The process of establishing a shared communication pattern lasted more than a year, and during this period they experimented with different approaches for how to communicate across geographical and temporal distance. Formalizing the communication pattern was a non-linear process that emerged over time as the project members experimented with different approaches. The end result created more visibility and accountability in the communication between the developers. Instead of having a loosely coupled structure they established a pattern of shared dependencies in the flow of communication as they moved closer to an offshore collaboration.

4.3.3 Evaluating the collaborative work

Towards the end of a development cycle in the Philippine office (Release C) the Danish project leader held two separate evaluation sessions of the current status. The Danish meeting lasted more than three hours with 20 participants form the Danish office. Most surprisingly was the fact that the collaborative work with the Philippine office was only mentioned once during the meeting. Instead people discussed a range of challenges that the Danish developers had experienced during the first year of the project. One of the main concerns was the lack of coordination between two offices in Denmark, namely the developers and the back office people. The back office people had not been prepared for the tasks expected of them and they got involved in the project at a time, which was considered too late by many of the developers. Moreover people were not located in the same office space, which created a disconnection between the two groups. The IT-developers did not know who to talk to in the back office department and the back office were not prepared for the task in terms of the time required to solve the complex tasks. Thus "us/them" issues had been a big issue for the Danish developers, but unexpectedly "us/them" feelings emerged among Danish

colleagues and not across geographical distance in distributed collaboration.

The evaluation session with the Philippine office was held as a video meeting with five attendees. The main concern at this meeting was the status of the collaborative work between Denmark and the Philippines. Although it was recognized that the collaboration had struggled during release B it was agreed by all participants that the collaboration was much better now. They even stated that the collaboration had been the best to date in their experience.

4.4 Emerging closely coupled work practices

Four months later a range of events in the project established the foundation for close collaborative work. The catalyst for these changes was the critical status of the project at the time. The project was severely delayed due to unforeseen challenges with the technical solutions as well as the complexity of the task. Moreover costs had accelerated due to these delays and the client had fined the project for not fulfilling the obligations in the contract. This situation called for changes in the organization of the work. A group of managers began to closely monitor the project mainly to ensure that no further delays would occur in the project. Thus management applied a key constraint of limiting the time available. Daily board meetings were established in the Danish office where key employees from the project participated. The purpose of these meetings was to enable the managers to react to current or future challenges and consequently the management group closely monitored the project members. The typical setup of these meetings was a stand-up meeting that lasted about an hour where the participants discussed the status of the project. A manager would lead the discussion and keep people updated by writing key points on a white board These meetings established visibility across the project areas and made people accountable for tasks. As the Danish project leader told us during an interview:

Being more integrated and having meetings often is a good idea in my opinion. The ordinary project leader meetings, where the project leader I drawing on a whiteboard and describes the status are not working as intended. Instead let us call it board meetings or stand-up meetings or whatever. These [meetings] are much more rewarding. We sit down together and address the issues when they occur. I think this is the reason why we succeeded – that constantly were ready to react to emerging issues.

Urgent challenges could be addressed directly by several members of the team and the access to managers helped the project because they enabled a flow of resources. One example of this was an update to the software used in the Philippine office or improving the bandwidth. The presence of the managers shortened the decision time and increased the speed of which decisions were taken.

4.4.1 Daily test meetings

Another example of the transition towards more closely work practices was the introduction of daily test meetings. These meetings had no agenda and the purpose was to create a common ground between the distributed testers and discuss current challenges in the test process. Although some of the testers felt it awkward to attend a meeting with no agenda they quickly got accustomed to the new format. The meeting served as an open space of interaction where information could flow seamlessly among the participants. For instance during one of the daily test meeting we observed the following:

They talk about test issues that has occurred since last meeting and pin point aspects which are need to be resolved to be able to continue. Diane mentions that she has been talking to John earlier today. Mary refers to her interaction with Mike while Sean refers to Jack about a task, which he must do on Release D, so that they can continue the work. However Diane informs her that Jack apparently is sick today, but may be working from home. She is unsure about this since received an email earlier today from him. (Obs. Denmark Oct 03. 2013)

Although Mary, Diane and Sean are the only people actively present at the meeting they still expand the flow of information to include members outside of the meeting by referring to other people's current status on different tasks. We also observed how these meeting allowed the testers to praise or critique each other directly and thus holding people accountable for their work. In the final stages of the project the Filipino testers became responsible for testing of Release D, which was the final release. It was rather remarkable event given the initial mistrust between the Danish and Philippine employees.

4.4.2 Project leader meetings
The critical situation and the involvement of the management level resulted in new emerging collaborative work practices that created more links between people in the project. At this point in time project leader meetings had been relatively were rare and had rarely happened in the first year of the project. This procedure was changed when a new project leader was assigned in Denmark. The new project leader quickly initiated weekly project leader meetings with the Philippine counterpart. Later these meetings also included people from the development group as well as key managers. The project leader began to have weekly project leader meetings with the project leader in the Philippines. Interestingly the project leader in Denmark also invited the IT-architects and managers from both the Danish and the Philippine offices to these meetings. The key difference from ordinary project leader meetings was that people from different organizational levels were able to meet and discuss the current status of the project. Thus the IT-architects could explain the challenges they were currently facing and the managers would be given a chance to better understand the complexity of the work. Moreover the managers were able to make quick decisions that would normally have to be confirmed at the monthly steering meeting. By having people from different organizational levels the project leader facilitated an effective forum for solving critical problems. Information could travel seamlessly between different levels in the organization and also to other employees in the project through the participants at the meeting. At one of these meetings the project leader successfully argued for more collocation between the developers and the back office people in Denmark. The project leader told us later that:

I think that the main factor [for succeeding] was allowing us to be collocated. I mean having the project members [in Denmark] sitting together and use the resources from the back office that was required. This has been really important for the project.

Being collocated greatly alleviated the disconnection between the developers in Denmark and the back office people. The project leader meeting established an easier access to resources and a shared understanding of the complexity and what needed to be done to solve challenges – both in Denmark and in the Philippines.

5. DISCUSSION
Why did the IT-developers shift towards more closely coupled work? First it became evident in the data analysis that the company initially still treated the Philippine office as an outsourcing capacity for example in terms of sticking to the fixed price setup despite being fully integrated into the same company. The collaborative aspect of the work was minimized and rather seemed to function as two separate entities that were merely solving a task together with little mutual responsibility. The two offices kept working as separate units even when after the fixed price setup had been abandoned. For example illustrated by the single point of contact between the two offices, which allowed for very little personal contact across the two teams. Another example of the separate nature of the work was the fact that the Philippine office implemented Scrum in the development process without the Danes even being aware of this change. Work practices were loosely coupled in terms little contact between the teams for example illustrated by the strict division of tasks with only a single-point of contact. Tasks were divided or decomposed into smaller pieces with the intention of minimizing interaction. The strategy of dividing tasks is typical in the software development business (Grinter 2003) and reducing interaction have been proposed as a viable strategy in global software development projects (Hertzum and Pries-Heje 2011). However we saw that in our case the separation of work practices subsequently created a perception of two separate entities. The loosely coupled work practices established a difference between how employees viewed themselves as one entity and then how the viewed their remote colleagues as another entity.

5.1 Alleviating the feeling of "us and them"
This distinction between 'us' and 'them' eliminated the possibility of perceiving the project as one system conducted with one team who just happens to be located at two different geographic sites. Instead the project seemed to consist of two teams with few shared relations and who had separate responsibility for clearly defined parts of the same system. Prior research has investigated the notion of "us and them" in terms of faultlines e.g. when key attributes of one group correlates without cross-cutting ties between other groups (Cramton and Hinds 2005). In our case we observed how the IT developers in the project initially shared few aligning attributes or were unaware of their existence. The developers located at the Danish office pointed to all the work they had put into the requirement specification and the lack of experience in the Philippine office as the reason for the poor quality of Release B. On the other hand the developers in Philippine office pointed to communication practices of the Danish office, which did not put enough emphasis on critical domain knowledge. Interestingly the IT-developers in Denmark also felt isolated from the Danish back office although they shared same cultural background and geographical location. Consequently the feeling of acting like "us and them" was an issue both between Denmark and the Philippines as well as between two groups of Danish employees located at the same site.

Release B, developed in the Philippines, did not meet contractual expectations. Failed expectations and lack of social interaction can result in lack of trust in virtual teams (Jarvenpaa and Leidner 1999) which also was apparent in this project. Interestingly the IT-developers managed to overcome the critical situation by choosing to engage in more closely coupled work. One example of the shift towards more closely coupled practices was the intensification of travels between the two offices. Travels allowed more face-to-face time building commitment in the project (Nardi,

2005) and created insight into local context and conditions. For instance the Danish IT-developers expressed their surprise of how cold the Philippine office was due to the air conditioning causing some Philippine developers to wear cloves during office hours. They also experienced the bandwidth problems that their Filipino colleagues had to deal with every day. Similarly the Filipino developers who travelled to Denmark felt the nerve and stressful environment in the Danish office. The travels enabled the IT developers to recognize context specific work conditions in each group. The travels were the first steps towards more closely coupled work practices because the IT-developers spent time together sharing knowledge and getting to know each other. Another similar change occurred when the Danish project leader decided to collocate the Danish Back office with the Danish developers. The benefit of being collocated was that they could see each other and knew that they were all working on the same project. While the importance of face-to-face time in global software development has been discussed at length in the literature (Oshri et al. 2007, Herbsleb et al. 2005), we point to these travels and the collocation of Danish employees as a turning point towards more closely coupled work in collaboration because it enabled the IT-developers to create closer connections to each other and begin to establish shared social norms. For instance during one of the travels the IT-architect spent time with the Filipino developers discussing the definition of "done" and finally decided that "done" meant tested and ready for implementation. Moreover seeing each other at the work place established a foundation for social translucence as people and their activities became mutually visible. We saw that the IT-developers managed to alleviate the feeling of "us and them" by intensifying the collaboration instead of continuing with loosely coupled work practices. The collocation greatly helped the collaborative work between the two Danish groups.

5.2 Creating connections across the project

The shift towards more closely coupled work also alleviated other challenges in the project. Initially the developers had trouble understanding each other while only sharing few links for instance illustrated by the failure to meet expectations of Release B. Although tasks (or Releases) were distributed between the Danish and Philippine office the different software components were highly dependent on each other and required coordination between the developers. This is what Grinter (2003) refers to as the recomposing aspect of the software. In time the work practices changed in several ways to overcome the challenge of recomposing the software. The developer teams introduced daily scrum meetings in the Philippines and the IT-architect formalized the communication pattern between developers in the Philippines and in Denmark. The testers on both sides began to have daily meetings and the project leaders also engaged in weekly meetings. These changes were often not planned but came as a reaction to discrepant (Majchrzak et al. 2000) events such as unexpected technical complexities or people suddenly leaving the project. Interestingly the developers chose more closely coupled work as a reaction to the discrepant events. Working closely together created more connections in the team allowing easier knowledge exchange and shared responsibility of the outcome. For instance sharing knowledge by presenting the requirement specification for the next release not only in written documents but also in face-to-face presentations where both Danish and Filipino developers engaged in discussions. The importance of meeting face-to-face cannot be understated in terms of establishing commitment and common ground as recent research has also argued (Nardi 2005, Olson and Olson 2000). However, the daily contact for instance

enabled through video meetings also contributed to greatly improving the collaboration by enabling visibility and awareness between project members across the geographical distance. Research have pointed to the concept of social translucence as a key factor for collaboration (Erickson and Kellogg 2000). In a collocated setting project members are easily visible and they are mutually aware of each other. The team members felt more connected to each other and the flow of communication became clearer. One Filipino developer specifically said that the communication was less "cloudy" after the daily meetings were established. In our case the developers worked distributed but we argue that the shift towards more closely coupled work practices also enabled mutual visibility of each other. By making more connections between people in the project they gained insight into the different tasks people were working on and allowing information to travel more freely between distributed members. The example with the daily test meetings illustrates how daily meetings created mutual visibility across different members. The closely coupled work practices thus created more connections across the project both in terms of spanning the geographical distance and locally. These connections enabled information to flow freely between members and creating insight in individual challenges of the project members.

5.3 Creating connections across hierarchies

Lastly we argue that closely coupled work practices enabled more connections between the traditional organizational hierarchies. Daily board meetings and the new project leader meetings spanned IT-architects, system analysts, project leaders and managers. Normally the project leader would report back to the steering group consisting of managers and later report back to the project members. However, we have described how for instance a Filipino system analyst or a Danish IT-architect were able to provide the necessary descriptions of current technical complexities in the development to both the project leader and the managers present at these meetings. Having these people in the project leader meetings made it easier for both project leaders and managers to understand the challenges in the project and acknowledge that action was needed. Bridging the gap between the organizational hierarchy greatly benefitted the project in the later stages especially when constrains such as time and money made conditions difficult. The managers provided decision-power and were able to react quickly to current issues based on the information received directly from the IT-developers. One example of this could be quickly adding new resources to the project in terms of necessary software updates or increasing the bandwidth in the Philippine office. Consequently having the project leader meeting and the daily board meetings allowed quick reactions to challenges that could be acknowledged by all parties at the meeting. Creating closer connections between the management group and the project members also increased the flow of information between people that would normally not work closely together. The close collaboration across hierarchies helped greatly in the later stages of the project when time became a critical factor. The meetings facilitated shared information between practitioners and managers and ensured that direct action would address the most problematic issues.

6. CONCLUSION

This paper presents an empirical observation from a longitudinal ethnographic study of a global software development company demonstrating why IT-developers chose to shift from loosely coupled to closely coupled work. We found that the IT-developers chose to engage in close collaboration to solve a complex and highly interdependent task while assessing the collaborative work as the best to date. We propose three key findings of why closely coupled work improved the collaborative practices in a geographically distributed setting. Firstly, working closely coupled work practices established many connections across the collaboration ensuring knowledge exchange and improving coordination for instance by establishing daily test meetings, collocating people and formalizing communication procedures between developers. Secondly, closely coupled work practices diminished the formation of sub-groups locally and established new faultlines across the geographical distance by removing the organizational constrains of the fixed price model and intensifying travels between the two locations. By collocating Danish employees and increasing the frequency of meetings between distributed members the IT-developers managed to moderate patterns of "us" and "them" in both locally and remotely in the company. Finally, closely coupled work created connections across organizational hierarchies by introducing daily board meetings and new project leader meetings. These meetings increased awareness of the complexities in the project, made people accountable and enabled shared responsibility the project outcome. Moreover the connections across organizational hierarchies allowed information to travel seamlessly between layers in the organization and consequently the practitioners could better anticipate issues and act accordingly for instance by adding more resources to the project. While it is impossible to generalize based on a single work place study, the data material showed that closely coupled work practices enabled productive collaboration in this particular project. This suggests that closely coupled work practices are useful for small to medium sized teams that collaborates over extended periods of time and operates in a field that requires specific domain knowledge. Further research is needed to investigate how closely coupled work practices scales to larger teams as well as how closely coupled work supports teams for shorter periods of time and in less domain specific projects.

In conclusion closely coupled work aided the IT-developers in solving the task despite being very challenging and suffering from delays and economic loss. Not only did they solve the task they also experienced that the collaborative work as the most successful to date. Thus transforming work practices from loosely coupled to closely coupled practices became a valuable learning process for doing global software development in the company.

7. ACKNOWLEDGMENTS

This research has been funded by the Danish Agency for Science, Technology and Innovation under the project "Next Generation Technology for Global Software Development", #10-092313. We would like to thank our study participants who generously spent time with us and shared their thoughts. We are grateful to anonymous reviewers for a close reading of the manuscript and their helpful suggestions.

8. REFERENCES

[1] Avram, G., Bannon, L., Bowers, J., Sheechan, A. and Sullivan, D. K. (2009) 'Bridging, Patching and Keeping the Work Flowing: Defect Resolution in Distributed Software Development', Computer Supported Cooperative Work (CSCW), 18, 477 - 507.

[2] Balakrishnan, A. D., Kiesler, S., Cummings, J. N., & Zadeh, R. (2011). 'Research Team Integration: What It Is and Why It Matters' (p. 523). in Conference on Computer Supported Cooperative Work (CSCW), New York, New York, USA. ACM Press, 523 -532.

[3] Bhat, J. M., Gupta, M. and Murthy, S. M. (2006) 'Overcoming Requirements Engineering Challenges: Lessons from Offshore Outsourcing', IEEE Software, 23(5), 38 - 44.

[4] Bjørn, P. and Ngwenyama, O. (2009) 'Virtual Team Collaboration: Building Shared Meaning, Resolving Breakdowns and Creating Translucence', Information Systems Journal, 19(3), 227 - 253.

[5] Boden, A., Avram, G., Bannon, L., & Wulf, V. (2012). 'Knowledge Sharing Practices and the Impact of Cultural Factors: Reflections on Two Case Studies of Offshoring in SME', Journal of Software Evolution and Process, 24(2), 139 - 152.

[6] Boden, A. and Avram, G. (2009) 'Knowledge Management in Distributed Software Development Teams: Does Culture Matter?', in International Conference on Global Software Engineering, Limerick, Ireland, IEEE Press, 18 - 27.

[7] Boden, A., Nett, B. and Wulf, V. (2009) 'Trust and Social Capital: Revisiting an Offshoring Failure Story of a Small German Software Company', in Wagner, I., Tellioğlu, H., Balka, E., Simone, C. and Ciolfi, L., eds., European Conference on Computer Supported Cooperative Work (ECSCW), Vienna, Austria, Springer, 123 - 142.

[8] Christensen, L. R. and Bjørn, P. (2014) 'Documentscape: Intertextuality, Sequentuality & Autonomy at Work', in ACM CHI Conference on Human Factors in Computing Systems, Toronto, Canada, ACM Press,

[9] Cramton, C. D. and Hinds, P. (2005) 'Subgroup Dynamics Internationally Distributed Teams. Ethnocentrism or Cross-National Learning?', Research in Organizational Behavior, 26, 233 - 265.

[10] Eisenhardt, K. M. (1989) 'Building Theories From Case Study Research', The Academy of Management Review, 14(4), 532 - 550.

[11] Erickson, T. and Kellogg, W. A. (2000) 'Social Translucence: An Approach to Designing Systems that Support Social Processes', ACM Transactions on Computer-Human Interaction, 7(1), 59 - 83.

[12] Gerson, E. M. (2008) 'Reach, Bracket, and the Limits of Rationalized Coordination: Some Challenges for CSCW' in Ackerman, M. S., Halverson, C. A., Erickson, T. and Kellogg, W. A., eds., Resources, Co-Evolution and Artifacts.Theory in CSCW, Springer 193 - 220.

[13] Grinter, R. E. (2003) 'Recomposition: Coordinating a Web of Software Dependencies', Journal of Computer Supported Cooperative Work, 12, 297 - 327.

[14] Heath, C. and Luff, P. (1992) 'Collaboration and Control: Crisis Management and Multimedia Technology in London Underground Line Control Rooms', Journal of Computer Supported Cooperative Work, 1(1), 24 - 48.

[15] Herbsleb, J., Paulish, D. and Bass, M. (2005) 'Global Software Development at Siemens: Experience from Nine Projects', in ICSE, St. Louis, Missouri, USA.,

[16] Herbsleb, J. D. (2007) 'Global Software Engineering: The Future of Socio-technical Coordination', in Future of Software Engineering, IEEE, 188 - 198.

[17] Herbsleb, J. D., Mockus, A., Finholt, T. A. and Grinter, R. E. (2000) 'Distance, Dependencies and Delay in a Global Collaboration', in Conference on Computer Supported Cooperative Work (CSCW), Philadelphia, Pennsylvania ACM Press, 319 - 328.

[18] Hertzum, M. and Pries-Heje, J. (2011) 'Is Minimizing Interaction a Solution to Cultural and Maturity Inequality in Offshore Outsourcing?' in Hertzum, M. and Jørgensen, C., eds., Balancing Sourcing and Innovation Systems Development, Trondheim, Norway: Tapir Academic Press, 77 - 97.

[19] Hofstede, G., & Hofstede, G. J. (2004). Cultures and Organizations: Software for the Mind. United States, McGraw-Hill Professional.

[20] Jarvenpaa, S. and Leidner, D. (1999) 'Communication and Trust in Global Virtual Teams', Organization Science, 10(6), 791 - 815.

[21] Jensen, R. E. and Bjørn, P. (2012) 'Divergence and Convergence in Global Software Development: Cultural Complexities as Social Worlds', in 10th International Conference on the Design of Cooperative Systems (COOP), Marseilles, France, Springer, 123 - 136.

[22] Krishna, S., Sahay, S. and Walsham, G. (2004) 'Communications of the ACM', International Conference on Intercultural Collaboration, 47(4), 62 - 66.

[23] Majchrzak, A., Rice, R. E., Malhotra, A., King, N. and Ba, S. (2000) 'Technology Adaption: The Case of a Computer-Supported Inter-Organizational Virtual Team', MIS Quarterly, 24(4), 569-600.

[24] Mark, G. (2002) 'Conventions and Commitments in Distributed CSCW Groups', Journal of Computer Supported Cooperative Work (CSCW), 11(3), 349 - 387.

[25] Marrewijk, A. v. (2010) 'Situational Construction of Dutch-Indian Cultural Differences in Global IT Projects', Scandinavian Journal of Management, 26(4), 368 - 380.

[26] Matthiessen, S., Bjørn, P. and Petersen, L. M. (2014) '"Figure Out How to Code with the Hands of Others": Recognizing Cultural Blind Spots in Global Software Development', in Conference on Computer Supported Cooperative Work (CSCW), Baltimore, USA, ACM Press,

[27] Metiu, A. (2006) 'Owning the Code: Status Closure in Distributed Groups', Organization Science, 17(4), 418 - 435.

[28] Mockus, A. and Weiss, D. M. (2001) 'Globalization by Chunking: A Quantitative Approach', IEEE Software, 18(2), 30 - 37.

[29] Nardi, B. (2005) 'Beyond Bandwidth: Dimensions of Connection in Interpersonal Communication', Journal of Computer Supported Cooperative Work (CSCW), 14, 91 - 130.

[30] Neale, D. C., Carroll, J. M. and Rosson, M. B. (2004) 'Evaluating Computer-Supported Cooperative Work: Models and Frameworks', in Conference on Computer Supported Cooperative Work (CSCW), Chicago, Illinois, ACM Press, 112 - 121.

[31] Noll, J., Beecham, S. and Richardson, I. (2010) 'Global Software Development and Collaboration: Barriers and Solutions', ACM Inroads, 66 - 78.

[32] Olson, G. M. and Olson, J. S. (2000) 'Distance Matters', Human-Computer Interaction, 15, 139 - 178.

[33] Oshri, I., Kotlarsky, J. and Willcocks, L. P. (2007) 'Global Software Development: Exploring Socialization and Face-to-Face Meetings in Distributed Strategic Projects', Journal of Strategic Information Systems, 16, 25 - 49.

[34] Pinelle, D. and Gutwin, C. (2003) 'Designing for Loose Coupling in Mobile Groups', in Conference on Supporting Group Work (GROUP), Sanibel Island, Florida, ACM Press, 75 - 84.

[35] Schmidt, K. (2011). Cooperative Work and Coordinative Practices. Springer Science & Business Media.

[36] Schmidt, K. (2002) 'The Problem with 'Awareness'', Journal of Computer Supported Cooperative Work, 11, 285 - 298.

[37] Schmidt, K. and Bannon, L. (1992) 'Taking CSCW Seriously: Supporting Articulation Work', Journal of Computer Supported Cooperative Work (CSCW), 1(1 - 2), 7 - 40.

[38] Søderberg, A.-M. and Holden, N. (2002) 'Rethinking Cross Cultural Management in a Globalizing Business World', International Journal of Cross Cultural Management, 2(1), 103 - 121.

[39] Søderberg, A.-M., Krishna, S. and Bjørn, P. (2013) 'Commitment, Trust and Cultural Sensitivity in Strategic Partnerships', Journal of International Management, 19(4), 347 - 361.

[40] Strauss, A. and Glaser, B. G. (1967) The Discovery of Grounded Theory: Strategies for Qualitative Research, United States: Rutgers.

Losing It Online: Characterizing Participation in an Online Weight Loss Community

Victor Li[1], David W. McDonald[2], Elizabeth V. Eikey[3], Jessica Sweeney[4], Janessa Escajeda[4],
Guarav Dubey[3], Kaitlin Riley[4], Erika S. Poole[3], and Eric B. Hekler[4]

mrvml@uw.edu, dwmc@uw.edu, exe145@ist.psu.edu, jssween2@asu.edu, jkfaust@asu.edu,
gxd176@psu.edu, ktriley13@gmail.com, epoole@ist.psu.edu, ehekler@asu.edu

[1] The Information School, University of Washington
[2] Department of Human Centered Design & Engineering, University of Washington
[3] College of Information Sciences and Technology, The Pennsylvania State University
[4] School of Nutrition and Health Promotion, Arizona State University

ABSTRACT

Many people struggle with their weight and are turning to online communities for social and informational support. The aim of this study is to understand the issues commonly discussed in online weight loss communities. Through observation and content analysis of threads in one specific weight loss community, we identified 17 distinct categories discussed by the participants. We detail four categories specifically: Personal Experience, Consumption Choices, Dieting Strategy, and Exercise. Our analysis describes some key user roles and states that often relate to different phases of a person's weight loss journey. We identify a set of transient states, which are not proper roles but are significant in an online community where individuals are attempting to change their own behaviors. We close with design suggestions for encouraging and maintaining participant engagement in an online health community.

Categories and Subject Descriptors

H.5.3. Group and Organization Interfaces

General Terms

Design, Human Factors

Keywords

Weight loss, online community, content analysis

1. INTRODUCTION

Kevin has struggled with his weight for years. When visiting his family physician, he was diagnosed with early stage heart disease and pre-diabetes, two conditions he had long suspected. The treatment was "simple." Kevin should eat better and lose his extra weight. His doctor recommended that he consider one of the many online weight loss communities but did not recommend one specifically. Kevin wondered, "what are these communities like? What kind of help do they really provide?"

Many people face Kevin's situation each year. They need to lose weight but wonder how to get the proper support to make the lifestyle changes necessary to achieve long-term weight loss and maintenance. Commercial programs tout success, but not everyone has the financial means to afford them. Thus free or low-cost online weight loss communities may be attractive ways help them meet their goals.

Current research regarding the success of online weight loss communities tells a mixed story. Studies within medical and public health literature demonstrate success for some communities and disappointment for others, where success is measured in terms of weight loss outcomes [1, 2, 10]. What these studies cannot answer is *why* some communities succeeded whereas others failed. Given the uncertainty surrounding these mixed results, a better understanding of participation in online weight loss communities is necessary.

In this study, we characterize participation in a successful online weight loss community. We aim to distinguish which design and participation features like forums and activity tracking are likely to lead to successful weight loss outcomes. To accomplish this aim, we conducted an inductive analysis of discussion threads in one popular online weight loss community. Based on this work, we can speak to the nature of participation and describe what happens in these threads. Further, given our grounded view of the community, we can speak to possible design features that could improve interaction and retention in online weight loss communities.

In the following sections, we review the relevant literature from the medical, public health, and human-computer interaction (HCI) tradition that specifically considers the experiential aspects and efficacy of online health communities. We briefly describe the weight loss community in our study and the methods that we used. The bulk of the paper focuses on the category scheme and the type of participation we saw across those categories. We follow up by considering some of the different roles that we have identified in the community, a little about how individuals appear to be integrated into the community, and a number of design directions that this specific community might take to help keep people involved.

2. RELATED WORK

The treatment of information technologies for weight loss in healthcare and HCI research literatures differ in focus. Medical and public health research primarily focus on weight loss as an end result, with a secondary interest in behavioral constructs that might drive the weight loss or usage (e.g., social support). In these studies, a technology's success is determined by the number of pounds lost. Alternatively, the HCI perspective focuses more on technology design processes and user experience, as opposed to health outcomes [9].

GROUP'14, November 9–12, 2014, Sanibel Island, Florida, USA.
Copyright © 2014 ACM 978-1-4503-3043-5/14/11...$15.00.
http://dx.doi.org/10.1145/2660398.2660416

Medical research about weight loss has been geared toward participant outcomes. However the methods for successful weight loss remain unclear. Two comprehensive meta-reviews [12, 18] reported that online weight loss programs can result in weight loss comparable to face-to-face programs, though with some caveats. These limitations included the use of heterogeneous samples limiting interpretability of the results. Another study [8] looked at randomized controlled trials, focusing on an informational approach to weight loss that disseminates information similar to that generated in an online community. Individuals in the intervention condition lost weight, but like other approaches, the intervention group was required to login and visit a particular website, where the control group was not required to participate in any online activities. A study by Hwang et al. [7] of SparkPeople.com, a weight loss online community, found a positive correlation between weight loss and participants who logged their weight at least four times. As well, some usage variables, such as posting at least once to the online forum, were also associated with weight loss. Finally, Tsai and Wadden [17] considered nine commercial weight loss programs, consisting of a mixture of face-to-face and online programs. They found that the success of programs varied depending on the types of services offered by the program and used by the participants. For example, by comparing WeightWatchers (known for face-to-face meetings) to other programs, they found those in WeightWatchers who did not participate in any services gained weight. Those in other programs who participated in face-to-face services, such as peer consulting, lost weight. Tsai and Wadden noted wide varying attrition rates across the programs that they studied, ranging from 2.5% to 67%.

This problem of attrition in online weight loss communities reflects the importance of user experience; people who have a positive experience as opposed to those who have a negative experience are more likely to return to a given site, and repeated use can impact weight loss outcomes. Studies from the HCI tradition largely focus on changing user attitudes and the impact of specific features on target populations but not always about the relationship between online communities and successful weight loss. Improving physical activity and healthy food choices can enhance social and cultural communities. The Eatwell and CommunityMosaic systems [3, 4, 14] provided social support networks for low income community members to characterize their healthy choices and activities. Eatwell relied on a phone based journal that let users call and share stories about their own experiences with food and consumption choices. CommunityMosaic allowed community members to share photos and text messages. Both systems were able to influence individuals to participate in the systems. The qualitative analysis characterizes how individuals see their participation in these communities through interviews. Purpura et al. [15] proposed a "critical design" of a system called Fit4Life. The system surfaced consequences and rewards through sensors and a phone application tracking food consumption, heart rate, and metabolic rate. Through the proposed design of Fit4Life, the researchers raised experiential and ethical issues about how individuals interact with sensing technologies and the associated social support systems (e.g., "support cloud"). Lastly, Newman et al. [13] examined the effects of social networks on weight loss by conducted interviews with people who interact with both online health communities and Facebook. They found that, in contrast to Facebook, within online health communities, it was easier to find emotional support since members were in a similar situation.

Personal preference and accountability were other reasons why online health communities were more desirable than Facebook.

We found no studies that explored the dynamics and interactions specific to weight loss communities. Improving our understanding of these specific types of online communities has potentially large social impacts and could also be helpful to other areas of research. Hwang et al. [5] noted that most primary care practitioners do not refer patients to online weight loss communities because of their unfamiliarity with these communities in general, not because of concerns about effectiveness.

Much of the community design for these weight loss programs are black boxed, making it difficult to describe what factors have the most influence on a participant's weight loss. These studies have approached online communities as a feature that a weight loss program has or a technology that can be improved. But the connection between health outcomes and user experience within these communities has not been tightly linked. There is still much to gain from understanding the information that is shared and the shape of participants' activities. Understanding participation in these communities could more effectively link what is known about the design of communities from the HCI and medical perspective can distinguish what design characteristics yield positive results.

3. A WEIGHT LOSS COMMUNITY

The technology described in this paper is DropPounds[1], a popular web- and mobile-based weight loss online community. Originally a mobile diet and activity tracking application, DropPounds quickly became one of the most downloaded "Health and Fitness" applications in the Apple iTunes Store. Two years after its initial release, DropPounds added a web-based version and online community as a companion to the mobile application. Both the website and the mobile application have been through revisions over the past few years. At this point there is effective feature parity. That is, the majority of the features of the system are available in some form through both the mobile application and the website.

Upon joining DropPounds, users create a weight loss plan based on one's height, weight, activity level, and desired weight loss per week. The plan consists of logging one's activity and diet to reach a maximum daily caloric target; there is no specific advice given on what to eat or what types of physical activities to do.

In this study, we focus on the online community associated with the DropPounds application. The community can provide additional ways for users to get assistance and support with the weight loss process. The community, which is like many online forums, features eight different forums that cover community announcements, exercise, nutrition, feature requests, technical support, an FAQ, community contests, and miscellany.

When users visit the forums within the community, they see a web page with a list of thread topics. The topics are typically listed based on recent activity, but forum moderators have administrative capabilities that can keep threads "sticky" at the top of a topic list. The moderators can also lock threads, remove or hide posts, or move threads between forum areas.

DropPounds provided us metadata from the online community. This included all thread titles, thread IDs, thread creation dates, total number of posts to the thread, and total number of thread

---

1. DropPounds is not the real name of the app or the online community and has been anonymized for privacy concerns.

views. We used the metadata to generate a random sample of threads for coding. In total, we have coded a little over 10% of the total threads represented by the metadata. The technical structure of the forum is based around thread ID. That is, given a thread ID, one can generate a URL (aka "permalink") to the specific thread in the community. We converted our random thread IDs to this URL structure and used the set of URLs to visit and code each of the randomly selected threads.

4. METHODS

The DropPounds online community is active with over 20,000 threads of discussion across eight different forums. Using the thread as a unit of analysis, we categorized topics of discussion by thread. Although the eight forums are topically named and each thread has a title as well, those names and titles may not correspond to what the participants are actually discussing. Hence our goal in this topical analysis is to understand the "what" and "how" of those discussions.

We created a set of grounded categories by selecting sets of threads and having two coders iteratively create codes and consolidate codes. We started with all threads having over 100 posts (222 total threads). After iterating through creation and consolidation, we had a total of 15 identifiable categories. The same two coders then took all threads having between 80 and 100 posts (92 total threads) to validate and clarify the category scheme. After the team completed coding, the "other" category was quite large (about 8%). The initial two coders reviewed all "other" threads to identify any latent categories not found during initial category creation. This effort yielded two additional categories. The following is a list of our final 17 categories and a brief description of those categories:

Consumption Choices - Discussion of favorite foods, drink, cooking, or eating habits such as vegetarian or vegan. Recipes, cooking methodology, and meal suggestions.

DropPounds Related - Technical support questions, feature suggestions, or discussion about the DropPounds system.

Personal Experience - Sharing stories, opinions, thoughts, rants, or advice. Social support threads, "Attaboy!", "Attagirl!", "I hear ya …", "Stay strong …", "Stick with the plan ..."

Health Information - Any thread discussing the medical or health benefits/disadvantages of diet or exercise. Typically users validate claims through external sources or focus the conversation around potential health outcomes. We do not validate the actual healthy/unhealthy claims.

Fitness Regimen - Structured fitness programs like P90X, Jillian Michaels, 30 Day Shred, BootCamp, and CrossFit. The program must have some type of progression or advancement between sessions.

Exercise - Unstructured activities that do not have an associated progression. Examples include running, aerobics, calisthenics, yoga class, spin class, Zumba, and group sports.

Dieting Strategy - Threads that include DropPounds philosophy, covering restricted calorie consumption, techniques such as substitutions, and strategies on how to stay with the DropPounds calorie restrictions. Includes threads of diet programs, or products such as Atkins, Paleo, WeightWatchers, SlimFast, or OptiFast.

Open Weight Loss/Exercise Challenge - Community event for all DropPounds forum users with daily or weekly check-ins to reach a defined goal or outcome in either weight loss or exercise. Should be accessible to all participants.

Team Weight Loss/Exercise Challenge - Community event for all DropPounds forum users who are part of a team, with daily or weekly check-ins to reach a defined goal or outcome in either weight loss or exercise. Teams can be preassembled or determined within the thread.

Gadgetry - Technology products and apps designed to aid in weight loss and exercise such as heart rate monitors, activity trackers like FitBit or Nike+, mobile and training applications like C25K, Endomondo, ZombiesRun.

Religion - Discussion about faith and belief relating to fitness, weight loss, or motivation.

Networking - Asking for accountability partners, trying to meet new people, or trying to find similar or like-minded individuals to become friends.

Love and Relationships - Discussion about dating, dating websites, meeting others, and relationships between family, spouses, and significant others. How these relationships impact success or failure of weight loss.

Workout Equipment – Something that is generally required for exercise. Differentiated from "Gadgetry" in that a gadget is not necessarily a requirement. In this category we specifically include threads on workout clothing (maybe not essential, but is clearly not a gadget), shoes, running shoes, bands, balance balls, and yoga mats. This category includes discussions of video games and video game equipment that facilitates exercise such as Wii, Wii Sports, XBOX, Kinect and associated fitness games, as having the console or game is essential to that specific form of exercise.

Quotes and Inspiration - Discussions initiated with detailed individual testimonial, stories about other users or celebrities, lists of inspirational quotes that are taken by the community as inspiring and motivating them to continue their weight loss journey. Responders often say that the post was "inspiring", "motivating", or include statements like "you are our inspiration", "you inspire us", "your story is my motivation".

Team Monthly Thread and Group Roll Call - Threads created each month for new and existing groups or teams, created monthly as a general discussion for team members. Team threads can have their own separate weigh-ins and challenges which are not Open or Team Weight Loss / Exercise Challenge.

Other - Online interactions or banter, generic talk or questions, and any other items not covered by the categories above.

We used a "tail sample" of the most popular threads to create our codes because we presume that the threads which have garnered the most posting activity have attracted the attention and contribution of the DropPounds community simply because the participants are most interested in those topics.

The process of coding threads weighted the named topic of the thread and the initial post most heavily. That is, the individual who starts the thread by naming it and contributing the first post is indicating something of what they want to talk about. The topic of the thread is what other participants will see, and it is likely to be what attracts them to the specific thread whether they just read it or post to it. We then consider one full web page of forum posts to see the topical direction of the thread and whether it is consistent with the initial post or whether the topic drifts to other issues. In the DropPounds forum implementation, the first page of posts to a thread will either be 10 or 15 posts. We did not investigate why the number of posts varies, but for each individual thread, the number of posts in the first page is invariant.

As much as possible, we attempted to code threads into one category, but we allowed for two categories to be assigned if there was a clear second topic. Secondary topics often arise as a function of topical drift. An initial post may start a thread in one direction but subsequent posts from participants take the thread in a different direction. Only 4.3% of our total sample of threads received two codes. In all of our subsequent reporting, we will report as a function of total codes applied.

Table 1 – Distribution of codes through all coding categories

Thread Category	Count	Percent
Personal Experiences	729	27.4
Consumption Choices	393	14.8
Dieting Strategy	261	9.8
Health Information	211	7.9
Exercise	209	7.8
Networking	171	6.4
DropPounds Related	154	5.8
Team Monthly Thread and Group Roll Call	75	2.8
Gadgetry	72	2.7
Open Weight Loss/Exercise Challenge	56	2.1
Fitness Regimen	47	1.8
Love and Relationships	42	1.6
Workout Equipment	33	1.2
Quotes and Inspiration	18	0.7
Team Weight Loss/Exercise Challenge	17	0.6
Religion	7	0.3
Other	168	6.3
Total	2663	100

We coded a random sample of threads using a consensus coding strategy. One primary coder was responsible for coding all threads. A set of secondary coders were given different non-overlapping samples of threads. The randomly selected threads came from threads with metadata indicating that they had from 10-80 posts to the topic. When both coders were finished with a set, the sets were compared for any differing codes. Threads that received different codes were debated between the primary and secondary coders until a consensus was reached. The primary coder acted as the authority control for judgment calls on edge cases. Coding consisted of multiple rounds over a 5 month period. The consensus coded threads were grouped together in a master spreadsheet to be processed by analytical software. We coded until we had surpassed a dual coded 10% sample of the total number of threads (2554 threads, 2663 total codes applied). Table 1 provides the distributions of codes across all of our categories.

5. FINDINGS

Among our 17 topical categories, we detail four categories that garnered a majority of the observed codes: Personal Experience (729; 27.4%), Consumption Choices (393; 14.8%), Dieting Strategy (261; 9.8%), and Health Information (211; 7.9%). Understanding the content of these categories and why these categories dominate conversation on DropPounds reveals much about how the community works and what it means to participate.

5.1 Personal Experience (729; 27.4%)

Much of the interaction that occurs on the forum is providing social support to others. Indeed, the term "Personal Experience"

inherently covers a broad range of content. Whether it is relating previous experiences a person has had, giving advice to another, or encouraging another user during a moment of struggle, users sharing their own thoughts with each other is the basis of forum interactions. Users often share events, both small and large in significance and often related to their weight loss journey, for other community members to read. Many threads announce personal victories or goals achieved, such as the user in this thread excerpt.

Thread 5.1.1[2]

> P#6205: I reached my goal a few weeks ago! I have never lost weight at such a consistent pace in my life before, so I want to share what has worked for me. Take whatever speaks to you and ignore the rest!
>
> P#6398: Absolutely fantastic! Congrats, dear!
>
> P#6552: Congrats <P#6205>! What a success story!
>
> P#6704: Welcome to the Maintenance Club! Awesome job! (And you are lucky to have a great chef as a husband!)

Posts like these often include a description of the participant's weight loss journey and offer some advice to others. The community typically replies with a series of congratulatory responses, showing the peer support function of online forums. Social support also occurs in the opposite instance when users are struggling. Participants share their frustrations and conflicts to release stress and to receive encouragement. An example here is of a person who is describing a setback on her weight loss plan while sharing her lack of confidence proceeding forward.

Thread 5.1.2

> P#6760: I've only been on a short time and watching my food intake for a short time. I feel myself giving up because I'm not losing weight very effectively. I always go through these cycles of dieting and giving up. I don't think I have ever achieved a weight loss goal. I would love to lose 40 pounds but I just don't think I have the willpower for it because I love food too much. Today, I was doing well until I went to the dollar store and bought myself a big bag of chips and my husband a big chocolate bar. Later I went home and ate both myself. I'm starting to think that nothing will help me lose weight. :(
>
> P#6999: It's a setback, not a relapse.
>
> P#6904: Don't give up! I've been there before and it so much easier to just stop than get back on the wagon. But getting healthy is important and you can do it! Do something that will make you feel better about the day like walking or eating a healthy dinner. You are worth it!
>
> P#6760: Thank you all! I had a healthy supper and feel a bit better about the day :)
>
> P#7845: Way to go, <P#6760>! Just keep at it and keep learning.

Responses are a mix of both reassurance and reminders on how to stay on schedule with the plan. Often users share their own stories

---

2. All of our example threads are text of the first few posts in order presented. In a few cases a small amount of text has been elided or modified to simplify presentation and clarify the message from users. User names have been replaced with random 4 digit IDs. In all of the examples the same ID always represents the same user.

when empathizing with others, creating a cycle where users can express their triumphs and struggles with one another.

Soliciting opinions on subjective matters about weight loss is also where personal experiences play a major role. The main point can be about whether to log or track atypical exercises, such as housecleaning or intercourse, or the times of day to weigh oneself. With no clearly defined answer, users can receive a wide variety of opinions.

5.2 Consumption Choices (393; 14.8%)

One of DropPounds' features is the ability to list what foods are eaten during a day. Successful weight loss through the DropPounds model is a combination of healthy eating and exercise. Consumption Choice threads are characterized by users' suggestions and questions about what to eat for a certain occasion, sharing recipes or cooking techniques for certain items, eating preferences, or favorite meals. Often users are focused less about the health benefits of the meal and focus instead on why the food is good for the situation presented. The example below is a user sharing his favorite salty snack to satisfy his cravings, followed by others sharing their own selections.

Thread 5.2.1

> **P#2324**: My downfall, for many years, has been SDMs (aka Salt Delivery Mechanisms, aka "chips"). Doesn't matter much which kind, potato chip, tortilla chip, Fritos, Doritos, etc. I probably ate the most tortilla chips with salsa over the years as I perceived them to be "least worst" We recently discovered a product named "Veggie Straws". Turns out the company, World Gourmet Marketing, sells a bunch of different products along this line. I understand that it would be better to eliminate SDMs completely...however on those occasions when I want to quench the craving rather than let it build, these seem to be a better choice than the stuff I used to eat.
>
> **P#4409**: My new thing is PopChips. I found them at Target and Meijer!"
>
> **P#2018**: I like the thin pretzel sticks. One 110 calorie serving is typically between 28 (Snyder's of Hanover) and 50 (Rold Gold) sticks. I treat them as my personal salt lick. Also, pumpkin seeds.

In other instances, learning how to cook a certain dish or even simply knowing how to handle a certain type of ingredient is the main focus of the discussion. Here in this instance a user is trying to find out the best methods on cooking buffalo meat. Respondents give general advice as well as asking where to procure buffalo. The discussion results in a recipe being adapted for buffalo meat.

Thread 5.2.2

> **P#4284**: On an impulse I bought a buffalo sirloin steak. How do I cook it? Any and all ideas are appreciated.
>
> **P#4693**: Grill it? That would be my best guess. Try seasoning it with something you like and grill it like any other steak.
>
> **P#2767**: I had steak tonight and tried out a new rub, it was amazing! I'm sure it would work with buffalo as well. Here's the recipe:
>
> 1 tbsp. smoked paprika
>
> 2 tsp. salt
>
> 1 tsp. brown sugar
>
> 2 tsp. chipotle chili powder

> 1/2 tsp. ground black pepper
>
> 1/2 tsp. onion powder
>
> 1/2 tsp. garlic powder
>
> 1/2 tsp. ground cumin
>
> Mix all the spices together and rub onto steaks. Let the steaks sit in the fridge for at least half an hour before cooking. Heat the grill to a very high temperature, at least 450 degrees F (232 degrees C). Grill for 3 minutes, turn, and grill for 3 more to achieve medium rare. Let the steaks rest for five minutes before cutting into them to prevent the juices from running out.

Finally, because vegans and vegetarians are making certain choices about specific foods, discussions around them are placed into Consumption Choice. This includes variations such as pescetarianism. Most users seek to understand the benefits of veganism and vegetarianism.

5.3 Dieting Strategy (261; 9.8%)

We call this category "Dieting Strategy" because many of the threads share concrete tips, techniques, and strategies for sticking with a weight loss plan. Since most of these plans require restricting calorie consumption, discussions around restrictions of calories also fall within this category. In this we are drawing a subtle distinction between Dieting Strategy and the concept of "dieting" which the community generally considers an undesirable, short-term practice that is not destined to solve individuals' real problems with weight.

DropPounds emphasizes the idea that healthy lifestyle changes are the key to losing and keeping weight off for the long term. Instead of short-term changes for quick weight loss that is commonly seen in a "diet", DropPounds encourages users to consistently log calories consumed and exercise over a longer period of time. The goal is to facilitate a type of self reflection and practices that reinforce changed behaviors. The following is an example of how DropPounds participants encourage each other to consider long-term weight loss and maintenance as a lifestyle change.

Thread 5.3.1

> **P#5147**: I read all over the internet where people say they gained their weight back! Why is this and how can you avoid it?
>
> **P#3068**: People gain their weight back because they lose the weight and stop trying. The only way to lose it and keep it off is not to diet but change your lifestyle. If you just stop eating and exercising properly then you're going to gain it back. That's why restrictive diets are bad because you need to be able to maintain that eating style for the rest of your life if you want to keep the weight off. If you are restricting yourself too much, it will become too challenging and not much fun. People fail because of these reasons.

The calculation of calorie limits for each person is based on a user's current weight, their goal weight, and the rate at which they want to lose weight. The results of this calculation in the system can generate unusually low calorie limits. As such, many discussions focus on calorie limits and the DropPounds process for losing weight. These discussions will surface safety issues surrounding low rates of calorie consumption. The community raises concerns when individuals appear to be eating so few calories that they are starving themselves. In the following example, the initial poster is asking about why they have stopped losing weight. In the interaction we see the initial poster pointing to the calorie allowance set by DropPounds.

Thread 5.3.2

> **P#1163**: I lost about 15 pounds but stopped. I feel like I've been on a diet for a year with a completely changed lifestyle. Yet I still can't get lower than 124-125 pounds unless I starve myself for a couple of days. I don't understand this. I eat less than or around 1000 calories everyday. Someone help! I just want to lose five more pounds.
>
> **P#1262**: You are probably not eating enough. Under 1000 calories isn't healthy for a person.
>
> **P#1163**: Oh trust me, I eat enough and my budget on this website is 980 calories. I also do ballet for two hours a day.
>
> **P#1434**: How tall are you? 125 pounds is thin to begin with.
>
> **P#1262**: Ask your doctor then.
>
> **P#1163**: 5 feet 5 inches. I want to be 118 pounds. It is still considered a healthy BMI.
>
> **P#1453**: Maybe your goals of "just another five pounds" and "ballet for 2 hours a day" are in conflict? Do you have a coach or nutritionist that might be able to make diet suggestions? Personally if you are really that close to your "goal", perhaps one based on inches or fitness levels might be more appropriate for you since you're so active. The scale is not a great measure of health or fitness and no number on the scale is worth starving yourself.

In this example, the community raises concerns regarding the low calorie rates and asks the original poster to consider other measures of success beyond simply the numbers on the scale. Often the DropPounds community expresses concern about how a new lifestyle is achieved and works to shape participants' attitudes toward techniques and approaches that are more likely to be safe and sustainable.

Many of the threads categorized as Dieting Strategy cover specific strategies that make weight loss successful. During our coding, we observed a range of strategies, many of which can be characterized in two different ways. First, there is a general calorie counting and calorie control strategy, which is the hallmark of the DropPounds approach. The second is a set of substitution strategies that help individuals handle times of weakness. The following two threads illustrate each of these strategies.

Thread 5.3.3

> **P#2070**: What are some views on meal planning? Does it really help keep nutrition on track? How would you even begin one?
>
> **P#4749**: I always plan my meals. I even plan my meal times. When he used to live in the states, my boyfriend would set his clock to 2 hours ahead (so, my time zone), and every 3-4 hours his alarm would go off and he'd text me to eat. (He also followed it for eating purposes).
>
> **P#5819**: I also plan my meals and meal times. Planning my meals ahead of time helps me stay on track and not be tempted to go out to lunch with co-workers or eat those 500 calorie donuts. If I already have my breakfast, lunch, and two healthy snacks, I can control my hunger better.

In this example thread, we see individuals discussing the control of calories by planning meals in advance. Through a planning approach, individuals can more accurately set calorie limits and know what is actually consumed. In other threads, posters describe strategies for substituting less calorie dense foods for other foods with too many calories. Both of these are key strategies for affecting weight loss and are part of changing long-term behaviors to support effective weight maintenance.

Dieting is a big business. Individuals and organizations spend money to advertise and make a name for their dieting strategy, products, and techniques. Many of these well known products and organizations are discussed by DropPounds participants. Many well known diet companies and products are mentioned. DropPounds does not have a blanket restriction around discussions that mention these other products, techniques, or services, but the community appears to be skeptical about anything that is being sold as the solution to weight loss problems.

Thread 5.3.4

> **P#7082**: I'm new on DropPounds. I was on Medifast for a while last year and lost 60 pounds, but decided to get back on the plan after trying everything else as it was the only plan that I was able to lose weight on. I would like to get down to 149 pounds and at the moment I'm 277 pounds. I started on Medifast again today and would love to find some new friends especially those on Medifast for support.
>
> **P#8974**: I am not on the full Medifast plan but I do always keep a supply of the protein shakes on hand. I find them very handy to use during the mid-morning, mid-afternoon, or if I am running late and need to catch up with breakfast.
>
> **P#8022**: To each his own and if you prefer this method more power to you but it really isn't teaching you how to be a healthy thin person. Learning to eat real food is an important part of maintaining a healthy weight and DropPounds can help you do that if you seriously log all your food. There's lots of support here and all the tools needed to make a healthy lifestyle change.
>
> **P# 4103**: I'm not a fan of meal replacers. They don't teach you how to live once you're off the diet, which is a recipe for gaining that weight back. Thin people don't live on shakes. You need to learn how to live as a thinner person. Forget "plans" to lose weight -- permanent weight loss isn't about plans or diets. It's about fundamental, lifestyle change.

Throughout this category, we see the different facets of Dieting Strategy. We can see how the participants focus on lifestyle, safe approaches to losing weight, and strategies that are likely to help participants become successful. The participants are wary of special diet programs. While they do not block or stop discussions of other structured diets, programs or products, the skeptical nature of responses will squelch discussion. The community is genuinely concerned for the safety of others and will cautiously challenge individuals who seem to engage in unsafe practices. Although we did not see them, there are allusions in some discussion threads to other threads that are hidden, blocked, or otherwise removed because they discuss or promote unsafe activity. The participants in DropPounds do not see magic in weight loss. Members of the community regularly say that the secret to long-term weight loss is to change behaviors to engage in a lifestyle that has a different relationship with food, calories, and exercise.

5.4 Health Information (211; 7.9%)

The correlations between weight and a wide range of behaviorally based medical conditions are well established. So, it is natural that DropPounds participants would discuss topics with medical and health implications. This category covered a wide range of topics from simple questions like "How do I manually calculate my heart rate?" to questions about managing diabetes during weight loss to complex questions that truly require a medical professional. Other aspects of a thread that put a discussion in this category included whether the participants were attempting to leverage evidence, such as a URL, a journal citation, or quoting text from a publication, and whether or not the participants in the discussion were attempting to diagnose something about the person or their situation through the types of questions they asked and the hypotheses they offered.

The discussions of Health Information exist on a dimension and participants are aware of that. As the questions become more complex, we see participants recommending medical consultation. This is not a role for DropPounds; it does not have paid medical staff to monitor the forums. And the forums are not suited to an appropriate medical consult interaction. Further, DropPounds is clear in several places on the website that individuals should seek medical advice when considering weight loss. In this first example thread, we see the threshold of recommending medical consultation crossed immediately:

Thread 5.4.1

P#1546: I recently started a diet where I am allotted 1,624 calories, but I tend to be only eating 500-600 calories a day while burning 300-500 with exercise everyday. What I am asking is how do I know if my body is in starvation mode? My body has been in ketosis for the last 4 days, and I am taking Phendimetrazine (3 a day) and Calcium Pyruvate (4 a day).

P#1833: I think you should call whatever doctor prescribed the Phendimetrazine and discuss with them. From the little amount of information you have given, I think you are eating a shockingly low amount of calories. Also since your case involves prescription weight loss medication, the only person that should be advising you on your diet should be your doctor, and your doctor needs ALL the facts to tell you what to do. I'm sorry that I can't be helpful but in your case I feel that it would be irresponsible to say anything other than to talk to your doctor, and I would do it ASAP.

P#1833: After looking into Phendimetrazine , I realized that this is a drug that can be obtained through other avenues than having a doctor prescribe it. If you chose to start this medication yourself, please know that it is chemically very similar to amphetamines, and is considered highly addictive. Similar to amphetamines (such as crystal meth) it suppresses the appetite and keeps you awake. Please, be very careful.

P#1992: What the heck are you eating?? (that would only be 2 meals for me) I am not a doctor, nor do I play one in this forum. However as <P#1833> stated, I would talk to your doctor. It certainly doesn't sound healthy to me. You may feel healthy, and your blood work may even reflect that, but I would be afraid of the long-term affect to your body. With that being said, I am not a fan of having to take a drug to curb your eating. This raises the question: What are you learning in your own eating habits if a drug is doing the work for you.

I had to look that drug up: so for others that don't (sic) know as well: Phendimetrazine is a sympathomimetic amine, which is similar to an amphetamine. It is also known as an "anorectic" or "anorexigenic" drug. Phendimetrazine stimulates the central nervous system (nerves and brain), which increases your heart rate, blood pressure and decreases appetite. <URL to drug info>

The DropPounds community takes Health Information questions very seriously and often work hard to understand what is happening to another participant so that they can point that

participant in a healthy and safe direction. This is similar to a study by Hwang et al. [6] that illustrated that questions to online health communities are answered with high quality information very frequently. Further, information that was inaccurate or dangerous was very quickly corrected..

Other Health Information threads concern debates about the truth or accuracy of some claims regarding health or weight loss. In this next example thread, we see the participants discussing information that comes from a lecture by a book author. The over 2 hour long lecture is comprised of a sequence of 10 minute videos which are embedded into the DropPounds website by the thread initiator.

Thread 5.4.2

P#2122: "Why We Get Fat" author Gary Taubes presentation. Hint: it's not because we eat too much and are lazy! <User supplied list of embedded videos>

P#2267: Very cool. Thanks for the video links.

P#1453: I will point out, as I have on other threads, that Gary Taubes is a great writer but a poor scientist. His conclusions are weak at best.

P#2122: Okay, links to back up your statement, please. His book cites references, where's yours? This is serious business.

P#1453: Here is one of the links. It clearly shows Taubes' pattern of misrepresenting both the remarks and research when he bothers to cite them at all. <User supplied links to article>

P#2622: My perspective is that there is not one approach that will work for everyone. To provide a blanket approach that is supposed to be applicable to us all just doesn't align with my views at all. There's a reason that my husband and I eat such different foods and quantities. There is definitely a problem with obesity in this country, but the result of equal diets does not produce equal results in everyone. Anyone who approaches weight loss as a one size fits all (no pun intended) solution loses credibility with me.

P#2122: With all due respect, we are actually talking about studies and facts. No one has credibility with me unless they back up what they are saying with facts. There is the traditional view promoting low-fat calorie restricted diets and there is evidence which promotes carbohydrate restrictions which reduces insulin production that regulates the fat stored in our cells. I think it's very important to get the facts out there regarding a different approach to health for people to see. I'm not presenting anything here that Taubes' hasn't shown where his information is from. If you don't like it, don't do it, but let's start discussing facts instead of beliefs. We all have a problem controlling our weight or maintaining it or we wouldn't be here. There is a lot of beneficial information for people who have not heard it before.

The conversational tone of these debates means that participants do not uniformly support their claims with evidence. Measuring the validity or trustworthiness of claims remains a challenge for many participants, as it is sometimes tough to differentiate between actual science and pseudoscience. Like most online communities, the reader should beware.

Not all Health Information threads are dire. Sometimes questions are important to the asker simply because they want to know about the topic. How the participants interact to understand the question and respond is one type of support that the community provides its members. In this next example, the initial post asks a question about a pending visit to the doctor, and the community works to figure out a reasonable answer.

Thread 5.4.3

> **P#3111**: I'm getting my blood drawn for a lab workup on Monday. That's also my morning for a long run (4-5 miles). I'm supposed to "fast" overnight as well; that's not a problem. I often run on an almost empty stomach. Is it okay to exert myself prior to getting blood work done?
>
> **P#3401**: Not sure, but I would play it safe and schedule the run for after the stick. I don't know what you're getting checked, but your glucose levels at least would probably be affected by heavy exercise.
>
> **P#3510**: <P#3111>, what are they testing for? If it's glucose, you probably shouldn't. On the other hand, if it's just cholesterol, then it's probably fine.
>
> **P#3111**: They are doing a complete metabolic panel (including glucose), a lipid panel w/ratios, and a CBC.
>
> **P#3510**: You know, I just don't know. Why not call them and ask?
>
> **P#3992**: I'd definitely recommend calling them, though they may not have a clear answer for you either (you might be the first person to ask). That said, given that exercise, especially fairly intense exercise, directly affects the metabolic functions you are testing for and that you are probably looking for a baseline, I'd run afterwards.
>
> **P#3111**: I was going to do that this morning (the lab happens to be on my mail route!) and it was the only day I've ever walked in there with no one in the waiting room and no one at the desk! I'll try again tomorrow.

The question in the example seems very reasonable. People get blood tests all the time and are commonly told to fast before the test, but what about a workout? While we end our example after only 7 posts to the thread, later in the thread other individuals chime in that exercise should not affect the results of the blood tests. This is confirmed later when participant P#3111 returns to the thread to say that the lab staff had said it was fine to exercise but that rehydration with water was important prior to the appointment.

6. DISCUSSION AND CONCLUSION

Naturally, the individual experience of DropPounds will vary from one participant to the next. Our study focused on a cross-section of the DropPounds forum as a way to gain insight into how individuals participate in an online weight loss community.

Our grounded topical category scheme provides one way to understand the shape of participation in an online weight loss community. In particular, the category of Personal Experience provides important social support to the participants. Personal Experience comprises a little over one quarter of the forum activity as a function of thread topics (see Table 1). This type of social support is important to keeping people engaged in the online community. Prior studies of online weight loss have shown that staying involved in the community is highly correlated with weight loss [12, 17, 18]. The other prominent categories that we have described above help us to understand the types of topical content that interest individuals in the community. The other high frequency topics include Dieting Strategies, Consumption Choices, Health Information, and Exercise, topics of which seem closely tied to weight loss.

The Networking category is interesting in that it reflects a concerted effort by members to find others who will serve to hold them accountable. In the DropPounds community, the notion of being accountable to oneself is a foundational notion of lifestyle behavior change. That is, in the long run, each person is ultimately accountable to herself for how she behaves and what she does or does not eat. But within this community, there is a need for people to transition from external (extrinsic) accountability to individual (intrinsic) accountability. The Networking category reflects one way the community helps facilitate that transition. Individuals seek accountability partners to help them change their lifestyle.

As a function of reading and categorizing threads, we have come to see a number of interesting aspects of the DropPounds community, which are not directly reflected in the category scheme. One thing is the range of participation roles that individuals take on at different times in the community. There are a few roles that are common to many online communities. DropPounds has "Moderators" who have added permissions in the system and who serve to maintain the social space and curate content among the different topic areas in DropPounds. Moderators are individuals who have been participating in DropPounds for a long period of time and are some of the most senior participants in the community. DropPounds also has newcomers ("Newbies") who join the community and express their inexperience in a wide range of ways. These two roles cross a wide range of other online communities.

DropPounds has a few roles which seem to be a function of the specific type of community. One commonly seen role is the "Shill". This role takes two slightly different forms. As we have mentioned, weight loss is a big business, and there are a wide range of products and services that claim to help individuals lose weight. There are many companies that would want to get their product in front of an audience like the participants in DropPounds. This is known and recognized by the community and the participants make an effort to police this in a reasonable way. Explicit marketing is called out, the account is banned, and the post removed. However, a reasonable question or discussion of a product may not be marketing, and the community is willing to discuss products even though they are often skeptical about any claims. This is the opening that the Shill is working to exploit. In one form, the Shill asks a question: "Say, I've been hearing very promising stories about <product_X>. Does anyone here know more about this product?" In response, there may be some community members who state that they have never heard about the product or that the product is not well respected by the community. Almost always, following a request for information, the other form of the Shill responds with something like: "Yeah, I love <product_X>! Here is where I get it for a great price: <link>." At that point, there is often heated discussion about whether or not this is marketing and should be allowed by DropPounds. The Shill will often respond by saying they were not marketing but rather just asking questions or providing information.

Another key role, which is promoted by the very idea of logging all calories and all exercise, is the "Quantified Self" role. We label this role after the broader Quantified Self movement made notable through websites such as quantifiedself.com, because the basic ideas are the same. People in DropPounds are encouraged to log everything. Some participants really enjoy that activity and seek to share the charts that they produce to help others understand the ways that calorie consumption, water intake, exercise, and weight fluctuate over time. Other than studies that have focused exclusively on the Quantified Self movement, we believe this is a new role that is likely to be found in the wider range of health and wellness online communities.

Identifying roles in online communities is important, but there are a number of states or attributes of participation which we believe should not formally be considered a role. These are somewhat temporary aspects of participation that can be observed in individual posts and are individually transient but persist in the community because different individuals will experience these states or attributes at different times. DropPounds highlights this because of the type of community it is: a weight loss community.

One of the most satisfying and important states or attributes that a person in an online weight loss community can have is what we call "Milestone." This is the sense of achievement and satisfaction stemming from reaching a goal that the individual set. The specific goals vary widely as does the time required to achieve the goals. This means that across a large number of participants there is always someone in a Milestone state. When people declare their Milestone state, the community often reaches out to celebrate and acknowledge their achievements. But for many in the community, Milestone is fleeting because often that state means it is time to set another, different goal.

Two other attributes or states bear mentioning, "Binged" and "Frustrated." In the Binged state, individuals come to the community to declare some type of failing. In DropPounds, it is often a failing due to excessive consumption, a binge. In the case of Frustrated, an individual describes a specific type of problem they have and cannot seem to overcome. In DropPounds, that problem is often a weight loss plateau or no effective weight loss for some period of time. Another common Frustrated state is when an individual declares inability to control consumption of a specific type of food or drink, like chips, beer, or ice cream. Like Milestone, Binged and Frustrated are considered temporary states of being not specific roles in the community.

Another aspect that we have come to see is the different ways that individuals approach the forums. For some people, the forums are more like a static repository of information to be searched. Individuals who come to the forums with this perspective engage these forums thinking something like "surely someone has had this issue/problem before and all I need to do is *search* for the answer." This mindset is evident in the wording and behavior of posters in two ways. First, we see some initial posters explicitly say they searched the forum for the content and could not find it. A more subtle version of this mindset is implicated in posts saying that they did not know how to describe something or what terms to call something. This apologetic approach is characteristic of newcomers learning some new domain or new practice [16]. This particular mindset is also evident in the behavior of individuals who are established in the community when responding tersely with a post like "see our FAQ on this topic: <link>."

The other mindset considers the forum as a place to work through an issue or question. These individuals come to the forums with the idea that interacting with people is the way for them to learn and understand what they need to know. These people see the forums as a social information process. They come to the forums thinking something like "surely someone has had this issue/problem before and all I need to do is *ask* them for the answer." These posters are more interested in the thoughts of the people who bother to respond.

The main point here is not to claim that a forum should be more of the former or the latter. The real issue is that the underlying assumptions which individuals bring to the forums are cause for a type of problematic interaction. When people come to the forum assuming it is a social information process and they are met with posts by individuals who assume the forum is an information repository, participants can feel as if the others in the community are brusque, prickly, or somewhat mean. While these conceptual views of forums and newsgroups may not be new, there is still little work that seeks to uncover the underlying assumptions of individual participants to smooth interaction between individuals who come to these discussion spaces with very different conceptual models.

The literature has shown a high correlation between individuals who participate in what an online community has to offer and weight loss [7, 8, 12, 18]. This suggests that efforts to attract participants to the social support, dieting strategies, and health information provided in forums could yield some benefits. Furthermore, the nature of roles in an online community has been explored in previous literature. Maloney-Krichmar and Preece found three primary roles users took in an online knee injury support group: Information Giver, Opinion Giver, and Encourager. These roles are important to facilitate the purpose of the support group to give advice and information to users [11]. The roles we discovered in DropPounds are analogous to some of the roles seen in the knee injury support group such as the role of quantified self being similar to the information giver. Many of the users take on the role of opinion giver in the community due to DropPounds lack of established rules. The Shill role can be thought of as an (unpopular) Opinion Giver. Encourager roles are also seen around the community especially in Personal Experience threads for users slogging through Binged or Frustrated states. The names for the roles may change between communities, but the concepts of information, opinion, and encourager exist in online support forums.

The DropPounds model itself played a role in the types of conversations that were observed. As previously mentioned, a large focus is placed on lifestyle changes through activity logging to achieve weight loss results. There are no set rules or methods listed from the application. This results in many interpretations of "the best way" to lose weight, leading to ideological clashes. This is most obvious in the disdain for product shills and debates around whether quantifying all aspects of the day is necessary. The design of the DropPounds forum also contributes to the types of discussion that occur. Of the eight sub-forums, only two of them are dedicated to certain weight loss activities such as "Fitness and Exercise" and "Diet and Nutrition" while the rest are for teams and miscellaneous discussion. There may be some confusion for users about where to post threads about their personal stories about eating behavior. The online forum system's search function is limited: all results of a specific term are shown but link back to the message where that term appears. This makes finding the original post of the thread more challenging. Certain threads are also permanently posted on the first page of each sub forum, which push down new topics and topics that receive responses to the middle of the page. Users may not immediately find threads pertaining to their interests and post a new thread to discuss their thoughts. This may have inflated the number of observances for certain topic types. These factors may have affected user discussions on DropPounds.

Effective support for newcomers is a common issue in online communities. One approach is to provide a forum space that allows new users to introduce themselves and receive responses from longtime members. By creating a welcoming experience, where newbies can share questions and receive answers from more credible community members, the barrier to participation can be lowered. Connections they make with other users can be enriched with the logging activity to create active social support. For instance, if the system sees a user fail to participate in any forum, or if the system sees a user exceed his caloric budget for a number of consecutive days, the system could notify friends that the user may be Frustrated or Binged. Friends could then intervene with questions, concerns, encouragement, and motivation, keeping the user engaged.

A more dynamic forum system would likely be needed to implement some of these proposed changes. By adding more options for users to describe their personal stories such as a blog per user, there can be a dedicated space for users to share their struggles and victories with others. These blogs won't get buried by other forum threads and can be viewed by others. These blogs can also be a safer area to share concerns or questions about the dieting process without the entire community chiming in. Combined with a more robust search function and a bookmarking feature to return to notables threads will help make the forum system curate and serve information to users more efficiently. The system could also work to provide more support for moderators. For example, when users ask questions about difficult topics or opaque features of the system, moderators will often just link to an FAQ. This type of response will result in some users feeling disconnected from the peer support that the community offers. Providing moderators better tools to tailor responses to each user could alleviate misunderstanding about the goals and role of moderators. Drawing on the user's weight loss progress and combined with sentiment analysis, a tool could suggest different responses that might address the user's issue more effectively. The goal is not to automate a response but to provide community moderators means to increase social support engendering a desire to return to the community.

This study has focused on the qualitative participation in one successful online weight loss community. Through a topical content analysis of the online forums, this study has shed light on the issues participants face and the types of activity that occur. Though the benefits of an online community have been previously documented, our work shows the many facets of user participation. We describe some of the significant content, how the community engages that content, and different roles that participants take. We identify a set of transient states, which are not proper roles but are significant in an online community where individuals are attempting to change their own behaviors. Lastly, we have provided concrete suggestions that could increase participation and engagement in an online community related to weight loss and healthy activity.

7. ACKNOWLEDGMENTS

We would like to acknowledge all of the participants of DropPounds. We have worked hard to describe their struggles and their successes. The work would not have been possible without support from FitNow Inc. We acknowledge the comments and reflections from the reviewers which we believe has improved the paper.

8. REFERENCES

[1] Bennett, G. G., R. E. Glasgow, "The Delivery of Public Health Interventions via the Internet: Actualizing Their Potential," *Annual Review of Public Health,* vol. 30, pp. 273-292, 2009.

[2] Eysenbach, G., Powell J., Englesakis, M., Rizo, C., Stern. A, "Health related virtual communities and electronic support groups: systematic review of the effects of online peer to peer interactions," *BMJ*, vol. 328, p. 1166, 2004.

[3] Grimes, A., Bednar, M., Bolter, J.D. and Grinter, R.E., EatWell: Sharing nutrition-related memories in a low-income community. in Proceedings of the ACM Conference on Computer-Supported Cooperative Work (CSCW'08), (2008) 87-96.

[4] Grimes, A., Landry, B.M. and Grinter, R.E., Characteristics of Shared Health Reflections in a Local Community. in Proceedings of the ACM Conference on Computer-Supported Cooperative Work (CSCW'10), (2010) 435-444.

[5] Hwang, K., Stuckey, H., Chen, M., Kraschnewski, J. Forjuoh, S., Poger, J., McTigue, K. and Sciamanna, C., Primary Care Providers' Perspective on Online Weight-Loss Programs: A Big Wish List, *Journal of Medical Internet Research (JMIR),* 14, 1 (Jan-Feb 2012).

[6] Hwang, K., Farheen, K., Johnson, C., Thomas, E., Barnes, A. and Bernstam, E., Quality of Weight Loss Advice on Internet Forums, *The American Journal of Medicine*, 120, 7, (July 2007)

[7] Hwang, K., Stuckey, Jing, N., Trickery, A. and Sciamanna, C.,Website usage and weight loss in a free commercial online weight loss program: Retrospective cohort study, *Journal of Medical Internet Research (JMIR),* 15, 1 (Jan 2013).

[8] Kraschnewski, Stuckey, Rovniak, Lehman, Reddy, Poger, Kephart, Coups, and Sciamanna. Efficacy of a Weight-Loss Website Based on Positive Deviance A Randomized Trial. *American Journal of Preventive Medicine,* 2011, 41(6), 610 – 614

[9] Klasnja, P., Consolvo, S. and Pratt, W. How to evaluate technologies for health behavior change in HCI research. in Proceedings of the ACM Conference on Human Factors in Computing Systems (CHI'11), (2011)

[10] Maher , C. A., Lewis, L. K., Ferrar, K., Marshall, S., De Bourdeaudhuij I., Vandelanotte C., "Are health behavior change interventions that use online social networks effective? a systematic review," *Journal of Medical Internet Research,* vol. 16, 2014.

[11] Maloney-Kirchmar and Preece. A Multilevel Analysis of Sociability, Usability, and Community Dynamics in an Online Health Community. ACM Transactions on Computer-Human Interaction, Vol. 12, No. 2, 201–232.

[12] Neve, M., Morgan, P., Jones, P. and Collins, C., Effectiveness of web-based interventions in achieving weight loss and weight loss maintenance in overweight and obese adults: a systematic review with meta-analysis, *Obesity Reviews,* 11, 4, (April 2010).

[13] Newman, M.W., Lauterbach, D., Munson, S.A., Resnick, P. and Morris, M.E. "It's not that I don't have problems, I'm just not putting them on Facebook": Challenges and Opportunities in Using Online Social Networks for Health. in Proceedings of the ACM Conference on Computer-Supported Cooperative Work (CSCW'11), (2011) 341-350.

[14] Parker, A., Kantroo, V., Lee, H.R., Osornio, M., Sharma, M. and Grinter, R.E., Health Promotion as Activism: Building Community Capacity to Effect Social Change. in

Proceedings of the ACM Conference on Human Factors in Computing Systems (CHI'12), (2012) 99-108

[15] Purpura, S., Schwanda, V., Williams, K., Stubler, W. and Sengers, P. Fit4Life: The Design of a Persuasive Technology Promoting Healthy Behavior and Ideal Weight. in Proceedings of the ACM Conference on Human Factors in Computing Systems (CHI'11), (2011) 423-432.

[16] Torrey, C., E. Churchill and D. W. McDonald (2009) Learning How: The Search for Craft Knowledge on the Internet. Proceedings of the ACM 2009 SIGCHI Conference on Human Factors in Computing Systems (CHI'09). Boston, MA.

[17] Tsai, A. and Wadden, T., Systematic Review: An Evaluation of Major Commercial Weight Loss Programs in the United States, *Annals of Internal Medicine*, 142, 1, (Jan 2005).

[18] Weinstein, K. A review of weight loss programs delivered via the Internet, *The Journal of Cardiovascular Nursing*, 21, (July-Aug 2006).

If It Is Funny, It Is Mean:

Understanding Social Perceptions of Yelp Online Reviews

Saeideh Bakhshi
Yahoo Labs
San Francisco, CA USA
sbakhshi@yahoo-inc.com

Partha Kanuparthy
Yahoo Labs
Sunnyvale, CA USA
parthak@yahoo-inc.com

David A. Shamma
Yahoo Labs
San Francisco, CA USA
aymans@acm.org

ABSTRACT

Online recommendation communities, like Yelp, are valuable information sources for people. Yet, we assert, review communities have their own dynamics behind the social interactions therein. In this work, we study the Yelp review votes of *useful*, *funny*, and/or *cool* to understand these social perceptions of the review. We examine the relationship between these social signals and the emotional valence of the review itself (text and rating). We aim to understand the community's perception of each of these signaling contributions. We construct a conditional inference tree of social signals from 230,000 Yelp reviews to study how social signals shape the deviance in review rating from the mean rating, an indicator of the overall business rating on Yelp. We find two effects of social signals. First, reviews voted as useful and funny are associated with lower user ratings and relatively negative tone in the review text. Second, reviews voted as cool tend to have a relatively positive tone and higher ratings. Our findings open a research direction for further understanding of perceptions of social signals and have implications for design of recommendation systems.

Categories and Subject Descriptors

H.4 [**Information Systems Applications**]: Miscellaneous; D.2.8 [**Software Engineering**]: Metrics—*complexity measures, performance measures*

Keywords

Yelp; Online Reviews; Social Signals; Votes; Social Feedback; Conditional Inference Trees; Funny, Cool, Useful Votes

1. INTRODUCTION

Online recommendation sites are important resources that enable sharing opinions among people. These communities enable members (users) to share their experiences with products, services and activities in the form of reviews and rat-

GROUP'14, November 9–12, 2014, Sanibel Island, Florida, USA.
Copyright 2014 ACM 978-1-4503-3043-5/14/11 ... $15.00.
http://dx.doi.org/10.1145/2660398.2660414.

ings, that may otherwise be difficult to find before receipt of a service or product. Consumers perceive online recommendation communities as unbiased sources of information as compared to business listing websites [10]. The presence of reviews for businesses has been shown to improve customer perception of the usefulness and social presence of the website [19].

Reviews have the potential to attract user visits, increase the time spent on the site, and create a sense of community among frequent users. However, as the availability of online reviews becomes widespread, the effectiveness of recommendation communities shifts from the mere presence of customer reviews to how community members evaluate and use the reviews.

To promote engagement between the minority of content creators and the majority of content consumers, many online communities provide users with voting and feedback systems. These systems serve an important purpose—they enable users to generate *social signals* in the community e.g. Facebook's *likes*, Twitter's *favorites* and *retweets* and Amazon's *helpful review votes*. In Yelp, each review can be voted as *useful*, *cool* and/or *funny* (in any combination) which provides three social signals that describe the different ways in which users perceive online reviews written by others.

Yelp indexed over one million recommendations from 100 million unique visitors in the month of January 2013[1]. Yelp members, or "Yelpers" add reviews as text with an integer rating score on a scale of one to five. The Yelpers can then vote on the review as one or more of useful, cool and funny. While the common perception is that these votes are proxies for quality of Yelp reviews, our understanding of each of these social signals is limited. In this work, we ask the question: What do these social signals for a review indicate about that review? Specifically, we ask two questions:

1. Are the social signals of a review indicative of how much the rating differs from the mean rating for that business?

2. Are the social signals of a review indicative of the polarity of the text?

We answer these questions by modeling the review's attributes (numeric rating and tone of the text) as functions of the social signals which that review receives. We construct a conditional inference tree of social signals, and use review attributes as the dependent variables. We study a large-scale

---

[1]http://officialblog.yelp.com/2013/02

Yelp dataset containing 230K reviews and their social signals.

In this paper, our hypothesis is that these voting signals have specific implications towards the reviews themselves which may not match the signal's label. To unravel such implications, we take a closer look at the relationship between these signals and the review content that is evaluated. We demonstrate two surprising observations, given that social signals for a review in Yelp are based on the review text, and have no relationship with the business that is under review. First, we find that social signals are associated with reviews whose ratings deviate from the mean rating. Second, we find that *useful* and *funny* signals are associated with reviews having a higher negative tone or lower positive tone, while *cool* signals are associated with reviews having a higher positive tone.

In the remainder of paper, we summarize related work, describe the data we obtained, and explain our statistical findings. We conclude our paper by discussing the results and describing some of the implications we can draw from this work. Finally we point out some of the limitations of this work and summarize possible future directions.

2. RELATED WORK

This paper on one hand, investigates the dynamics of behavior on online review site, Yelp, and on the other hand is focused on differentiating between various social signals communicated by users. In an effort to understand what has been done in this scope and what is missing, we summarize the relevant literature on perceptions of online reviews and the prior studies on understanding helpful votes.

2.1 Perceptions and Social Feedback

Understanding people's perceptions of web based information systems, or social media sites is a complex phenomenon, requiring a series of systematic studies. There has been a significant amount of work on how members of online communities perceive content. Prior work has shown that attributes of review text, reviewer and social context can shape user response to reviews [2, 12, 13, 21, 27]. Lu et al. [21] use a latent topic approach to extract rated quality aspects (corresponding to concepts such as price or shipping) from comments on eBay. Harper et al. [16] studied the helpfulness of answers on the Yahoo Answers site and the influence of variables such as the type of answer and the topic domain of the question. Siersdorfer et al. [25] looked at prediction of community ratings for comments and discussions of video content on YouTube. Another study on YouTube [28] predicted the genre categorization of YouTube videos based on people's interactions around media content without recourse to meta-data.

A body of work studied how members of online communities use review content. For example, studies have examined the role of expert reviews [6], the role of online recommendation systems [3, 5, 15], and the positive effect of social signals (and feedback mechanisms) on buyer trust [22]. Clemons et al. [7] found that positive ratings can positively influence the growth of product sales, and Chen et al. [6] found that the quality of the review as measured by helpfulness votes also positively influences sales.

A primary objective of online communities is that of user engagement. General aspects of online user engagement have been discussed in detail in prior work [20, 29]. A common way to study user engagement is through online behavior metrics that assess the extent of users' engagement with content on the site. For instance, Peterson and Carrabis [23] describe engagement metrics that are related to consumption time on the site, users' return to the site or subscription to the site's feed. A study of web content by Amento et al. [1] investigated the utility of various metrics in estimating the quality of web documents. Further, Wu et al. [27] study the temporal development of product ratings and their helpfulness, and dependencies on factors such number of reviews and the effort required (writing review versus just assigning a rating).

2.2 Helpful Votes

To encourage both creators of content and the readers to engage with the site, many online communities provide users with a feedback system. Facebook likes, twitter's favorites or retweets, Amazon's helpful votes on reviews and Yelp's useful, cool and funny votes are all examples of such systems. Prior research suggests that perceived attributes of the review text, reviewer and social context may all shape consumer response to reviews [2, 12, 13, 21, 27].

There is a body of work on analyzing product reviews and postings in forums. Lu et al. [21] use a latent topic approach to extract rated quality aspects (corresponding to concepts such as "price" or "shipping") from comments in ebay. The temporal development of product ratings and their helpfulness and dependencies on factors such number of reviews or effort required (writing review vs. just assigning a rating) are studied [27]. The helpfulness of answers on the Yahoo! Answers site and the influence of variables such as required type of answer, topic domain of the question is manually analyzed [16]. Siersdorfer et al. [25] focused on community ratings for comments and discussions rather than product ratings on Youtube. Another study on Amazon reviews [8] studied the helpfulness scores on Amazon site and found that the helpfulness scores are not only dependent on the content of the review but also on other reviews posted for the product.

While there has been studies on understanding and predicting helpful votes, we don't know much about other useful feedback mechanisms than can encourage engagement. Yelp provides users with two new voting concepts, funny and cool. Not only it is important to know what users in general perceive as *funny* or *cool*, but also better understandings of how social feedback system relates to conventional text analysis such as sentiment can give us insights in building more effective recommender systems.

3. DATA

Founded in 2004, Yelp is a large online recommendation community that is also a user-maintained business and service directory to help people find local businesses. According to their website[2], Yelp had an average of about 102 million monthly unique visitors in 2013 and the community members have written over 39 million reviews. Members of Yelp make millions of contributions to the community a month. Many regular Yelpers, maintain profiles with pictures, their interests, favorite places, friends and location. Yelpers can friend or follow other people on site, as well as the aforementioned reviewing and voting features. We acquired our data

---

[2]http://officialblog.yelp.com/

Variable	Description	Distribution
business stars	The average number of Yelp stars for the business.	
review stars	The number of stars attributed to the review. The star scale is between 1 to 5.	
review cool votes†	The number of review's cool votes.	
review funny votes†	The number of review's funny votes.	
review useful votes†	The number of review's useful votes.	
review polarity	Polarity score of review text, in range of (-1,1).	
review subjectivity	Subjectivity score of review text, in range of (0,1).	

Table 1: Distributions of variables used in this paper. Variables marked with † are log-transformed. The red and blue lines identify mean and median of the distribution respectively.

from the Yelp Dataset Challenge[3] which consists of a sample of Yelp data from the Greater Phoenix, AZ metropolitan area. It includes 11,537 *businesses*, 43,873 *reviewers* and 229,907 *reviews*. The data spans from 2005 to 2013. Table 1 summarizes the description and distributions of the numerical variables used in this paper.

As in any online recommendation community, Yelp members contribute reviews for businesses. A review consists of a stars rating and a review text. In order to understand the effect of review text, we process the text for each review to quantify the *subjectivity* (between 0 and 1) and *polarity* (between -1 and 1) of the text using the Pattern Toolkit[4]. We use the *funny*, *cool* and *useful* votes counts as measures of review's social feedback.

We construct variables for our model as follows. Our dependent variable is a binary attribute that denotes whether a review's rating was larger than the overall rating for that business (across all reviews). This measures the difference between review's rating and the average rating on Yelp for that business. We use the difference between these two ratings, as opposed to the actual review's rating to control for the average rating of the business being reviewed.

We use the *funny*, *cool* and *useful* votes as predictors of the rating deviance (defined as the difference between the review rating and the average rating for that business). Instead of using numerical values of votes for *funny*, *cool* and *useful* votes, we define a binary variable for each type of signal. The binary variable is based on whether there were more than three votes on the signal. We chose three as the threshold to control for noise and weak community feedback. We checked the results with thresholds of 0, 1, 2, 4 and 5, and found the results to be similar.

4. METHOD

In this paper, we wish to understand the relationship between each social feedback signal and the review's rating, controlling for the rating of the business. We first perform a group comparison between *funny* and *not-funny* reviews[5],

cool and *not-cool* reviews and *useful* and *not-useful* reviews. We use a Chi-Square (χ^2) test with the null hypothesis that both groups of *funny* reviews and *not-funny* voted reviews come from the same distribution. The test rejects the null hypothesis, indicating that they are not coming from the same distribution, with p-value smaller than 2.2×10^{-16}. We repeated this test on *cool* and *useful* votes and both tests rejected the null hypothesis with p-value smaller than 2.2×10^{-16}. Therefore, we proceed with analyzing the interaction between these social signals and understanding how they might impact the deviance in the rating.

We use conditional inference trees [17] to study the role of social feedback on deviation in a review's rating. This method is particularly useful in the case of this study, because the trees not only tell us the extent to which each variable is important, but also help us to better interpret the results. The common splitting criterion used in conditional inference trees is the Gini Index. The Gini Index checks for the "purity" of resulting children nodes in the tree. For a given node t with estimated class probabilities $p(j|t)$, $j = 1, \ldots, J$ [4], the node impurity $i(t)$ is given by:

$$i(t) = \phi(p(1|t), \ldots, p(J|t))$$

The most favorable split is the one that reduces the node or equivalently the tree impurity. The most favorable split is identified by search. Adopting the Gini diversity index, $i(t)$ takes the form:

$$i(t) = \Sigma_{j \neq i} p(j|t)p(i|t)$$

The Gini index, defined as a function $\phi(p_1, \ldots, p_J)$ of the $p_1, \ldots, p_J$, is a quadratic polynomial with nonnegative coefficients. In conditional inference trees, the node split is selected based on how good the association is. The resulting node should have a higher association with the observed value of the dependent variable. The conditional inference tree uses a χ^2 test to test the association. Therefore, it not only removes the bias due to categories but also chooses those variables that are informative.

The key to this algorithm is based on the separation of variable selection and the splitting procedure. The recursive binary partitioning is as follows. The response Y comes from sample space Y, which may be multivariate. The m dimensional covariate vector $X = (X_1, \ldots, X_m)$ is taken from a

---

[3] https://www.yelp.com/dataset_challenge

[4] http://www.clips.ua.ac.be/pattern

[5] We consider a review to be funny if it has at least 4 funny votes (see Section 3).

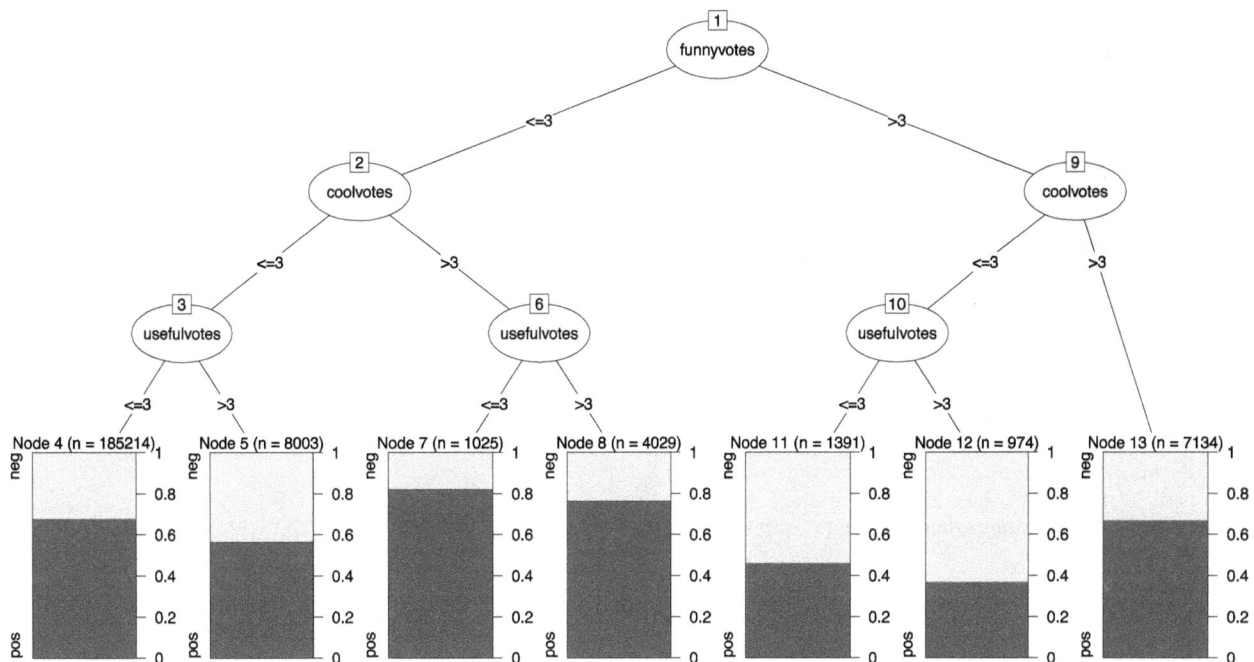

Figure 1: Conditional inference tree with difference in review's rating and business's rating as dependent variable. For each inner node, the Bonferroni-adjusted *p-values* for all splits are less than 0.001, the number of data points in each group is displayed for each terminal node. The black color in the bar plots quantifies the likelihood of the review's rating being greater than the business review, and the gray area shows the likelihood of the review's rating being lower than the business's collective average rating.

sample space $X = X_1 \times \cdots \times X_m$. Both the response variables and the dependent variable may be measured at any arbitrary scale. The conditional distribution of the response variable given the covariates depends on the function of covariates:

$$D(Y|X) = D(Y|X_1, \ldots, X_m)$$
$$= D(Y|f(X_1, \ldots, X_m))$$

For a given learning sample of n iid observations a generic algorithm can be formulated using nonnegative integer of case weights $w = (w_1, w_2, \ldots, w_n)$. Each node of a tree is represented by a vector of case weights having non-zero elements when the corresponding observations are significant for that node, and zero otherwise. The generic algorithm is:

1. For case weights w, we test the global null hypothesis of independence between any of the covariates and the response. The step terminates if the hypothesis cannot be rejected at a pre-specified nominal level α. Otherwise, we select the j'th covariate X_j with the strongest association to the response variable.

2. Set $A \subset X_j$ is chosen to split X_j, into two disjoint sets. The case weights w_{left} and w_{right} determine the two subgroups with

$$w_{left,i} = w_i I(X_{ji} \in A)$$

and

$$w_{right,i} = w_i I(X_{ji} \notin A)$$

for all $i = 1, \ldots, n$, where $I()$ denotes the indicator function, which indicates the membership of an element in a subset.

3. We repeat the steps 1 and 2 with modified case weights w_{left} and w_{right}, respectively.

The separation of variable selection and splitting procedures is essential for the development of trees with no tendency toward covariates with many possible splits [17].

5. RESULTS

Figure 1 visualizes the conditional inference tree for our dependent variable (the difference in review's rating and the business's rating). The terminal nodes show different distributions of the dependent variable (the deviance from mean rating) in each case. Also, we can see that on the right side of the tree where the number of *funny* votes is greater than three, there is higher density of negative deviance from the mean. This means the reviews written for the business with more *funny* votes are usually rated lower than the mean business rating. In other words, the *funny* votes are usually given to the more critical reviews that have lower ratings. The negative tendency of the ratings compared to the collective business rating shows that the concept of *funny* is perceived negatively by the Yelp users. Table 2 summarizes the mean, standard deviation and standard error of sentiment polarity for reviews considered *funny* or *not-funny*. We can see that the funny reviews are -0.39 units more negative than the not-funny ones.

We find that when the *funny* votes are high but the *cool* votes are low (Figure 1), we see the most negative deviance in the ratings from the mean business's rating. When the useful votes are low as well, the likelihood of having a negative deviance rating is equal to 0.5 but when the useful votes are high, the negative deviance likelihood is as high as 0.6, meaning that 60% of the reviews with higher *funny* votes, lower *cool* votes and higher *useful* votes are rated lower than the collective business's rating. We show an example of parts of a review that was voted funny and useful but did not receive many cool votes:

> "...Upon arrival, we were immediately greeted by a smell that can accurately be described as 'Fat, grease, and charred death.'" ...
>
> As far as decor, the restaurant does a good job of sticking to an anti-doctor theme, with signs plastered all over the restaurant warning you of the unhealthy nature of their food, mandatory patient gowns for all diners, and waitresses dressed as cute nurses.
>
> But the food itself could be summed up with the word 'Sickening,' which actually works metaphorically and literally. Their shakes are incredibly sweet, but actually filled with ice cream, pure cream, and butter. Their fries are cooked in lard, and their burgers are excessively heavy and fattening. A burger and fries is really enough to fill up a fully-grown man, but the sensation of being completely filled by lard, meat, and grease is almost as disgusting as seeing one of the obese regulars scarf down a triple-bypass burger for free. ...
>
> Disgusting? Yes. Necessary? No. Immoral? Decidedly no, since they clearly warn you about what you're getting in to.
>
> I'd eat here once, and NEVER again. It's a place fueled by novelty- go there only if you're inspired after watching Epic Meal Time on youtube."
>
> (*2 cool votes, 17 funny votes, 11 useful votes*)

While *funny* votes are given to more critical reviews (lower ratings), the *cool* votes seem to enforce a positive perception on the users. On the other hand the *useful* votes when accompanied by *funny* votes, seem to be related to lower ratings. We see that in the case of high *funny* votes and high *cool* votes the likelihood of a review rating being smaller than the collective business review is 0.3, see Figure 1.

When the *funny* votes are low and *cool* votes are high, we see the highest likelihood of positive change in ratings. In the case that *useful* votes are low, the likelihood of positive change is the highest among all, i.e. 0.8. When the *useful* votes are high, the likelihood is slightly lower but still close to 0.8. This shows the positive perception of *cool* votes and negative perception of *funny* votes. An example review, where the cool votes were high and useful and funny votes were low is provided below:

> "Ode to Trader Joe's
>
> Seasonal produce of mellow fruitfulness!
>
> Island themed friend of the tropical sun;
>
> Conspired to load the shopping cart

Condition	Mean Polarity	Std.Dev	Std.Err
Funny > 3	-0.17	0.16	0.002
Funny ≤ 3	0.26	0.22	0.000
Cool > 3	0.46	0.22	0.001
Cool ≤ 3	0.21	0.15	0.001
Useful > 3	0.09	0.16	0.001
Useful ≤ 3	0.26	0.22	0.001

Table 2: Mean, Standard Deviation and Standard Error values of polarity for reviews voted with each of the social feedback signals. We can see the mean polarity for funny reviews is around 0.4 less than not-funny ones. The cool reviews are more positive in 0.25 units in their polarity and the useful votes are 0.17 less positive than the not-useful ones.

> With fruit and veggies that round the table run;
>
> Oft whoever seeks tasty may find. ...
>
> Where are thy Joe-O's? Ay, where are they?
>
> Think of them, and thy hast cheeses too,
>
> Then in a clanging call the young cashiers beseech
>
> Open yet another among the checkout stands
>
> And gathering shoppers swoon in the lot.
>
> WIth a nod to Keats"
>
> (*11 cool votes, 1 funny votes, 3 useful votes*)

Table 2 shows that the difference among the sentiment polarity of cool reviews and the ones without *cool* votes is substantial—indicating that both the ratings and polarity of the reviews are higher among the ones with cool votes. The *useful* votes are also slightly negatively perceived. When the *funny* votes are low and the *cool* votes and *useful* votes are low as well, we have the most common case happening ($n = 185214$). In this case, the chance of negative change is 0.3 and the chance of positive deviance is 0.7. We can see from Figure 1 that in the case of low *funny* and *cool* votes but higher *useful* votes, the chances of negative change increases to 0.4, indicating that the perception of *useful* signal on Yelp is negative. The polarity of the sentiments on *useful* reviews is around 0.17 units less than the ones without *useful* votes, which emphasizes on the negative tone of useful reviews.

6. DISCUSSION

In this paper, we have shown how different social signals, used as feedback votes, demonstrates the differences of review ratings and their sentiments. We started with a limited understanding of what users perceive as *cool*, *funny* or *useful* and took a first step towards understanding the relative relationship of each of these social signals with respect to the changes in the review ratings. We were able to point out significant differences in review rating patterns and emotional valence of the review text across these social signals. We summarize our findings and discuss implications below.

Funny votes imply lower ratings and higher negativity in the tone.

Our results show that the funny votes are related to higher likelihood of negative changes in the ratings. This means that the population of Yelp users perceive those reviews as funny that are lower in ratings. This can be explained in two ways. First, it might be that the general audience on the review sites such as Yelp, enjoy reading the reviews with sarcastic tone or those reviews that criticize the business with some humor. The second explanation goes back to the perception of the reader and the votes. It could be that the users find the lower rated reviews and those with negative tone more funny or humorous. Either way, the fact that the higher funny votes are related to the lower rated reviews illuminates the opinion of the general Yelp user of what is considered funny. Further, it's worth mentioning that negativity of funny reviews can help with crowd-generated content that may be identified as sarcasm. Previous research has investigated ways to detect sarcasm through natural language models [9, 26].

Useful votes imply lower ratings and lower positivity in the tone.

The same pattern that is observable with funny votes also applies to useful votes, but in a smaller scale. Our results show that the reviews that are rated as useful are on average more likely to be rated lower than those without useful votes. This finding suggests that users find the more critical reviews more useful. While, useful reviews are usually perceived as high quality reviews on review sites, here our findings emphasizes its relationship with lower ratings and higher negative sentiment.

Cool votes imply higher ratings and higher positivity in the tones.

Unlike the perceptions of funny and useful on the reviews, we find that reviews that are perceived as cool are more likely to be highly rated. This suggests that the cool perception is usually tied with the higher rated reviews of businesses. The lower rated reviews are less likely to be perceived as cool. We also find that the level of polarity in the review is higher in positivity among cool reviews, which makes the argument of positive perception of cool reviews stronger.

Community signals carry implied meaning beyond their specific labels.

Online recommendation communities rely on member contributions to index and serve recommendations [11, 14, 18]. The findings of our research suggest that there is deeper meanings and interaction forms than the generic votes. The specific community of Yelp, for example, judges and communicates meaning through its own interpretation of the signal labels, which is congruent to similar finding in the multimedia community [24]. Future work can elaborate on the use of these labels and their corresponding social perceptions in other communities. For example, what do *likes* on Facebook mean in different contexts and by different people? Is it some form of social confirmation, do users support the content of the post? Do they find it cool or funny? Deeper understandings of forms of user feedbacks can enable us with better recommendation and social network design.

This study is based on Yelp and further work is needed to ascertain whether our findings apply to other review com-

munities. For example the negative tone in funny reviews might not be appreciated in other types of communities. Further, our data was limited to certain variables and the statistical methods we used examine only a small segment of behavior on Yelp. A possible direction for future work is to look closely into the language that is used in funny, cool and useful reviews. For example, are there certain phrases or types of writing that contribute to funny votes? Another possible research direction is to complement this work with a qualitative study. One could find what users perceive as cool or funny by interviewing Yelp users.

7. CONCLUSION

Online recommendation communities such as Yelp enable people to find right businesses and services, and enable businesses to find new customers. Hence, it is critical for such communities to maximize social interactions around reviews. Yelp, as a pioneer in online review communities, has provided users with several ways to evaluate content. In this paper, we took a first step to better understand the underlying review patterns associated with each of these social signals. We found that useful and funny signals are mostly associated with lower ratings and more negative sentiment, while cool signal is associated with higher ratings and positive sentiment.

8. REFERENCES

[1] B. Amento, L. Terveen, and W. Hill. Does "authority" mean quality? predicting expert quality ratings of web documents. In *Proceedings of the 23rd annual international ACM SIGIR conference on Research and development in information retrieval*, pages 296–303. ACM, 2000.

[2] N. Archak, A. Ghose, and P. G. Ipeirotis. Show me the money!: deriving the pricing power of product features by mining consumer reviews. In *Proceedings of the 13th ACM SIGKDD international conference on Knowledge discovery and data mining*, pages 56–65. ACM, 2007.

[3] J. Y. Bakos. Reducing buyer search costs: implications for electronic marketplaces. *Management science*, 43(12):1676–1692, 1997.

[4] L. Breiman. *Classification and regression trees*. CRC press, 1993.

[5] P.-Y. Chen, S.-y. Wu, and J. Yoon. The impact of online recommendations and consumer feedback on sales. 2004.

[6] Y. Chen and J. Xie. Online consumer review: Word-of-mouth as a new element of marketing communication mix. *Management Science*, 54(3):477–491, 2008.

[7] E. K. Clemons, G. G. Gao, and L. M. Hitt. When online reviews meet hyperdifferentiation: A study of the craft beer industry. *Journal of Management Information Systems*, 23(2):149–171, 2006.

[8] C. Danescu-Niculescu-Mizil, G. Kossinets, J. Kleinberg, and L. Lee. How opinions are received by online communities: a case study on amazon. com helpfulness votes. In *Proceedings of the 18th international conference on World wide web*, pages 141–150. ACM, 2009.

[9] D. Davidov, O. Tsur, and A. Rappoport. Semi-supervised recognition of sarcastic sentences in twitter and amazon. In *Proceedings of the Fourteenth Conference on Computational Natural Language Learning*, pages 107–116. Association for Computational Linguistics, 2010.

[10] C. Dellarocas. The digitization of word of mouth: Promise and challenges of online feedback mechanisms. *Management science*, 49(10):1407–1424, 2003.

[11] K. E. Finn, A. J. Sellen, and S. B. Wilbur. *Video-mediated communication*. L. Erlbaum Associates Inc., 1997.

[12] C. Forman, A. Ghose, and B. Wiesenfeld. Examining the relationship between reviews and sales: The role of reviewer identity disclosure in electronic markets. *Information Systems Research*, 19(3):291–313, 2008.

[13] A. Ghose, P. G. Ipeirotis, and A. Sundararajan. Opinion mining using econometrics: A case study on reputation systems. 45(1):416, 2007.

[14] A. Girgensohn and A. Lee. Making web sites be places for social interaction. In *Proceedings of the 2002 ACM conference on Computer supported cooperative work*, CSCW '02, pages 136–145, New York, NY, USA, 2002. ACM.

[15] U. Gretzel and D. R. Fesenmaier. Persuasion in recommender systems. *International Journal of Electronic Commerce*, 11(2):81–100, 2006.

[16] F. M. Harper, D. Raban, S. Rafaeli, and J. A. Konstan. Predictors of answer quality in online q&a sites. In *Proceedings of the SIGCHI Conference on Human Factors in Computing Systems*, pages 865–874. ACM, 2008.

[17] T. Hothorn, K. Hornik, and A. Zeileis. Unbiased recursive partitioning: A conditional inference framework. *Journal of Computational and Graphical Statistics*, 15(3), 2006.

[18] J. Koh, Y.-G. Kim, B. Butler, and G.-W. Bock. Encouraging participation in virtual communities. *Commun. ACM*, Feb. 2007.

[19] N. Kumar and I. Benbasat. Research note: the influence of recommendations and consumer reviews on evaluations of websites. *Information Systems Research*, 17(4):425–439, 2006.

[20] J. Lehmann, M. Lalmas, E. Yom-Tov, and G. Dupret. Models of user engagement. In *User Modeling, Adaptation, and Personalization*, pages 164–175. Springer, 2012.

[21] Y. Lu, C. Zhai, and N. Sundaresan. Rated aspect summarization of short comments. In *Proceedings of the 18th international conference on World wide web*, pages 131–140. ACM, 2009.

[22] P. A. Pavlou and A. Dimoka. The nature and role of feedback text comments in online marketplaces: Implications for trust building, price premiums, and seller differentiation. *Information Systems Research*, 17(4):392–414, 2006.

[23] E. T. Peterson and J. Carrabis. Measuring the immeasurable: Visitor engagement. *Web Analytics Demystified*, 2008.

[24] D. A. Shamma, R. Shaw, P. L. Shafton, and Y. Liu. Watch what i watch: using community activity to understand content. In *MIR '07: Proceedings of the international workshop on Workshop on multimedia information retrieval*, pages 275–284, New York, NY, USA, 2007. ACM.

[25] S. Siersdorfer, S. Chelaru, W. Nejdl, and J. San Pedro. How useful are your comments?: analyzing and predicting youtube comments and comment ratings. In *Proceedings of the 19th international conference on World wide web*, pages 891–900. ACM, 2010.

[26] O. Tsur, D. Davidov, and A. Rappoport. Icwsm-a great catchy name: Semi-supervised recognition of sarcastic sentences in online product reviews. In *ICWSM*, 2010.

[27] F. Wu and B. A. Huberman. How public opinion forms. In *Internet and Network Economics*, pages 334–341. Springer, 2008.

[28] J. Yew, D. A. Shamma, and E. F. Churchill. Knowing funny: genre perception and categorization in social video sharing. In *Proceedings of the SIGCHI Conference on Human Factors in Computing Systems*, pages 297–306. ACM, 2011.

[29] E. Yom-Tov, M. Lalmas, R. Baeza-Yates, G. Dupret, J. Lehmann, and P. Donmez. Measuring inter-site engagement. *IEEE International Conference on Big Data*, 2013.

Impression Management Struggles in Online Dating

Doug Zytko
New Jersey Institute of Technology
Newark, NJ 07301
daz2@njit.edu

Sukeshini A. Grandhi
Eastern Connecticut State University
Willimantic, CT 06226
grandhis@easternct.edu

Quentin Jones
New Jersey Institute of Technology
Newark, NJ 07301
quentin.jones@njit.edu

ABSTRACT

Online dating systems are now widely used to search for romance and yet there is little research on how people use these systems to manage their impressions with potential romantic partners. To address this issue we conducted an interview study of 41 online dating users, revealing that—contrary to prior work—online daters largely do not want to intentionally deceive their online dating partners because they think such lies would quickly be discovered face-to-face. Nevertheless, bad first dates were a norm rather than an exception for this study's participants. In this paper we present various frustrations online daters associate with conveying and forming impressions of potential romantic partners before meeting face-to-face. We discuss the implications of these findings for the design of online dating systems.

Categories and Subject Descriptors

H.5.3. Group and Organization Interfaces; Asynchronous interaction; Web-based interaction.

General Terms

Design, Economics, Human Factors

Keywords

Online dating, online introductions, impression management, impression formation, social matching, social computing

1. INTRODUCTION

In 2008 one out of thirty single Americans had used an online dating system [36]. By 2013 that number had risen to one in ten, making online dating a significant part of our social fabric. The number of commercially available online dating systems has significantly risen in recent years. In spite of this wide scale availability and adoption, user frustrations are still quite prevalent in online dating [9]. In this paper we explore the nature of online daters' experiences in such systems in order to obtain a rich understanding of how their needs can be better supported.

User frustration with online dating is often spoken about in popular press as well as academic research [17, 44, 45]. Both men and women struggle to find a suitable romantic partner online, driving some to quit online dating entirely [44, 45]. Women are inundated with messages from men that they find unattractive at best, and terrifying at worst [15]. The time users spend looking for and evaluating potential partners also significantly outweighs time

GROUP'14, November 9–12, 2014, Sanibel Island, Florida, USA.
Copyright © 2014 ACM 978-1-4503-3043-5/14/11...$15.00.
http://dx.doi.org/10.1145/2660398.2660410

they spend on face-to-face dates with users they meet online [17]. In spite of this general awareness of online dating issues, our knowledge of the processes involved in online dating interactions is limited. While it is not clear why users find the online dating process so frustrating, one popular belief held by users and researchers is that online daters intentionally deceive their potential partners in an attempt to appear more attractive [23]. Studies support the claim that a majority of online daters lie or exaggerate aspects of themselves through their profile pages [15, 18], but these studies focus solely on demographic qualities as listed on profile pages and seldom take into account personality traits that are also important to the evaluation of potential romantic partners [14, 17, 22, 32]. Challenges in identifying and interacting with a compatible dating partner online can be tied to impression management and formation. Impression management in online dating entails the ways users present themselves to fellow online daters, while impression formation involves the evaluation of fellow online daters to decide whether to continue communication and eventually meet face-to-face.

In this research we explore both impression management (self-presentation) and impression formation practices in online dating through profile pages and private messaging conversations. We begin by reviewing relevant background literature and then present an interview study with 41 online dating users about how they self-present and form impressions of other users through the entire online dating process—from browsing and crafting their own profile pages, to private messaging, to face-to-face meetings. We discuss our findings and their implications for the design of online dating systems.

2. BACKGROUND

Previous online dating research has primarily followed two paths — algorithm development to improve matching, and understanding user behavior with respect to impression management. Research concerning matching algorithms views online dating as a subset of recommender systems [6] and typically measures matching success based on a dataset of predetermined correct matches or users' initial reactions to the profile pages they are matched with [1, 6, 34]. Such research has not evaluated the outcome of a match after an initial profile page view in terms of interaction between matched users, nor has it analyzed self-presentation practices. For the purposes of the research presented in this paper, we will focus our background review on impression management-related literature in online dating. We first begin with a short review of social matching and online dating systems. We continue with a review of research investigating romantic attraction, and how attractiveness is evaluated in online dating systems today. Then we discuss traditional impression management literature before delving into impression management within online dating. We end with a review of literature pertaining to misrepresentation—an issue frequently highlighted in existing research about impression management in online dating.

2.1 Social Matching and Online Dating Systems

In recent years a steady flow of web sites and mobile applications that facilitate online introductions between unknown individuals have emerged to satiate our need for new interpersonal attachments [3]. Online introductions are a key component of many social networking, social matching, and social discovery systems. For example, the social networking system *LinkedIn* uses its in-mail system to facilitate business introductions and networking. Online dating systems are a form of social matching system, or a type of system that aims to bring unknown parties together in both physical and online spaces [39]. Most online dating systems incorporate social matching algorithms that determine compatibility between users based on pre-determined sets of variables. The premise of matching in online dating systems is simple: match two users that are statistically likely to be romantically attracted to one another. Proprietary algorithms to unearth these romantic matches are often the main selling point for online dating systems. *OkCupid* and *Zoosk*, for instance, both promote their matching algorithms to differentiate themselves from competing online dating systems. Numerous non-dating social matching systems also exist. For example, *CoFoundersLab* connects budding entrepreneurs together to found a business, *Couch Surfing* helps match people with residences they can live in for free while on vacation, *Tennisopolis* helps people find tennis partners, and *Tastebuds.fm* and *Alikewise* find people with similar music or reading interests.

Online dating systems are "Internet services designed to facilitate interactions between potential romantic partners" [26]. Online dating now lays claim to one third of marriages in the United States [28] and major brands such as *match.com* and *eHarmony* boast millions of users. These major brands try to facilitate long-term relationships, but there are now a myriad of new online dating systems that hone on other user bases. *Grindr*, for example, caters to homosexual men, *JDate* to Jewish singles, and *How About We*, which matches users based on activities they want to do in the real world. There has also been explosive growth in mobile-only online dating systems such as *Tinder*, *Charm*, and *Blendr*, which use geo-location to match users. Online dating systems that began as browser-based systems now also have mobile app versions, such as *OkCupid* and *Plenty of Fish*.

2.2 Romantic Attraction and Online Dating

Research has produced a list of qualities and traits that determine physical attraction. For example, we are more attracted to people with symmetrical faces [31] and body odors that exert particular pheromones [21]. Men are more attracted to women that prominently wear the color red [10], and women are more attracted to men that are "prosocial," altruistic, and dominant [7]. Humor has also been found to be a common predictor of desirability for women [5]. Some research even makes the argument that we are more attracted to a person when we have limited information about them, because additional information we gain may include qualities we deem to be unattractive [33].

Online dating systems try to explicate as many qualities about a potential mate as possible through information located on public profile pages. Research has shown that profile pictures are the biggest determinant of attraction [16, 24, 25, 39, 42], but other qualities exhibited in free-text components of the profile page are also important. Specifically, females find male online daters attractive when their free-text components suggest the man is "genuine, trustworthy, extraverted, feminine, and not too warm and kind" [16]. Women were considered attractive when perceived as being feminine and possessing of high self-esteem through free-text components. Profiles pages that exhibited similarities to the profile viewer through factors such as height were also generally deemed more attractive [15, 27, 43].

2.3 Impression Management

"Virtually everyone is attentive to, if not explicitly concerned about how he or she is perceived and evaluated by other people" [30]. This concern is the basis of impression management, or the act of self-presentation. Goffman theorized impression management as a way to explain the "theatrical performances" that we undertake in our everyday social interactions in real life to shape the way people see us [20]. According to Goffman, people attempt to manage their impressions through their actions and words because they want people to perceive them a certain way.

Bozeman and Kacmar's self-regulation model [4] depicts impression management as a process where each person (an "actor") has a reference goal, which is the desired impression that the actor wants to convey during face-to-face interactions. Actors then use the feedback they receive from their communication partners during face-to-face interactions to evaluate how they are being perceived and if they are achieving their reference goal. If such feedback indicates that the actor is not being perceived as intended, the actor will alter his or her behavior in an attempt to better convey the intended impression in future interactions.

Several theories have also focused on impression formation, which entails the evaluation of communication partners during social interactions. Predicted Outcome Value Theory posits that a primary goal during initial interactions with strangers is to evaluate their value for future interactions [37]. If we predict a positive outcome value for a new acquaintance, it means we expect to extract value from future interactions with this person. If we predict a negative outcome value for this new person, we will end the relationship because we do not expect to gain additional value from it in the future.

Together, impression management theory and Predicted Outcome Value Theory suggest that our goal during social interactions with newly introduced people is two-fold. We want to 1) influence the way our communication partners perceive us (impression management), while we 2) evaluate our communication partners to determine their value for future interactions (impression formation).

2.4 Impression Management and Formation in Online Dating

Traditional impression management theory is based on face-to-face interactions. While the goal of online dating is typically to meet a fellow user face-to-face at some point [12, 22, 40], a bulk of interaction—and thus impression management—is done online before meeting in person. Online daters communicate with each other in public and private ways on these systems. Most online dating systems require every user to have a public profile page, which other users can view and use as a basis for instigating private communication. Private communication between two users is facilitated with messaging capabilities. For example, *Tinder*, a mobile online dating app, provides a private messaging interface similar to text messaging for two users to communicate once they have indicated mutual attraction. On top of messaging capabilities, some online dating systems feature generic forms of private communication, such as sending "virtual gifts" to other users on the site (e.g. *PlentyofFish.com*), or "winking" at a user of interest (*match.com*).

While some online dating research indicates that users engage in private communication [8, 17], it seldom identifies and reports on the specific nature or content of such communication. A majority of online dating research has focused exclusively on public profile pages for impression management purposes [11, 15, 25, 39, 40, 42], with some of these studies being based on artificial profile pages or profiles built by participants purely for research purposes [2, 22]. Patterns have emerged between profile content and private messaging, such as that women often receive many more private messages than men [16]. But the impression management and formation processes that occur during private messaging are largely under researched.

There are two types of information that online daters can convey and interpret through public and private communication channels: searchable attributes and experiential attributes [17]. *Searchable attributes* are demographic qualities like height or ethnicity that are objective in nature and unambiguous. Several online dating systems such as *OkCupid* and *Ashley Madison* let users search for others based on searchable attributes, i.e. – "white men over 6 feet tall and younger than 30 years old." Searchable attributes typically comprise a series of questions on public profile pages where users can choose fixed-choice answers about their height, ethnicity, sexual orientation, and other demographic qualities. Users also want to convey and interpret *experiential attributes,* which are personality traits that often need to be experienced in order to be conveyed, as the name implies. Experiential traits, like sense of humor, are integral when evaluating a potential online dating partner [14, 17, 22, 32], yet these traits are inherently subjective and tacit. This means they cannot be succinctly conveyed in fixed-choice profile questions. We consider "chemistry" and other vaguely defined qualities that daters often demand in their partners to be experiential attributes.

Most online dating research on impression management has focused only on searchable attributes and public profile pages. Existing research has seldom included experiential attributes in its scope despite being important to impression formation.

2.5 Misrepresentation in Online Dating

Social Information Processing Theory posits that online communications suffer from reduced social cues relative to face-to-face communication [41]. As a result, previous literature concludes that online daters frequently take advantage of stifled impression formation abilities to intentionally misrepresent themselves in an attempt to appear more attractive [23]. Studies have shown that a majority of online daters believe their fellow users lie, and studies comparing self-presentations online to attributes actually possessed support that belief [15, 18]. However, research around intentional misrepresentation has dealt almost exclusively with searchable attributes and their portrayals on public profile pages. We do not know if or how users adopt private communication methods to intentionally misrepresent themselves, or if and how they intentionally misrepresent experiential attributes. Furthermore, while online daters believe most of their fellow users deceive, they tend to consider themselves to be truthful [12, 42]. These users claim that intentional misrepresentation would not be conducive to their goals, which typically involve meeting other online daters in person and having successful romantic relationships in the physical world.

If online daters consider themselves to be truthful, why has existing research largely concluded that they lie? Recent studies suggest that much of this intentional misrepresentation comes in the form of exaggerations about one's qualities instead of blatant lies [11, 41]. These users attempt to convey a form of their "ideal future self," characterized by qualities they expect to one day possess, but currently do not. An example would be an overweight user listing his body type as fit on his profile page because he goes to the gym several times a week and expects to be in better physical shape in the future.

Despite this explanation, existing research implies that users actually know how to self-present their intended impressions. In other words, it has been largely assumed that all misrepresentation in online dating is intentional. The possibility of unintentional misrepresentation—that a truthful user does not know how to clearly convey him or herself—has not been entertained, which could explain the disconnect between findings that most users misrepresent despite self-identifying as truthful.

Confusion between potentially unintentional and intentional misrepresentation becomes compounded when experiential attributes are introduced to the impression formation process. While a searchable attribute such as one's height can be objectively validated, how does one validate sense of humor, or confidence? Subjectivity in one's self-presentation and the possibility of unintentional misrepresentation have not been accounted for in existing research.

3. RESEARCH QUESTIONS

Our research questions revolved around understanding how online daters present themselves and evaluate other users within the system, with an emphasis on experiential attributes and private communication. We also explored if and how relationship goals influenced these two processes. Additionally, we aimed to investigate the severity of intentional misrepresentation (deception), particularly in terms of experiential attributes. Our broad research question was:

RQ1: How do users adopt public and private methods of communication in online dating systems to 1) present themselves and 2) form impressions of other users?

With respect to self-presentation we also asked:

RQ2: What are users' relationship goals when joining the online dating system? Do these goals affect self-presentation?

RQ3: What feedback do users receive about their conveyed impressions?

RQ4: Do users intentionally misrepresent their experiential or searchable attributes? If so, what traits do they intentionally misrepresent and why?

With respect to impression management we also asked:

RQ5: Do relationship goals affect how users form impressions of others?

RQ6: How do impressions formed online compare to those formed once two users meet in person?

4. METHOD

A qualitative approach was used to investigate the above research questions. Specifically, we conducted semi-structured interviews with 41 users of a popular online dating system and used an open coding scheme to derive themes and theoretical constructs [19].

4.1 The Online Dating System

We chose a popular, free online dating system in the United States as the context for our interview study. All users in the chosen system have a public profile page as well as four different methods of private communication available to them. These methods include private messaging (asynchronous like e-mail), "live chat" for instant/synchronous messaging, profile ratings (similar to a Facebook "poke"), and anonymous messaging between two randomly paired users to schedule a blind date.

4.2 Participants

Participants were found using the search feature available on the chosen online dating system. This search feature allows users to search for other users based on specific demographic criteria such as ethnicity, height, or location. We created a profile on the system in the lead researcher's likeness—with our research intent clearly described in the profile—and sent a private message to users found through the search feature, inviting them to participate in an interview. Interview participants were searched for based on a combination of location (within 25 miles of the lead researcher's university), gender, and ethnicity. Because the chosen system had eight different ethnicity choices that users could identify with, this yielded 16 different combinations of search criteria (2 genders x 8 ethnicities).

The top six profiles returned for each ethnicity/gender combination were messaged each week, inviting them to an interview. This led to 96 users being messaged each week—48 men and 48 women. We engaged in this interview invitation process for eight weeks, resulting in 864 total users being private messaged with an interview invitation. Of these users, 62 responded to the initial interview request and 41 of those resulted in an interview. Of the 21 that did not, 13 responded merely to decline the interview offer, 2 responded with overt sexual advances, and 6 failed to respond after a time and location for the interview were suggested.

Twenty-eight of the 41 interviews were conducted in-person at a location of the participant's choosing, namely coffee shops (13), a bar (1), universities (12), and restaurants (2). The other 13 interviews were conducted online using Skype video chat because logistic and scheduling issues rendered an in-person interview impossible. Interview lengths ranged from 22 minutes to 72 minutes. Twenty of the participants were male, 21 were female, and ages ranged from 19 to 37. In terms of sexual orientation, 34 participants were straight, 5 were bisexual, and 2 were gay. Breakdown of ethnicities was as follows: 18 white, 9 black, 5 Hispanic, 3 Native American, 6 Asian, 8 Indian, 2 Middle Eastern, and 1 Pacific Islander. Six participants identified with multiple ethnicities.

4.3 Data Collection and Analysis

All interviews were voice recorded and summaries of each interview were written with 24 hours of the interview ending. A Grounded Theory approach was used for the qualitative analysis of interview data. Grounded Theory entails an iterative independent coding process to allow themes in the data to emerge naturally, and theory to emerge from these themes [19]. Our interview guide went through 3 iterations to reflect and hone in on emerging themes identified in completed interviews.

The first interview guide sought to grasp a broad understanding of participants' communication habits, including what forms of communication they favor. The second iteration placed a tighter focus on self-presentation and impression formation practices.

The third and final iteration explored impression validation during face-to-face meetings in more detail and how relationship goals influenced self-presentation and impression formation practices. Interviews were initially coded using the themes discovered from our interview notes and debriefing discussions with the research team. Based on our coding scheme, a series of the most informative interviews were selected for full transcription and additional rounds of analysis and theory generation. The findings of this study are the end result of this iterative coding process. Representative quotes of the emergent themes are presented below. Participants' names were changed for privacy.

5. FINDINGS

Several themes regarding communication preferences and frustrations with impression formation and management emerged early on in this study as we reported in a Research In Progress paper [44] prior to the completion of our interviews and the full transcription and analysis process. These findings were that:

1. Participants use both profile pages and private messaging to decide whether to meet other users face-to-face, making private messaging an essential step in self-presentation and impression formation.
2. The initiators of private conversation—usually men—try to emphasize positive affinities they have with their communication partner. However, they do not fabricate affinities to appear more attractive.
3. Users are not confident with the impressions they form online of other users before meeting in person and primary frustrations with online dating stem from inadequate feedback about conveyed impressions.

In this paper's Findings section, we delve more deeply into relationship goals and their influence on communication behavior, as well as take a closer look into the dynamics of private messaging and how it contributes to self-presentation and impression formation. We also revisit the severity—or lack thereof—of intentional misrepresentation.

5.1 Self-Presentation

5.1.1 Users exhibit tremendous anxiety and fear of rejection when trying to convey complex experiential traits.

A majority of participants felt they were not being interpreted as intended by their communication partners on the system. Several of these participants believed misinterpretation could not be avoided online and is an expected side effect of the online dating process.

Larry, 32: "There's a part of one's personality that can't be replicated online. You need the [in-person] dates to understand chemistry in a way that the Internet can't do."

Participants tended to describe their intended impression in terms of experiential attributes instead of searchable attributes. When asked to describe the general intended impression they wanted to convey to communication partners, participants often spoke of negative experiential qualities they try to avoid being associated with. Kenneth, a 33-year old single father who is looking for a committed relationship while juggling college courses and a full time job explained his intended impression:

Kenneth, 33: "Girls on the system tend to think everyone is a douchebag. I try to steer away from things that would give that impression [...] Most of the guys want to get a girl in bed. I'm not like that."

Dissatisfaction with communication methods available on the system for self-presentation was common. Participants felt hindered in their ability to convey complex experiential traits. Participants opted to present simpler versions of themselves in the open-ended sections of their profile pages because they discovered through face-to-face dates that their subtle experiential traits were often being misinterpreted online.

William, 35: "I find it so hard to accurately represent yourself. I feel that what I end up putting out there is a very extreme version of myself. I'm a far more complicated person than you can put out there in one little profile."

Jackie, 37: "I try to keep [my profile] honest as possible, but keep something open for the conversation."

Private messaging was considered an opportunity to convey complex experiential traits that were left out of profile pages, yet this was also the communication method that participants struggled with the most. Participants exhibited visible frustration when recounting how communication partners abruptly stop responding to a private messaging conversation. They were not necessarily bothered by the idea that a communication partner did not want to continue the conversation. Rather, frustration stemmed from not knowing why the conversation ended. Participants could not learn what behavior or information resulted in the conversation ending. They did not know if they were interpreted as intended and, if not, how they could correct their behavior to avoid future misinterpretation.

Jack, 28: "You think they would be such a great match [...] I took a good amount of time to write out this message, you couldn't take three seconds to say no?"

Amanda, 28: "[My private message conversations end abruptly] all the time. For a long time it was mostly the guy. Some guys like to blow me off, and it makes me so angry, ridiculously angry."

Feedback about conveyed impressions was most desired for the private messaging phase, as opposed to profile pages. Some participants even explicitly suggested it as a system improvement during interviews. Several also admitted that their primary motivation for agreeing to an interview was to solicit feedback from the lead researcher about their private messaging conversations.

Jason, 26: "What really sucks is that I don't get any feedback as to what is bad about my profile and messages. If you could look into putting in a freaking random suggestion box for the site that would be cool."

Evelyn, 30: "I get about three to five messages a day. Is that normal? What have the other girls said?"

Explicit feedback in the online dating system was scarce. Participants were not happy with system-provided feedback, which came in the form of a list of users that viewed their profile page, notifications when a user rated their profile highly, and timestamps that showed when a communication partner read their message. This feedback did not inform participants about their conveyed impressions, which led many to seek feedback through other informal ways. Straight men, in particular, described randomly changing their messaging habits to coax a response from their communication partners. They would use reactions (or the absence of responses) to these random messages as feedback

to inform their future messages with new communication partners. Others recounted messaging the same user multiple times in a row directly asking for feedback about how they were perceived.

Kenneth, 33: "Once in a blue moon, after a couple days, I'll go 'hey why didn't you respond to my message?' [...] That's something I want to know!"

Brian, 24: "I used canned lines from the Internet for a couple weeks, and then I started sending deeper messages. I ask a lot of questions in my messages now too."

Male participants frequently reported having a fear of rejection that developed from a lack of private message responses. For some of them, private message responses were so infrequent that they interpreted this to mean they were universally unattractive to the system's user base. This kept them from messaging the women they were most attracted to and led them to lower their participation levels on the system or leave the system entirely for extended periods of time.

Jack, 28: "Girls stop responding all the time. I'm kind of just un-phased by it now. I actually think that's incredibly depressing. [...] I never contact a girl first anymore. I wouldn't consider myself an active user anymore."

Jason, 26: "If the girl is supremely attractive, I won't message her. I'll only go for the average looking girls because my chance of a response is higher."

Arnold, 24: "I don't message more than three new girls a day because when they don't respond, it kind of hurts."

5.1.2 Users seldom want to intentionally deceive their communication partners because they believe such deception would not help their face-to-face relationships.

Participants tried to self-promote themselves to users they initiated private messaging with by emphasizing similarities they shared or qualities they believed the user would find attractive. This was true for both genders, regardless of sexual orientation. Perceived similarities were based on information found on the user's profile page, such as hobbies and careers mentioned in open-ended profile sections. Re-usable message content and response time behavior — such as waiting a minimum amount of time to respond in order to appear non-needy — were used by several participants in attempts to appear more attractive.

Malcolm, 24: "Seventy-two hours, that's my rule. I wait 72 hours before I respond to a message, always. I don't want to come off as needy."

Kenneth, 33: "There might be something in their profile about their favorite movies, so I'll quote those movies [in my private messages to them]."

Recipients of private messages liked it when their communication partner highlighted such affinities because it suggested the user took the time to read their profile page. This was particularly true when the affinities were based on information that was not explicitly stated in the participant's profile page. For example, Lara recounted a man she met face-to-face from the online dating system whose initial message referenced the college campus they both lived on. He had inferred this from information in her profile page.

Lara, 21: "A guy recently messaged me saying 'oh you must live on [her college campus]. I thought, 'oh cool, what gave me away?' He made the connection because I said I like trees and nature."

John, 25: "It's nice when they talk about programming with me or computer things. I'll spend a little more time on those messages because it's an interest we share."

Despite the desire to self-promote and maximize attractiveness, almost all participants considered themselves to be truthful in self-presentation on their profile page and through their private messages. This they said was due to their desire for successful relationships in the physical world where false presentation would quickly be discovered.

Jackie, 37: "I keep it 100% real. I don't want to portray myself as anything, I just want to be myself."

Only 2 participants reported intentionally misrepresenting an experiential attribute, and another 2 admitted to intentionally misrepresenting a searchable attribute. Barry joined the online dating system because he was insecure and wanted to work on his confidence, an experiential attribute. As such, he described how he acted more confident during his private messages than he really believed himself to be. The other example of intentional experiential misrepresentation was by Lauren, who used a fake profile picture during her first couple weeks on the system because of privacy concerns. She later changed it to a real picture of herself before meeting a man she was interested in from the system face-to-face.

Barry, 24: "I used to send long paragraphs, but now I send short messages where I try to make fun of the girls. Honestly, I have no idea what's working, I just don't want them to think I'm insecure."

Lauren, 19: "In the first few weeks I didn't even use my real picture. I still got a date. I mean I told him and sent him a real picture before we met."

The 2 participants that intentionally misrepresented a searchable attribute did so with their weight and sexual orientation, respectively. Jack exaggerated his weight by listing himself as "average" while considering his actual body type to be overweight. Elisa listed her sexual orientation as bisexual because she wanted to meet more platonic friends of the same sex face-to-face.

Jack, 28: "I do lie about my body weight. I say 'average' [on my profile page] because I think the average American is overweight."

Elisa, 27: "I'm listed as bisexual, but I'm not really into girls sexually [...] I went out with one girl. I think she could tell that I wasn't a real lesbian."

5.2 Impression Formation

5.2.1 Impression formation involves searchable attributes for immediate decision-making, and experiential attributes for gradual qualification towards a face-to-face meeting.

Physical attraction based on profile pictures was a requirement for most participants to meet another user in person for romantic purposes. However, searchable and experiential attributes also played integral roles in this decision process. Some participants had specific searchable attributes as "deal breakers"—such as smoking or a minimum height—that they used to immediately disqualify a potential partner. Profile pages were used to evaluate

these searchable disqualifiers. Most participants then used experiential traits to decide if the user qualified for a private messaging conversation (based on open-ended profile content), and then if they qualified for an in-person meeting based on the private message conversation. This means that while most relied on profile pages to form preliminary impressions, a bulk of impression formation for the purpose of face-to-face meetings was done during private messaging.

Amanda, 28: "First I read his message. If it's a one-liner like 'hi,' I won't even bother with the profile. [...] Then I'm looking for immediate disqualifiers on his profile—religion, politics, and height. [...] During messaging [...] I want to see his conversational abilities too."

Michael, 24: "I'll look at the profile first. If their physical features catch my eye I'll look for grammatical errors [in the open-ended profile elements]. This tells me a lot about a girl's intelligence."

Rose, 24: "I'm tall, 5'9", so I check that. But the message has to be good first. [...] Then we'll have a conversation [through messaging] and schedule a date through that."

Aside from searchable "deal breakers," recipients of the initial private message often judged message content more harshly than profile content. Most participants, especially female and gay users, discussed how they would not respond to a communication partner if the content of the initial message received did not immediately catch their attention. This was because our female and gay participants were receiving considerably more private messages than straight males (often 20-60 weekly, versus 0-5 for straight men). Several participants complained that profile pages felt like generic advertisements that could not be used to adequately assist in their evaluation of a communication partner.

Jonathan, 32: "I almost didn't message [my current boyfriend] back. He didn't have good pictures, but I liked his message. I'm generally more interested in the message."

Carry, 19: "I don't like long messages, or ones that are immediately sexual, or bring up an ex, or sound like they're not taking it seriously. [...] Yeah, I'll reject a guy purely on this."

Straight men expressed a great amount of anxiety when it came to private messaging because they knew one "bad" message could end the conversation abruptly. This anxiety was most pronounced when attempting to move communication off the system to text messaging, phone calls, or an in-person meeting. Some men were so wary of rejection that they would stop responding permanently during a private messaging conversation if they could not think of something funny or witty to say.

Barry, 24: "If I don't know what to say, I just don't respond. [...] It's my fear of failure. I'm trying to work on that."

Moving communication to a phone conversation or in-person meeting was a "moment of truth" in private messaging, in which a private messaging conversation would immediately end if a phone number or date idea was given too soon. "Too soon" did not coincide with a fixed time frame or number of messages, but rather the comfort level of the participant during the messaging conversation. This made private messaging an intense focus for most users. Female participants said a phone number given too early was a sign of poor social skills and made them feel uncomfortable. They seldom responded to any future messages from a man if this happened. Conversely, female participants recalled feeling annoyed when men took too long to give their phone number. They did not feel it was the woman's role to escalate communication off the system and would stop responding if the man waited too long to give a phone number or propose a date.

Rachel, 28: "Sometimes the conversation can get really long—as many as 57 messages this one time—because I'm waiting for the guy to pull the trigger [and ask me out on a date]. I can't bring myself to do it. That's his role."

Rebecca, 25: "Some guys take too long. By the time he gives his number, I'm not actually interested anymore. But if it's too early, I'll stop responding completely. Either way the messaging is done."

5.2.2 Users feel limited in their abilities to form impressions of experiential attributes online.

A majority of participants felt limited by existing communication methods on the system for impression formation. Many of them did not expect to have interpreted their communication partners accurately before meeting them face-to-face, especially in terms of experiential attributes.

Connor, 24: "The people you meet in person, they're always a little off. That's always going to happen."

All but 4 participants met at least one other user face-to-face. A majority of their first face-to-face meetings, however, did not result in a second meeting. Seldom did participants consider their first face-to-face meeting with another user to be a "date," but rather a chance to validate and build on impressions formed online. Participants often planned their first face-to-face meetings to be non-committal, in which they could easily leave early if they determined their online-based impression to be too inaccurate. Common first meeting plans involved coffee shops and similar public areas because these locations afforded a "quick exit" for participants without a significant time investment.

Ben, 26: "I hate calling it a 'date date.' I like it to start as friends first and see if we have things in common."

Javier, 24: "It's not really a date. More like a pseudo-date because it's more like an interview. I'll schedule something more romantic for the second date if it goes well."

Marissa, 19: "We'll pick places that don't require much commitment, like coffee. [...] Definitely not dinner. I don't want them to look at me eating."

If the first meeting was going well, however, participants explained how they would alter the meeting in real time to incorporate more romantic activities.

Connor, 24: "I go into it like we're just hanging out. But during that first hang out, if I'm attracted, okay now it's a date. It's really after it started do I determine if it's a first date."

Most online-based impressions were deemed incorrect once participants met their partner face-to-face. Impressions deemed incorrect during face-to-face meetings were commonly due to experiential attributes rather than searchable attributes. Most found their partners to be less attractive than their online impression led them to expect, but a few participants recounted finding some partners to be more attractive or compatible than they were expecting based on the impression they formed online.

Lara, 21: "The second guy I met was very reserved in-person. Our personalities didn't jive. [...] We never spoke again."

Jack, 28: "There was one date that just went horrifically. She was just dumb. We went out to dinner and she was like 'what's a scallion?' I had no hint of that online, that she was that stupid."

Connor, 24: "She came off as really cool and nonchalant [in her messages]. She's not really like that [in person], but I like her for totally different reasons now."

Some participants had a tendency to attribute an unexpected face-to-face impression to intentional deception, even if their partner did not admit to deceiving purposely. They assumed their partner had intentionally lied about particular qualities, which included both searchable and experiential qualities.

Jackie, 37: "They're trying to portray themselves as looking for a relationship, when they're just looking to get physical."

Carry, 19: "He said he was in law school, but he was totally still in college, I'm sure of it. [...] He kept denying it the whole time."

Other participants acknowledged the possibility that a misinterpretation could have been unintentional, recalling reverse instances in which their partners admitted to misinterpreting them once they met face-to-face.

William, 35: "I'm not sure if it was a misrepresentation on their part, or a miscalculation on my part."

Javier, 24: "The one girl that didn't turn into a relationship, I was too intimidating she said, and too nice. [laughing] Yeah that doesn't make sense, but that's what she thought."

5.3 Relationship Goals

5.3.1 Despite primary goals being of a romantic nature, users also join the online dating system to improve their social skills and make friends.

The majority of our interview participants viewed online dating as a general online introduction platform to meet new people for both romantic and platonic reasons. More than half of the participants were open to meeting friends on the system for platonic reasons and considered it an important reason for why they joined the online dating system. For example, Hannah explained that she and her college friends use online dating as their primary way to meet new people.

Hannah, 19: "This [online dating system] has literally become our way of life. This is how we communicate with people now."

Participants both male and female reported exchanging private messages with and meeting face-to-face with users because they had similar interests, despite not being romantically attracted. Some male participants discussed having trouble talking to women in the real world and felt platonic social interaction online would improve their dating skills. Four male participants had never met another online dater face-to-face and each one of them considered general social interaction with female users online and off line to be their immediate goal for using the system. Arnold and Isaac were two such participants.

Arnold, 24: "I love talking about Obama and politics [in my private messages]. I also ask a lot of questions at the end of my messages. I want to make it easier for them to respond."

Isaac, 37: "I'm looking for real talk. I don't like talking to people in bars because you can't have conversations...online dating is so empowering because I can send these longer, deeper messages."

Other participants joined the online dating system to find new friends when they moved to a new area. Erica, for example, relocated to be a nurse. She worked 12-hour shifts, which made meeting new people in real life difficult. Mark also used the online dating system to find new friends and romantic partners when he moved to an unfamiliar city for a job.

Erica, 28: "I moved here almost a year ago. I didn't know anybody. [...] And I wanted to meet people outside my direct social circle. So I figured a really good way to meet some people and get to know the area a little bit was to go on online dating."

Mark, 25: "After coming here three months ago, I started using [the online dating system] because I don't really know anyone yet."

None of the participants with platonic interests were against sexual or romantic relationships. When pursuing platonic relationships, participants used only experiential traits and common interests to evaluate their communication partners. Physical attraction was not a requirement for exchanging private messages or meeting face-to-face. When the primary goal was to build platonic relationships, participants also tended to respond to every private message sent to them and sometimes did not even read the profile page of a user they were conversing with for platonic reasons.

Edward, 25: "I met four girls just to hang out. I usually invite them to parties at my bar. [...] I met one girl where I didn't even look at her profile."

Lara, 21: I really like Star Trek and Lord of the Rings. If you want to talk about that, I will respond, even if I'm not interested [romantically] at all."

Platonic relationship goals sometimes led to unintentional misinterpretations during in-person meetings if participants did not explicitly clarify their platonic interest. Connor said most of the women he met on the system only had romantic relationship goals and assumed his willingness to meet face-to-face meant he was romantically attracted.

Connor, 24: "I think she thought it was a date, but I wasn't attracted to her like that. We never messaged each other again after that."

6. DISCUSSION

Our data from interviewing 41 online daters indicate that there are several frustrations and struggles they face concerning impression management and impression formation. While technology enables daters to reach out to more people, it also increases the likelihood of unanticipated communication breakdown.

Participants expressed considerable frustration regarding private messaging conversations that ended abruptly without explicit understanding of why they ended. Aside from a ratings feature and a list of users that visited one's profile, users were left to speculate implied feedback on their own. While this implicit feedback may tell the user the valence of the impression formed about them—i.e. a lack of a response implies a negative impression—it fails to help the user understand what information contributed to that impression. Online dating systems do not provide explicit feedback to users about their conveyed impressions, therefore hindering their impression management abilities. Users do not know if and how they are being misinterpreted or what behavior is contributing to these interpretations. As a result, users are largely missing the type of feedback integral to Bozeman and Kacmar's model of impression management, which can guide them in altering their behavior to better achieve their desired impression.

Social Exchange Theory explains human relationships in terms of cost-benefit analysis [12]. The two people involved in a social exchange weigh the costs and rewards of that given exchange. If they deem the costs to be higher than the rewards, the exchange is discontinued. If we view a private messaging conversation in online dating as a social exchange, a discontinued conversation would be the result of one user evaluating the costs of the conversation to be higher than the rewards. It was typically women who discontinued conversations according to our interviews. This makes sense considering women receive considerably more messages than men, often to the point of being overwhelmed. Women can thus afford to judge the rewards of a given conversation more stringently because they will have a number of new men messaging them in the near future. Conversely, users who do not receive many messages—often straight men—will rarely consider the costs of continuing a conversation to outweigh the expected benefits. Unfortunately, social exchange is discontinued as soon as one user's perceived costs outweigh the expected rewards, meaning the other user has no opportunity to gather feedback as to what contributed to this decision.

Challenges of self-presentation seem to directly affect impression formation capabilities. Users misjudge the online daters they meet in person so often that they have come to expect a disconnect between impressions formed online and impressions formed in person. If self-presentation abilities can be improved through more informative feedback, impression formation would benefit as well because users could learn how to avoid the behavior that tends to result in misinterpretation and/or perceived costs during social exchange. The key design implication of this study is thus the need for system mechanisms that deliver explicit and consistent feedback about conveyed impressions to online daters. A potential argument against this design implication is that users could use such feedback to intentionally misrepresent themselves in an attempt to create a more attractive impression. However, we have found that users largely do not want to misrepresent themselves because they want their online introductions to lead to a successful relationship in real life, whether that be platonic or romantic. They do not believe deception will help them form relationships in the physical world because intentionally misrepresented qualities would be exposed during face-to-face meetings.

The large number of participants that exhibited a strong desire to meet other users for platonic reasons suggests that individuals turn to online dating systems to meet a variety of social needs. As a result, design implications derived from online dating research are germane to a variety of social needs besides romance. Online dating systems can be considered a subset of online introduction systems geared to facilitate face-to-face meetings with newly introduced users. The findings described in this paper have generalizable benefits to this online introduction domain at large. Popular systems for online introductions, as mentioned in the background section, permeate many different markets including business, sports, and traveling. The design implication of providing feedback mechanisms can readily be applied to other domains for helping job seekers better convey their marketable skills on *LinkedIn*, or helping travellers form clearer impressions of strangers they are about to spend the night with from *Couch Surfing*, among other examples.

Despite the wealth of insight into online dating perceptions and self-presentation practices that this interview study has provided, it stills leaves us with a major question: when and how often are users getting misinterpreted in online dating? Most of our participants say they misinterpret the people they meet, but we do not know where in the communication process this misinterpretation is occurring or what behavior contributes to it. We do know that users are frustrated when their communication partners stop responding, but misinterpretation may not be the only reason for a lack of response. Some users may actually be getting interpreted as they intended, with this interpretation simply being deemed unattractive. Unfortunately, this interview study cannot differentiate between conversations that end based on correctly interpreted information, incorrectly interpreted information, or other circumstances external to the system such as life events that prevent a user from continuing communication.

This study is one of the first to investigate impression management and formation behavior throughout the entire online dating process. It reveals that impression management goes beyond the profile page and relies heavily on private messaging, yet users find neither of these tools satisfactory for their impression management and formation needs. Our future work aims to analyze impression management and formation from the perspective of both users in a given communication. This will allow us to directly compare the intended impression and perceived impression of the same user, revealing if misinterpretation is indeed occurring, and where in the online dating process this misinterpretation is happening.

7. REFERENCES

[1] Akehurst, J., Koprinska, I., Yacef, K., Pizzato, L., Kay, J., and Rej, T., 2012. Explicit and implicit user preferences in online dating, in: *New Frontiers in Applied Data Mining*. Springer, Berlin Heidelberg, 15-27.

[2] Bak, P., 2010. Sex Differences in the Attractiveness Halo Effect in the Online Dating Environment *Journal of Business and Media Psychology* 1, 1-7.

[3] Baumeister, R. F. and Leary, M. R. 1995. The need to belong: desire for interpersonal attachments as a fundamental human motivation *Psychological bulletin*, 117(3), 497-529.

[4] Bozeman, D. P., and Kacmar, K. M. 1997. A cybernetic model of impression management processes in organizations. *Organizational behavior and human decision processes*, 69(1), 9-30.

[5] Bressler, E. R., & Balshine, S. 2006. The influence of humor on desirability *Evolution and Human Behavior*, 27(1), 29-39.

[6] Brozovsky, L. and Petricek, V. Recommender System for Online Dating Service. Retrieved February 12, 2014. http://arxiv.org/abs/cs/0703042.

[7] Buss, D. M. 1988. The evolution of human intrasexual competition: tactics of mate attraction *Journal of personality and social psychology*, 54(4), 616.

[8] Couch, D. and Liamputtong, P., 2008. Online dating and mating: The use of the internet to meet sexual partners *Qualitative Health Research*, 18(2), 268-279.

[9] Darne, K. June 8, 2013. Six reasons why many people become frustrated with online dating. Retrieved February 12, 2014. http://www.examiner.com/article/six-reasons-why-many-people-become-frustrated-with-online-dating.

[10] Elliot, A. J., & Niesta, D. 2008. Romantic red: red enhances men's attraction to women *Journal of personality and social psychology*, 95(5), 1150.

[11] Ellison, N. B., Hancock, J. T., and Toma, C. L., 2012. Profile as promise: A framework for conceptualizing veracity in online dating self-presentations *New Media & Society* 14(1), 45-62.

[12] Ellison, N., Heino, R., and Gibbs, J., 2006. Managing impressions online: Self presentation processes in the online dating environment *Journal of Computer Mediated Communication* 11(2), 415-441.

[13] Emerson, R. M. 1976. Social exchange theory. *Annual review of sociology*, 335-362.

[14] Finkel, E. J., Eastwick, P. W., Karney, B. R., Reis, H. T., andSprecher, S. 2012. Online Dating A Critical Analysis From the Perspective of Psychological Science *Psychological Science in the Public Interest*, 13(1), 3-66.

[15] Fiore, A. and Donath, J.S. 2005. Homophily in online dating: when do you like someone like yourself? In *CHI'05 Extended Abstracts on Human Factors in Computing Systems*. ACM, New York, NY, 1371-1374. DOI= http://dx.doi.org/10.1145/1056808.1056919.

[16] Fiore, A. T., Taylor, L. S., Mendelsohn, G. A., and Hearst, M. 2008. Assessing attractiveness in online dating profiles. In *Proceedings of the SIGCHI Conference on Human Factors in Computing Systems*. ACM, New York, NY, 797-806). DOI= http://dx.doi.org/10.1145/1357054.1357181.

[17] Frost, J. H., Chance, Z., Norton, M. I., and Ariely, D., 2008. People are experience goods: Improving online dating with virtual dates *Journal of Interactive Marketing*, 22(1), 51-61.

[18] Gibbs, J. L., Ellison, N. B., and Heino, R. D., 2006. Self-presentation in online personals the role of anticipated future interaction, self-disclosure, and perceived success in Internet dating *Communication Research*, 33(2), 152-177.

[19] Glaser, B., Strauss, A., 1967. The Discovery of Grounded Theory: Strategies for Qualitative Research. Aldine Transaction.

[20] Goffman, E., 1959. The presentation of self in everyday life. Doubleday, New York.

[21] Grammer, K., Fink, B., and Neave, N. 2005. Human pheromones and sexual attraction *European journal of obstetrics & gynecology and reproductive biology*, 118(2), 135-142.

[22] Guadagno, R. E., Okdie, B. M., and Kruse, S. A. 2012. Dating deception: Gender, online dating, and exaggerated self-presentation *Computers in Human Behavior*, 28(2), 642-647.

[23] Hall, J. A., Park, N., Song, H., Cody, M. J., 2010. Strategic misrepresentation in online dating: The effects of gender, self-monitoring, and personality traits *Journal of Social and Personal Relationships*, 27(1), 117-135.

[24] Hancock, J. T., and Toma, C. L. 2009. Putting your best face forward: The accuracy of online dating photographs *Journal of Communication*, 59(2), 367-386.

[25] Hancock, J. T., Toma, C., and Ellison, N., 2007. The truth about lying in online dating profiles. In *Proceedings of the SIGCHI conference on Human factors in computing systems*.

ACM, New York, NY, 449-452. DOI= http://dx.doi.org/10.1145/1240624.1240697.

[26] Heino, R. D., Ellison, N. B., and Gibbs, J. L., 2010. Relationshopping: Investigating the market metaphor in online dating *Journal of Social and Personal Relationships,* 27(4), 427-447.

[27] Hitsch, G. J., Hortaçsu, A., and Ariely, D. 2010. What makes you click?—Mate preferences in online dating *Quantitative Marketing and Economics,* 8(4), 393-427.

[28] Jayson, S. University of Chicago study: One-third of recent marriages began online. Retrieved February 12, 2014. http://www.suntimes.com/lifestyles/family/20557420-423/university-of-chicago-study-one-third-of-recent-marriages-began-online.html.

[29] Katz, E.M. How Do I Survive The Frustration of Online dating? Retrieved February 12, 2014. http://www.evanmarckatz.com/blog/online-dating-tips-advice/how-do-i-survive-the-frustration-of-online-dating/.

[30] Leary, M. R., and Kowalski, R. M. 1990. Impression management: A literature review and two-component model. *Psychological bulletin,* 107(1), 34.

[31] Little, A. C., Burt, D. M., Penton-Voak, I. S., and Perrett, D. I. 2001. Self-perceived attractiveness influences human female preferences for sexual dimorphism and symmetry in male faces *Proceedings of the Royal Society of London. Series B: Biological Sciences,* 268(1462), 39-44.

[32] McCrae, R. R. and Costa, P. T. 1987. Validation of the five-factor model of personality across instruments and observers *Journal of personality and social psychology* 52(1), 81.

[33] Norton, M. I., Frost, J. H., and Ariely, D. 2007. Less is more: the lure of ambiguity, or why familiarity breeds contempt. *Journal of personality and social psychology,* 92(1), 97-105.

[34] Pizzato, L., Rej T., Chung T., Koprinska I., and Kay J. RECON: a reciprocal recommender for online dating. In *Proceedings of the fourth ACM conference on Recommender systems.* ACM, 2010, 207-214.

[35] Ries, E. 2011. The Lean Startup: How Today's Entrepreneurs Use Continuous Innovation to Create Radically Successful Businesses. Random House Digital.

[36] Smith, A. and Duggan, M. October 21, 2013. Online Dating and Relationships. Retrieved February 12, 2014. http://www.pewinternet.org/2013/10/21/main-report/.

[37] Sunnafrank, M. 1986. Predicted outcome value during initial interactions: A reformulation of uncertainty reduction theory *Human Communication Research,* 13(1), 3-33.

[38] Terveen, L. and McDonald, D. W. 2005. Social matching: A framework and research agenda *ACM transactions on computer-human interaction (TOCHI),* 12(3), 401-434.

[39] Toma, C. L., and Hancock, J. T. 2010. Looks and lies: The role of physical attractiveness in online dating self-presentation and deception *Communication Research,* 37(3), 335-351.

[40] Toma, C. L., Hancock, J. T., and Ellison, N. B. 2008. Separating fact from fiction: An examination of deceptive self-presentation in online dating profiles *Personality and Social Psychology Bulletin,* 34(8), 1023-1036.

[41] Walther, Joseph B. 1996. Computer-mediated communication impersonal, interpersonal, and hyperpersonal interaction *Communication research* 23(1), 3-43.

[42] Whitty, M. T., 2008. Revealing the 'real'me, searching for the 'actual' you: Presentations of self on an internet dating site *Computers in Human Behavior,* 24(4), 1707-1723.

[43] Yancey, G., and Emerson, M. O. 2014. Does Height Matter? An Examination of Height Preferences in Romantic Coupling. *Journal of Family Issues.*

[44] Zytko, D., Grandhi S.A., and Jones, Q. 2014. Impression Management and Formation in Online Dating Systems. In *Proceedings of European Conference on Information Systems.* AIS.

[45] Zytko, D., Grandhi, S. A., and Jones, Q. G. 2014. Impression management through communication in online dating. In Proceedings of the companion publication of the 17th ACM conference on Computer supported cooperative work & social computing, ACM, New York, NY, 277-280. DOI= http://dx.doi.org/10.1145/2556420.2556487.

Investigating the use of a Simulator to Support Users in Anticipating Impact of Privacy Settings in Facebook

Manoel Pereira Junior
Dept. of Computer Science
UFMG / IFMG – Campus Formiga
R. Padre Alberico, 440 – 35570-000
Formiga – Minas Gerais – Brazil
manoel.pereira@ifmg.edu.br

Simone I. R. Xavier
Dept. of Computer Science - UFMG
Av. Antônio Carlos 6627
31270-010 Belo Horizonte
Minas Gerais - Brazil
simone.xavier@dcc.ufmg.br

Raquel Oliveira Prates
Dept. of Computer Science - UFMG
Av. Antônio Carlos 6627
31270-010 Belo Horizonte
Minas Gerais - Brazil
rprates@dcc.ufmg.br

ABSTRACT

One of the challenges faced by Facebook users is that privacy settings change not only the visibility of the information, but also impact actions other users can take on a piece of information. These actions on their turn can also create changes to the visibility of that piece of information, sometimes granting access to people originally unintended by the user who posted the information. In this paper we investigate how a simulator that allows users to explore the different situations that can result from privacy settings may support them in anticipating the impact of their decisions. To do so, we have implemented a privacy setting simulator prototype, and evaluated it through a qualitative case-study which involved 12 regular Facebook users. Our findings indicate that the simulator improved users understanding of the effects of their privacy settings and allowed them to identify misunderstandings they had about the visibility of their information.

Categories and Subject Descriptors

H.1.2. [**Information Systems**]: User/Machine Systems - *human factors, human information processing*; K.4.1. [**Computers and Society**]: Public Policy Issues - *privacy*.

General Terms

Human Factors, Design, Experimentation.

Keywords

Privacy; Facebook; social network sites; user experience; collaborative systems; configuration; settings; simulation.

1. INTRODUCTION

Social network sites are nowadays one of the most popular applications among internet users. People use them to stay in touch with friends, to find people to date, to meet new people [11, 12] or to collaborate amongst themselves [8]. In other words, these systems are used to achieve a broad range of goals [11, 12]. Facebook is currently the most popular social network site, according to alexa.com (http://www.alexa.com). In June 2014 it achieved 1.32 billion active users per month (http://newsroom.fb.com/company-info/). However, this broad use of social network sites brings new challenges to researchers of social sciences and collaborative systems [2]. One of the issues

that researchers have focused on is privacy, which has been investigated under different perspectives, such as analyzing users' concern with privacy issues [7, 13] and which aspects (e.g. gender or age) impact privacy setting [17, 21] or even inferring new information about users based on public information [14, 22].

One of the reasons that privacy raises so much interest is because it falls into what Ackerman has coined as the social-technical gap of collaborative systems [1]. The social-technical gap has been defined as the divide between what we know we must support socially and what can be done to support it technically. One of the issues regarding privacy is that socially people make decisions based on who is involved and in which context, making fine distinctions between people and situations and switching between them. Social network sites have been trying to create flexible settings in order to accommodate these different situations. For instance, in Facebook, users can define access to information to all people in a role (e.g. friends or friends of friends) or for a specific piece of information (e.g. only one specific friend can see a photo).

Although the flexibility of privacy settings have increased and included some of the suggestions of earlier works [1], it still presents challenges to users, developers and researchers. In an investigation that included an analysis of feedback issues, de Souza et al. [5] have pointed out that the feedback regarding the meaning of configuration parameters in collaborative systems requires users to be able to anticipate how their decisions influence group processes. In order to do so they suggest that users should be able to simulate the communicative and social processes affected by such decisions.

We believe that one of the challenges regarding privacy is the difficulty users have in anticipating the effects their decisions regarding the parameters associated to privacy will have on the available access to their information. Taking Facebook as an example, access to information depends not only on configuration of privacy settings, but also on actions that others can take over pieces of information. Therefore, in this paper we intend to investigate: (1) Can users understand the effects of their privacy settings on the access they grant other users to their information? (2) Would a simulator that presented the impact of their settings in the access to their information increase their understanding of the effects of their decisions?

In order to answer these questions we have chosen to investigate Facebook through a case study. The reason for choosing Facebook is its high popularity, as well as the large number of articles analyzing its privacy. The case study focused on privacy regarding photos, since this has been identified as one of the pieces of information users are most worried about [15]. The case study involved two steps. The first one required Facebook users to interact with Facebook and perform certain privacy settings and explain what they believed the impacts of their decisions were. In the second moment they interacted with a Facebook Privacy Simulator developed for this investigation and simulated the impact of the settings they had defined in step one in Facebook.

The case study involved 12 Facebook users, half of them with background in technology. The results showed that users had great difficulties in understanding the effects of privacy settings on the access they granted to their information. Sometimes they realized they were not sure of what the impacts were, but in other situations they believed they knew what the effects were, only to find out through the use of the simulator that it was not what they had expected.

Our results show that users in fact have great difficulty in translating the combination of settings into the actual social situation it creates for them. Allowing users to simulate the range of situations that may result from their decisions supports their understanding of the systems' rules. This solution does not intend to close the social-technical gap in collaborative systems' settings, but to show its potential as a tool to help users bridge it.

In the next section, we present recent works regarding privacy in Facebook. Then we discuss the problem we are focusing on in this paper. Next we present the Facebook Privacy Simulator (PrivSim) developed for our case study. We then describe the case study and discuss the results obtained. Finally, we go over the paper's contribution and next steps in this research.

2. RELATED WORK

Recently, a number of studies that investigate different problems and issues related to privacy have been published. The issues vary from the difficulties that users have in representing the level of privacy desired [17] or understanding how the settings affect the availability of information [13] to legal aspects of privacy policies [10] or the generation of new information about users by crossing public information available about them [14, 22]. Since our goal is to analyze the challenge of anticipating impacts of configuration settings, in this section we will focus on the articles related to the difficulties users have in setting privacy and understanding their effects.

Some works have shown that users often tend to keep the default settings provided by the system, without making any changes to increase their privacy [7, 13]. Even when users claim to be concerned about their privacy they do not take the necessary measures to ensure the privacy of their information [17]. Furthermore, privacy concerns may differ according to users' profiles, for instance according to their genre [15, 20]. Women tend to worry more about privacy, but they post more often and with less attention to access to these posts than men [14]. Besides, types of information people are willing to share may also differ according to genre [21].

Lack of concern is not the only problem regarding privacy. Often users will try to define settings to achieve the desired privacy, but have difficulties managing them [13]. Sometimes specific situations or pieces of information require users to define differentiated settings for them. Johnson et al. [9] have collected data about contents that users had posted and their levels of comfort in sharing content with randomly selected people from their friendship network. Results indicated that users could set privacy to prevent access by people who were not among their friends, but they failed when defining different access to subgroups of friends, for instance, defining that only a subgroup

of their friends could see a post. Furthermore, other outside factors may add to the complicating factors, such as when a new update restores the original settings [19].

Facebook privacy settings provide users with the possibility to create different access levels to people or to a specific piece of information. However, Liu et al. [13] have shown that users do not always understand how the settings impact access to their information, and that there are disparities between the levels of privacy users expected to have and their actual privacy settings. Results show that only in 37% of the cases do users succeed in setting privacy correctly to achieve the desired effect on access to their information. In the remaining cases users often reveal more information than expected. Furthermore, the authors explored whether friend lists could be automatically populated using community detection algorithms as a potential way for assisting users in managing their privacy.

Razavi & Iverson [16] argue that a better model to the common public/private model would be to let users create their own classification of their contacts. To do so, they proposed a mechanism that allows users to categorize their social network into groups by using tags. These tags are then used to control access to certain pieces of information in their personal space.

Besmer & Lipford [3] examined users' privacy concerns regarding photo tagging on Facebook. To do so, they conducted three focus groups and, based on the results, they suggest nine design considerations regarding photo tagging. They then developed a tool called Restrict Others that allows users tagged in a photo to open a negotiation with the user who posted the photo about people they would not like to have access to the photo. The photo is untagged while the negotiation takes place. According to them, the tool complements the untag feature available at Facebook and helps users get a more desired level of privacy while maintaining the social value of sharing photos.

de Paula et al. [4] argue that the effectiveness of security systems, such as those that ensure privacy, do not depend only on cryptographic algorithms and advanced computers, but rather involve technical, human and social resources. Therefore, they attempt to understand what would be the best approach to design usable technologies to support security. According to the authors, users must (1) view the status of the system, and (2) understand the integration of configuration and action. To support their proposal, they developed an application called Impromptu. It provides users with a space for sharing peer-to-peer files. Each user's files are represented by points in a slice of a circular region. Users move their files in the circle to define access to the file, ranging from not shared (outer ring) to for persistently available to read and write (inner ring). Any changes are quickly perceived by the whole group. Thus, the real-time visualization of system state and integration between configuration and action can create a collective experience of sharing information. That way people can understand the activities of a distributed system and anticipate the consequences of their actions within that system.

Gilbert [6] goes beyond visibility and argues that although social translucence has shown its relevance in supporting the design of social technologies, social network sites have not been able to incorporate it, due to their structure. To deal with the challenge, he proposes a way to incorporate social translucence concepts in triadic relations. Using the triad relation associated to awareness he implements a web-based application (Link Different) that lets Twitter users know how many of their followers have already seen a link from someone else they follow. The high adoption of

Link Different by users indicates the value of including social translucence in social network sites. Nonetheless, how to apply the proposed triads to higher order structures that connect more people is still an open challenge.

The works discussed in this section focus on analyzing the difficulties users have in setting the desired privacy and some of them propose a solution on how to support users in dealing with this difficulty. Liu et al. [13] have suggested that users can use automatically generated list of friends' as a way to facilitate managing privacy. Razavi & Iverson [16] on their turn suggest that users create their own classification by the use of tags. Although these solutions may support users in managing the many levels of privacy, it does not seem to help them understand the impact of their privacy settings.

Gilbert's [6] solution provides awareness on how many users related to the posting user have seen a piece of information in Tweeter, helping him/her decide whether or not share it. Besmer & Lipford's [3] tool focuses on preventing undesirable impacts of photo sharing to tagged users, by allowing users to negotiate its visibility. Their solutions support users taking into consideration their social relations when deciding upon specific actions, but not in anticipating different scenarios that can be generated by their decisions.

de Paula et al. [4] propose a visual interactive solution for users to define and understand sharing levels of files. However, in this case, the sharing definition depends only upon the decision made by the file owner, and is not impacted by other users' actions on the file. In Facebook, often visibility of a piece of information depends not only on settings defined by the user posting the information, but also on actions other users are entailed (by these settings) to take on that piece of information. In this work, we focus on allowing users to preview what access other users may have to their information by exploring how users' roles and actions may change this access.

3. THE PROBLEM

The challenge in understanding the effects of users' decisions in many collaborative system settings, including Facebook privacy settings, is that the available parameters are not the only aspects considered in the final outcome. For instance, in Facebook users can choose who they would like to have access to a photo by choosing a category of users (e.g. Friends) or specific individuals. The interface in this case could be considered straightforward, as shown in Figure 1.

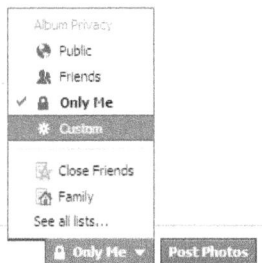

Figure 1 – Facebook photo album privacy settings

However, what is not clear in the interface is that there are other aspects involved in the final visibility of that piece of information. In this example, if someone who has access to the photo (the user who posted it or someone he/she has granted access to) tags someone who had not been given permission to see it, that person immediately gains access to the photo. Thus, often the final result

of a specific parameter depends not only on the value chosen for it, but also on other parameters or actions taken by the users themselves or other users they have relationships with.

Thus, we believe that in such situations allowing users to simulate the different scenarios that may be generated by considering the different combination possibilities would be an efficient way for them to understand and anticipate the possible effects of their decisions regarding settings.

4. FACEBOOK PRIVACY SIMULATOR – PRIVSIM

The Facebook Privacy Simulator (PrivSim) is a prototype created specially to investigate whether a simulator would support users in having a better understanding of the impact of settings and actions on the access others have to their information[1]. The prototype focused on photos and their visibility by others, since photos seem to raise more concerns from users regarding their access by others [15]. Photos were also chosen because their visibility in Facebook depends on settings defined by users, but also on actions that other users who have given access to the photo can take on it, as illustrated in the example in the previous section.

The prototype uses a model relationship network in which it represents possible roles users may have in the network. The relationship network depicts roles that are present in Facebook friendship network (e.g. friends or friends of friends). Since the model network does not represent users' real network, known character names were chosen to represent users.

Figure 2 (a) shows how the network is depicted in the prototype's interface[2]. PrivSim was modeled based on Facebook's functionalities available to users from February to April 2013. It included all the possible scenarios that could be generated based on combination of possible photo privacy settings and actions performed on photos. To identify all these possible scenarios a systematic inspection of Facebook was conducted and experimentation of the possible different scenarios made. In the prototype the user does not actually post a photo, but simulates it. He takes the role of the user depicted as the root node of the relationship network and defines the privacy settings he would like for a photo. Based on the setting, the prototype visually indicates (through the use of colors) which members of the network would be able to see the photo. If the user clicks on one of these users, he would also see what actions this other user could take regarding the photo (e.g. like or tag). The user may explore the various scenarios by simulating actions the different users in the network could take and visualizing their impact. The prototype also presents explanations regarding the impact of the simulated actions.

Figure 2 presents the interface for PrivSim. The user always takes the role of the root node of the relationship network, in the case Mickey. He can then explore the different scenarios considering distinct settings for the photo, as well as actions he or others who have access can take on the photo. To do so, he will interact with PrivSim interface that provides him with:

---

[1] Notice that PrivSim is a single-user system, not integrated to Facebook which was developed for the sole purpose of this investigation.
[2] It is worth emphasizing that the prototype's interface is in Portuguese, and was translated to English for this article.

Figure (PrivSim Interface screenshot):

.: Privacy on Facebook :.

Possible relationships within Facebook - Lines indicate relation of friendship:

(a)

Clarabelle — Horace
Minnie
Mickey — Donald — Daisy — Gladstone Gandar
Goofy
Max Goof — Pluto

Any Facebook user

Legend
Cannot see
Can see
Was tagged in the picture
Received a share

Note: Click on the above users to learn what they can do or see in Facebook regarding a photo. You can only select users who can view the photo and are depicted in colors different from grey.

Note: All users who are not colored in grey can see the photo.

Post picture with the setup:
○ Public
● Friends   (b)
○ Only me
○ Custom

The selected user can:
☐ Change date
☑ Like
☐ Comment
☐ Edit location
☑ Tag photo
☑ Share   (d)
☐ Remove tag
☐ Download
☐ Delete this photo
☐ Change privacy setting

How to use this simulator:
For instructions on using this simulator, move the slider below. Each degree corresponds to a step. To remove the tips from screen, slide the slider to one end.   (g)

Selected User (See above):
Mickey   (c)

Details
As the photo owner, you (Mickey) can take all the actions on the left. Select them to view comments.

User (Mickey) tagged users: Daisy

User (Mickey) shared the photo with: Goofy

Comments about the selected scenario:
--> Like: you (Mickey) can like your photo. Only you, your friends (Minnie, Donald, Goofy, etc.) or other tagged users will see your like.
--> Tag photo: you (Mickey) can tag your friends (Minnie, Donald, Goofy, etc.) or friends of your friends (Clarabelle, Daisy, Max Goofy, etc.). Only you, your friends (Minnie, Donald, Goofy, etc.) or other tagged users will see the tags.
--> Share: you (Mickey) can share your photo on your own timeline or on the timeline of your friends (Minnie, Donald, Goofy, etc.). The user who receives the sharing of your photo can remove it from your timeline without noticing you.

(e)

WARNING: Although Daisy is not a friend of yours, Daisy has been tagged and thus has access to your photo, which violates your privacy setting (Friends)   (f)

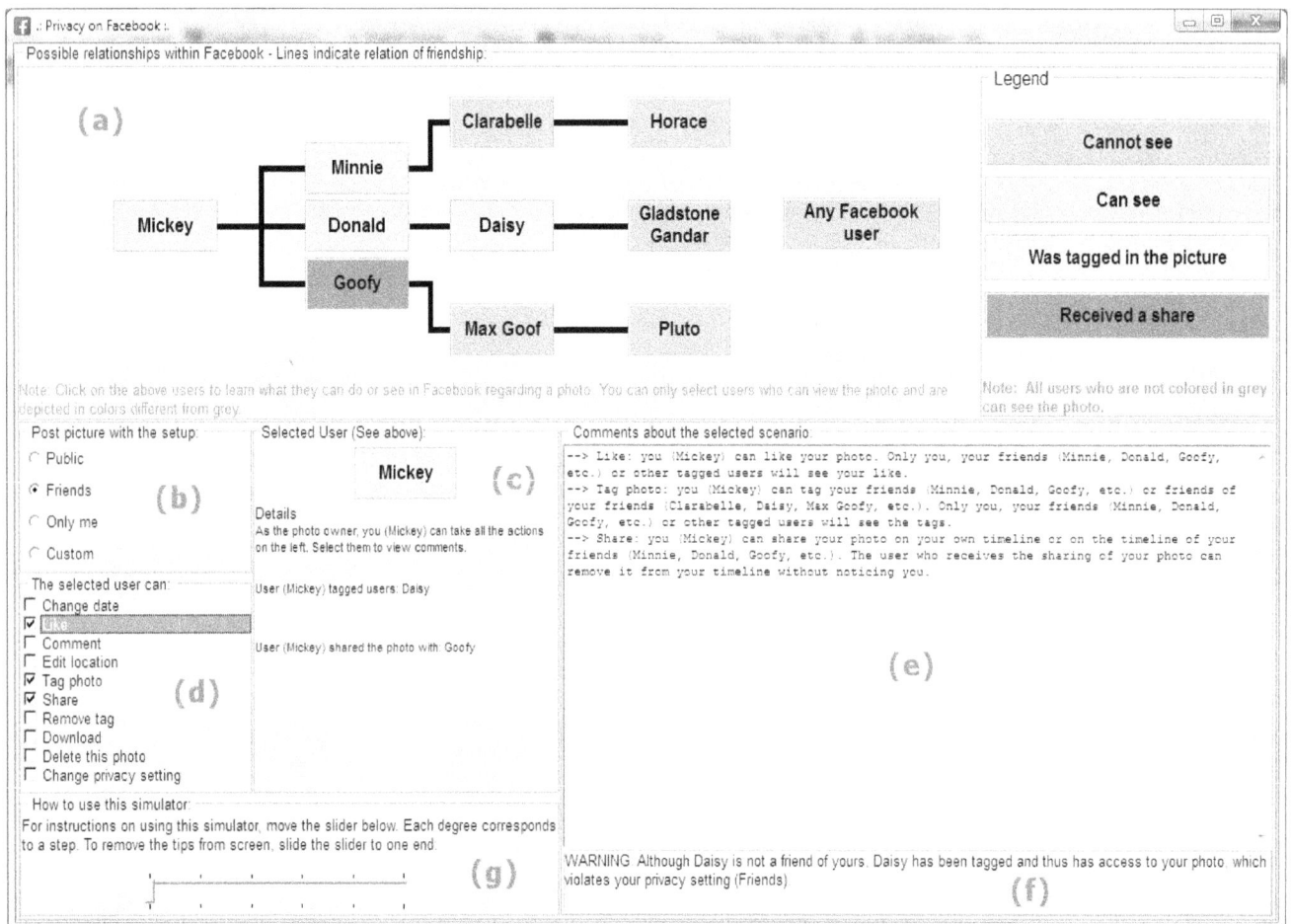

Figure 2 - PrivSim Interface

(a) Visual representation of the relationship network using characters' names to depict users. To select a member of the network, the user must click on its node. On the right, a legend indicating the meaning of the colors of the nodes of the network.

(b) Options of possible privacy settings that the user can choose to simulate and explore. The options regarding Friends of Friends or a specific set of people are available in the Custom setting.

(c) Indicates which user of the network is selected and the actions involving other users that have been chosen to be explored. In Figure 2 the user posting the photo, Mickey, is selected, and it shows that he has tagged Daisy in the photo and has shared it with Goofy.

(d) Presents the actions available for the selected user. By choosing an action, the system simulates how it would impact the access to the photo, and an explanation of the action and its impact is presented in (e). In Figure 2 it shows the actions the posting user, Mickey, can take on the photo. The user could choose any of the other users who have access to the photo to check what actions they would be able to take, and explore their effects.

(e) Presents explanation in natural language of all actions that have been chosen in (d).

(f) If users' actions generate inconsistencies according to the intended privacy setting selected in (b), a warning informing the user is presented. In Figure 2, in the explored scenario Mickey had defined that the photo should be visible by his friends. However, he has tagged Daisy (who is not a friend) in the photo, and as a result she gains access to it. Since she was not in the set of intended users (friends) a warning is presented to the user.

(g) Short step-by-step about how to use PrivSim. As the user drags the slide bar, callouts about how to use PrivSim are displayed on the screen.

In order to simulate and explore scenarios of how privacy settings and possible actions impact access to information, users interact with PrivSim as if they were posting a photo. They can choose different members of the network structure and select actions they could take and see their impact. Users can only choose members who have access to the photo (node color different from grey), since only they can take any action on the photo. It is interesting to note that the action that grants a member of the network access to the photo, also defines the actions that are available to him/her regarding the photo. For instance, a member who has been tagged (e.g. Daisy in Figure 2) will be able to edit its date, whereas others with whom the picture has been shared (e.g. Goofy) will not have that action available to them. Figure 3 illustrates the actions Mickey took that have defined the actions Daisy and Goofy would have available to them regarding the photo, and the difference between the set of actions available to each one of them.

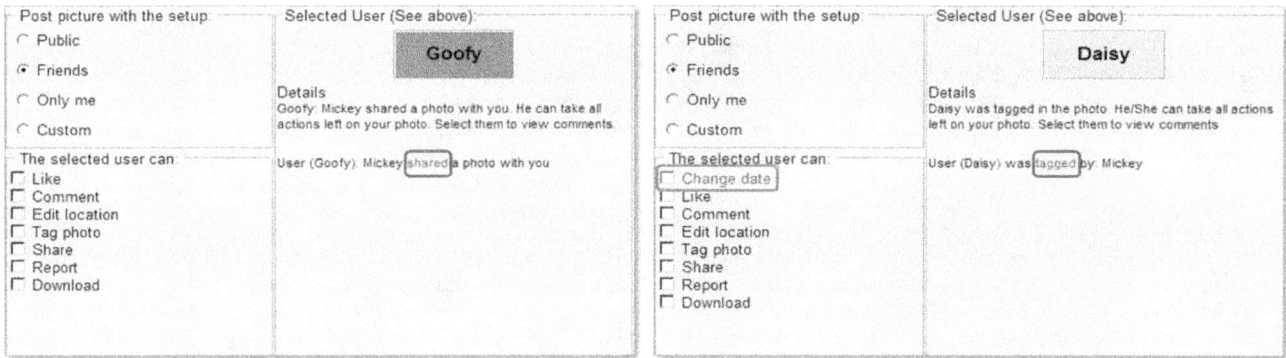

Figure 3 - Part of PrivSim interface showing the different actions available to users according to how they gained access to photo

Furthermore, when an action that involves other members is chosen by a member of the network, PrivSim indicates which other members can be involved in the action. For instance, in Figure 2 both Minnie and Donald can tag a photo, however, the set of people they can tag in the photo is different (e.g. Minnie can tag Clarabelle, but Donald cannot). Besides, the natural language explanation describes the consequences of an action, involving other aspects that are not shown visually. For instance, if Mickey chose a "Public" setting for his photo, and selected the Share action, PrivSim would present the following explanation:

"--> Share: you (Mickey) can share your photo on your own timeline or on the timeline of your friends (Minnie, Donald, Goofy, etc.). The users who you share your photo with can remove it from their timeline without informing you. Your friends (Minnie, Donald, Goofy, etc.) can share your photo on their timelines with their friends. You have no control over the sharing of your photo, but you receive a warning whenever it is shared."

Notice that the explanation presents not only who he could choose to share the photo with, but what other actions it would, as consequence, entail other members to take. In the example, when Mickey chooses to share a photo, it informs him about users being able to remove the photo from their timeline or to share it with their friends.

The number of combinations of possible settings and possible actions is considerable, even just for the model network. Thus, by simulating different scenarios, settings and actions, users can understand the impact of their actions. PrivSim allows users to explore what-if questions regarding the impact of the combination of settings and actions.

In Facebook's interface users can only see the privacy settings they can choose from (see Figure 1). They have to actually set them in order to try and understand their effects. Once they have set the privacy settings, they can see what actions they can take on it. To understand how a specific friend or the general public (a member that has no relation to the user) would see the photo, users may use the "View as" functionality. However, they still would not be able to simulate other users' actions and their impacts, but rather visualize the **actual** effects of their decisions. Thus, if they identify some undesirable effect, it might have already generated unwanted consequences. For instance, if users notice in the "View as" that they have unwillingly granted access to a photo to someone they did not intend to, they could go back and change their settings. However, there are no guarantees that in that time frame (between defining the settings and checking their effects) the unintended person would not have already seen the photo. Furthermore, the "View as" functionality does not allow users to

explore the consequences of other users' actions. That is, Mickey may view his info as Donald would, but not the consequences of Donald tagging Daisy in a photo he (Mickey) has posted. The information is also available at the help system, but reading the descriptions of all the possible scenarios may not be very appealing to users, and may not be easily understandable.

In order to investigate how a simulator, such as PrivSim, can support users in understanding the impact of configuration in settings that affect group social processes, we conducted a case-study for Facebook. We next describe the methodology used and the results obtained.

5. CASE STUDY

PrivSim allows Facebook users to simulate various scenarios relating how photos' privacy settings and possible actions upon these photos impact who would have access to them. Thus, PrivSim allowed us to make an initial evaluation of how the availability of simulations could support users in understanding the many possible scenarios involved in the combination of settings and possible actions. In this section, we present the methodology that was used in this case study and the results obtained from it

5.1. Methodology

In this case study we contrasted the understanding regarding information access that users had from using only Facebook, from what they perceived with the help of PrivSim. The study had two steps, in the first step participants interacted with Facebook, and in the second with PrivSim.

The goal of the first step (interacting with Facebook) was to collect data to answer our first research question – *"Can users understand the effects of their privacy settings on the access they grant other users to their information?"*. Whereas the second step (interacting with PrivSim) aimed at collecting data to our second question – *"Would a simulator that presented the impact of their settings in the access to their information increase their understanding of the effects of their decisions?"*. For that reason, we chose participants who were frequent Facebook users, and thus could be considered to have a good knowledge of Facebook interface and functionality. All participants performed the steps in the same order, since the goal of step 2 was to investigate whether the simulator could improve the understanding of privacy settings effects in Facebook that users already had based on their former experience with Facebook. In other words, we were more interested to see if there were impacts users could not perceive through the interaction with Facebook, and that PrivSim conveyed to them.

Twelve real Facebook users participated in the evaluation performed in May 2013. All of them were previously informed of the goal and conditions of the evaluation, participated voluntarily and signed a consent form. An initial interview about users' privacy concerns and their experience with Facebook was conducted.

Participants were Brazilians and had their accounts on Facebook for at least one and a half years. They were all undergraduate or graduate students with ages ranging from 19 to 29 years old. Of these, six people had a background in information technology (IT) and six had backgrounds in other fields. The reason for selecting these two user groups was to be able to verify whether people with an IT background had a better understanding of how Facebook behaved regarding access to information, and if PrivSim could help improve their understanding of the impacts of privacy settings and actions on Facebook. Also participants were equally distributed between males and females.

Regarding users' experience with Facebook, the time they had been using the system varied from one and a half to four years. All users access Facebook at least once a day and seven of them claimed to enter the system more than ten times a day. Furthermore, only four participants reported never having changed their privacy settings on Facebook and only two said they do not post personal photos and that they have in their accounts only profile pictures or photos in which they have been tagged.

Table 1 - Summary of tasks and related questions

#	Tasks / Questions
1	Post a photo with privacy setting "Friends".
1.1	*Who can view the photo after posted?*
1.2	*With whom can your friend Donald share the photo?*
1.3	*Who can Donald tag in the photo?*
2	Tag Minnie in the photo posted in the first task.
2.1	*After tagging your friend Minnie, someone besides you and your friends will have access to the photo?*
2.2	*Can Minnie tag people who did not gain access to the photo through the settings in the first task?*
3	Post a photo to only yourself and "Minnie".
3.1	*May Minnie (who has access to photo) tag her friends? If so, will they have access to the photo? If not, explain your answer.*
4	Post a picture with the setting "Friends of Friends".
4.1	*Could Minnie tag her friend Clarabelle, who is not your friend?*
4.2	*Could Minnie share the photo with Horace, who is a friend of a friend of hers?*
4.3	*Could Clarabelle, a friend of a friend of yours, tag Horace, who is her friend?*

For the evaluation, a scenario was prepared, and a test profile for Facebook was created, which made use of the same characters used in PrivSim, with the user taking the role of Mickey. The evaluation consisted basically of a set of tasks related to photo posting and defining their privacy settings. The tasks chosen represented privacy settings and actions users frequently perform on photos (posting to friends or friends of friends, tagging[3] and

sharing), and also that could generate changes to the original settings. After each task, the participant was asked to answer an electronic form containing multiple choice and open-ended questions regarding their understanding of who would have access to the photo and the expected impact of certain actions on this access. Audio of the whole test was recorded, as well as users' interaction with the systems. Table 1 shows a summary of the tasks and the questions related to them.

Before interacting with Facebook, users were informed that during the test they could ask about any doubts that might come up regarding how to perform the requested tasks on Facebook interface. They were also told that they could explore any of Facebook's features and when answering questions they could go back to the system if they wanted to. After executing the tasks in Facebook, users were interviewed briefly to know if they had had trouble answering the questions related to the tasks.

In the next evaluation step, PrivSim's interface was explained in a brief presentation, which lasted about 5 minutes. Once again, users were informed that they could ask for help if they had doubts about PrivSim's interface or about how to execute any of the tasks on PrivSim. At the end of their interaction with PrivSim, a post-test interview was conducted, regarding their opinion about PrivSim and which moments of the whole test they felt they had had more difficulties in answering the questions.

In the next section, we present the results obtained for the interaction with each one of the systems. In order to reference tasks and questions presented in Table 1 we will use task number "T" to reference tasks, and the questions will be referenced by the format "T.Q", where "T" is the task number and "Q" the question number for that task, for instance "1.2" refers to the second question of the first task.

5.2. Results Achieved

5.2.1. Interaction with Facebook

From the nine questions users were asked, there were only two that all participants got right: question 1.1 and 4.1. Whereas question 1.1 they all responded promptly, in answering question 4.1 five participants said they were not sure if their answer was correct.

Table 2 presents the information on the successes and doubts users had in each of the questions answered by them. The first two columns show the number of correct answers in each question grouped by participants background (or not) on IT. Column "Had no doubts but were wrong" shows the total number of participants in each question who felt confident about their answer, but were wrong. Finally, in column "Had doubts" indicates, for each question, the total number of participants who expressed their doubts about the correct answer, or did not know how to answer.

An independent-samples t-test was conducted to compare the hit rate between non-IT and IT background groups. There was not a significant difference in the hit rate for non-IT (M=2.1111, SD=2.36878) and IT groups (M=3.0, SD=2.17945); t (16)=-0.828, p = 0.42. These results suggest that users, independently of their IT background, had equivalent difficulties to answer the questions asked. Column "Had doubts" draws attention to the fact that with the exception of question 1.1, in all other questions at least half of

---

[3] Facebook has acknowledged the popularity of tagging and sharing photos. See: http://www.facebook.com/notes/facebook/making-photo-tagging-easier/467145887130 and

https://www.facebook.com/notes/facebook-data-science/the-anatomy-of-large-facebook-cascades/10151549884868859 the participants felt insecure about how Facebook would behave in the situation at hand. Comments such as "*I have doubts.*" or "*I don't know*" followed by pauses in which users thought about what to expect were common during the test. One participant (IT background) to try and find out the answer for a couple of questions explored the explicative texts available at the privacy settings interface, but claimed that they did not help him answer the questions.

Table 2 - Results of interaction with Facebook

#	Non-IT Hits	IT Hits	Had no doubts but were wrong	Had doubts
1.1	6	6	0	0
1.2	0	0	4	8
1.3	0	2	5	6
2.1	1	1	5	6
2.2	1	3	2	10
3.1	1	5	0	10
4.1	6	6	0	5
4.2	3	2	3	8
4.3	1	2	0	11

One other important aspect identified is that in several cases participants felt confident about their answer, but the answer was actually wrong, as is shown in the column "Had no doubts but were wrong". This situation is even worse than the participants being aware that they did not know how Facebook would behave, because it means that users have a misunderstanding about the system's behavior, but do not realize it. This combination is prone to lead to undesired situations, such as people who are not meant to have access to a piece of information accessing it, or not everyone who is supposed to access it being aware of it. Both cases could potentially lead to social inconveniences or problems for users.

During the tests, an example of such a situation was observed regarding question 2.2. This question was whether someone who had been tagged in a photo could tag someone else who was not in the set of people who the photo posting user had given access to. Eight of the participants got the answer wrong, that is they believed that the tagged user would not be able to tag someone who did not already have access to the photo (when in fact he would be able to tag any of his friends or friends of friends, regardless of them having access to the photo or not). Among them, two were certain of their answers and that only the users who the photo posting user had intended would be allowed to have access to the photo, independently of who was tagged. In other words, in this case users were not aware that unintended users could gain access to that piece of information as a result of other users' actions.

In the interview, after having interacted with Facebook, all participants reported having had difficulties in answering the questions. They referred to the tag or share features as a major source of doubt. When asked about what they thought could be the cause of these difficulties, some stated that they had never thought about it, or had never sought to find out, or even that it could be a problem of lack of practice. For instance, one of the participants said "*Because I never looked it up, nor is it clear anywhere, you'd*

have to look it up, and I never did"[4]. When we asked him and two others, who had given a similar answer, where they thought they could find this information, if it would be through the interface, or through the help page, they all said they believed they would only be able to find it at Facebook's Help system. However, none of them used the help system to try and answer the questions.

Another participant, when asked about where he expected to find explanations regarding the doubts he had, answered that "*With just one account I could not [find out], maybe I would need to have an extra Facebook profile or ask a brother, a cousin or a friend*". In addition, seven users also indicated explicitly that Facebook's interface is not clear regarding its behavior on users' privacy such as the situations that were addressed in the questions. For instance, another participant said "*Actually the interface is not very clear. At least if it had some warning messages [...]. Sometimes you end up doing something that is not quite what you want due to the lack of knowledge, then it becomes trial and error, you do it and see what happens*".

It is interesting to notice that participants' comments were not about **how to do** what had been asked of them, but rather about the difficulties they have in getting information about the **impact** of privacy settings and actions. One of them said he resorts to a strategy of simulation to understand the impact of these settings. To do so he either uses a dummy profile for testing or counts with another user who is willing to help him understand the effects of his actions. Notice, however, that this strategy would not be enough to cover all the possible scenarios, since doing so would require involving several people or several fictitious accounts, each having a different relationship to his actual profile. One other user acknowledges using a trial and error strategy. Nonetheless, this strategy may cause problems in situations in which by the time the user realizes the effect achieved was not the desired one he had already disclosed more information than he would have wished to or to people he had not intended to.

5.2.2. Interaction with PrivSim

In analyzing the execution of the same tasks with PrivSim, it is noticeable that none of the participants had doubts in answering the questions and the accuracy of responses was approximately 97%. There were only three errors throughout the test apparently due to some difficulty in understanding PrivSim's interface. The results of the evaluation with PrivSim are depicted in Table 3.

After the evaluation with PrivSim, a post-test interview was conducted. In this interview all participants said they had more difficulties in answering the questions when interacting with Facebook than with PrivSim. Also, they all stated that PrivSim had helped them understand the impact of privacy settings and actions, and thus, answer the questions. Some of them also commented that during the interaction with PrivSim they had realized that some of the answers they had given during the interaction with Facebook were wrong. One participant said: "*I know what will happen [with the use of PrivSim]. I realized that Facebook is full of mistakes, full of things that make no sense. I think I have gotten right most of the questions that I had gotten wrong before. So I know who will be able to see the photos and what possibilities the person will have*". Another participant's

---

[4] This quote was actually said in Portuguese, the participant's first language, and was translated by authors. This is the case for all quotes presented in the article.

comment indicated that PrivSim allowed her to become aware of how she might be more exposed than she had thought. In answering whether she would use PrivSim she said: *"I would be interested in using it [PrivSim] once I have found out today that I am not as safe as I believed I was."*.

Table 3 - Results of interaction with PrivSim

#	Non-IT Hits	IT Hits	Had no doubts but were wrong	Had doubts
1.1	6	6	0	0
1.2	6	5	1	0
1.3	5	6	1	0
2.1	6	6	0	0
2.2	6	6	0	0
3.1	6	6	0	0
4.1	6	5	1	0
4.2	6	6	0	0
4.3	6	6	0	0

Except for three of the users who said that they are not concerned with privacy, all the others said they would like if Facebook had a simulator of the effects of privacy configurations and that they would use it. They also said it would be better if it was native to Facebook and not an app, because they tend not to trust apps.

At the end of the interview, participants were asked if they would like to use a simulator if it was available on Facebook. Those participants who had declared to worry about privacy on social networks sites showed more interest in using the feature. Furthermore, some of them answered that they would use it, since during the experiment they had realized they did not quite understand all the possible impacts of the settings. The others said that they would not use it or would use it only in specific cases. For instance, one user said that one specific situation he would be interested in using PrivSim would be when he wanted to post photos he would not want his girlfriends' relatives to see.

6. DISCUSSION

The first research question we were set out to investigate in this work was *"Can users understand the effects of their privacy setting in the access others have to their information?"* The reason for raising this question is motivated by the fact that access to information depends not exclusively on the privacy settings defined by users. One of the results of the setting is the definition of the subset of actions that will be available for all users who have access to the information. Furthermore, the actions themselves, if taken by users, can generate changes to the group of people who have access to the photo. In other words, privacy settings in fact define a number of paths (or social processes) that are possible to be taken. Different paths may or may not give access to a distinct set of people. Therefore, making this process and all possible resulting scenarios clear to users at the interface is a very hard task, if not impossible. Of course, a description in natural language of all of them could be a way to explain all scenarios to users, but it would require users to be interested in reading the whole text.

The results described in the previous section showed that not only did users have doubts about how Facebook would behave, but also they had misunderstandings that they were unaware of. As discussed, the latter is even a less desirable situation than the former. However, these results do not come as a surprise. Understanding how decisions regarding configuration settings made at a given moment will impact group processes and access rights along a period of time is a complex problem. This is even more the case when other conditions (e.g. other users' actions) can change the final results. We believe that this problem is not specific to Facebook privacy settings or interface, but that it is faced whenever a set of parameters is used to configure group collaborative processes [5].

In order to deal with this challenge, it would be necessary to allow users to simulate the processes and how they are impacted by parameter configuration and actions. Thus, our second question was *"Would a simulator that presented the impact of their settings in the access to their information increase their understanding of the effects of their decisions?"*. PrivSim interaction results showed that users had a thorough understanding of how the settings and actions associated with them could impact photo visibility. Furthermore, they realized during the use of PrivSim that many of the expectations they had built through Facebook interface were wrong. Notice that these expectations were based not only on their interaction during the test, but on their whole experience with Facebook. Graph 1 shows a comparison between the correct responses obtained through the interaction with Facebook and PrivSim. These results can be taken as a sign of how an interface that allows users to simulate and explore the possible scenarios (before making decisions) could be a good solution for the problem raised.

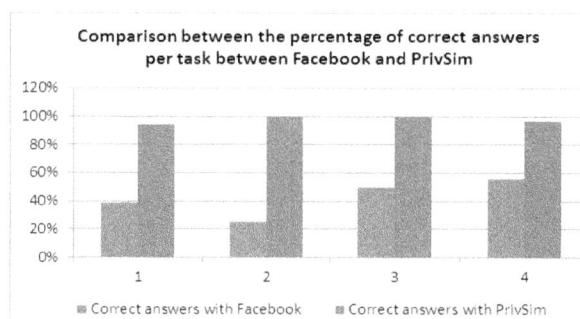

Graph 1 - Percentage of correct answers per task for Facebook and PrivSim

A paired-samples t-test was conducted to compare the hit rate using PrivSim and Facebook. To do so, the total number of hits for each question was compared. There was a significant difference in the hit rate for PrivSim (M=11.6667, SD=0.5) and Facebook (M=5.1111, SD=4.28799); t(8) = 4.6, p = 0.002. These results suggest that when using PrivSim, users had a mean value of correct answers greater than when they interacted with Facebook.

Although our study has generated interesting findings supporting the usefulness of a simulator in conveying to users impact of their privacy settings in Facebook, some limitations of the study should be noted. First of all, some participants reported using the "View as" function to understand the effects of privacy settings, as well as accessing Facebook through different accounts or through the support of friends. In our case-study none of them made use of such strategies, even though they could explore the interface to find out. The decision not to use these strategies could be due to the controlled setting of the experiment. First of all, there were no real effects that mattered to the participants, since a test profile was being used. Second, they might not have had at the time access to their usual resources – other accounts that related to the test profile that they could use to understand the impact of their settings or friends they could ask.

Furthermore, some participants said they expected the information about the impact of the settings to be available at Facebook help. Once more, although one user inspected the local explicative texts at the privacy settings interface, none of them interacted with the help system to answer the questions. Again this could have been because they did not really care about the final results of the settings or even that it may not have been clear to them that they could resort to the help system in case of doubts. In the methodology, in cases where users expressed doubts they could have been explicitly asked to do whatever they would normally do to solve them.

Evaluating whether the information was in the help system and if users could find it was not relevant in determining whether the simulator could or not support users in anticipating the impact of settings configuration. Nevertheless, having found that the simulator can be an interesting solution to the problem, comparing the user experience and efficiency in using it versus the help system could be relevant in analyzing its cost and benefits.

One may argue that another limitation would be the small size and simplicity of the network used in the evaluation. However, in the first step in which participants interacted with Facebook, as our results showed, even for such a simplified network users had little understanding of the impacts photo settings and actions. Furthermore, participants were frequent Facebook users for over an year, and most posted photos (even the two who said they did not post photos said that they had shared photos in which they had been tagged) so they could have obtained this knowledge from their previous experience with Facebook in real context.

Even if the simplified network depicted could have acted in favor of the understanding of the simulation in PrivSim, results still mean that the simulator improved users' understanding of configuration and actions impacts. Furthermore, it was not our goal to explore what would be the best way to represent the simulation (in the prototype or real systems). In order to evaluate whether a simplified version of the network would be able to allow users to generalize Facebook behavior and apply it to their own network would require further investigation to be conducted.

7. CONCLUSIONS AND NEXT STEPS

In this article we have investigated the challenges for users to understand the possible impacts of Facebook privacy settings. We also examined the proposal to offer as a solution a simulator that can emulate the impacts generated, and that allows users to explore the different scenarios.

Through the case-study in Facebook we have illustrated through users' experience that often they are not sure of what to expect as results of privacy settings taking into account the actions they enable, or they have misunderstandings about it. Also, their interaction with PrivSim has shown that given the opportunity to simulate the different scenarios resulting from specific settings and actions, users were able to understand rules of how Facebook worked, and even discuss whether they believed they were adequate or not.

The case-study involved 12 users and was not intended to generate quantitative results about the issues at hand, but rather allow for qualitative and interpretative investigation of them. The tasks and scenarios chosen to be investigated were representative of situations in which access permissions could change along time according to what actions were performed upon the pieces of information, and thus were challenging for users to anticipate. The

results obtained were able to illustrate the difference in the perception of the cause-effect relation between settings, actions and information access provided by the interface and with the help of the simulator.

As discussed, we argue that the problem is not specific to Facebook interface, but is faced in any situation in collaborative systems in which parameter setting is used to define how social processes will work. The gist of the problem is at the social-technical gap that is inherent to collaborative systems [1]. According to Ackerman, technology may never account for all nuances that are involved in social processes. A solution to deal with this problem is providing users with systems that are highly configurable. If on the one hand, this allows users to narrow the social-technical gap, on the other, it creates a large number of resulting scenarios that users should be able to anticipate in order to achieve the desired results. Allowing users to simulate and explore the effects of parameter configuration supports them in anticipating all of the possible scenarios. Nonetheless, simulation does not close the social-technical gap, but supports users in understanding the rules created in the system to represent social processes, that is supports them in bridging the existing gap.

The results of this article contribute to the investigation of the challenges involved in making clear to users the cause-effect of configuration and the impacted processes. Although PrivSim itself was not meant to be directly integrated to an existing system, the results indicate that a simulator is a viable solution that could be incorporated by designers of collaborative systems. We do not claim to contribute to a discussion about what would be the best way to incorporate simulation to social network sites or collaborative systems in general. Nonetheless, we have come across indicators of aspects to be considered in such an effort. First of all, the simulation should be incorporated into the system, so that whenever the system behavior is changed, the simulation would automatically change as well. Besides, regarding privacy in social network sites, some participants of our study pointed out that they probably would not trust an application that was not native to the system.

Also we have not explored what would be the best representation to depict the social relations network. In our study users understood well the simplified network and, as a result of their interaction with PrivSim, the rules of Facebook behavior. An interesting next step would be to investigate whether users would be able to transfer this understanding of Facebook behavior to their real relationships' network. If so, a model network could be an interesting option to avoid an overly complex visualization of the users' real networks [18].

In this paper it was not our goal to compare different ways to convey Facebook behavior rules to users. Nonetheless, it might also be interesting to investigate other possible representations of systems' behavior rules and compare how each one of them impacts users' understanding.

The results have shown that simulation supported users in understanding the social processes. As a next step in our research we are developing a simulator as an integrated part of a collaborative system (in a different domain than social network sites). Our goal is to analyze if and how users interact with it in a real context of use.

Although we discussed in this article the challenges faced by users of collaborative systems, it is interesting to note that a similar challenge is faced by collaborative system designers. Designers must choose the parameters, and the rules that define which aspects of collaboration they will impact and how. Often, the large number of possible combinations means that a broad range of scenarios is possible. Anticipating these scenarios at design time is not an easy task. Therefore, creating a modeling language and tool that would allow designers to describe their decisions and explore the possible scenarios that they would entail could be useful to support their decision making. We believe that the results discussed in this paper are valuable to advancing in this direction.

8. ACKNOWLEDGEMENTS

Authors are grateful to all participants of the case-study. They also thank INWeb (MCT/CNPq/ grant 57.3871/2008-6) for partially supporting this work.

9. REFERENCES

[1] Ackerman, M. 2000. The Intellectual Challenge of CSCW: The Gap Between Social Requirements and Technical Feasibility. Human-Computer Interaction. 15, 2 (2000), 179–203.

[2] Bernstein, M.S., Ackerman, M.S., Chi, E.H. and Miller, R.C. 2011. The trouble with social computing systems research. CHI '11 Extended Abstracts on Human Factors in Computing Systems (New York, NY, USA, 2011), 389–398.

[3] Besmer, A. and Richter Lipford, H. 2010. Moving beyond untagging: photo privacy in a tagged world. Proceedings of the SIGCHI Conference on Human Factors in Computing Systems (New York, NY, USA, 2010), 1563–1572.

[4] de Paula, R., Ding, X., Dourish, P., Nies, K., Pillet, B., Redmiles, D.F., Ren, J., Rode, J.A. and Filho, R.S. 2005. In the eye of the beholder: a visualization-based approach to information system security. International Journal of Human-Computer Studies. 63, 1-2 (2005), 5–24.

[5] de Souza, C.S., Leitão, C.F., Prates, R.O., Amélia Bim, S., da Silva, E.J. and DaSilva, E.J. 2010. Can inspection methods generate valid new knowledge in HCI? The case of semiotic inspection. International Journal of Human-Computer Studies. 68, 1-2 (Jan. 2010), 22–40.

[6] Gilbert, E. 2012. Designing social translucence over social networks. Proceedings of the 2012 ACM annual conference on Human Factors in Computing Systems - CHI '12 (New York, New York, USA, May 2012), 2731.

[7] Gross, R. and Acquisti, A. 2005. Information revelation and privacy in online social networks. Proceedings of the 2005 ACM workshop on Privacy in the electronic society (New York, NY, USA, 2005), 71–80.

[8] Hamidi, F. and Baljko, M. 2012. Using social networks for multicultural creative collaboration. Proceedings of the 4th international conference on Intercultural Collaboration (New York, NY, USA, 2012), 39–46.

[9] Johnson, M., Egelman, S. and Bellovin, S.M. 2012. Facebook and privacy: it's complicated. Proceedings of the Eighth Symposium on Usable Privacy and Security (New York, NY, USA, 2012), 9:1–9:15.

[10] Johnston, A. and Wilson, S. 2012. Privacy Compliance Risks for Facebook. Technology and Society Magazine, IEEE. 31, 2 (2012), 59–64.

[11] Joinson, A.N. 2008. Looking at, looking up or keeping up with people?: motives and use of facebook. Proceedings of the SIGCHI Conference on Human Factors in Computing Systems (New York, NY, USA, 2008), 1027–1036.

[12] Lampe, C., Ellison, N.B. and Steinfield, C. 2008. Changes in use and perception of facebook. Proceedings of the 2008 ACM conference on Computer supported cooperative work (New York, NY, USA, 2008), 721–730.

[13] Liu, Y., Gummadi, K.P., Krishnamurthy, B. and Mislove, A. 2011. Analyzing facebook privacy settings: user expectations vs. reality. Proceedings of the 2011 ACM SIGCOMM conference on Internet measurement conference (New York, NY, USA, 2011), 61–70.

[14] Pontes, T., Magno, G., Vasconcelos, M., Gupta, A., Almeida, J., Kumaraguru, P. and Almeida, V. 2012. Beware of What You Share: Inferring Home Location in Social Networks. 12th International Conference on Data Mining Workshops (ICDMW), 2012 IEEE (2012), 571–578.

[15] Rauber, G., Almeida, V. and Kumaraguru, P. 2011. Privacy Albeit Late. Accepted at WEBMEDIA, Brazilian Symposium on Multimedia and the Web. (2011).

[16] Razavi, M.N. and Iverson, L. 2009. Improving personal privacy in social systems with people-tagging. Proceedinfs of the ACM 2009 international conference on Supporting group work - GROUP '09 (New York, New York, USA, May 2009), 11.

[17] Reynolds, B., Venkatanathan, J., Gonçalves, J. and Kostakos, V. 2011. Sharing ephemeral information in online social networks: privacy perceptions and behaviours. Proceedings of the 13th IFIP TC 13 international conference on Human-computer interaction - Volume Part III (Berlin, Heidelberg, 2011), 204–215.

[18] Shen, Z., Ma, K.-L. and Eliassi-Rad, T. Visual analysis of large heterogeneous social networks by semantic and structural abstraction. IEEE transactions on visualization and computer graphics. 12, 6, 1427–39.

[19] Strater, K. and Lipford, H.R. 2008. Strategies and struggles with privacy in an online social networking community. Proceedings of the 22nd British HCI Group Annual Conference on People and Computers: Culture, Creativity, Interaction - Volume 1 (Swinton, UK, UK, 2008), 111–119.

[20] Stutzman, F. and Kramer-Duffield, J. 2010. Friends only: examining a privacy-enhancing behavior in facebook. Proceedings of the SIGCHI Conference on Human Factors in Computing Systems (New York, NY, USA, 2010), 1553–1562.

[21] Tufekci, Z. 2007. Can You See Me Now? Audience and Disclosure Regulation in Online Social Network Sites. Bulletin of Science, Technology & Society. 28, 1 (Dec. 2007), 20–36.

[22] Zheleva, E. and Getoor, L. 2009. To join or not to join: the illusion of privacy in social networks with mixed public and private user profiles. Proceedings of the 18th international conference on World wide web (New York, NY, USA, 2009), 531–540.

Designing Better Location Fields in User Profiles

Ting-Yu Wang
GroupLens Research
University of Minnesota
twang@cs.umn.edu

F. Maxwell Harper
GroupLens Research
University of Minnesota
harper@cs.umn.edu

Brent Hecht
GroupLens Research
University of Minnesota
bhecht@cs.umn.edu

ABSTRACT

Twitter, Facebook, Pinterest and many other online communities ask their users to populate a *location field* in their user profiles. The information that is entered into this field has many uses in both industry and academia, with location field data providing valuable geographic context for operators of online communities and playing key roles in numerous research projects. However, despite the importance of location field entries, we know little about how to design location fields effectively. In this paper, we report the results of the first controlled study of the design of location fields in user profiles. After presenting a survey of location field design decisions in use across many online communities, we show that certain design decisions can lead to more granular location information or a higher percentage of users that fill out the field, but that there is a trade-off between granularity and the percent of non-empty fields. We also add context to previous work that found that location fields tend to have a high rate of non-geographic information (e.g. Location: "Justin Bieber's Heart"), showing that this result may be site-specific rather than endemic to all location fields. Finally, we provide evidence that verifying users' location field entries against a database of known-valid locations can eliminate toponym (place name) ambiguity and any non-geographic location field entries while at the same time having little effect on field population rate and granularity.

Categories and Subject Descriptors

H5.m. [Information interfaces and presentation (e.g., HCI)]: Miscellaneous.

Keywords

Location field, user profile, geotagging, geographic user-generated content, volunteered geographic information

1. INTRODUCTION

User profiles in online communities very often contain what is known as a *location field* [11]. This is true of many popular social media sites such as Twitter, Pinterest, Flickr, and Foursquare, but also of other types of communities like eBay and Github (see Figure 1 for examples). Moreover, the use of the location field spans Eastern and Western cultures, with popular Eastern communities like Kaixinwang, Renren, and Cyworld also incorporating these fields into their user profiles.

Researchers and operators of online communities have found location field entries to be invaluable in a number of ways. First and foremost, members of many communities are reluctant to tag individual pieces of content with their specific location; only 1.5-3.2% of tweets have geotags, for instance [19]. Location field entries can provide a rough estimate of the location of users who are not among the small group of people that frequently post or update their location. Indeed, in order to provide users of its Search API with geographic context for the 96.8-98.5% of tweets that are not geotagged, Twitter mines the location field in its users' profiles [29]. Moreover, many research projects have taken a similar approach, with the toponyms (i.e. place names) in location fields being used to assign geographic references to social media (e.g. [9,11,17]).

Location field entries can also help researchers avoid major confounds introduced by user mobility. Given that a person's geotagged social media (e.g. photos, tweets) may be widely

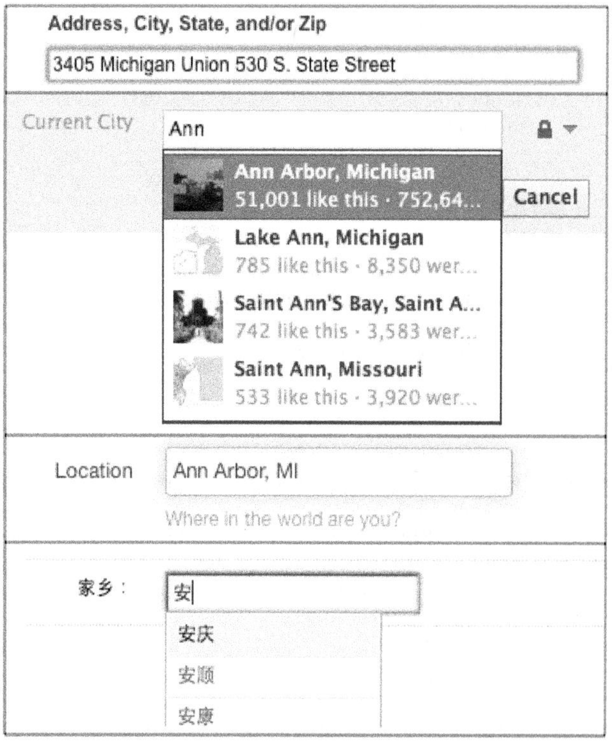

Figure 1. Examples of location fields from a number of online communities (top to bottom: Yelp, Facebook, Twitter, Kaixinwang). Note that all use different prompts, have different lengths, and take different approaches to validation. (Kaixinwang's prompt translates to "Hometown").

GROUP'14, November 9–12, 2014, Sanibel Island, Florida, USA.

ACM 978-1-4503-3043-5/14/11...$15.00
http://dx.doi.org/10.1145/2660398.2660424

dispersed due to vacations, business trips, and other forms of travel, the information in the location field is frequently used as a simple heuristic for determining the location(s) in which a social media user can be considered a "local" [10]. For instance, this approach has been utilized for studying the demographic makeup of social media communities (e.g. [12,18]), understanding geographic patterns in social networks (e.g. [14,15,22]), and inferring the home locations of the online community members from the content (e.g. tweets) they produce (e.g. [20,23]).

However, data from location fields also has a number of important disadvantages. Research has shown that the toponyms in location fields tend to be of relatively course geographic *granularity*, with most field entries being city names [11,20]. In addition, far from all users fill out their location field (i.e. there is a low field *population rate*) and many users input non-geographic information like "Justin Bieber's Heart" and "preferably anywhere but here" [11] (i.e. low *geographicness*).

The goal of this paper is to inform the design of location fields that can minimize these disadvantages, thereby providing more and higher quality location information to online community operators and researchers alike. Despite the importance of the information entered into location fields, no work has examined the relationship between location field design and the quality of the information entered into them. Indeed, as we will show, there is extensive variation across online communities in location field design, with sites using different prompts, having different verification strategies, and using fields of highly varied length, among other differences (Figure 1).

Below, we report the results of a series of controlled experiments targeted at identifying the most effective approaches to location field design. Our objective was to understand the relationship between the design of location fields and the three major limitations of location field data that have been identified in the literature:

1) *Population Rate*, or the percent of users who fill out the location field in their user profile.

2) *Granularity*, or the geographic scale of the location information that is entered (e.g. city-level, address, country-level).

3) *Geographicness*, or the percent of location field entries that contain valid geographic information rather than non-geographic entries like 'Justin Bieber's Heart' and 'preferably anywhere but here'.

Through these experiments, we are able to establish that simple changes in location field design can increase the amount or the granularity of location field entries, but that online community operators must generally negotiate a trade-off between the two. In addition, we show that concerns about geographicness in location fields may only be valid in certain online communities rather than being endemic to location fields as a whole. However, we also report findings that can inform the design of location fields in communities where geographicness is indeed a problem. Namely, validating users' entries against a database of legal places had no effect on population rate or granularity, but completely removes concerns about geographicness. Validation has the added benefit of a-priori disambiguation of place names, reducing the need for and error introduced by geocoding.

Below, we begin with a discussion of related work. In the subsequent section, we discuss the results of a survey of location field design decisions made in 18 different online communities.

Next, we introduce our overall experimental approach and walk the reader through our three controlled studies on location field design. Finally, we conclude with a discussion of design implications and future work.

2. RELATED WORK

The work most related to our research can largely be grouped into two areas: (1) studies of location disclosure behavior and (2) research that utilizes location field data.

The rapid increase in the popularity of location-aware technologies like smartphones has led to a strong interest in location disclosure behavior in the literature. For instance, Consolvo et al. [6] and Wiese et al. [30] used questionnaires to understand why and with whom people share their locations. Tsai et al. [28] identified that feedback can improve user comfort levels with location sharing. Other researchers have studied the effect of incentives (e.g. [27]) and place naming strategies (e.g. [16]) on location sharing behavior.

No existing work has investigated the effect of location field design on location disclosure in location fields. In addition to the applied utility of a study directly targeted at location fields as outlined above, our work also sheds light on location sharing behavior in the context of a categorically different type of location information: low temporal resolution location information. Several schema of location information in online communities exist, and all of them distinguish between *high temporal resolution* information and *low temporal resolution* information. High temporal resolution information (e.g. Hecht and Gergle's [10] "Contribution" location type and Schultz et al.'s [24] "Tweet Location" type) is the focus of existing location disclosure work, which tends to look at phenomena like Foursquare check-ins and the sharing of real-time locations. Location fields, on the other hand, are infrequently updated and contain low temporal resolution location information (e.g. Hecht and Gergle's "Contributor" location type and Schultz et al.'s "User's Residence" location type).

Location field data is used in a wide variety of research projects from a number of different disciplines. In addition to the work noted above on geographic social networks, demographic analysis, and location inference, other researchers have used location field data to, for instance, study online activism surrounding major political events (e.g. [9,17]), examine the prevalence of local perspectives in user-generated content (e.g. [10]), and monitor public health [3,4,7]. Further, the inference attack problem – in which a user's location is predicted from her social media – has attracted considerable interest beyond the papers cited above, with location field data frequently serving as ground truth (e.g. [2,5,11,13,21]). Much of this location field-based inference work involves using location field entries to ground *geographic topic models*, which have a number of other uses such as modeling linguistic variation across space [8]. Finally, it is important to note that *any* study (or application) that uses the Twitter Search API implicitly uses location field information.

All of the above work (including studies and applications that use the Twitter Search API) could benefit from more and higher quality location field entries, the end goal of this paper. For instance, with more granular entries, those who study the geographic properties of online social networks would be able to understand these properties at a more local scale. The same can be said for research that takes a geographic approach to understanding the demographics of online community members and uses tweets to monitor public health. Along the same lines, the Twitter Search API could provide more precise geographic context for more tweets if more Twitter users populated their location fields with more granular toponyms. In addition, increasing the geographicness of location field entries could open up new applications for location field data. Researchers have eschewed the use of location field data out of concern for geographicness in a number of areas (e.g. emergency management [25]).

3. LOCATION FIELD DESIGN SPACE

Our first step in understanding the effect of location field design decisions on the field's population rate and the granularity and geographicness of its entries was to survey the design space of location fields in a variety of online communities. Examining 18 communities that are popular in Eastern and Western cultures, we identified five key location field design dimensions:

- *Prompt:* the text that appears to the top or the left of the location field.

- *Length:* the length of the field in number of characters, as measured by the number of "0" characters one can enter before one of the "0" characters is not fully visible.

- *Verification*: whether or not entries are validated against a dataset of known-valid locations (e.g. using a gazetteer).

- *Visibility*: whether the information placed in the location field is public, private, or whether users have control over the extent to which the information is shared with others.

- *Number of fields*: whether the user profile contained a single or multiple location fields. For instance, Twitter

uses a single field ("Location") while Kaixinwang uses two ("Current City" and "Hometown"[1]).

Table 1 describes the design choices made by each of the 18 surveyed communities (on their non-mobile websites) along each of these dimensions as of Fall 2013. The table reveals that there is a great deal of diversity in all five dimensions. For instance, Yelp prompts its field with "Address, City, State, and/or Zip", while Twitter uses "Location" (see Figure 1). Location field lengths also range widely, for example, with Twitter adopting a 29-character field and Pinterest using a 49-character field. A similar lack of consensus can be seen with regard to whether or not location fields are verified against known place names, how widely location field information is shared within an online community, and the number of location fields in a user profile.

Using the results of our survey of the location field design space, we developed three experiments to identify the design choices that result in (1) the highest location field population rates, (2) the most granular location information, and (3) the highest degree of geographicness. In these experiments, which are described immediately below, we evaluated the effect of a range of design decisions along all of the key design dimensions outlined above with the exception of the number of fields. Most of the online communities whose location field data has been used in the literature utilize single fields (e.g. Twitter, Foursquare) and we anticipate that our conclusions about single fields will also apply to individual fields on multiple-field profiles.

4. EXPERIMENTS

All experiments were performed in MovieLens[2], a movie-focused online community that has over 100,000 users and, as of Fall

Community	Entry Prompt	Field Length	Verification	Visibility
Pinterest	Location	49	No	Public
Twitter	Location	29	No	Public
Yelp	(1) Address, City, State, and/or Zip (2) My Hometown	(1) 49, (2) 45	(1) Yes, (2) No	(all) Public
Facebook	(1) Current City, (2) Hometown	(1) 27, (2) 27	(1) Yes, (2) Yes	(all) User-Controlled
Foursquare	Location	23	No	Public
LinkedIn	Postal Code	39	Yes	Public
Flickr	(1) Your Hometown, (2) City you live now, (3) Country, (4) 3 letter Airport Code	(1) 26, (2) 26, (3) 26, (4)7	(1) No, (2) No, (3) No, (4) No	(1) Public, (2) (3) User-Controlled, (4) Private
G+	Place lived	57	No	User-Controlled
Bitbucket	Location	49	No	User-Controlled
MeetUp	(1) ZIP, (2) Hometown	(1) 17, (2) 20	(1) Yes, (2) No	(all) Public
Lang-8	Location	Drop-down	Yes	User-Controlled
Ebay	(1) Address, (2) City, (3) Postal Code	(1) 40, (2) 40, (3) 20	(1) No, (2) Yes, (3) Yes	(all) Private
Renren	(1) Location, (2) Hometown	(1) Drop-down, (2) Drop-down	(1) Yes, (2) Yes	(all) User-Controlled
Cyworld	Current City	31	No	User-Controlled
Weibo	Location	Drop-down	Yes	Public
Ameba	(1) Hometown, (2) Haunt, (3) Region In Which You Live	(1) 39 and Drop-down* (2) 39, (3) Drop-down	(1) Hybrid*, (2) No, (3) Yes	(all) User-Controlled
Skype	(1) City, (2) State/Province	(1) 31, (2) 31	(1) No, (2) No	(all) Public
Kaixinwang	(1) Current Location, (2) Hometown	(1) 20, (2) 20	(1) No, (2) No	(all) Public

Table 1. The variation in location field design decisions across 18 online communities. In communities with multiple fields, each field is numbered. Lang-8, Renren, and Weibo use drop-down menus that allow users to select cities in China (drop-down menus implicitly use verification by our definition). *The Ameba "Hometown" field is a hybrid field, with a 39-character free text field and a prefecture(state)-level drop-down menu.

2013, received about 20 registrations per day. When a user signs up for MovieLens, they are invited to input information for their online profile. We manipulated the design of the location field in this process (Figure 3). All experiments were performed between November 2013 and February 2014 and a total of 1,673 users took part.

In our first experiment, we examined the effect of prompt and length on the quality metrics outlined above: population rate, granularity, and geographicness. Next, we looked at the effect of verification against a database of known-valid locations. Finally, we conducted a third experiment that examined the role of visibility on the quality metrics.

When analyzing the location field entries recorded during our experiment for granularity and geographicness, we followed the approach of Hecht et al. [11] in which two coders independently assessed granularity and geographicness. Each entry was assigned granularity codes from the following set: {address, neighborhood, city, intrastate region, state, interstate region, country}. To afford ordinal analysis, the granularity codes were ranked from 0 (address) to 6 (country). Geographicness was treated as a binary. Interrater agreement was above 97% in all cases for both granularity and geographicness. Conflicts were resolved through negotiation between the two coders.

4.1 Experiment 1: Length and Prompt

We analyzed the effect of location field length and prompt on the quantity and quality of location field entries using a between-subjects 3x3 experiment. The three levels of the length factor were set to 30 characters, 50 characters, and 70 characters so as to explore the short, medium, and long areas of the field length spectrum. The levels of the prompt factor were "Location" (e.g. Twitter, Pinterest, Foursquare), "Current City" (e.g. Facebook, Cyworld), and "Address, City, State, and/or Zip" (Yelp). These levels were selected to (1) cover the most common prompts (i.e. the first two) and (2) to span the spectrum of requested granularity. New users of our experiment online community were randomly assigned to one of the nine conditions.

The online movie community received 663 new registrations during the one-month period Experiment 1 was active[3]. Looking at our data a high-level, we saw that overall, 44.0% of users entered a value into the location field. 67.1% of geographic entries were at the city-level. Country was the next most common granularity (16.3%), followed by state (6.0%). 4.6% of users who entered a valid geographic location entered an address.

While research has shown that many users input non-geographic information into the Twitter location field [11,26], we observed a much smaller percentage of non-geographic entries. A total of *four* entries (0.7%) were non-geographic (e.g. "Sears", "here") as opposed to the 16% reported by Hecht et al. [11]. As we will discuss below, this result was not limited to Experiment 1; we saw very little in the way of non-geographic location field entries from the over 1,600 users in our entire study. Because there were so few non-geographic location field entries, we did not consider geographicness in our subsequent analyses.

To understand the effect of field length and field prompt on population rate and granularity, we performed logistic regressions with length and prompt as independent variables. A nominal

---

[3] The location field entries from six users had to be omitted from granularity and geographicness analysis due to data corruption likely related to character encoding issues.

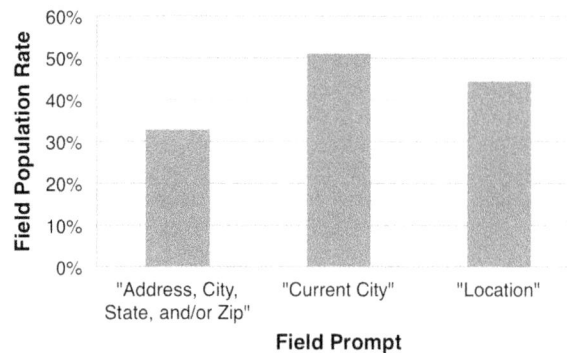

Figure 2. The population rates for each prompt considered. The Facebook-style "Current City" had a rate approximately 1.5 times higher than that for the Yelp-style "Address, City, State, and/or Zip".

logistic regression with field population (has entry / does not have entry) as the dependent variable indicates that prompt has a significant effect on population rate ($\chi^2(2,N=663) = 17.97$, $p < 0.01$). No significant effect could be detected for field length ($\chi^2(2,N=663) = 0.30$, $p = 0.86$) or for a prompt by length interaction ($\chi^2 (4,N=663) = 2.43$, $p = 0.66$).

Looking at the relationship between prompt and population rate more closely (Figure 2), a clear trend emerges: while the "Current City" and "Location" prompts have population rates of around 50%, the population rate for "Address, City, State, and/or Zip" – the prompt that requests the most granular information – is only 32.8%.

With regard to granularity, an ordinal logistic regression indicates that prompt has a significant effect on ordinal granularity ($\chi^2(2,N=283) = 73.68$, $p < 0.001$). The regression also indicates a marginal effect for both length ($\chi^2 (2,N=283) = 4.80$, $p = 0.09$) and a prompt by length interaction ($\chi^2 (4,N=283) = 8.83$, $p = 0.07$).

It is not unexpected that prompts that request different levels of granularity get location field entries of different granularities. For instance, *all* of the address-scale entries in this experiment came from the "Address, City, State, and/or Zip" prompt, making up 19.4% of entries for this prompt. Similarly, 95.1% of "Current City" entries were at the city-scale. "Location" received a much more balanced distribution.

While the prompt main effect may not be surprising, it is revealing of an important larger implication. Namely, while designers of online communities can significantly increase location field granularity using the Yelp-style "Address, City, State, and/or Zip" prompt over the Twitter-style "Location" and Facebook-style "Current City" prompts, our results related to input rate indicate that by requesting an address, input rates will drop. As such, designers of online communities must negotiate a trade-off between granularity and input rate and choose a location field approach that maximizes the outcome that is most important to them.

Returning to the results of the granularity regression, the marginal main effect for length can likely be explained by the drop-off of country-scale entries as soon as length gets longer than 30 characters. 20.8% of locations entered into the 30-character field were country-scale while 13.2% and 14.3% were country-scale for the 50- and 70-character fields, respectively. We also saw a steady increase in addresses as the field length got longer, although the numbers are sufficiently small to prevent us from drawing major

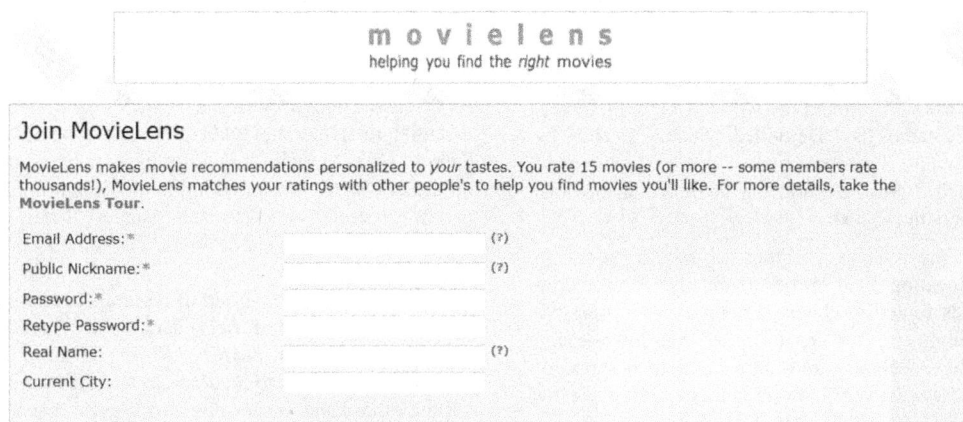

Figure 3. An example of the MovieLens registration page under the 30-character, "Current City" condition in Experiment 1. (Note: By the time of publication, MovieLens will have undergone a major redesign).

conclusions. Both of these findings can likely be explained by there simply being enough room to write a full address in a 70-character field, while a country will nearly always fit in a 30-character field. The marginal interaction effect is likely due to the fact that the country drop-off occurs almost entirely in the "Location" prompt and the address increase occurs entirely in the "Address, City, State, and/or Zip" prompt.

4.2 Verification

In our second experiment, we looked at the effect of verification on the quantity and quality of location field entries. Verification, which is employed by Facebook, Yelp and others, involves checking location field entries against a database of locations (e.g. cities, addresses, etc.) known to be valid. This process is typically executed using a drop-down auto-complete functionality, with users not being allowed to save entries that do not match a valid location.

The necessary result of verification is that 100% of location field entries will be of a geographic nature ("Justin Bieber's Heart" is not likely included in any database of valid locations). However, the effect of verification on population rate and granularity is not clear. For instance, users may shy away from entering information if they cannot enter a colloquial name for a location (e.g. "Singa" for Singapore) or if they are forced to fully disambiguate their entries (e.g. writing "Springfield, IL" versus just "Springfield"). Similarly, they may change the information they enter due to verification, for instance writing "Illinois" instead of "Springfield, IL".

To test the effect of verification on location field population rate and granularity, we conducted a 2x3 between-subjects experiment similar to Experiment 1. The verification factor had two levels: verification and no verification. Our verification implementation was modeled closely on Facebook's but we extended the database of known valid locations to include location types other than cities (e.g. addresses, states, countries) using Google's Geocoding API[4]. We also considered the prompt factor (and the same three levels) in this experiment due to its strong effects in the previous experiment. Length was fixed at 50. Our verification experiment ran for one month, during which time 819 users registered for the online movie community.

Examining the effect of verification on location field population rate, we performed a nominal logistic regression with field population (has entry / does not have entry) as the dependent variable and both field prompt and verification as independent variables. No significant effect could be detected for either verification (χ^2(1,N=819) = 0.31, p = 0.58) or a verification by prompt interaction (χ^2(2,N=819) = 2.95, p = 0.23). (A significant main effect for prompt was found again, providing additional support for our conclusions from the first experiment, χ^2(2,N=819) = 9.76, p < 0.01.) At a descriptive level, we found that the population rate was 58.6% for the no verification condition and about 1.4% lower (57.2%) for the verification condition.

We identified a similar result with regard to the relationship between verification and granularity. An ordinal logistic regression with ordinal granularity as the dependent variable and the same two independent variables revealed no significant effect for verification (χ^2(1,N=329) = 1.70, p = 0.19) or for a verification by prompt interaction (χ^2(2,N=329) = 0.71, p = 0.70). For instance, considering the "Location" prompt, in the verification condition, 44.8% of users provided city-level entries and 48.2% of users provided country-level entries. The equivalent numbers for the no verification condition were 48.2% and 46.6%, respectively. We did see a moderate (non-significant) effect for verification in one prompt: in "current city" fields, 72.9% of entries were city-level or more local in the verification condition, while 90.1% were in the no verification condition.

These findings have potentially important implications for the design of location fields. Most obviously, they indicate that operators of online communities may be able to achieve 100% geographicness without drastically affecting the location field population rate or the granularity of location field entries, although research on a larger online community is needed to increase confidence in this conclusion.

If indeed verification has little effect on population rate and granularity, the benefits would extend beyond geographicness. Namely, verification eliminates the issue of *toponym ambiguity* (i.e. place name ambiguity), a well-known challenge in the natural language processing and geographic information retrieval communities. A critical preprocessing step in the use of location field entries by both researchers and practitioners involves the use of a *geocoder*, which converts place names into machine-readable geospatial representations (e.g. latitude and longitude coordinates). One of the fundamental challenges in the development of geocoders is handling toponym ambiguity. For instance, if a

---

[4] https://developers.google.com/maps/documentation/geocoding/

member of an online community enters "London" into their location field (as many of our users did), the geocoder must figure out whether they are referring to the London in England, the London in Canada (with over 300K people), or one of the many other places named "London" around the world. The problem gets even worse with place names like "Danville", which is an entry by a user in this experiment. There are over a dozen cities named Danville in the United States, and none of them are an obvious first choice for a geocoding system.

Verification allows the system designer to require users to disambiguate their location field entries manually. A user who types in "Danville" is forced to choose among a list of possible senses of the toponym in, for instance, a drop-down menu (employed in both Facebook and our implementation of verification). In other words, verification reduces to zero the error introduced by geocoders due to toponym ambiguity. As such, our results suggest that, like non-geographic entries, toponym ambiguity in the processing of location field entries may be able to be entirely eliminated without drastic effects on population rates or granularity.

4.3 Visibility

Our final experiment examined the effect of the visibility of location field information on population rate and granularity. In this experiment, we tested whether users would change their location field entries if they were told these entries would be shared. This experiment had three visibility conditions: *publicly visible*, *not visible*, and *no information*. In the *publicly visible* condition, text appeared below the location field box that informed the user that the information in the field would be publicly accessible on their user profile. In the *not visible* condition, the text instead informed the user explicitly that the location information would remain private. Finally, in the *no information* condition, users were not told anything related to the visibility of the location information. The experiment ran for one week and 191 users participated. In order to capture any interaction effects with location field prompt, we also varied the prompt using the same three levels as before.

Just as was the case with verification, visibility played little role in population rate. A nominal logistic regression predicting whether or not a user entered information into the field (field population) revealed no significant main effect for visibility ($\chi^2(2,N=191) = 0.78$, $p = 0.68$) or for a visibility by prompt interaction ($\chi^2(4,N=191) = 4.04$, $p = 0.40$).

We did, however, see marginally significant results when examining the relationship between visibility and granularity. An ordinal logistic regression indicated that visibility ($\chi^2(2,N=86) = 4.53$, $p = 0.10$) and a visibility by prompt interaction ($\chi^2(4,N=86) = 9.11$, $p = 0.06$) have a marginally significant effect on the granularity of location field entries[5].

Examining the main effect more closely, we saw that the *publicly visible condition* had more low-granularity entries. For instance, while 54% percent of entries in that condition were less granular than the less city-level (e.g. country-level), the equivalent numbers for the *not visible* and *no information* conditions were 27% and 38% respectively. This result echoes what has been seen with high temporal resolution location sharing, where Lin et al.

[16] found that participants will share less granular locations with people with whom they have fewer connections, e.g. strangers.

5. DISCUSSION AND FUTURE WORK

As discussed above, entries in Twitter's location field have proven essential to numerous studies and systems (including Twitter's Search API). As such, it is a useful thought experiment to reflect on the effects of Twitter adopting the design implications of each of our experiments. Our results suggest that if Twitter were to change its location field prompt ("Location") to one that requests more granular information like Yelp's ("Address, City, State, and/or Zip"), the large group of researchers and practitioners who use Twitter's location field data either directly or implicitly through the Twitter Search API would have access to more granular information to incorporate into their studies and systems. On the other hand, our results also suggest that this would reduce the percent of users who fill out the location field.

Our results also suggest that the incorporation of verification into Twitter's location field (like Facebook has done) would not have an enormous cost in terms of granularity and field population rate, but would eliminate non-geographic location field entries (16% of entries on Twitter [11]) and all issues with toponym ambiguity. This would result in a large increase in the accuracy of geocoders when they are applied to Twitter location field entries. Since the application of a geocoder is a nearly universal step in the pre-processing of these entries, verification would result in significant improvements to the many research projects and technologies that rely on Twitter location field data.

This paper takes a traditional (non-critical) geographic information perspective on location field design. That is, it is concerned with increasing the quantity and quality of location field entries so that they may be more useful for a wide variety of studies and systems. However, designers of certain online communities may want to consider factors other than quantity and quality of geographic information. For instance, some designers may not want to disallow users from entering non-geographic information like "Justin Bieber's Heart" into their location fields, for instance to allow for greater self-expression in user profiles. Examining users' motivations for entering non-geographic information and developing approaches to support this behavior while reducing the large problems related to non-geographic information in location fields [11] (e.g. geocoders' tendency to return real latitude and longitude coordinates for non-geographic entries) is an important direction of future research.

As our work is the first investigation of location field design, there are several additional important directions of future work. Existing location disclosure research on high temporal resolution location information has found that people's location sharing preferences vary depending on the group of people with whom their location is shared (e.g. [1,16]). It would be useful to see whether the same occurs with low temporal resolution information, and if so, whether the behaviors are different than those that have been observed with high temporal resolution information. The online movie community that supported this study does not have social network features, but our study could be easily repeated and extended to look at difference audiences in online communities such as Facebook (e.g. share with "Public", "Your Friends) and Google Plus (e.g. share with certain circles versus others).

Finally, another important area of future work relates to multiple location fields. Many sites include multiple location fields in their user profiles, and this study did not examine the interaction between these fields. Does having more than one field affect

---

[5] We again saw a significant main effect for prompt ($\chi^2(2,N=191) = 15.45$, $p < 0.001$).

population rates? Granularity? Geographicness? In addition, some of these multiple location field communities often request information that may be outside of the current temporal context (e.g. Flickr and Facebook's "Hometown" field). Examining the effect of "currentness" would shed additional light on location field design.

7. CONCLUSION

In this paper, we demonstrated that the design of a location field in a user profile has an effect on the field's population rate and the granularity of its entries, which are critical to many systems and studies. In particular, through a series of controlled experiments, we demonstrated that the choice of location field prompt can result in higher granularity or higher field population rates, but that there is a trade-off between the two. We also saw evidence that designers of online communities can include verification in location fields without having a large negative effect on population rate or granularity. This suggests that toponym ambiguity and non-geographic entries can be eliminated without huge costs. Finally, as opposed to what has been found on Twitter, we identified only a few location field entries that were non-geographic in nature, suggesting that the geographicness issue found by Hecht et al. [11] is online community-specific rather than endemic to location fields in general.

8. ACKNOWLEDGEMENTS

The authors would like to thank our colleagues in GroupLens Research, and particularly Loren Terveen, Joe Konstan, and the MovieLens development team. This work was supported in part by NSF IIS-0808692, a 3M Non-Tenured Faculty Award (NTFA), and a Yahoo! ACE Award.

9. REFERENCES

1. Benisch, M., Kelley, P.G., Sadeh, N., and Cranor, L.F. Capturing Location-privacy Preferences: Quantifying Accuracy and User-burden Tradeoffs. *Personal Ubiquitous Comput. 15*, 7 (2011), 679–694.

2. Bergsma, S., Dredze, M., Durme, B.V., Wilson, T., and Yarowsky, D. Broadly improving user classification via communication-based name and location clustering on twitter. *NAACL-HLT '13*, (2013).

3. Broniatowski, D.A., Paul, M.J., and Dredze, M. National and Local Influenza Surveillance through Twitter: An Analysis of the 2012-2013 Influenza Epidemic. *PLoS ONE 8*, 12 (2013), e83672.

4. Burton, S.H., Tanner, K.W., Giraud-Carrier, C.G., West, J.H., and Barnes, M.D. "Right Time, Right Place" Health Communication on Twitter: Value and Accuracy of Location Information. *Journal of Medical Internet Research 14*, 6 (2012), e156.

5. Cheng, Z., Caverlee, J., and Lee, K. You Are Where You Tweet: A Content-Based Approach to Geo-locating Twitter Users. *CIKM '10: 19th ACM International Conference on Information and Knowledge Management*, (2010).

6. Consolvo, S., Smith, I.E., Matthews, T., LaMarca, A., Tabert, J., and Powledge, P. Location Disclosure to Social Relations: Why, When, & What People Want to Share. *CHI '05*, (2005), 81–90.

7. Dredze, M., Paul, M.J., Bergsma, S., and Tran, H. Carmen: A Twitter Geolocation System with Applications to Public Health. *AAAI-13 Workshop on Expanding the Boundaries of Health Informatics Using AI (HIAI)*, (2013).

8. Eisenstein, J., O'Connor, B., Smith, N.A., and Xing, Eric P. A Latent Variable Model for Geographic Lexical Variation. *EMNLP '10: 2010 Conference on Empirical Methods in Natural Language Processing*, (2010), 1277–1287.

9. Gaffney, D. #iranElection: quantifying online activism. (2010).

10. Hecht, B. and Gergle, D. On The "Localness" of User-Generated Content. *CSCW '10: 2010 ACM Conference on Computer Supported Cooperative Work*, (2010), 229–232.

11. Hecht, B., Hong, L., Suh, B., and Chi, E.H. Tweets from Justin Bieber's Heart: The Dynamics of the "Location" Field in User Profiles. *CHI '11: 29th ACM Conference on Human Factors in Computing Systems*, (2011), 237–246.

12. Java, A., Song, X., Finin, T., and Tseng, B. Why We Twitter: Understanding Microblogging Usage and Communities. *Proceedings of the 9th WebKDD and 1st SNA-KDD 2007 Workshop on Web Mining and Social Network Analysis*, ACM (2007), 56–65.

13. Kinsella, S., Murdock, V., and O'Hare, N. "I'M Eating a Sandwich in Glasgow": Modeling Locations with Tweets. *Proceedings of the 3rd International Workshop on Search and Mining User-generated Contents*, ACM (2011), 61–68.

14. Kulshrestha, J., Kooti, F., Nikravesh, A., and Gummadi, K.P. Geographic Dissection of the Twitter Network. *ICWSM '12: Sixth International AAAI Conference on Weblogs and Social Media*, (2012).

15. Liben-Nowell, D., Novak, J., Kumar, R., Raghavan, P., and Tomkins, A. Geographic routing in social networks. *Proceedings of the National Academy of Sciences 102*, 33 (2005), 11623–11628.

16. Lin, J., Xiang, G., Hong, J.I., and Sadeh, N. Modeling People's Place Naming Preferences in Location Sharing. *UbiComp '10*, (2010).

17. Lotan, G., Graeff, E., Ananny, M., Gaffney, D., Pearce, I., and Boyd, D. The Revolutions Were Tweeted: Information Flows during the 2011 Tunisian and Egyptian Revolutions. *International Journal of Communication 5*, 0 (2011), 31.

18. Mislove, A., Lehmann, S., Ahn, Y.-Y., Onnela, J.-P., and Rosenquist, J.N. Understanding the Demographics of Twitter Users. *ICWSM '11: 5th International AAAI Conference on Weblogs and Social Media*, (2011), 554–557.

19. Morstatter, F., Pfeffer, J., Liu, H., and Carley, K.M. Is the Sample Good Enough? Comparing Data from Twitter's Streaming API with Twitter's Firehose. *ICWSM '13: Seventh International AAAI Conference on Weblogs and Social Media*, (2013).

20. Pontes, T., Vasconcelos, M., Almeida, J., Kumaraguru, P., and Almeida, V. We Know Where You Live: Privacy Characterization of Foursquare Behavior. *Proceedings of the 2012 ACM Conference on Ubiquitous Computing*, ACM (2012), 898–905.

21. Popescu, A. and Grefenstette, G. Mining User Home Location and Gender from Flickr Tags. *ICSWM '10: 4th International AAAI Conference on Weblogs and Social Media*, (2010).

22. Quercia, D., Capra, L., and Crowcroft, J. The Social World of Twitter: Topics, Geography, and Emotions. *ICWSM '12: Sixth International AAAI Conference on Weblogs and Social Media*, (2012).

23. Rout, D., Bontcheva, K., Preotiuc-Pietro, D., and Cohn, T. Where's@ wally?: a classification approach to geolocating users based on their social ties. *HT '13*, (2013).

24. Schulz, A., Hadjakos, A., Paulheim, H., Nachtwey, J., and Mühlhäuser, M. A Multi-Indicator Approach for Geolocalization of Tweets. *ICWSM '13: Seventh International AAAI Conference on Weblogs and Social Media*, (2013).

25. Starbird, K., Muzny, G., and Palen, L. Learning from the Crowd: Collaborative Filtering Techniques for Identifying On-the-Ground Twitters during Mass Disruptions. *ISCRAM '12*, (2012).

26. Takhteyev, Y., Gruzd, A., and Wellman, B. Geography of Twitter networks. *Social Networks 34*, 1 (2012), 73–81.

27. Tang, K.P., Lin, J., Hong, J.I., Siewiorek, D.P., and Sadeh, N. Rethinking Location Sharing: Exploring the Implications of Social-driven vs. Purpose-driven Location Sharing. *Proceedings of the 12th ACM International Conference on Ubiquitous Computing*, ACM (2010), 85–94.

28. Tsai, J.Y., Kelley, P., Drielsma, P., Cranor, L.F., Hong, J., and Sadeh, N. Who's Viewed You?: The Impact of Feedback in a Mobile Location-sharing Application. *Proceedings of the SIGCHI Conference on Human Factors in Computing Systems*, ACM (2009), 2003–2012.

29. Twitter Inc. Twitter Streaming API. *Twitter Developers*, 2013. https://dev.twitter.com/docs/api/1.1/get/search/tweets.

30. Wiese, J., Kelley, P.G., Cranor, L.F., Dabbish, L., Hong, J.I., and Zimmerman, J. Are You Close with Me? Are You Nearby?: Investigating Social Groups, Closeness, and Willingness to Share. *Proceedings of the 13th International Conference on Ubiquitous Computing*, ACM (2011), 197–206.

Exploring How a Co-dependent Tangible Tool Design Supports Collaboration in a Tabletop Activity

Min Fan[1], Alissa N. Antle[1], Carman Neustaedter[1], Alyssa F. Wise[2]

[1]School of Interactive Arts + Technology
Simon Fraser University
250-13450 102 Avenue
Surrey, B.C. Canada
V3T 0A3

[2]Faculty of Education
Simon Fraser University
250 -13450 102 Avenue
Surrey, B.C., Canada
V3T 2W1

[minf, aantle, carman_neustaedter, afw3]@sfu.ca

ABSTRACT

Many studies suggest that tangibles and digital tabletops have potential to support collaborative interaction. However, previous findings show that users often work in parallel with such systems. One design strategy that may encourage collaboration rather than parallel use involves creating a system that responds to co-dependent access points in which more than one action is required to create a successful system response. To better understand how co-dependent access points support collaboration, we designed a comparative study with 12 young adults using the same application with a co-dependent and an independent access point design. We collected and analyzed categories of both verbal and behavioural data in the two conditions. Our results show support for the co-dependent strategy and suggest ways that the co-dependent design can be used to support flexible collaboration on tangible tabletops for young adults.

Author Keywords

Tangible user interfaces; digital tabletop; interactive surfaces; co-dependent access points; collaboration; young adults.

ACM Classification Keywords

H.5.3 [Information interfaces and presentation]: Group and Organization; H.5.2. Information interfaces and presentation: User interfaces.

1. INTRODUCTION

Much research has been conducted to explore how to better support collaboration on digital tabletops. The large size of digital tabletops enables users to view and work on tasks together, which supports collaborative activities [23]. More recently, tangible user interfaces have been used in conjunction with digital tabletops to facilitate collaborative activity [25]. Using tangible objects on tabletops allows people to share, view, place and manipulate physical objects as tools and representations in collaborative activity. The physicality of objects has been shown to support awareness of each other's actions in collaborative activity [25].

However, studies of tangible tabletop collaborative activity reveal disparate results [17, 20]. For example, multiple physical access points offered by tangible tabletops have been shown to promote

synchronous collaboration [25]. However, in another paper, researchers reported that this strategy resulted in parallel, independent work rather than collaborative activity [17, 21]. In order to support collaborative activity, some researchers from the collaborative learning field have suggested distributing information, skills, roles or tools among learners in a way that requires them to work together. This is called a collaboration jigsaw script [1]. Another approach is to hard-code system constraints (e.g. enforcing turn-taking) to force collaboration [19]. The drawback of these approaches is their inflexible nature. The challenge is to design tabletop systems that enable and encourage collaborative activity but do not enforce it [1,13, 21].

Antle and Wise suggest a variant of the jigsaw script that utilizes a system design that recognizes sequences of actions and involves a unique set of tangible input objects that can be split up and assigned to different users -- resulting in a system/physical/social configuration that either enables, encourages or enforces collaboration as the situation warrants [1]. In a system with co-dependent access points, inputs are sensed separately but processed together by the system [1,13]. That is, two or more input actions are required for a successful response. If the design also includes a unique set of tangible input objects, then the set can be split into groups and assigned to different users. The co-dependent access points enable users to collaborate by enacting sequences together. The assignment can be done to encourage (but not enforce) users to collaborate. Antle and Wise also propose that using tangible rather than touch-input objects reduces the chances of one user ignoring the assignments and taking over, or undoing another's actions because of social norms around object ownership and use (based on [24]). Taken together a set of unique co-dependently sensed, tangible, and user-assigned input objects may encourage flexible opportunities for collaboration. For brevity we call this approach co-dependent access (CD) and an unconstrained variation independent access (ID). Our research explores the strategy proposed by Antle and Wise. Our research questions are, *(RQ1) Does a CD design on a tabletop encourage young adults to collaborate more than a similar design that is ID? (RQ2) What kinds of collaborative behaviours and interactional patterns emerge for each design strategy?* Answering these questions will provide guidance for designers looking for alternative ways to encourage tabletop collaboration without enforcing it.

In order to address our questions, we conducted an exploratory, comparative study with 12 young adults who used a tangible, multi-touch tabletop application for collaborative land use planning, called *Youtopia*. In this paper, we present the results of our analysis comparing quantities and types (qualities) of verbal negotiation and physical collaboration in two conditions, which we call co-dependent (CD) and independent access (ID) points.

We provide a summary of quantitative data, and then focus on a detailed analysis of the qualities of behaviours and interactions to better understand how our design strategies may facilitate collaborative activity. We discuss the implications of our results and propose four ways in which the CD approach may be beneficial for the design of collaborative, tangible digital tabletop applications.

2. RELATED WORK

There is no one single definition of collaboration or collaborative activity. According to Goos *et al.* [10], collaboration is a reciprocal, coordinated interaction in which ideas and perspectives are explored and exchanged. Dillenbourg [7] views collaboration as a situation in which interaction and negotiation must happen between participants to successfully complete a task. This definition stands in contrast to cooperation, in which people may still work together to accomplish a task but negotiation and interaction are not necessary. Negotiation plays an essential role in collaboration [26]. Collaborative activity needs the negotiation not only of task-related content, but also of task structure in terms of roles, activities, and sub-task allocations [6]. Dillenbourg's definition also suggests the importance of equitable participation – both verbal and physical -- for hands-on tasks. Equitable participation helps team members to better understand each other, adjust plans, and achieve the shared goals.

2.1 Designing for Tabletop Collaboration

Multi-touch and tangible digital tabletops have been suggested as one way of encouraging productive synchronous collaboration. However, the empirical findings of previous studies are contradictory [17, 21, 24]. Several studies suggest that multi-touch tabletops enable more synchronous collaboration than traditional user interfaces [22, 24]. Traditional computer technologies, such as a single mouse with PC, do not allow synchronous activity for multiple users [20]. The single-mouse situation forces users to share a single input and often results in frustration and reduced engagement [14, 22]. In contrast, multi-touch tabletops enable multiple users to simultaneously engage in the same activity, which may simulate synchronous collaboration and avoid conflict over input controls (i.e., 'cursor wars'). For example, the multi-touch system *DiamondTouch* [8] allows for synchronous collaboration among multiple users as well as multiple simultaneous touches from a single user. *CollabDraw* [18] uses cooperative gesture interaction techniques to support collaborative art and photo manipulation.

Benford *et al.* [4] present different approaches to interface designs that *enable, encourage* or *enforce* collaboration. *Enabling* collaboration refers to providing multiple access points that allow users to participate simultaneously. *Encouraging* collaboration refers to offering an incentive or functionality that encourages collaborative work. *Enforcing* collaboration refers to functionality that enforces specific collaborative actions, such as turn-taking. Encouraging collaboration is more proactive than only enabling collaboration, but not as inflexible as enforcement [17].

Combining tangible objects with multi-touch tabletop interaction may improve users' awareness of each other's actions and tool use [12, 24]. For example, Speelpenning *et al.* [24] conducted an exploratory study to compare the differences between tangible and multi-touch tool use and the impact of tool use on collaboration in a digital tabletop game. Observational findings suggested that the physicality of the tangible tools facilitated individual ownership and announcement of tool use, which in turn supported awareness of each other's actions, and therefore more effective support for collaboration.

Tangible objects provide multiple access points to a tabletop application, which may lead to parallel rather than collaborative activity [17, 21]. Several design strategies have been explored to avoid parallel use. For example, in a tabletop computing game called *SIDES* [19], turn-taking was used to regulate and ensure each individual's equitable participation in collaboration. However, this approach forces people to work together rather than encouraging them to collaborate, which results in less flexible collaboration.

The literature [1,13,20] illustrates we do not yet understand how to reliably design tabletop systems that enable and encourage collaboration but do not force collaboration. Antle and Wise [1] suggest that *positive interdependence*, which will encourage collaboration, may be achieved through a combination of system, physical and social design. They suggest creating a system with co-dependent access points in which more than one input action must be taken in order to create a successful system response. Access points may be any potential input elements that enable users to interact and participate in a collaborative activity [11, 13]. They suggest using a unique set of tangible input objects – which may be tools or representations – that are essential to task(s) completion. Lastly, they suggest assigning the tangible objects to different users to *encourage* collaboration. If objects are not assigned (ID), the collaboration is enabled because the system still requires sequences of actions – which may be taken by one or more users. Conversely, authoritative assignment instructions (e.g. teacher in a classroom) can lean towards enforced collaboration (e.g. children are told not to exchange tangible objects). In this paper, we focus on the strategy that *encourages* equitable collaboration without restricting it. We implement Antle and Wise's approach for a land use planning activity to explore *whether* a CD design is more effective for encouraging collaboration than an ID design and to understand *how* these two design strategies effect collaboration in a tabletop activity for young adults.

2.2 Analyzing Tabletop Collaboration

Analysis of collaboration tends to focus on verbal and physical behaviours that people use to mediate collaborative activity [11, 15, 20]. The amount and type of explicit communication can indicate the degree of collaboration [9]. For example, verbal negotiation, such as talk or dialogue, plays an essential role in sharing mutual understanding among participants in face-to-face collaboration. Studies [11, 15] suggest various types of talk patterns are important in collaborative activities around tabletops. Jamil *et al.* [15] discuss how different tabletop designs lead to different talk patterns during collaborative activity. Similarly, Harris *et al.* [11] present results from a comparative study of multiple-touch and single-touch collaborative interaction on a tabletop activity, wherein a coding system of talk types was developed to measure the level of collaboration.

Physical interaction is also important in collaboration analysis. In a study presented by Hornecker *et al.* [12], they demonstrated that large surfaces provided users with opportunities to organize objects physically in space in order to support collaborative activity. The size of the surface also allowed each member to be visually aware of other members' activities.

3. SYSTEM DESCRIPTION

Youtopia is a collaborative, tangible, multi-touch tabletop sustainable land use planning activity (Figure 1). It was designed to support users to experience the challenges of sustainable land use planning. We implemented Antle and Wise's three tier (system/physical/social) design strategy. The system recognizes sequences of inputs made with a unique set of tangible stamps, which can be assigned in sets to each user, or left unassigned.

3.1 Youtopia

The system of Youtopia consists of a set of tangible stamps used for input onto a multi-touch tabletop map display (Figure 1). The main form of interaction with the map is through stamping land uses onto the map with the tangible stamps. There are two kinds of stamps: land uses and tools. Touch is used for basic system controls such as choosing a map or population size. A complete description of Youtopia can be found in [2].

Figure 1. Youtopia: a collaborative hybrid tangible multi-touch tabletop sustainable land use planning activity.

3.1.1 Land use Stamps

Land use stamps can be used either to designate natural resources as usable for human development or as development stamps to designate spaces for food, shelter or energy production facilities. Human developments cannot be built without first designating natural resources as usable. For example, in order to create a housing unit, a user must stamp the lumber stamp onto an area of forest to designate the lumber from the forest as usable. Then s/he can use the housing stamp to place a housing unit somewhere in the available grasslands (Figure 2). Youtopia requires co-dependent input: first lumber, then housing in order to create a shelter unit.

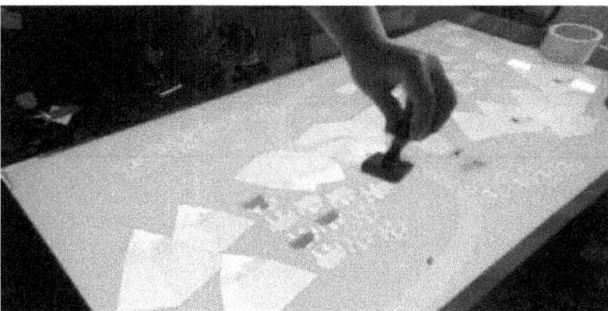

Figure 2. Stamping trees into lumber units.

3.1.2 Tool Stamps

A set of three additional stamps provide tool functionality, including *erase*, *impact* (which shows the current state of the world), and *info* (which shows information about each land use type). The eraser stamp undoes previous stamp actions. When placed anywhere on the map, the impact stamp displays an information overlay about the current state of the world in terms of the proportion of the population's needs being met for food, shelter and energy, as well as displaying the world's pollution level. Placing any stamp in the information ring displays a detailed information overlay about that stamp including what the land use is, which other stamps it is co-dependent on and what it produces. Users can rotate or scale the information overlay to share it using multi-touch. Both impact and information tools provide a freezing screen feature whereby all other functions are inactive when these stamps are in use (Figure 3).

Figure 3. Impact tool and Information tool – freeze the display.

3.2 Scenario of Use: Co-dependent and Independent Modes

Youtopia can be used in two modes based on the instructions given to the users. In the *co-dependent mode*, the natural resource stamps (labelled with a tree on top of the handle) are given to one person assigned the role of natural resource planner, and the development stamps (labelled with a wrench) to another assigned the role of developer. In the *independent mode*, users do not have any roles and they can use any stamp.

The application begins with an undeveloped landscape that contains areas of natural resources (e.g. trees, river, coal reserves in mountains) and other "open" areas (e.g. grasslands). Participants use the stamps to designate what use will be made of each specific space on the interactive map. They can designate natural resources for preservation or use, and build food, shelter or energy sources to try to support either a small or large population's needs. The balance of preserving the natural environment while meeting the population's needs is up to the participants. Youtopia provides no explicit feedback on winning or losing in order to allow participants to explore options according to their values.

4. STUDY METHODOLOGY

4.1 Study Design

In our study we explore how the CD strategy compares to the ID strategy. We also explore how the two designs affect negotiation and decision making about the domain topic (sustainability). Youtopia only responds when resources are stamped before development stamps are used. In the co-dependent configuration (CD) we use this system rule AND social conventions to set up the condition where each person "owns" either resources or developments. Both users must act to create anything. This has the potential to set up conflict, which leads to the need to negotiate. In the independent group (ID), we remove the social constraint of assigning tools; this configuration represents a typical tabletop system in which a single user can take a series of actions with different objects to control interaction at any given time.

An exploratory comparative study was conducted. In the CD condition, pairs were asked to use their own stamp tools. In the ID condition, pairs could use any of the stamp tools. A within-subjects design was used because group dynamics can influence collaboration [16]. To control for order effects, conditions were counterbalanced.

4.2 Participants
We collected data from 12 participants (four males and eight females) who played the activity in pairs. The participants were university students (aged 20 to 28). All participants had used a touch surface before (e.g. smart board, iPhone, iPod). Most participants had used a digital tabletop (eight of 12) and a TUI (eight of 12) before. However, none of them had played our system before. The groups were randomly assigned and participants knew each other to different degrees: some were classmates or friends (eight of 12) while others did not know each other at all (four of 12). Pairs in four groups were a male and a female while in two groups there were two females. Participants were rewarded with $5 for participating in our study.

4.3 Task
The task was to *"Create a world that you like to live in, which includes creating enough food, shelter and energy for a small population."* The task was challenging because there were not enough resources to meet the needs of the population and keep the environment pristine. Users needed to discuss trade-offs, negotiate and use stamps and tools to designate land uses. This approach reflects typical planning activities in the real world. Participants used a different but equivalent map in the second condition to control for learning effects. In each condition, participants had 10 minutes for this task. The decision of 10 minutes was based on our previous experience of pilot studies. There was no fixed approach or "winning state" for the task. Participants could use different stamp tools to achieve the goal. For example, in order to make shelters for a small population, participants could use any combination of apartments, townhouses or single-family dwellings.

4.4 Procedure
Our land use planning application was set up on a Microsoft Surface table in a controlled lab space. The session began with a demographic survey. We gave participants a basic system tutorial. The pair then had five minutes to familiarize themselves with Youtopia. When they felt ready to begin, they were given the task. Each pair worked on the same task in each condition, changing conditions after 10 minutes. Post-task interviews of each participant were conducted after each of the two tasks. Sessions lasted about 30 minutes in total.

4.5 Data Collection and Analysis
Our mixed-methods approach involved collecting data including video (V.), structured observations (S.O.), system logs (S.L.), and post-interviews (P.I) in order to analyze verbal negotiation (V. & S.O.), physical actions (V. & S.L.), interactional patterns (V. & S.O.) and participants' opinions (P.I.). We used quantitative methods to address our first research question (*RQ1*). Quantitative methods consisted of measuring the level (duration) and equity of verbal negotiation and level (duration) and equity of physical interaction in both conditions. We analyzed data with descriptive statistics depending on data type (median/range for ordinal, mean/standard deviation for interval). We used qualitative methods to address our second research question (*RQ2*). Two researchers observed and recorded different types of verbal negotiation and physical actions, identified interactional patterns, and asked for participant's opinions about their collaborative work after each condition.

4.5.1 Level of verbal negotiation
Level of verbal negotiation refers to the amount of task-related utterances that either participant made during the task session [11]. To avoid the challenges of time-consuming video coding which are not warranted by an exploratory study, we used structured observational sheets with four options to categorize the level of each pair's utterances (none, few, some, many). One researcher observed each participant, collected categorical utterance data which was then summed for the pair, and assigned a value 0 (none) to 4 (many/a lot). For example, if the pair did not talk in the entire gameplay, then 'none' was chosen. If they talked almost constantly to each other about the task - for at least 7.5/10 minutes - then 'many' was chosen. While we lose precision with our approach, we can easily and reliably identify large differences between groups, which is a suitable approach for an exploratory study.

4.5.2 Equity of verbal participation
Equity of verbal participation refers to the differences in the duration of utterances between two participants during the task session [11]. The equity of utterances can reflect the degree of an individual's participation. We calculated the difference of the duration in terms of each participant's utterances. If the difference was less than approximately two minutes (10%), it was considered most equitable. If the difference was more than five minutes, then we considered it unequal. Categorical data about equitable participation (unequal, some equity, most equity) was collected for each task in each session. We then coded this data from 1 to 3, with 3 being most equitable.

4.5.3 Level of physical interaction
Level of physical interaction refers to the total number of touches and tangible object uses during the task session. System logs were used to record interval data including the total number of stamp uses; tool uses (eraser, impact and information tool); touches on feedback tabs; and touches on the impact tool display.

4.5.4 Equity of physical participation
Data sets from system logs could not indicate which participant took each action. We used a video camera to record participants' actions and distinguish each participant's stamping actions and touching actions based on both video and system log datasets. By counting the number of stamping and touching actions per participant, we could compare two participants' frequency of physical participation in each condition.

4.5.5 Types of verbal negotiation
We were also interested in the content of verbal utterances about the task as well as the similarities and differences between the CD and ID conditions. Researchers iteratively developed a coding scheme of types of verbal negotiations based on the literature review [11, 15] and pilot studies before the experiment. The final categories were:
1. Task-focused discussion and negotiation (e.g., strategies)
2. Information exchange (e.g. instructions)
3. Conflict dialogues (e.g. disagreement)

Structured observational sheets and video data were used to collect the number of instances of each types of utterance and write descriptive notes about when they occurred.

4.5.6 Type of physical action

Type of physical interaction refers to different physical patterns that emerged during system use. We focused on physical actions between participants. The coding themes were developed prior to the experiment [11]. The main patterns of physical interaction were:

1. Purposeful actions or gestures (e.g. pointing to a place on the map, passing tools to each other)
2. Contents sharing through tools and multi-touch (e.g. rotating or scaling contents for the other)
3. Conflict over use of tools (e.g. grab tools at the same time)

We analyzed *which* type of physical actions emerged during the CD and ID conditions and *how* participants used these actions during collaboration in the different conditions.

4.5.7 Interactional patterns

Interactional patterns refer to how participants worked with each other during the task. We hypothesized that co-dependent access points might support collaborative rather than parallel work. We were interested in the interactional patterns that participants developed to coordinate their work in tasks. We used observational notes, video data and post-interviews (with one open-ended question for each participant: *How do you think the different setups impacted your collaboration?*) to help us understand interaction.

5. RESULTS

Our results provide insight into the similarities and differences in collaborative behaviours between the CD and ID conditions. Quantitative results provide information about levels of verbal negotiation and physical interaction while qualitative findings reveal types of verbal negotiation, physical interaction and working strategies.

5.1 Level and Equity of Verbal Negotiation

There was no difference in verbal negotiation between two conditions (Table 1). However, we noticed that when participants started parallel work in the ID condition they stopped verbal negotiation, perhaps because they did not need group awareness for independent work.

More pairs in the CD condition participated equally in verbal negotiation than in the ID condition (Table 1). Participants in both conditions usually had turn-taking talk patterns. Yet we found the duration of their verbal utterances was different. Since participants had their own roles and tools in the CD condition, they had to discuss with the partner in order to complete tasks. As shown in the following excerpt, we found that co-dependent use of tools promoted more equitable contributions.

```
[P9 is the natural resource planner and P10 is the
developer. Relationship: Friends]

P9: We have to do some shelters?
P10: Yes. We can do them at that area [pointing to a
certain place on the map].
P9: Okay. But as for the lumber, we have to do (them)
here [stamping lumber in the forest]. I will have three
for, for…
P10: for a townhouse [stamping a townhouse on the map]
```

In the ID condition, we often observed that one participant played a "dominant role" by proposing strategies or offering information to the other participant. Conversely, the non-dominant participant often asked the dominant person for suggestions or confirmations in the decision-making process. The "no roles" configuration decreased the equitable participation from both players.

	CD Median (Range)	ID Median (Range)
Level of verbal negotiation *(median level per session)*	4(2)	4 (3)
Equity of verbal participation *(median level per session*	3(1)	2 (1)

Table1. Level (0-4) of verbal negotiation and participation

5.2 Level and Equity of Physical Interaction

The mean number of physical interactions in the CD condition was a little higher than in the ID condition. We also found that pairs used the impact tool more often in the CD condition than in the ID condition (Table 2). It is possible that encouraging co-dependent use of tools may make pairs focus more on checking progress as part of their world-building strategy.

	CD: Mean (SD)	ID: Mean (SD)
Level of physical interaction *(mean # events per session)*	94 (24.1)	85 (14.9)
Level of the impact tool use *(mean #uses per session)*	10 (8.2)	6 (5.2)

Table 2. Level of physical interaction and impact tool use

The equity of physical participation between pairs in the CD condition was much better than that in the ID condition (Table 3). The results were also consistent with our observational findings. In the ID condition we found that it was common for one participant to conduct all the actions while the other only offered verbal suggestions without physical involvement. An example is presented below:

```
[No role. Relationship: Strangers]
P2: What do you want, houses or townhouses?
P1: Houses. We need houses, but probably not close to
here [pointing to the hydro dam] because… Why don't we
move the hydro to here [erasing the hydro in the center
and rebuilding it on the edge of the map].
P2: Okay.
P1: Far away (from the forest).
P2: Now where do you want to build the house?
P1: Both these areas will be fine. Here [pointing to the
forest] or here [pointing to grasslands close to forest].
```

	CD: Mean (SD)		ID: Mean (SD)	
Equity of physical participation *(mean # events per session)*	P1	P2	P1	P2
	50 (12.4)	44 (17.0)	50 (14.7)	35 (13)

Table 3. Equity of physical participation between players

5.3 Types of Verbal Negotiation

5.3.1 Task focused negotiation

People in both CD and ID conditions spent a large amount of time discussing their vision and strategies. The most common themes were what kind of a world they intended to have (the overall vision) and how specifically they planned to build it (their strategies). Although people in both conditions talked about their tasks and strategies, we found there was a slight difference in the ways they spoke about them. In the CD condition, we noticed that in three of six groups both players used declarative sentences to state their opinions. Participants were more deliberative about their decisions when they controlled their own tools, which gave their contributions more equal weight in the decision-making process.

```
[P1 is the natural resource planner and P2 is the
developer. Relationship: Strangers]
P2: Then let's have some garden.
P1: So (we need) irrigations.
P2: Gardens. Garden is three or farm is three… Oh, three
[checking the feedback tab].
P1: I will give you four.
P2: We need more water. (But) we don't have enough water.
P1: Take this one off [pointing to the hydro dam].
P2: Yes, and then use (coalmine)[pointing to the
coalmine].
```

In contrast, when people (three out of six) worked together in the ID condition, they tended to ask for confirmation first before conducting the next action. It was common to see a non-dominant participant ask the other for suggestions in the decision-making process. Similarly, when the dominant participant attempted to make any movement, he/she also informed the other one. Actions were more tentative.

```
[No role. P1: dominant role P2: non-dominant role]
P1: As for the energy, let's do hydro because it is clean
enough. Coalmine [pointing to the stamp] is not clean.
Right?
P2: Okay.
P1: We probably do here [pointing to a certain place on
the map]?
P2: Yes.
P1: Hydro can be built only on the river [reading the
feedback tab for P1].
P2: And, then, we need house. You want the house or the
townhouse?
P1: Probably house. We want [to] build a house. Maybe not
close to here [hydro].
P2: Yeah.
```

5.3.2 Information exchange

We observed that participants sometimes exchanged information or taught each other about how to use Youtopia in both conditions. Compared to the task-focused discussion, there was a low level of discussion related to information exchange. We did not observe any obvious difference between two conditions. Instead, order affected the levels of information exchange. Most of the information exchange occurred during the first session of the experiment. There were several types of information exchange. The most common way was directly asking. If one participant had doubts or concerns, they simply proposed questions to the other player. We also found that people used "reading aloud" to exchange information. For example, if they were reading the texts on feedback tabs, they often read it aloud (Figure 4). When participants intended to make an action, they tended to verbalize it first.

5.3.3 Conflict

We found that two groups had some conflict in the CD condition, while none occurred in the ID condition. The conflict stemmed from their different thoughts about how to make decisions based

on their own roles. In part, this may be because participants were more dedicated to their own roles in the CD condition, which encouraged more negotiation. Sometimes the negotiations involved conflict, which was not always resolved.

```
[P5 is the natural resource planner and P6 is the
developer. Relationship: Friends. Conflict: Resolved.]
P5: Do you want to destroy the world (after seeing P6
stamped a hydro dam)?
P6: Destroy the world? No, I make the world a more
livable space.
P5: [Checking about the impact tool]. All people have
shelter. All people have energy. Most people have food.
There is some pollution for a small population. Is this
the world you want to live in [reading it from the impact
tool]? Okay.
```

```
[P1 is the natural resource planner and P2 is the
developer. Relationship: Strangers. Conflict: unresolved]
P2 kept building irrigations and then the river level
decreased.
P1: Oh, see the river! I think the pollution is (heavy).
P2 checked about the impact tool.
P1: Oh, lots of pollution [pointing to the pollution
category on the impact tool]!
P2: [Checking about all the categories and focusing on
the food one] (We should have) more food.
P1: More food? (Do) we need more food?
P2 already started to stamp irrigations.
```

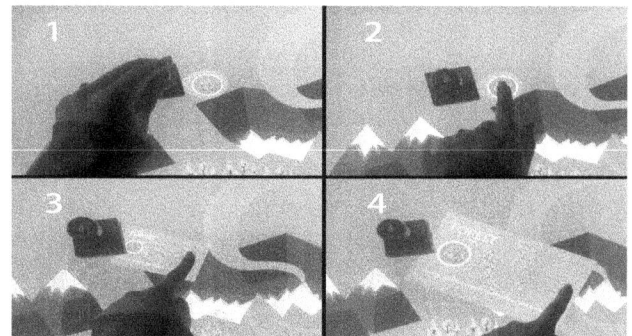

Figure 4. Dragging feedback tab reveals error massage.

5.4 Types of Physical Action

5.4.1 Purposeful actions and gestures

Participants in both CD and ID conditions used many pointing gestures to indicate a particular place on the map or a specific stamp on the table. We observed that people used more pointing gestures in the CD condition than in the ID condition. When one participant attempted to create a unit at a particular place on the map, they often informed the other participant through verbal sentences with a pointing gesture.

```
[No role. Relationship: Strangers]
P1: let's do (here) [pointing to a pace on the grass].
P2: yes [pointing to the same place]!
```

We found there were several factors that seemed to be related to people to use pointing gestures. The most common was the use of the impact tool. It was common for participants to point to each category of the world state display (shelter, food, energy, pollution) when discussing their strategies (Figure 5). Pairs used the impact tool 62 times in the CD condition, while it was used only 39 times in the ID condition, which influenced the levels of pointing gestures.

Another common use of pointing gestures was to indicate a particular place on the map. We observed this behaviour in both conditions. Participants often used it when giving suggestions or discussing strategies. In the ID condition, there were many gestures related to participants managing and sorting stamps together. In contrast, the role assignment in the CD condition contributed to less need to organize and manage tools. This is a secondary advantage of the CD strategy – it enables users to focus less on tool management and more on the task at hand.

Figure 5. Pointing to the category of the world state display (impact tool) when discussing strategies.

5.4.2 Content sharing through tools

In Youtopia, the impact and information tools provide a freezing screen feature whereby all other functions are inactive when these stamps are in use.

It is important to note that people started to concentrate on the same content and discussed their strategies when using the impact and information tools (Figure 6). We infer that the freezing feature might provide external tensions that force people to share group awareness.

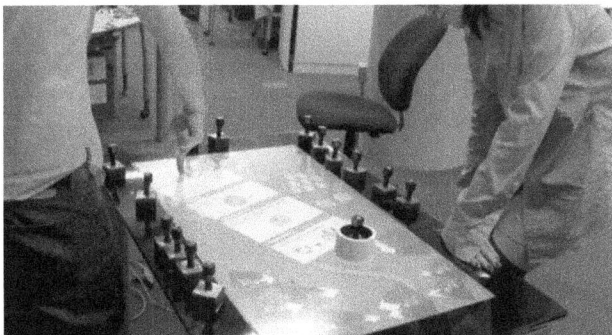

Figure 6. Sharing content through the Information tool.

5.4.3 Conflicting uses of tools and space

We observed conflicting uses of tools in both CD and ID conditions, but the types of conflicts were completely different. In the ID condition, players reached for the same stamp by accident (Figure 7). When they realized it, they usually let the other use it first. We suggest that this is due to a strong social constraint in young adults about not taking objects out of another person's hands (as found in [24]). However, in the CD condition, when one group turned their collaboration into competition, we observed them intentionally stealing the other's tools and using them as a part of their task.

```
[P5 is the natural resource planner and P6 is the
developer. Relationship: Friends]
P6: My job is to destroy the world. You see.
P5: I don't want you to build the factories here [holding
the eraser tool to erase factories]. Why not (to do
something else)?
P6: That's the point! This game for me is to create the
pollution. Ha-ha!
P5: No! You destroy the world!
```

```
P6: I really want to do this [directly picking up P5's
lumber stamp to use it].
```

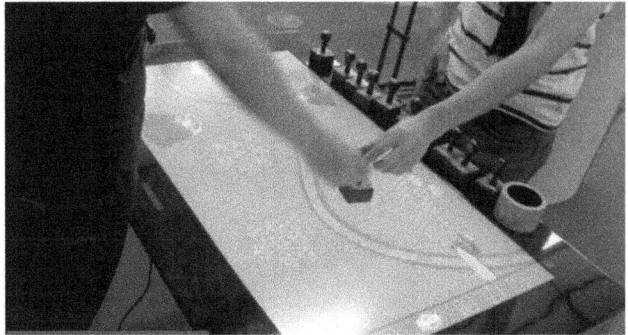

Figure 7. Reaching the same stamp in the ID condition.

Conflict over use of space only occurred during parallel work in the ID condition. We noticed that sometimes the two participants would use their stamps at the same place on the map or their actions would impact the other's actions (Figure 8). For example, when one participant (P2) was creating houses (lumber->house) and the other participant (P1) was creating gardens (irrigation->garden) in the ID condition, they had some conflict over use of space on the map.

```
[No role. Relationship: Strangers]
P2 created a house close the irrigation.
P1 kept trying to stamp the garden but fails.
P1: Sorry. It is too close to (my irrigation)[pointing to
the house that P1 just created]. Where is the eraser
tool? I have to erase (it).
P2: Okay. It doesn't matter.
P1: You can build it here [pointing to another place
which is a little bit offset from the original place].
```

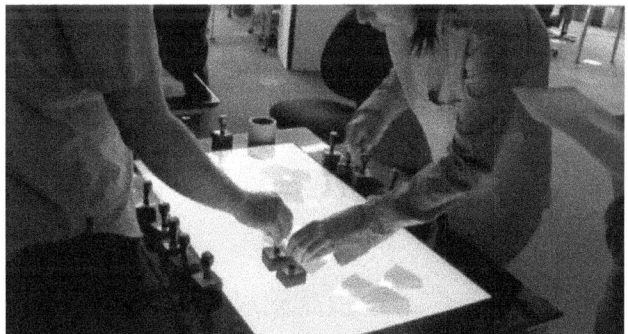

Figure 8. Conflict over use of space in the ID condition.

We found that the conflict over use of space was an effective trigger point for people to switch from parallel work to collaborative or cooperative modes. It significantly encouraged people to start verbal negotiation and physical interaction.

5.5 Interactional Patterns

There was a significant difference in the interactional patterns between the CD and ID conditions. We identified four main patterns: (a) collaboration with shared goals and co-dependent uses of tools; (b) collaboration with shared goals but with only one person executing actions; (c) cooperation with separate sub-tasks and parallel uses of tools; and (d) no collaboration or cooperation with parallel uses of tools.

5.5.1 Co-dependent condition

The dominant interactional pattern in the CD condition was collaboration with co-dependent use of tools. In this case, participants discussed and performed the task together. Five of six groups adopted this strategy during the whole process.

Similar behaviours were found in the five groups that adopted the actively collaborative pattern. They first talked with each other about *which* units they wanted to create, *why* they had to create them as well as *how* or *where* to build on the map. Then each participant manipulated their own stamp to create a specific unit.

```
[P4 is the natural resource planner and P3 is the
developer. Relationship: Friends]
P4: No people have shelter. Oh, we don't have shelter
[looking for and picking up the lumber stamp]. Oh my god!
P3: [Laughing].
P4: Where do they want to live [looking for the specific
place on the map]? I think in the forest. Not here
[pointing to the hydro dam] because we have [a] dam.
P4: First we need to do this (create lumber)[pointing to
the lumber on the map] and then?
P3: Yeah. It's basically this (single house) takes one
lumber [holding the single house stamp]. This (townhouse)
takes two lumbers [holding the town house stamp] and this
(apartment) takes three lumbers [holding the apartment
stamp].
```

Rather than actively discussing strategies, we observed that participants in one group (out of six) *only* asked for basic help from each other in order to complete their stamping actions during the whole activity.

```
[P11 is the natural resource planner and P12 is the
developer. Relationship: Strangers. They did not have any
conversation for almost three minutes before the
following talk]
P11: Oh, I can't have a farm because I need two these
(irrigations).
P12: You need more these irrigations?
P11: Yes.
P12: [Stamping two irrigations for P12].
```

Another interesting observation in the CD condition was that in one group, one participant stole tools from the other during the activity, which caused conflict over the tools. P6 who acted as the developer stole tools from P5 who was the natural resource planner. However, the independent uses of tool did not lead to subsequent parallel work. They still continued to verbally argue and negotiate with each other.

5.5.2 Independent condition

Compared to the CD condition, there was no single dominant interactional pattern in the ID condition. Participants appeared to adjust their interactional patterns from time to time. In general, we observed three patterns in the ID condition. In the first pattern, pairs cooperated to perform tasks with parallel uses of tools. They first broke down the task and assigned different sub-tasks to each person. Then, each person focused on his or her own part with parallel uses of tools to achieve their shared goals. We observed this pattern in two groups.

```
[No role. Relationship: Strangers]
P1: Let's do houses here [pointing to a place close to
forests].
P2: We are going to cut these trees [holding both lumber
and house stamps to create a single house].
P1: I will sow some more gardens [picking up both
irrigation and garden stamps to build gardens].
```

A second pattern involved pairs working in parallel but not coordinating their activity beforehand. The independent use of tools made it possible for each person to concentrate his/her own subtasks. In one group, participants worked individually with little verbal or physical interaction during the whole activity.

A third pattern involved one person physically controlling and using the stamps, while the other person passively watched or offered verbal suggestions. Both participants were involved in verbal collaboration, but only one participant physically manipulated tools and executed tasks. Two (out of six) groups interacted this way many times in their collaboration.

In the ID condition, most groups had two or three interactional patterns, with one dominant pattern. They switched between patterns several times during the activity. Based on observation, we found three possible motivations for their switches: (a) conflicting use of space on the map; (b) frozen screen; and (c) familiarity with the system and activity.

5.5.3 Post-interviews: experiences between two conditions

Participants responded in a variety of ways to the post-task question: *How do you think the different set-ups impacted your collaboration?* One group reported that they really enjoyed learning together in the CD condition. They also indicated that the CD use of tool made them feel like a team. Two other groups reported that they preferred the ID use of tools because it made their collaborative work more efficient and gave them more freedom to explore different tools. Three groups mentioned that they preferred to use the CD configuration early while learning about the activity. They said that after becoming familiar with the activity, they would like to switch to the ID configuration because it gave them more freedom and ability to explore.

6. LIMITATIONS

We do not make strong claims in this exploratory study for several reasons. First, we have a small number of participants, which is suitable to an exploratory study with detailed qualitative analysis, but limits generalization. We categorized our quantitative data coarsely, which means we may not have picked up small effects. In addition, four groups of the pairs knew each other while the other two groups of pairs were strangers. This difference typically influences the dynamics of collaboration. Participants also had different experiences using tangible and multi-touch technologies. Although participants were given time to explore Youtopia and familiarize themselves with it, we found there was still a learning curve for a few participants, which may have contributed to inequitable participation. While we used two observers for data collection, we did not do a detailed inter-rater analysis for coding video data for counts of individual's physical actions so we use this data cautiously.

7. DISCUSSION

Our results provide some evidence that the CD design strategy encouraged more equitable verbal participation and physical interaction compared to the ID strategy. Our work is consistent with findings that having multiple input objects rather than single objects reduces discussion about tool organization or turn-taking (e.g. [11]), However, we have the best of both worlds in that users have their own tool set and a few shared tools that can be used to synchronize activity. The design of a CD system enables collaboration. By using physical grouping and social context (object assignment/instructions) the nature of the interaction can be changed in real time. Thus an additional benefit of the CD approach is that it is more flexible for encouraging collaborative activity because it can be adapted in real time to suit the dynamics of the group, task or context. The analysis of video, observational and interview data led us to suggest four ways the CD design can be used to encourage flexible collaboration.

7.1 Supporting Different Group Dynamics

We hypothesized that people would work independently without collaborating in the ID condition. Our results indicated that some pairs did just that. However, pairs also enacted other interactional patterns, such as cooperatively splitting up work into separate tasks. The flexible nature of the CD design means that a group or group leader could decide to use a cooperative "divide and conquer" approach simply by reassigning the input objects or roles. Thus, our CD approach can be modified to support different group dynamics and strategies as needed. On the other hand, if one or more users are not participating then they can be assigned tools or roles to encourage more equitable verbal and physical participation. Our approach is consistent with findings in [20] that suggest hybrid digital-physical interfaces enable equitable participation. The CD approach to digital-physical tabletops may be particularly useful in contexts where participation by all group members is paramount (e.g. learning, community land use planning).

7.2 Supporting Productive Conflict

The CD groups had more conflict over ideas (rather than tools) which can be beneficial in eliciting each user's values around land use priorities, and lead to negotiation and compromise necessary in land use planning. Thus, in a situation that requires conflict to elicit values, or conflict to learn or negotiate or trigger reflection, shifting the object assignment to a CD strategy will likely encourage productive conflict. The ID group exhibited more evidence of non-collaborative behaviours involving non-productive conflict (e.g. dominance) and parallel activity. In these cases the group leader or instructor or possibly even the system could suggest or mandate shift to a CD mode through object assignment. The design of a unique set of tangible input objects which are recognized individually but processed by the system co-dependently creates a system that encourages productive conflict over the domain or activity rather than unproductive conflict over input or tool use. This relation between interaction technique and the nature of productive dialogue about the application domain versus application itself has been noted by others (e.g. [15]).

7.3 Supporting Different Phases of Interaction

Our post-task interview revealed that people use different patterns of interaction at different points in the task. At the beginning, people may need to learn and explore Youtopia together so they can also learn from each other, scaffolding or accelerating their learning process (as suggested in [10]). However, as people become familiar with the system and tools, they may want to interact more independently depending on their goals, ideas, personalities and strategies. Much previous work has treated collaborative activity as an all-or-nothing phenomenon. We suggest that the CD strategy, which can be used to support different ways of interacting, and can be configured in real time, may be more beneficial than strategies (e.g. hard coding turn taking (e.g. [19]) or roles (e.g. [3]) or tasks (e.g. [7,18]) that enforce collaboration throughout an activity. For example, at the beginning of a session, participants may be instructed (by a facilitator, teacher or the system) to take on roles to support the CD mode and encourage equitable learning participation. Later on in the session, participants could be enabled to drop their roles and switch to the ID mode to enable independent work or divide-and-conquer approaches, and then later come back together to further collaborate. However, if collaboration is desired, then the CD mode can remain intact for the duration of the task.

7.4 Supporting Shared Check in Points

An additional feature of our system that we have found beneficial is when various tools disabled interaction and displayed an overlay on the map. Since the Information and Impact tools were not assigned to any one user, any user can decide its time to "check in" and create a shared check in point. We found that our system promoted the kind of group sharing and awareness that is essential to collaborative work through this functionality. By disabling interaction when one participant displays important information, the other participant is encouraged to attend to that information and possibly discuss it with his/her partner. This enables participants to maintain a shared awareness and helps them to coordinate their subsequent interactional patterns. We observed that in both conditions when pairs employed the impact or information tools, they tended to talk and work together after they resumed interaction with Youtopia. We suggest this might be more beneficial in the ID as a means to get team members to "check in" with each other. This observation is consistent with results from the work on a tabletop game called *Futura* [3]. We suggest that freezing the map screen to display important information enables that information to act as a referential anchor [5]. The map and information provide a common reference that anchors the participants' attention to a shared representation of the world state or other important information. Letting any user use a check in tool or alternatively giving each user such a tool is another important way that the system and social design can enable effective collaboration. Although this feature is unrelated to the CD strategy, it is complementary and enhances the benefits of this approach.

8. CONCLUSION

We present the results of an exploratory study that compared the similarities and differences in collaborative behaviours of young adults between CD and ID design strategies for a tangible tabletop activity. We found that the CD design supported more equitable verbal and physical participation. It encouraged participants to discuss their goals and decisions. The ID design sometimes led to parallel interaction. It also enabled a variety of working strategies and purposeful gestures. In both cases, freezing the display with informational tools encouraged subsequent collaborative behaviours. Overall, our results support the benefits of using the CD approach to support collaboration. We also found secondary benefits in that CD can be adapted easily, through social context, to be responsive to group dynamics, different goals around productive conflict, task phases and working approaches. We suggest that this approach will be applicable to any tabletop system in which multiple inputs can be processed co-dependently and input objects can be divided into unique groups. Further research is needed to test out these claims with other tabletop applications.

9. ACNOWLEDGMENTS

Thanks to NSERC, SSHRC, PICS and the GRAND NCE for funding to pursue this project. Thanks to Rachael Eckersley, Saba Nowroozi, Perry Tan, Amanda Willis, Jillian Warren and Allen Bevans for the design of Youtopia.

10. REFERENCES

[1] Antle, A. N. and Wise, A.F. (2013). Getting down to details: Using learning theory to inform tangibles research and design for children. *Interacting with Computers 25*, 1. 1-20.

[2] Antle, A. N., Wise, A.F., Hall, A., Nowroozi, S., Tan, P., Warren, J., Eckersley, R., Fan, M. (2013). Youtopia: a collaborative, tangible, multi-touch, sustainability learning activity. In *Proceedings of the 12th International Conference on Interaction Design and Children (IDC)*, ACM. 565-568.

[3] Antle, A. N. Tanenbaum, J., Bevans, A., Seaborn, K., and Wang, S. (2011). Balancing Art: Enabling public engagement with sustainability issues through a multi-touch tabletop collaborative game. In P. Campos, N. Graham, J. Jorge, N. Nunes, P. Palanque, M. Winckler (Eds.) *INTERACT 2011-Lecture Notes in Computer Science*, vol 6947, Springer Berlin/Heidelberg. 194-211.

[4] Benford, S., Bederson, B., Akesson, K., Bayon, V., Druin,A., Hansson, P., &Taxen ,G. (2000, April). Designing storytelling technologies to encourage collaboration between young children. In *Proceedings of the SIGCHI Conference on Human Factors in Computing Systems (CHI)*, ACM. 556-563.

[5] Clark, H.H., Brennan, S.E. (1991). Grounding in communication. In *Perspectives on Socially Shared Cognition, American Psychological Association*, Washington, DC. 127–149.

[6] Churchill, E. F., & Snowdon, D. (1998). Collaborative virtual environments: an introductory review of issues and systems. *Virtual Reality*, 3(1). 3-15.

[7] Dillenbourg, P. (1999). What do you mean by collaborative learning?. *Collaborative-learning: Cognitive and Computational Approaches*. Oxford: Elsevier. 1-19.

[8] Deitz, P. and Leigh, D. (2001). DiamondTouch: A Multi-User Touch Technology. In *Proceedings of the 14th annual ACM symposium on User Interface Software and Technology (UIST)*, ACM. 219- 226.

[9] Gutwin, C., & Greenberg, S. (2000). The Mechanics of Collaboration: Developing Low Cost Usability Evaluation Methods for Shared Workspaces. In *IEEE Workshop on Enabling Technologies: Infrastructure for Collaborative Enterprises (WETICE 2000). Proceedings. IEEE 9th International workshops on*. 98-103.

[10] Goos, M., Galbraith, P., & Renshaw, P. (2002). Socially mediated metacognition: Creating collaborative zones of proximal development in small group problem solving. *Educational Studies in Mathematics*, 49, 193-223.

[11] Harris, A., Rick, J., Bonnett, V., Yuill, N., Fleck, R, Marshall, P, & Rogers, Y. (2009). Around the table: Are multiple-touch surfaces better than single-touch for children's collaborative interactions? In *Proceedings of the 9th international conference on Computer Supported Collaborative Learning (CSCL)- vol 1*. International Society of the Learning Sciences. 335-344.

[12] Hornecker, E., Buur, J. (2006). Getting a grip on tangible interaction: A framework on physical space and social interactions. In *Proceedings of CHI'06*, ACM. 437–446.

[13] Hornecker, E., Marshall, P., & Rogers, Y. (2007). From entry to access: how shareability comes about. In *Proceedings of Designing pleasurable products and interfaces*, ACM. 328-342.

[14] Inkpen, K., Booth, K.S., Klawe, M., Upitis, R. (1995). Playing together beats playing apart, especially for girls. In *CSCL'95*, L.Erlbaum Associates Inc. 177-181.

[15] Jamil I., O'Hara, K., Perry, M., Karnik, A., & Subramanian, S. (2011). The Effects of Interaction Techniques on Talk Patterns in Collaborative Peer Learning around Interactive Tables. In *Proceedings of CHI'11*, ACM. 3043-3052.

[16] Meerbeek, B., Bingley, P., Rijnen, W., Hoven van den, E.Pipet. (2010). A Design Concept Supporting Photo Sharing. *NordiCHI'10*, Reykjavik, Iceland.335-342.

[17] Marshall.P., Hornecker, E., Morris, R., Sheep Dalton, N., & Rogers, Y. (2008).When the fingers do the talking: a study of group participation with varying constraints to a tabletop interface. In *Horizontal Interactive Human Computer Systems, TABLETOP 2008, 3rd IEEE International Workshop*. 33-40.

[18] Morris, M. R., Huang, A., Paepcke, A., & Winograd, T. (2006). Cooperative gestures: multi-user gestural interactions for co-located groupware. In *Proceedings of CHI'06*, ACM. 1201-1210.

[19] Piper, A. M O'Brien, E., Morris, M.R. & Winograd, T. (2006). SIDES: A cooperative tabletop computer game for social skills development. In *Proceedings of the 20th anniversary conference on Computer Supported Cooperative Work (CSCW)*. Banff, Canada: ACM. 1-10.

[20] Rogers, Y., Lim, Y., Hazlewood, W., Marshall, P. (2009). Equal Opportunities: Do Shareable Interfaces Promote More Group Participation Than Single User Displays? *Human Computer Interaction 24(1/2)*. 79–116.

[21] Stanton, D., & Neale, H. (2003). The effect of multiple mice on children's talk and interaction. *Journal of Computer Assisted Learning, 19(2)*. 229-238.

[22] Stewart, J.,Raybourn, E.M, Bederson, B., &Druin, A.(1998). When Two Hands are Better Than One. In *Proceedings of CHI'98*, ACM. 287-288.

[23] Subramanian S., Pinelle D., Korst J., Buil V.(2007). Tabletop collaboration through tangible interactions. *Enabling Technologies: Infrastructure for Collaborative Enterprises'07. WETICE' 07. 16th IEEE International Workshop*. 412-417.

[24] Speelpenning, T., Antle N. A., Doering, T. and van den Hoven, E. (2011). Exploring how tangible tools enable collaboration in a multi-touch tabletop game. In *Human-Computer Interaction-INTERACT'11*. Springer Berlin Heidelberg, 605-621.

[25] Waldner, M., Hauber J., Zauner J., Haller M., Billinghurst M. (2006). Tangible Tiles: Design and Evaluation of a Tangible User Interface in a Collaborative Tabletop Setup. In *Proceedings of the 18th Australia conference on Computer-Human Interaction: Design: Activities Artefacts and Environments*, ACM. 151-158.

[26] Wardhaugh, R (1985). How Conversation Works, *Basil Blackwell*, USA. 1-230.

Metrics for Cooperative Systems

Nils Jeners
Fraunhofer FIT
Schloss Birlinghoven
53754 Sankt Augustin, Germany
nils.jeners@rwth-aachen.de

Wolfgang Prinz
Fraunhofer FIT
Schloss Birlinghoven
53754 Sankt Augustin, Germany
wolfgang.prinz@fit.fraunhofer.de

ABSTRACT

This paper proposes performance indicators and metrics for the analysis of shared workspaces. We investigate user activity in various electronic workspaces of a shared workspace system and compare these on the basis of the proposed metrics: activity, productivity and cooperativity. Based on these results we further investigate the intensity of cooperation on shared documents. The investigations show that the proposed metrics permit an identification of the current cooperation status of a workspace as well as a classification of workspaces and benchmarking of the cooperation maturity.

Categories and Subject Descriptors

H.5.3 [**Information Interfaces and Presentation**]: Group and Organization Interfaces – *Asynchronous interaction; Web-based interaction; Collaborative computing; Computer-supported cooperative work.*

General Terms

Measurement, Performance, Experimentation, Human Factors.

Keywords

Metrics, evaluation, cooperativity, shared workspaces, cooperation analysis.

1. INTRODUCTION

Electronic media for communication and collaboration has been used for many years in business. Although there are critical considerations whether these media have a positive impact on the productivity of employees [4, 5], there are many advocates for the use of modern media cooperation. For knowledge workers [7] and virtual teams [8] groupware systems in general and especially shared workspace systems are indispensable in the context of today's work [20]. In order to make a statement about the use of the systems and in particular on the productivity and the cooperativity of the actors within these systems, it is necessary to identify indicators that meet the requirements of operational performance measurement systems [19].

Previous evaluations over workspace systems were intended to gain knowledge about a specific system, with the question in mind: how is it used? By using these statistical evaluation methods, these systems have been improved and developed [1, 9]. But, these results are not yet used to characterize groups and to make a statement on their cooperation.

Social networks and their analysis are well researched and widely

used [18, 23]. The social network analysis (SNA) is a method of social research and defines for example the edge density metrics, node degree centrality and clique analysis. The statements of these numbers refer to individual actors within the network, their relationships with each other and also to the entire network. Some approaches already exist to adopt this kind of analysis for groups and shared workspaces [10, 16]. The focus of the SNA lies in the description of the static network. Therefore, dynamic processes and activities of the members are not considered.

Another field of investigation is the classification of individual participants into productive workers and so-called lurkers [13, 15]. The classification of knowledge workers in these role categories is based on the performed actions. The decisive factors are both quantitatively and qualitatively and serve the productivity evaluated [7]. According to Drucker, there are six factors that affect productivity: (1) knowledge of the task, (2) knowledge and self-organization, (3) continuous innovation, (4) continuous learning and teaching, (5) the quantity and quality of work, and (6) identification with the company. These factors put their focus on an individual knowledge worker and are difficult to measure. It is obvious that most of the results of knowledge workers arise in a group in which each group member occupies one or more specific roles [21].

The metrics proposed by Koch and Richter [12] are suitable for measuring the success of the introduction of social media in the enterprise and expand the perspective from an individual to a broader view of the whole group. The mentioned figures are e.g. the change of the communication behavior (number of emails), number of documents, activity, level of participation in individual documents, degree of crosslinking of employees and employee satisfaction. The use of these indicators is often limited to a before-and-after comparison in the introduction of tools to determine the effect on the behavior of a group. Although a large body of quantitative research on Wikis and in particular Wikipedia exists, a measuring and benchmarking approach for the performance history of a group in a shared workspaces environment is missing. In [14] 188 communities are analyzed to investigate the use of social media within different communities. This study is primarily based on a comparison of the different media types produced by the community members. Our research extends this by focusing on the cooperative activities performed by the group members.

The aim of this work is to define meaningful metrics that enable comparability and characterization of different workspaces and the observation of these over time. It is obvious that cooperative work is not happening within a single system, but rather in a set of systems. Other studies have shown, that the tools used for collaboration are very diverse [9]. The used tools range from e-mail, telephone conferences, collaborative editors, to lightweight specialized tools, such as Doodle. The use of all these tools happens in parallel within a work context. All these activities, as well as the physical cooperation in the same room, cannot be taken into account in the approach presented here. Therefore, the authors limit their view on a single monolithic system that allows covering a huge amount of cooperation log file data, but with the knowledge not being able to capture all types of cooperation. The considered system is BSCW, a shared workspace system which will be presented in the following chapter. Chapter 3 defines the proposed indicators and metrics. In chapter 4, we present the result of applying the metrics to different workspaces.

2. SHARED WORKSPACE SYSTEMS

The shared workspace system BSCW (Basic Support for Cooperative Work) is a groupware that supports collaboration of several users on the internet [2]. The BSCW system is developed as a groupware system to support distributed work since 1995 at Fraunhofer FIT (former GMD FIT) and the spin-off OrbiTeam Gmbh & Co KG. The focus of the system lies on the self-organized coordination of distributed teams through a shared workspace. BSCW offers extensive facilities for document management, for registering and managing users and groups, discussion forums, as well as calendar and task management. Currently, about 1,000 servers of BSCW have been installed worldwide and the fifth major version has recently been released. The number of users is estimated at over 1 million. On the public server operated by FIT (http://public.bscw.de) more than 200,000 users are registered.

The BSCW system captures and stores all user actions on shared objects to provide users the information on the collaboration history and the current object state. Among additional technical details, the following meta-information is logged for each user action:

- **Timestamp** of the certain action
- **Action type**, e.g. read, create, modify, versioning, delete, etc.
- **Object ID**, unique identifier of the target of the action
- **Object type** of the target, e.g. document, folder, etc.
- **User ID**, unique identifier of the user performing the action

This information is provided by BSCW within the user interface by corresponding icons, but it can also be downloaded as a CSV file (comma separated values). This makes it possible to evaluate the behavior of cooperation in a workspace for an extended period of time.

For the analysis described in this article several work spaces were selected with different characteristics according to the different application domains of BSCW:

- **Project related workspaces (P)** serve the organization of cross-organizational projects. These are typically national or international research projects with 5-20 partners and a total of 10-70 project members over a period of several months or a few years.
- **Organizational workspaces (O)** support the cooperation within a specific department of an organization over several years.
- **Task related workspaces (T)** support the completion of a specified task, such as exchange of documents for a course over a short period of about six months or the joint development of a paper or a proposal.

We have selected these types of workspaces because they represent the major application domain of the shared workspace platform [9, 20].

3. NUMBERS AND METRICS

The indicators and metrics developed in this work are based on the participant-artifact-framework [6] and the meta-model of cooperative systems [11]. For the data analysis we transform the log data into the *Activity Streams* format [22], which shows a specific event at a specific time with its *actor*, a *verb*, an *object* and a *target*. By using this open format, it is also possible to analyze event data from other systems and to compare them with those of BSCW at a later stage of research. The log data of BSCW is exported as comma separated values (CSV) per workspace and then converted to the appropriate format. Different workspaces are first analyzed individually and then compared with each other.

For each work area elementary metrics are determined first. These include the duration of the activities or the project (in days), the number of active members, the number of objects or documents in the workspace and the number of individual events. These events are divided into three different categories: *create*, *edit*, and *read* (cf. Figure 1). This categorization achieves an abstraction in order to enable an adaptation of these metrics to other systems. *createEvents* are events in which people invest objects or documents. People who create the objects have the role of an author. *editEvents* are events in which a person modifies an existing object. A distinction is made here between changes to the metadata (name, description, tags, etc.) of the object, and the content of the object. People that edit the objects have the role of an editor. *readEvents* are events in which people consume objects or documents. The role of these people is called reader.

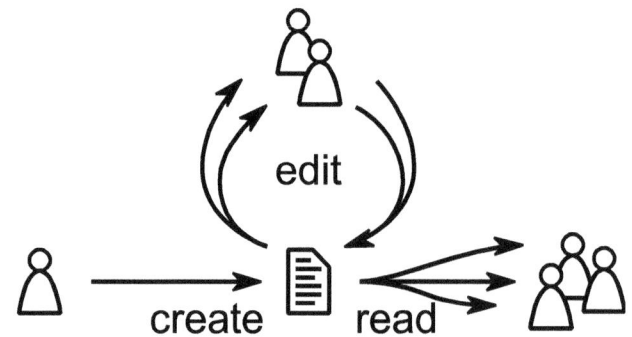

Figure 1. Model of cooperation

Three basic metrics were derived from the ratios: activity, productivity and cooperativity.

The activity metric describes the overall activity within a workspace: sum of all actions in a workspaces per member per day on average.

$$activity := \frac{\# \text{ events}}{\# \text{ members} \cdot \# \text{ days}}$$

The productivity metric shows the number of productive activities, i.e. how many objects or documents have been created per member per day on average.

$$productivity := \frac{\# \text{ createEvents}}{\# \text{ members} \cdot \# \text{ days}}$$

The cooperativity metric describes the degree of cooperation, i.e. how many edits per member have been performed per day on average.

$$\text{cooperativity} := \frac{\#\ editEvents}{\#\ members \cdot \#\ days}$$

The above mentioned metrics are typically represented on a time basis. Dynamic considerations of the workspaces are playing a major role in projects. They allow an assessment of the nature of the workspaces and the group of employees. The metrics can be applied to any time interval (days, weeks, months, years) or even over the whole project duration. Our evaluations have shown that these values have a high variance over a longer time period. Thus shorter intervals are more useful for monitoring and evaluation.

In addition to these three basic metrics, additional metrics were developed to investigate the cooperative behavior on the objects in a workspace. The division of labor metric considers the allocation of activities to members and investigates the question: "What percentage of the workspace activity is performed by what ratio of active people in a workspace?" This metric is presented in a diagram with the axes of people and activities, in each case in per cent, so that a normalized representation can be achieved. This allows the comparison of different workspaces

The responsiveness of a workspace answers the question: "After how many days is a certain percentage of the documents at least once considered or processed by a person (besides the author)?" This metric shows on the one hand how quickly members react on created objects of others, but also what percentage of the objects are never read. In the following section, we apply the presented metrics on different workspaces.

4. RESULTS AND EVALUATIONS

To apply and evaluate the usefulness of the metrics we analyzed ten different workspaces. Four belong to the category of project workspaces (P), three to the category of organizational workspaces (O), and three to the category of task related workspaces (T). The criteria for the selection of these workspaces were:

- Content: the workspaces contained a considerable amount of shared documents
- Group size: all workspaces had a group size of more than 40 people from different organizations
- Duration: all workspaces were in used for at least 2 years.

Applying these criteria we ensured that our analysis is both based on a broad spectrum of data as well as on longitudinal data. A total of nearly 50,000 events on nearly 7,500 objects from more than 600 persons were analyzed, which have occurred in different lengths of time between six months and several years.

Table 1 shows the basic data of the investigated areas. P1-P3 are medium sized projects with several project partners, whereas P4 clearly is a larger project. Similarly, O1 and O2 workspaces are within smaller working groups and O3 is a workspace of an entire organization area, which includes three working groups. T1-T3 are workspaces of lectures.

In the remaining of this section we analyze the event data of these workspace by different criteria and metrics.

4.1 Distribution of read, create and edit activities

The individual workspaces also differ in the type of events (Figure 2). As introduced above, we distinguish between three event types (*create*, *edit*, *read*).

Table 1. Basic figures of the investigated workspaces.

Workspace	People	Objects	Events	Days
P1	55	593	3139	981
P2	47	384	1465	1840
P3	52	814	4153	923
P4	105	1668	10427	2493
O1	32	74	390	3928
O2	9	57	182	497
O3	247	3749	22108	4547
T1	28	48	549	238
T2	89	82	730	553
T3	27	18	298	411

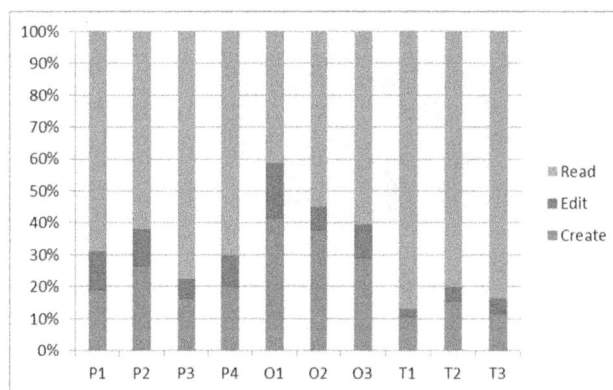

Figure 2: Ratio of events for each workspace

The results of the event type analysis by proportion become more visible by the representation as pie charts in the following figure.

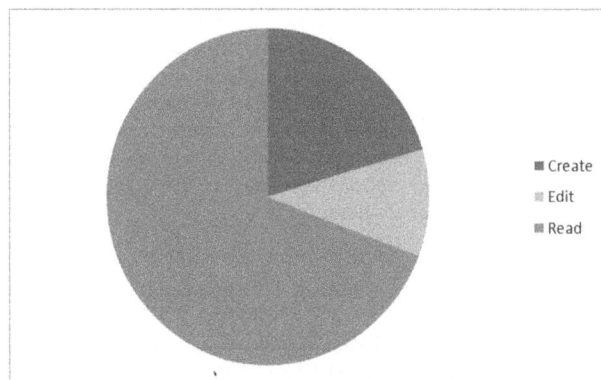

Figure 3: Average event ratio for project workspaces

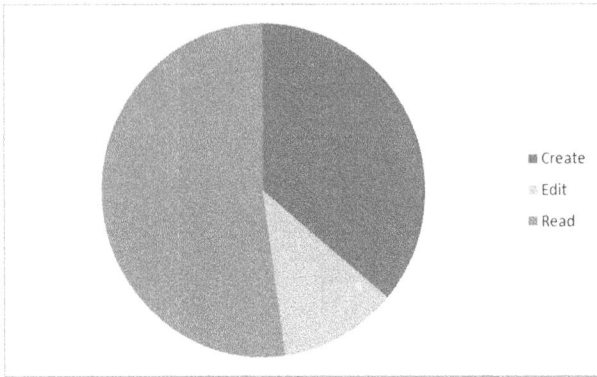

Figure 4: Average event ratio for organizational workspaces

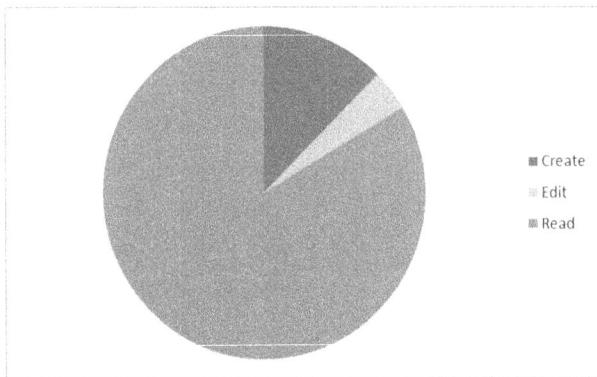

Figure 5: Average event ratio for task workspaces

Figure 3-5 can be explained with the nature of the workspaces. Organizational work areas are mainly used for documentation and archiving of documents (project proposals, photos, company outings). Therefore, these workspaces have a relatively high proportion of create events (Figure 4). The task specific workspaces that have been used here for tuition, are used for the distribution of documents (lecture slides, scientific articles), which should be read by each participants of a course. This explains the very high proportion of read events for these kind of workspaces (Figure 5). The project-related work areas are used for the actual cooperation of the individual members. Here we can observe a more even distribution between create and edit events compared to the organizational workspaces while the ration of edit activities is similar for both.

From this analysis we can derive that the nature of a workspace has a direct consequence on the activity events produced within this workspace. While this conclusion appears straightforward, the reverse interpretation is more relevant. This means that we can identify the nature of a workspace by analyzing the activity events over time:

- Workspaces with a ratio of more than 75% of read events are typically distribution oriented information spaces.
- Workspaces with a high ratio of create events (>33%) compared to read events are typically oriented towards archiving information and providing information spaces within a long term organizational environment

- Workspaces with a more balanced ratio of create and edit events point to a more cooperation oriented workspace that is typical for project work.

4.2 Activity, Productivity and Cooperativity

In the previous section we introduced activity, productivity and cooperativity as cooperation metrics. Figure 6 presents the monthly analysis of the activity, productivity and cooperativity metrics for a large project workspace over 24 months.

It can be easily recognized that the values have a high variance. Actually the maximum value is 1.5, but the presentation is clipped for better readability. The fact that phases with stronger or weaker activity exist is hardly surprising for such a long term project. Focusing on a single metric such as productivity provides an indication of that metric over time, but it is not possible to identify a characteristic pattern.

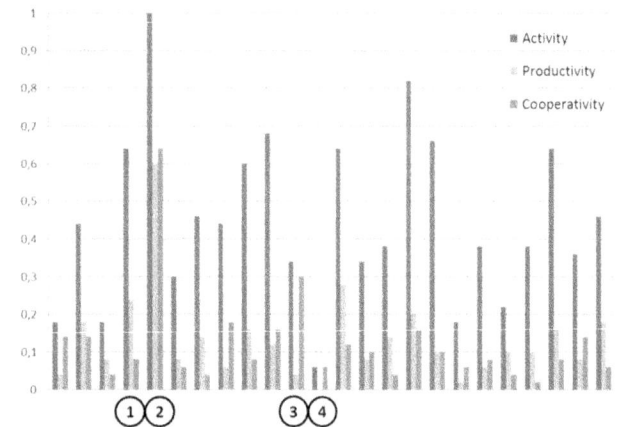

Figure 6: Activity, Productivity and Cooperativity of a project workspace over a period of 24 month. (Each group of 3 bars representing one month)

However, a comparison of the three metrics among each other is very interesting since it can be used to depict different working situations during the project lifetime. The following table identifies characteristic working situations and the corresponding metrics.

Table 2: Working situations and corresponding metrics

	Activity	Productivity (P)	Cooperativity (C)
Archive	$\sim$ (P)	high	low
Co-Creation③	high	$<$ (C)	high
Re-Use ①	N*(C)	high	low
Deadline ②	high	high	high
No Activity ④	low	low	low

In the archive situation, users produce a lot of content that is not further edited nor read by many other users. Thus the activity level is almost equal to the productivity level and the cooperativity level is low as not many edit events are produced. Such a situation does not appear in Figure 6.

In a co-creation phase the number of edit events increases resulting in a high cooperativity. The productivity level is actually below the cooperativity level as users concentrate more on the cooperation of existing content than the production of new. The activity level is also high since users need to read other users content before they start editing it. We can find a typical co-creation month at position (3) as well as at the project start (1st column bar) in Figure 6.

A situation in which the productivity level is high while the activity is significantly higher than the productivity and the cooperativity is low, indicates a phase in which a lot of content is produced and read by many users, but not further edited. This indicates a phase of information distribution and re-use (1).

A phase in which all metrics are high is likely to correlate with a deadline situation in which all project members become active in producing, reading and contributing (editing) content. We can find such a situation at position (2) which actually correlates to a real project review date. The fact that a re-use phase (1) precedes the deadline phase (2) in Figure 6 can be explained by the fact that the project members first start reading the existing content to become up-to-date before they start contributing new and working on existing content.

We can learn from this analysis that a situated and comparative analysis of the activity, productivity and cooperative metrics is useful to identify specific cooperation patterns and their corresponding project phases.

Using the data gathered for this analysis we further calculated the percentage of active, productive and cooperative days in Table 3,

Table 3. Active, productive and cooperative days of the project with and without weekends.

Active days:	46% / **64%**
Productive days:	19% / **26%**
Cooperative days:	13% / **19%**

Actually only at 20%-26% of all working days the project members produced new content or have been cooperatively working on the content, while definitely on more every 2nd day activities took place.

4.3 The division of labor

After the investigations of the proposed cooperation metrics we analyzed the division of labor within the workspace. For this purpose we calculated the ratio of the events that are produced by a certain ratio of users. The result is shown in Figure 7 to Figure 9.

The division of labor is relatively identical for the different project and organizational workspaces (Figure 7, Figure 8). It is interesting to note that approx. 20% of the group members are responsible for 80% of all events. On the other hand, the figures also indicate that already 70-80% of the members produce almost 100% of all events. The consequence is that 20-30% of all members are almost not active at all. A possible reason for this observation is that often people are invited into a workspace

similar to being addressed by cc: in an email. I.e. they are receiving access to the workspace "just in case", i.e. as observers or to prepare for these case that they need to become active in the project. Another reason is that project members often change between projects while there membership in past project workspaces is not revoked.

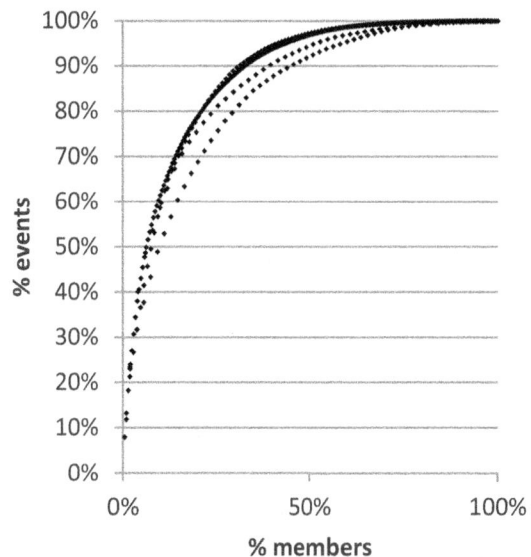

Figure 7: Division of labor in project workspaces

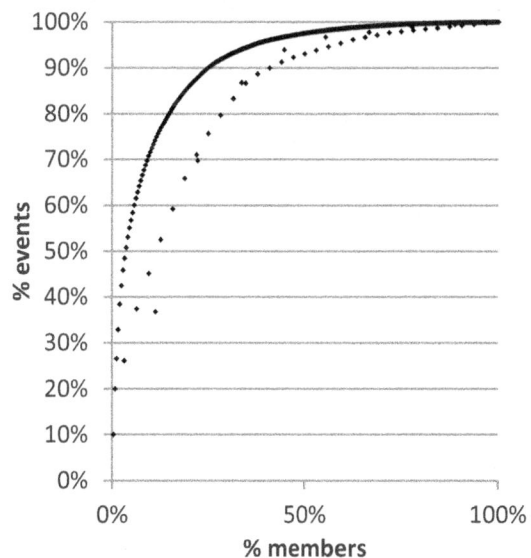

Figure 8: Division of labor in organizational workspaces

The analysis of task oriented workspaces yields a flatter curve (Figure 9) which indicates a more even division of labor among the participants. This can be explained by the fact that in this specific case were these workspaces were used to organize a lecture the participation and contribution by the students was more evenly distributed as in the project or organization workspaces which furthermore provides a good indication of the students' engagement.

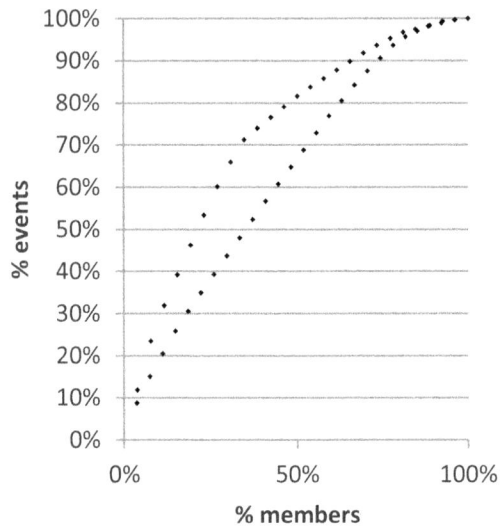

Figure 9: Division of labor in task specific workspaces

The division of labor analysis cannot easily be used to classify workspaces as in the previous sections. However it provides an interesting insight into the group structure and their participation in the cooperation process. The steeper the curve, the less equal is the division of labor. This indicator can be used to evaluate the group structure and membership.

The findings of the division of labor analysis are confirmed by analyzing the individual contribution of the workspace members. Figure 10 presents on the x-axis the 20 most active users of the 4 different project workspaces. In total these workspaces had a membership count between 43 and 62. The y-axis shows the ratio of the activity for these users.

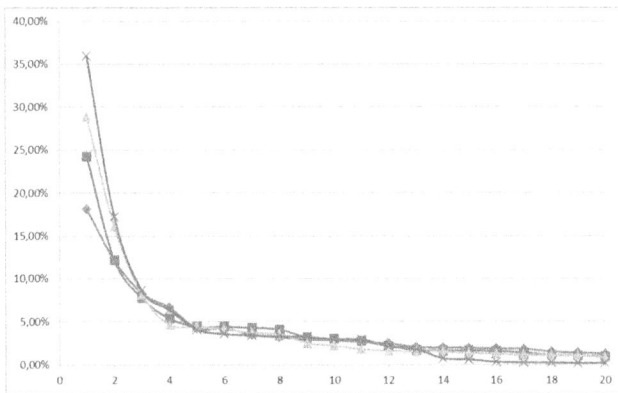

Figure 10: The long tail of user participation

We see a steep drop from the most active to the 5th most active user who contributes approximately 5% of all activity events. From then on, the participation drops slowly and beyond position 13 the activity level corresponds to user who only very occasional became active in the shared workspace.

A more closer and user specific look at the participation confirms the findings of M. Muller in [13]. Among the 4 project workspaces we could identify 27 users who participated at least in 2 different workspaces.

For each user we calculated the activity position within the respective workspace. This position was then normalized using the total numbers of users in the workspace to enable a comparison. The result of this analysis is shown in Figure 11.

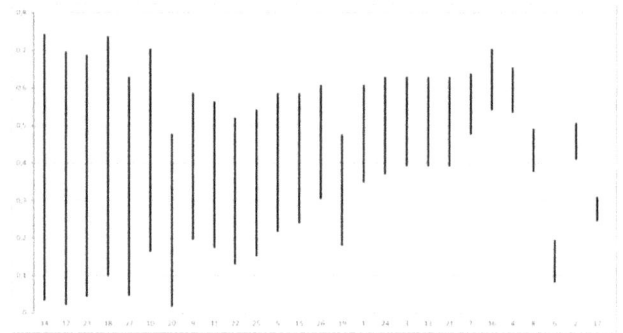

Figure 11: Variance of activities for user who participated at least in two workspaces

The x- axis lists the users anonymized by a user id. The y-axis indicates the normalized position in the activity list, were 0 indicates a high activity ranking and 1 a low activity ranking[1]. The graphic demonstrates that at least 50% of the users have a high variance of their activities in different workspaces, i.e. they are very active in one workspace (~ 0.1) and almost not active in the other workspace (~0.7). This very much confirms the findings in [11] that the user participation is determined by the situational disposition and not simply by the fact of a general user attitude.

4.4 Responsiveness within a workspace

Another important indicator of a workspace and its associated group is it responsiveness. We determine the responsiveness of a workspace as the duration until a certain percentage of documents has been part of an activity. The following figures show the responsiveness as a graph in which the x-axis denotes the days after creation and the y-axis the percentage of read documents. The curve then indicates the ratio of documents that have become part of an activity (mostly read activities) within the range of days.

The responsiveness of project (Figure 12) and organization-related (Figure 13) workspaces differ only slightly. In both cases the workspace members respond within the first day on 30% to 45% of all objects. I.e. 30-45% of all objects become part of an activity within the first day. The steep start of the curve can be considered as the cooperation phase in which several users become active by reading or contributing to an object. After approximately one week the curve becomes more shallow indication a phase in which objects turn to archives. Further activity is them often initiated by a search by explicitly pointing users to the object. Both types of workspaces reach a response rate of 50% to 75% of the objects within 30 days. In turn this means that 25% - 50% of the objects have never been used during this period. The higher this value is, the higher is the archive nature of this workspace.

---

[1] This value is calculated by $\dfrac{activity-position}{number\ of\ workspace\ members}$

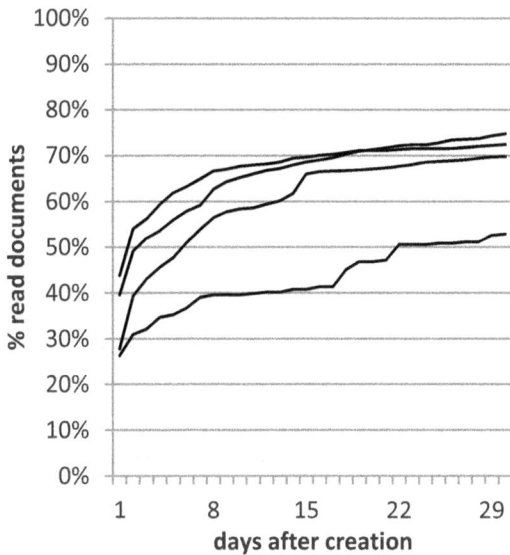

Figure 12: Responsiveness of the project workspaces

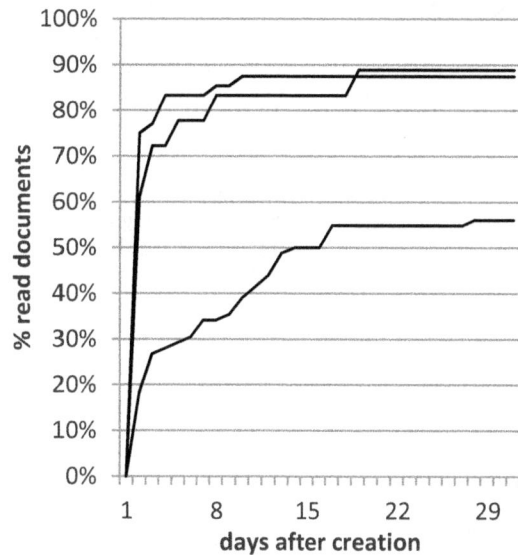

Figure 13: Responsiveness of the organizational workspaces

The responsiveness of task-related workspaces (Figure 14) is different form the other workspaces. On the one hand, it is striking that in principle there is no reaction within the first day. Thereafter, the response rate rises quickly to 80% reaching even almost 90%. This means the proportion of unread items is just over 10%. One reason for this probably lies in the fact that many users are aware of the new objects only through the overnight sent activity report via e-mail and then read the newly provided documents the next day. The high response rate of almost 90% corresponds to observations in the previous section.

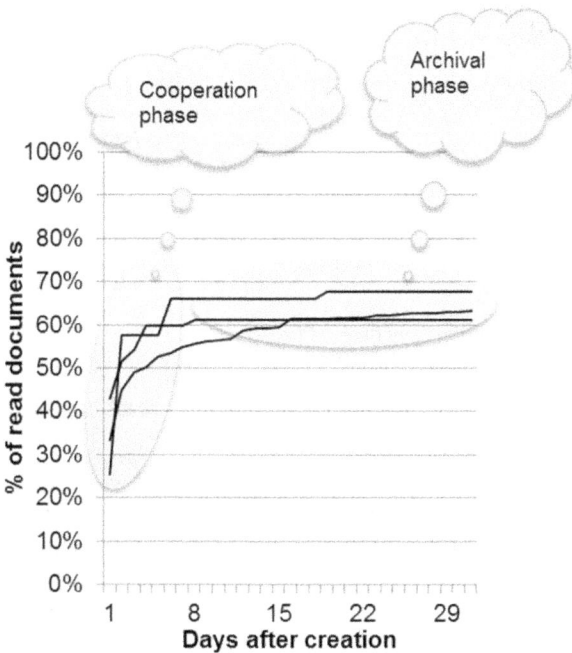

Figure 14: Responsiveness of the task workspaces

The division of labor as well as the responsiveness analysis indicates that the shared workspaces contain a significant number of objects that are never read by any user of the group nor become part of a cooperative activity, i.e. they are only read by other users but they are never edited and revised.

Therefore we performed a deeper analysis of the read and cooperation activities per object. The results are shown in the following table.

Table 4: Ratio of objects that become part of an activity

Workspace	% of read documents	% of revised documents
P1	84%	34%
P2	91%	28%
P3	87%	11%

We can learn from Table 4 that between 84 and 91% of all created documents are read at least once by another user. Furthermore between 11% and 34% of all documents are revised, i.e. they became part of a cooperative activity. This indicates that the shared workspaces are mainly used as information and document sharing tools and less as a cooperation media in which documents are produced cooperatively. From our experience with the system we can identify two reasons for this observation. The first is that often the cooperative document production phase takes place outside of the system using email as the primary exchange media. Only when documents have reached a more stable status they are then shared with the overall project. The second reason is indicated by the ratio of revised documents on P3 compared to P1 and P2. Actually the ratio of revised documents in P3 is less than 50% of the other workspaces. P3 represents a project in which the majority of users were not IT-literate. They also used a cooperation platform for the first time. The membership of P2 and P3 consisted mainly of IT-professionals who are experienced in collaboration. Thus these metrics can also be used to determine the maturity of a user group with respect to the use of cooperation tools and platforms.

5. CONCLUSION AND OUTLOOK

This paper proposes several new metrics for the analysis of shared workspaces and it applies these metrics on a large body of activity logs produced within an operational shared workspace platform over a period between 2 and 3 years.

The quantitative analysis demonstrates that different work spaces of the same category often produce similar values, while they are different between the categories. Thus the following observations can be made: The statistical analysis of the group behavior in a work space can be used to indicate the type of usage. This can trigger appropriate configurations or adjustments to the system can be triggered. Furthermore we have shown that the combined consideration of the proposed metrics activity, productivity and cooperativity yields interesting insights into the current cooperation situation of a workspace such as a re-use, archival, co-creation or deadline phase.

The investigation of the division of labor lead to the interesting finding that the use of shared workspaces follows the Pareto principle [3, 17] (80-20 rule). Thus, we found that 20% of users perform 80% of the activities. Furthermore the cooperative activities only took place on 20% of the days of a cooperative project in a workspace. In addition the analysis of the user behavior across different workspaces confirmed Mullers finding from the analysis of communities with respect to the situational disposition between been a lurker and a producer.

The responsiveness analysis clearly shows that we can distinguish between a cooperation and an archival phase for shared documents. It is interesting to note that the cooperation phase has a typical duration of 5-7 days. The subsequent analysis of the ratio of objects that become part of an activity shows clear differences between workspaces used by unexperienced and more experienced users.

These finding can now be used to inform the design of shared workspace systems and even cooperation support systems in general. Today, most shared workspace systems provide visual representations to indicate recent activities on shared documents such as the awareness icons in Figure 15 or on the presence or activity of a single user.

2014-02-13 12:58   2013-11-20 15:28

Figure 15: Different awareness icons of BSCW that indicate recent user activities

Based on the proposed metrics is becomes possible to indicate the overall behavior of a group as well as the current cooperation situation of a workspace. This can include indications of:

- The type (project, organizational, task-oriented) of workspace based on the ratio of the recent event types (Figure 3 - Figure 5)

- The current working situation of a group based on a comparative analysis of the metrics (Table 2).

- The structure and homogeneity of a group based on the analysis of the division of labor (Figure 7 - Figure 9)

- The time until which users can expect a reaction of the group on new contributions based on the responsiveness analysis (Figure 12 - Figure 14).

In a next step we will design appropriate means to visualize and present this information within the user interfec of the shared workspaces system. It will be interesting to see whether this feedback will have effects on the individual and group behavior.

We hope that these studies and the proposed performance indicators and metrics help to understand the cooperative behavior in shared electronic workspaces. In the next step we will extend the studies to other workspaces, with the aim to obtain a broader data base for the determination of metrics of shared workspaces. Often organizations that apply cooperative systems require baseline data to benchmark their own behavior. The research and quantitative results presented in this paper provide a first step towards this baseline. If the intended usage of a work space is known, a comparison of the workspace metrics with the benchmark data provides an interesting insight in the cooperation maturity of a group and its organization. Appropriate training or change management processes to improve the team and group collaboration can then be triggered based on solid indicators.

6. REFERENCES

[1] Appelt, W. 2001. What groupware functionality do users really use? Analysis of the usage of the BSCW system. *Ninth Euromicro Workshop on Parallel and Distributed Processing* (2001), 337–341.

[2] Appelt, W. and Busbach, U. 1996. The BSCW system: a WWW-based application to support cooperation of distributed groups. *Enabling Technologies: Infrastructure for Collaborative Enterprises, 1996. Proceedings of the 5th Workshop on* (1996), 304–309.

[3] Arnold, B.C. 1983. *Pareto distributions*. International Co-operative Publishing House.

[4] Brynjolfsson, E. 1993. The productivity paradox of information technology. *Communications of the ACM*. 36, 12 (1993), 66–77.

[5] Carr, N.G. 2003. IT doesn't matter. *Educause Review*. 38, (2003), 24–38.

[6] Dix, A. 1994. Computer Supported Cooperative Work - A Framework. *Design issues in CSCW*. Springer-Verlag.

[7] Drucker, P.F. 1999. Knowledge-worker productivity: The Biggest Challenge. *California management review*. 41, 2 (1999), 79–94.

[8] Duarte, D.L. 2006. *Mastering virtual teams: strategies, tools, and techniques that succeed*. Jossey-Bass.

[9] Jeners, N., Lobunets, O. and Prinz, W. 2013. What Groupware Functionality Do Users Really Use? (A study of collaboration within digital ecosystems). *7th IEEE International Conference on Digital Ecosystems and Technologies (DEST)* (2013), 49–54.

[10] Jeners, N., Nicolaescu, P. and Prinz, W. 2012. Analyzing Tie-Strength across Different Media. *On the Move to Meaningful Internet Systems: OTM 2012 Workshops* (2012), 554–563.

[11] Jeners, N., Prinz, W. and Franken, S. 2013. A Meta-Model for Cooperation Systems. *PRO-VE* (Berlin, Heidelberg, 2013).

[12] Koch, M. and Richter, A. 2009. *Enterprise 2.0 Planung, Einführung und erfolgreicher Einsatz von Social-Software in Unternehmen.* Oldenbourg.

[13] Muller, M. 2012. Lurking as personal trait or situational disposition. *Computer Supported Cooperative Work* (2012), 253.

[14] Muller, M., Ehrlich, K., Matthews, T., Perer, A., Ronen, I. and Guy, I. 2012. Diversity Among Enterprise Online Communities: Collaborating, Teaming, and Innovating Through Social Media. *Proceedings of the SIGCHI Conference on Human Factors in Computing Systems* (New York, NY, USA, 2012), 2815–2824.

[15] Muller, M., Shami, N.S., Millen, D.R. and Feinberg, J. 2010. We are all lurkers: consuming behaviors among authors and readers in an enterprise file-sharing service. *Computer Supported Cooperative Work 2010 Workshop on Collective Intelligence* (2010), 201.

[16] Nasirifard, P., Peristeras, V., Hayes, C. and Decker, S. 2009. Extracting and utilizing social networks from log files of shared workspaces. *Leveraging Knowledge for Innovation in Collaborative Networks.* Springer. 643–650.

[17] Newman, M. 2005. Power laws, Pareto distributions and Zipf's law. *Contemporary Physics.* 46, 5 (Sep. 2005), 323–351.

[18] O'Brien, G. 1968. The measurement of cooperation. *Organizational Behavior and Human Performance.* 3, 4 (1968), 427–439.

[19] Preißler, P.R. 2008. *Betriebswirtschaftliche Kennzahlen: Formeln, Aussagekraft, Sollwerte, Ermittlungsintervalle.* Oldenbourg Verlag.

[20] Prinz, W., Loh, H., Pallot, M., Schaffers, H., Skarmeta, A. and Decker, S. 2006. ECOSPACE - Towards an Integrated Collaboration Space for eProfessionals. *Collaborative Computing: Networking, Applications and Worksharing* (Atlanta, Nov. 2006), 1–7.

[21] Reinhardt, W., Schmidt, B., Sloep, P. and Drachsler, H. 2011. Knowledge Worker Roles and Actions-Results of Two Empirical Studies. *Knowledge and Process Management.* 18, 3 (Jul. 2011), 150–174.

[22] Snell, J., Atkins, M., Norris, W., Messina, C., Wilkinson, M. and Dolin, R. 2011. JSON Activity Streams 1.0.

[23] Wasserman, S. and Faust, K. 1994. *Social network analysis: methods and applications.* Cambridge University Press.

The Dream About the Magic Silver Bullet – the Complexity of Designing for Tablet-Mediated Learning

Isa Jahnke
Umea University
Dept. Applied Educational Sciences
Interactive Media and Learning
+46 70 2278870
isa.jahnke@umu.se

Niels V. Svendsen
Aalborg University
Dept. Communication & Psychology
eLearningLab
+45 4059 2874
nielsv@hum.aau.dk

Simon K. Johansen
Aalborg University
Dept. Communication & Psychology
eLearningLab
+45 6078 8895
smn.k.jhnsn@gmail.com

Pär-Ola Zander
Aalborg University
Dept. of Communication & Psychology
eLearningLab
+45 4151 3256
poz@hum.aau.dk

ABSTRACT

In this paper, we report three cases of the integration of technology, such as web-enabled media tablets in Scandinavian schools. Both qualitative and quantitative data have been applied. A daily challenge for teachers is to coordinate their group of students in a way that enables collaborative learning. We report the gaps and interrelations between the dreams and the practice of the teachers. They dream about an interconnected praxis – the magic silver bullet – and establish their visions of inter-connectivity because of their breakdown experiences of media tablets aiding complexity instead of reducing it. The teachers must learn how to navigate during the breakdowns before media tablets reduce complexity and reach a state in which the tablets take part in the classroom ecology as functional organs. The teachers have to deal with complex situations during class *in situ*. In order to be able to continue with the class, the teachers become *jongleurs* of different design elements including the handling of the didactical designs and the breakdowns caused by the integration of media tablets; the teaching practice in classrooms moves away from a common routine activity and turns into a *design project*.

Categories and Subject Descriptors

K.3.1 Computer Uses in Education

General Terms

Design; Human Factors; Theory

Keywords

Media tablets; Educational technology; Cooperation; Design

1. INTRODUCTION

The omnipresence of mobile technology has lead to new situations in educational institutions in the western countries. In early times, Information and Communication Technology (ICT) has been segregated from the classrooms and placed in computer labs [17]. This has changed with the invention of smaller devices like tablet computers and smart phones. Now, instead of segregation, a shift is happening to co-located settings in which ICT becomes part of the classroom. The teachers' acceptance on mobile technologies in the classrooms is changing from a negative attitude towards traditional ICT into a more positive attitude towards media tablets [20].

As any new technology, media tablets do not lead to a better or worse practice, but the adoption of new technology matters and can lead to different metamorphoses and situated actions ([43], [56]). "Technology will probably not change what it takes to learn (…) but it may change how the process of learning is facilitated" [31]. The adoption of new technology in education affects existing teaching practices. It could be that media tablets serve as substitutes for textbooks and laptops or the teachers create new designs for cooperative learning [21].

In three studies of Danish classrooms, this paper aims to explore teaching practices enhanced by media tablets. Mobile technologies, e.g. media tablets, might be adjusted to the existing teaching practice or a re-design is required. When using technology, different elements, for example teaching objectives, learning activities and assessments, require a reflection, a new balance, and a new adjustment in what could be called a new form of "constructive alignment" [3] in which the elements fit to each other to support student learning. A constructive alignment is like a house with building blocks or pieces of a bigger puzzle that fits with the other pieces. The model of digital didactical designs [22] is one possible approach to study the complexity of teaching as social practice. To plan teaching and to do it in practice is a matter of coordination. We demonstrate the ecological complexity from a close ethnographical study supported by in-depth interviews and an online survey.

The paper reveals a gap between the digital didactical design *thinking* (what the teachers wish for) and the application of the designs in social *practices* – especially the increasing complexity and breakdowns that teachers have to deal with.

2. THEORETICAL PERSPECTIVE

Prior research on ICT, mobile technology and media tablets in education reports that the use of mobile devices improved student engagement and the achievement of learning [41], [54], [55], [50]. In 2010, Melhuish & Falloon's study [40] show that media tablets are useful for a) utilizing and creating content in a collaborative, interactive way [19], b) it is useful for student-centered activities [37], [44] and c) the devices improve teaching practices [9].

International research on mobile technology in education reveals that such devices create a new quality of online presence and open access to information [53] while sitting in the classroom [21], useful for user-generated contexts [45], and can change the ownership and power relations [58] towards learner-centered concepts [37]. Mobile technology potentially fosters student creativity [4] and student collaboration [5].

Highly relevant is whether the devices are integrated into the pedagogical design or not [39]. Educational technologies can have implications ranging from being mere substitutes with only limited effects, up to completely redefining the pedagogy [47]. A focus on tools alone cannot explain the emergence of new teaching designs and "is hard to convert into a pedagogy for teaching and learning since tools are always specific to tasks" [60], p. 155.

Studies on integrating technology, pedagogical and content/subject knowledge by teachers, known as TPCK models, show how these dimensions affect each other [28]. This points toward a lack of the aforementioned existing studies on a mobile learning focus. They focus on micro levels of learning from a learner's perspective; they neglect that teaching is also a *design project* developed and carried by teachers. The discourse surrounding TPCK is in our view largely blackboxing how teachers appropriate, coordinate and collaborate through educational technology at the level of *practice* [29]. Still under-explored and under-researched is how the new situation of co-located spaces, created through the use of media tablets, affects the teacher's practice for enabling learning.

In our research, we study the integration of mobile technology in teaching practices in co-located settings; where media tablets and teaching spaces merged together to new expanded communication spaces. We define teaching practices as the creation and doing of sociotechnical-pedagogical processes in classrooms.

2.1 What is a "design" in teaching practices?

The word 'design' focuses on specific actions and parts of activities by the teachers in schools. Design is the act of giving a form; the act of modeling the teaching practices by shaping a focus and key points. A design focuses on certain elements but does not take all of the reality into consideration. A design has both a planned component and an operative doing – it is process and product at once. The teachers design teaching activities for enabling students' learning. We call these didactical designs. The word Didaktik (didactics) comes from a Greek term that means the theory of teaching. The European approach of Didaktik does not only include the methods of 'how to' teach, but also embraces the question of 'what to' learn (curriculum and content), 'why', 'when/where', and in what kinds of situations.

A digital didactical design is a design that focuses on fostering students' learning, in particular technology- and tablet-enhanced learning. It involves a formulation of teaching objectives by the teachers and the plan for achieving those objectives by creating learning activities for students. It also includes forms of process-based assessment, especially guided reflections in order to enable student development. The enablement of learning is the central concept. Teachers can enable learning by applying different instructions that help to increase the likelihood that learning really takes place [61]. Following the concept of "informed choices" [42], the approach of digital didactical designs is an attempt to make the relation between design, education and technology visible [8].

2.2 Digital Didactical Design approach

The term Digital Didactical Design draws inspiration from the European concept of Didaktik [27] – the "content-student-teacher" relation. It is enhanced by a digital didactical design grounded on different concepts ([12], [18], [12]) that stress the differences of teaching activities and learning activities. This view on didactics, activities *and* design puts teaching and learning into a new light. Learning is not only a cognitive effort and teaching is not only a tool to reach the cognitive dimension. Instead, teaching is rather an activity-driven design, and learning is an on-going activity of knowledge production instead of consumption. An elaborated example of "activity designs for learning" is published in [16], which shows that designing teaching and learning needs a "multimodal perspective" [52]. A digital didactical design includes different design elements and their relations. In an ideal world, a teacher does design and shape these elements below:

1. Teaching objectives (and expected learning outcomes).
2. Forms of learning activities in order to foster the intended learning outcomes.
3. Process-based feedback and assessment (peer-reflections, teacher's feedback, self-assessment) [2] [24].
4. Social relations and dynamics of roles [23].
5. Integration of technology (e.g. media tablets).

The teacher constructively aligns these elements to support learning ([3], [49]); see the middle layer in Figure 1 (on next page). The assumption is that the better these five elements align to each other, the higher the likelihood that the students really learn. In our research, we study how the teachers *design* such digital didactical designs for media-tablet learning. Are the teachers "'bowling alone" or do they create digital didactical designs in cooperation with each other? How do they coordinate and juggle the different design elements? What do the teachers design (what not), how and why? We studied the choices and the design rationales the teachers made, and it became clear how complex the situation is for the teachers.

2.3 Complexity and Improvisation

The integration of mobile technologies and media tablets in teaching practice is more complex than it seems. Koehler et al. [28] show that the interrelation of content, technical and pedagogical knowledge creates different types of knowledge that are important when teaching with ICT. Loveless [33] illustrates by the example of primary schools how the co-evolutionary development of subject knowledge and didactics needs the support of "improvisation". Media tablets enable student collaboration in classrooms and monitor class activities in hitherto unseen ways. However, such new modes of activity can produce counterintuitive developments on the classroom level in what Grudin [13] called "the breakdown of intuitive decision-making". The complexity of utilizing ICT for education is also studied by Kirschner and Davis [26], which reveals rubrics of how technology should be used and integrated in training programs for teachers.

The requirement for teachers today is not only to use technologies, it is also to design competence development, learning activities, social roles and assessment, together with the integration of new technologies. The complexity increases substantially. It is not enough to design teaching as content delivery (see Figure 1, the inner layer). Teachers have an increasing toolbox of didactical means to choose between, but these tools are not alternatives to each other. They may be used in concert and orchestration, which is, on the other hand, a driver of complexity. In addition, the teachers' performances are increasingly compared to the outside world, see Figure 1, the outer layer (e.g. the Danish schools have recently been under tremendous pressure in popular media because they are perceived as loosing out against Chinese schools). Thirdly, schools are increasingly competing, and the pressure on both management and pedagogues to be innovative, is increasing. The innovator has to consider how his innovation is perceived from the viewpoint of different stakeholders like school management, parents, students, and colleagues ([51], [48]).

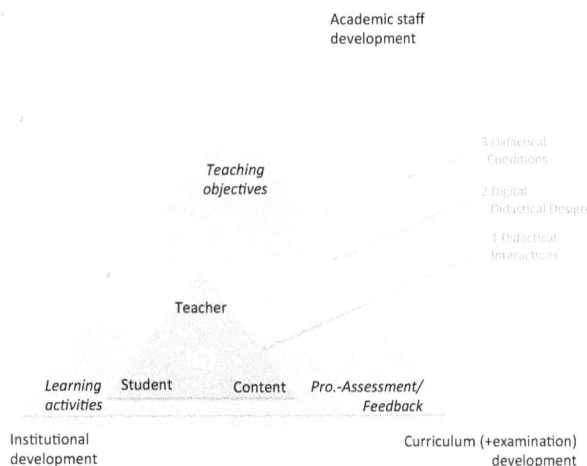

Figure 1. The three layers of education affect each other (influenced by innovation such as technology).

This adds to a setting that has arguably always been complex. Learning and development arises from a number of actions and operations on the micro level [32], and is the reason for why there is such a large research field on the learning sciences that the relationship between these micro levels are complex and difficult to disentangle.

In sum, when we refer to complexity, we refer to it on the middle layer (Figure 1) of teacher and student activities as well as to the fact that innovation of learning activities often takes place in an open system outside the classroom.

We formulate it like this:

Complexity in the classroom is constituted by a multitude of choices for the individual change agent, where some of the choices are not known, and it is a complexity that is mediated by the observation and feedback of a community outside of the learning activity.

3. RESEARCH METHODS

The research study took place in Danish K-9 schools from fall 2012 to winter 2013. The cases did not use the same methods. We provide an overview below.

The different methods were related to the timeline of the schools' adoption of the devices and this paper aimed to combine the varied approaches in a fruitful manner. The different methods followed the approach of triangulation to establish the validity of the qualitative study [14]; data triangulation (different sources and stakeholders), methodological triangulation (different methods), investigator triangulation (different researchers in the same field), environmental triangulation (different locations, different times).

Case I was design-driven, employing a future workshop (see 3.1 for details). In case II, the researchers applied a qualitative, ethnographical approach for exploring the use of mobile technology in classrooms, in particular to understand the choices by the teachers, and how they design teaching activities for fostering students' learning in co-located settings. The respondent selection was based on voluntary sampling [10] and included those classrooms where teachers agreed voluntarily to be part of the research and to be observed and interviewed. We further analysed teaching situations in which the media tablets were adjusted to several different learning objectives and activities. For further methodological details, read 3.1 for case I, read 3.2 for case II, and 3.3 for Case III. Case III took a mixed methods approach and was part of a bigger study with classroom observations.

3.1 Description of Case I

This case took place at a small primary and lower secondary school of Mou in Northern Jutland, Denmark in October 2012. The case was a student-led semester-project, which aimed to envision design principles that could help to facilitate collaborative learning. To achieve this, a future workshop was conducted with 7 teachers in October 2012 [35]. The workshop included three phases: critique, fantasy, and implementation [25]. The purpose of the future workshop was to support the teachers to externalize the experiences that they made with the use of media tablets in their teachings. In the *critique phase* the teachers discussed the media tablet as a functional learning tool. In the *fantasy phase*, it helped them to visioning and discussing solutions to the critiques they created during the first phase (e.g. how software incompatibility issues could be resolved by hiring a tablet supervisor on the school). The teachers retained their knowledge by drawing the situations they discussed in the two first phases. Then, the teachers used their externalized knowledge in order to form strategies for implementing them into their classroom teachings [36]. To ensure a steady retention of the teachers' externalization, the future workshop progressed through the utilization of inspiration cards [15]. The inspiration cards were divided into three categories: Technology, Domain and Action. The technology cards represented all types of technologies – not just the digital kind. The domain cards represented information on the domains in which the given technologies were physically present, e.g. "The Classroom" or "Common Areas". The action cards were familiar to the domain cards but focused more specifically on the actions and the utterances that were directly connected to the use of technologies in the domains. The use of inspiration cards ensured both facilitation of discussion amongst the teachers, and documentation of their externalisations (Figure 2). The inspiration cards also allowed a range of flexibility and creativity during the discussions, since the different combinations of the cards could take the discussion in different directions and possibly uncover valuable tacit knowledge [35]. The result of the future workshop was roughly three hours of teacher-teacher discussion about the praxis with media tablets in teaching.

Figure 2. Inspirations cards and drawings ensured retention of externalizations on the future workshop.

In order to process this data we used a general inductive approach to label and categorize through open coding and abstraction [11]. Open coding involved reading through the transcripts several times whilst applying headings that would describe the content of sections of text. The headings were then put into separate coding sheets in which they were placed under higher order categories. This effectively resulted in a level of abstraction that made it possible to describe what each category represented. The result of this process was 37 labels across three generic categories (Table 1). The labels refer to topics and situations of designing teaching in each of their respective generic categories. By describing these generic categories, we describe our findings.

Table 1. Generic categories and their labels.

Praxis with tablets	Problems	Dreams / visions
- Compatibility. - Hardware limitations. - Learning by doing. - Long learning curve. - The younger the more teacher control. - Apps with rewards. - Administrator rights. - Fragile hardware. - Writing on a tablet. - Game narration. - Overhead backup. - Creation. - Software quality. - Tablet as reward. - Extra-curricular activity.	- Expensive. - Pupils guess and remember. - Reward can become an issue. - Ability to skip tasks can be problematic. - Outdated software. - Internet issues.	- Internet based. - Using the tablet as a remote. - Tablets for all. - Knowledge sharing. - Shared-area for learning. - Immersion. - Parental involvement. - Teacher training. - A tablet supervisor. - Total access. - The tablet lesson. - Replace all the books. - Replace paper. - Inclusion. - Teacher supervision in app. - An app that provides all the needed shortcuts.

3.2 Description of Case II

This case took place in March 2013 at the primary and lower secondary school of of Gug in Northern Jutland, Denmark. In 2012, the school decided to buy iPads for teachers and students. All 62 teachers were given the opportunity to receive a media tablet on behalf of the school if they attended eight teaching courses about the iPad, which they all accepted. The case was a student-led semester-project, which studied how the media tablet was used in the complex ecology that constitute classroom teaching, and more specifically, situations in which the media tablet became a teaching tool and/or learning device [36] (Fig. 3).

Figure 3. Young students working with media tablets.

A close scope ethnographic study was performed in a class of 20 students at the age of 6-7 with two teachers involved. The form was participant observation with the roles of the observers being openly recognised to all involved as researchers [46]. The observers followed the class in the subjects of native language and math lessons. The study lasted 18 hours in total. The observers used field notes along with pictures and videos during observations. Small semi-structured post interviews were conducted with the teachers after each lesson [30].

First, the data was processed by identifying patterns as singularities, regularities, and variations [46]. These patterns, that were identified across different phases of the observed lessons, were organized in "settings" relating to the observed activity with the media tablets, undertaken by the class, e.g. students solving math puzzles with the media tablet [36].

Each setting was then subjected to a second analysis with the Human-Artefact Model (HAM), an activity theory based thinking tool, drawing upon Leontiev's hierarchies of activity to divide user activity into layers according to the users perceptual orientation within the use situation [7]. The creation of each individual HAM model was done by arranging the data in different categories, according to the layer of the activity addressed within the data. The data analysis involved five steps:

1. Identifying the user(s) activity and the goal(s) of the user(s) in the specific use situation.

2. Forming a hypothesis regarding the motivation governing the user activity.

3. Identifying handling and learned aspects within the data.

4. Identifying elements of adaption in the data.

5. Identifying tensions within the different layers of the user activities and the relation to the contextual setting [7].

This analysis provided a different perspective in relation to the tensions in the handling of the media tablets on a user-device level, especially how this tension evolves into breakdowns, as well as reasons for implementing recovery strategies and learning situations, as the result of interactions between human(s) and artefact that become too complex to handle [7].

3.3 Description of Case III

The case III took place at the municipality of Odder in Denmark; the main survey was conducted in September 2013. The community implemented iPads for all their 7 schools; ca. 170 teachers and 2,000 students from preschool class to year 9 (K-9) got media tablets. The students got the tablets in January 2012. Instead of using new laptops, the politicians in Odder decided to use iPads. The headteachers and the local department of the teachers union were consulted to make sure that the parties agreed. We applied an explorative qualitative approach with mixed methods, particularly a) classroom observations, b) teacher interviews and school visits (usually 1 school per day), and c) online questionnaires and meetings with head teachers as part of a larger study about media tablets and Nordic countries didactics (Denmark, Sweden, Finland).

a) 24 classroom observations (45-90 mins. each) and interviews with the teachers (approx. 60 mins. each) were conducted in six schools in April 2012, August 2012 and August 2013, all based on a voluntary and purposeful sampling [10]; 7 male teachers and 17 female teachers. The teaching subjects comprised Native Language (Danish), Math, English, Art, Music, Chemistry and Physics. The classes ranged from preschool class to 9th grade with different class sizes of 10 to 27 students (a mix of male and female students). Two to five researchers conducted the classroom observations. With the teachers' permission, they took notes, photos and made video recordings. The classroom observations were guided by the theoretical model of the Digital Didactical Design, including teaching aims, learning activities, forms of process-based feedback and assessment, and the degree of technology integration, the linking of teaching and learning in the practice.

b) The interviews were conducted by a total of three researchers and audio recorded. The interview guide was divided into five parts and contained 12 questions. Data from the observations and interviews were first analyzed according to each classroom and then open coded ([1], [6]). For the data analysis we created a scheme adopted from the theoretical framework of Digital Didactical Design. The aim was to make the digital didactical design for each classroom visible. The data were coming from the observations and the interviewed teachers of the classroom. We analyzed the teachers' didactical design practice including the integration of the tablet-use according to the extent of usage: a low extent (tablet as pen and paper substitute), a medium extent (tablet as laptop substitute) and a high extent (a new multimodal device). The analyzed data were checked by content validation and peer-review validation, where at least three researchers checked the analysis of the data. Such a *communicative* validation was done by using intersubjective methods, which is important to proof the quality of the research outcomes [1].

c) The online survey, which regarded all teachers, comprised 22 items; closed questions on the teaching practice using media tablets. It was conducted in September 2013 and pre-tested in the summer of 2013. From a total of 170 teachers in the Odder schools, the online survey was answered by n=148 teachers from all seven schools in the municipality, who started to use media tablets in January 2012. Some of the teachers skipped some questions. 85 were completed; response rate was 50.2 percent, 30% male and 70% female teachers. The teaching practice ranged from less than 1 year to 35 years (mean = 17-18 years; median: 16-17 years, standard-dev. 11). The results from the observations, the interviews, and the online survey, were presented and discussed with all of the teachers, see Fig. 4.

Figure 4. Discussing the results with the teachers.

4. FINDINGS

First, we present the results of the teachers' visions, and then we present our findings from the studying of the teachers' design practice.

4.1 Case I: Visions of the Teachers

Table 1 (section 3.1) gives an overview about the clustered teachers' expression under "dreams/visions". The ideas, that the teachers expressed mostly, referred to the media tablet as a complexity-reducing medium with greater interconnectivity. One cognitive conception of the teachers is that the media tablet could potentially replace all books and whatever paperwork the teachers usually have to deal with:

"FWT1 – 1:29:10: No, but it would be fine if it could replace all the books, because a bag like this gets quite heavy."

"FWT1 – 1:44:54: And then we must replace the books."

"FWT2 – 48:54: And that is also the explanation as to why we do not just discard all those damn books and only use apps."

The teachers seem to know the technical possibilities, but they are also quite aware that there are obstacles in the way of ever achieving such paperless practice. They all agree that it would be most beneficial if everyone had a media tablet each, because otherwise the paperless idea would fall short. In connection to the idea about paperless practice, the teachers dream about a practice that draws on the benefits of interconnectivity:

"FWT1 – 1:09:46: Well, regarding that app, it would be nice if you could sit and work in it, and then the next time it was able to find a network out here on the countryside, then it would automatically connect. Everything that you would have worked on would still be saved and it would not have been in vain. And the kids would not feel frustrated because their work suddenly did not look like it did when they were working on it here at the school."

"FWT2 – 1:00:00: [...] there you can create them and you can create their email addresses, which means that their results will automatically be sent to you. And then I can sit at home and watch that 'Patrick' has made these and those math-equations and he has progressed like this and so on."

The teachers understand that, in a perfect world, it would be possible to have everyone connected to the Internet. They explain their dream as a dream of total access, in which interconnectivity allows them to ensure greater inclusion, not only of students, but also of parents. They are not dreaming about a particular app to include all functions, but rather a diverse eco-system of apps that all interconnect to allow for greater monitoring and retention, as well as a faster way to plan curriculum and spend more time teaching than planning. A very low-practical wish is for example the ability to use the media tablet as a remote control, allowing the teacher to be physically positioned anywhere in the domain. The dream of interconnectivity derives from bitter experiences with software and hardware incompatibility issues, administrator rights and out-dated software, all of which causes common activity breakdowns that result in media aiding complexity instead of reducing it. The teachers realize that these are issues that need to be efficiently addressed in order for their praxis to become less complex. The teachers see the Internet and the promise of a web-based ecosystem of apps that allows for greater interconnectivity as a dream solution that could remove most of these issues.

4.2 Case II: Breakdowns

Table 1 (section 3.1) gives an overview of the clustered teachers' expression labelled as "problems". The teachers had concerns regarding the technology such as "expensive" and "internet issues". On the other hand they expressed concerns with regard how the pupils would use the tablet, "pupils guess and remember" and "the ability to skip tasks can be problematic" when using the tablet in the classroom. In detail, case II aims to demonstrate the *complexity* of the artefact ecology of a classroom, from a close ethnographical study. During the observational period, several incidents of unforeseen interaction issues were documented, that developed from simple obstacles for the shared activity of the class, to causing breakdowns in the workflow within the classroom, hereby resulting in either the teacher revising her teaching strategy and students losing focus, braking away and engaging in wild fire activity [36].

In two specific settings, we observed how the teacher introduced what could be considered as secondary artifacts to support her activity of directing the class members towards a specific outcome. In both cases, the motive of the teacher was to manage the class activity by breaking it into a chain of separate actions that could be seen and copied by the students.

A) This setting is based on observations from two occasions, where the teacher extended the functionality of the media tablet by connecting it to a projector. In the first instance, this was done in order to guide the pupils through the task of installing an application on the tablet, and later to move an icon to the front page of the media tablet. In both cases, the teacher introduces her tablet into the teaching situation as an illustrative tool, allowing her to direct the activity of the class as a whole, by breaking a complex activity into smaller manageable sub goals through visualizations of her activity. When functional, the addition of the projector enabled her to successfully maintain the individual student's attention focused on the different interactive aspects of the downloading process, by allowing the students to monitor and mirror her actions when in doubt. During the second instance, we experienced how the failure of the secondary artifact (projector) ended up causing a significant breakdown in the teacher's activity, while complicating her possibilities of recovering. The teacher made several attempts to master the breakdown in one device (projector), only to experience another breakdown (Internet connection failed), and she eventually had to abandon her initial goal, and move on to a different activity in the classroom.

B) During the second setting, the students were instructed to login to "*infuse learning*" – an online teaching application that allows the teacher to create interactive quizzes and monitor the progress of the individual pupils in real time on her own media tablet via a special teacher dashboard application. Instructions consisted of a URL, written on the blackboard for the pupils to copy into the media tablets Internet browser. We observed how the login-procedure caused a sudden rise in the complexity of the situation, resulting in several students experiencing tensions and breakdowns in their activity. Judging from the insights gathered in the previous project (on the future workshop), few teachers assumed that the simple task of login would cause significant problems for teachers and affect the whole class. The teacher had to troubleshoot several pupils, who were unable to recover from their breakdowns during this activity. The breakdowns were usually simple spelling errors that might have occurred because the students had to shift their attention between the blackboard and their media tablets. Furthermore, students that were able to overcome the obstacle on their own had to wait for everyone to log in before they were allowed to complete the curriculum. Some of those who were already logged in and who were just waiting for everyone else to get help from the teacher, ended up wasting the time by talking, fooling around and wrestling, which actually did not seem to be a disturbance to anyone, including the teacher, because she was busy helping the other students recover from their breakdowns.

By analyzing both settings through the HAM analysis model, it became clear that a sudden rise in the complexity caused the students to shift their operational orientation towards the breakdowns, hereby losing their focus on the current task at hand. In both cases, the underlying cause of the breakdowns could be identified as a rise in tension between the users adapted strategy for creating desired outcomes (goals), their chosen path of action (handling), and their ability to adapt these to the conditions offered by the tablet, e.g. students have to switch the focus to and from the blackboard during the login procedure in setting B. The tension caused when encountering obstacles, would eventually bring students to a point where they had to reevaluate their activity on a procedural level in order to keep up, creating grounds for disturbances in the classroom. We equally observed that, once all the students were logged in to infuse learning, the teacher regained control of the classroom. The complexity had been reduced, and the students had no trouble navigating the system once they were past the login-screen. The added functionalities in the system did not add noticeably to the complexity of the teaching situation.

Especially in setting A it becomes visible how the extensions such as a projector, adds to the potential of a sudden rise in complexity, due to a break in the chain of connected devices. From the HAM analysis, it becomes apparent how an unanticipated rise in complexity, due to a breakdown, impacts the margin of maneuver of the teacher by significantly reducing her possibilities of facilitating the shared activity of the class.

One significant post analysis finding was how the inclusion of the media tablets, when interpreted through the complexity lens, becomes a double-edged sword, with one side relating to the complexity found within the artifact, and the other relating to the addition of further complexity of the classroom ecology itself. From a student perspective, the media tablet adds a form of inner complexity, by offering the students multiple paths to follow in the student-tablet situation. This inner complexity causes tensions for the students, when tasks become too complex, like for instance, navigating through a serious breakdown. From a teacher's perspective, the inclusion of the tablet opens new possibilities in regards to facilitating an ongoing exchanging and transformation of material between the teacher and the students. We see how an unforeseen rise in complexity means the teacher's attention is diverted from the goal fulfillment towards the operational aspects of engaging with the technology, with the consequence, that the teacher-student-exchange of material comes to a halt. From a teacher perspective, the challenge to successfully integrating the tablet into her teaching practice rests on her ability to manipulate the device into states, in which the tablet takes on the role as a functional organ. The criteria for a successful use therefore becomes a question of the tablet supporting the teacher in framing the activities of the class community on a meta level, while equally facilitating learning on a one-to-one basis through e.g. visualizations.

The cases show how the implementation of media tablets into the classroom means that the teacher's role takes a leap in the direction of a didactical designer. The teacher creates a sociotechnical-pedagogical scenario and prototype for tablet-enhanced teaching and learning, put these into practice, improvise during practice, manipulate the technology for their needs, and change the scenario for the next time. The teaching practice moved away from a common routine and turned into a *design project*.

4.3 Case III: Teachers are Jongleurs

The findings of case III support the qualitative data from cases I and II. It shows the complexity of designing teaching practices where the tablet integration is aligned to the teaching and learning activities. In addition, case III shows in what domains the teachers struggle while carrying out such a digital didactical design in practice.

The survey findings of case III show that the teachers have a strong belief that media tablets are useful to support learning. The majority of the teachers (around 80%; Q18) believe that media tablets are able to improve teaching practice and student learning. This confirms a recent study on technology belief [20], which showed that the acceptance on media tablets is increasing. Usually the majority of the teachers show a weak acceptance of computing in education but with the invention of the media tablet, the acceptance rates have increased significantly. The amount of teachers who do belief in the tablets is high, but how many really do re-align their teaching practices?

Around half of the teachers actively integrate the media tablets in learning activities (they can give specific examples about innovative usage, Q2). This is also supported by our classroom observations where 16 of 24 cases are constructively aligned designs to support tablet-enhanced learning; 8 cases are not, which means that they did not re-design their teaching practices. Around 40% of the teachers want to integrate media tablets better than they do but do not know exactly how to do it and around 10% do not believe in tablets, and therefore do not use them in their classrooms (Q1, Q2, Q4, Q6). The SAMR model [47] is useful to understand the level of technology use from low to high extent of ICT-integration merging into a digital didactical design:

- **S**ubstitution: "Technology is used as a direct substitute for what you might do already, with no functional change" – low extent of tablet use
- **A**ugmentation: "Technology is a direct substitute, but there is functional improvement over what you did without the technology" – low-medium extent of media tablet use
- **M**odification: "Technology allows you to significantly redesign the task" – high-medium extent of tablet use
- **R**edefinition: "Technology allows you to do what was previously not possible" – high extent of tablet use

Whereas 11 of 24 in-depth observed classrooms illustrate that the teachers integrated the tablet into the didactical design of teaching

and learning in high extent (R=11; M=5), the other 8 classrooms did integrate the media tablets in a medium or low level (A=5; S=3).

The potential of integrating media tablets into classrooms can be seen in the teachers' responses towards collaboration, didactical integration, and different functionalities for student learning activities:

- Around 35% of the teachers say that they include the media tablets into teaching and learning truthfully, "*I can give you some examples of how I design teaching and learning in a way that the tablets support collaboration among my students*" (Q1). Whereas, around 55% think media tablets are useful but do not use them for student collaboration. The other teachers say that such devices have no effects (4%) or "*they are not good for collaboration*" (6%).

- The teachers use the tablets in a wide range of different activities for meaningful learning (Q3); "*my students use the iPads for...*" creating presentations, writing texts, reading, recording and editing videos, note-taking (around 80% each), creating and editing images, controlling the interactive whiteboard (tablet as remote control), recording/editing audio files (around 60% each), listening to audio books, creating digital stories, and sharing/demonstrating their knowledge (50% each). The teachers say that they do not use the media tablet as a student response system and do not use it for online conferences.

- 80% of the teachers say the students use the media tablets for presenting their learning outcomes in a new form (Q5); to some extent (52%) and to a large extent (29%).

The teachers mention that they experience some social changes over the last two years from since they started using media tablets. Almost 90% said that the teachers role was changing – especially the planning of activities; "*The way I plan the activities on the classroom has changed*" and "*the way I act in the classroom*" (41%) (Q7). The teachers also perceive a change of human interaction since they use media tablets; the student-teacher-interaction changed in a useful way (76%, Q8) and student-student-interaction changed in a useful way (75%, Q9) these interaction forms have been assigned a positive change since the media tablet has been launched. The use of different multimodal resources increased (80%, Q13). The teachers say that this is the main difference to the traditional classroom. The majority says that there is a huge need on training for both technical issues but more importantly, training for digital didactical design thinking (80% Q12).

We followed some of the innovative teachers (33% in 2012/13) and aimed to understand how they handle the increase of complexity. From our in-depth-interviews, the data informs a kind of passion towards teaching and learning. Their teaching philosophy is based on activating the students' potential. The following quotes support this:

"*I want to set the knowledge of my students free.*"

"*I'm supporting learning by foster my pupils doing mistakes.*"

"*I tell my students: make mistakes, that's good.*"

"*I tell my students: be creative.*"

"*I want to challenge my students.*"

The innovative teachers use the media tablet like a "*booster*" to foster student learning. We wanted to know if the teachers thought the media tablet made a difference. This was interesting, because the schools had laptops before they purchased media tablets. All interviewee's said that they liked the tablets more than laptops. The problem with the laptops was that they were often out of energy, the software was not updated, or software bugs prevented them from working. One teacher said; *"You don't waste time like with the laptops where the batteries where out of energy or the software wasn't installed"*.

The teachers argued that the laptops wasted a lot of teaching time in classrooms whereas tablets reduced those problems. One innovative teacher said; *"Now, with the iPads, I have more time for my students"*. The interview data shows that for the teachers the media tablets differ from laptops in many aspects, but the most important difference is that different teachers made the following statements:

"The iPad works - you open it and it works."

"It's easy... my old father and mother use it too."

"It's mobile... pupils can bring it home."

"It isn't time consuming like the laptops."

"I have more time for my students for individual guiding."

"The students are equal now. All of them now have access to knowledge."

The quote; *"...my old father/mother use it too"* is very interesting. Some years ago, quotes like *"my young daughter/son uses the new technology"* was used. Since the young generations grow up with the new mobile technology, it seems to be normal that they are able to use it (it does not mean that they really can). Nowadays, it is a sign for 'easy-to-use' when the old generations, who never tried to use computers before, use them too. Making something easy to use is not only an individual usability issue; it also enables the limited resource of teacher attention to be focused on issues of collaboration rather on making up for bad usability.

The teachers also mentioned challenges. They observed that the students perceived tablets as a tool for playing and that they did not accept it as a *"working machine"* in the beginning of the project in 2012. Some teachers mentioned that this view changed after some weeks of using the tablets in the lessons. Others were afraid that the students did other things and that they did not focus on the assignments in the classroom. The media tablet is easy to use for chatting and using other forms of social media during class. For the teachers, it is not clear what the students do when they use the media tablet. The teachers asked themselves; *"Is the iPad for note-taking or are they using Facebook?"*. The majority of the interviewees argued that this problem of distraction had always been present, even before they started using tablets. Years ago, the students wrote letters on a piece of paper or just had oral chats. Contrary to common complaints, we did not find any support to the fear that media tablets increased complexity by bringing non-school social life into the classroom through social media.

One teacher mentioned another challenge:

"The biggest challenge for us teachers is to know when to shut off the iPads; when do we use iPads? When do we use other things?"

This quote makes clear that the implementation of new technology does not mean to banish other technologies, tools or materials. Instead of focusing on tablets only, a mix of different tools for different classes might be useful to enhance learning. It also reveals that the situation becomes complex for the teachers. The design of teaching gets more and more complex nowadays; from textbook

learning (one design element) to many different possibilities of enabling learning using different kinds of technologies, choosing between different online open resources, creating learning activities where the student becomes a pro-sumer, and creating guided reflections for collaborative learning. The teacher becomes a juggler (jongleur) of many different design elements.

Despite of cases I and II, which show the increase of complexity for teachers, the early-adopters in case III have a different viewpoint. They say that the media tablet has one advantage in comparison to other technologies like laptops and stationary computers: "There is no technology in there!" (the teacher who gave this statement pointed her finger to the media tablet). Of course, a media tablet is made of electronics and it is a purely technological device. However, with this quote, we understood the innovative teachers' point of view. They perceive the media tablet as a device that is easier to use than the complicated older PC programs. Years ago, technology in teaching was seen as being very complicated, but there has been a change with media tablets. The tablets *"just work"*. Therefore, to the innovative teachers, the media tablet is not perceived as being challenging in itself, but the complex interplay of different technologies, didactical designs, educational resources and the breakdowns that derives from these contextual elements becomes the challenges they are learning to navigate.

5. DISCUSSION AND CONCLUSION

In an empirical study about media tablets at Scandinavian schools, the research aim was to explore the teachers' strategies and their (re-)designs in the teaching practice of integrating new technology in the classrooms moving to a new practice of Digital Didactical Designing.

In this paper, we provided a multifaceted view into the use and consideration of tablet devices in the context of primary school settings. In many ways, the study redefines and reveals the nature of the classroom from the teacher being a simple tablet-enhanced instructor to one of handling both instruction and technical support. The paper highlighted the various ways in which teachers dealt with this complexity. Such co-located tablet-mediated communication spaces "require teachers to undertake more complex pedagogical reasoning than before in their planning and teaching" [59]. While this is a manner that runs incongruent to teacher perceptions of classroom possibilities with tablets, our study provides evidence that these perceptions are markedly different with tablets as the technological intervention than with other tools (e.g., laptops).

Moreover, the model of the classroom and interactions between teachers and students is *in constant motion*, swayed by the expectations and perceived potential of digital technologies and grounded by the realities of the digital technologies in use. The teacher in co-located spaces becomes a juggler and a digital didactical designer; the teaching practice moves away from a common routine activity and turns into a *design project*.

The teacher creates sociotechnical-pedagogical scenarios and prototype for tablet-enhanced teaching and learning, put these into practice, improvise during practice, manipulate the technology for their needs, and change the scenario for the next time. The issue is not merely to look at some teacher strategy and see if pedagogy, technology and content (as in TPCK) is connected, but to be attentive towards how the teachers combine these *in situ*.

When social complexity through technology integration rises, one coping strategy is to search for a reduction of complexity. For the teachers, the media tablets and their apps are targets for a projection of that wish for reducing complexity, which is clearly visible in our workshops, classroom observations, and interviews. Teachers tend to assign *interconnectivity* as their wish of a solution.

The magic silver bullet is the teachers' wish and belief that interconnectivity can help solve many of their problems on the floor. First, the teachers are able to envision the benefits of an interconnected praxis in which media tablets are justified through their mobile traits. Secondly, they establish this vision because of their breakdown experiences of media tablets aiding complexity instead of reducing it. The teachers' dream of interconnectivity comprises the following:

• Open or total access, in which interconnectivity allows them to ensure greater inclusion, not only of students, but also of parents.

• They are not dreaming about a particular app to include all functions, but rather a diverse eco-system of apps that all interconnect to allow for greater monitoring and retention, as well as a faster way to plan curriculum and spend more time teaching than planning.

The teachers share a common understanding in their dream of an interconnected praxis that prevents common activity breakdowns, regardless of teaching subject. Such an interconnected praxis would for example be useful for didactical designs and would remove the need to extend the functionality of the media tablet in order to teach. Sufficient reduction of breakdowns is a prerequisite for collaboration that is sometimes being overlooked in CSCW research.

The teachers exhibit a rich understanding of the variety and vastness of technological possibilities. They are not thinking about media tablets as technology per se, but its interrelation with content and pedagogy (new wicked forms of digital didactical designs), and they dream about realizing the potential which technology has created for this potential. We speculate that it is because *their* reality has proven that the present praxis with media tablets is prone to increase complexity.

The general promise that the use of technology helps to 'make life easier' and reduces complexity was not what the teachers experienced. Instead, the teachers experience breakdowns, which they must learn how to navigate before the media tablets will aid in the reduction of complexity and reach a state in which they take part in the classroom ecology as functional organs. The media tablet is thought of as a tool, but is not easily functional as such, in Leontiev's [32] terms, a "functional organ" where the users do not experience the technology, but perceives it as an integrated extension of their thoughts and bodies.

The study has some limitations through its heterogeneous methods across the cases, trading rigorous inter-case comparability for inter-method triangulation. Despite different types of data, there is basis for the importance of interconnectivity, whose vastness we try to describe. However, we must remain open for the possibility that there are sectors in Scandinavian schools where media tablets are experienced differently. For instance, even if there is much talk of the "New Nordic School", there may be strong national differences between media tablet use in Denmark and the other Scandinavian countries, as educational systems sometimes become quite nationally idiosyncratic. Furthermore, we have not focused our observations on beforehand on "interconnectivity". Close studies on whether and how teachers use it as a concept in their didactic practice would add to this study.

We studied how the innovative teachers handle the increasing complexity. These explorative characteristics are not seen in the previous empirically based literature of media tablets. We learned that they have the same problems and plenty of breakdowns during the teaching practices in classrooms – not only technical problems, but also design challenges related to teaching aims, learning activities and assessment. The difference is that the innovative teachers see themselves as *jongleurs* of different didactical and technical elements; they test their ideas and try them during the teaching practice. When they have technical problems they ask their students to help them. They do not see themselves as experts of everything; they know that sometimes their students have the knowledge to solve a breakdown.

Our data reminds us of the fact that there will be plenty of breakdowns already in the social situation of a classroom itself. Students will make errors, forget their material, and so on. In the Scandinavian classroom there is a tradition of relative "frihed under ansvar" (it means teaching within a degree of freedom with responsibility), and this will also lead to some breakdowns of disciplinary nature. So any situation where complexity is successfully managed is not characterized of smooth flow of conflict-free activity. Rather, it will be characterised by activity where breakdowns of collective activity occur, which are then reinstated or even reconstructed, either by the teacher, by the students, or in combination. We have demonstrated how this complexity increases when media tablets are used in classroom teaching.

6. ACKNOWLEDGMENTS

We are indebted to Marianne Georgsen, who commented on the paper in an early version and we are very grateful to the reviewers who helped to improve the takeaway message. Many thanks go to the PhD students, Lars Norqvist and Andreas Olsson for their great research participation and critical-constructive reflections in the cases of Odder/DK. We are deeply grateful and want to thank the participating schools of Mou and Gug in Northern Jutland in Denmark as well as the school, teachers and pupils in the municipality of Odder in Denmark. Lise Gammelby always did and does support the research. Tusen tak!

7. REFERENCES

[1] Bauer, M. and Gaskell, G. 2000. Qualitative Researching with text, image and sound. London: Sage.

[2] Bergström, P. 2012. Designing for the Unknown. Didactical Design for Process-based Assessment in Technology-Rich Learning Environments. Umeå University Press.

[3] Biggs, J. and Tang, C. 2007. *Teaching for Quality Learning at University*. 3rd, New York.

[4] Buchem, I., Jahnke, I. and Pachler, N. 2013. Guest editorial preface. In. Special Issue on Mobile Learning and Creativity. In. International Journal of Mobile and Blended Learning. July-Sept 2013, Vol 5., No. 3.

[5] Buchem, I., Cochrane, T., Gordon, A., and Keegan, H. 2012. M-Learning 2.0: The potential and challenges of collaborative mobile learning in participatory curriculum development. In *Proceedings of the IADIS Mobile Learning Conference 2012*, Berlin, Germany.

[6] Bryman, A. 2008. *Social research methods* (Third Edition). New York: Oxford University Press.

[7] Bødker, S. and Klokmose, C. N. 2011. The Human–Artifact Model: An Activity Theoretical Approach to Artifact Ecologies. *Human–Computer Interaction, 26(4)*, 315–371. doi:10.1080/07370024.2011.626709

[8] Caputo, J. D. 1997. *Deconstruction in a Nutshell: A Conversation with Jacques Derrida*. New York: Fordham University Press.

[9] Chou, C.C., Block, L. and Jesness, R. 2012. A case study of mobile learning pilot project in K-12 schools. In *Journal of Educational Technology Development and Exchange*, 5(2), pp11-26.

[10] Cohen, L., Manion, L. and Morrison K. 2011. *Research methods in education*. 7th edition. New York: Routledge.

[11] Elo, S. and Kyngäs, H. 2008. The qualitative content analysis process. *Journal of Advanced Nursing, 62(1)*, 107–115.

[12] Fink, D. L. 2003. *Integrated Course Design*. Idea paper #42. Idea Center, Kansas.

[13] Grudin, J. 1994. Groupware and social dynamics: Eight challenges for developers. *Communications of the ACM*, 34, 93–105.

[14] Guion, L., Diehl, D. and McDonald, D. 2002. Triangulation: Establishing the Validity of Qualitative Studies. In: 4 pages. (FCS6014). Retrieved 24 March 2014 from http://edis.ifas.ufl.edu/fy394

[15] Halskov, K. and Dalsgaard, P. 2006. Inspiration Card Workshops. In *DIS 2006*. University Park, Pennsylvania, USA.

[16] Hauge, T. E. and Dolonen, J. 2012. Towards an Activity-Driven Design Method for Online Learning Resources. In A. D. Olofsson & O.J. Lindberg (Eds). *Informed Design of Educational Technologies in Higher Education: Enhanced Learning and Teaching*. Hershey: IGI Global, pp. 101-117.

[17] Henderson, S. and Yeow, J. 2012. iPad in Education: A Case Study of iPad Adoption and Use in a Primary School. In *System Science (HICSS)*, 2012, 45th Hawaii International Conference, pp.78-87. DOI: 10.1109/HICSS.2012.390.

[18] Hudson, B. 2008. A Didactical Design Perspective on Teacher Presence in an International Online Learning Community. *Journal of Research in Teacher Education*, 2008 Umeå University, Vol. 15, Issue 3-4, pp. 93-112.

[19] Hutchison, A., Beschorner, B., Schmidt-Crawford, D. 2012. Exploring the Use of the iPad for Literacy Learning in. *The Reading Teacher*. Vol 66, issue 1, pp. 15-23 DOI: 10.1002/TRTR.01090

[20] Ifenthaler, D. and Schweinbenz, V. 2013. The acceptance of Tablet-PCs in classroom instruction: The teachers' perspectives In *Computers in Human Behavior*, Vol 29. Issue 3, pp. 525-534.

[21] Jahnke, I., Bergström, P., Lindwall, K., Marell-Olsson, E., Olsson, A., Paulsson, F. and Vinnervik, P. 2012. Understanding, Reflecting and Designing Learning Spaces of Tomorrow. In: I. Arnedillo Sanchez & P. Isaias (Eds.). *Proceedings of IADIS Mobile Learning 2012*. Berlin, pp. 147-156.

[22] Jahnke, I. and Kumar, S. 2014. Digital Didactical Designs: Teachers' Integration of iPads for Learning-Centered Processes. In: *Journal of Digital Learning in Teacher Education*, Vol. 30, Issue 3. pp. 81-88. DOI:10.1080/21532974.2014.891876

[23] Jahnke, I. 2010. Dynamics of social roles in a knowledge management community. In *Computers in Human Behavior*, Vol. 26, DOI 10.1016/j.chb.2009.08.010.

[24] Jahnke, I., Ritterskamp, C. and Herrmann, T. 2005. Sociotechnical Roles for Sociotechnical Systems: a perspective from social and computer science. In: 2005 AAAi Fall Symposium, 8. Symposium: Roles, an interdisciplinary perspective. Arlington, Virgina. Washington DC, November 3-6, 2005.

[25] Jungk, R. and Müllert, N., 1987. Future Workshops - how to create desirable futures. London: the Institute for Social Inventions.

[26] Kirschner, P. and Davis, N. 2003. Pedagogic benchmarks for information and communications technology in teacher education, Journal *Technology, Pedagogy and Education*, 12:1, DOI:10.1080/14759390300200149, pp. 125-147.

[27] Klafki, W. 1963. *Studien zur Bildungstheorie und Didaktik*. Weinheim: Beltz.

[28] Koehler, M.J., Mishra P., and Yahya, K. 2007. Tracing the development of teacher knowledge in a design seminar: Integrating content, pedagogy and technology. *Computers & Education*, 49, pp. 740–762.

[29] Kuutti, K. 2013. "practice turn" and CSCW identity. In M. Korn, T. Colombino, & M. Lewkovicz (eds.) *Adjunct proceedings of ECSCW*. ECSCW'13. Paphos, Cyprus: Dept. of Computer Science, Aarhus University, pp. 39–45.

[30] Kvale, S., and Brinkmann, S. 2009. *InterView: introduktion til et håndværk* (2nd ed.). Kbh.: Hans Reitzel.

[31] Laurillard, D. 2008. Technology enhanced learning as a tool for pedagogical innovation. *Journal of Philosophy of Education, 42(3-4)*, 521-533.

[32] Leontiev, A. N. 1978. Activity, consciousness, and personality. Hillsdale: Prentice-Hall.

[33] Loveless, A. 2007. Preparing to teach with ICT: subject knowledge, Didaktik and improvisation, *Curriculum Journal, 18:4*, DOI:10.1080/09585170701687951, pp. 509-522.

[34] Lund, A. and Hauge, T. E. 2011. Designs for teaching and learning in technology-rich learning environments. *Nordic journal of digital literacy. (4)*, pp 258-272.

[35] Marchev, G., Rønn, L., Johansen, S., Nielsen, T. and Svendsen, N. 2012. *Designing for Participation: A Social Approach to Technology Enhanced Learning in the Classroom* (Semester project) (p. 72). Aalborg University. Retrieved from http://projekter.aau.dk/projekter/da/studentthesis/designing-for-participation(0c09df93-0ad2-4867-bb9e-185b09d84755).html.

[36] Marchev, G., Rønn, L., Johansen, S., Nielsen, T. and Svendsen, N. 2013. *Designing for Participation Part 2*: Studying the use of iPads by observing a classroom ecology (Semester project) (p. 88). Aalborg University.

[37] McCombs, S. and Liu, Y. 2011. Channeling the channel: Can iPad meet the needs of today's M-Learner. In *Proceedings of*

Society for Information Technology & Teacher Education (pp. 522-526). Chesapeake, VA.

[38] McCombs, B. 2000. Assessing the Role of Educational Technology in the Teaching and Learning Process: A Learner-Centered Perspective. In: The Secretary's Conference on Educational Technology: Measuring Impacts and Shaping the Future; Proceedings (Alexandria, VA, September1-12, 2000).

[39] McCormick, R. & Scrimshaw, P. 2001. Information and Communications Technology, Knowledge and Pedagogy. In. *Education, Communication and Information*, Vol. 1, No. 1, 2001, pp. 37-57

[40] Melhuish, K. & Falloon, G. 2010. Looking to the future: M-learning with the iPad. In *Computers in New Zealand Schools,* 22(3), 1-16.

[41] Ng, W. and Nicholas, H. 2009. Introducing pocket PC's in schools: Attitudes and beliefs in the first year. In *Computers & Education, (52)*, 470-480.

[42] Olofsson, A.D. and Lindberg, O. J. 2012. *Informed Design of Educational Technologies in Higher Education: Enhanced Learning and Teaching*, Hershey: IGI Global.

[43] Orlikowski, W. 1996. *Improvising Organizational Transformation over Time: A Situated Change Perspective.* Information Systems Research, 7/1, pp. 63-92.

[44] Ostashewski, N. & Reid, D. 2010. iPod, iPhone, and now iPad: The evolution of multimedia access in a mobile teaching context. In *Proceedings of World Conference on Educational Multimedia, Hypermedia and Telecommunications* 2010 (pp. 2862-2864). Chesapeake, VA: AACE.

[45] Pachler, N., Bachmair, B., & Cook, J. 2010. *Mobile learning: Structures, agency, practices*. New York, NY: Springer. doi:10.1007/978-1-4419-0585-7

[46] Pole, C. and Morrison, M. 2003. *Ethnography For Education*. England: Open University Press.

[47] Puentedura, R. 2014. SAMR model. Retrieved 20 May 2014 from https://sites.google.com/a/msad60.org/technology-is-learning/samr-model

[48] Qvortrup, L. 2001. *Skolen i et hyperkomplekst samfund. Uddannelse* "Fremtidens folkeskole"*, 2.

[49] Reeves, T. 2006. How do you know they learn? The importance of alignment in higher education. In: International Journal Learning Technology, Vol. 2, No. 4, 2006, pp. 294-309

[50] Roschelle, J., Penuel, W. R., Yarnall, L., Shechtman, N. and Tatar, D. 2005. Handheld tools that "informate" assessment of student learning in science. *Journal of Computer Assisted Learning, 21*(3) 190–203.

[51] Rutenbeck, J. 2006. *Bit by Bit by Bit: Hypercomplexity and Digital Media Studies.*

[52] Selander, S. and Kress, G. 2010. *Design för lärande - ett multimodalt perspektiv.* (Designing for learning - a multimodal approach). Norstedts.

[53] Sharples, M., McAndrew, P., Weller, M., Ferguson, R., FitzGerald, E., Hirst, T. and Gaved, M. 2013. *Innovating Pedagogy 2013:* Open University Innovation Report 2. Milton Keynes: The Open University.

[54] Song, Y. 2007. Educational uses of handheld devices: What are the consequences? *TechTrends: Linking Research and Practice to Improve Learning, 51*(5), 38-45.

[55] Staudt, C. 2005. Changing how we teach and learn with handheld computers. Thousand Oaks, CA: Corwin.

[56] Suchman, L. 1987. P*lans and Situated Actions: The Problem of Human-Machine Communication.* Cambridge Press.

[57] Thomas, D. R. 2006. A General Inductive Approach for Analyzing Qualitative Evaluation Data. *American Journal of Evaluation, 27*, 237–246.

[58] Traxler, J. 2011. Context in a wider context. Medienpädagogik. *Mobile Learning in Widening Contexts: Concepts and Cases,* 19.

[59] Webb, M. & Cox, M. 2004. A Review of Pedagogy Related to Information and Communications Technology. In: Technology, Pedagogy and Education, Vol. 13, No. 3, 2004, pp. 235-286.

[60] Wegerif, R. 2005. A dialogic understanding of the relationship between CSCL and teaching thinking skills. In Computer Supported Collaborative Learning (2006) 1, pp. 143–157. DOI 10.1007/s11412-006-6840-8

[61] Wildt, J. 2007. On the Way from Teaching to Learning by Competences as Learning Outcomes. In Pausits, A., & Pellert, A. (Eds.): *Higher Education Management and Development in Central, Southern and Eastern Europe*. Münster: Waxmann, pp. 115-123.

Community Code Engagements: Summer of Code & Hackathons for Community Building in Scientific Software

Erik H. Trainer, Chalalai Chaihirunkarn, Arun Kalyanasundaram, James D. Herbsleb
Institute for Software Research
Carnegie Mellon University
5000 Forbes Avenue, Pittsburgh, PA 15213
{etrainer, cchaihir, arunkaly, jdh}@cs.cmu.edu

ABSTRACT

Community code engagements — short-term, intensive software development events — are used by some scientific communities to create new software features and promote community building. But there is as yet little empirical support for their effectiveness. This paper presents a qualitative study of two types of community code engagements: Google Summer of Code (GSoC) and hackathons. We investigated the range of outcomes these engagements produce and the underlying practices that lead to these outcomes. In GSoC, the vision and experience of core members of the community influence project selection, and the intensive mentoring process facilitates creation of strong ties. Most GSoC projects result in stable features. The agenda setting phase of hackathons reveals high priority issues perceived by the community. Social events among the relatively large numbers of participants over brief engagements tend to create weak ties. Most hackathons result in prototypes rather than finished tools. We discuss themes and tradeoffs that suggest directions for future empirical work around designing community code engagements.

Categories and Subject Descriptors

H.5.3 [**Information Interfaces and Presentation (e.g., HCI)**]: Group and Organization Interfaces – *computer supported cooperative work, organizational design.*

Keywords

Community code engagements, Google Summer of Code (GSoC), hackathons, scientific software.

1. INTRODUCTION

How do you go from a small number of people with a common interest to a full-fledged community? The active body of research on this problem (e.g., [17, 30, 31]) is a testament to the role of community building in collaborative work practices.

Active communities are essential to the sustainability of software. Without a community around the code distribution, key issues of the software's future may not be addressed, e.g.: in 4 years' time, will the software still be available? Will it work? Will there be pool of participants with the right set of technical skills who can

respond to bug reports and feature requests? Successful communities find ways to get code contributions from their members and to incorporate successive generations of newcomers after the original developers leave [30].

There is an additional twist for software that scientists write. Although scientists are directly funded to produce new knowledge, they spend significant time searching for, using, and developing software that enables those results. The sustainability of scientific software – the ability to maintain the software in a state where scientists can understand, replicate, and extend prior reported results that depend on that software – has sometimes been an afterthought because scientists are rewarded for the publications they write, not the software they create and support [25, 26]. This software, however, is a critical link in the chain of evidence establishing new scientific knowledge, and thus other scientists need to be able to run this software in order to understand and replicate this new knowledge, and apply it to new problems.

A few scientific communities in the life sciences have begun experimenting with short-term focused community engagements, such as Google Summer of Code (GSoC) and hackathons. Although there is reason to believe from previous research on online communities (e.g., [30]) that these engagements may enhance the sustainability of scientific software, there is as yet little empirical support. Moreover, evidence about when various types of engagements are likely to succeed is scant.

In this paper, we aim to understand the range of outcomes these engagements produce and the underlying practices that lead to these outcomes. We hope to highlight concrete engagement design issues that community leaders and funding agencies might consider in order to optimize the outcomes they desire.

2. BACKGROUND

2.1 Sustainability of Scientific Software

Software is of vital importance to science. The role of software in data analysis, simulation, and visualization is widely acknowledged [9, 27, 38]. A 2005 NSF Workshop Report [5] clarified the importance of software in cyberinfrastructure, which is the "infrastructure based upon distributed computer, information, and communication technology"[2]. Much scientific software, however, is not infrastructural. For instance, there are many "workbench" applications for end user scientists (e.g., Dan Gezelter's directory [34] lists almost 500 programs). This list does not even include the myriad scripts and data conversion utilities scientists write to translate data into intermediate forms required by tools in the later stages of workflows [26]. Although NSF sponsored workshops have repeatedly called attention to cyberinfrastructure maintenance [5], there is less clarity into how scientific software more generally can be sustained over time, even though it is a crucial part of scientific research, development, and delivery [44].

Informal evidence suggests that scientific software is increasingly a key problem of interest to individual researchers and research institutions. For example, the First Workshop on Sustainable Software for Science [51] was recently held collocated with an annual conference on High Performance Computing. A simple head count revealed that one third of the workshop participants only attended the conference for the workshop. As further evidence, the Water Science Software Institute has developed a model for software development specifically aimed to support the maintenance of scientific software [6].

Scientific software exists in a variety of states from "as persistent as the next grant supporting maintenance" to "supported by a very small community of volunteers" [44]. But if that software has gained widespread use outside of the lab and served a valuable role in assisting other scientists in making new discoveries, it should be able to be refined and extended for use by other scientists who can use it to produce new knowledge.

2.2 The Promise of Open-Source
In discussions of software sustainability, the open-source software model is invariably held up as a promising approach. For instance, position papers from the 2009 NSF funded workshop on "Cyberinfrastructure Software Sustainability and Reusability" [44] led to the report's recommendation that cyberinfrastructure software should be released under an open-source license.

Directly applying the open-source model to scientific software development, however, neglects crucial differences between open-source scientific software and open-source software in general. The primary difference is in the incentive structure for contribution [25, 26]. For open-source developers, reputation in the open-source community is a primary motivation, where the number of "followers" a developer has is a symbol of social status [13]. Scientists who write software, in contrast, operate in a "reputation economy of science" that rewards software production only indirectly through publication [26].

Because scientists need tools for their own work, however, there is built-in motivation to put time and effort into developing them. Although scientist developers are reluctant to build software they themselves do not need, scientists are, under certain conditions, willing to undertake extra work needed to turn their personal tools into a community resource [48]. For example, if scientists understand users' needs well enough, they will be more inclined to devote effort to building features that meet those needs.

Newcomers, however, will likely face multiple barriers to entry: for example, installing the tools, learning technical aspects of the codebase, and learning social conventions, such as where to post questions or issues and how to contribute code. As we review below, research suggests that a healthy community can help lower the barriers to participation and contribution. The reverse is also true: lowering the barriers helps grow a healthy community.

2.3 Online Communities
At a recent workshop on the sustainability of scientific software [51], over half of the 57 papers accepted mentioned *community* as a crucial ingredient in the recipe for success of scientific software sustainability. A community is a group of people who share a common interest, purpose, or goal. Practitioners who learn from each other to develop themselves personally and professionally (e.g., a less experienced scientist developer works with a more experienced developer to develop features of increasing difficulty)

constitute a community of practice [33], whereas people who share information with others but who are not necessarily practitioners themselves (e.g., an end user scientist answers a question about the tool's installation procedure on the mailing list) constitute a community of interest [24]. In a community of practice, learning is always situated in practice. Prior studies of open-source software communities have used *situated learning* to describe the socialization and sustained participation of newcomers [17]. This suggests that community of practice is the type of community important for the sustainability of scientific software.

The literature on communities suggests that in order to be successful, communities must address two primary challenges: receiving contributions and attracting newcomers.

2.3.1 Contributions
Communities need contributions from participants ([30], p. 2-5). In software development, contributions might comprise a working base of source code that serves people significantly better than the competition. For example, BLAST, the widely used open-source tool for comparing biological sequence information [1] achieved such early success because it was so much faster than previous algorithms available at the time. Assuming a newcomer is at least interested in modifying or contributing to the software, the barrier to entry must be low to modify and extend the existing contributions to meet their own needs. Because most contributors to open-source software projects leave after their personal needs are met [41], it is important to attract enough newcomers in order to find those who will continue to contribute and act as stewards of the code base.

2.3.2 Attracting Newcomers
To survive over the long-term, **communities must find ways to attract new generations of members** to replace the ones who leave ([30], p. 179). For example, in recent years leaders of the online encyclopedia Wikipedia have expressed discontent over the fact that the growth rate of new contributors does not compensate for the number of experienced article editors who drop out [3]. Incorporating newcomers can be challenging for three reasons. First, newcomers have not yet developed the same commitment to the group as older members. Second, newcomers will not know how to contribute as effectively as older members. Third, they will not be aware of the norms and objectives guiding the group. In open-source software projects, learning how to contribute to the codebase is often informal and undocumented, placing the onus on the would-be developer instead of the group [15, 31].

2.3.3 Designing Communities
Research on online communities also tells us that **the features of online communities can be designed and managed to achieve the goals that their members desire** ([30], p. 6). For example, designers of communities can encourage new participants and prepare them to make contributions by providing them with welcoming activities, safe spaces for exploration, and formal training opportunities. The size of the community can make a difference as well; more participants can potentially contribute more content. Furthermore, tasks taken on by members can be independent or interdependent, and they can be embedded in social experiences. Rewarding or sanctioning users in response to the actions they take can motivate or demotivate them to make additional contributions.

The fact that communities are so important to software sustainability, and that they are amenable to management and design, suggests that we can improve the sustainability of scientific software by intervening to improve the state of its community.

2.4 Community Code Engagements

Prior studies suggest that there is reason to believe that *community code engagements* – short term, intensive, software development events – may be an effective way to put scientific software projects on sustainable trajectories [6, 47]. Open-source scientific software communities, particularly those in the life sciences, have started employing two types of engagements: Google Summer of Code (GSoC) and hackathons.

2.4.1 Google Summer of Code (GSoC)

Google Summer of Code (GSoC) is an annual program that pays university students stipends to develop features for various open-source software projects. It aims to familiarize students with open-source software development and enable projects to more easily identify and bring in new contributors [20].

The GSoC application requires mentoring organizations, individuals or organizations running an active open-source software development project, to provide details about the organization, previous participation in GSoC, communication methods, plans for project management and participant engagement, and a URL to their project "idea list." The idea list contains descriptions of potential projects, potential mentors, and required skills for students. Mentors are community members who volunteer to provide students technical and social support.

If Google accepts an organization's application, students then submit proposals to the organization describing features they wish to develop. Students can expand on projects in the idea lists, or propose new projects. The organization reviews and ranks student proposals, assigns project mentors and students, and requests project slots from Google.

Google allocates each accepted organization a certain number of project slots, and the organization assigns students and mentors to those slots. Before coding begins, mentors introduce students to the community's culture and practices, select communication channels to use, and decide on the frequency and form of status reports. Throughout the coding period, mentors oversee their students, providing help and guidance. Coding lasts three months, after which students submit their final projects to Google. Google pays students once at the beginning of the coding period, and at the middle and end, provided that they pass mid-term and final evaluations.

2.4.2 Hackathons

Hackathons are events typically lasting two to seven days where people meet face to face and collaborate intensively on software. Hackathon experience reports tend to place emphasis on the number of new tools, prototype functionality, and lines of code produced (e.g., [28, 29, 32]). Because the number of participants at hackathons can be high (having at least 30 participants is common, according to papers in our review), these events have the potential to significantly contribute to a codebase. Hackathons also provide opportunities for networking and relationship building, which may facilitate incorporating new generations of newcomers.

Hackathon organizers typically solicit participants, who may be developers of scientific software, or end user scientists, through private invitation or open calls on mailing lists. Before the event starts, organizers may hold "bootcamps," short tutorials designed to help developers new to a toolkit get acquainted with the codebase and the functionality it offers. When the hackathon starts, participants make presentations on topics they would like to work on. Based on these presentations, participants collectively consolidate and prioritize development tasks and then form sub-groups of about five people based on common interests and project affiliations. For the duration of the hackathon, sub-groups work collocated in a large room on their respective tasks and hold short meetings at the beginning of every day in which group members give status updates on their work. At the end of each day, there is often a dinner, reception, or short excursion where participants eat, drink, and socialize with each other.

We note that hackathons have been widely applied in areas outside of science, such as Yahoo! Open Hack Day, where developers create applications using Yahoo! APIs. For a fairly comprehensive list of the varieties of hackathons, see [22]. In this paper, we focus on hackathons used in the sciences.

3. METHOD

To understand the range of outcomes GSoC and hackathons produce and the underlying practices that lead to these outcomes, we performed a multiple case study of 22 GSoC projects within 6 different scientific software projects across 3 different domains (Table 1). Searching the project lists on the GSoC home page [20] for scientific software, we found that the proportion of bioinformatics GSoC projects is high compared with other scientific domains, which is reflected in our sample. Another criterion was to pick projects with a track record of participation in GSoC so that we could tell if participants' project activities carried over into subsequent years. Our last criterion was to pick active projects, which would indicate that the software serves a current scientific need.

We found very active projects in Biopython, Cytoscape, Wikipathways, CGAL, Bioconductor, and VTK. Each project has consistent development activity, a well-used wiki for documentation and discussion and publicly available mailing lists. Biopython is a set of Python libraries for biological computation [7]. Cytoscape is a software platform for visualizing molecular interaction networks [42]. Wikipathways is a wiki for contributing and maintaining content related to biological pathways [36]. The Computational Geometry Algorithms Library (CGAL) is a software library that provides access to efficient algorithms for computational geometry [16]. Bioconductor provides R packages for analysis and comprehension of genomic data [19]. Visualization Toolkit (VTK) is a software tool for 3D computer graphics, image processing, and visualization [39]. For each project in our sample, we looked at the software community's website and mailing list archives in order to identify the mentors and students and discussions of project ideas and feedback.

3.1 Data Collection

To find instances of hackathons, we conducted a review of the research literature on hackathons using Google Scholar and regular web searches. If we found a publication describing a particular hackathon, we triangulated information about the number and types of participants, activities, objectives, and outcomes described in the publication with information from any planning documents (e.g., agendas, calls for participation, write-ups of work accomplished) linked to on the engagement's web page. This process resulted in a list of 42 hackathons.

In addition to collecting archival data, we conducted semi-structured interviews with 38 scientific software developers.

Scientific Software Name	Scientific Domain	Number of GSoC Projects
Biopython	Bioinformatics	8
Cytoscape	Scientific Visualization	3
Wikipathways	Bioinformatics	3
CGAL	Mathematics	4
Bioconductor	Bioinformatics	2
VTK	Scientific Visualization	2

We also targeted scientist developers who attended hackathons, some of whom attended the same hackathon, and some of whom attended different ones, in order to see variations in their perceptions of the benefits, challenges, and outcomes. We conducted interviews using either Google Hangout or Skype. Each interview lasted 45 minutes on average. If participants could not commit to an interview, we e-mailed them questions from our interview protocol. Twenty-four people participated in GSoC; 15 participated as students, 5 participated as mentors, and 4 participated as both students and mentors. Six of our 38 participants participated in hackathons. Two participated in the 2012 and 2013 OpenBio Codefest Hackathons [8], 2 participated in the 2013 RMassBank Hackathon, 1 participated in the 2012 NESCent Phylotastic Hackathon [35], and 1 participated in the 2012 SWAT4LS Hackathon [46]. Three people participated in both GSoC and hackathons.

3.2 Data Analysis

We applied a grounded approach [10] to analyze our interview data, and started analysis while the data was being collected. All interviews were recorded, transcribed, and prepared for analysis in the Dedoose qualitative data analysis software [43]. We began analysis by conducting open coding on statements about practices and outcomes associated with GSoC and hackathons. Our research group met weekly to define and discuss codes, compare instances of coded excerpts to previously examined examples, and unify them where there was commonality. Moreover, we triangulated statements in the interviews, such as references to mentors, students, and project status with the archival data we collected on GSoC and hackathons. In the next phase of analysis, we wrote, shared, and discussed descriptive memos about the role of GSoC and hackathons.

4. RESULTS

We found that each engagement has periods where participants define development targets and interact with other community members. These phases result in similar outcomes, but in different ways. We describe these processes and their outcomes in the sections below.

4.1 GSoC

A GSoC project is often structured such that the student works on a particular module that is independent of the rest of the codebase. For example, in the Biopython project, we observed that students created a separate GitHub branch for their code. In the Bioconductor project, students worked on a standalone package that contained all the code necessary to implement one piece of functionality. GSoC projects proceed without concerns that the development will break functionality in the existing code distribution.

4.1.1 Defining Development Targets

Among other things, the GSoC application requires each mentoring organization to submit an idea list. The idea list is meant to introduce contributors to the needs of the project and to provide inspiration to would-be students. It is framed as a starting point for student applications, but we observed a range of projects, from those expanding on a proposed idea, to those not mentioning items in the idea list at all.

We investigated where the ideas in the idea list came from, how those ideas were prioritized, and how student projects were established.

4.1.1.1 Creating the Idea List

The decision for participating in GSoC usually emerged from discussion among core community members, those who were actively involved in project management, or who contributed the majority of the code. Because of their experience and expertise, they were sometimes quite sure about what ideas should be implemented as part of GSoC:

"...we did it in a controlled kind of a way, that we discussed it internally and amongst the [group name], which are, say a group of power users that...And from there we identified projects that would be useful to pursue." (P31)

One member of the core team informed us that most projects will have a to-do list or wish list that community members would like people to work on. GSoC provides an opportunity to get these ideas rolling. As he said:

"...there are some ideas on the Wiki, and also in the bug tracker, and sometimes they just sort of get passed around on the project mailing lists. But the developers, in general, have more ideas than time on their hands..." (P4)

Those initial ideas generated by the core team members would be placed on a webpage designed for showing existing ideas and providing details about them[1]. Core team members also encouraged community members and potential student applicants to contribute their ideas, or build on the existing ideas presented on the webpage.

We found that sometimes the core team member would send the call for ideas to the community mailing lists. Biopython also used a Wiki page to facilitate contribution of ideas [4]. The ideas reflected the visions and needs of individuals. Most ideas came from their own research, problems they faced, lack of certain features in the software, new things they wanted to explore, or common needs that were discussed among members.

4.1.1.2 Prioritizing Ideas and Establishing Projects

Since only a few proposals will be accepted, the task of ranking and prioritizing the proposals becomes important. The criteria to prioritize these ideas depend on the views of the core team members. Typically, ideas must be generally useful, practical, and able to be completed within the GSoC time frame.

The availability of mentors and the potential of student applicants were also taken into account. We found that, in general, the match between mentors and students had a big influence on which ideas were prioritized over others. Ideas proposed by experienced

---

[1] For an example of a project idea page, see https://www.cgal.org/project_ideas.html

mentors that attracted students who showed a strong promise to complete the work and potential to continue to make contributions after GSoC, were assigned high priority.

The number of ideas that would be selected depended on the slots allocated by Google for the mentoring organization. Once the mentoring organization selected ideas based on the number of project slots, the mentors and the students could define the directions of the project by themselves. The code of the student projects was usually visible and the community members were welcome to give them feedback.

4.1.2 Relationship Building: Interactions with Mentors Create Strong Ties; Sharing Updates Creates Weak Ties

GSoC students build relationships with mentors as well as other members of the community. We use the term *strong tie* to refer to relationships that involve frequent communication, which may lead to bonding. We use *weak tie* refer to relationships that involve occasional communication, which may lead to exposure to novel information [21].

4.1.2.1 Strong Ties

One of the recurring themes among GSoC students was the strength of the mentor-student relationship. Almost all students we interviewed expressed a deep sense of bonding with their mentor. Students begin their interaction with mentors during the proposal phase of the project, usually via private emails or video chats. There are usually very few face-to-face interactions and yet we found that over time, students developed a strong relationship with their mentor. One student expressed this as follows:

"Communication with my mentor was great, initially it was email communication and in July I attended the Bioconductor's conference that they have every year. After the conference we kind of transitioned into this Google hangouts weekly. And now he is actually going to serve on my thesis committee." (P48)

We found that GSoC students get direct feedback from their mentors on a frequent basis, which supplements our previous findings from a quantitative analysis of communications between students and mentors in Biopython GSoC projects [47]. As such, students are able to focus more on getting work done instead of collating feedback from different members of the community, which is typical of open-source software communities [15].

Prior to GSoC, a number of students had only limited software development experience (e.g., P5, P27) and others had none at all (e.g., P34). Mentors help these students develop skills around unit testing, APIs, GitHub, object-oriented programming, and reading others' code.

We found that mentoring is often far-ranging, not just about developing source-code. For example, mentors give GSoC students advice on choosing career paths:

"A lot of the students that we get are probably in the middle of grad school, which is the time when you're most like I don't know what's going on. So people have asked me about career paths and those sort of questions. So definitely I've tried to help people in that way too. And because I had all those same experiences. So it's like I can at least relate to them." (P1)

We also found evidence that students are likely to stay in touch with their mentors after GSoC ends. Students across different projects in our sample (e.g., P33, P38, P40, P43) mentioned that they were only in touch with their mentors, suggesting that they did not continue to communicate with other project members.

4.1.2.2 Weak Ties

The way students interact with other members of the community during the course of their project depends on how their progress is shared. We found two distinct ways in which this was done: private communication and announcement of updates on mailing lists. In the case of private communication, students typically maintain their code in a private repository shared only with mentors. In such cases, sharing updates on their progress is sometimes implicit, which involves submitting changes to the shared repository without explicitly updating their progress via emails, as one participant from Bioconductor described:

"Most of the updates went to either <mentor>(P26) or <a core member>, basically everything was done through SVN. So, at any point they could come and check what changes I have made." (P48)

Upon probing further about receiving any requests or feedback from other members, the participant (P48) mentioned that there was not much engagement on the mailing list except for a short period after his package was included in a Bioconductor release.

On the other hand, in Biopython, we found that in addition to private communication between students and mentors, it was mandatory for students to share their progress on mailing lists and blogs. This increased visibility and the potential to garner feedback and different points of view from other members. Making the code available on a public repository like GitHub during the development phase was also another way of increasing community engagement. One of the Biopython participants who was also a GSoC mentor, explained this process as follows:

"Some discussion actually happens on Github itself through the commenting on there. And we also wanted our students to do a weekly blog post. So every week they would try and summarize what they'd been doing. And then post the link on the mailing list, and post it up on our blog as well." (P7)

In sum, we observed that establishing a formal protocol of making GSoC project updates available to the community allowed students to form weak ties with other community members.

4.1.3 Project Outcomes

4.1.3.1 Actively Used Software

The primary objective of GSoC projects is to produce code. However, it is unclear how this code is used and maintained few years after a GSoC project ends. Fourteen of the 22 GSoC students responded that their code written as part of GSoC was still being used and maintained. The most common way to gauge the usefulness of the code was by identifying if it was included in the official release. We saw instances, however, where the project resulted in scientific publications (e.g. P46) and in one case the software itself was being cited in other scientific publications (e.g. P42). All 14 participants who expressed positively that their code was being used were also aware of how their code was currently being maintained, and in some cases the participants continued to maintain the code after GSoC.

Some of the reasons why the participants thought their code was not useful or were not aware if their code was being maintained were change in field of work and re-implementing their code using a different technology:

"Once GSOC finished I had almost zero contact with the project. This was also because my line of work after graduating did not fall in line with the project (am doing clinical instead of research-related work). A few months after GSOC, there was an email thread going on regarding how to best deploy the work done after

my mentor made several improvements on it, but by then my interest on the project had faded so I did not look much into it." (P43)

4.1.3.2 Student Retention

One of the motivations of this process of facilitating ties between newcomers and other members of the community is to retain their engagement and future contributions. We found that the possibility of students continuing to be involved in the community was also one of the criteria in selecting students. The following quote summarizes the rationale behind student selection:

"Sometimes people just work for the summer and that's it. And then sometimes they continue. And we really try to keep this in mind when people are selected. You really want someone that's going to keep going and keep contributing to the community." (P1)

While some students ramped down their involvement post GSoC, other students went on to become mentors, active contributors and users. Among the 22 GSoC projects we studied we found that 18% of students went on to become mentors later, a reasonably strong indication of retaining new comers in a community. One participant who has been actively involved in the community for several years since being a student said:

"I am still involved. I co-mentored and mentored some Cytoscape projects from 2009-2011, joined a couple of retreats, published a book on Cytoscape, and some of my other research are still closely related to Cytoscape though I am not part of the core development." (P46)

There were few participants who mentioned their involvement with the community stopped after their GSoC project ended, although we found that they had still retained some of their ties that they formed during course of their project:

"No contact once GSOC ended. Shortly after the GSOC though, a professor in close relationship to the project came to visit Singapore and I met him plus one other GSOC student and had a chit-chat together. It was nice, but no activity after that." (P43)

4.2 Hackathons

Whereas the GSoC format works well for independent work, the hackathon format seems more designed for interdependent work. Participants recalled that hackathon organizers purposefully select objectives that require intensive coordination and collaboration because it is maybe the only time they will be able to do this kind of work (e.g., P7, P20). For example the goals of the 2008 DBCLS Biohackathon [29], and the 2006 NESCent Phyloinformatics Hackathon [32] were to increase the level of interoperability and standardization of bioinformatics databases, services, and tools. By their nature, standardization and interoperability require cooperation from independent tool builders, database providers, and standards bodies. These stakeholders, however, are often geographically dispersed across multiple time zones, and live interactions such as conference calls would have to be scheduled outside normal office hours.

Hackathons last up to several days in length (the average length in our sample was 3.3 days), which provides a long but limited span of uninterrupted time to work. A short period of issue prioritization and development target identification precedes intensive and focused coding sessions.

4.2.1 Defining Development Targets

Hackathons begin with an agenda setting phase in a large shared room, where the output is a list of tasks that participants will work on for the duration of the event. Each participant who wants to raise an issue gets the opportunity to speak before the group. One participant summarized the process as follows:

"...the very first day, we had a few presentations to kind of give the scope of the hackathon, what we wanted to accomplish... [presenters] would say, 'I think that would further our goals would be to develop this. And I'm looking for collaborators to work on this with me.'" (P30)

After hearing from presenters, attendees collectively consolidate the total number of issues, translate them into development targets, and prioritize them into two categories: (1) issues that can be directly addressed at the event and (2) issues that cannot be addressed in the time allotted. For example, a hackathon planning document from the 2006 NESCent Phyloinformatics Hackathon [32] indicates that 6 out of the original 19 "use cases" proposed by participants were ultimately selected for development targets. The following comment on the "Population Analysis" use case seems to indicate that, while not selected for the hackathon, it is still of value to the community:

"This [use case] is outside the scope of the current hackathon but will be addressed in a future one --Tjv 10:26, 21 October 2006 (EDT)" [49]

Through this process, participants can effectively identify and prioritize the common challenges facing the community. When otherwise geographically and temporally dispersed from their closest collaborators, scientists may wonder whether the issues they struggle with matter to others in the same way. The hackathon answers this question with clarity. Once participants sort these issues out, they break into sub-groups and work intensively on the development targets they identified.

4.2.2 Relationship Building: Sub-group Work Creates Strong Ties; Social Events Create Weak Ties

Hackathon participants gather together from all over the world. While they may know the names of their colleagues and something about the kinds and level of their activities from project mailing lists, issue trackers, and source-code repositories, they have fewer opportunities to get to know them. We found that working in sub-groups creates few strong ties among members, and that social events create weak ties among a relatively larger number of people.

4.2.2.1 Strong Ties

The number of people who attend the hackathon can influence the degree to which participants build upon their current relationships, because there is a limit to the time they can interact outside of sub-groups. As one participant described:

"At larger hackathons, like the BioHackathon series which has had about 80 participants, inevitably as with a similarly sized workshop/conference I am unlikely to get to speak to everyone. I would hope at least to remember key people giving talks or representing a sub group in progress meetings/wrap-up sessions." (P7)

We found that sub-group work creates strong ties among group members. Participants spend the majority of their time working together in sub-groups. During this time, debugging code, explaining thought processes, asking for feedback, and offering tips and suggestions lead to frequent interactions. Working together allows participants to develop deeper relationships with individuals within the group:

"I find you get to know the people better if you actually work together with them and see how they react to problems along the

116

way. I really need to know this about a person to be able to work with them well." (P36)

4.2.2.2 Weak Ties

Outside of sub-group interactions, social events provide social networking opportunities with the larger group. Of the hackathons in our sample, 79% (33/42) included short social events, such as coffee breaks, group dinners, and group excursions to nearby landmarks of interest. These events provide participants with opportunities to chat informally with other hackathon attendees, creating weak ties that expose them to information about:

Interesting tool developments or research in one's area. Several of the developers we talked with spent a lot of time discussing technologies and tools that might benefit their research. We interviewed a developer (P20) who introduced an end-user (P36) to an online community that distributes R packages for conducting analyses of genomic data. The end-user is now an active reader of that community's forums and user of the packages that the developer writes. They have also co- authored articles, worked together at subsequent hackathons, and provided feedback on each other's work.

Suggestions for future conferences of interest. Participants reported hearing about conferences and people working on related things through researchers that they met at hackathons (P7, P23, P36). In some cases, they led participants to whole software communities. One of our participants, for example, reported that a developer she met at a hackathon introduced her to the Bioconductor community (P36).

News of job vacancies. The participants we spoke with also told us that hackathons are a useful way to hear about job openings that open up, both academic positions and positions in industry (e.g., P7).

Invitations to tutor or speak at other conferences. One participant told us that he just got back from contributing to a Python part of a workshop tutorial on "keystone skills for bioinformatics." (P7) Another scientist who he had first met at a hackathon invited him.

4.2.3 Project Outcomes: Limited Time Results in Unfinished but Promising Outcomes

Participants we spoke with indicated that it is rare that "finished" software is produced as a result of the hackathon. As one participant recalled, *"we did a lot of programming in that meeting but had a long way to go still." (P36).* We found that participants often attributed the reason for this to the limited time allotted for the hackathon:

"Of course we came across more problems than anticipated and didn't get as much done as we wanted…the task was much bigger than 1 day." (P36)

Instead, software outcomes ranged from *"not anything to write home about" (P31)* to *"discarded—serving as inspiration for a second attempt"* to something *"useful enough that the authors can polish it afterward." (P7)*

We found that the most common software products were:

4.2.3.1 Integration of Existing Tools, Web Services, and Databases

Outcomes improved the interoperability of existing tools with other tools, services, and databases. For example, at the NESCent 2006 hackathon [32], developers of the Bio* toolkits (i.e., BioPerl, BioJava, and Biopython), expanded their coverage of data types and analyses commonly used in phylogenetics. At BioHackathon 2009 [28], developers of the G-language project implemented web service interfaces so that the G-language functions would be available to workflows available in the popular workflow workbench application Taverna.

4.2.3.2 Proof-of-Concept

Some tools only demonstrated a concept's feasibility, but motivated the authors to develop a more sophisticated version after the hackathon. One example from the O|B|F CodeFest 2013 report was a visualization tool that made it possible to visualize an RNA sequence analysis while browsing the genome. This prototype later inspired a version of the tool that scheduled animation updates more efficiently, leading to smoother animations and more accurate windows.

Other useful community resources included:

4.2.3.3 Mailing Lists

In some instances, hackathon participants created mailing lists to sustain the energy of the hackathon after the event. For instance, after the NESCent hackathon for comparative methods in R, a hackathon that aimed to ensure compatibility and data flow between R packages, the participants created a mailing list for users and developers of the packages. Five years after the hackathon, the mailing list has 962 subscribers and an average of over 50 posts per month [11].

4.2.3.4 Documentation

Documentation is an additional important outcome of a hackathon. We observed that there is both documentation in the form of "records of the event" and documentation in terms of how to use the software that is produced. Examples of activities that participants document include use cases, the names of sub-groups, their progress in addressing the use cases, and future work [14].

Participants also created extensive documentation of the tools themselves, both for tools already in wide use, and for tools created at the hackathon. For instance, due to increased interest in using CloudBioLinux, a project providing machine images for bioinformatics on cloud computing platforms participants from the "Infrastructure management" group at Codefest 2013 created extensive documentation on the ReadTheDocs website [37].

4.2.3.5 Training and Tutorials on New Tools

Some developers we spoke with attended "bootcamps," short tutorials designed to help developers new to a toolkit to get acquainted with its basic design and coding principles (P7, P23, P36). We found evidence that these tutorials enabled some effective cross-project interactions. For instance, a developer from the HyPhy project added an interface to the Biopython codebase. In another example, a creator of PhyloXML contributed a NEXUS parser to the BioRuby project [32].

5. DISCUSSION

Below, we draw on our results to suggest how four different themes that cross-cut our work may have implications for organizing community code engagements: *task interdependence, ties, transparency of contributions,* and *appropriate mix of experts and novices.* We place these themes in the context of community growth and code contributions. We also discuss other possible forms of community code engagements, additional outcomes of interest beyond contributions and community growth, how the type of community results in different outcomes, and implications for Information and Communication Technologies (ICTs).

5.1 Community Growth

5.1.1 Task Interdependence

In the hackathon format, large groups of participants engage in face-to-face interactions. Face-to-face is an effective medium for highly interdependent tasks. Previous research by others has found that groups whose members work cooperatively on interdependent tasks tend to be more cohesive and committed to the group [18, 50]. Commitment may increase in these interdependent tasks as individuals see evidence that the group depends on them and values their work ([30], p. 85). Our findings indicate that a GSoC project, in contrast, involves a single student who works remotely on an isolated task. We speculate that independent tasks may make it difficult for students to understand the value of their contributions, which may lead to lower levels of commitment. It may also partly explain our finding that some students were unaware of how their code was being used after GSoC. Future study would investigate the relationship between task interdependence and community growth.

5.1.2 Ties

The benefits of completing highly interdependent work, however, may need to be balanced against the creation of strong ties in GSoC. Although GSoC tasks are isolated, our findings indicate that the longer, intensive mentoring facilitates the creation of strong ties between student and mentor. According to previous research, people who develop connections to others in a group work harder, do more, and tend to stick with the group longer ([30], p. 77). Therefore, the relative benefit of community growth will require more research to assess.

5.1.3 Transparency of Contributions

We suggest that the extent to which participants make their contributions visible to others will have a positive impact on community growth. We found that some Biopython GSoC students, for example, created blogs to promote their projects and posted links to their source-code on the blogs. Students also posted updates on their projects to the mailing list. These behaviors prompted other community members to comment on students' projects and help solve problems [47]. In contrast, the majority of Bioconductor GSoC students neither shared updates on their projects over the mailing list nor created materials promoting their projects. We found that Bioconductor community members (other than the project mentors) were often unaware of students' GSoC projects altogether.

Based on this evidence, we propose that if other community members do not see students' work, they will be less likely to provide feedback or offer suggestions for improvement. If this is true, students will not know if others value their work and may not feel strong enough commitment to stick with the community.

5.1.4 Appropriate Mix of Experts and Novices

Our findings indicate that community code engagements often provide opportunities for mentoring and learning, as novices and experts collaborate. GSoC mentors teach students about the codebase and community norms, and expose them to other community members through blog and mailing list posts. During hackathon tutorials, experts teach new contributors about a tool's codebase. According to Lave and Wenger [33], people join communities by being present and participating along with experts and learning while doing actual work, as "Legitimate peripheral participants" (LPP). Not only is it typical for peripheral participants to become core members through situated learning, it is apparently an important motivation for the learner to continue participating in the community [17].

There is presumably some ratio where mentoring and learning are most efficient, as the ratio influences the number of opportunities for situated learning. Future work around this topic is needed.

5.2 Code Contributions

5.2.1 Appropriate Mix of Experts and Novices

Before newcomers can contribute to open-source software, a socialization process is triggered [15, 17]. GSoC students, for example, go through a process of introducing themselves to the community, formulating project ideas, and learning the technical aspects of the code base with their mentors. As hackathon tutorials illustrate, even experienced developers must learn about how to contribute to other tools.

Seasoned *core members* of the community are likely to be the most expert contributors [12]. We found that these members are also aware of what contributions are needed. In GSoC, for instance, mentors often seed project idea lists. Moreover, student projects are heavily influenced by the vision of mentors. We speculate that, all other things (including number of participants and engagement duration) being equal, an engagement involving only core members would likely contribute more code than an engagement with more novices. A mixture of attendees including novices not only decreases the mean productivity of participants, but may cause the experts to devote time to assisting novices instead of coding.

This suggests a tension between the goals of *code contribution* **and** *community growth*: the greater proportion of experts present, the more code that will be produced, but the greater the ratio of novices present, up to some optimum, the more newcomers will join.

We suggest that **there are important tradeoffs involving both** *appropriate mix of experts and novices* **and** *task interdependence*. An engagement in which many novice participants are included (up to some optimal number), and/or in which highly interdependent tasks are chosen, will contribute more to community growth but less to the codebase; and conversely an event in which experts work on independent tasks will be likely to grow the source code without doing as much to grow the community.

5.3 Hybrid Forms of Community Code Engagements

There are likely hybrid forms of engagements worth exploring that mix aspects of GSoC and hackathons. For instance, one issue we raised in this work is that GSoC students are seldom exposed to other students, mentors, and the larger community. A possible variation on GSoC would be, at the midpoint of the project, to send the student to a community conference. In addition to receiving feedback on their projects, the student could get exposure to the networking and relationship building benefits of hackathons, such as hearing about job opportunities and meeting potential users of their software. On completion of the GSoC project, they may feel more connected to the community, feel that others value their work, and perhaps be more likely to stick around.

As another example, a variation on the hackathon format would be to invite students to a hackathon and pair them off with more experienced members of the community. This configuration might be a way for the engagement designer to strike a balance between code contributions and community growth. As they work side-by-side with mentors in the sub-group, students would not only learn by doing, but also get a sense of real issues that matter to the community that they aspire to join. Working on interdependent tasks would enhance students' perceptions that their work has value. Mentors could delegate simpler tasks to students therefore freeing them up to work on more difficult tasks. Students would see how their contributions matter in the "big picture" while mentors would be able to devote more of their time to coding.

5.4 Other Outcomes

We suggest that there are two important outcomes in addition to community growth and code contributions: visibility of community needs, and training.

5.4.1 Visibility of Community Needs

Both GSoC and hackathons provide the community with an occasion to identify, discuss, and prioritize needs in a way that is generally visible to everyone. The creation of the idea list in GSoC facilitates discussion with potentially new community members and existing community members, who may normally not have the interest or need to engage one another. The agenda setting phase of the hackathon facilitates real-time interactions and discussions with community members who may normally have a willingness to collaborate, but who otherwise face obstacles of geographical and temporal dispersion. Participants can therefore establish a common vocabulary for talking about the work and develop shared goals before development begins. These mechanisms may play an important role in bringing the community together around common goals, regardless of what is accomplished by any particular engagement.

5.4.2 Training

We find that for some students, GSoC is not only their first exposure to the project's codebase, but also to software engineering practices in general such as versioning, unit testing, and object-oriented programming. During hackathons, participants receive training on other software tools and projects of interest. This training seems an important component for the sustainability of scientific software, since new generations of newcomers will need a certain set of technical skills to fill the roles of the original authors. Unfortunately, research shows that scientists tend to undervalue important software engineering concepts like modularity, test-driven development, versioning, and tend to underestimate the amount of time required to develop the software [40]. This not surprising, as scientists are trained in their domain of science, not software engineering. Future work should therefore examine how to structure engagements around optimizing for training, not just code contributions and community growth.

5.5 Impact of Community Type on Outcomes

Our findings suggest that situated learning, a concept from communities of practice [33], may help explain GSoC outcomes. Students learn throughout the process, from introducing themselves to the community, proposing project ideas, discussing project plans, and resolving issues related to the code they write, all with support from their mentors and other community members. In general, upon project completion, their code is added to the codebase. Afterward, they may continue to develop new features (e.g., P4, P5, P8), mentor future students (e.g., P4, P5), or both (e.g., P4, P5). Students thus *become* contributors, they do not simply *learn about* how to contribute.

The hackathons in our sample, in contrast, had more of a flavor of scientific software communities of interest. GSoC involved pairing up newcomers who had scientific domain knowledge and at least some knowledge of software development with mentors, whereas hackathons involved experienced developers working with end user scientists who had the domain knowledge. The presence of both groups was mutually beneficial; end users played an important role in determining requirements for the software (i.e., providing use cases), and the developers played an important role in demonstrating what software was possible using prototypes and proof-of-concepts. Developers often ran tutorial sessions to teach other developers, which are examples of knowledge being codified and then transferred to others, not situated learning. As we discussed previously, there may be promise, however, for facilitating situated learning by investigating hybrid forms of community code engagements.

5.6 Implications for Information and Communication Technologies (ICTs)

Although community code engagements have several positive outcomes, we also found evidence of many technological challenges that participants faced. Among them, there are two major issues that we discuss here.

Ranking Proposals. During the student application period in GSoC, mentoring organizations receive a huge number of project proposals from students. Since only a few can be accepted, the task of ranking these proposals becomes important. Also each proposal requires a mentor to be assigned, however, the availability of mentors is usually limited. Therefore, the use of software tools can assist in the process of ranking proposals, sharing with other members and assigning mentors. The Biopython community does this by having lots of discussions on the mailing list. One Biopython participant (P1) mentioned that this results in a flurry of emails and is often difficult to keep up. The participant suggested that developing a tool with a Reddit[2] like interface where members can up / down vote proposals, sort, comment and share them, could facilitate this process.

Video Chats as a Substitute for Face to Face Interaction. We found that in GSoC, students and mentors almost always coordinated remotely. Some of them used emails whereas others relied heavily on real time video chat tools such as Google Hangouts and Skype. While some mentors (P29) found it comfortable to communicate via emails when students were able to work independently, other students (P48) and mentors (P26) felt they needed more face-to-face interaction. In the latter cases, the use of video chat technologies was found to be an appropriate substitute for working from the same physical location. One participant (P48) acknowledged that this helped them get a better sense of what they were trying to communicate and therefore, sped up the process.

6. CONCLUSION

In this work we examined two community code engagements: Google Summer of Code and hackathons. We sought to understand the range of outcomes these engagements produce and the underlying practices that lead to those outcomes. We found that in GSoC, the vision and experience of core team members influences project selection and the mentoring process facilitates creation of strong ties. Most GSoC projects result in stable features. The agenda setting phase of hackathons reveals high priority issues perceived by the community, and social events create weak ties. Most hackathons result in promising prototypes rather than finished tools. Our findings point to several themes and tradeoffs around community code engagement design that we hope to explore in future empirical work.

---

[2] http://www.reddit.com/

As is common with case studies, the generalizability of our results is limited. On the one hand, some elements from community code engagements seem applicable to other types of collaborative groups, not just open-source software. For instance, mentorship, which facilitates the socialization of newcomers, seems useful to explore in Wikipedia, where contributions from newcomers are disproportionally rejected due to not following standard policies [23]. Moreover, articulating and prioritizing user needs seems fundamental to eliciting contributions in any community, because contributors will know what to do. On the other hand, these elements are likely impractical for software shared only within local laboratories, tailored to a particular purpose, and limited to a few developers and users. Numerical simulations, for example, are difficult to make generally useful, and many scientists are reluctant to share, or open up development of the code, lest others use it incorrectly and produce spurious results [45]. In addition, different scientific fields may value individual skill and reputation in developing software over collective achievements. Future work could thus elaborate on the conditions under which community code engagements are appropriate and likely to have impact.

7. ACKNOWLEDGMENTS

This work was supported by a grant from the Alfred P. Sloan Foundation, the Google Open Source Programs Office, and NSF awards IIS-1111750, SMA-1064209, and ACI-0943168. We thank our participants for taking time out of their busy schedules to collaborate with us.

8. REFERENCES

[1] Altschul, S.F., Gish, W., Miller, W., Myers, E.W. and Lipman, D.J. 1990. Basic local alignment search tool. *Journal of Molecular Biology*. 215, (1990), 403–410.

[2] Atkins, D., Droegemeier, K., Feldman, S., Garcia-Molina, H., Klein, M., Messerschmitt, D., Messina, P., Ostriker, J. and Wright, M. 2003. *Revolutionizing Science and Engineering Through Cyberinfrastructure: Report of the National Science Foundation Blue-Ribbon Advisory Panel on Cyberinfrastructure*.

[3] Attracting and Retaining Participants: 2010. *http://strategy.wikimedia.org/wiki/Attracting_and_retaining_participants*. Accessed: 2014-02-02.

[4] Biopython Google Summer of Code: *http://biopython.org/wiki/Google_Summer_of_Code*. Accessed: 2014-06-13.

[5] Blatecky, A. and Messerschmitt, D. 2005. *Planning for Cyberinfrastructure Software*.

[6] Christopherson, L., Idaszak, R. and Ahalt, S. 2013. *Developing Scientific Software through the Open Community Engagement Process*.

[7] Cock, P.J. a, Antao, T., Chang, J.T., Chapman, B. a, Cox, C.J., Dalke, A., Friedberg, I., Hamelryck, T., Kauff, F., Wilczynski, B. and de Hoon, M.J.L. 2009. Biopython: freely available Python tools for computational molecular biology and bioinformatics. *Bioinformatics (Oxford, England)*. 25, 11 (Jun. 2009), 1422–3.

[8] Codefest: *http://www.open-bio.org/wiki/Codefest*. Accessed: 2014-06-13.

[9] Colwell, R. 2000. Information Technology: Ariadne's Thread Through the Research and Education Labyrinth. *Educause*. June (2000), 15–18.

[10] Corbin, J. and Strauss, J. 2008. *Basics of Qualitative Research: Techniques and Procedures for Developing Grounded Theory*. Sage.

[11] Cranston, K. and Evolutionary, N. 2013. A grassroots approach to software sustainability. *Proc. Workshop in Sustainable Software for Science: Practice and Experience (WSSSPE)* (2013).

[12] Crowston, K., Wei, K., Howison, J. and Wiggins, A. 2012. Free/Libre open-source software development: what we know and what we do not know. *ACM Computing Surveys*. 44, 2 (Feb. 2012), 1–35.

[13] Dabbish, L., Stuart, C., Tsay, J. and Herbsleb, J. 2012. Social Coding in GitHub: Transparency and Collaboration in an Open Software Repository. *Proceedings of the ACM 2012 conference on Computer Supported Cooperative Work* (2012), 1277–1286.

[14] Database Interop Hackathon: *https://www.nescent.org/wg/evoinfo/index.php?title=Database_Interop_Hackathon*. Accessed: 2014-06-13.

[15] Ducheneaut, N. 2005. Socialization in an Open Source Software Community: A Socio-Technical Analysis. *Computer Supported Cooperative Work (CSCW)*. 14, 4 (Jul. 2005), 323–368.

[16] Fabri, A. and Pion, S. 2009. CGAL: the Computational Geometry Algorithms Library. *Proceedings of the 17th ACM SIGSPATIAL International Conference on Advances in Geographic Information Systems* (2009), 538–539.

[17] Fang, Y. and Neufeld, D. 2009. Understanding Sustained Participation in Open Source Software Projects. *Journal of Management Information Systems*. 25, 4 (Apr. 2009), 9–50.

[18] Gaertner, S. and Dovidio, J. 2000. Reducing intergroup conflict: From superordinate goals to decategorization, recategorization, and mutual differentiation. *Group Dynamics: Theory, Research, and Practice*. 4, 1 (2000), 98–114.

[19] Gentleman, R.C. et al. 2004. Bioconductor: open software development for computational biology and bioinformatics. *Genome biology*. 5, 10 (Jan. 2004), R80.

[20] Google Summer of Code: 2013. *https://developers.google.com/open-source/soc/?csw=1*. Accessed: 2014-01-31.

[21] Granovetter, M. 1973. The Strength of Weak Ties. *American journal of sociology*. 78, 6 (1973).

[22] Hackathon: *http://en.wikipedia.org/wiki/Hackathon*. Accessed: 2014-02-12.

[23] Halfaker, A., Kittur, A. and Riedl, J. 2011. Don't Bite the Newbies: How Reverts Affect the Quantity and Quality of Wikipedia Work. *Proceedings of the 7th International Symposium on Wikis and Open Collaboration* (2011), 163–172.

[24] Henri, F. and Pudelko, B. 2003. Understanding and analysing activity and learning in virtual communities. *Journal of Computer Assisted Learning*. October 2002 (2003), 474–487.

[25] Howison, J. and Herbsleb, J.D. 2013. Incentives and integration in scientific software production. *Proceedings of the ACM 2013 conference on Computer Supported Cooperative Work* (New York, New York, USA, 2013), 459–468.

[26] Howison, J. and Herbsleb, J.D. 2011. Scientific software production : incentives and collaboration. *Proceedings of the ACM 2011 conference on Computer Supported Cooperative Work* (2011), 513–522.

[27] Jirotka, M., Procter, R., Rodden, T. and Bowker, G.C. 2006. Special Issue: Collaboration in e-Research. *Computer Supported Cooperative Work (CSCW)*. 15, (Sep. 2006), 251–255.

[28] Katayama, T. et al. 2011. The 2nd DBCLS BioHackathon: interoperable bioinformatics Web services for integrated applications. *Journal of biomedical semantics*. 2, 4 (Jan. 2011), 1–18.

[29] Katayama, T. et al. 2010. The DBCLS BioHackathon: standardization and interoperability for bioinformatics web services and workflows. *Journal of Biomedical Semantics*. 1, 8 (2010), 1–19.

[30] Kraut, R.E. and Resnick, P. 2011. *Building Successful Online Communities*. MIT Press.

[31] Von Krogh, G., Spaeth, S. and Lakhani, K.R. 2003. Community, joining, and specialization in open source software innovation: a case study. *Research Policy*. 32, 7 (Jul. 2003), 1217–1241.

[32] Lapp, H., Bala, S., Balhoff, J.P., Bouck, A., Goto, N., Holland, R., Holloway, A., Katayama, T., Lewis, P.O., Mackey, A.J., Osborne, B.I., Piel, W.H. and Pond, S.L.K. 2007. The 2006 NESCent Phyloinformatics Hackathon: A Field Report. *Evolutionary Bioinformatics*. 3, (2007), 287–296.

[33] Lave, J. and Wenger, E. 1990. *Situated Learning: Legitimate Peripheral Participation*. Cambridge University Press.

[34] OpenScience Software: *http://openscience.org/links/*. Accessed: 2014-01-31.

[35] Phylotastic1: *http://www.evoio.org/wiki/Phylotastic1*. Accessed: 2014-06-13.

[36] Pico, A.R., Kelder, T., van Iersel, M.P., Hanspers, K., Conklin, B.R. and Evelo, C. 2008. WikiPathways: Pathway Editing for the People. *PLoS Biology*. 6, 7 (2008), e184.

[37] Proteomics Data Analysis with CloudBioLinux: *http://mass-spec-data-analysis-with-cloudbiolinux.readthedocs.org/en/latest/*. Accessed: 2014-06-13.

[38] Ribes, D. and Lee, C.P. 2010. Sociotechnical Studies of Cyberinfrastructure and e-Research: Current Themes and Future Trajectories. *Computer Supported Cooperative Work (CSCW)*. 19, 3-4 (Sep. 2010), 231–244.

[39] Schroeder, W.J., Martin, K.M. and Lorensen, W.E. The design and implementation of an object-oriented toolkit for

3D graphics and visualization. *Proceedings of the 7th conference on Visualization* 93–100.

[40] Segal, J. 2009. Software Development Cultures and Cooperation Problems: A Field Study of the Early Stages of Development of Software for a Scientific Community. *Computer Supported Cooperative Work (CSCW)*. 18, 5-6 (Sep. 2009), 581–606.

[41] Shah, S. 2006. Motivation, Governance, and the Viability of Hybrid Forms in Open Source Software Development. *Management Science*. 52, 7 (2006), 1000–1014.

[42] Shannon, P., Markiel, A., Ozier, O., Baliga, N.S., Wang, J.T., Ramage, D., Amin, N., Schwikowski, B. and Ideker, T. 2003. Cytoscape: a software environment for integrated models of biomolecular interaction networks. *Genome research*. 13, 11 (Nov. 2003), 2498–504.

[43] SocioCultural Research Consultants, L. 2013. Dedoose Version 4.5, web application for managing, analyzing, and presenting qualitative and mixed method research data.

[44] Stewart, C.A., Almes, G.T., McCaulay, S. and Wheeler, B.C. eds. 2010. *Cyberinfrastructure Software Sustainability and Reusability*. Indiana University.

[45] Sundberg, M. 2010. Organizing Simulation Code Collectives. *Science studies: an interdisciplinary journal for science and technology studies*. 23, 1 (2010), 37–57.

[46] SWAT4LS 2012: *http://www.w3.org/wiki/HCLS/SWAT4LS2012/Hackathon*. Accessed: 2014-06-13.

[47] Trainer, E., Chaihirunkarn, C. and Herbsleb, J. 2013. The big effects of short-term efforts: A catalyst for community engagement in scientific software. *Proc. Workshop in Sustainable Software for Science: Practice and Experience (WSSSPE)*. (2013).

[48] Trainer, E.H., Chaihirunkarn, C., Kalyanasundaram, A. and Herbsleb, J.D. 2015. From Personal Tool to Community Resource: What's the Extra Work and Who Will Do It? *Proceedings of the ACM 2015 Conference on Computer Supported Cooperative Work & Social Computing* (2015), to appear.

[49] Use Cases: *http://informatics.nescent.org/wiki/UseCases*. Accessed: 2014-06-13.

[50] Worchel, S., Rothgerber, H., Day, E., Hart, D. and Butemeyer, J. 1998. Social identity and individual productivity within groups. *British Journal of Social Psychology*. 37, (1998), 389–414.

[51] Working towards Sustainable Software for Science: Practice and Experiences: 2013. *http://wssspe.researchcomputing.org.uk*. Accessed: 2014-01-31.

Anyone for Bowling? Coalescing for Shared Activities

Stephen Ricken
New Jersey Institute of Technology
Newark, NJ, USA
sr82@njit.edu

Sukeshini Grandhi
Eastern Connecticut State University
Willimantic, CT
grandhis@easternct.edu

Doug Zytko
New Jersey Institute of Technology
Newark, NJ, USA
daz2@njit.edu

Starr Roxanne Hiltz
New Jersey Institute of Technology
Newark, NJ, USA
hiltz@njit.edu

Quentin Jones
New Jersey Institute of Technology
Newark, NJ, USA
qgjones@acm.org

ABSTRACT

Despite the importance of individuals coming together for social group-activities (e.g. pick-up volleyball, chess clubs), the process by which such groups coalesce is poorly understood. Existing theories focus on adoption and contribution rates, group types, and the formation of group norms, as opposed to the processes involved in initial group coalescence. We address this gap in the literature through an interview study examining: 1) how well people's needs for social group activity engagement are being met; 2) the challenges they face in finding and participating in, and; 3) leading interest-based group activities. Our findings highlight how people's needs are not being addressed by current technologies. In particular, they place a heavy burden on individuals to step forward into leadership positions where the return they will receive for their efforts is often unknown, or extremely limited. We discuss the implications of our findings for the design of interest-based group coalescing technology.

Categories and Subject Descriptors

H.5.m. Information interfaces and presentation (e.g., HCI): Miscellaneous.

General Terms

Design, Human Factors, Theory.

Keywords

Social Activities, Critical Mass, Social Capital, MeetUp

1. INTRODUCTION

Humans are fundamentally social beings, and routinely engage in a range of group activities. "Bowling alone," rather than as a member of a league or club, was used by Putnam [32] as an example of how U.S. citizens' participation in social group

GROUP'14, November 9–12, 2014, Sanibel Island, Florida, USA.
Copyright © 2014 ACM 978-1-4503-3043-5/14/11...$15.00
http://dx.doi.org/10.1145/2660398.2660421

activities has waned during the second half of the 20th century, thereby causing social capital to decline. Social capital is gained when people strengthen their connections through socializing with others, including participating in interest-based group activities (e.g. bowling leagues, pick-up soccer, car clubs) [9]. In sports, a "pick-up" game is a game that has been spontaneously started by a group of players, and is usually less structured than normal games. Social capital is an indicator of social wellbeing that measures the amount of reciprocal connections and mutual benefits people have within their social networks [10]. The decline of social capital noted by Putnam was particularly acute in diverse urban environments with high in-migration, where people can find it hard to make new friends and discover new interest groups in which to participate.

The extent to which the widespread use and adoption of social media has reversed the trend toward lower group activity participation observed by Putnam is unclear [29], [30]. People are routinely adding others they meet offline to their list of online social ties on social network sites [21]. However, those who use the Internet the most, also visit friends and family face-to-face the least [12]. People are using the Internet to seek out others for a range of social activities including discussion forums, philanthropy, and online multiplayer games. In addition, numerous existing systems aim to help people move from online discovery to offline social events. For example, Meetup.com boasts nearly 500,000 monthly 'meetups.' Even so, there is little evidence that these systems are effectively addressing the needs of people and the communities they inhabit to engage with others. Loneliness and social isolation routinely occur in places such as college campuses where it is likely that there are actually a significant number of other like-minded individuals with similar interests in geographic proximity [26], [41]. Clearly, in many environments the current state of affairs is suboptimal.

Increasing the extent and quality of individual participation in social group activities is a complex undertaking. This is because participation requires: 1) shared interests related to a potential group activity; 2) knowledge of others with whom that interest is shared; 3) the existence of relevant social activities; 4) their discovery by the interested people; 5) one or more individuals who are willing and able to perform a leadership role to organize the group activities; and 6) a critical mass of individuals deciding to socially engage in a particular activity group. At present, there is a significant gap in our knowledge regarding how these factors are conducive for participation.

The process of group coalescence is poorly understood, and many of the existing theories of current social practice focus on groups after they have been formed. There is limited understanding of the relationship between people's interests and the challenges they face in finding, participating in, and leading interest-based group activities. The study presented in this paper examines the relationship between people's interests and activities – 1) where they are finding interest-based activity groups, and where they are missing out; and 2) what were their impressions of the opportunities to participate in interest-based group activities.

To address these questions we conducted interviews on an ethnically and nationally diverse urban technical college campus. Such environments are good places to explore group coalescing thanks to the high number of individuals in geographic proximity, with few or no strong social ties, who are eager to find interest-based activities in their locale. The vast majority of the denizens of such places go online each day "for no particular reason, just for fun" [34]. If any environment and associated population is likely to shed light on the challenges people face using today's social media to facilitate participating in group activities it is that of urban U.S. college campuses.

In the remainder of this paper, we first review foundational concepts and theories that frame this research, including social capital, group coalescence, critical mass, pluralistic ignorance, and event-based social networks. Research questions and method lead into findings, which are organized according to themes extracted from interviews. We conclude with discussion of these findings, design considerations, limitations, and future research plans.

2. BACKGROUND
This section begins by explaining what social capital is and why it is an indicator of social wellbeing. Next, we define what social groups are and our current understanding of how groups form. Then, the concepts of critical mass and pluralistic ignorance are described, as they relate to the conditions necessary for the formation of activity-based groups that could help members build social capital. Finally, we discuss current technologies used to form groups that meet offline.

2.1 Social Capital
Social capital refers to the individual and collective benefits accumulated through social networks or social structures [9], [32]. It is the amount of opportunity to gain (socially, economically, etc.) by using one's social-ties or "connections". These can lead to helping hands, job offers, and party invites, among other social engagements. People gain social capital through interactions with each other and developing strong ties (building upon established relationships). The importance of social capital is two-fold, as it has been linked to a variety of positive community outcomes (e.g. better public health, lower crime rates, and more efficient financial markets) [1], [18]. Also, on an individual level, social capital has been found to be related to positive psychological well-being (e.g. higher self esteem and satisfaction with life) [5], [16].

Putnam's cumulative research suggested social capital decreased during the course of the twentieth century [32]. The argument laid out that people have been participating in less social activities and social clubs with each other, including participating in community service, turning to their checkbooks as service instead. Since then,

research has investigated the effects of social media on social capital – as people now spend time in virtual communities (e.g. web forums [11], [22], email lists [20], social network sites [8], [24], virtual worlds, video games). Lampe and Ellison, in studying college students' use of Facebook, have discovered that Facebook is used more for maintaining offline contacts by bringing them online (becoming Facebook 'friends'), rather than for creating new contacts [21]. People who use Facebook the most for social interaction also tend to visit friends and family less [36]. It is clear that new social ties can be made through the Internet, and that people are using new social tools to come together face-to-face but the extent to which new technologies have reversed the decline is unclear.

2.2 Groups, Coalescing, and Formation
A group is colloquially understood to be a cluster of two or more individuals. When individuals come together to participate in an interest-based activity (e.g. pick-up basketball, card games, etc.) over time they may coalesce into a "social group". Social Categorization Theory (SCT) [40] indicates that social groups are defined through a process of classification of the self – individuals identify with a group that matches his or her view (in-group), and reinforce this identity partly through excluding themselves from groups they have no affinity for (out-groups) [3]. Over time, these social groups develop "group norms" that consist of goals and behaviors (e.g. actions/discussion topics) that are part of the group [37]. These norms also create boundaries between the in- and out-groups, describing what is and is not acceptable to the group. For example, the individuals playing pick-up basketball together can be identified as part of a group, with a specific goal (to play basketball), and specific behaviors (level of competitiveness, playing styles, etc.). Social groups can emerge not only as a result of repeated shared participation in a particular class of group activity, but also because the individuals come to recognize mutual friendships, family or work ties.

Social groups are often categorized as bond-based or identity-based [31]. Members of bond-based [35] social groups feel connected with the individuals within the group more so than with the whole group itself. These groups typically do not have a specific shared activity centric goal. For example, Fraternity members are "brothers" and create life-long friendships with each other. Unlike bond-based groups, interest-based activity groups can generally be considered "identity-based". Individuals care about the group as a whole rather than the individuals involved. For example, members of a pick-up basketball group will change over time, but the group will continue to exist. The group survives no matter who is a member, and if one individual leaves, there is not necessarily a mass exodus of players. Some interest-based activity groups are initially formed with a tight-knit group of friends, and would be considered more bond-based, as they are less likely to include outsiders. The focus of this research is less on nature of the groups that do exist, but on the challenges faced by individuals wishing to participate in group activities.

Currently, there is a lack of literature on the process individuals go through to coalesce for groups. In fact, the seminal model of group development, Tuckman's Stages of Group Development [38], focuses on groups that have already formed, rather than on the emergence of new social groups. By this we mean social groups that result from free association and shared participation in an interest-based group activity. The research in this paper is focused on participation in interest-based group activities, and the associated "emergent social groups". A modified version of Tuckman's Stages of Group Development model can be used to reflect on the group activity coalescing process. Tuckman's model describes five stages: 1) forming, 2) storming, 3) norming, 4) performing, and 5) adjourning [7]. The first three stages of this model can be modified to explain the coalescing process of emergent social groups: 1) discovery, 2) introduction, and 3) membership. Tuckman's "Forming" stage is an initial stage where people learn who is in the group, the goal, and test their dependence. Little is known about each other. This relates to "discovery" in group formation - individuals must form a mutual awareness of each other's existence. For example, two individuals who are independently practicing shooting hoops at a basketball court become aware of each other's existence. The only information they have is their shared interest in basketball. Tuckman's "Storming" stage is filled with conflict. At this stage, members discuss individual goals, argue ideas, and feel out each other's place within the group. This relates to the "introduction" step where individuals reveal self-information to judge whether or not they want to continue their relationship [33]. For example, if two individuals begin to play 'pick-up' basketball with each other, they will take note of each other's levels of skill and competitiveness in order to decide if they want to continue their relationship (to play each other again) in the future. During Tuckman's "Norming" phase, the collective forms a single goal, establishes roles, and begins to work efficiently. In group formation, this third step is where the group forms a membership, where individuals self-identify with others' mutual goals/views to form mutual goals/views of the group.

2.3 Social Engagement and Critical Mass

While interest-based group activities enable members to share their interest with others, it creates the opportunity to gain social capital through relationships. This is even more evident on college campuses where students can afford to build new social foundations as well as further their career opportunities through social networking. Based on the Theory of Collective Action, two conditions need to converge for a successful interest-based group activity: 1) a critical mass of members; and 2) a shared vision of collective action (collective action goal) [28]. If only the former condition is met, an ineffective "all talk, no action" group may result (e.g. online cat lover discussion community). If a collective action goal is articulated ("let's form a basketball team") but an inadequate cohort of members has been accrued, the group will have no chance of achieving its collective goal.

The concept of 'critical mass' was used by Hiltz & Turoff [17], to refer to a sufficient number of individuals who adopt an idea or innovation so that the rate of adoption becomes self-sustaining and creates further growth. In the absence of a critical mass, the idea or innovation is not only unlikely to spread, but to be deserted altogether. Olson, in The Logic of Collective Action, describes the "exploitation of the great by the small," in which a small group of individuals (critical mass) who have the most interest in the public good will invest the most resources (e.g. time, energy, money) toward its success, compared to the majority. Since the critical mass are so interested, he argues, they will provide the good themselves, regardless of the actions of the less interested parties. The latter exploit the "great" by not contributing at all: they know they will get the good anyway, because the "great" will provide it [28]. Leaders/organizers of activity groups are part of the critical mass, and face the challenge of doing the legwork (e.g. finding interested individuals, posting flyers, providing equipment) to push for activities to take place.

Oliver, Marwell, and Teixiera, in relating critical mass to collective action, argue that while the critical mass of interested

individuals contribute the most resources initially, there is a scale or 'production function' that others who are less interested do contribute, albeit less, and the ones who do not contribute at all are free-riders [27]. Their theory states that once the critical mass has provided enough towards the goal, an "explosion" of attendance will rise from others who want to participate, but who are less interested (and therefore provide fewer resources than the critical mass). These less interested participants are of course necessary for a successful activity.

Collective action goals are necessary for group members to collaborate towards success. Gold and Sugden's [15] observation that the theoretically challenging prisoner's dilemmas and other "public good" puzzles can be rationally and optimally solved by agents who adopt the "team reasoning" stance ("we should" rather than "I should") illuminates the ways in which membership ("we") and collective goals ("should") are intertwined for successful collective action. Collective action goals are often referred to as "we-intentions" [39]. We-intentions are specifically group-centric goals that everyone involved agrees to accomplish with the same motive.

2.4 Pluralistic Ignorance

In order for an interest-based group activity to successfully take place, social groups must have both a critical mass of interested members willing to put forth the effort and a shared goal to accomplish. Often, a critical mass is never achieved because the members needed for an emergent group are not found. The problem that needs to be solved is to help interested people identify others who share their interests. "Pluralistic ignorance" was originally defined by Floyd Allport [2] as a pattern in which individual members of a social group assume that they are alone in holding the social attitudes and expectations they do, all unknowing that others privately share them. As Merton (1968, p. 431) points out, "there are two patterns of pluralistic ignorance- the unfounded assumption that one's own attitudes and expectations are unshared and the unfounded assumption that they are uniformly shared" [25]. Latané and Darley [23] suggested that pluralistic ignorance leads to inaction; an individual believes they do not need to act or react under the assumption that someone else will. In this study, we are interested in discovering and identifying how we can alleviate the extent to which people are unaware of others sharing their interests in specific types of group activities such as a sport or music. Here though we are not only interested a general belief that others share an activity interest, but that others with that interest can be discovered and identified.

2.5 Event-based Social Networks

Over the past few years Event-based Social Networks (EBSN), have become increasingly popular [24]. Examples of such systems include Meetup (www.MeetUp.com), Plancast (www.Plancast.com) and Eventbrite (www.EventBrite.com). They provide an online platform for users to create, distribute and organize social events, which are generally face-to-face. Research to date on these systems has focused on enhancing social engagement through recommending individuals to events or public event-focused groups through an analysis of a profile of user's interests, user social-ties, and co-presence data [4], [8].

Commercial EBSB applications generally adopt one of three commercial models – pay for the ability to lead/organize groups (e.g. MeetUp), sell event tickets (e.g. Eventbrite), or push commercial venues through advertising and getting users to make private group planning a fairly public activity (e.g. Plancast). Each of these models pushes the support focus towards social structures where there is 1) a main organizer of an activity (leader) who is willing to make significant investment to actualize the event; and/or 2) an existing social group interested in using a commercial venue of one sort or another. We conjecture that in the real world, many social group-activities are less structured and more ad hoc than those currently supported by EBSN. Consequently, a motivation for this research was to see if a paradigm shift for EBSNs away from their current focus on 'leaders' and 'events' towards 'activities' and 'people's activity affinities' would be of value.

3. RESEARCH QUESTIONS

As noted in our background section existing theories focus on social group-activities in terms of adoption/membership and contribution rates (e.g. Critical Mass Theory), group types (e.g. Social Categorization theory,), and the formation of group norms (e.g. Tuckman's Stages), as opposed to the processes involved in initial group coalescence. To address this concern we explore the following broad research questions focusing specifically on our exemplar campus:

RQ1: How do individuals perceive their needs for social group activity engagement are being met?

RQ2: What challenges do individuals face in regards to searching for, participating in, and leading interest-based group activities?

RQ3: How does technology impact the process of coalescing social group activity?

4. METHOD
4.1 Study Procedure

To address the above research questions we conducted an interview study on an urban school campus of a technological university with approximately 10,000 students. Students were randomly approached in locations of the university known for social activity and requested to participate in a short interview about their participation in various interest-based activities. In order to ensure that we collected data from various social contexts, locations, and times of day, we conducted interviews in 16 unique locations (e.g. gym, basketball court, game room, racquet ball court, hallways of buildings with classrooms, student lounges, cafeteria, outdoor lawns, coffee shop) between 11am and 6:30pm on weekdays. Two types of locations were targeted: 1) locations that had a reputation for certain activities (e.g. playing basketball at the basketball court) and 2) locations that are open for interpretation (e.g. playing Frisbee on the campus green or hanging out in the student lounge).

When approached, interview respondents were first asked about their current activity and then our semi-structured interview guide was used to obtain data on other activities they were involved in, how they gathered information about activities they participate in, and how they make decisions to participate or not participate in these activities. Summaries of each interview with key insights on data and trends were cataloged within 24 hours of being conducted. Early versions of the interview guide focused on understanding people's interests and activities that they participated in. As insights were gained, later guides focused on deeper understanding of the underlying motivations and challenges in finding, participating in, and sustaining participation in interest-based group activities. Each interview was audio recorded for transcription and further analysis. The summaries created for each interview highlighted several themes. Interviews were then transcribed for coding.

4.2 Coding Procedure

The initial coding was informed by the trends found in the summaries of each interview, followed by an iterative open coding process that was used to enable the discovery of emergent themes [6]. Once coding was complete, quotes were extracted from the transcripts for evidence of each theme's existence.

4.3 Participants

Interview data were collected from a total of 60 respondents (23% female – approximating the student population distribution) between 18 and 36 years of age. The majority of students (90%) were undergraduates and belonged to engineering (34%) or computer science (30%) fields while the rest were from a range of disciplines such as math, science, architecture, and management. Interview times ranged from 5 to 40 minutes with an average of 15 minutes each.

5. FINDINGS

The following themes emerged from our interviews:

1) Missing Opportunities: Most respondents felt they were missing out on activities that directly related to their interests. Students use a "satisficing" strategy in order to find the "next best thing" so they can socialize and make friends. They typically experimented by joining at least one club on campus, but that club often did not relate directly to an important personal interest.

2) Information Not Getting to Target Audience: Current methods of communicating and advertising upcoming events are ineffective and not reaching the intended audience. Signs advertising events hung around campus are often ignored by passersby because too many cause information overload. Electronic means of advertising (e.g. Facebook invites, online calendar, etc.) also lead to information overload. When overburdened by too many irrelevant invites, people tend to ignore them all and miss potentially relevant invites.

3) Burden of Leadership: There is a burden of leadership that prevents interest-based activities from occurring and interest-groups forming. The task of coalescing a critical mass of individuals for an activity to occur for the first time is seen as daunting, and is a major deterrence to most individuals.

Below we explain and illustrate these themes in more detail.

5.1 Missing Opportunities

Our respondents typically mentioned four to five primary interests (e.g. comics, gaming), but on further probing also mentioned one or two secondary interests. While most of our respondents actively sought others to participate in primary interests, they pursued secondary interests if they had "extra time." For example, one graduate student enjoyed technology news and played team handball, but if she had the time, she would be willing to play basketball – only if others invited her. While she has been a student at the university for a number of years, she had not once played basketball on campus. Respondents reported joining at least one club on campus, however the clubs joined were not necessarily directly related to their interests but were a way for them to socialize.

A common sentiment expressed by most respondents was that they felt they were missing out on activities related to their interests. Several reasons were cited for this: 1) a club for a particular interest did not not exist and there was no easy way to find others who liked the same interest 2) respondents did not have the time to search for or participate in an activity, or 3) previous bad experiences keep respondents away from pursuing activities of interest. Respondents mentioned it is not easily possible to find others who share their interests to participate in group-activities together.

5.1.1 There is No Easy Way to Find Others Who Share the Same Interest

Respondents often had unfulfilled wishes to participate in specific interests because the people they knew did not share similar interests. Anthony, a 21-year-old male CS student, mentioned that he liked to party, but *"My friends don't like to party. I want to go but I don't really want to go by myself and I don't know where to go."* Needing a friend who shared the interest was important for many respondents. Jenny, a 20-year-old female biology student said, *"I want to take an airplane lesson, and go to a gun club. But my friends don't like this. They aren't interested; they don't want to go [...] I want them to go with me. I won't do it by myself."*

Respondents shared a desire to find a club that consisted of members who share their interest. They reported that often no such club existed. John, an 18-year-old male IT student, said, *"We were at the club fair looking around for clubs to join. I asked if there was a snowboarder club. They said 'no.' It was a joke at the time, but it is something that I want to do."* Kate, an 18-year-old female architecture student, said, *"My friends have no interest in what I want to do. I want a club that shows my interest and people who share my interest. People I can have conversations with."*

5.1.2 Perceived Time Commitment

Some interviewees reported that with school and/or work, their load was too full for many activities they wanted to participate in. Neal, an 18-year-old male CS student, said, *"If I had more time I would be in more clubs. Originally I was in three clubs but I was like nah, it's way too much. So I cut back to one, the one I liked the most. I'll probably join them back later, but I don't have the time right now."* Others exclaimed that they did not have enough time to join a club. Julius, a 22-year-old male CS student, said, *"I just don't have time. I heard about the TED talks recently. Which is something I would have liked to do, but I wouldn't have gone because I don't have enough time."* James, a 21-year-old male civil engineering student, expressed a similar sentiment, *"Like yesterday, there were a bunch of people who went on the tour of the new buildings. I signed up for it but didn't have time. I had work to do so I need to work instead."* Ben, an 18-year-old male ECET student, said, *"I want to stay focused on my major right now…just trying to survive through the semester. I actually joined [the anime club]. I kind of joined last semester but never really participated because it's my first semester at college. I freak out about my schedule so I don't participate in any clubs now."*

5.1.3 Previous Experiences Affect Later Participation

Respondents became frustrated with clubs that participated in activities outside of what respondents expected. Several respondents shared stories of going to a club meeting and being turned off by what they saw. Shawn, an 18-year-old male biology student, mentioned his experience with the anime club, *"I went to a couple of meetings. I didn't really like it because they didn't really do anything. I walked in and people were playing Magic [the card game]."* A similar problem happened to Kevin, a 19-year-old male IS student, *"I went to a sci-fi club meeting once. I sat there and realized they only watched anime."*

Bad experiences also affect respondents' motivation to participate in similar activities in the future. Leonard, a 20-year-old male civil engineering student, complained about a Frisbee group, *"they are really selective about who they throw their Frisbee at. They would only throw it to people they knew."* Anne, an 18-year-old female biology student, felt more comfortable playing basketball with her friends than with strangers in a pick-up game. She said, *"it is usually a group of boys at the gym, because girls don't usually play. That's why they don't pass me the ball or afraid to block me, because I'm a girl."* In light of such experiences, both respondents reported being reluctant to join pick-up games in their respective sports.

5.2 Information Not Getting to Target Audience

Respondents felt they were not receiving information about activities they were wanted to participate in. Fliers were posted around campus in public locations: on bulletin boards, on walls, and near elevators (Figure 1), respondents reported not being able to gather information relevant to them. Respondents gave reasons as to why they don't get this information. Kate, an 18-year-old female architecture student, revealed, *"I've seen fliers everywhere. I read the big letters, but I don't get up close. I'm always on the way to somewhere."* Ben, a 21-year-old male biomedical engineering student, agreed, *"I can choose to read them, or I can continue on my day. I'd rather not waste my time."* The main reason for respondents ignoring these signs was information overload – there were too many signs about activities not relevant to their interests.

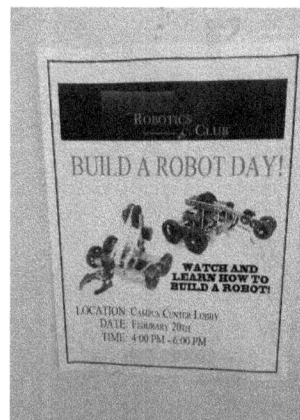

Figure 1: Wall flier advertising an activity

Current technological solutions were also ineffective. Students used Facebook invites for activities, but as Sam, a 20-year-old female architecture student, said, *"I get invited to a lot of things but that gets annoying. Most of the time its stuff I have no interest in. I end up ignoring things I would be interested in."* When asked about using Meetup.com, all respondents gave a similar answer as John, an 18-year-old male IT student, *"This is the first time I'm hearing about meetup.com"* Students did not know about or use this system built specifically for interest-based group coalescing.

126

Sam, a 20-year-old female architecture student, wished, *"I feel like there should be a better way to communicate. I feel that other campuses have some kind of Facebook."*

While respondents were aware of the university electronic calendar, they said did not find much use for it. Jillian, a 19-year-old female architecture student, said, *"You finally get to the calendar and it is listed in a way that is not intuitive. [...] A well-coordinated calendar would be nice."* Respondents also mentioned the University Facebook app, which was not a very good resource for activities. As shown in figures 2 and 3, messages asking about activities do not receive useful or accurate replies.

5.3 The Burden of Leadership

Many respondents said they were hesitant to start their own club for an interest if it did not already exist. They expected the task to be too time-consuming or difficult, especially since they did not know many others with the same interest. Shawn, an 18-year-old male biology student, said, *"I don't have time [to start a kickboxing club]. I just wish they had something like that. I wish that someone else would initiate it, not me. It's too much effort."*

The process for becoming a sanctioned club at the University required having a roster of at least 10 people, creating a constitution with club rules, and announcing/planning four events outside of a weekly meeting. John, an 18-year-old male IT student, who decided to create his own snowboarder club, explained how he gave up after finding that it was too much effort to start a club, in spite of finding enough people with the same interest. *"It was myself and a few friends who wanted to start it, because we had a president, secretary, treasurer, the positions you need for the club. So we needed 10 people. It was 4 of us, we needed 6 other people. Within a week we had 40 people who said they were interested in joining the snowboard club. The main problem was no one followed through. I gave everyone many chances to give me an application, even made it downloadable (on Facebook). I think I got 3 back out of 40 people. And then, I tried to set up a trip for us to go on, but it ended up me and one other person. So, based on all that, it didn't go well."*

Groups that started small had issues with continued membership and gaining critical mass. This lack of critical mass was also a factor in weaning enthusiasm among group leaders. Jimmy, a 21-year-old CS student, said, *"There used to be a guitar club on campus. We got together and played, and just talking too. I think the organizers were hoping more people would come. After the first couple meetings we stopped getting new people and they weren't enthusiastic anymore, the organizers. [...] It kind of just fell apart."*

6. DISCUSSION

This interview study sought to gain an understanding of the extent to which college students were participating in activities related to their interests in the current technological environment. In so doing, we discovered the challenges they face and factors that affect their finding, participating in, and leading interest-based group activities.

Many definitions of "community" exist [19], here we consider community to be a group of people living in the same place or having a particular characteristic in common. Local communities can be made up of small towns or neighborhoods. College campuses are akin to residential communities, residents move in with little to no knowledge of the other inhabitants, and waves of people enter, exit, and interact daily, nightly, and weekly. College campuses are unique in that 18-22 year olds usually populate them, and the residents are primarily students. While we believe our results are generalizable to small communities, further research is clearly needed to confirm this conjecture.

6.1 Lack of Optimal Social Activity Engagement

Our study shows that students' social needs are not being met within the college community. When we asked about their interests and the types of group activities they would like to participate in, and their level of involvement in such activities on campus, the disparity between activity interests and participatory engagement became immediately apparent. The main reason for this appears to be 1) the inability to easily find individuals who share the same interests and 2) there exists no established organizations/clubs for those interests.

While one would expect a small campus community to be close and tight knit we found that college students found it very hard to learn about the interests of its inhabitants. Several students expressed interest in participating in certain activities that their friends were not interested in but did not know others who shared their interests, and did not have a way to find them. Students only find out about others' interests after meeting them. Having no system that gives students the ability to seek and find others based on shared interests leads to missed opportunities to participate in interest-based group activities. This finding is further corroborated in our interviews where we found that even within the sample of respondents in the study, several reported similar interests, yet were not aware of others with those shared interests. For example, eight respondents were interested in dance, but only one participated with a dance group.

The college community under study boasts of a "club culture" where groups form school-sanctioned clubs based on interests. However there is mismatch between what students want and what the clubs offer. The school hosts a club fair one afternoon at the beginning of each semester, where clubs occupy booths to recruit new members. Many respondents mentioned finding a club they were interested in at the club fair, making this an easy method for students to find clubs on campus. While this allows students to participate in some social activities, they are often "satisficing" (sacrificing to satisfy needs) by participating in groups and activities that are not directly related to their interests in order to socialize. Joining a club because their friends are involved or because it is something to do does not satisfy respondents' needs for finding others who share similar interests, specifically their primary interests.

Overall, while students do participate in some social activities, they are not necessarily optimizing the number of activities they participate in, or participating in activities that match their interests. The need for social activity engagement on campus is currently not being met with several students expressing a desire to be involved with more clubs or activities that related to their interest.

6.2 Process Challenges of Social Activity Engagement

The inability to optimally participate in activities based on one's interests is tightly linked to the inability to find others who share the same interests or find ongoing activities on campus based on interests. There are a variety of activity advertising methods available to students (e.g. posters hung in public locations, Facebook groups/apps, an events calendar), but they are ineffective in reaching the target audience. Too often, influx of irrelevant activity advertisements cause individuals to ignore most of the ads they receive or see.

Finding others who enjoy a similar interest is an exhilarating feeling, and being accepted into a group gives students the chance to create bonds. There are occasions, however, where joining an interest-based activity can have negative consequences. There are instances where respondents participated in interest-based group activities that became less than ideal situations. Several respondents mentioned participating in a group where they felt like outsiders to the others. In these situations, the respondents' reactions were to not partake in an activity with that group again, or to dismiss participating in that activity with strangers anymore.

There is an issue of expectation versus reality that forms between group organizers and participants. Some groups advertise a specific interest, but are created to serve ulterior motives (e.g. a ski club created for the purpose of socializing). This often turns off individuals who seek out an interest-based group for the purpose of sharing their interest with like-minded individuals. The anime club is an example, where respondents expected to watch Japanese animated cartoons and movies, but in reality, they witnessed other unrelated activities instead. Explicitly expressing the purpose of a group leads to the target audience joining and staying with particular groups. Initially stating the true purpose of a group could reduce the disenchantment we have seen.

Some respondents who left the anime club because their expectations were not met ended up satisficing their needs with groups of others who had a minority interest in anime. Others were not so lucky, and have no way of finding other interested parties who are not part of the anime club. This again reaffirms that individuals have difficulty finding others who share the same interest. If a major group cannot satisfy their needs, where can they go? These individuals could benefit greatly from meeting each other.

While our respondents had a range of significant unmet social group activity interests, most were unwilling to step forward and lead an effort to coalesce a critical mass of participants. Reasons given included a lack of knowledge of the existence of a critical mass of potential participants, personal preferences, and the uncertainty regarding the effort required and likelihood of success. This appears to be the main barrier to the coalescing of emergent groups, which is highly dependent on one individual or a very small group of individuals doing a significant amount of legwork to find and organize the other individuals who are willing to participate in a group activity. The result is that the majority of individuals (who find this burden too great) decide to simply wait and hope that somebody else does the work required.

6.3 Technological Challenges of Social Activity Engagement

Use of technology by social group activity organizers appears to be driven by a desire to inform as many potential participants as possible about an upcoming event. However, the technology used to notify people such as Facebook Invites and email nearly always goes out to a large number of people with little interest in the activity in question. The result is that people feel that they are being spammed, suffer from information overload, and as a consequence ignore the majority of activity related messages, which may or may not be of personal relevance. The school also

implemented a Facebook App for students to converse. Students tried to repurpose the app for finding others who share interests (using discussion threads to advertise their interests), but the low population of users and inability to alert others using the app reduced its effectiveness. Figures 2 and 3 show instances where students used the Facebook app to find soccer activities, but in both cases the answer did not help them find a group activity. While students try to use technology to find others with shared interests, the inability to find, alert, or recommend others hinders the coalescing process.

Figure 2: Missed opportunity due to lack of awareness

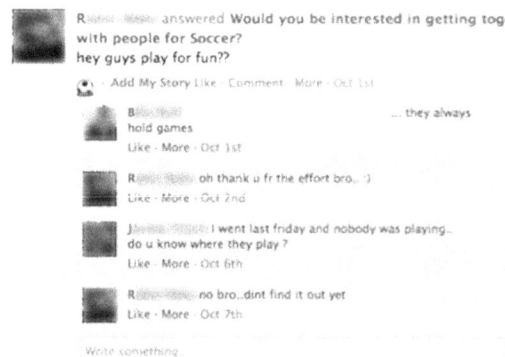

Figure 3: Looking for soccer players on Facebook

Systems such as *Meetup.com*, which are designed specifically for interest-based group activity coalescing are unused and largely unknown by the student campus community. Although Meetup is designed to bring individuals together who share common interests, it is not ideal for use in small communities or college campuses. The issues brought up by respondents exist in Meetup's current configuration. Meetup is focused on individual organizers/leaders making the payment, time, and effort to create Meetup groups.

Meetup's system of using a single organizer to create groups and activities leads to the same problem as above; individuals must step forward to begin the coalescing process without knowledge of shared community interest, or "how many people share my interest, and are willing to participate in an activity?" The only indication is if there are similar groups already in existence, but creating multiple groups for the same purpose leads to reduction in critical mass by spreading those who share the same interest into several groups. Also, Meetup is designed such that groups are created to host activities. Activities cannot be created on their own. This makes ac hoc activities and emergent groups (e.g. "pick-up basketball now", "card game tournament today") difficult to use and naturally form through the system.

6.4 Design Considerations

Our examination of the challenges faced by students wishing to participate in social group-activities provides us with new insights into the extent to which the current state of participation is sub-optimal. In an ideal world, interest-based activity group formation would be optimized in such a way that every person is satisfied by the quality and quantity of groups they participate in. Every person would participate in the optimum number of interest-based activities, which are in dependent on their interests. In parallel, there would be a balance between individual and community needs, with a community also having the optimum number of activities occurring at any given time with the optimum number of participants (e.g. never too few or too many to hinder success). For example, if a person was interested in both playing volleyball and "arts and crafts", and 9 others were willing to play volleyball right now, but only one person was willing to craft, a system taking into account both community and individual needs would recommend the volleyball activity to the 10 willing individuals.

Gale and Shapley shared the Nobel Prize in Economics for their work on Stable Market Theory [14], developing an algorithm that pairs members of two groups in such a way that no other pairing would be better [13]. If we re-conceptualize community based social group-activities as occurring within an 'activity market', then we can use the notion of "Stable Markets" to understand the extent to which the current situation is far from the optimal. Unfortunately, we cannot simply apply Gale and Shapley's solutions to activity markets because 1) coalescing groups is more complex than pairs; 2) communities are dynamic, people enter and leave often (e.g. commuters come to campus for a certain number of hours per day); and 3) there are unknown variables (e.g. every member's interests, availability, and willingness to participate. That said, we can start to think of the coalescing problem not as that of individuals, but of the community in which the individual operates.

This more holistic interpretation of coalescing challenges leads us to call for new system designs that take into account the population of interests of the community as a whole and availability of willing participants (the activity marketplace). This would allow for 1) highly targeted outreach without the overload that currently results in people ignoring potentially relevant information; and 2) a reduction in the burden and risks associated with helping to organize social group activities, as greater information would be available regarding the pool of potential participations and how to reach them. Of course, capturing the overall real-time participatory interest levels of members of a community is not an easy task. Research must be conducted to understand how user search behavior can reflect their interests and level of willingness to find others who share that interest.

One major issue that survey respondents brought up was the difficulty in finding others who share interests. Currently, interest-based group activity systems have a similar problem. Systems wait for an individual to create a group, then use keywords in the group description to recommend the group to individuals who share that interest. Having a database of individuals' interests has the potential to recommend individuals to each other in a group setting to facilitate the coalescing process. By opening communication between these individuals, they could discuss their interest as well as collaborate on forming a group or organizing an activity. The system could give the group a forum/chat room or simply the option to send a message to the individuals – e.g. there are five others who like anime. Why don't you start a group for anime?" Showing that other individuals have

the same interest lowers the barrier of finding others, and increases the possibility that one person will step forward to start a new group. Putting a group together may create the immediate critical mass of interested individuals needed to form a new group.

6.5 Limitations and Future Work

This research set out to explore activity leadership and participation, rather than answer precisely framed questions. To achieve this we adopted a semi-structured interview method that had both benefits and costs associated with it. In this study the interviews were powerful means of gathering insight into the context of wants and needs of the community, but the small sample cannot indicate the number of people who share interests across the entire community. The community that was studied is of a very specific type – a college campus community. While we believe the similarity between members of the college campus and members of local communities is close enough to validate generalizability, we need further research on people's interest-based group activity- seeking behavior to claim that this is truly generalizable.

A natural extension of this work is to consider the use of technology in finding activities. We plan to execute a qualitative study that focuses on users of *Meetup.com*, and specifically, looking at organizers and their attempts (failed and successful) to create *Meetup* groups on specific activities.

From this, we will continue the research by using quantitative methods to understand how current coalescing methods affect both online and offline experiences. The surveys will be sent to samples of both the university and Meetup.com populations in an effort to compare the two. This will lead to an elucidation of the problems people face in becoming leaders and an understanding of what needs to be done in order to support emergent leaders in future applications.

7. CONCLUSION

This paper presents findings of an interview study that focused on the interests and activities of college students. These results represent a first step towards understanding the coalescing process of interest-based group activities. We found that the process of finding and leading such activities is currently not optimal and barriers prevent groups from forming. These findings point towards a need to better understand the coalescing process in small communities in order to build better systems to support successful coalescing for interest-based group activities.

8. REFERENCES

[1] Adger, W.N. 2010. Social capital, collective action, and adaptation to climate change. *Der Klimawandel*. Oxford University Press for Social Sciences. 327–345.

[2] Allport, F. 1924. *Social Psychology*. Houghton Mifflin.

[3] Ashforth, B.E. and Mael, F. 1989. Social identity theory and the organization. *Academy of management review*. (1989), 20–39.

[4] Ashida, S. and Heaney, C.A. 2008. Social Networks and Participation in Social Activities at a New Senior Center: Reaching Out to Older Adults Who Could Benefit the Most. *Adaptation & Aging*. 32, 1 (2008), 40–58.

[5] Bargh, J. A. and McKenna, K. Y. A. 2004. The Internet and Social Life. *Annual Review of Psychology*. 55, (Feb. 2004), 573–590.

[6] Blum, F.H. 1955. Action research--A scientific approach? *Philosophy of science*. 22, 1 (1955), 1–7.

[7] Bruce W. Tuckman and Mary Ann C. Jensen 1977. Stages of Small-Group Development Revisited. *Group Organization Management*. 2, 4 (Dec. 1977), 419–427.

[8] Burke, R. et al. 2011. Experience Discovery: hybrid recommendation of student activities using social network data. *Proceedings of the 2nd International Workshop on Information Heterogeneity and Fusion in Recommender Systems* (2011), 49–52.

[9] Coleman, J.S. 1966. Foundations for a Theory of Collective Decisions. *American Journal of Sociology*. (1966), 615–627.

[10] Coleman, S. 1988. Social Capital in the Creation of Human Capital. *American Journal of Sociology*. 94, (1988), 95–120.

[11] Dennen, V.P. 2008. Pedagogical lurking: Student engagement in non-posting discussion behavior. *Computers in Human Behavior*. 24, 4 (2008), 1624–1633.

[12] Ellison, N. B. et al. Social network sites and society: current trends and future possibilities. *interactions*. 16, 1, 6–9.

[13] Gale, D. and Shapley, L. S. 1962. College Admissions and the Stability of Marriage. *The American Mathematical Monthly*. 69, 1 (Jan. 1962), 9–15.

[14] Gale, D. and Shapley, L. S. Stable Allocations and the Practice of Market Design. *The Royal Swedish Academy of Sciences*.

[15] Gold, N. and Sugden, R. 2007. Collective intentions and team agency. *Journal of Philosophy*. 104, 3 (2007), 109–37.

[16] Helliwell, J.F. and Putnam, R. The Social Context of Well-Being. *Philosophical Transactions of the Royal Society*. 359, 1449, 1435–1446.

[17] Hiltz, S. R. and Turoff, M. 1978. *The Network Nation: Human Communication Via Computer*. Addison Wesley.

[18] Hurlbert, J. et al. 2001. Social Networks and Social Capital in Extreme Environments. *Social Capital: Theory and Research*. Transaction Publishers. 209–231.

[19] Jones, Q. 1997. Virtual-Communities, Virtual Settlements & Cyber-Archaeology: A Theoretical Outline. *Journal of Computer-Mediated Communication*. 3, 3 (Dec. 1997).

[20] Joyce, E. and Kraut, R. 2006. Predicting Continued Participation in Newsgroups. *Journal of Computer•Mediated Communication*. 11, 3 (2006), 723–747.

[21] Lampe, C. et al. 2006. A Face (book) in the crowd: Social searching vs. social browsing. (2006), 167–170.

[22] Lampe, C. and Johnston, E. 2005. Follow the (slash) dot: effects of feedback on new members in an online community. *Proceedings of the 2005 international ACM SIGGROUP conference on Supporting group work* (2005), 11–20.

[23] Latane, B. and Darley, J. 1970. *The unresponsive bystander: Why doesn't he help?* Prentice Hall.

[24] Liu, X. et al. 2012. Event-based social networks: linking the online and offline social worlds. *Proceedings of the 18th ACM SIGKDD international conference on Knowledge discovery and data mining* (2012), 1032–1040.

[25] Merton, R. K. 1968. *Social Theory and Social Structure*. The Free Press.

[26] Moreno, M. A. et al. 2013. Exploring Depression Symptom References on Facebook among College Freshmen: A Mixed Methods Approach. *Open Journal of Depression*. 2, 3 (2013), 35–41.

[27] Oliver, P. et al. 1985. A theory of the critical mass. I. Interdependence, group heterogeneity, and the production of collective action. *American Journal of Sociology*. (1985), 522–556.

[28] Olson, M. 1965. *The Logic of Collective Action: Public Goods and the Theory of Group*. Harvard University Press.

[29] Park, N. et al. 2009. Being Immersed in Social Networking Environment: Facebook Groups, Uses and Gratifications, and Social Outcomes. *Cyberpsychology & Behavior*. 12, 6 (2009), 729–733.

[30] Pempek, T. A. et al. 2009. College students' social networking experiences on Facebook. *Journal of Applied Developmental Psychology*. 30, 3 (2009), 227–238.

[31] Prentice, D.A. et al. 1994. Asymmetries in attachments to groups and to their members: Distinguishing between common-identity and common-bond groups. *Key Readings in Social Psychology*. (1994), 83.

[32] Putnam, R. 2000. *Bowling Alone*. Simon & Schuster.

[33] Raban, D.R. et al. 2009. Hello Stranger! A Study of Introductory Communication Structure and Social Match Success. (2009), 1–9.

[34] Rainie, L. 2013. *The internet is a Diversion and Destination*. Pew Research Center.

[35] Ren, Y. et al. 2007. Applying Common Identity and Bond Theory to Design of Online Communities. *Organization Studies*. 28, 377 (2007).

[36] Shklovski, I. et al. 2004. The Internet and Social Participation: Contrasting Cross-Sectional and Longitudinal Analyses. *Journal of Computer-Mediated Communication*. 10, 1 (Nov. 2004).

[37] Tajfel, H. 1981. *Human Groups and Social Categories: Studies in Social Psychology*. Cambridge University Press.

[38] Tuckman, B. W. 1965. Developmental sequence in small groups. *Psychological bulletin*. 63, 6 (1965).

[39] Tuomela, R. 2005. We-Intentions Revisited. *Philosophical Studies*. 125, 3 (2005), 327–369.

[40] Turner, J.C. et al. 1987. *Rediscovering the social group: A self-categorization theory*. Basil Blackwell.

[41] Wei, M. et al. Adult Attachment, Social Self-Efficacy, Self-Disclosure, Loneliness, and Subsequent Depression for Freshman College Students: A Longitudinal Study. *Journal of Counseling Psychology*. 52, 4, 602–614.

Exploring How Parents in Economically Depressed Communities Access Learning Resources

Parisa Khanipour Roshan, Maia Jacobs, Michaelanne Dye, and Betsy DiSalvo

Georgia Institute of Technology
College of Computing, GVU
Atlanta GA 30332 USA
khanipour@gatech.edu, mjacobs30@gatech.edu, mdye@cc.gatech.edu, bdisalvo@cc.gatech.edu

ABSTRACT

This qualitative study of parents in financially depressed communities in westside Atlanta examines parents' access to information technology and out-of-school learning resources through five dimensions of digital divide: technical apparatus, autonomy, social support, skill, and purpose. The context of this study is a broader research agenda to explore how technology impacts parents' knowledge and use of out-of-school learning resources for their children in low socioeconomic status neighborhoods. The findings contribute to a growing body of research on marginalized groups and provide a rich description of parents' digital access and technology practices in the context of education. Finally, we identify design implications that are specific to this community and can be extended to similar populations to support parents in finding more learning opportunities.

Author Keywords

Digital Inequalities; Digital Divide; Access; Informal Learning; Education; Social Capital; African American; Marginalized Communities; ICTD

ACM Classification Keywords

K.4.2. Social Issues

1. INTRODUCTION

I feel like good resources are always like a needle in a haystack. We always have to look for those resources. Like resources aren't out there being advertised like McDonald's - Maria (all names are pseudonyms)

This quote represents a problem many parents in financially depressed communities are facing when trying to find out-of-school, informal learning resources for their children. Parents are important facilitators for informal learning among their children [3], and how parents utilize technology to find resources and ideas for informal learning impacts a child's exposure and interest in education [16]. However, there is a gap in the literature about parents' use of technology in low-income families and their role as resource brokers for supporting their children's education.

In this study, we focus on the access of African American parents in low-income neighborhoods in metro Atlanta, and reflect on the design opportunities to empower this audience to gain access to a broader array of educational resources for improving their children's educational attainment.

We propose that the first step towards understanding and designing for parents' access to informal educational resources is to move beyond a binary view of access (i.e., whether or not one has the technical means to access the internet). Instead, we seek to address this issue as a complex sociotechnical problem embedded in one's skill, practices, and cultural settings. Therefore, we adopt a multi-dimensional lens at digital inequality, as outlined by DiMaggio et al.'s five dimensions of access [13]. In their paper, authors argue that in addition to having the technical means of getting online, researchers also need to examine the degree of autonomy one has over their technology use, the social support they receive for continuous use, whether one has the required skills to effectively use the system to its full potential, and finally, whether they use it for the purposes that increase their financial, educational, or social capital.

Investigating the complex sociotechnical barriers of access through the lens of these dimensions, as well as investigating parents' roles in their children's education through interviewing 28 parents, this research provides insight on parents' use of information technologies, their everyday practices, cultural values, and the role of technology in finding learning opportunities.

Beyond issues of access, through the interviews emerged participants' current ways of exchanging information; the most significant of which was a close sense of community among parents and the focal role of parent-to-parent communications in finding and sharing information about the opportunities available.

We propose that a large portion of current informal learning resources and methods of accessing them have not been designed for the specific needs of low-income families who have traditions of low educational attainment. By investigating the design of accessible, culturally relevant sociotechnical systems that are specifically targeted at this audience, we seek to increase a more equalized access to the rich array of free and inexpensive informal learning opportunities.

While our research focuses on the realm of learning, it has broader implications for the Human-Computer Interaction (HCI) community. The main contributions of this paper are twofold:

1. We examine parents' access in financially depressed communities beyond a binary look at their "have" and "have-nots". Our findings contribute to a growing body of research on technically underserved groups and provide a rich description of their technology practices, cultural beliefs, and

perspectives on using technology as a way to access learning resources.

2. We argue that the design that would help increase parents' access to learning resources should be embedded in their current practices and needs. Our analysis of parents' technology-use along the five dimensions of access reveals several everyday practices woven in their local culture that can inform the design of new technologies. We identify design implications that are specific to this community and provide details for transferring the results to similar populations to support parents in finding learning opportunities.

We begin this paper by providing the motivation for our work and reviewing previous research regarding the digital divide, technology access among marginalized groups, and the role of parents in education and technology use. Secondly, we describe our research methodology and participants. Then, we present our findings through a framework of five dimensions of inequalities in access to information technology and emerging themes in parents' current practices. We conclude by framing the findings in a discussion of implications for the context of this paper: increasing parents' access to out-of-school learning resources for their children

2. MOTIVATION

Recently, there has been an explosion of courses and learning resources offered online. Khan Academy, Coursera, and Udacity are a few examples of Massively Open Online Courses (MOOCs) that have gained attention. There are also sandbox activities, educational games, and a broad expanse of news, blogs and other media that provide access to online play and discovery, important skills in shaping learners for the 21's century [23].

While these learning resources are frequently free, research suggests that due to unequal awareness of online informal learning tools, the way they are marketed, differences in cultural values of audiences, and their different levels of access, these free resources may be increasing the educational gap, privileging well-educated and the wealthy populations, and therefore, further broadening the gap between the rich and poor in terms of education and income [30,31].

However, there is a lack of research focusing on parents' role in facilitating access to these free learning resources for their children. We argue for the importance of addressing this topic since, while some audiences are able to navigate and critically evaluate online resources, the groups that may be in the greatest need (i.e., low-income and low-educational families), may have problems finding appropriate and effective learning resources [14]. We believe that this issue can be addressed through research on issues of access and technology use, and the design of systems that specifically speak to marginalized communities.

3. BACKGROUND

Access to information technology has gained attention from several different research areas. Social scientists have been reviewing the concept of digital divide for many years. Within the HCI community, researchers have sought to better understand access issues and their potential for impacting technology design among underserved populations. Parents, especially in the context of education, are among one of the most important emerging audience within the HCI research, and examining their technology use remains to be further investigated. In all of these contexts, social support and access to extended networks play an important role in shaping one's access to information technologies. In these sections, we reflect on some the previous studies along these lines and situate our work in the current research.

3.1 The Problem Formerly Known As The Digital Divide

Traditionally, digital divide has contrasted those who do and do not have access to computers with internet connection. However, this issue carries far more complexities [35]. By classifying technology users into one of these two groups, important factors such as context, language, education, community, and social resources are overlooked. The binary framing of the digital divide overemphasizes the presence of computing devices, instead of examining other important factors that contribute to the problem [35]. For example, in deploying low-cost laptop use in Mexican schools, HCI researchers found that creating the infrastructures needed to sustain the laptop use goes beyond simply providing the devices, and is dependent upon various sociotechnical issues around the context of community [8].

In their paper, *From Unequal Access to Differentiated Use*, DiMaggio et al. have framed digital divide by redefining the definition of "access" to include people's quality of information technology use from five aspects [13]:

1. *Technical apparatus* by which people access the Internet,
2. *Autonomy of use* when they get online,
3. *Social support* on which they can draw when facing technical difficulties,
4. *Skill* in effectively using the affordances of technology, and,
5. *Purposes* they use the technology for

This framework has been broadly adopted by social scientists and policy makers as a substitute for the previous binary view. Therefore, we positioned our research on parents' access through this lens as it provides a valuable tool in revealing hidden aspects of information technology use, especially among underprivileged communities.

Our work builds upon the existing research on underserved populations in the HCI community. Various researchers have begun to examine the effects of culturally relevant technology designs on marginalized communities both within the US (e.g., [26]), and in developing countries (e.g., [32]). In these cases, an in-depth analysis of the complex sociotechnical context of the community is crucial in the success of design. For example, when designing video games for children in rural India, Kam et al. [24] discovered that the game's design had to rely heavily on the values of the community in order for it to effectively engage the population. Additionally, this research emphasized the role that parents played in the adoption of certain games among their children.

Recent efforts have started to address the issues of digital divide by providing physical public spaces where young people can access computers. For instance, the Intel computer clubhouse network[1] provides access to computers and mentors to youth from underserved communities. The Come_IN project in Germany also addresses this issue by creating an intercultural computer clubhouse to provide physical access to computers for underprivileged social groups, particularly immigrant families [33]. Moreover, this project emphasizes the importance of integrating parents in the process as informal learning partners, for achieving a socio-cultural learning experience.

3.2 Parents Access to Information Technology

Parents play an important part in the kinds of learning opportunities children are exposed to. When studying children from suburban

---

[1] http://www.computerclubhouse.org

neighborhoods in the San Francisco Bay Area, Forssell et al. discovered that parents play a crucial role in supporting their children's adoption of new media technologies. Interestingly, the study revealed that, although parents may not be adept users of technological services, they still affect their children's degree of technological literacy [16]. However, constraints and attitudes toward technology differ among parents across different populations, further stressing the need for close assessment of variations in behavior and use [34]. For instance, in a study of teens' use of technology for informal learning, authors discovered that parents' distrust toward technology may restrain teens from finding informal learning opportunities in their extended networks [27]. Therefore, authors call for more investigations in parent's practices and values toward technology as a worthwhile research direction.

While parents are an emergent audience within the HCI community, to date research has explored parents' understanding and mediation of their child's digital lives [[1], [9], 38, 39] rather than their technology and information seeking practices to access learning resources for their children. In a study of parents acting as learning partners in the development of technological fluency, Barron and colleagues [3] found that parents play a critical role in creating learning opportunities for their children. Two parenting roles identified in the study, (1) *Learning Broker*, when parents seek learning opportunities for the child; and (2) *Resource Provider*, when parents supply resources beyond the family computer to the child, are closely tied to the parent's ability to effectively seek educational resources. Contrasting the findings from this research, which is focused on parents with high levels of educational attainment and income, with our findings on parent's access to informal learning resources in underprivileged communities, highlights the need to address differential access to online learning based upon education and income.

3.3 Social Support and Networks

The benefits of maintaining and drawing on a network of strong and weak ties have been well studied. Learning new information is more likely to happen through connections that are not embedded in one's close network [18]. This is because individuals within the same network are most likely to be exposed to the same sources of information. Therefore, establishing ties that would bridge the structural holes would increase one's chances of being exposed to new information and build social capital [18]. Social capital, commonly defined as benefits made possible by the existence of an aggregate social interactions and social structure, allows individuals to draw on resources from other members within their networks [11]. These resources can take the form of useful information, personal relationships, or the capacity to organize groups. Previous research has linked the ability to form strong and weak ties online to increased emotional and economic support [17]. Moreover, Burke et al. associate active use of online social networks with increased social capital and reduced loneliness [7]. In the context of learning, examining the effect of parents' social capital on their children's educational achievements shows that the ability to bridge social capital through parents' weak ties increases the opportunities available to children [14].

While some audiences are able to navigate and critically evaluate online learning resources, low-income and low-educational families' ability to access these resources is less explored. Thus far, neither research nor educational providers have deeply addressed these families' need to access online learning resources. A first step toward addressing this gap is to examine the issues of inequality beyond a binary view to unfold the cultural values and current technology practices present among parents.

4. METHODS

In order to study the detailed practices of this population, semi-structured interviews were conducted with parents attending different events at two different sites located in financially depressed neighborhoods in Atlanta. The locations, a middle school and a parent resource center, were visited during 2012 and 2013. We chose qualitative approach as this study was exploratory in nature. We wanted to examine parents' access to information technologies as well as their perspective and practices participating in their children's education. The five researchers conducting the interviews were all female and self-identified as white American, African American, or Middle Eastern.

4.1 Recruitment and Participants

Interviews were conducted with participants from similar populations at two locations. The first location was a public middle school whose population is 99% African-American and approximately 80% of them are economically disadvantaged. The second location was a parent resource center located in a public elementary school, where parents regularly dropped in to use computers, get information, and attend workshops. To recruit participants we introduced ourselves and asked if they would be interested in talking about their children's education and technology use for approximately 30 minutes. We informed them they would receive $15 in compensation. We interviewed 28 individuals who were acting as parents for children, but also included grandmothers and aunts. Of the 28 participants, there were 26 females and two males, all self-identified as African American. The greater number of female participants followed the same pattern of imbalance in parents' participation at the center and at school events. Recruited parents represented a diverse range of engagement level, from presidents of Parent Teacher Associations, to parents who rarely visited their child's school.

Interviews lasted between 20 and 90 minutes depending on the topics brought up by the participants, their availability, and interest in continuing the conversation. At the beginning of the interviews, participants were asked about the number of children they have and their ages. After this introduction, researchers asked a series of questions about technical access issues outlined by the five dimension of digital inequality introduced earlier. Participants were further asked a series of questions about their involvement in formal and informal education with their children, the role that technology plays in their child's education, and their expectations for their child's future. At the end of the session, we asked parents to answer a survey about demographic information such as their employment and relationship status, partners in parenting, and number of children.

Although we collected the data on the percentage of participants who were single or did not have a partner in parenting, we refrain from providing a numerical break down of this data. This is because during the interviews, we realized that the family structures and the division of parenting roles were often too complex to be captured by a quantitative representation. We realize that there is no single normal way to define what makes up a family, and therefore, believe that presenting the statistics may portray a flawed image of the community.

Interviews were audio recorded, transcribed, and coded based upon five aspects of digital inequality [12]. Table 1 outlines these five aspects of digital inequality with a description, an example of what qualified as an utterance relevant to that code, and the number of times that code was used in our analysis.

Title	Description	Example	# of codes
Technical apparatus	Talk concerning access to or limited access to technical means.	*"We really need another computer to get back online so he can get back to learning."*	122
Autonomy /Child Autonomy	Talk concerning institutional, social or parental limitations, or open use of technology.	*"So, he doesn't [use Facebook] because I know how to check."*	206
Skill	Talk concerning skill in using and trouble shooting problems with technology.	*"The computer has a different system you have to update. That gives me a hard time."*	167
Social Support	Talk concerning social support for using or trouble shooting technology.	*"They were real good with me, because momma's the dummy right here."*	115
Variation in Use	Talk concerning varied or limited purposes for using technology.	*"I might use it for shopping and just to look up general information."*	309

Table 1. Code descriptors for inequality in digital access

Two researchers coded, refined codes, and trained on coding reaching .80+ inter-rater reliability on 20% of the interviews. Inter-rater reliability is reported using Cohen's Kappa statistic—Cohen [10]. Landis and Koch [25], suggest that kappa values of: <.20 = poor agreement, .21-.4 = fair agreement, .41-.6 = moderate agreement, .61-.8 = good agreement, and .81-1.0 = very good agreement. The authors then reviewed the groups of excerpts for each code in order to identify patterns in the context of digital access.

5. FINDINGS

In this section, we first present our findings organized by DiMaggio et. al's five dimensions of digital access as a framework to investigate digital inequality among a community of parents in a financially depressed neighborhood. Then we move forward by reflecting on some of the emergent themes that came up in the interviews when we asked parents about the way they usually find out about out-of-school resources.

While our participants are all African American parents from the west side Atlanta, they represent a diversity of ages and levels of expertise regarding technology. Our findings serve to provide empirical evidence to present a rich and realistic account of the community's online practices, and help us avoid making assumptions about the community. These descriptions are presented to inform future design for financially depressed communities. It is important to note that all of the parents who interviewed with us, even when they did not or could not access learning resources, expressed a great desire to help their children, and education was a big part of the goals they had for their children. We would like to emphasize that our findings do not present a critique of parenting skills. Instead, we are trying to provide a realistic image of how

technology practices impact a population's access to learning resources.

5.1 Technical Apparatus

DiMaggio et al.'s first dimension of digital inequality, technical apparatus, deals with the physical availability of suitable technical means that provide effective access to online tools. In this section, we examine the technologies currently in use by participants, their access to suitable hardware and software for connecting to the internet, and the speed and bandwidth of their connection. Examining this dimension reveals more than basic accessibility of technical means and provides us with insights into unique characteristics of the community, which are discussed in the following sections.

5.1.1 Technical Mediums of Access

One of the aspects of technical apparatus is having access to the necessary hardware to get online. Participants reported a widespread adoption of smartphones. Twenty-four (85.7%) of the participants we interviewed owned smartphones and twenty-two of them (78.6%) discussed having internet connectivity on their phones. Five participants mentioned connecting to the internet on portable devices other than cellphones (such as tablets); in these cases the portable device was mostly used by the children. Finally, all but three of the participants had a laptop or desktop computers at home (89%), although the device was usually shared among the members of the family (this is discussed in following sections).

Several of the participants mentioned a higher level of comfort and preference connecting to the internet on laptop or desktops. Issues such as difficulty of interacting with a small display were among the reasons mentioned. However, all three participants who did not own a computer at home owned smartphones with internet connectivity which they used as their primary means of connecting to the internet. In these cases, the smartphone was often used as a shared device for the family, specially the children who used the smartphone to browse websites or play games. One of the participants who shares her smartphone with her two preschoolers describes this issue in the following quote, and further explains that she is often forced to use the computers at the parent center as a result:

> *My kids will be on my phone trying to do technology, pull up games, YouTube, and all that other stuff... They're always on my phone.* (Quinn)

Interviews show that, cell phones, which are often considered a personal device, are frequently used as a shared device among participants and their families.

5.1.2 Technical Apparatus and Security

In addition to having access to physical means of connecting to the internet, access to effective software constitutes another aspect of technical apparatus. One issue that limited the use of internet services among many of our participants was the fear of cyber attacks and unwanted malwares. The fear of these threats was intensified by the fact that the majority of our participants did not have appropriate antivirus software to protect their devices against such threats. This concern often deterred them from visiting unfamiliar websites. This was especially important in situations where participants' families owned one computer system, a common situation for several families with low income. In these situations, the participant could not afford to lose their system, and therefore, restricted their use of computer to avoid possible attacks.

One example of this self-regulation of services can be seen in *Mandy*'s reflection on her activities online. Mandy is a mother of five school-age children, she is working toward an online degree, and the whole family shares a desktop computer.

> *I have to be careful and mindful who's on my computer and what they're getting on in the internet, because my Norton Antivirus Protection is expired. I no longer take emails that I don't know anything about, because that's like the only computer we have.* (Mandy)

This example, and other participants' experiences, demonstrates the limitations that participants may impose on themselves and their children, even when the means for connection were available.

5.1.3 Internet Connectivity
The third aspect of technical apparatus is the quality of internet connection (e.g., speed or bandwidth). Despite the diverse age range and technical experiences among participants, the majority of them discussed having high-speed internet connectivity in their homes, and the majority of them used the internet on a daily basis. One participant also mentioned having a hotspot that they used to have internet connectivity in different places.

5.2 Autonomy
Although having the technical means is necessary for connecting to the internet, it does not guarantee an effective use. Autonomy of use refers to the degree of control and flexibility one has over their internet use. The more autonomy one enjoys, the more one has power over where, when, and how she wants to access the internet. Issues such as time limitations on a shared device, using public devices, and filtering on the kinds of services available on a network impose restrictions on one's autonomy.

5.2.1 Use of shared devices
Owning a device that is exclusively used by an individual increases one's degree of autonomy. Participants indicated that it was not always possible, due to financial issues, to provide personal devices for each member of the family. A majority of participants shared a computer (or sometimes their smartphones) with their children. This is inline with the findings of previous studies on the technology use of low socioeconomic status families [39]. Although all participants had the technical means to get online, only two parents had a computer they could use exclusively. Therefore, a majority of participants were not able to use these devices whenever and however they needed to. This issue was brought up in several of our interviews:

> *I'm like the odd man out. 'I'll get it when you all have gone to bed or I can use it when you're at school or something like that.'* (Tessa)

> *Everybody* [uses the computer]. *(Laughter) Family of six people!...(Laughter) It's a fight for it. The children use it more than the adults.* (Veronica)

These excerpts are a subset of numerous stories shared with us explaining the challenges and tensions cause by sharing devices among family members.

5.2.2 Use of Public devices
Several of the participants interviewed used the computers at the public spaces such as libraries or parent centers. This use of public devices was prevalent even among the participants who owned a computer at home. Using public devices enforces various restrictions on when, where, and how one is able to use online services, which consequently decreases the autonomy in use. This issue was particularly intensified in this community, as many parents do not own a car and rely on public transportation. Furthermore, most of the parents interviewed worked outside the home, which imposes further limitations on the time they can visit such facilities during their hours of operation.

Sylvia, a working mother of two, talks about the issues she faces using the computers at the library as she does not own a computer at home:

> *I do some time* [go to the library]. *It depends, you know, on what time the library closes... it is much better than on your phone.* (Sylvia)

Sylvia goes on to explain that she tries to go to the library twice a week and she is able to use the computers for 30 minutes each time. The issue of limited time was brought up by other parents as well. Sherri, a full-time working mother with 4 children, explains this issue in the following quote:

> *You go to Atlanta Public Library and you only get like an hour. So, you're maybe lucky to get maybe extended time at some periods of the day if people are not in the library waiting to use the computer* (Sherri)

However, not every parent is able to incorporate regular visits to public facilities into their busy schedules. For instance, Mandy has one computer at home, which she relies on for taking online courses. Therefore, she does not trust her children with her computer due to the danger of cyber attacks mentioned in the previous section. She explains that she often faces difficulty taking her children to the library to use the computer facilities:

> *If we have time, we go to the library. But normally, I call the teachers and say, 'Look, their access is limited,' because he has a lot of stuff he has to type up.* (Mandy)

In addition to the issues surrounding the accessibility of these places, participants face limitations while using the computers as well. Several online resources, including social networking sites and online games, are restricted on public networks at libraries or schools. This imposes further limitations on the autonomy of use among participants who rely on using these services to get online.

5.2.3 Limiting Children's Access
One finding from our interviews was the percentage of participants (75%), who shared the concern to limit their children's access to online services. Part of this was regarding their concern about the vulnerability of their children toward online threats and the desire to keep them safe, and the other part was due to the risks of viruses and malwares that could affect the performance of their devices. The following examples illuminate participants' feeling of mistrust towards different online services that are available to their children:

> *They really don't recognize the dangers that are out there as far as predators and things like that. . . I'm pretty vigilant about walking past to glance and see what site they're on. If I'm unsure, I will even stop and take the mouse and navigate to see what's there.* (Teresa)

Olive, a working single mother of four, expresses her concern about viruses as her primary reason she does not allow freedom of use to her children regarding their only computer at home:

> *They have to come ask me first and tell me what site they're going on. So, if they want to play a game or anything, because viruses picks up easily.* (Olive)

However, the restrictions imposed on children due to these concerns were sometimes very broad:

> *I try to oversee the sites that they try to navigate on, from downloading material they know nothing about. I try to explain to them what a warning certificate is all about. I just had to get*

rid of a virus twenty days ago. My whole computer crashed. So, it was one of those sites that offers all of these games or whatever. As soon as you clicked on it, the viruses just like, Boom! (Teresa)

In these cases, participants restricted their children's access to a broad range of online services that would include several educational websites and games as well. This is inline with research on teens' use of internet and social media that shows parents' concerns toward technology may work as a barrier for some teens to reach into extended networks and support their informal learning activities [27].

5.3 Skill

In addition to technical apparatuses and autonomy, technical competency plays an important role in understanding online inequality. Having the right technical skills closely affects the degree to which people successfully find information online [19], in addition to impacting the types of activities they perform [20].

5.3.1 Identity and Technical Competency

Although the majority of participants used the internet on a daily basis and demonstrated technical skills in various tasks, most of them chose to identify themselves as "not a tech person" during their interviews. For example, Vanessa, a working single mother of one, uses online tools to find math problems for her fifth grader and is on both Instagram and Twitter. Although she demonstrates good search skills and often helps other parents at the center with computer-related issues, she does not think that she "knows much".

I'm the go-to person. Little does she (another parent) *know, I'm not even the one that actually knows much. But I just end up figuring it out all the time* (Vanessa)

This instance represents a common theme among the participants and help us understand the disconnect that may exist between participants' perceived technical literacy and their actual capabilities. This was particularly significant in using tools that carried a *high-tech* profile or was commonly associated with a younger user audience with a higher level of technical skills. For instance, Instagram was among the social networking tools several of the participants associated with their children and did not consider themselves capable of using.

In addition to Vanessa, seven other female participants who demonstrated strong technical skills identified themselves as novice users. However, we did not observe the same issue in either of the male participants. We had far too few male participants to draw a conclusion, but these findings are in line with prior studies that show women often have a lower estimation of their technical skills [21], which negatively affects their online behavior and the extent to which they use different online services.

5.4 Social Support

Social support is an important factor in continued use of online services. This is particularly important for non-expert users who may need help with the tasks they perform. In these situations, receiving help with technical problems may decrease participants' frustration and guarantee a rewarding experience that motivates them to continue using the technology. In this section, we examine participants' support with regards to this dimension.

5.4.1 Relying on Strong Ties and Peer Support

The majority of participants mentioned experiencing technical problems with their devices at some point or needing help with performing certain tasks. However, few participants mentioned seeking help from professional technicians. The majority of

participants stated relying primary on their strong ties (i.e., family members including their children, or close friends) as their go-to-person when in need of technical support:

[About her children] *They're teaching me...they were showing me how to go to different websites. I was able to order some stuff, like I was able to get on that Walmart website and order something.* (Karin)

My older brother. I call him a lot. He's a programmer. So, anything that I need as far as technology is concerned I can call him. (Teresa)

However, the circle of immediate friends and family may not be enough to support participants, since they may have the same level of expertise. As Alicia, a working mother of one, puts it, "everybody's pretty much the same". This lack of support may result in frustration, and discourage parents to continue using services they have problems with.

I haven't even really looked into asking anybody for help. If I have an issue, it's just that I really don't do anything. I don't have anybody to go to. (Mandy)

However, it seems that the main source of support, outside the immediate circles, is drawn from other parents at places like the parent center.

[The parent center] *is just somewhere you would come like if you just need a little help with the computer.* (Pattie)

5.5 Variations in Use

Although individuals may have the same level of technical apparatus, autonomy, skill, and social support, they may use the internet for completely different purposes. Different uses of internet services vary greatly in the amount they increase or decrease one's opportunities. To this end, DiMaggio et al. put a particular emphasis on distinguishing between various uses that increase economic welfare and political or social capital, and those that are merely recreational.

5.5.1 Information Seeking and Education

Nearly all participants mentioned using search engines for finding information online. However, although all participants cared deeply for their children's education and expressed high educational and career goals for them, when asked how they found learning resources for their children, only a few mentioned searching for them online.

Based on the interviews, the number one source for finding new learning opportunities was through teachers at schools or via informal word-of-mouth through interacting with other parents and parent liaisons at the parent center. Thirteen participants (46.4%), mentioned educational websites such as *Study Island*, a school district endorsed website providing exercises, quizzes, and games categorized by subject and the student's grade level. Study Island was introduced to parents through the public school system as the primary online educational tool used by their children.

One of my daughters was having problems in social studies. I watched her grade improve a little. It's by her studying every day for an hour extra. So, that's what I really do, Study Island. It helps a lot with the kid. (Joyce)

Parent Portal, introduced by the Atlanta Public Schools system, is another tool for tracking children's performance at school. However, most of the parents seemed to lack motivation to use the portal regularly. In several cases, participants reported allowing their children to log on the parent portal instead and self-report their grades. Alternatively, most parents preferred to monitor their children's performance through direct interactions with their teachers and asking them how their child is doing.

5.5.2 Social Networking Sites

Social networking websites play an important role in expanding one's social capital and exposing them to new resources. Studies have demonstrated that taking advantage of the ties on social networking sites may expose individuals to a broader range of opportunities [5], and research on teens' use of social media suggests the same pattern in the contex of informal learning resources [27].

A high percentage of participants (82.1%) used social networking websites, with Facebook being the most frequently used. However, their reported use of these sites does not indicate they are engaging in developing social capital. Many of the participants used social networks mainly for passive consumption of information.

> *I might just glance to see what's up. I'll be on there looking at what folks wrote down. I look at the people's pictures on Facebook. I look at everybody's stuff and I'll be like, "Okay."* (Quinn)

> *I just browse. I don't do anything with it, but I do have a Facebook page. Yeah. Go through and see what's going on.* (Olive)

Studies on the role of Facebook on social capital show that passive consumption of information has no effect on bridging social capital [6]. On the other hand, active engagement in these services has the potential to facilitate networking, expand one's social capital, and increase one's access to different opportunities. For instance, Yazmeen, a widowed mother of two, explained to us that she was able to find a job through Facebook, after three years of searching through job-searching websites.

> *I have my job websites linked up to my Facebook and they'll link jobs to me that they're not linking to my email or they're not posting.* (Yazmeen)

However, such uses of social media were very rare among participants. Studies on a similar population in Detroit also show the same under-use of social platforms for increasing financial mobility among economically distressed populations [12]. Authors suggest lack of social connections, or the mental model that would link these platforms to such uses, as possible reasons.

Among participants, there were multiple instances where parents wanted to advocate for their community. For instance, Tillie is very involved with her children's school and is concerned about the educational inequalities at school. She is often trying to figure out what services are available to the schools in more financially advantaged neighborhoods that are lacking at her child's school, and demanding them from the principals.

> *I could spend the whole day on the computer just checking. I'm one of those kinds of people that will email you to death! If something's going on at school that I see, I'll email the principal or his boss. My girlfriends have kids who go to school on the north side [a wealthier part of the town]. They have a whole different issue than kids on the south side of town. Why is that? It's the same school system.* (Tillie)

However, Tillie does not use social networking sites as a platform to reach out to the community about these issues.

> *I don't understand that whole concept [of Facebook]... Or that LinkedIn. They're just too much. When I see it, I just delete it. I don't even go check it.* (Tillie)

Similar advocacy incentives were mentioned by other participants, which closely match the affordances of social networking sites, yet there were not any mentions of such uses by participants.

5.6 Parenting and Education: It is a Collaborative Process

One of the main emerging themes in the interviews was the degree to which information about educational resources was received and shared through informal, often face-to-face, interactions with the members of the community. In this section, we reflect on this theme from two different aspects: the communication dynamics between parents and the school system, and the interactions among parents within the community.

5.6.1 Dynamics of Parent-Teacher Communication

As described earlier, teachers can serve as important resources for learning about educational tools. Most parents described having regular communications with their children's teacher to monitor their child's progress, which exposed them to educational resources for their children as well. However, a subset of parents indicated anxiety about communicating with teachers in the higher grades such as high school. Joyce highlighted this feeling by comparing her communication with her daughters' elementary school teachers and her son's high school teacher:

> *Well, my son is in high school. I'm not pretty much as hands-on as much as I am with the girls, because I just feel like I just can't have a relationship with some of his teachers because they're different to me than the elementary teachers.* (Joyce)

Parents suggested that one reason for this difficulty in communication is a perceived difference in education. Parents indicated they consider themselves to have less authority or knowledge than the teachers. During her interview, Tillie described this situation:

> [Parents] *get intimidated when they don't know. When the teacher's talking to them and they say certain words, they can't figure it out. Or the kid comes home with homework and they can't do it, and they can't figure it out, they don't know how to get the help.* (Tillie)

However, as demonstrated in the following section, these tensions were contrary to the feelings expressed regarding interactions with other parents.

5.6.2 Parent-to-Parent Ties

One of the characteristics we observed among participants was the close ties among the members of the community at the parent resource center. Several of our participants mentioned coming to or volunteering at the parenting centers at their children's school while their children were in class. Furthermore, participants were very welcoming toward outsiders like us and it did not take long before the researchers were receiving warm hugs upon each visit and getting invited to their workshops and neighborhood events:

> [The Parent Center] *is really like a family. We call it 'the house'. You do have that support system, because as we go through this thing called parenting, peer support is important... When it's another parent talked to a parent, we can relate on a whole different level.* (Amanda)

As Amanda, a working mother of six, points out, parents within the community value support from their peers. Peer-support and informal interactions are important ways participants learn about new resources available to them. Twenty-three participants (82.1%) mentioned learning about educational resources through offline word-of-mouth. Many participants mentioned exchanging parenting advice, as well as technical support, with other parents they met through the centers. They were often eager to reach out to other parents to share their knowledge and expertise about issues that were of common importance to them.

6. DISCUSSION

The goal of this study was to provide a rich description of parents' access to information technology and learning resources in economically depressed communities in westside Atlanta. Using the framework for examining digital inequality in terms of technical apparatus, autonomy, social support, skill, and purpose, we not only gained insight into issues of online access, but also learned about participants' broader technical and educational needs. In examining the findings, we found significant trends that may help researchers design more customized resources for this, or similar, communities. In this section, we discuss some of these trends before moving on to the design inspirations they carry.

6.1 Technology and Trust

One of the most common trends observed among participants was the extent to which they limited their use of online services, as well as their children's access to different websites, not only because of the content of those services, but also because of their concern about unwanted viruses and malwares that could break their devices. These concerns were warranted because their devices were not robust and there is a high cost associated with losing a device. However, we did find that participants would utilize resources introduced to them through other parents or trusted entities such as their child's school.

For educational resources to become embedded in participants' lives, future designs should consider this sensitivity and incorporate features that gain the trust of the community. In addition to providing resources through trusted groups within the community, one possible solution for gaining trust is to model the design of online resources after the sites participants already use and trust. Ensuring that new services designed for participants will not damage their devices increases their willingness to adopt newly introduced resources.

6.2 Finding the Right Medium

We argue that finding the right medium of communication that closely matches the specific needs and the cultural values of the community is the key aspect in designing a useful and viable platform of communication that would be broadly adopted by the parents. Here, we examine this issue from two aspects: finding the right *technological medium* or platform, and finding the right *communication medium* that supports the type of communication needed or valued by the community.

Based on our analysis of parents' access, smartphones are among the most largely adopted devices within the community. In some cases, the smartphone is the only means of getting online and is used as a shared device among the family. This is inline with patterns reported among other low-income communities in urban areas [[26], 37]. However, despite this broad adoption of smartphones, an exclusive mobile solution might not be the right means of reaching this audience. While many parents had smartphones, few used them as their primary means of accessing information online due to the phones' smaller screens. Even among parents who did not own a personal computer, there was a tendency towards using computers at public facilities rather than a smart phone. Furthermore, mobile devices were frequently used as shared devices, hence they may afford limited autonomy, including less privacy than a computer system where one can create multiple individual accounts. This capability is usually not supported in mobile devices because they are designed for personal use. Therefore, while designing for a smartphone platform is promising because of the broad use, the information seeking practices of our audiences with smartphones and computers suggest that desktop computers have great potential as well and should not be overlooked by the designers for this audience.

Beyond technological medium of communication, the study brought forward the type of communication (the communication medium) that parents preferred when communicating about parenting. Parents expressed a strong interest to share and learn from each other about parenting. The parents also indicated they would prefer to communicate their parenting expertise in narratives and stories of their own experiences.

In many cases, the motivation behind this interest was to advocate for change for the community. Parents were invested in the prosperity of their community and saw sharing their narratives as a step toward solving community issues. This is inline with the critical role of story telling in similar social justice efforts [4]. Further evidence for a desire to share narratives showed itself through parents' enthusiasm to discuss parenting topics in our interviews. Several of the interview sessions lasted far longer than we anticipated due to the participants sharing stories about their everyday lives, reflecting on parenting, and the importance and challenges of being involved in their children's education.

In Come_IN clubhouses, similar interests in telling stories of the neighborhood were used to motivate engagement [36]. Future design within this community, and similar ones, should also build upon this interest for sharing narratives and provide a platform that supports collective story telling in a safe and collaborative environment. This may be an additional reason for the importance of personal computers in the design (compared to a mobile-only solution or app), as they may provide greater affordances for sharing long narratives for some users.

6.3 Motivation

As one of the parents puts it, "It's not as much the ease of the tool as the motivation behind using the tool". As described in the findings, parents were reluctant to check the parent portal on a regular basis. Further research is needed to find the reasons behind this reluctance; however, one possible reason may be that the parent portal is a one-way channel from schools to parents, which does not provide a channel for further interactions or deeper engagement by parents. Furthermore, Parent portal is frequently a list of assignments and grades that are sometimes weeks behind students' progress. The lack of consistent and meaningful content may contribute to limited engagement from parents as well. This is inline with previous research that shows community members must be active participants in content production in order for technology to engage low-income communities [29].

Another reason why the parent portal is not adopted broadly among parent could be parents' concerns with other, more basic aspects of the everyday life. As one of the parents puts it, it may be hard for parents to "focus on the things that they desire to do as opposed to something that they have to do" in an economically challenging situation. When one's mind is occupied with concerns about providing basic needs of their family, other things are inevitably pushed to second priority, no matter how important they may be. This is inline with the findings from a similar group of parents in low income families where researchers found that although parents perceive monitoring their child's social media use to be very important, they were often too constrained by first order necessities of life to put a high priority on the issue [39].

Therefore, designs for this and similar communities should put a great emphasis on two-way engagement and build itself around the everyday needs and practices of the parents and the values they hold. The parent center is a good model for this. It is a public school initiative with an academic agenda, but they offer much in terms of social services and resources to parents as well. This engages parents based upon their needs and interests, and further provides a space for them to share learning resources as well.

6.4 Mediating Teacher to Parent Communication

In addition to other parents, teachers constitute an important part of participants' social networks and are an important source for finding about learning opportunities. While many participants communicated regularly with their children's teacher, some also mentioned feeling apprehensive about this relationship. This was particularly true for communicating with high school teachers.

Similar to enhancing parent-to-parent communication, empowering participants to communicate with teachers may serve as a critical strategy for connecting parents with more learning resources. One possible strategy to enhance this communication may be to provide a platform that mediates information flow from teachers to parents and allows parents to engage in conversations with teachers and other parents in the community while being able to choose customized level of anonymity toward each group. Future research should address balancing the power dynamics by investigating platforms that provide parents with a safe and comfortable space to participate.

7. DESIGN INSPIRATIONS AND FUTURE WORK

In this section, we reflect on the design inspirations gained from our study, justify why they might address the specific needs and challenges this community is faced with, and elaborate on some of possible directions for future work. We believe that improving parents' access to a broader set of learning opportunities calls for technological interventions and design efforts from information retrieval experts and educational technology designers, as well as developing a platform for more systematic engagement from within the community where parents can find more information through story sharing and informal communications. We further elaborate on these two directions in the following sections as *top-down* and *bottom-up* design inspirations.

7.1 Top-down: The Role of Learning Providers

Most of the participants mentioned using search engines and social network sites on a regular basis, yet very few parents found educational opportunities through independent online searches or from their extended networks. While parents showed great investment in their role concerning children's education, in most cases, they were not seeking resources for out-of-school learning; resources that make up a critical part of children's learning experience [2].

While further research is needed to examine why parents are not taking advantage of resources out of their immediate network, issues of access indicate some factors. Previous research shows that low-income and low-educational families are not able to find the broad array of online resources for technical fluency, such as computer science related courses or programming languages, because the search terms they most commonly use are not the same as the terms that informal learning providers use in meta tags or keywords for their products [14]. This difficulty in finding related

resources was reflected in interviews as well, such as the quote from Maria at the beginning of this paper.

These disconnections in vocabulary and communication highlight the type of changes that need to be made in the design of such resources. Design implications from these findings suggest investigating the search keywords parents are most likely to use when searching for learning resources for their children's interest, and creating custom tag labeling structures for online educational datasets that matches parents' keywords. This change would be top-down, in that it would be dependent upon developing a stronger communication among informal learning providers such as museums, afterschool programs, online tutorial providers, and educational technology producers. It would also be dependent upon a shared goal of reaching a diverse audience of users. We further see value in providing tools that would facilitate parents' search practices by automatically augmenting their keywords through suggesting terms that would provide them with a broader array of resources in their search results.

7.2 Bottom-Up: The Role of Community

Our analysis of this community shows that parents currently find learning opportunities through their relationship with the school system (e.g., teachers) or other parents within the community. One unique characteristic in this community is a close bond among parents. Particularly the parent center we worked with fostered a feeling of family among visitors and even toward us as outsiders. Many parents come to these centers to use the computer facilities, participate in workshops, or just chat to the other parents and parent liaisons at the center. Parents within the community are willing to both provide and receive advice and peer support about parenting related topics. While this openness to sharing parenting practices and receiving advice from other parents may be unique to this parent center, it serves as a model for culturally relevant design solutions with other parents who do not visit the center or other communities that have similar values.

Currently there is no specialized online community for these parents. An online platform could leverage the community ties and provide asynchronous and documented discussions that do not suffer from the shortfalls of relying on informal, accidental encounters for sharing information. In addition, an online community may reach more parents that are currently left out of offline discussions.

Based on the close bond among the community, and the willingness to communicate, we see a great opportunity for platforms such as online hyper-local networks that build upon the existing ties among the community. We envision a hyper-local network that is geographically based, serving as a way to increase parents' ability to create and utilize the affordances of weak ties, as well as enforcing their existing strong ties.

In recent studies of hyper-local social networks, such as Nextdoor (a social network for neighborhoods), researchers found that these networks have a positive role in enhancing existing community engagement already present among members [28]. Therefore, to support current gatherings and in-person interactions which are necessary for the strength of community, developing an online space where parents can share their stories and expertise with each other may help make the process more systematic and documented. Furthermore, it would reach a broader group of parents beyond those who participate in offline gatherings.

This solution may overcome the chaos associated with general-purpose social networking sites as well. Although having access to a wide range of information through the social networking sites such as Twitter and Facebook is valuable and well studied, the abundance of information in these general-purpose social networks may be "just too much" for parents. A more specialized network focused on the issues surrounding the community may be more desirable. Studies have shown that using Whooly, "a web service that provides neighborhood-specific information based on Twitter posts" was both easier and more desirable for finding hyper-local information [22].

Moreover, the locality of information in a hyper-local network helps parents to find information that is geographically accessible, which is particularly important for low-income families with limited transportation access.

We believe that this solution may also address parents' concerns toward security and trust when interacting online. Based on our findings, parents are more likely to use the services that are introduced to them through other parents or the school system. In addition, research has suggested that the close match between the online and offline profiles in a hyper-local network provides a degree of accountability that may result in higher level of trust among the members [27].

The design and deployment of a local social networking site may conquer the deficits associated with school districts' current parent portals. An online community provides a two-way, interactive communication channel where parents can actively engage in conversations around parenting topics and contribute to them, as well as receive information from other members. This may provide a more natural setting as it is augmenting what is currently happening offline.

Studies on ways social capital can be fostered in low socioeconomic status communities where little or zero social capital exist underline the importance of connecting people with bridging ties to those with more resources [12]. In the context of our study, teachers and parent liaisons are among key people who know about a broader set of learning opportunities. As discussed earlier in the paper, there is already a great reciprocal motivation to connect and a high level of trust between parents and parent liaisons, but in some cases there are tensions communicating with school systems or vertical links with higher authority levels. Accounting for power dynamic issues in parent-teacher relations discussed earlier, the role and position of teachers should be further examined in this space. Teachers can provide a great added value to the quality of resources shared in the community and their presence in the online community may be of value. However, there may be trade-offs for teachers' participation that calls for further research.

Finally, to support for the needs and concerns of the community, the designed online community should provide an infrastructure for discussions around learning resources, and yet be flexible to be appropriated by parents for other discussions around parenting, community change efforts, and social services that may be of value to the community.

8. CONCLUSION

Access to information technology plays a critical role in improving one's educational attainment, economic status or social capital. It is often assumed that, beyond technical means, access to information technology is free; however, this is far from the case. The five dimensions of access to the digital world highlight that access can come at a high cost. Issues that surfaced in our analysis, such as reliability of technology, social support from strong and weak ties, and finding a medium matching the practices of their everyday lives, have design implications for our broader research goals as well as others working with similar communities. In addition to

revealing significant trends that may contribute to design, the findings revealed that this population would greatly benefit from technologies that have been customized to meet their specific needs.

As all researchers and designers do, we came to this project with some biases and a goal, to develop an online resource built upon previous research and our experiences. In conducting this study many of our findings validate previous research with similar audiences and may not be surprising. In other cases, such as our original hunch that smartphones would be the centerpiece of the design, the findings such as the desire for narrative communication directed us to unexpected inspirations. We argue for the importance of both of these types of findings when designing for less traditional audiences and populations that have been historically understudied within the field of HCI.

9. REFERENCES

[1] Ames, M.G., Go, J., Kaye, J.J., and Spasojevic, M., 2011. Understanding Technology Choices and Values through Social Class. In *Proceedings of the ACM 2011 conference on Computer supported cooperative work* ACM, 55-64.

[2] Banks, J.A., 2007. *Learning in and out of School in Diverse Environments: Life-Long, Life-Wide, Life-Deep*. LIFE Center, University of Washington, Stanford University, and SRI International.

[3] Barron, B., Martin, C.K., Takeuchi, L., and Fithian, R., 2009. Parents as Learning Partners in the Development of Technological Fluency. *International Journal of Learning and Media 1*, 2, 55-77.

[4] Bell, L.A., 2010. *Storytelling for Social Justice: Connecting Narrative and the Arts in Antiracist Teaching*. Taylor & Francis.

[5] Burke, M. and Kraut, R., 2013. Using Facebook after Losing a Job: Differential Benefits of Strong and Weak Ties. In *Proceedings of the 2013 conference on Computer supported cooperative work* ACM, 1419-1430.

[6] Burke, M., Kraut, R., and Marlow, C., 2011. Social Capital on Facebook: Differentiating Uses and Users. In *Proceedings of the SIGCHI Conference on Human Factors in Computing Systems* ACM, 571-580.

[7] Burke, M., Marlow, C., and Lento, T., 2010. Social Network Activity and Social Well-Being. In *Proceedings of the SIGCHI Conference on Human Factors in Computing Systems* ACM, 1909-1912.

[8] Cervantes, R., Warschauer, M., Nardi, B., and Sambasivan, N., 2011. Infrastructures for Low-Cost Laptop Use in Mexican Schools. In *Proceedings of the SIGCHI Conference on Human Factors in Computing Systems* ACM, 945-954.

[9] Clark, L.S., 2012. The Parent App: Understanding Families in the Digital Age. Oxford University Press.

[10] Cohen, J., 1960. A Coefficient of Agreement for Nominal Scales. *Educational and psychological measurement 20*, 1, 37-46.

[11] Coleman, J.S., 1988. Social Capital in the Creation of Human Capital. *American journal of sociology*, S95-S120.

[12] Dillahunt, T.R., 2014. Fostering social capital in economically distressed communities. *Proceedings of the 32nd annual ACM conference on Human factors in computing systems*, ACM, 531–540.

[13] DiMaggio, P., Hargittai, E., Celeste, C., and Shafer, S., 2004. Digital Inequality: From Unequal Access to Differentiated Use. *Social inequality*, 355-400.

[14] DiSalvo, B., Reid, C., and Khanipour Roshan, P., 2014. They

can't find us: the search for informal CS education. *Proceedings of the 45th ACM technical symposium on Computer science education*, ACM, 487–492.

[15] Dufur, M.J., Parcel, T.L., and Troutman, K.P., 2012. Does Capital at Home Matter More Than Capital at School?: Social Capital Effects on Academic Achievement*. *Research in Social Stratification and Mobility*.

[16] Forssell, K.S., Barron, B., Martin, C.K., Takeuchi, L., and Fithian, R., 2008. Roles of Parents in Fostering Technological Fluency. In *Proceedings of the 8th international conference on International conference for the learning sciences-Volume 3* International Society of the Learning Sciences, 33-34.

[17] Gilbert, E. and Karahalios, K., 2009. Predicting Tie Strength with Social Media. In *Proceedings of the SIGCHI Conference on Human Factors in Computing Systems* ACM, 211-220.

[18] Granovetter, M.S., 1973. The Strength of Weak Ties. *American journal of sociology*, 1360-1380.

[19] Hargittai, E., 2002. Second-Level Digital Divide: Differences in People's Online Skills. *First monday 7*, 4.

[20] Hargittai, E., 2010. Digital Na (T) Ives? Variation in Internet Skills and Uses among Members of the "Net Generation"*. *Sociological Inquiry 80*, 1, 92-113.

[21] Hargittai, E. and Shafer, S., 2006. Differences in Actual and Perceived Online Skills: The Role of Gender*. *Social Science Quarterly 87*, 2, 432-448.

[22] Hu, Y., Farnham, S.D., and Monroy-Hernández, A., 2013. Whoo. Ly: Facilitating Information Seeking for Hyperlocal Communities Using Social Media. In *Proceedings of the 2013 ACM annual conference on Human factors in computing systems* ACM, 3481-3490.

[23] Jenkins, H., 2009. Confronting the Challenges of Participatory Culture: Media Education for the 21st Century. The MIT Press.

[24] Kam, M., Agarwal, A., Kumar, A., Lal, S., Mathur, A., Tewari, A., and Canny, J., 2008. Designing E-Learning Games for Rural Children in India: A Format for Balancing Learning with Fun. In *Proceedings of the 7th ACM conference on Designing interactive systems* ACM, 58-67.

[25] Landis, J.R. and Koch, G.G., 1977. The Measurement of Observer Agreement for Categorical Data. *biometrics*, 159-174.

[26] Le Dantec, C., 2012. Participation and Publics: Supporting Community Engagement. In *Proceedings of the 2012 ACM annual conference on Human Factors in Computing Systems* ACM, 1351-1360.

[27] Lin, P., and Farnham, S.D., 2013. Opportunities via extended networks for teens' informal learning, In *Proceedings of the 2013 ACM conference on Computer supported cooperative work*, 1341-1352.

[28] Masden, C., Grevet, C., Grinter, R., Gilbert, E., Edwards, W.k., 2014. Tensions in Scaling-up Community Social Media: A Multi-Neighborhood Study of Nextdoor, In *Proceedings of the SIGCHI conference on Human factors in computing systems*.

[29] Pinkett, R., and O'Bryant, R., 2003. Building community, empowerment and self-sufficiency. *Information, Communication & Society*, 6, 2, 187-210.

[30] Reardon, S.F., 2011. The widening academic achievement gap between the rich and the poor: New evidence and possible explanations. *Whither opportunity*, 91-116.

[31] Reich, J., 2011. Open Educational Resources Expand Educational Inequalities. In *Educational Technology Debate*.

[32] Shroff, G. and Kam, M., 2011. Towards a Design Model for Women's Empowerment in the Developing World. In *Proceedings of the SIGCHI Conference on Human Factors in Computing Systems* ACM, 2867-2876.

[33] Stevens, G., Veith, M., and Wulf, V., 2003. Come_IN: Using Computers to Foster the Integration of Migrant Communities. *SIGGROUP Bull.* 24, 3, 66–72.

[34] Walker, S.K., Dworkin, J., and Connell, J., 2011. Variation in Parent Use of Information and Communications Technology: Does Quanitiy Matter? *Family and Consumer Sciences Research Journal 40*, 2 (December 4, 2011), 106-119.

[35] Warschauer, M., 2004. Technology and Social Inclusion: Rethinking the Digital Divide. the MIT Press.

[36] Weibert, A. and Schubert, K., 2010. How the Social Structure of Intercultural Computer Clubs Fosters Interactive Storytelling. *Proceedings of the 9th International Conference on Interaction Design and Children*, ACM, 368–371.

[37] Woelfer, J.P. and Hendry, D.G., 2010. Homeless Young People's Experiences with Information Systems: Life and Work in a Community Technology Center. In *Proceedings of the SIGCHI Conference on Human Factors in Computing Systems* ACM, 1291-1300.

[38] Yardi, S. and Bruckman, A., 2011. Social and Technical Challenges in Parenting Teens' Social Media Use. In *Proceedings of the SIGCHI Conference on Human Factors in Computing Systems* ACM, 3237-3246.

[39] Yardi, S. and Bruckman, A., 2012. Income, Race, and Class: Exploring Socioeconomic Differences in Family Technology Use. In *Proceedings of the SIGCHI Conference on Human Factors in Computing Systems* ACM, 3041-3050.

Media2gether: Sharing Media During a Call

Azadeh Forghani[1, 2], Gina Venolia[2], and Kori Inkpen[2]

School of Interactive Arts and Technology[1]
Simon Fraser University
Surrey, BC, Canada, V3T 0A3
azadehf@sfu.ca

Microsoft Research[2]
1 Microsoft Way
Redmond, WA, USA, 98052
[ginav, kori]@microsoft.com

ABSTRACT

Telephone calls and videoconferencing are ubiquitous parts of everyday life. As the content of the call may extend beyond just words, people share applications and media using techniques such as screen sharing and email attachments. Little is known about the prevalence of this behavior and the benefits it can provide. We conducted a survey and a lab study to examine media sharing during a video call and found that it can be useful as well as emotionally engaging. Participants indicated that they would be more likely to have more frequent and longer calls if media sharing were easy. Overall, this work demonstrates the importance of exploring communication media that augment and enrich our everyday activities.

Categories and Subject Descriptors

H.4.3. Information Systems Applications: Communications Applications – Computer conferencing, teleconferencing and videoconferencing

Keywords

Shared experiences, telepresence, video-mediated communication

1. INTRODUCTION

People have a strong need and desire to maintain connections and awareness with their family, friends and loved ones, whether they live nearby or far away [25]. It is understandable then, that telephone calls and videoconferencing have become ubiquitous parts of everyday life because these communication channels help people stay in touch with each other and maintain social bonds for both personal and professional reasons. Different types of technology such as video chat applications, social networking and media sharing web sites have added more variety to the ways that people can grow and maintain their social ties. Among all of these, audio and video communication applications are rich and easy tools for sharing everyday life, maintaining awareness, and supporting a feeling of togetherness in order to compensate limited face-to-face interactions. Video communication can mediate closeness in a domestic environment. This feeling of intimacy is coming from being mutually aware of each other's life as well as the content that is being shared [17].

Audio and video chatting has also become mundane in domestic environments and as a result the content of the call may go beyond only conversation, as people may want to share different aspects of their life with one another and move beyond exchanging verbal

GROUP '14, November 9–12, 2014, Sanibel Island, FL, USA.
Copyright 2014 ACM 978-1-4503-3043-5/14/11…$15.00
http://dx.doi.org/10.1145/2660398.2660417

information. This could include sharing media for different purposes such as entertainment, awareness, excitement or organizing some activities together. For example, one may want to share the photos of his recent trip with his family during video conversation and tell detailed stories about exciting places he visited or his different adventures. People may also aim to organize activities together such as planning for a group trip during a call by sharing map and calendar. As another example of the usefulness of media sharing: it is easier to browse the web page together during a phone call rather than sending back and forth several pictures of online items to a friend to see whether we should buy it or not. It would also be more fun to watch some personal or humorous video with a remote family member or friend and see their facial reactions. Similarly, there are many scenarios that show the desire of adding media to a regular video or audio call.

As people desire to increase the level of communication and sharing within their close social circles [1], technology has offered a variety of ways for people to share different kinds of media such as photos, calendars, videos, blog entries, and other personal or professional information. However, in comparison to the huge expansion of technology offering different ways of sharing media and information, less effort has been put forth in integrating information and media sharing with communication channels such as audio and video chat applications.

Currently, people usually share media during an audio/video call using techniques such as email attachments, picture/video messaging and screen sharing. However, there is still no simple way of embedded media sharing in a call offering mutual interactions where both sides can take the control simultaneously and interact with the media. In fact, supporting higher level of mutual interactions and collaboration in domestic communication channels can make the experience more engaging and useful and also provide more opportunities to do some collaborative activities such as web browsing during a call. Despite a high desire for sharing different types of media in a call and different techniques for the current practices of sharing media, little is known about the prevalence of this behavior, the benefits it can provide and the way it can enrich a regular call.

On the other hand, the existing options for communication channels benefit our ability to share media by providing live information and supporting a feeling of presence in absence. Without co-presence, we view our photos or other types of media such as our personal video or social posts alone. As a result, there are fewer opportunities for social interactions around media that is usually limited to asynchronous comment threads left by our family or friends. As stated above, communication channels can provide a feeling of togetherness and have potential to support social interactions. In addition, they can provide more emotional content and detailed stories for presented media compared to media sharing without accompanying video and audio communication channels. Yet the integration of the existing options for communication channels and the possibilities for media sharing has not been explored. The integration of these two components of social technology has the potential to create an experience similar to a traditional way of browsing our physical photo album with our family or friends where we talk about the stories behind the photo together. In fact, the mutual benefits of coupling different kinds of media sharing with audio/video mediated communication channels makes this topic an important area to explore, which has not been studied in domestic environments.

Our goal is to understand the benefits of sharing media in a call, how and why people currently share media in a call and how to best design for this situation. To meet this goal we conducted a survey and a lab study. The survey looked at the current and desired practices of media sharing during a call. For our lab study, we developed our prototype, *Media2gether* following the WYSIWIS approach. Our prototype offers two-way mutual simultaneous interaction with media for sharing photos and Facebook posts by mutual friends. We also used an existing feature of Windows for sharing browsers. In our lab study, we studied how media sharing can enhance video-mediated communication in terms of emotional connection, engagement, enjoyment and utility. In this regard, we evaluated the benefits and costs of using media with video-mediated communication in different design modalities.

2. RELATED WORK

2.1 Social Dynamics and Media Sharing

People intensively engage in the process of creation and sharing different types of media for several purposes such as entertainment, awareness, collaboration and reminiscing [9,20]. Photo sharing is increasingly being used as every day social activity [1]. Photographs are important in domestic life as a way to represent family traditions, identity and values [6]. Tee et al. found that people enjoy sharing photos together and photos are considered as a good way of connecting with extended families [1].Due to the popularity of this topic, there has been significant amount of research focused on designing tools for people to share and present photos in order to provide more social connections [1,14,20,28]. Sharing photographs supports reminiscing and collaboration and has outcomes for closeness, togetherness and awareness [30,37]. Reminiscing also supports several social and emotional purposes such as developing relationships and increasing intimacy between people [36].

Social networks also have potential to support reminiscing. Cosley et al. designed a tool for everyday reminiscing and found the potential value of Facebook posts and status updates for this purpose especially with geographically distant people [7].There are also several designs to provide collaborative browsing to support some collaborative online activities such as searching, shopping or organizing social events [22,24].

Although having a communication channel seems vital to make sharing experiences more engaging and useful, there is less effort to embed these sharing practices within video mediated communication.

2.2 Media for Supporting Conversation and Storytelling

Mementos can trigger memory practices which might shape and evoke conversation, reminiscence, stories and could also facilitate engagement in story telling talk aka "phototalk" around personal photos [29,33,35,40]. O'Hara et al. explored "phototalk" in the context of sharing a meal and they found that the mementoes can provide opportunities for several social practices in gatherings [29].

Balabanovic et al. found the potential of using digital photos to support some kind of story sharing by designing an interface for sharing and recording stories [1]. Zancanaro et al. built a non-interactive tabletop at a museum café providing relevant context to encourage collocated visitors to engage in a conversation 0.

Photos can also engage children in communication with remote family members through video or audio and also help them participate in every day family conversation [1]. In addition, supporting retrospective storytelling of personal experiences through digital media could benefit people sharing their experiences with both collocated and distant audiences [19].

2.3 Enriching Audio/Video Communication

As people are becoming more and more geographically separated, teleconferencing and video mediated communication (VMC) is gaining popularity. Regardless of distance separation, family and friends still desire to be in touch and involved in each other's lives [17]. Accessibility, reasonable quality and variety of uses have caused teleconferencing and VMC to become very popular in both work and domestic domains [3,17].

In domestic domains, video mediated communication has been rapidly adopted by home users and is usually considered intimate behavior which is very popular among different groups of audience such as teenagers, couples, remote family members, grandchildren and grandparents [5,8,17,27]. Mass adoption of video applications in domestic environments has brought the need and desire to move beyond verbal conversation and focus on sharing activities through video links [1]. As a result, many HCI researchers have explored systems that go beyond simple audio/video communication to include shared experiences [13]

Neustaedter et al. [27] studied how distance-separated couples keep intimacy and they found that they share diverse activities such as watching television or videos, sharing meals and playing video games. Brubaker et al. found similar behaviors in their interviews of the use of VMC in personal and workplace contexts [1]. In their diary study of mobile VMC, O'Hara et al. [1] found that people used the visual channel to show objects or environments.

There have been several attempts to enhance teleconferencing and VMC [3,13,16,39]. Some studies tried to enhance video communication by enabling people to share an environment [16,18], while others tried to support sharing life experiences in video chat [4,13]. All of these attempts aim to move beyond "talking heads" and present a mutual common ground in communication. In fact, as part of our adjustment with distance separation we have to move beyond talking heads in order to experience more feeling of presence in absence and togetherness [1].

In spite of the mentioned benefits of using media in domestic daily practices, the benefits that it can provide for video communication has never been studied. In this work we explore enriching the VMC experience by providing new opportunities for rich engagement around media. We study the benefits and costs of adding media to the video communication and assess whether sharing media during a call can increase enjoyment, emotional connection and usefulness.

Similarly, some systems such as [1] and [35] have been using photos as a way to facilitate communication and provide more context between remote families and particularly children and remote family members; however, prior works have focused less on the integration of communication channels with shared media. In [35] an audio channel provided a way for grandparents and grandchildren to communicate while sharing photos. Watching video and TV in addition to communication channels such as video and instant messaging has been investigated in [21] and [31] but the use of video communication while sharing different types of media has not been explored yet. Our study fills this research gap.

Our work has the same concept as [1] and [29], where photographic materials and personal memory have been used to facilitate reminiscing and conversation in a co-located social gathering. Here, however, we are trying to benefit from using media for a somewhat similar purpose but in remote gathering over video conferencing. While there are several works such as [20], [1] and [33], which explored the culture of media sharing either in collocated situations or online, none have considered the integration of sharing media with existing communication.

3. SEMI-STRUCTURED INTERVIEW

To have some initial insights, and to better understand the field and design of our survey, we conducted semi-formal, semi-structured interviews with 20 people including full time employees and interns in our global software engineering company. The interview session took around 20-30 minutes and was mainly about their recent and current practices of viewing media with some one else during a call as well as the desired feature that they need but they think current technology cannot support.

We found that distance-separated families and friends tend to share media together during videoconferencing in order to share their experiences with each other. This media sharing mainly consisted of viewing photos together during video talk with their close family or friends. However, some interesting usage was also revealed as one participant used to share his calendar and also a road map to schedule a trip with his father who was living in another country.

Our participants mainly believed that the current technology cannot support mutual interactions easily and they either applied some intuitive techniques to solve this problem or have used other applications to accompany video chat application. For example, during video chat with her mom, *Abby* wanted to show her some photos of her visit to a recent festival. As there were so many details on the picture she had a difficult time showing different things to her mom even after screen sharing. She made this easier by opening the photo in paint software and circling different areas in the photo that she wanted to show her mom while her screen was shared with her. However, at certain times her mom wanted to refer to some areas in the photo but she had no control and had to give her clue verbally.

This example highlights the features our participants mentioned as desirable: synchronization, the ability to see where the other person is looking or pointing, synchronous manipulation, annotating, facial recognition and tagging. Having the insights about current and desired practices, we designed our survey for a general audience as well as our own prototype for our lab study.

4. SURVEY AND LAB STUDY

We conducted a two-phase study to explore the current and desired practices of viewing media collaboratively during a call as well as the benefits that this practices can provide to enrich the call.

4.1 Survey Method

We designed a survey to understand and assess users' current and desired practices of sharing media in audio and video calls. The survey was distributed to a general population of 125 participants (provided by Cint.com). Our participants were equally distributed across five different age groups between 18 and 65. Our survey

participants were approximately equally distributed by gender (44% Male and 56% Female).

The survey consisted of 32 questions on recent practices, desired practices and demographic information. Recent and desired practices explored the types of media viewed during a call and the frequency of viewing each type of media (e.g. photos, videos, maps, social posts, search engines, and calendars). We were also interested in media sharing practices for different relationships (e.g. significant others, immediate family, friends, colleagues). Picturing an ideal system to view media with someone else easily with all required and desired features and interactions, we also asked about participants' desired practices of sharing media during a call in an ideal situation. A discussion of survey's findings can be found in the result section.

4.2 Lab Study Method

We conducted a lab study to explore first-hand how people share different types of media during a video call, and the challenges and opportunities of this practice.

In particular we had two questions in mind:

Can sharing media during a call increase users' enjoyment and sense of connectedness?

Can sharing media during a call add significant value in terms of usefulness?

4.2.1 Media Sharing Prototype

The goal of the study was to explore three different types of media sharing during a video call: photos, Facebook posts by mutual friends, and web browsing. Media sharing was supported on a touch-enabled surface computer, while the video call was established using a laptop computer running Skype. We ran our prototype in a separate device as we felt this better reflected a future scenario where devices are plentiful and a secondary device, such as a tablet, might naturally be used for photo viewing. This is akin to how someone might look at a physical photo album while having a Skype call on a laptop. Figure 1 shows a participant using this configuration.

Sharing photos and Facebook posts were enabled through a custom application we developed, while shared browsing was supported using windows remote assistance to establish a peer-to-peer connection over a LAN or Internet. Remote assistance allows remote users to easily share their desktop where both parties can have full control over the shared browser.

Figure 1. Skype window is being shown on laptop while the shared media is being displayed on a surface tablet.

Our custom Photo/Facebook Viewing application consisted of two separate views: Photo View and Facebook View. In Photo View (see Figure 2), each participant's photos are shown in a vertical side bar down either side of the screen.

Users can jointly view photos by tapping on a photo (either their own photo or their partner's), which will cause it to appear full-size in the middle of the screen (e.g., the cooking photo in Figure 2). We followed the WYSIWIS approach. In addition, both users have full control and users have their own telepointer (distinguished by different colors), which enables them to point and gesture to any part of the photo simultaneously. The telepointer approach was different from screen sharing approach where only one person can take the control and interact with the presented media. The Facebook View (Figure 3) displays a scrolling list of posts from mutual friends. Similar to Photo View, telepointers are provided to enable users to point and gesture to items on the Facebook list.

Figure 3. Facebook View app.

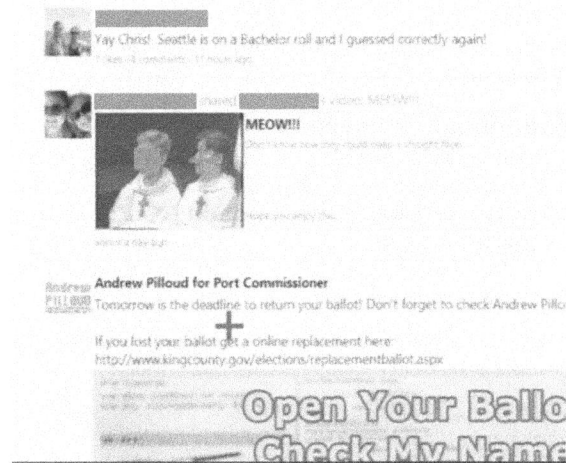

Figure 2. Photo View app.

4.2.2 Study Design

The study was a within-subject design with 20 participants. Ten participants were recruited through a centralized recruiting service at our company and each person was asked to recruit a friend or family member as their study partner. To be eligible for the study, participants needed to be Facebook users, be Facebook friends with their partner, have at least 10 mutual Facebook friends, and talk to their partner at least once a week (either in person, on the phone, or via video).

All 10 pairs of participants were from the Puget Sound area (10 female, 10 male) between 23 and 66 years old. Three pairs were Female-Female (2 were friends, 1 was mother-daughter), 4 were Female-Male (2 were friends, 2 were couples) and 3 were Male-Male (friends).

4.2.3 Preparation

Before the study, we asked each participant to select ten photos that they would like to talk about with their study partner. Half of the photos were supposed to be about both people such as a shared event, a common interest, or mutual friends. The other half were supposed to be about something the participant wanted to show the other person. We were aware that because of the nature of the lab study, the situation might be different from an actual video call. In order to make it more similar to an actual video or phone call, we asked them to preferably arrive independently and not talk together the day before the study.

We counterbalanced the four conditions (Skype Only, Photo Sharing, Facebook Sharing, Browser Sharing) using a partial Latin square design, which resulted in four different orderings. Each pair was given 10-minutes to experience each condition and was then moved on to the next condition. All sessions were video recorded for later analysis.

4.2.4 Procedure

Participants were welcomed by two researchers, given a short summary about the study, and placed in separate rooms. A Skype video call was established and used for the whole session while the relevant prototype features were described at the beginning of each section. After 10 minutes, the participants were interrupted to answer a questionnaire and the next condition was set up. After completing all four conditions, the participants were given a final questionnaire to evaluate all four conditions together. They were instructed to converse over Skype and use the prototype as much or as little as they desired. However, all participants kept communicating over Skype for the whole time of all sessions and used the prototype for the whole time of three sessions that they had it available.

4.2.5 Questionnaire

We used the modified Affective Benefits and Costs of Communication Technology (ABCCT) questionnaire 0 for the purposes of our study. The ABCCT is designed for assessing long-term field studies. To use it in the lab study we eliminated several questions that were not relevant in this context and slightly reworded some others. The resulting questionnaire consisted of 23 questions to measure four "benefit" scales including emotional expressiveness, engage and play, presence in absence, opportunity for social support and two "costs" scales including unmet expectations and threat to privacy.

We also asked the participants whether adding these features to a video call would increase their usage in terms of making more or longer calls. At the end of the study we also asked participants to rank each condition in terms of enjoyment, emotionally connection, and usefulness.

4.2.6 Exit Interview

At the end of each session we had a short (15 minute) unstructured interview with both participants together during which we asked about their opinions, experiences and the challenges they faced during each condition.

5. RESULTS

In this section we combine the results of the survey and lab study, grouped by themes.

5.1 Emotional Connection

Sharing media during a call can be more emotionally engaging than a call without media sharing. 48% of survey participants who had experienced viewing media with someone during a call believed that this practice increased the emotional connection of the call (Figure 4). Likewise, several survey respondents expressed the emotional impact of sharing media during a call:

"It makes the calls more emotionally involved due to being able to see and discuss what we are viewing." [Survey P100]

"[Sharing media] made the call deeper emotionally, enhanced the overall depth of the conversation." [Survey P60]

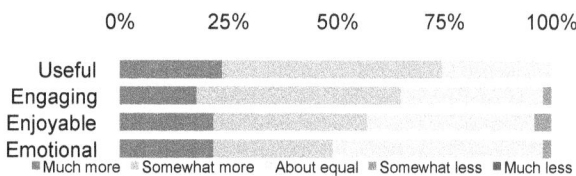

Figure 4. Responses to the survey question, "In the last six months, how _____ was it when you viewed and discussed a media item during a phone or video call, compared to not sharing?" (n=51).

In our lab study, 15 of 20 participants ranked the media sharing conditions as the most "emotionally connecting." Ten ranked the Photo condition first, four ranked the Browser condition first, and one ranked the Facebook condition first (Figure 5).

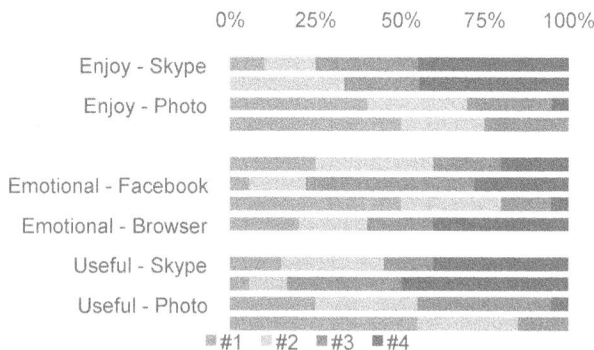

Figure 5. Responses to the lab study final questionnaire ranking the four conditions on three aspects (n=20).

These findings are in line with findings in [21], [31] and 0. Macaranas et. al. showed that remotely watching video during video mediated communication provided a strong sense of connection and co-presence [21]. Weisz et al. in 0 found that watching media synchronously with others promotes connection and people feel closer to the remote person. Shamma et. al. found that simultaneous video sharing online in addition to the ability to communicate through text messaging or video chat can help people feel togetherness while being apart and support feeling of intimacy and closeness [31]. Observations from the lab sessions suggested that the most emotionally meaningful moments came from storytelling and reminiscing that was triggered by the shared media. Some stories were directly related to the media, while others were triggered by the media but only tangentially related to it.

Some stories were directly related to the media, while others were triggered by the media but only tangentially related to it. Although very little emotional storytelling was observed in the Browser condition, it was especially apparent in the Photo condition, and to a lesser extent in the Facebook condition. As one survey respondent commented:

"We were able to reminisce about a point in our lives together." [Survey P158]

In fact, one of the most touching moments was in the Photo condition when one participant shared a Google Street View photo of her grandparent's house in Hawaii (). This photo and the stories it triggered for both her and her partner evoked strong emotions in both women.

"Your grandfather's house - I had never physically seen it but I could also see the emotion you put into it. And that's where the emotion came in – because of the car. That's your dad's car, and your dad's been passed away for quite a while. I picked up the emotion – are you going to cry? I'm sorry – that came along with the pictures." [Lab P1b]

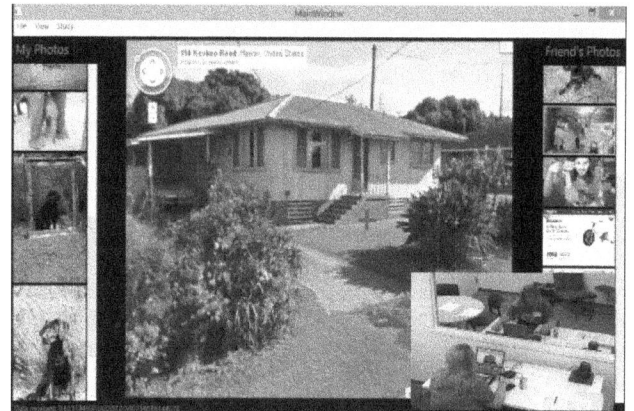

Figure 6. During the Photo condition, one participant showed a Google Street View screen shots of her grandfather's house to her study partner.

While there are many ways to share photos asynchronously online, the combination of synchronous communication with media sharing seemed conducive to storytelling and reminiscing. One lab study participant said:

"I would prefer video and pictures because I liked seeing her reaction when she looked at the picture, because you can take a picture of anything but what is the real reasons behind those pictures, so we were talking about that and I liked that part and we understand why we took that picture." [Lab P1b]

Many of the stories were reminiscent of a shared event, while others were stories about events that only one of the participants experienced. Both types appeared engaging for the participants. Many participants liked the fact that they were able to reminisce about themselves, things that they had done together, as well as share about their friends and family members. Sometimes this reminiscing could lead to planning for repeating the mutual memories. For example, after viewing a photo showing one participant swimming with dolphins on a trip that both study participants experienced, they started to reminisce about that trip, share stories about dolphins and then started planning another trip together.

"A lot of things are missed during text, or they can be misinterpreted, but when we have the face, the expression and there is also the energy that is transmitted." [Lab P2b]

This value of reminiscing is echoed in previous work by O'Hara et al. [29] who also found that synchronous photo viewing provided opportunities for people to share their stories, talk about themselves, reminisce, show empathy. It also helped augment emotional bonds between people in the context of adding media to a mealtime. In addition, the personalized nature of the photos shared during the lab study was another factor that added emotional impact. Participants knew that their study partner selected these photos particularly to show to them as opposed to sharing them in social media where photos are chosen for a larger audience.

"I was really interested to see [my study partner's] pictures and what he would bring because I knew that they were really important to him because he picked specifically those ones to show me." [Lab P9a]

"The way she picked up certain pictures in our history was great, selecting it beforehand made it special because it wasn't like browsing my [Facebook] feed." [Lab P9b]

The Facebook condition also evoked some emotional moments as posts prompted reminiscing and storytelling. However, participants ranked the Facebook condition as the least emotionally engaging by far (Figure 5). In fact, the spontaneous and less personalized nature of Facebook posts by mutual friends changed the nature of the conversation to gossiping rather than personal emotional stories.

The Browser condition had very few instances of storytelling or reminiscing. Sharing some activities such as trip planning created some opportunities for storytelling or reminiscing about the previous similar experiences but most engagement took the form of exchanging information, so it didn't evoke emotional connection that much. As one lab study participant commented, the somewhat generic activities they did in the Browser condition made them feel emotionally disconnected.

"It was the most fun and open but it was emotionally disconnected us, if my study partner was worried about something, I wouldn't be able to tell." [Lab P9b]

> **Insight:** Sharing media especially photos during a call create opportunities for emotional connections by triggering storytelling and reminiscing.

5.2 Emotion and Visual Attention

Interestingly, the emotional expressiveness scale in the ABCCT questionnaire used in our lab study revealed that the Skype Only condition was rated higher than all of the other media-sharing conditions (Figure 7). However, this section of the questionnaire is comprised of questions related to users' ability to read emotions over the communication system 0. From this perspective, media sharing introduces the potential for divided attention, likely diminishing the participant's focus on their partner, making it harder to interpret their facial expressions. As one survey respondent noted:

"The focus would be on the 'media item' and not the conversation." [Survey P124]

Another lab participant commented that:

"Anytime that anything was in front of us even the Facebook that [had] given us something to talk about, I did pay attention less to my study partner but during video talk I was reading her emotion and I felt more connected to her ..." [Lab P9b]

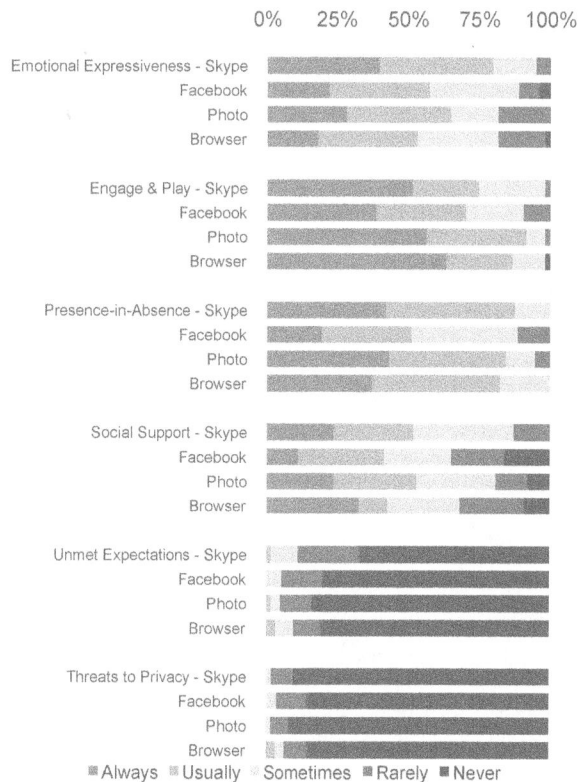

Figure 7. Lab study responses to the ABCCT questions.

However, the Photo and Browser condition appear as strong as the Skype Only condition in the ABCCT Presence-in-Absence scale, which is comprised of questions about feeling increased emotional connection with their partner through the communication technology (Figure 7). In addition, the Photo condition stands close to the Skype Only condition on the Social Support scale. This feeling of Presence-in-Absence provided by shared visual context has also been found in [1] and [31]. This suggests that the shared media adds a degree of emotional connection that compensates for the reduced ability to read facial expressions. One of the lab study participants expressed feelings of co-presence engendered by the Photo condition.

"It was like I'm here with you with the photo" (posing as she has a photo album in her hand showing it to her friend who was her study partner). [Lab P2b]

Insight: Sharing media draws visual attention away from video, but this is made up for by the addition of triggers for emotionally significant topics.

5.3 Utility of Media Sharing

The usefulness of media sharing is what was most apparent to our survey and lab study participants. 54% of our survey respondents had shared media during a phone or video call in the prior six months. 73% of this group responded that sharing media made the call more useful compared to a call where no media was being shared (Figure 4).

We asked our lab participants to rank the usefulness of each prototype that they used during the study from best (#1) to worst (#4) (Figure 5). Adding media to a call appeared to greatly enhance the utility of video-mediated communication as only three of 20 participants ranked the Skype condition as the most useful. The most useful condition was the browser, with 11 of 20 participants ranking it first, while six ranked it second. Many of our lab study participants mentioned the open nature of the Browser condition and the variety of activities that they could do together as an important reason for preferring it.

> *"It was my favorite because you could do anything, for example my daughter is going to get help from your husband [referring to her friend and study partner], they can talk and have the math work, go to web sites or go to the others, where you can find a math help."* [Lab P1b]

In addition, the flexibility of the Browser condition introduces the potential to support the need of single, multi-purpose integrated design for sharing media.

> *"I would spend more time on this because you can also share pictures on that"* [Lab P2a]

Our lab participants were allowed to choose any online activity for Browser condition. We observed several different shared activities, categorized as follows: entertainment, information seeking, show and tell, activity planning and shopping.

Interestingly, the most common activity was watching humorous videos together. In some cases one participant played a YouTube video he had seen before to show to his study partner or they browsed collaboratively for funny YouTube video not already seen. This finding supports Macaranas et al. [21], who found that watching TV with someone remotely is engaging and fun. Some categories such as activity planning and shopping, benefited more from augmenting by audio and video communication channels because the other person's feedback seemed more necessary.

> *"I wanted to buy a birthday gift for her kid so we could browse together and at least I could have a visual idea what to get for her."* [Lab P1b]

Insight: Sharing media adds utility over a normal call. The shared browser is particularly useful due to its flexibility.

5.4 Tool Usage

People who share media during a call today for domestic purposes are doing it by repurposing existing technologies, e.g., sending media (or links to it) via a messaging system (Figure 8). People sharing media in this way do not have the benefits of a WYSIWIS experience or the ability to point and gesture, and must do all co-navigation and deixis through voice. There are some tools where users can interact via multiple media types but as these features

have not been proposed and integrated into domestic video chat applications, they have been rarely used by a general audience during a home video conferencing session.

Our survey results show that a minority of respondents (35%) have used screen sharing for media sharing, however, most screen sharing tools do not provide shared control or telepointers. Through interviews, our participants indicated several desired practices of sharing media during a call, which are not supported by current technology offered in video chat application. These mainly included the ability to have two-way, mutual interaction with the media as well as synchronous manipulation. As a result, extra effort and some intuitive techniques were applied. The WYSIWIS approach in our prototype along with two-way simultaneous interaction and ease of use was appreciated by some of our lab participants. As one lab participant commented:

> *"No extra effort was needed, clicking back and forth was great it wasn't like oh go to this link or open this file, everything was there and I could scroll and see what she was talking about or queue up the next one."* [Lab P9b]

Another lab study participant compared the ease of the shared web browser to browsing in parallel on separate computers.

> *"We both wanted to look at the cruise and she wanted to show me a ship that she had researched on, and sometimes when the website has many different places to go then it is easy to get lost, when you are talking on the phone and talking about the web site even if you are on the same web site you might not see the same screen so that's kind of cool when you say oh this is so cool you see what she is talking about."* [Lab P5a]

Insight: Media sharing during a call is currently not well supported because of lack of two-way simultaneous interaction.

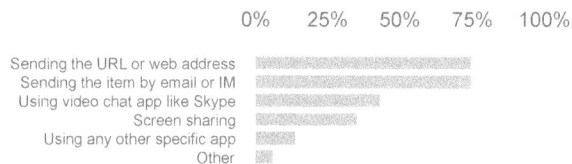

Figure 8. Responses to the survey question, "Which tools have you used to view media together during a call?" (n=51).

5.5 Enjoyment and Increase in Usage

Of the 51 survey respondents who had prior experience sharing media during a call, 65% found the experience more engaging and 57% enjoyed the call more when they viewed or discussed media (Figure 4). One respondent said,

> *"It just made it a lot more fun, didn't have those awkward silences and made the call more worthwhile."* [Survey P122]

These results are consistent with findings in [21] and 0. Macaranas et. al. found that the communication enhanced the enjoyment of the content for some participants [21]. Similarly, Weisz, et al. showed that people found it more enjoyable when they have the ability to communicate with each other during the synchronous media watching session 0.

148

The ABCCT questions in the "Engage and Play" group ask about engagement, excitement, and fun. The lab study participants' responses to these questions were highest for the Photo and Browser conditions (Figure 7)

As part of the lab study post-task questionnaire we asked if having a tool that made it easy to have that experience would make the participant call more frequently or encourage longer calls (Figure 9). The results were strongest for the Browser and Photo conditions, though even the Facebook condition had positive responses.

"I think there would be more calls instead of just messaging each other." [Survey P122]

"If I had a device that could easily do that with my family and friends I would talk to them more about videos or photos, over the phone, than I do now." [Survey P165]

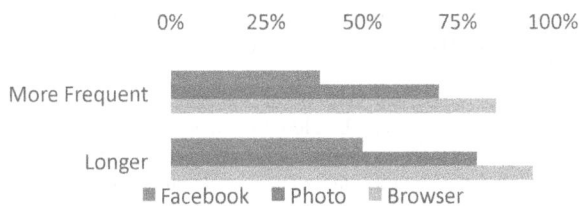

Figure 9: Responses to the lab study questions, "If you had a tool that made it easy for you to have this experience, would it make your calls _____?" (n=20).

Although the Skype condition was still engaging for our participants, some of them reported in the interview that it was somewhat boring in comparison to the other conditions. When they were asked about their experience, one participant found the Skype Only session difficult because of the undirected nature of the activity, and believed that her study partner seemed bored because he started to sneak glances at his cell phone although he paid full attention to her in other sessions. [Lab P7b]. We also observed some other forms of boredom in some of our participants such as yawning, looking around and not maintaining the eye contact and playing with some other objects.

"Skype was almost the most boring one because we used it and there was no other interaction." [Lab P3a]

"I liked it when we have a mutual goal, the browser stuff or pointing at things on the pictures and we had a task instead of just looking at each other. I think it was fun." [Lab P8b]

> **Insight:** Sharing media during a call makes the experience more engaging and enjoyable and encourages for more frequent and longer communication.

6. DISCUSSION

Home video communication is not only about exchanging information. In fact, conveying affection is also an important part of communication. Studies show that many of the non-verbal cues that are important parts of showing our emotions, such as gesture and gaze directions are distorted over video link [10, 17]. In this regard, sharing media during video conversation could compensate for this shortcoming of expressing our emotions in video chat compared to face-to-face communication. We saw that users are able to share more personal stories and to emotionally connect with others over

video chat while sharing media during a call. These show a clear need to go beyond talking heads in video communication and repurpose video to engage in shared activities. This need is echoed in [1], [15] and [17]. However, there is limited support for shared activities augmented with present-day video communication technology [1]. Our findings further illustrate the synergy between different types of media and communication channels, especially video-mediated communication. Sharing media can enhance video-mediated communication since it can potentially create opportunities for emotional connection, utility, enjoyment and engagement.

We found that media sharing has a high potential to emotionally connect people during video-mediated communication by triggering story telling and reminiscing. Emotional storytelling and reminiscing were apparent in the Photo condition, to a lesser extent in the Facebook condition and very little in the Browser condition. The personalized nature of the Photo condition and preparation made each user feel very special to the remote person and increased the emotional content of the conversation as a consequence. This suggests providing a secure personalized shared space attached to each contact in the video chat contact list where users can upload media specified for that person. Such design features would be desirable and provide more opportunities to share life moments in the middle of conversations.

Colsey et al. in [7] showed the potential value of Facebook content including status updates and wall posts for reminiscing. Similarly, we showed that social networks such as Facebook can support reminiscing and emotional connection during video-conferencing by focusing on one's personal 'stuff' and on a limited circle of his close mutual friends and family. In this regard, integrating some mutual interests from social media in the video chat application could also offer several reminiscing opportunities and conversation topics and lead to more enjoyable communication.

While Harboe et al. speculate that the combination of video chat and audiovisual entertainment such as a TV program will be distracting [12], Macaranas et al. found that augmenting synchronous watching with video-mediated communication does not cause divided attention [21]. However, we found that media sharing introduces the potential for divided attention. Diminishing the user's focus on the remote partner is seemingly inevitable in current practices of synchronous media sharing, since users usually have to minimize their video chat application and open the attached file. Even in screen sharing, only one person has the control for the video feed window. In addition, this concern of drawing visual attention away from the partner to the media was echoed for our participants who found that they did not pay enough attention to their remote partner. This cost suggests that in future design for sharing media during a video communication, space should be divided equally between the video feed and media presentation space. Despite this drawback of diminished focus, we found through our lab study that that Photo and Browser conditions provided the same level of Presence-in-Absence as Skype by itself. This result is similar to findings in [1] and [31] that showed shared visual context during video chat can support a feeling of co-presence. Thus, the emotional connection provided by media is strong enough to compensate for the distraction that occurs when media is added.

Sharing media adds utility over a normal call. Several studies have shown the importance of video as data in work environments [4][1]. Kirk et al. [17] saw the benefit in integrating messaging with utilities like file sharing and web browsing. 73% of our survey participants believed that sharing media makes the call more useful. This result shows the importance of integrating sharing media with audio and video communication channels with more features for collaboration and interaction. In our lab study, we also found that media including Photo and Browser have the potential of adding utility to a domestic video communication. However, Facebook was not successful in enhancing the utility of the Skype call. The open nature of the Browser condition and its flexibility, provided the opportunity for a variety of shared activities while the communication channel created a suitable environment for collaboration, better decision making and the exchange ideas about a mutual shared goal. These findings demonstrate the value in providing a multi-purpose, flexible, collaborative and personalized environment that enables users to do a wide variety of online activities together for different purposes such as entertainment, education, information seeking, show and tell, activity planning and shopping.

Despite the fact that people rated the Skype Only condition as being very engaging and enjoyable, we observed several signs of boredom in our participants during the Skype Only condition. Such behaviors were never observed in other conditions. Thus, according to our data, Photo and Browser sharing could engage participants to the same extent as Skype, and possibly more. According to our observations, participants enjoyed Photo and Browser sharing to a greater extent than the Skype Only condition. The Facebook condition provided the same level of joy as the Skype Only condition. This higher level of enjoyment that media encourages can potentially lead to more frequent and longer communication between people. This possibility shows the importance of embedding media sharing in designing future communication tools for distance-separated families, especially for young children and teenagers who lack communication with their families, which may make them emotionally disconnect from their remote family members.

Sharing media could help to facilitate conversation and could be a good catalyst for reducing awkward silences and providing context for those that like to chat but may not always have something to say. Yet, it is unlikely that more frequent and longer calls are desired by all demographics especially those that have enough in-person contact on a daily basis, but it could be regarded as an asset for those family and friends that lack communication exchanges. Providing an easy and accessible platform for sharing daily life in a call could facilitate being a part of daily life of each other and support more feelings of togetherness.

Regardless of all of these benefits that augmenting media sharing can offer to video-mediated communication, media sharing is currently not well supported in this type of communication. Sharing the exact same experience needs a WYSIWIS design that also supports simultaneous, mutual two-way interactions. We also evaluated the costs of adding media to a video call in two scales: unmet expectations and threat to privacy. We did not find any considerable costs compared to the Skype Only condition.

7. LIMITATION

While valuable, our research also had several limitations. We believe that we would have more detailed data about the long-term real practices of media sharing during calls if we had done a field-based study. In addition, we are also aware that a lab study and associated observations may cause behavior changes and may not be truly indicative of actual practices. In addition, for this work we were more focused on the benefits of adding media to a video call than potential drawbacks. Trying this approach in an everyday situation could reveal drawbacks such as feelings of obligation to share personal data during a conversation. We will focus on this drawback in our future work.

8. CONCLUSION

Our survey and our lab study show that media sharing in video mediated communication is desirable because it is useful, emotionally fulfilling, and enjoyable. We found that people have a desire to share the experience of viewing media together during a video chat. However, this practice is not well supported in the current communication systems. The results from our work demonstrate that shared browsing fulfilled utilitarian needs, while sharing photos supported emotional connection.

We also found that audiovisual calls are enhanced by viewing media in terms of increasing users' enjoyment and sense of connectedness. We learned that viewing media during a call can add significant values in terms of usefulness. Our participants felt that adding media to calls would encourage them to make more calls, and have longer calls. Our study also revealed that people want to share many different activities during a call. The collaborative and open nature of shared browsing during a call made the call very useful in comparison to regular calls. Adding media to a call increased the emotional content of the call and made it more engaging for remote users. In addition, adding media often triggers more stories, which supported emotional connections between users. We believe that this emotional connection is strong enough to compensate for the distraction that occurs when media is added. Considering the benefits of and desire for sharing media during a call, we believe that this integration of technologies is an area that is worth investing in future audio/video chat applications.

9. REFERENCES

[1] Balabanović, M., Chu, L. L., and Wolff, G. J. 2000. Storytelling with digital photographs. In *Proceedings of the SIGCHI conference on Human factors in computing systems,* CHI '00. ACM, New York, NY, 564-571.

[2] Banks, R., Kirk, D., and Sellen, A. 2012. A design perspective on three technology heirlooms. In *Human–Computer Interaction,* 27,1-2, 63-91.

[3] Bly, S.A., Harrison, S.R., and Irwin, S. 1993. Media spaces: bringing people together in a video audio and computing environment. Communication of the ACM, 36, 1, 28-46.

[4] Brubaker, J, R., Venolia, G., and Tang, J. C. 2012. Focusing on shared experiences: moving beyond the camera in video communication. In *Proceedings of the Designing Interactive Systems Conference,* DIS'12. ACM, New York, NY, 96-105.

[5] Buhler, T., Neustaedter, C., and Hillman, S. 2013. How and why teenagers use video chat. *In Proceedings of the conference on computer supported cooperative work.* CSCW'13. ACM, New York, NY, 759-768.

[6] Chalfen, R. 1987. *Snapshot versions of life.* Bowling Green, KY: Bowling Green State University Press.

[7] Cosley, D., Sosik, V. S., Schultz, J., Peesapati, S. T., and Lee, S. 2012. Experiences with designing tools for everyday reminiscing. In *Human-Computer Interaction* 27,1-2, 175-198.

[8] Forghani, A. and Neustaedter, C. 2014. The Routines and Needs of Grandparents and Parents for Grandparent-Grandchild Conversations Over Distance, In *Proceedings of the SIGCHI Conference on Human Factors in Computing Systems.* CHI '14. ACM, New York, NY, 4177-4186.

[9] Frohlich D.M., Wall S. and Kiddle G. 2013. Re-discovery of forgotten images in domestic photo collections. *Personal and Ubiquitous Computing,* 17,4, 729-740.

[10] Grayson, D. & Monk, A. 2003. Are you looking at me? Eye contact and desktop video conferencing. TOCHI, 10,3, 221-243.

[11] Greaves, A., and Rukzio, E. 2009. View & share: supporting co-present viewing and sharing of media using personal projection. In *Proceedings of the 11th International Conference on Human-Computer Interaction with Mobile Devices and Service*, MobileHCI'09. ACM, New York, NY, 44.

[12] Harboe, G., Massey, N., Metcalf, C., Wheatley, D., and Romano, G. 2008. The uses of social television. *Computers in Entertainment*, 6, 1, 8.

[13] Inkpen, K., Taylor, B., Tang, J., Junozovic, S., and Venolia, G. 2013. Experiences2Go: Sharing Kid's Activities Outside the Home with Remote Family Members. *In Proceedings of the 2013 conference on Computer supported cooperative work*, CSCW'13. 1329-1340.

[14] Jansen M., van den Hoven E., and Frohlich D. 2013. Pearl: living media enabled by interactive photo projection. *Personal and Ubiquitous Computing*, 18, 5, 1259-1275.

[15] Judge, T, K., and Neustaedter, C. 2010. Sharing conversation and sharing life: video conferencing in the home. In *Proceedings of the SIGCHI Conference on Human Factors in Computing Systems*, CHI'10. *ACM, 655-658.*

[16] Junozovic, S., Inkpen Quinn, K., Blank, T., and Gupta, A. 2012. IllumiShare: Sharing any surface. In *Proceedings of the SIGCHI Conference on Human Factors in Computing Systems,*CHI '12. ACM, 1919–1928.

[17] Kirk, D., Sellen, A., and Cao, X. 2010. Home Video Communication: Mediating 'Closeness'. In *Proceedings of the 2010 conference on Computer supported cooperative work*, CSCW'10. 135–144.

[18] Kraut, R. E., Gergle, D., and Fussell, S. R. 2002. The use of visual information in shared visual spaces: Informing the development of virtual co-presence. In *Proceedings of the 2002 conference on Computer supported cooperative work*, CSCW '02. 31-40.

[19] Landry, B. M., and Guzdial, M. 2006. iTell: Supporting retrospective storytelling with digital photos. In *Proceedings of the Designing Interactive Systems*, DIS '06.160-168.

[20] Lucero, A., Holopainen, J., and Jokela, T. 2011. Pass-them-around: Collaborative use of mobile phones for photo sharing. In *Proceedings of the SIGCHI Conference on Human Factors in Computing Systems*, CHI '11. ACM, 1787-1796.

[21] Macaranas, A., Venolia, G., Inkpen, K., and Tang, J. 2013. Sharing Experiences over Video: Watching Video Programs Together at a Distance. In *Human-Computer Interaction*, INTERACT'13. springer Berlin Heidelberg, 73-90.

[22] Maekawa, T., Hara, T., and Nishio, S. 2006. A collaborative web browsing system for multiple mobile users. In *Pervasive Computing and Communications*. PerCom'06. IEEE, 22-35.

[23] Miller, A. D., and Edwards, W. K. 2007. Give and take: a study of consumer photo-sharing culture and practice. In *Proceedings of the SIGCHI Conference on Human Factors in Computing Systems*, CHI'07. ACM, 347-356.

[24] Morris, M. R., and Horvitz, E. 2007. Search Together: An interface for collaborative web search. In *Proceedings of the 20th annual ACM symposium on User interface software and technology*, UIST '07. ACM, 3-12.

[25] Neustaedter, C., Elliot, K. and Greenberg, S. 2006. Interpersonal awareness in the domestic realm. In *Proceedings of Australia conference on Computer Interaction: Design, Activities, Artifacts and Environments*, OzCHI'06. ACM, 15-22.

[26] Neustaedter, C. and Fedorovskava, E. 2009. Understanding and improving flow in digital photo ecosystems. In *Proceedings of Graphics Interface 2009*, GI'09. 191-198.

[27] Neustaedter, C., and Greenberg, S. 2012. Intimacy in long-distance relationships over video chat. In *Proceedings of the SIGCHI Conference on Human Factors in Computing Systems*, CHI '12. ACM, 753-762.

[28] O'Hara, K., Black, A., and Lipson, M. 2006. Everyday practices with mobile video telephony. In *Proceedings of the SIGCHI Conference on Human Factors in Computing Systems*, CHI'06. ACM, 871-880.

[29] O'Hara, K., Helmes, J., Sellen, A., Harper, R., ten Bhömer, M., and van den Hoven, E. 2012. Food for talk: Phototalk in the context of sharing a meal. *Human-Computer Interaction*, 27,1-2, 124-150.

[30] Rose, G. 2004. Everyone's cuddled up and it just looks really nice: An emotional geography of some mums and their family photos. *Social & Cultural Geography*. 5, 4, 549-564.

[31] Shamma, D.A., Bastea-Forte, M., Joubert, N., and Liu, Y. 2008. Enhancing Online Personal Connections through the Synchronized Sharing of Online Video. In *Ext. Abstracts of* CHI'08. ACM, 2931–2936.

[32] Tee, K. Brush, A. J. and Inkpen, K. M. 2009. Exploring communication and sharing between extended families. *International Journal of Human-Computer Studies*. 67,2, 128-138.

[33] Van House, Nancy A. 2009. Collocated photo sharing, story-telling, and the performance of self. In *International Journal of Human-Computer Studies*. 67, 12, 1073-1086.

[34] Vetere, F. Davis, H., Gibbs, M. and Howard, S. 2009. The Magic Box and Collages: Responding to the challenges of distributed intergenerational play. *International Journal of Human-Computer Studies*. 67,2, 165-178.

[35] Vutborg, R., Kjeldskov, J., Paay, J., Pedell, S., and Vetere, F. 201. Supporting young children's communication with adult relatives across time zones. In *Proceedings of Australia conference on Computer Interaction: Design, Activities, Artifacts and* Environments, OzCHI'11. 291-300.

[36] Webster, J. D., and McCall, M. E. 1999. Reminiscence functions across adulthood: A replication and extension, *Journal of Adult Development*. 6,1, 73-85.

[37] Weisz, J.D., Erickson, T., and Kellogg, W. A. 2006. Synchronous broadcast messaging: the use of ICT. In *Proceedings of the SIGCHI conference on Human factors in computing systems*, CHI'06. ACM, 1293-1302.

[38] Wiese, J., Kelley, P. G., Cranor, L. F., Dabbish, L., Hong, J. I., and Zimmerman, J. 2011. Are you close with me? Are you nearby? Investigating social groups, closeness, and willingness to share. In *Proceedings of the 13th international conference on Ubiquitous computing*, UbiComp '11. ACM, 197-206.

[39] Yarosh, S., Markopoulos, P., and Abowd, G.D. 2014. Towards a Questionnaire for Measuring Affective Benefits and Costs of Communication Technologies. In *Proceedings of the 2014 conference on Computer supported cooperative work*, CSCW '14. ACM, 84-96.

[40] Zancanaro, M., Oliviero, S., Tomasini, D., and Pianesi, F. 2011. A socially aware persuasive system for supporting conversations at the museum café. In the *Proceedings of the 16th international conference on intelligent user interface*, IUI '11. ACM, 395-398.

The Backstage Work of Data Sharing

Karina E. Kervin
University of Michigan
Ann Arbor, MI, USA
kkervin@umich.edu

Robert B. Cook
Oak Ridge National Laboratory
Oak Ridge, TN, USA
cookrb@ornl.gov

William K. Michener
University of New Mexico
Albuquerque, NM, USA
wmichene@lternet.edu

ABSTRACT

Conventional wisdom suggests that there are benefits to the creation of shared repositories of scientific data. Funding agencies require that the data from sponsored projects be shared publicly, but individual researchers often see little personal benefit to offset the work of creating easily sharable data. These conflicting forces have led to the emergence of a new role to support researchers: data managers. This paper identifies key differences between the socio-technical context of data managers and other "human infrastructure" roles articulated previously in Computer Supported Cooperative Work (CSCW) literature and summarizes the challenges that data managers face when accepting data for archival and reuse. While data managers' work is critical for advancing science and science policy, their work is often invisible and under-appreciated since it takes place behind the scenes.

Categories and Subject Descriptors

K.4.3 [**Organizational Impacts**]: Computer-supported collaborative work; H.3.5 [**Online Information Services**]: Data sharing

General Terms: Human Factors.

Keywords: Cyberinfrastructure, data managers.

1. INTRODUCTION

Conventional wisdom suggests that there are benefits to the creation of shared repositories of scientific data. For example, Earth observation data are critical to deepen our understanding of factors and processes controlling life on Earth and for use by policy makers, resource managers and others to make decisions that affect sustainability of life within a context of global change and increasing population [9,10]. Recognition of these advantages to archiving data has led the NIH, NSF, and NASA to require researchers to submit data management plans that include whether and how data will be made available publically [16,17,18].

Given the importance of data sharing, reuse, and integration and synthesis, an open question is why are we not advancing more rapidly to the promise of fully curated, metadata-complete, publicly-accessible repositories [8]. At first glance, it would seem that the influence of grant agencies and publication venues would force more widespread data deposition. Certainly, international and US agencies have implemented data sharing practices that are partially effective. A deeper look reveals that researchers' data practices,

including data sharing, are more often guided by individual benefit [11]. The reality is that many researchers do not budget adequate time for metadata generation, and perceive that this task is not a high priority. Nor are researchers compensated for producing data products—they are evaluated for advancing science through research publications.

Data repositories have emerged as a key enabling infrastructure to mediate these opposing forces by providing organized, indexed, and well-documented data products that are easily found and independently understandable [5,14]. Some repositories have addressed the issue of individual benefit by treating data publication as another form of peer-reviewed journal publication, such as the Ecological Society of America (ESA) Ecological Archives and Scientific Data from Nature Publication Group. Even when researchers gain professional recognition through peer-reviewed data publication, many data collection activities are not targeted for archives, and often the resulting data products are not well documented or formatted for others to use [12]. Data managers help to bridge this gap between data creators and data users by creating clear and understandable data documentation.

Data managers must successfully straddle multiple worlds. First, they must be up to date with the technical aspects of data archives. Second, they must maintain an in-depth knowledge of advances in data curation, and preservation since a key service of data centers is supporting long-term access and use of the data stored in the repository. In addition, just as research librarians have expertise in their client's disciplines, so should data managers [15].

2. BACKGROUND

"Human infrastructure" was described by Lee, et al. as the social context that enables and sustains the work of creating and maintaining cyberinfrastructure (CI) [13]. Lee, et al. further articulate the importance of human infrastructure to the process of creating a data sharing infrastructure, namely data repositories. The key to maintaining data repositories is to identify and understand the key stakeholders, including research organizations and individual researchers, as well as the interactions between those stakeholders and the tools and standards that they use [3].

Some of the most challenging and important questions regarding data reuse revolve around specific details of data collection and how those details directly affect new analyses [4]. Understanding the original context of data stored in repositories is especially important when the original purpose differs from the purpose for reuse [1,2]. These challenges become even more pronounced when data is used across different communities of practice, organizations, or technical systems [6]. Every time data moves across any of these boundaries there is potential for that data to become misinterpreted or lost [6]. To complicate matters, the creation of metadata to effectively describe data is time consuming and is often viewed as unrewarding by the data creator. These challenges are complicated by the natural tendency of the person collecting data to document that data based on their own anticipated future uses [4].

All this implies the need for data managers to assist researchers in overcoming the challenges of data sharing and reuse. For example, data managers help to address the challenge of understanding the original context in which data was collected by ensuring the metadata associated with published data is clear and complete. Data managers are a critical, but overlooked, component of the human infrastructure that makes data sharing possible [13]. Despite their important role in the human infrastructure of cyberinfrastructure, these gatekeepers have been largely left out of CSCW literature. These observations led to two research questions: 1) *What challenges do data managers face, and 2) How does this role compare to the CI roles studied in the past?*

3. RESEARCH METHODS

This survey of data repository managers examined components related to preparing data for publication for which individual researchers are typically responsible. Additionally, the survey sought to understand what types of errors data managers were most likely to encounter when receiving data for publication.

3.1 Methodology

This survey was distributed as an online survey, and was open for responses from July 2012 through November 2012. We sent the survey request email in two waves. First, we sent an email with the survey link and later reminders to data managers in each author's respective communities, which had a 79.5% response rate. For the second wave, we extracted data manager email addresses from the Databib website (http://databib.org), a directory of research data repositories and sent an email request with the survey link to the resulting list. The response rate for this portion of the sample was 37.8%. Overall, the survey was sent to a total of 113 data managers, with 59 responses for a total response rate of 52%..

3.2 Survey Instrument

The focus of the survey was on the interaction between data managers at scientific data repositories and the researchers in the community served by that data repository. Initial survey questions identified the nature of the community each data repository primarily serves. The remainder of the survey focused on the Data Center Stewardship and Archive Functions proposed by Author 2 (acquire, document, archive, provide citation, distribute, provide outreach and user support, and provide long-term stewardship) [5]. For each of these services, the survey asked respondents about the data related services offered at their repository and some of the common errors they saw in relation to these services [12]. The final few questions attempted to understand the motivations and challenges data repositories face when asking researchers to deposit data into the repository. These questions were phrased in the form of a list of motivations and constraints gathered from previous studies on data publication [7]. Respondents had the opportunity to offer an open-ended response to these questions in addition to selecting multiple items from the list provided.

4. RESULTS

Many of the repositories included in this survey served researchers from multiple subject areas. A large percentage of those who responded served fields related to ecology and environmental science, because of the communities represented by Authors 2 and 3. Repositories for fields related to the physical and social sciences

were also well represented. While most repositories served communities of a few hundred to a few thousand researchers, a reasonable portion also served research communities of 10,000 or more. Again, this distribution reflects the higher response rate from authors' repositories.

4.1 Common Errors Seen by Data Managers

According to our survey, data managers regularly encountered a wide variety of data management errors. Most data managers who responded to the survey reported planning errors (93%) in the data submitted by researchers (Table 1). The most common problem was neglecting to review and update data management plans (DMP) after they were written. Data managers also mentioned a variety of related planning errors, including not involving data centers until data were produced, researchers not having a plan for the long-term archive process, and researchers not making themselves familiar with data deposition requirements.

Table 1. Data Management Plan errors reported by repository data managers. *n=24; **n=29; †n=16.

Errors	Rarely (<= 5%)	Sometimes (5-25%)	Frequent (26-75%)
Do not make *	29%	25%	46%
Do not implement **	7%	45%	48%
Make and implement after data collection **	10%	24%	66%
Do not review and update †	13%	0%	88%

Fewer data managers (86%) saw errors in the description of data collection methods, but this was still common. The most common methodological errors data managers observed were a lack of description of the data limitations and quality control (Table 2). Other errors related to the methodology description include: lack of temporal and spatial coverage (e.g. exact dates and site coordinates), neglecting to update method and instrumentation descriptions, and omitting details that are common knowledge within a researcher's own sub-discipline but not to outsiders.

Table 2: Methodological documentation errors reported by repository data managers. * n=31; **n=22.

Errors	Sometimes (<= 25%)	Frequent (26-75%)	Almost always (>=76%)
Insufficient description of method protocol *	41%	48%	10%
Insufficient description of quality control procedures *	33%	48%	19%
Insufficient description of data limitations *	21%	48%	29%

Another class of errors that most data mangers (83%) observed regularly was in data organization. The majority of data managers reported non-descriptive labels (Table 3). Other errors reported by the data managers include: incomplete descriptions of data codes and units, as well as missing files,and incorrect file names.

Table 3: Data organization errors commonly seen by repository data managers. * n=39; **n=36; †n=30.

Errors	Rarely (<= 5%)	Sometimes (5-25%)	Frequent (>=25%)
Non-descriptive labels *	6%	28%	67%
Insufficient description of missing or incomplete data codes *	20%	41%	38%
Inconsistent labels or units **	28%	31%	42%

The data managers surveyed also reported that metadata errors were also common (79%). The most common error reported was neglecting to describe the potential uses of the deposited data followed by lack of data provenance (Table 4). About a third frequently reported lack of definitions and lack of descriptions of variables. Other metadata errors mentioned by data managers were inaccurate information, esoteric descriptions, and no descriptions at all.

Table 4: Metadata errors commonly seen by repository data managers. *n=37; **n=36; †n=39; ††n=30.

Errors	Rarely (<= 5%)	Sometimes (5-25%)	Frequent (>=25%)
Lack of accurate definitions *	27%	41%	32%
Descriptions of variables do not match actual variables *	44%	22%	35%
No data provenance †	21%	38%	41%
Do not describe contributions of data††	20%	17%	63%

Data managers (79%) reported seeing errors or omissions in the integration of multiple data sets. Of those, 47% (22) reported that researchers do not include the scripts or workflows used to integrate data sets. Data managers also mentioned that researchers did not include metadata from original data sets, or researchers would integrate data sets with inconsistent taxonomy or methodology. A similar problem existed for the analysis and visualization of data sets, and many data managers (21 out of 47) reported that researchers did not include the scripts or workflows used to analyze or visualize their data sets. Other difficulties mentioned by data managers were researchers neglecting to include the equations used in data analysis, and incorrect cartographic methods for visualization.

4.2 Attitudes Toward Depositing Data

Most data managers reported that researchers were willing to deposit data, with 77% (36 out of 47) saying researchers were frequently or always willing to share data. Data managers reported that researchers had a variety of reasons for depositing data in repositories. The most common were: the greater good of the scientific community (74%); greater visibility for the researcher's own work (80%); and funding source requirements (80%). Other reasons for data deposition were extra services provided by the data repository and easier access to and discovery of data.

Data managers also reported a variety of reasons that researchers were reluctant to deposit their data, with lack of experience in data management (79%) being the most common reason. Other common reasons were a lack of resources (65%) and fear the data would be misused or misunderstood (60%). Data managers also reported that there was a lack of funding for data archival. On the other hand, some data managers said that while these factors had influenced data deposition in the past, they were less important considerations now. Another factor mentioned was the growing prevalence of institutional repositories, which give researchers more choices as to where to deposit their data.

5. DISCUSSION

Data managers encountered a variety of problems when data was submitted to a repository, which are unique to data managers, although there are parallels to other groups studied previously.

5.1 The Context of Data Managers

Data managers are similar to librarians, in that the work they perform is often taken for granted, and therefore invisible [19]. Like CI software developers, the final product is set out for public use and critique, which Star & Strauss called "embedded background work", or "going backstage" [19].

Both librarians and data managers manage and share information, but what differs is when they perform these tasks. A librarians' job is to give clients the information they need, often by bringing a nebulous request into focus [15]. Along the same lines, data managers often acquire data with nebulous metadata and make it clearer through their knowledge of a certain field or their client. Both data managers and research librarians need to have an in-depth knowledge of the data in their holdings in order to help direct clients to the most relevant, complete, and accurate data sets or references [15]. Essentially, data managers act as critical intermediaries both when data is deposited in the repository and when people are looking for data to use.

Another way data managers parallel research librarians is that the effort required to offer research data services is often invisible to clients requesting the work [15]. Researchers rarely see the work that goes into making the data they deposit in a repository usable to a wider audience. Unfortunately, this invisibility can lead to those roles being perceived as unnecessary and therefore able to be eliminated and replaced by software [15].

Unlike librarians, the end result of data managers' work is highly visible. In this fashion, data managers are closer to CI software developers. Data managers curate raw data into usable data while typically working on multiple projects in parallel. Where CI software developers typically only have researchers as end users, data managers must first help researchers who create new data for the repository, as well as assist researchers and policy makers who are looking for data to answer a potentially wide range of questions that did not occur to the person creating the data.

A good data manager is rather like an entrepreneur—able to take on different roles as needed. Some of these roles are obvious, like maintaining the domain knowledge and technical skills necessary to serve the repository's clients effectively. These requirements alone mandate extensive and continuing education. Data managers also need expertise in areas that are harder to pin down. On one hand, data managers must be able to listen to and adapt to their clients' requirements. On the other side, data managers need to be advocates for their repository in order to procure both funding to maintain the repository and to convince researchers to archive their data in the repository. These skills are harder to teach, and often come with experience.

5.2 Challenges Data Managers Face

Data managers face challenges on multiple fronts, most of which center around carefully balancing the needs and requirements of various stakeholders that may not always mesh seamlessly, including relationships with researchers, maintaining domain knowledge, and larger organizational pressures [3]. At the center of these challenges is the need to address the social context of data creation and reuse, specifically choosing the right data and metadata to preserve so those reusing the data can assess the data's quality and usefulness for their own purposes, and the politics of funding ongoing maintenance [1].

Many of the most immediate challenges originate with the idiosyncratic data received from researchers. In terms of data ingest, the first challenge is that while researchers may write a data management plan, they fail to maintain and adhere to that plan. This is illustrated by our finding that over half (54%) of the data managers reported that researchers make a data management plan, but do not regularly review and update that plan. While researchers are starting to recognize the importance of effective data management, updating the data management plan to reflect changes to a research project is still a low priority [7]. This creates a problem, because when researchers decide to share their data without following a data management plan throughout the research project, the result is often poorly documented and unusable data.

Another challenge related to receiving archival data is the lack of clear descriptions of the data. A clear description of data collection, quality control, and data analysis methods and the data is critical for re-using data after the data is deposited in a repository [14]. This type of knowledge is so common within a given discipline that it may not occur to researchers that the procedures need to be documented. One data manager described the challenge as, "Often they omit details which are common knowledge within their own sub-discipline … but not known to outsiders. These details are too obvious to mention, for them, but if I have to ask, I assume others not in their field would have to ask." This can lead to titles and labels for data columns and variables that are obvious to those who generate the data, but can be confusing to others.

More challenges present themselves when data managers document data after it has been deposited. Some of these challenges can be addressed through intimate domain knowledge, but maintaining this is part of the backstage work that often goes unrecognized [15]. Some data repositories address this concern by creating metadata as a service to their depositors, but this requires expertise in the field of the data creator. The challenge repositories face in offering these services is that they handle data that is extremely heterogeneous. Many data repositories serve such a wide variety of scientific fields that maintaining enough expertise in any one field to add accurate metadata to every data set is impossible.

This leads to the final challenge: navigating the requirements of larger research organizations and funding agencies. The final set of challenges center around research organizations and funding agencies. Many research organizations do not recognize the importance of research data services and data managers [21]. The result is that these organizations relegate data services to already overworked librarians, often without offering librarians the training

they need to offer expanded research data services [21]. Funding organizations also fall short when recognizing the importance of data sharing. Most data managers said the best way to encourage researchers to deposit data is increased funding for data management (82%). In open ended responses, data managers suggested funding agencies could do more to encourage data sharing by giving grants for researchers to use existing data, and research institutions should encourage and reward data sharing.

5.3 Implications

Researchers should view data managers as a key resource for throughout the research life cycle. Ideally, researchers will start working with repository data managers in the research planning stages, prior to data collection. The advantage of this is that data managers can help researchers understand what aspects of the data collection context are important to record and preserve. Data managers can offer advice to researchers regarding what metadata is most important to record during data collection. Once the data is collected, data managers can help researchers review the data and existing metadata, and determine what additional information is necessary while the data collection processes are still fresh in the researchers' memory.

While data mangers can offer critical advice, metadata is best when created by the researchers who gathered the data. All too often, detailed knowledge of how data is generated and organized is lost when students employed on a research project graduate or move on to other projects [6]. As one data manager put it, "Research is not often run by a single party but by many PIs and graduate students, so the knowledge that is needed to fully document a data set is often distributed between all of the researchers, which just adds to the difficulty of gathering the needed information." Requiring all members of a research team to document their individual knowledge before, during, and after the data collection process can mitigate the problems generated by this distribution of knowledge [12]. Tools to remind and aid researchers to take detailed notes would allow researchers to generate the methodological metadata that is critical to later re-use.

Many of the challenges mentioned stem from researchers' lack of knowledge regarding good data management practices [21]. As data sets become larger, this knowledge becomes more important. For example, a basic knowledge of computer programming provides a complement to data organization, since programming can automate and standardize many of the tedious and error-prone aspects of data management and processing. Unfortunately, this type of technical knowledge is not emphasized in early career training, which forces researchers to pick up the knowledge on the job, where errors are much more costly [20]. To address this, about half of the data managers surveyed (51%) offered training and assistance regarding data management best practices, including data management, data documentation, data organization, file structure, and storage.

Most data managers (85%) performed a variety of quality checks on the data they received from researchers. Data managers reported using a large variety of means to check the quality of ingested data, the most common method being logical consistency checks. The most thorough data managers will read every submitted file from beginning to end to discover inconsistencies in metadata and missing data. Others give the submitted data to experts for review or compare submitted data to published literature. With this level of quality checking, researchers should keep in mind that data publication is similar to publication of results in that there may be multiple iterations prior to final publication in order to address issues with data and metadata.

Universities and other research institutions need to take an active role in encouraging data publication. Unfortunately, research institutions often lag behind the needs of researchers in providing research data services, such as data management and storage [21]. While some fields such as biochemistry have well-established data repositories, researchers in other fields such as materials science must search long and hard for a reasonable place to publish their data. On the policy side, researchers will be more likely to publish data if data publication is taken into account during promotion and tenure cases.

6. Conclusion

This paper articulates the role of data managers. We present key differences between the socio-technical context of data managers and other "human infrastructure" roles articulated previously in CSCW literature. We provide a summary of challenges that data managers across a variety of fields face when accepting data for archival and reuse. These challenges include: out of date or non-existent data management plans, lack of description of data collection and analysis methods, and descriptive metadata that is not understandable to those outside a scientific field.

In the design implications, we focused on the two opposing forces pushing on data managers. First, we suggested designing tools to help reduce the burden of generating accurate methodological descriptions on individual researchers. Second, we suggested policy changes that research organizations and funding agencies could implement to encourage data sharing and reuse. Future work will explore the experience of being a data manager in order to answer the remaining question: what tools or policies can more directly assist the data managers in effectively generating and maintaining accurate and useful data products?

Currently, researchers across disciplines have access to larger amounts of data than in the past, due to advances in data collection and analysis technology, as well as data centers that can curate, store, and distribute these data. While these technological improvements have dramatically increased the possibilities available to researchers, the increased data collection and analysis capabilities also present researchers with new data management challenges that many are not properly trained to face. This means that the role of data managers and data centers will become even more important, one that CSCW cannot afford to ignore.

7. ACKNOWLEDGMENTS

This research was supported by the National Science Foundation's DataONE award (ACI-0830944). We would like to thank to our respondents for their time and insights, as well as Thomas Finholt and the anonymous reviewers for their feedback on this paper.

8. REFERENCES

[1] Ackerman, M.S., Dachtera, J., Pipek, V., and Wulf, V. Sharing knowledge and expertise: The CSCW view of knowledge management. *Computer Supported Cooperative Work 22*, 4-6 (2013), 531-573.

[2] Bannon, L.J. and Kuutti, K. Shifting perspectives on organizational memory: from storage to active remembering. *Proc. 1996 HICSS (1196),* 156-167.

[3] Bietz, M.J., Paine, D., and Lee, C.P. The work of developing cyberinfrastructure middleware projects. *Proc ACM 2013 CSCW* (2013), 1527–1538.

[4] Birnholtz, J. and Bietz, M. Data at work: supporting sharing in science and engineering. *Proc. 2003 ACM GROUP*, (2003), 348.

[5] Cook, R.B., Olson, R.J., Kanciruk, P., and Hook, L.A. Best Practices for Preparing Ecological and Ground-Based Data Sets to Share and Archive. *Bull. of the Ecological Soc. of Am. 822*, (2001), 138–141.

[6] Edwards, P.N., Mayernik, M.S., Batcheller, A.L., Bowker, G.C., and Borgman, C.L. Science friction: Data, metadata, and collaboration. *Social Studies of Science 41*, 5 (2011), 667–690.

[7] Griffiths, A. The publication of research data: Researcher attitudes and behaviour. *Intl J of Digital Curation 4*, 1 (2009).

[8] Hampton, S., Strasser, C., Gram, W.K., et al. Big Data and The Future for Ecology. *Frontiers in Ecology and the Environment*, (2012), 1–34.

[9] Holdren, J.P. *Increasing Access to the Results of Federally Funded Scientific Research*. US OSTP, Washington, DC, 2013

[10] ICSU, I.C.F.S. *Annual Report 2010*. ICSU, 2011.

[11] Kervin, K., Finholt, T., and Hedstrom, M. Macro and micro pressures in data sharing. *Proc 2012 IEEE IRI* (2012), 525–532.

[12] Kervin, K., Michener, W., and Cook, R. Common Errors in Ecological Data Sharing. *J of eScience Librarianship*, (2013).

[13] Lee, C., Dourish, P., and Mark, G. The human infrastructure of cyberinfrastructure. *Proc 2006 ACM CSCW*, (2006), 483–492.

[14] Michener, W.K., Brunt, J.W., Helly, J.J., Kirchner, T.B., and Stafford, S.G. Nongeospatial metadata for the ecological sciences. *Ecological Applications 7*, 1 (1997), 330–342.

[15] Nardi, B.A. and O'Day, V. Intelligent agents: what we learned at the library. *Libri 46*, 2 (1996), 59–88.

[16] NASA. *Guidebook for Proposers Responding to a NASA Research Announcement (NRA) or Cooperative Agreement (CAN)*. NASA, 2010.

[17] NIH. *NIH Data Sharing Policy and Implementation Guidance*. NIH, Bethesda, MD, 2003.

[18] NSF. *CHAPTER II PROPOSAL PREPARATION INSTRUCTIONS*. NSF, Arlington, VA, 2011.

[19] Star, S. and Strauss, A. Layers of silence, arenas of voice: The ecology of visible and invisible work. *CSCW 8*, 1 (1998), 9–30.

[20] Tenopir, C., Birch, B., and Allard, S. *Academic Libraries and Research Data Services: Current Practices and Plans for the Future*. Association of College & Research Libraries, 2012.

Revisiting Corporate Social Media:
Challenges and Implications from a Long-Term Study

Alina Krischkowsky, Verena Fuchsberger, Manfred Tscheligi
Christian Doppler Laboratory for "Contextual Interfaces"
ICT&S Center, University of Salzburg
Salzburg, Austria
{firstname.lastname}@sbg.ac.at

ABSTRACT

In a multi-step assessment of a corporate social media platform, which has been implemented in a large company for internal collaboration, we identified three major challenges regarding acceptance and adoption of the platform: (1) diverging perspectives & uncertain top-down communication, (2) functionality jungle & high usage complexity, and (3) lacking collaboration & customization. Based on these challenges, we discuss potential implications for design and implementation of corporate social media. The challenges and implications were derived from data gathered in two rounds of polling employees of the company, where we found that the surveyed employees tended to initially accept the internally implemented social media platform. Nevertheless, by assessing their attitude one and a half years later, we came to understand that the employees have rarely adopted the platform into their daily work practices. This finding led us to analyze in detail the qualitative data gathered along with the survey, as it holds valuable examples and explanations to better understand this phenomenon. Besides presenting the results of the surveys, this paper focuses on the discussion of challenges and implications for enhancing collaboration and supporting adoption processes of social media in workplaces.

Categories and Subject Descriptors

H.5.3 [Group and Organization Interfaces]: Collaborative computing and Computer-supported cooperative work

General Terms

Human Factors.

Keywords

Corporate Social Media; CSCW; Cooperative System Evaluation; Collaboration.

1. INTRODUCTION

Social media not only pervade our private lives, but also change the landscape of corporate technologies (e.g., [19], [41]). On one hand, they enter work through the use of private social media during work hours. On the other hand, corporations themselves acknowledge the potential of functions and features in social media and increasingly use them for external communication (e.g., Facebook pages) as well as internal collaboration. However, the

GROUP '14, November 9–12, 2014, Sanibel Island, FL, USA.
Copyright 2014 ACM 978-1-4503-3043-5/14/11...$15.00.
http://dx.doi.org/10.1145/2660398.2660411

process of implementing social media for internal collaboration into corporations is complex. It is challenging to decide for a tool, to roll it out, and actually use it, especially for a longer period of time. In our work we focus on researching social media as tools for *internal* collaboration, i.e., dedicated tools to facilitate internal networking and innovation processes. Thereby, we are specifically interested in the *social* of corporate social media (i.e., how it contributes to and constitutes collaboration through the usage of social media). We had the opportunity to not only accompany the introduction of such a social media tool in a large corporation (approximately 26.000 employees), but also to observe its usage repeatedly within a period of two years. Our role, as researchers, was to investigate the social media usage throughout the implementation process. We investigated the employees' experiences at the end of the pilot-phase by means of a questionnaire. One and a half years later, we again distributed the questionnaire to the employees, this time including a set of open questions to focus on further facets that we found to be relevant in the previous studies.

Even though the platform was one and a half years in the field between the first and the second poll, the findings surprisingly showed that the corporate social media platform did not increase in popularity within this timeframe, as it was rated slightly worse, (e.g., in terms of internal collaboration potential of the corporate social media). This indicates that the employees rarely integrated the social media platform into their daily work practices, i.e., the platform was not entirely adopted. In order to explore the reasons, we looked at the qualitative data in detail – and found that the employees acknowledged the potential of the platform, but did not know how to actually make use of that potential.

In this paper, we start by giving an overview of literature related to corporate social media in the field of Computer Supported Cooperative Work (CSCW) and Human Computer Interaction (HCI) in which our work is positioned. Then, we outline our research objectives and briefly present the quantitative outcomes of our questionnaires that illustrate the acceptance and (non)adoption processes of the social media platform. Afterwards, we discuss those findings on basis of the qualitative results. Finally, we derive challenges and implications for the design and implementation of social media for company internal collaboration, which constitute the main contribution of this paper.

2. CORPORATE SOCIAL MEDIA

2.1 Positioning in Related Work

The technology that is used for company internal collaboration is, in literature, either labeled enterprise social media (e.g., [34], [35]), or enterprise social networks/network sites (e.g., [13], [26], [42]). However, those terms are not selectively used. In this paper we decided to use the term corporate social media, emphasizing that we are referring to any technology that facilitates social interactions, such as collaboration and networking within an enterprise. In academic research, very valuable and influential work has been done at IBM (e.g., [34]), wherein their internal corporate social media platform was investigated. This example shows "early adopters" of social media in large enterprises, therefore representing a valuable source for our research. We add to this research by investigating social media in a company, wherein social media are considered exclusively a tool for internal collaboration and potentially innovation, from the implementation phase of the platform onwards, as we regard longitudinal studies as providing a great potential to investigate organizational behavior and its dynamics in greater detail. Besides academic research, there is also related work in the area of business consulting, which focuses, for instance, on success factors of enterprise social networks (ESN) [26].

However, there are hardly scientific research findings that combine academic and industrial perspectives on social media integration in a long-term study. One of the few exceptions is the work from Archambault and Grudin [1], who conducted a longitudinal study of Facebook, LinkedIn, and Twitter use with employees working at Microsoft, aiming to investigate attitudes and behaviors around social networking sites and communication technologies in general, through carrying out four in-depth surveys. Also Holtzblatt et al. [16] discuss the benefits of multi-step investigations to study and evaluate individuals' social media usage patterns. They conducted a long-term study at MITRE and its social business platform called Handshake. Tierney and Drury [43] likewise investigated improvement potentials regarding the innovation management through social media in the case of MITRE. However, Handshake was not only designed to enable employees, but also trusted external partners to improve social ties and create their own profiles, rather than a tool that is exclusively meant for company internal collaboration purposes.

In the following, we give a brief overview of what social media are in general. Afterwards, we illustrate related work on corporate social media (including Intranet, which we consider being a pre-form of corporate social media) and social network sites followed by related research on acceptance, adoption and appropriation.

2.2 Social media

In brief, social media may be defined as "the media we use to be social." ([41], p. 3). However, this very broad definition may not particularly address and uncover all aspects that are related to social media, such as content sharing sites, blogs, social networking, and wikis, in order to actually create, find, share, modify, discuss, and make sense of the mass of information available online ([15], [19]). Boyd and Ellison ([1], p. 211), for example, define social media "as web-based services that allow individuals to (1) construct a public or semi-public profile within a bounded system, (2) articulate a list of other users with whom they share a connection, and (3) view and traverse their list of connections and those by others within a system." This definition lays an emphasis on social networking, in terms of enabling users to articulate but also make their social networks visible.

In contrast to this definition, Kaplan and Haenlein ([18]) rather refer to the notion that social media provides the capability to create and exchange User Generated Content (UGC). In their view "Social Media is a group of Internet-based applications that build on the ideological and technological foundations of Web 2.0, and that allow the creation and exchange of User Generated Content." ([18], p. 61).

2.3 Corporate Social Media

Social media have recently begun to pervade corporations to, for instance, lightweight internal, and maybe also support informal communication and collaboration among employees.

Contrary to traditional corporate communication media such as email, social media allow employees "to circumvent traditional organizational hierarchies and to connect with geographically distant readers." ([5], p. 61) Before the initiation of social media, corporations already used computer-based tools for these purposes, such as Intranets (e.g., [27], [29]). Lai [27] found in a survey with 500 organizations in Hong Kong that organizations with a greater extent of Intranet-based collaborations had significantly better employee and organizational performance. The author concluded that collaboration is rather not about the technology, but about how it is used to increase the employees' performance. Therefore, positive input from the employees is needed, as well as a good fit between task and technology.

Even though Intranet might be considered a pre-form of social media, the terminology, and connected to that, the notion has changed. Referring to the terminology of *social* media, companies express their emphasis on pursuing something *social*, something that has not been in the focus when using earlier collaboration tools. In reference to social media literature that is in line with our understanding, "social" refers to humans' instinctual needs to connect with other humans (e.g., [40], [41]) and addresses basic needs to be around and included in groups of like-minded individuals in order to feel at home and comfortable in sharing thoughts, experiences, and ideas. The second part of the terminology, "media", refers to the actual medium used in order to make those connections with other individuals [41]. Consequently, social media incorporate several aspects (or building blocks), such as presence, sharing, conversations, groups, identity, relationships, and reputation [19].

Social media are thus not only an instrument with specific features and functions, but also express the focus on the sociality of employees being an integral part of collaboration. For instance, Kaplan and Haenlein [18] reviewed social media for business purposes and stated regarding collaborative projects that "The main idea underlying collaborative projects is that the joint effort of many actors leads to a better outcome than any actor could achieve individually." ([18], p. 62) In terms of social structures in enterprises, "the use of social and open technologies, like a wiki at the workplace, represents a dynamic social production of new structures and reproduction or reflection of existing structures." ([30], p. 14) Consequently, the use of social media is governed by both emergent and reflected social structures [30]. Also, the remote participation in geographically distributed work through social media has been researched, revealing that even if people work alone, the distributed work is actually very social [22].

Muller et al. [34] investigated 188 very active online communities at IBM. They found that different types of communities differed in their appropriation of social media tools to create and use shared resources and build relationships within these networks. They concluded, for instance, that different types of communities with a different number of community members seem to require different extents of efforts from their leaders. DiMicco et al. [8] interviewed people at IBM regarding their social media usage and found that personal profiles have a crucial role. They argue that profiles need to be dynamic, changing according to a user's activity elsewhere on the site (e.g., when writing a comment or creating content) and they need to be customizable, allowing the user to choose which information to display where on the page.

Geyer et al. [13] have conducted a study at IBM with 2.000 users regarding a recommender system for profiles, which "recommends" content for users to create, rather than consume. Further research in this area has shown that online profiles are very important when it comes to the formation of personality impressions and that users also intentionally craft their profiles to convey a desired impression (e.g., [11]). In order to create a social media experience, profiles are thus an essential feature.

Furthermore, Thom et al. [42] investigated the effect of rewards and gamification on users' activity and found that removing gamification features from their social network led to a negative impact on users' activities on the site. Based on six case studies in small and medium sized enterprises, Zeiller and Schauer [46] emphasized the necessity of additional activities (e.g., training sessions for inexperienced employees) to have satisfactory user acceptance rates.

2.4 Acceptance, Adoption and Appropriation
The above-mentioned aspects found in related work may contribute to the employees' acceptance, adoption and appropriation of corporate social media. Generally spoken, acceptance is an attitude towards technology, which is influenced by a variety of factors (see e.g., [7], [38], [39], [44]). Technology adoption is a process that ends with a user embracing a technology, making full use of it [39]. Appropriation, i.e., individuals using technology in their own ways, indicates that users understand and are comfortable with the technology [9]. It is an active process of incorporation and co-evolution of technologies, practices and settings [10], such as influences of cultural processes or negotiations between social practices and technological features [2].

Analyzing acceptance as well as adoption and appropriation processes of Information and Communication Technology (ICT) has become a common agenda for practitioners as well as researchers in the field of information studies [24]. However, there are still challenges the field faces in understanding and designing for these processes [33]. Furthermore, the concepts are not strictly distinct to one another.

In this paper, we thus investigate acceptance, meaning the employees' attitude towards the corporate media at a specific point in time, as well as adoption, which we consider the process of actually integrating the social media into daily work practices. In reference to Dix [9], we are not focusing on technology appropriation, as we need to understand the employees' acceptance and adoption before looking specifically at the employees' own ways of using corporate social media.

3. RESEARCH GOALS
With our research, we aim to better understand what the *social* aspect of social media in enterprises is, i.e., how it contributes to and constitutes collaboration through the usage of social media. Hence, our research focuses on

- investigating social aspects that contribute to collaboration
- identifying collaborative capabilities of corporate social media
- increasing the acceptance of the corporate social media platform
- facilitating adoption processes of corporate social media

We had the opportunity to cooperate with a large enterprise where we could actually study and investigate the collaborative capabilities of corporate social media. We conducted several quantitative, but also qualitative driven research activities, which are presented in the following.

4. STUDY CONTEXT
Our industrial partner is a leading system solutions manufacturer for the automotive and industrial electronics sector. The company employs about 26.000 people in locations throughout the USA, Europe, and the Asia-Pacific region, focusing on the development of new and innovative products for the market. Therefore, they considered corporate social media being appropriate to make use of the employees' communication and collaboration potential in order to support innovation processes within and across the different departments and sites. Regarding our different research activities, we mainly cooperated with the innovation management of the company and frequently organized knowledge-exchange sessions with their respective representatives. To make use of the employees' collaboration potential, they particularly aim to (1) organize all sites within the company, (2) establish information and knowledge exchange across multiple sites, (3) support the formation of online communities, and (4) enable the employees to search (e.g., colleagues, communities, documents) for what they need within their specific working area.

They decided to use Microsoft SharePoint 2010, which is a web application platform. Usually, SharePoint is strongly associated with document systems and web content, but it actually offers a broad platform of web technologies to suit a high variety of solutions. It provides a multi-purpose design, which allows the management, scaling, but also provisioning of business applications. Additionally, SharePoint provides pre-defined 'applications' for commonly requested functionalities (e.g., file and document management, collaboration spaces, social tools)[1]. Based on these pre-defined 'applications', our industrial partner had selected a high variety of different features and functionalities (e.g., newsfeed and expertise browser) in order to achieve the four above-mentioned aims.

5. METHODS AND PROCEDURE
In order to provide an overview of our research activities, the following section describes the different steps, including methods and instruments used. The pilot-phase of the platform (i.e., the release of the platform for selected users, such as community members and volunteers from selected departments) lasted from April 2011 until June 2012. Therein, we accompanied the initial release, for example, by means of heuristic expert evaluations and the definition of use cases (step 1). Afterwards, we evaluated the pilot-phase with a first questionnaire round (step 2). The final rollout (to all employees of the company) was also evaluated with an extended version of the questionnaire (step 3) in June 2013.

5.1 Step 1: Accompanying the Pilot-Phase
Within the pilot-phase, we defined objectives and goals for our research activities, which was done in close collaboration with our partner to shape and support the introduction of the social media. Therefore, several methodological approaches had been applied: (1) knowledge-exchange workshops together with representatives of our industrial partner to raise awareness, (2) a success criteria survey in order to define aspects characterizing a successful

---

[1] http://technet.microsoft.com/de-AT/sharepoint/

implementation of corporate social media, (3) an heuristic expert evaluation to identify major usability issues, and (4) the definition of use-cases together with our industrial partner to shape the intended interaction with the platform. More detailed descriptions about the approach and related results can be found in previous publications (see [20] and [21]).

5.2 Step 2: Evaluating the Pilot-Phase

Based on the findings from step 1, a questionnaire had been developed in order to assess the initial perception of the social media platform [20]. In addition to the gathered findings in step 1, we conducted knowledge-exchange sessions together with 20 community managers at two different sites of our industrial partner in order to discuss the most important themes regarding their corporate social media.

The questionnaire: Based on the findings from step 1, we developed items for evaluating corporate social media, resulting in 17 items. They covered aspects of expectations towards the usage of social media in terms of hopes and wishes for the implementation, barriers the employees see when introducing social media for collaboration as well as potentials and capabilities for the use of the platform in the future. The items were measured on four-point Likert scales (1 = strongly disagree, 2 = disagree, 3 = agree, 4 = strongly agree) with an additional option to indicate "don't know", which was excluded from further calculations (due to limitations to indicate an agreement on a certain statement at present).

In total, around 2.000 selected employees (e.g., community managers und selected users mainly from departments in Munich and Villach) were part of the pilot-phase and thereby invited to complete the first run of the questionnaire. This represents the whole population of pilot-phase participants at this time as only selected departments of our cooperation partner were involved in the test-phase of the platform. The questionnaire was distributed for 10 days via an online survey tool that was internally provided by our industrial partner. Based on inclusion criteria (e.g., having experience with the platform), 224 filled in questionnaires (11,2%) could finally be used for the analysis.

5.3 Step 3: Evaluating the Final Rollout

In January 2013, the social media platform was rolled out to the entire company. Since then, it was intended for employees around the globe to use the platform within their daily work in order to collaborate and communicate within and across the different departments and sites. We decided to reassess the employees' attitude towards the platform by distributing the questionnaire (in an extended version) for a second time.

The modified questionnaire: In addition to the 17 items that we developed for the questionnaire, we included further items into the questionnaire to be assessed in the second round. As the acceptance of the platform was rather neutral in the first round (stated in more detail in the next section), we wanted to extend the questionnaire to better understand influences on this phenomenon. In literature, we identified trust as a potential complementing factor on acceptance and the actual intention to use a system [3]. Consequently, we included trust related aspects in the second deployment by following McKnight and Harrison's [32] approach, as they distinguish between trust in people (interpersonal trust) and trust in technology (system trust). Various questionnaires have been developed to measure interpersonal and system trust (e.g., [17], [31], [32], [34]), whereof we extracted 6 items considered as the most relevant items for our questionnaire (e.g., helpfulness,

functionality, integrity). We also included six items related to the innovation potential of the platform in terms of how the social media platform supports or strengthens the generation of innovations, as this was one of the main purposes of introducing the social media platform. Besides the quantitative items, the questionnaire also held an additional set of three qualitative, open-ended questions. This time they aimed to explore underlying reasons and opinions as well as further facets of collaboration that were found to be of relevance in the first round. Two of these questions addressed the employees' collaboration needs in terms of most important functions on the platform, first regarding the already available functions, and second, further required functions for the future. The third question focused on the social media's potential to foster innovation, explicitly asking for the employees' estimations about what the innovation management might expect from the usage of social media in order to identify innovation capabilities on the platform that foster innovation. For the innovation managements' general prospects see section 4.

The deployment of the questionnaire lasted for two weeks and was sent via email to a random sample of 2.300 community members on the platform from departments around the globe. As it was not distributed to the same sample (i.e., pilot-phase users in the first round and actual end-users within the second round), a within-subject comparison between the first and second round was not possible. In order to increase the response rate, a reminder was sent out after one week. Overall, we received 303 questionnaires, whereby based on pre-defined exclusion criteria (e.g., having no experience with the usage of the platform), 144 responses (6,3%) were finally taken into consideration for further quantitative and qualitative analysis.

6. RESULTS

In this section, we first give an overview of the results gathered throughout our quantitative analysis to illustrate how the employees assessed and valued the platform within the first and second round. The quantitative results revealed that the employees have rarely adopted the corporate social media into their daily work practices (see section 6.1). Therefore, we present our qualitative explorations gathered along with the quantitative data in more detail, in order to investigate underlying reasons and opinions (see section 6.2). In a subsequent section (see section 7), we discuss and reflect upon these findings by means of derived challenges and general implications for the design and implementation of corporate social media.

6.1 Questionnaire (Step 2 and 3)

As the sample differed for the two measurements (i.e., pilot-phase users in the first round and actual end-users within the second round), independent sample t-tests were conducted. Thereby, we aimed to assess how the employees accepted the social media platform at the two instances in time to find out whether they adopted the social media platform into their daily work practices (see Table 1).

All items from the second point of measurement were rated slightly worse than in the first round, whereof eight differences in the scores for single items between the first and the second round were statistically significant. Three relate to expectations, two to barriers and the final three to potentials of the platform. This means that the employees' expectations regarding the usage of the platform and the identified potentials for using corporate social media in the future were significantly considered worse within the second round. Table 1 provides an overview of selected items, which illustrate the tendency that the social media platform has not really become part of the employees' daily work. As an example, the item "The social media platform simplifies day-to-day business" was rated significantly worse in the second questionnaire round than in the first one. Even though not different by statistical significance on a 5 % significance level, by tendency the employees seemed to less expect that the platform simplifies internal collaboration in the second round than in the first round, where we found this aspect having the third most positive rating.

Thus, when reassessing the employees' attitude in the second round, the employees were not as sure about the internal collaboration potential of corporate social media any more.

In addition to the statistically significant differences, we also came to understand throughout the quantitative analysis that, within both rounds, the employees agreed with the item "I update my profile infrequently." Still, personal profiles would play a crucial role for corporate social media to be successful [7], as humans have the fundamental need to belong and connect to others [40]. Thus, we will come back to this aspect within the discussion section (see section 7).

Even though the employees' attitude towards the inherent expectations, barriers and potentials were decidedly rated worse within the second round, it has to be noted that the mean values for both rounds are mostly located around the middle. This means that the employees' opinions were on average rather neutral than specifically positive or negative at both instances indicating that the employees have not completely rejected the social media platform, but they were also not really convinced that it would benefit their internal collaboration.

Complementary to these results, we now want to outline the findings gathered with the additional six quantitative items on interpersonal and system trust, that were part of the second deployment, as trust might be a complementing factor to acceptance and adoption and therefore might enrich a deeper understanding of these processes [3]. The mean value (M=2,78) of the trust construct suggests that employees tend to trust in the platform as well as in the present communities and their community members. This slight positive tendency can be supported through research in this area as "an enterprise provides a shared context in addition to the context of the community, which can contribute to a level of trust and common ground" ([34], p. 2815). On basis of the single items, the highest agreement rate was found for the item "The social media platform is trustworthy" (M = 2,95). This is important, as a low level of trust in a system constitutes a tremendous barrier to actually use a system or even use a system for the first time [38]. As the employees tended to trust the platform but also the individuals on the platform, the rather rare adoption of the corporate social media might not be explained by a lack of trust building strategies.

6.2 Collaboration Needs and Innovation Capabilities

The gathered results within the first round showed that the employees, taking part in the pilot-phase, at that time had rather accepted the newly implemented corporate social media platform, or at least not rejected it. However, the second deployment of the questionnaire after the final rollout (i.e., one and a half years later) revealed that the employees had rarely adopted the corporate social media into their daily work practices. Hence, we wondered what had happened since we first evaluated the platform. In order to identify the underlying reasons, we analyzed the qualitative data gathered along with the questionnaire, by means of content analyses [23] (i.e., the data was condensed and categorized according to its relevance for our research goal). We followed an explorative, open categorization approach, meaning that we did not strive for generalizable results, but aimed to identify motivations and challenges regarding the adoption of the platform. In the following, we outline our qualitative findings in more detail, starting with the description of the results gathered with the first two qualitative questions on employees' collaboration needs regarding the corporate social media (section 6.2.1). Subsequently, we present the qualitative results from the third open question on innovation capabilities on the platform to foster innovation (section 6.2.2).

Table 1. Selected items of the questionnaire (1= strongly disagree, 2= disagree, 3= agree, 4= strongly agree)

	Item	M_{t1}	SD_{t1}	M_{t2}	SD_{t2}	Mean dif.	t	Sig. (p)
1	The social media platform simplifies day-to-day business.	2.47	0.90	2.18	0.87	0.29	2.41	.016
2	The social media platform promotes communication.	3.12	0.84	2.86	0.89	0.26	2.31	.022
3	I'm confident about using the social media platform.	2.88	0.91	2.60	0.93	0.28	2.31	.022
4	The social media platform simplifies internal collaboration.	3.02	0.85	2.80	0.88	0.22	1.86	.064
5	I update my profile infrequently.	3.27	0.84	3.22	0.83	0.05	0.65	.517

6.2.1 Collaboration Needs

Even though specifically asked for the most important functions on the platform, the employees also made use of this question to express their general attitudes and opinions towards the platform. They expressed their wishes and needs from a more generic perspective to highlight what they consider as crucial for corporate social media and, therefore, what they find important to actually use the platform within their day-to-day business.

Most relevant functions on the platform: The majority of the statements concern 'sharing/exchange', capturing general aspects that were mentioned by the employees. The employees considered the possibility to share and exchange information as the most important function on the platform and, therefore, that collaboration on various levels and topics is the most important capability of corporate social media. They expressed their wish to collaborate within and across sites and within and across communities and colleagues, including unknown people. As many employees used this question to express their general attitude towards the platform, we believe that even though sharing and exchanging information is intended and already supported by a high variety of different functionalities on the platform, open issues still exist to fulfill the users' collaboration needs.

Throughout knowledge-exchange sessions with representatives from the innovation management, we came to understand that it might be less an issue of availability of specific functions, but rather how they are actually used and introduced to the employees. Until then, no specific introductory trainings or strategies have been comprehensively applied to make the employees familiar with the platform. Additionally, the large number of pre-defined 'applications' provided by SharePoint seemed to have made it difficult to choose from, without any pre-selection according to the employees' needs. Maybe also more information for the employees might have been beneficial on which functions to use for which collaboration purpose, and what added value the usage of the platform generates for day-to-day business. Similarly, one employee stated, *"In the past two years I did not find a good use for the social media platform"* (original quote). This impression can also be supported through our quantitative findings, as the employees, who were part of the second round, less expected that the usage of corporate social media promoted communication than in the first round (see Table 1).

Additional functions to be included in the future: These findings align with the answers regarding additional functions the employees wanted to have on the platform in the future, which are outlined in more detail in the following. The employees' responses mainly either addressed both high quality and additional content on the platform, or a better overview of already existing content by reducing the platform's complexity. The employees wanted to share and exchange information on the platform; however, regarding the design (e.g., complexity) of the platform they were not completely satisfied. As outlined before, the high variety of different functionalities available on SharePoint led to a rather high usage complexity.

The majority of additional functions mentioned by the employees aimed at reducing this high complexity and, therefore, provided a better overview of the platform (e.g., receive emails in case of updates on the platform). Consequently, the employees require a simpler usage of the social media platform. This goes in line with the quantitative finding that employees, who were part of the second round, found the platform less simplifying their day-to-day business, than the ones polled in the first round (see Table 1).

In addition, the employees also explicitly outlined the need for a consistent interface design and representation of content, a better navigation through all pages, and a general advancement of the platform's usability. The employees also emphasized the request for an appropriate extent of content and, in particular, high-quality content on the platform. The employees stated a particular need to increase the quality of the content within the different online communities, but also within discussions about problems they sought a solution for (e.g., discussions within online communities, but also within the 'question-answer' function). With regard to the extent of content provided on the platform, the employees wanted additional information about colleagues, their respective working areas, the different sites and new technologies. In order to actually collaborate with each other, this information was considered a prerequisite.

The aspect of extensive information about colleagues and working areas might also be related to the results regarding personal profile pages of the employees. As identified with the questionnaire, the employees did not regularly update their profiles. Still, they highlighted the importance of the personal profile pages within the qualitative part. In particular, they outlined that profile pictures and short pieces of information would be very helpful. Some employees mentioned that they occasionally looked at profile pictures to be able to identify colleagues when meeting them face-to-face (e.g., in a meeting with colleagues, whom they have not physically met before). Also the possibility to gather more information about the competencies of colleagues, as well as the details and content provided on the profile pages of how to contact someone, were considered as very useful.

6.2.2 Capabilities to Foster Innovation

To further investigate the innovation potential of the platform we included a respective open question. This question targeted to investigate the employees' perspectives and attitudes towards various innovation activities on the platform (e.g., specific innovation online communities or voting's on the platform to award innovative ideas). For the innovation managements' general prospects see section 4.

Overall, we identified three main aspects within the gathered data. The employees believed that the innovation management expects (1) better, faster and easier communication through the usage of the platform; (2) advancing networking capabilities through the platform; and (3) that ideas on certain topics and issues are shared and exchanged on the platform. Based on this overall perspective, communication seemed to be the basis for networking, idea generation and innovations, as the employees believed that the innovation management expected to establish networks through and across employees, sites, and communities. By building stronger networks via the platform, the innovation management intended to ease the discussion on complex topics and reduce time needed for generating innovations.

They also believed that the innovation management expected to advance the way ideas are shared and exchanged by using the social media platform. Networking might be considered a precondition for sharing and exchanging ideas, both needed for a successful use of corporate social media to support the generation of and discussion about innovations. The employees emphasized the following potentials of the social media platform to facilitate innovation: (1) involving different people with different backgrounds, (2) involving not just experts in discussions, but also novices, (3) using the platform to be faster and more spontaneous, and (4) also sharing thoughts and not just elaborated ideas. These answers reveal that the platform supported innovation processes that are less complex, hierarchical, time consuming, and more open as it was previously within their company. One employee emphasized that the innovation management might expect an *"Improved cross-functional networking to get a higher level of communication within the org [sic] and to avoid re-creating the wheel. To improve and speed up innovation, brainstorming and creating networks."* (original quote)

7. DISCUSSION: CHALLENGES & IMPLICATIONS

Figure 1 provides a visualization of the above presented findings and their mapping to the challenges, which we derived. However, as visualized in the figure, the mappings are not completely distinct, as some findings may be interpreted in several ways. In the following, we summarize the results and reflect upon the challenge that is inherent to these findings linking them to related work. After each identified challenge, we describe the general implications for corporate social media, derived from these results and challenges.

7.1 Diverging perspectives & uncertain top-down communication

By tendency, the results from the second round suggest that the employees less expected that the platform simplifies internal collaboration, compared to the first round (see section 6.1). Furthermore, even though the employees considered the sharing/exchanging of information, and hence collaboration on various levels and topics as the most important capability of corporate social media, the users' collaboration needs (e.g., on basis of the provided functionalities) were not fulfilled yet (see 6.2.1). A high variety of different collaboration functions were already available on the platform as intended by the innovation management (see section 6.2.2).

Nevertheless, the employees might not have been appropriately introduced to how to use them and in particular what for (see

section 6.2.1). These findings lead us to discuss the (mis-) match between the employees and the (innovation) management, including uncertain top-down communication channels, which will be outlined in more detail in the following.

While the intended purpose of the corporate social media platform was to support collaboration, the employees' actual usage did not match this intention. Furthermore, the top-down targets of how to use the corporate social media platform (and what for) were either not articulated clearly enough or employees simply did not completely comply with those. Here, a problematic situation evolves. On the one hand, hierarchical top-down structures are needed to give instructions on how to use the corporate social media platform to start its integration into daily work (to "get it going"). On the other hand, hierarchical structures might counteract using the platform, as many activities can be easily monitored by the management via the corporate social media platform, which might make employees be skeptical about its usage.

This impression can be supported through other research in this area. For instance, Orlikowski [36] highlighted that if the underlying premises of social media (e.g., shared effort, cooperation, collaboration) are counter-cultural to the structural properties of an organization (e.g., rigid hierarchy) the technology is unlikely to be used collectively. Majumdar et al. [28] considered issues such as privacy and security, and the awareness of being watched by the organization, as major concerns of users when using corporate social media. Furthermore, Orlikowski and Gash [37] derived three core domains of individuals' technological frames; i.e., different interpretations of technological artifacts by multiple user groups.

The three frame domains embody understandings that reflect what the technology is (nature of technology), why it was introduced (technology strategy), and how it is used to create various changes in work (technology in use).

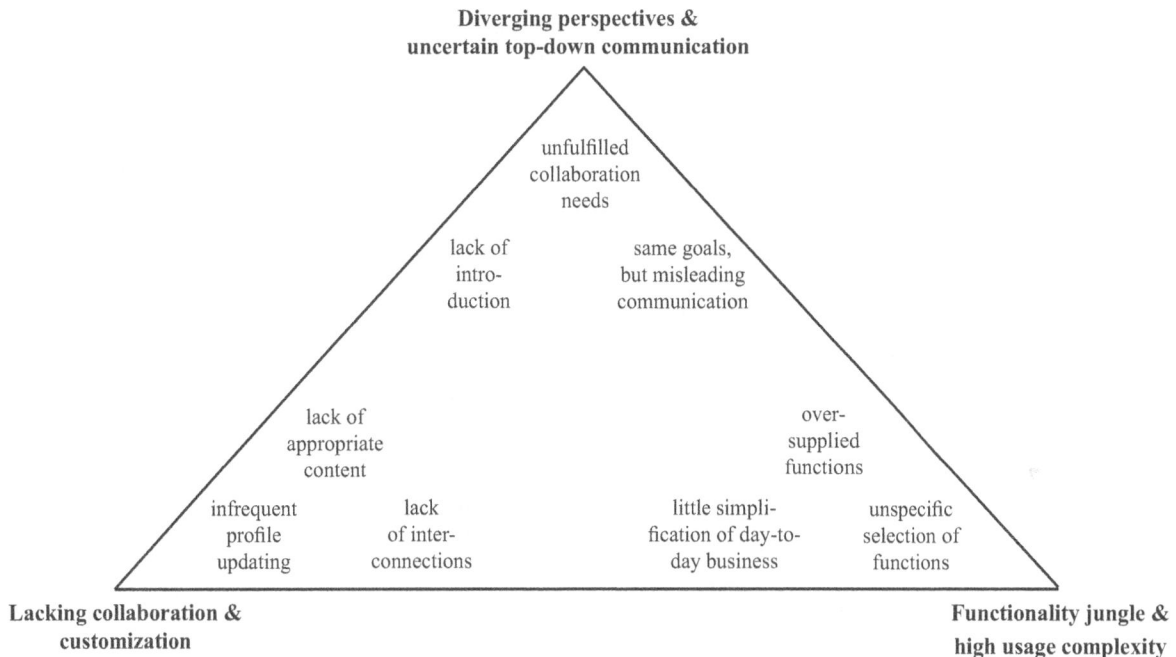

Figure 1. Mapping of findings according to extracted challenges

Here, similar to our findings, they found out that expectations (and actions) about a technology between different user groups (e.g., technologists and managers) are distinct due to diverging technological frames. They emphasized the need to identify the means through which technology frames become shared or divergent.

For example, it may be useful to examine how much difference in assumptions, knowledge, and expectations about technology constitute frame incongruence, and if the notion about incongruence varies by context and time [37].

Furthermore, Faste et al. [12] emphasized that communities need to be open and accessible for all employees to increase the innovation potential and, therefore, the collaboration on the platform. However, this process requires the company not only to commit itself to openness on the platform, but also within offline collaboration to avoid being perceived ambiguously by the employees and, thus, not being taken seriously.

Implication: Articulate top-down intentions and requirements clearly and address potential fears of employees regarding the usage of the corporate social media. Here, it is particularly important to understand the employees' perspectives (e.g., fears), as the perceived benefits of corporate social media are motivated at a 'personal level' [28]. Be honest in what the management will monitor and what they expect from the employees. Follow a consequent strategy that holds true for online and offline collaboration. Promote co-design approaches to actively involve employees from all hierarchical levels to be part of an open, creative, interpretative and social process that facilitates social interaction and hence co-experience. Furthermore, support the engagement with the social media platform also in uncommon ways to make the employees curious, (e.g., through gamified, ludic approaches). A certain degree of curiosity and interest might be needed to start engaging with the platform at all. Thom et al. [42], for instance, described gamified elements as supporting the usage of a corporate social network site.

7.2 Functionality jungle & high usage complexity

The high varieties of pre-defined 'applications' provided by SharePoint (see section 4) were not optimally chosen according to the employees collaboration needs. The cluttered interface, by this time, made most of the collaborative capabilities of the platform accessible for all employees. Therefore, the employees explicitly outlined their desire for a better overview and structuring of available tools and content as they saw the inherent need to reduce the platform's usage complexity, e.g., receive emails in case of updates on the platform (see section 6.2.1). This impression can be supported by the finding that the employees considered the social media platform as less simplifying their day-to-day business (in terms of collaborative tasks) as in the first point of measurement (see section 6.1). Hence, our second identified challenge deals with the high availability of collaboration supporting functions resulting in a high usage complexity of the corporate social media platform.

The multitude of functions on the platform overwhelmed the employees, resulting in a kind of cluelessness on which functions to use for which purposes. In relation to this aspect, Muller et al. [34] address communities' appropriation and use practices of corporate technologies and developed implications for the fit of community goals and needed functions (e.g., community recommendation service, templates for different types of communities). Furthermore, our results showed that the social media platform required efforts

from the employees to learn and effectively use the platform for internal collaboration, requiring time and help. Some surveyed employees, for instance, claimed to improve search functions according to the Intranet they were used to. *"Googling in the old Intranet gave better results."* (original quote). Not only does this refer to the need for adequate outcomes and benefits of using the corporate social media platform, but also for relying on activities and strategies, which the employees were already familiar with in order to decrease barriers and rejections. Regarding search engines, Grudin [14] emphasizes that people use search engines to find answers to questions more efficiently than they can by directly searching the pertinent online document that actually contains the answers. He outlines that the reason why Google was so effective is that searching worked out well even when using non-expert terminology.

Implication: Guide the online communities on what functions to use for what purpose by, for example, reducing the number of choices in the beginning to ease the start for the communities and step-by-step releasing of functions (e.g., in terms of a social media "starter-set" to make the employees familiar with the platform and hence reduce initial usage barriers). Furthermore, allow the employees to dedicate time for getting familiar with the platform (instead of just being an add-on activity) and provide them with help, for instance, through trainings or trained colleagues. Finally, create familiarity, such as relying on conventions known from previously used Intranets or else.

7.3 Lacking collaboration & customization

As outlined before (see section 6.2.1), the employees indicated the need to share and exchange information and knowledge across communities and sites. This aspect implies also the need to have appropriate information and access to information about colleagues, working areas and sites to establish a basis for corporate collaboration (see section 6.2.1). The employees wanted to involve different people with different backgrounds. They did not only require experts, but also novices for sharing thoughts. Additionally, less elaborated ideas may also be part of these discussions, allowing faster and much more spontaneous collaborations. This would advance currently common collaboration practices in order to make use of the innovation capabilities of corporate social media (see section 6.2.2). However, counterproductive to these needs, the employees did not regularly update their profiles (see section 6.1), which made it hard to network internally. Based on these findings, our third derived challenge focuses on lacking collaboration and customization.

Even though the employees were seeking for comprehensive company internal collaboration, the provided resources (e.g., functions) for this purpose were not used. This might be due to several reasons such as limited access to content (e.g., through not having a computer available continuously), lacking quality of the content (e.g., Who makes sure that the shared content is correct and complies with the companies regulations? What is high quality content?), or rarely updated profiles, which would be needed to benefit from the social ties that are intended in social media. Regarding the lacking quality of content, Venkatesh and Bala [44] highlight the importance of information-related characteristics of a system as positively influencing user acceptance and system success. They outline that "If a system can provide users relevant information on a timely manner, accurately, and in an understandable format and help them make better decisions, it is more likely that users will perceive greater job relevance of the system, high output quality, and greater result demonstrability." ([44], p. 294). DiMicco et al. [8] found that personal profiles play a crucial, but at the same time challenging, role. They furthermore argue that profiles need to be dynamic, changing according to a user's activity elsewhere on the site (e.g., when writing a comment or creating content), and they need to be customizable, allowing the user to choose which information to display where on the page [8]. Holtzblatt et al. [16] consider personal profiles and pictures as particularly relevant for strengthening connections across organizational boundaries and geographic distances. Regarding information and content, Geyer et al. [13] have developed a recommender system for profiles at IBM, which actually "recommends" content for users to create and therefore encourages users to actively involve themselves as contributors rather than as passive consumers.

The emphasis on and potential of the "social" when introducing social media in companies needs to be taken seriously. Besides the personal profiles that add social clues, the matching of specific people to collaborate is also part of this social potential, such as finding experts to support novices. Yarosh et al. [45] investigated in depth how and in what situations people looked for help in a large enterprise. What was found, for instance, is that selection criteria for finding the right helper are crucial to be supported by a tool, such as experience, group affiliation, or "someone like X".

Implication: Let the communities define and explicitly indicate what they consider meaningful content (e.g., through recommendations of content). Nevertheless, the management might also provide examples or "role models" of what they think is meaningful content to support employees who prefer having examples to relate to. Furthermore, avoid redundant information (e.g., do not provide the same information via email, Intranet and social media to the employees), but decide carefully how to distribute the information. For instance, urgent information might be best communicated via email, but information that is meant to inspire ideation or feedback might be better articulated via a forum on the social media platform. Furthermore, emphasize that such a platform offers the possibility to get multiple perspectives on a topic and facilitate possibilities to socially connect to others in meaningful ways (e.g., through expert-novice matching support).

8. CONCLUSION

With the studies presented here, we want to draw attention to the complexity of corporate social media, their potentials, as well as pitfalls that might come with the integration. The extensive assessment of opinions (both quantitative and qualitative) over a period of two years enabled us to uncover a variety of aspects related to everyday work with social media in companies. Based on the reflection of the results, complemented with findings from related work, we were able to identify three challenges: (1) diverging perspectives & uncertain top-down communication, (2) functionality jungle & high usage complexity, and (3) lacking collaboration & customization.

In the context of corporate social media, addressing those challenges and considering our proposed implications might imply a variety of strategies a company might pursue. However, as our presented studies were conducted within a very specific organization by evaluating the adoption of a particular corporate social media platform, the findings might not be directly transferred to other organizations or platforms. Nevertheless, our implications can provide valuable guidance to support smooth adoption processes, and hence might lead to successful collaborations via corporate social media as part of day-to-day collaboration practices.

However, with these challenges further questions arise that we will investigate as part of our future work, such as how social ties can be

better supported (beside profiles), or how the employees can be further motivated to contribute with meaningful content. Furthermore, we will address the identified challenges in technology acceptance and adoption, by broadening our perspective in terms of investigating technology appropriation (practices) for meeting *social purposes* (i.e., communication and collaboration). All this will support us in achieving our overall research goal, i.e., to understand what the *social* is that companies emphasize when referring to social media for their internal collaboration.

9. ACKNOWLEDGMENTS

The financial support by the Austrian Federal Ministry of Science, Research and Economy and the National Foundation for Research, Technology and Development is gratefully acknowledged (Christian Doppler Laboratory for "Contextual Interfaces").

10. REFERENCES

[1] Archambault A, Grudin J (2012) A longitudinal Study of Facebook, LinkedIn, & Twitter Use. In Proc. CHI 2012, ACM, 2741-2750.

[2] Becvar L.A, Hollan J.D (2007) Transparency and technology appropriation: social impacts of a video blogging system in dental hygiene clinical instruction. In Proc. GROUP 2007, ACM, 311-320.

[3] Benamati J, Fuller M, Serva M, Baroudi J (2010) Clarifying the integration of trust and tam in e-commerce environments: implications for systems design and management. In: IEEE Transactions on Engineering Management, volume 57, number 3, 380–393.

[4] Boyd D.M, Ellison N.B (2007) Social Network Sites: Definition, History, and Scholarship. In: Journal of Computer-Mediated Communication, volume 13, 210-230.

[5] Brzozowski M.J, Sandholm T, Hogg T (2009) Effects of feedback and peer pressure on contributions to enterprise social media. In Proc. GROUP 2009, ACM, 61-70.

[6] Ciborra C (1996) Groupware and Teamwork. What Does Groupware Mean for the Organizations Hosting It? John Wiley & Sons, 1-19.

[7] Davis F, Bagozzi R, Warshaw P (1989) User Acceptance of Computer Technology: A Comparison of Two Theoretical Models. In: Journal of Management Science, volume 35, number 8, 982-1003.

[8] DiMicco J, Millen D.R, Geyer W, Dugan C, Brownholtz B, Muller M (2008) Motivations for Social Networking at Work. In Proc. CSCW 2008, 711-720.

[9] Dix A (2007) Designing for Appropriation. In Proc. 21st BCS HCI Group Conference.

[10] Dourish P (2006) Implications for Design. In Proc. CHI 2006, ACM, 541-550.

[11] Farrell S, Lau T, Wilcox E, Muller M (2007) Socially augmenting employee profiles with people-tagging. In Proc. UIST 2007, 91-100.

[12] Faste H, Rachmel N, Essary R, Sheehan E (2013) Brainstorm, Chainstorm, Cheatstrom, Tweetstorm: New Ideation Strategies for Distributed HCI Design. In Proc. CHI 2013, ACM, 1343-1352.

[13] Geyer W, Dugan C, Millen D.R, Muller M, Freyne J (2008) Recommending topics for self-descriptions in online user profiles. In Proc. RecSys, ACM, 59-66.

[14] Grudin J (2006) Enterprise Knowledge Management and Emerging Technologies. In Proc. HICSS 2006, IEEE, 1-10.

[15] Hansen D, Shneiderman B, Smith M.A (2010) Analyzing Social Media Networks with NodeXL: Insights from a Connected World. Morgan Kaufmann.

[16] Holtzblatt L, Drury J.L, Weiss D, Damianos L.E, Cuomo D (2013) Evaluating the Uses and Benefits of an Enterprise Social Media. In: Journal of Social Media for Organizations, volume 1, number 1, 1-21.

[17] Jarvenpaa S, Knoll K, Leidner D (1998) Is anybody out there?: antecedents of trust in global virtual teams. In: Journal of Management Information Systems, volume 14, number 4, 29–64.

[18] Kaplan AM, Haenlein M (2010) Users of the world, unite! The challenges and opportunities of Social Media. In: Business Horizons, volume 53, Elsevier, 59-68.

[19] Kietzmann JH, Hermkens K, McCarty IP, Silvestre BS (2011) Social media? Get serious. In: Business Horizons, volume 54, 241-251.

[20] Krischkowsky A, Weiss A, Osswald S, Tscheligi M (2013) Evaluating a social media platform in a large-scale international company: A five action approach. In Proc. CTS'13, 99-106.

[21] Krischkowsky A, Weiss A, Osswald S, Tscheligi M (2013) Enhancing company communication: The case of a social media platform. In Proc. CHI EA '13.

[22] Koehne B, Shih PC, Olson JS (2012) Remote and alone: coping with being the remote member on the team. In Proc. CSCW 2012, ACM, 1257-1266.

[23] Krippendorff K (2008) Content Analysis. An Introduction to Its Methodology. Sage Publications, California.

[24] Leclercq A, Isaac H, Besseyre des Horts C (2006) Adoption and appropriation: towards a new theoretical framework. An exploratory research on mobile technologies in French companies. In: Journal of Systèmes d´information, volume 11, number 2, 9-50.

[25] Li X, Hess T, Valacich J (2008) Why do we trust new technology? A study of initial trust formation with organizational information systems. In: The Journal of Strategic Information Systems, volume 17, number 1, 39-71.

[26] Li C (2012). Making the business case for enterprise social networks. Retrieved from: http://www.altimetergroup.com/2012/02/making-the-business-case-for-enterprise-social-networks.html.

[27] Lai VS (2001) Intraorganizational communication with intranets. In: Communications of the ACM, volume 44, number 7, ACM, 95-100.

[28] Majumdar A, Krishna S, Bjorn P (2013) Managers' Perceptions of Social Software Use in the Workplace: Identifying the Benefits of Social Software and Emerging Patterns of its Use. In Proc. AMCIS, AIS, 1-8.

[29] Mani G, Byun J, Cocca P (2013) Enhancing communication and collaboration through integrated internet and intranet architecture. In Proc. ACM international conference on Design of communication, ACM, 91-100.

[30] Mansour O (2012) The Not-So-Open Wikis: Structures of Collaboration At Work. In From Research to Practice in the Design of Cooperative Systems: Results and Open Challenges. Springer, 65-80.

[31] McKnight D, Carter M, Thatcher J, Clay P (2011) Trust in a specific technology: An investigation of its components and measures. In Proc. ACM Transactions on Management Information Systems (TMIS), volume 2, number 2.

[32] McKnight D, Harrison D (2005) Trust in information technology. In The Blackwell Encyclopedia of Management, volume 7, 329–331.

[33] Moore GC, Benbasat I (1991) Development of an Instrument to measure the perceptions of adopting an Information Technology Innovation. In: Information Systems Research, volume 2, number 3, 192-222.

[34] Muller M, Ehrlich K, Matthews T, Perer A, Ronan I, Guy I (2012) Diversity among enterprise online communities: collaborating, teaming, and innovating through social media. In Proc. CHI 2012, ACM, 2815-2824.

[35] Muller M (2012). Lurking as personal trait or situational disposition: lurking and contributing in enterprise social media. In Proc. CSCW 2012, ACM, 253-256.

[36] Orlikowski W (1992) Learning from Notes: Organizational Issues in Groupware Implementation. In Proc. CSCW 1992, ACM, 362-369.

[37] Orlikowski W, Gash D (1994) Technological frames: making sense of information technology in organizations. In ACM Transactions of Information Systems, volume 12, number 2, 174-207.

[38] Pavlou P (2003) Consumer acceptance of electronic commerce: Integrating trust and risk with the technology acceptance model. In: International journal of electronic commerce, volume 7, number 3, 101–134.

[39] Renaud K, Van Biljon J (2008) Predicting technology acceptance and adoption by the elderly: a qualitative study. In Proc. SAICSIT 2008, ACM, 2008, 210-219.

[40] Rettie R (2003) Connectedness, Awareness and Social Presence. In Proc. PRESENCE, 2003.

[41] Safko L (2010) The social media bible: tactics, tools, and strategies for business success. John Wiley & Sons.

[42] Thom J, Millen D, DiMicco J (2012) Removing gamification from an enterprise sns. In Proc. CSCW 2012, ACM, 1067-1070.

[43] Tierney ML, Drury J (2013) Continuously Improving Innovation Management through Enterprise Social Media. In: Journal of Social Media for Organizations, volume 1, number 1, 1-16

[44] Venkatesh V, Bala H (2008) Technology Acceptance Model 3 and a Research Agenda on Interventions. In: Journal of Decision Science, volume 39, number 2, 273-315.

[45] Yarosh S, Matthews T, Zhou M, Ehrlich K (2013) I need someone to help!: a taxonomy of helper-finding activities in the enterprise. In Proc. CSCW 2013, ACM, 1375-1386.

[46] Zeiller M, Schauer B (2011) Adoption, motivation and success factors of social media for team collaboration in SMEs. In Proc. I-KNOW 2011, ACM.

The Nomad and the Couch Potato: Enriching Mobile Shared Experiences with Contextual Information

Seungwon Kim[1,2], Sasa Junuzovic[1], Kori Inkpen[1]

[1]Microsoft Research
Redmond, WA 98052, USA
{sasajun | kori}@microsoft.com

[2]HITLab NZ, University of Canterbury
Christchurch, 8140 New Zealand
seungwon.kim@pg.canterbury.ac.nz

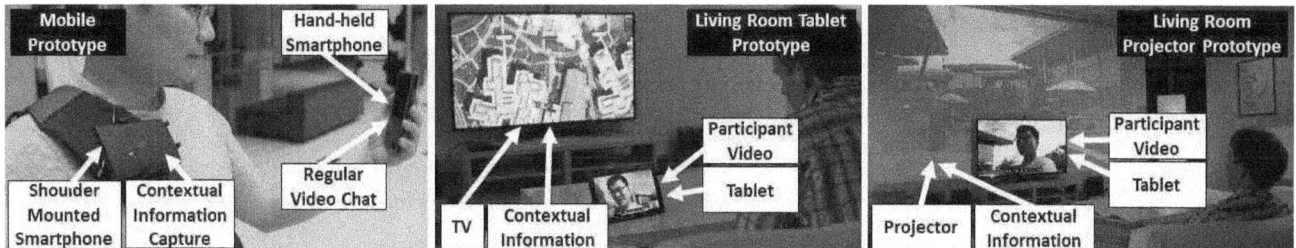

Figure 1. Mobile prototype (left); living room TV-Tablet prototype (center); living room Projector-TV prototype (right).

ABSTRACT

Mobile videoconferencing is increasingly being used to bring remote friends or family along to an activity happening outside the home, such as shopping or visiting a tourist attraction. We explored how including contextual information of the event, in addition to audio and video of the person at the event, impacts the shared experience. We studied three kinds of information: a map showing the position of the person at the activity, a second live video showing what was in front of that person, and periodic high quality images showing what was in front of the person. We carried out a field study with twelve pairs of participants, where one participant (the nomad) was at a self-selected activity while the other (the couch potato) joined the activity from our living room lab. The study results show that including contextual information significantly improved connectedness and the sense of presence for both participants. Each type of contextual information offered unique benefits. The map was used for orientation and to provide directions, the live video for "do you see this" moments and to maintain a sense of liveliness, and the periodic images for "did you see that" moments and to see greater detail. Together they led to smooth view negotiation, activity input from the couch potato, and high levels of engagement.

Categories and Subject Descriptors

H.4.3 [Information Systems Applications]: Communications Applications – computer conferencing, teleconferencing, and videoconferencing.

General Terms

Human Factors.

Keywords

Telepresence; consumer; mobile; wearable; video; periodic snapshots; map; field study; connectedness; sense of presence.

1. INTRODUCTION

People are increasingly using mobile devices to capture and share events with friends or family who could not be there in person. For example, they share shopping trips with friends to get advice on what to buy, kids' soccer games with grandma so that she can attend from across the country, and visits to tourist attractions with loved ones back at home. They share events asynchronously through social media and text messages, and synchronously using mobile video chat apps. In this paper, we focus on synchronous shared mobile experiences.

Synchronous shared mobile experiences go beyond the traditional "talking head" conversations over video chat by enabling people to share rich experiences as they do something together. Two important shared experience factors are connectedness and the sense of presence. *Connectedness* can be defined as the degree to which participants relate to each other in terms of what they are experiencing and feeling. Meanwhile, the *sense of presence* can be defined as the degree to which participants feel as if they are physically side by side during the experience.

We were interested in exploring how to increase connectedness and the sense of presence in shared mobile experiences. Our approach was to provide the person joining the experience remotely with additional live views showing the context of the activity in combination with the live audio and video of the person at the activity. As people already frequently share videos and photos, and sometimes geo-tag them, we wanted to study the benefits of providing contextual views that convey these types of information. We focused on three views: a map showing the position of the person at the activity, a second live video showing what was in front of that person, and periodic high quality images showing what was in front of the person.

To better understand the impact of adding contextual information to mobile shared experiences, we built and field-tested a prototype system that shared contextual views of an activity, as well as, audio and video of the person at the activity. The field study had twelve pairs of participants, where one participant was at a self-selected outside location while the other was in our living room lab. The field test results showed that including contextual information significantly improved connectedness and the sense of presence for both participants. Each kind of contextual information offered unique benefits. The map was used for orientation and to provide directions, the second live video for "do you see this" moments and to maintain a sense of liveliness, and the periodic images for "did you see that" moments and to see greater detail. Together the different sources of context led to smooth view negotiation, activity input from the couch potato, and high engagement levels.

The rest of this paper is organized as follows. First, we present prior work. Then we describe our prototype and the field study. We end with a discussion, conclusions, and directions for future work.

2. RELATED WORK

The use of mobile videoconferencing is on the rise, and as O'Hara et al. [13] discovered, many mobile video calls occur on the go, outside home and work settings. People are increasingly going beyond video calls that primarily focus on conversations (talking heads) to video calls that enable people to do things together or share rich experiences. Recently, shared experiences have attracted significant media attention, such as the iPad Bridesmaid [9] and a deployed soldier who watched the birth of his son on Skype [18].

Current mobile devices are well suited to sharing experiences because they can capture both video of the participant at the event (front-facing camera) and contextual video of the activity (rear-facing camera). They also support switching between the cameras during a call, which is important for collaboration scenarios. Prior research in the workspace supports this notion with Olson et al. [15] reporting that people like seeing each other during remote collaborations, and Gaver et al. [7] demonstrating that in some situations, they prefer seeing video of the activity rather than video of the people. Generalizing these results to mobile shared experiences suggests that would be useful for a remote attendee to have a view of the person at the event, additional contextual views of the event, and the ability to switch among these views.

Inkpen et al. [8] experimented with contextual information in the form of a second live video stream of an activity. They created and field tested a device that could stream front and rear-facing camera videos at the same time and found that this increased the remote attendee's engagement and feelings of being together and at the activity. Recently, Procyk et al. [16] explored sharing live head-mounted video in addition to audio between two remote geocaching partners. They found that the video was useful for coarse-grained navigation but not for fine-grained search. The issues with using video for fine-grained tasks were low resolution (640x480) and difficulties with framing. The GestureCam by Kuzuoka et al. [12] and other prior work have addressed the video framing issue by allowing the remote person to direct the camera. The video quality issue remains, however, and is largely dependent on infrastructure.

In addition to live data, contextual information may be synthetic, such as websites relevant to the shared activity, as well as, mash-ups of live and synthetic data, such as a live video annotated with digital content. The Chili system by Jo and Hwang [10] supports a mash-up view in which both users can annotate a shared live video. In addition, Stafford et al. [19] created a system in which a non-mobile user can help give directions to a mobile user. The non-mobile user places pins on locations in a digital map, and the mobile user sees that data superimposed on a mobile device when the device's camera sees those locations. Prior work has also enriched the real world with participants' videos. For instance, Billinghurst and Kato [1] show videos of remote participants overlaid on the real world when looking at the world through a head mounted display.

These previous works studied contextual information for shared activities. Contextual information has also been studied and applied differently in other research areas. For instance, in ubiquitous computing, devices compute decisions by sensing and responding to the environment around them, which forms the context for the computation [5]. Meanwhile, in studies of organizational processes and meetings, context has been used to describe relationships between people and entities, such as documents and devices, within the institution [4]. We focus on the notion of context for shared experiences, where context of a shared activity conveys additional awareness of the activity to remote attendees.

As a final note on prior work, while we focused on connectedness and the sense of presence, there are other factors that also impact remote shared experiences. At a low level, these factors include aspects such as the richness of the communication channels [2][6], mutual and directional gaze [14][17], and referential awareness [3]. These low-level factors drive high-level experience metrics such as task completion time [6], trust [2], and others, including the two we focused on, the sense of presence [14] and connectedness.

To summarize prior work, some systems have provided contextual activity information to a remote participant, but there have been few studies of this information, especially in the wild. Even fewer of these evaluations were carried out for activities that users themselves chose as something they would like to share remotely. Finally, prior work has not studied how users manage multiple types of contextual information when they are available simultaneously. Our work addresses these outstanding issues.

3. PREPARING FOR FIELD STUDY

To better understand how contextual activity information impacts connectedness and the sense of presence during a shared experience, we needed to observe it in the wild rather than in a lab. In a lab, it is not practical to replicate multiple real world shared events because of costs and scale. Thus, a lab could support only a few shared activities, which may not be reflective of the types of activities people actually want to share in their everyday life. As a result, we decided to run a field study in which the activity and the person at the activity were out in the wild while the remote attendee joined from our lab. While ideally the remote attendees should have joined from their own homes, having them in the lab made both administrative and data collection tasks more manageable.

By taking the shared activity out of the lab, the equipment and software that we could use for the study were limited. In particular, we could not rely on super-high resolution cameras, virtually unlimited bandwidth, and high-quality audio that exists in lab settings. Instead, we had to use mobile devices to capture both the person at the event and the contextual information of the event. We also had to rely on cellular networks for connecting the lab and the activity. The use of real-world devices and networks undeniably impacted the quality of the shared audio, video, and data. However, and more importantly, this quality was realistic.

The preparation complexity was further increased by the fact that no existing applications share contextual information of an activity together with the audio and video of the person at the activity. Thus, we built our own prototype to support this kind of sharing. To reduce the prototype build time, we leveraged a combination of existing commercial products and added custom components where required. The result was a prototype with a mobile and a living room end-point that connected our lab to an event in the wild.

3.1 Mobile Prototype

The mobile prototype had to perform three tasks: present the audio and video of the remote attendee; capture the audio and video of the person at the activity; and capture contextual information.

Standard video chat applications on a smartphone with a front-facing camera already accomplish the first two tasks. As a result, one part of the mobile prototype was a *handheld smartphone* (Figure 1 left), in our instance a Lumia 920 Windows Phone 8, running Skype mobile. As with most video chat applications and smartphones today, users could switch to the rear-facing camera if they wanted to use the phone to show a video of something in front of them. To reduce the impact of noise in outdoor settings, a headset was connected to the phone. The headset also made it possible to have audio when users placed the phone in a pocket or purse to free up their hands.

Standard video chat applications, however, do not currently capture contextual information in the form of live video, snapshot history, and user location together with the audio and video of the person using the phone. For this, we created a new system. Since a smartphone could capture photos and videos using one of its cameras and user location using the built in GPS sensor, we used a *second, shoulder-mounted, wearable smartphone* to capture the contextual information. We again used a Lumia 920. We mounted it in landscape orientation at shoulder level using a sash-like belt so that the rear camera was facing forward (Figure 1 left). Thus, users could not see or use the wearable phone's screen as it was pressed flush against their bodies.

The wearable smartphone captured three types of contextual information: **Map** – GPS location at one second intervals; **Video** – a video showing what was in front of the user wearing the phone; and **Images** – automated high-quality images taken every five seconds and capturing what was in front of the user. Because only one application at a time can use the camera on the Lumia 920, we used the rear camera to capture Video and screenshots of the camera preview window as Images. Thus, the resolution of the images matched the 800x480 resolution of the Lumia 920 screen.

To share the contextual information with the remote attendee, we used two separate channels. To share Video information, we setup a second Skype session with one-way muted video stream from the wearable phone. To share the Images and Map information, the wearable smartphone uploaded data to an Azure cloud service that could serve that data on demand.

3.2 Living Room Prototype

The living room prototype space needed to look like a living room so that users in the room could at least partially forget that they were in a lab. Thus, we created a space that had a couch, a 55" TV placed a comfortable distance from the couch, a coffee table, and some simple living room décor, such as rug, floor lamps, fake plants, and wall hangings (Figure 1 center and left).

Figure 2. The context view stretches across the TV and the projector when the hand-held phone is put away.

The prototype had to execute three tasks: capture the audio and video of the person in the room; present the audio and video of the person at the activity; present contextual information of the activity.

To capture the video of the person in the living room, we placed an HD webcam on top of the TV and digitally zoomed it in on the person. To capture the audio, we placed a ClearOne speakerphone on the coffee table. The speakerphone also played back the audio of the person at the activity.

Displaying content is more complex in the living room than in the mobile case. The mobile prototype had to display only the video of the remote attendee, while the room prototype had to show both contextual information and the video of the person at the activity.

An important question was whether to display contextual information and video of the person at the activity on a single display or multiple displays. With a single display, both could have been shown at the same time using a tiled or picture-in-picture view. However, this could have made some things difficult to see. Another possibility was to let users choose what to show on the display. However, switching between the views would have been burdensome to users. We instead chose to utilize two displays, so that the video of the person at the activity and the contextual information could be shown simultaneously on different displays. We used a TV and one additional display in the living room.

A related question was what size display should be used to show contextual information. Intuitively, a larger display should increase connectedness and the sense of presence because it brings the person in the living room closer to the action. To test this intuition, we explored two dual-display configurations with drastically different display sizes. In the *TV-Tablet condition*, a Surface Pro tablet was placed on the coffee table to serve as the second display (Figure 1 center). In the *Projector-TV condition*, we placed an In-Focus IN126ST short-throw projector under the coffee table and it projected a 14' diagonal image to the sides and above the TV (Figure 1 right). In both conditions, the video of the person at the activity was shown on the smaller display and the contextual views were shown on the larger display.

In order to display the participant video and contextual information on the two displays, the living room used two desktop computers. One computer joined the Skype session with the handheld phone in the mobile prototype and showed the participant video from that phone on the smaller display that was being used. The second computer joined the Skype session with the wearable phone and displayed the context video from that phone on the larger display that was being used. This desktop did not transmit any audio or video back to the wearable phone. In addition, it downloaded the Images and Map contextual information from the Azure cloud service. For the Map data, it converted the GPS location to a pin on a Bing map and a line showing the path of the person at the activity.

The living room prototype allowed users to choose which context view to show and then interact with it. In the Map view, users could change the zoom level and clear the movement history. Map tilting, panning, and searching were disabled for simplicity. In the Images view, users could navigate through image history and jump to the latest image. The system did not provide any ways to interact with the Video view other than to watch it.

Finally, the living room prototype was mindful of the times when the people at the activity put their handheld phone away (e.g., into a pocket or purse) to free up their hands. When the handheld phone was put away, the video captured by the phone was simply black and not useful. In the Projector-TV condition, this meant that the TV occluded a part of the projected image for no reason. To improve this experience, when the system detected that the handheld phone was put away, it made things appear as if the TV and the projector were one large contiguous screen (Figure 2). The prototype accomplished this by determining the part of the projected image that was occluded by the TV and sending that part of the image to the TV. The prototype also enabled users to manually activate or deactivate this behavior.

4. FIELD STUDY

With the prototype system in place, we were ready to evaluate the impact of contextual information for activities people want to share. To identify these activities, we decided to allow the study participants to choose their own events to share, people to share them with, and their preferred time and location. While affording this freedom to the participants made our study more realistic, it also added some complexity.

4.1 Complexity

While the use of a field study was beneficial in terms of ecological validity, it also introduced additional complexity. First, there were cross-session differences since participants were allowed to choose their activity. This enabled us to observe different activities that took place in a variety of settings with different levels of ambient noise, lighting, and network coverage. However, it was difficult to compare results across the sessions. Second, our study design introduced a within-session difference because the participants out in the wild and those in the lab had asymmetric experiences. Thus, we had to analyze their feedback separately. Third, our use of two different display setups and multiple forms of contextual information in the living room added another layer of complexity. Therefore, we had to tease out the impact of each of these factors as we analyzed the study results. Finally, it is also important to recognize the overall quality and potential variability in the cellular network for connectivity. In particular, the quality of mobile video chat over 4G/LTE is still poor and will continue to be so in the near future. In the rest of this section, we describe our methodology.

4.2 Participants

For our field study, it was important to recruit participants who were already familiar with standard video chat features. Otherwise, their feedback could have been influenced by the novelty of using video chat rather than focusing on feedback about contextual information in mobile shared experiences. Therefore, we recruited twelve pairs of people who had used video chat at least once a month during the last six months. Our participant pairs were family members, couples, and good friends.

During recruitment, the recruits were told that one of them would attend an activity in person while the other would join them remotely. We provided some suggestions for activities (e.g., visiting a museum, attending a child's soccer game, etc.) but left it up to them to choose the event and who would attend it remotely.

4.3 Procedure

At the start of each session, one participant came to our lab while the other participant went to the event. We refer to the participants in the lab and at the event as *inside* and *outside participants*, respectively. One study administrator met with the outside participant while two administrators met the inside participant.

We started each session by explaining the purpose of the study. Then we demonstrated basic Skype features to the outside participant, such as switching between front and rear-facing cameras (on the handheld phone). We also explained that they can put the phone away in their pocket or purse any time they desired, and that if they did so, they could still talk to their partner through the headset. We then mounted the wearable smartphone on the participant and started the shared experience.

Each shared experience was divided into three sections: warm-up, familiarization, and free play.

Warm-up: Each shared experience started with a five-minute warm-up period of regular Skype video chat. Even though the outside user was wearing the second smartphone, we told them that it was not active. Meanwhile, the inside user could see video of the outside user on either the tablet or the TV, depending on which living room condition they were using. We used the warm up period to work out connection issues and get the participants talking. At this point, they were using a system that they were comfortable with since it was just basic Skype video chat.

Familiarization: Following the warm-up period, the participants spent three five-minute periods using each type of contextual information our system could provide. We explained each view to them as they started to use it. Since the outside participant could not see the living room, the administrator showed them what the current condition looked like using photographs. We used these five-minute periods to get the participants familiar with the contextual information. They could not choose what information they were seeing or otherwise interact with it. Of the twelve pairs in our study, six used the TV-Tablet condition in the living room and six used the Projector-TV condition. Within each condition, the order in which the contextual information views were used during the familiarization stage was counterbalanced.

Free-play: After the familiarization period, the participants entered a twenty-minute free-play period during which the inside user could control what contextual information was shown. We explained to the user how to 1) switch between Map, Video, and Images views; 2) zoom and clear the location history in the Map view; 3) navigate through image history in Image view; and 4) turn the "phone in pocket" feature on and off in any view. The free-play period was the period we were most interested in. We felt that it could help us better understand user preference for the contextual information, inform us of whether they would switch among the different views, and when a particular view is better than the others. Most of our data collection, analysis, and reported results are with respect to the twenty minute free-play period.

4.4 Data Collection

To assist in managing the study complexity, we collected multiple forms of data.

Questionnaires and interviews: We collected subjective data via two questionnaires and a debrief interview at the end of each session. The first questionnaire was completed at the start of each session and included demographic questions. At the end of the free-play phase, the participants completed the second questionnaire, which asked them to rate the usefulness, enjoyment, feeling of connectedness, feeling of being together, and the feeling of being a part of the activity for each contextual view. It also asked them to rank the views from best to worst and included two open ended questions about their likes and dislikes for each view. Once they completed the questionnaire, we conducted a semi-structured interview with the inside and outside participants separately.

Logs of inside user activity: To complement the subjective data, we also logged the inside users' interactions with the contextual views. These logs included times at which the participants changed their contextual views, their interactions with the Map and Images views, and if the phone in pocket feature was on or off. From this data, we can obtain information such as the number and frequency of view changes and total time spent in each contextual view.

Observations, pictures, and screen and video recordings: To help us better understand the questionnaire and log data, we took notes and pictures during the sessions. Moreover, we video recorded the inside participant and screen captured their screens, while the outside admin captured the outside user's activity with a GoPro. From this data, we could get information that we could not get otherwise, such as whether the front or rear-facing camera was being used on the handheld phone.

4.5 Results

Despite our best efforts, the video quality during the study was fairly poor. As a result, Video quality was lower than Images quality. Unfortunately, our participants expected very good video because of two reasons they mentioned in their comments. First, they thought that mobile video on 4G/LTE would have similar quality as on their home Wi-Fi. Second, they believed that the quality of live mobile video should be similar to that of pre-recorded content, such as videos from a GoPro camera. These expectations influenced the feedback about the live video streams.

As predicted, our participants chose to share a variety of activities which resulted in many differences across the sessions. To help us understand the overall data, we first qualitatively analyzed what activities people shared and how our prototype system was used to share them. This initial analysis provided the scope for a deeper investigation into the usefulness of contextual information. Therefore, we start by presenting an in-depth description of what the participants did during the sessions.

4.6 Descriptions of Individual Sessions

The shared activities included two playtime sessions in a park, three shopping excursions, three tours, hanging out on the beach, walking the dog, visiting a farmers market, and fly fishing. We describe six unique activities in detail as we observed them to be representative of the remaining six, for which we provide only a brief summary. Three of the session we describe used the Projector-TV condition in the living room and three used the TV-Tablet condition. We focus on the twenty minute free-play periods in our descriptions.

Playtime in park (Group 2): In this session, a mom used the Projector-TV condition to join her husband as he took their young son to play in a park. The father and son walked around, climbed

Figure 3. (left) view of snack time from living room: front cam on TV and snapshots on projector; (right) outside view.

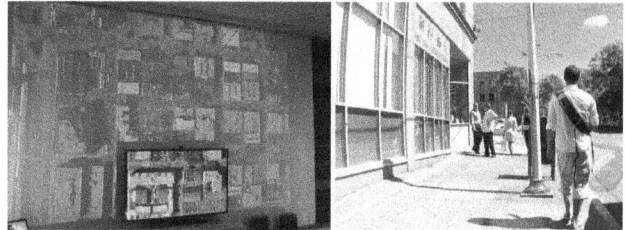

Figure 4. China Town from living room showing full screen map (left); walking around outside (right).

Figure 5. Shopping from living room: snapshot on TV with front cam (left); view from inside a store (right).

tables, visited a gazebo, and ate some snacks. Mom continuously interacted with them and suggested things to do in the park.

The mom spent almost the entire time in Map and Images views. She used Map mostly when the father and son were walking and often told them what was nearby: "*at the end of that little curved road you're going to be on, there's going to be something, I don't know what it is, but it's an oval thing that's green.*" When the dad and son were stationary, she used mostly Images, which worked especially well when the father put the hand-held phone in front of their son (Figure 3). The son liked seeing his mom, while the mother enjoyed watching him stuff food into his mouth. She frequently navigated through the snapshot history until she found the photo she liked best. Her comments reflected her usage pattern: "*I liked the map the best because I can zoom in and out and see where they were*" and "*I liked the snapshots because I could choose to go back and forth*". She did not feel the context video was useful because "*that's what Skype was already doing.*" She also liked the ability to change views: "*sitting and watching just the plain video is not as fun as when I have control.*"

The dad enjoyed experience because "*[the mom] could see around us, and what we were doing, and she could see us*"; however, he found the system cumbersome to manage while also taking care of his son: "*it was hard because there was gear strapped to me, and the headphones, and the other camera*".

China Town tour (Group 5): In this session, one participant gave a tour of Seattle's China Town to one of his friends. The inside participant joined using the Projector-TV condition. They talked about nearby restaurants and the history and future of China Town.

The inside participant used all of the contextual views and frequently switched among them. Overall, he used Video and Images the most, and he used the Map for location references and to ask location specific questions. At times, he surprised his friend by asking questions about things he could see in the Images or Map views. For example, he asked "*Hey, are you walking towards the big arch thing?*" when he saw the China Town Gate on the map (Figure 4), or "*Hey what's that Gossip restaurant on the corner there?*" when the sign appeared in a snapshot. In both cases, the friend in China Town paused in surprise at these questions because he did not expect his friend could see these things. However, even though the inside user was actively participating in the tour, when asked if the system helped him feel like he was there, he said "*not at all, it's no substitute for being there.*" He added that "*I found myself gravitating toward the existing technology, like a basic Skype camera that you can switch between front and back views as being more familiar and comfortable.*" He liked that because "[the outside user] *could control it and focus my attention on something.*"

Interestingly, the perspective from the outside user was completely opposite. He felt that providing the additional contextual views automatically from the wearable phone made it feel like his partner was there: "*when I had regular Skype it didn't feel like he was right next to me. I knew I was talking to him over Skype. No major difference over phone call. When I had the other camera I was more inclined to show him things, because I was able to gesture freely, because I had this one in my pocket. I knew he could see what I was seeing. He is getting the same experience, or a similar experience, to that if he were standing right next to me.*"

Shopping at a mall (Group 6): In this session, a boyfriend remotely joined his girlfriend for a shopping trip. He used the TV-Tablet living room condition. They shopped for clothes and vitamins.

The boyfriend used all contextual information, although he used Images the most and Video the least. He generally enjoyed the experience. At one point he said "*you know normally I hate shopping but this experience has been great sitting here on the couch.*" Once she held up a shirt for him to see, and he could see details such as the price tag because he was using the Images view: "*I can see a white shirt. For $19*". Later on, when shopping for vitamins, he used the Images view to find them himself. When she looked at the shelf, he said "*oh yes I can see something there*" (Figure 5). During the debrief interview, he said that "*overall, I was a bit surprised that I did have a feeling of being present.*" He mentioned that "*Skype by itself is not enough, but when you add more things that you can see at the same time, that gives a better feeling of the activity to the person.*"

The girlfriend wanted to see her boyfriend while shopping so she kept the front camera active on the handheld phone most of the time. She explained that she liked that she "*could see his reaction, if he liked it or not*". One challenge this pair had was that the she walked very fast, which made the video difficult for him to watch.

Beach (Group 7): In this session, two friends went to a farmers market and then walked along a beach. The inside participant joined using the Projector-TV condition.

The inside participant used all contextual information. Initially, she used Images and Map views interchangeably to get a sense of where her friend was. Later, she used Video and Images to see what her friend could see, such as a beautiful sunset (Figure 6).

Figure 6. Sunset at beach from living room: front cam on TV and snapshot (left) and (right) outside view.

Figure 7. Hanging out in the living room: no video on tablet and snapshots on TV (left); outside view (right).

Figure 8. Farmers market from the living room: rear cam on TV and snapshot on projector (left); outside view (right).

She used Video when she wanted to see something that was currently happening, such as people walking by or paddle boarders in the water. According to her, what she liked best was "*switching between the videos and the images and Skype with her so that I could really see what she was talking about*".

The outside participant also liked that "[my friend] *could switch between what worked for her … which was nice as well for me to not have to be turning the camera back and forth. That made it feel like she was here*".

Walking the dog (Group 8): In this session, a teenage girl walked her dog while a friend joined using the TV-Tablet living room condition. They generally just hung out during the session.

The teenager outside felt self-conscious about holding the phone out in front of her, so she kept it in her pocket the entire time. She explained that "*I like being able to see the person, but I don't like when you walk around you have to hold it up*".

The inside teenager used only Video and Images, so that she could see what her friend could see. At one point, the girl outside asked her friend "*can you see Seduce right now?*" to which she responded "*yeah, I saw it in the pictures*" and then she switched to Images (Figure 7). When asked how much the system helped her feel like they were together, she said "*a lot, I really liked the picture and video a lot just because I could see if there was a place there … and it was really cool to talk to her about it while we look at it.*"

Farmers market (Group 11): In this session, two friends visited a farmers market. The one in the living room joined using the TV-

Tablet condition. They visited booths, tried samples, and generally enjoyed the market.

The inside friend briefly used the Map view a few times to see where her friend had been. For instance, one time she looked at the map, she commented "*it looks like you've been around the entire place!*" She spent the majority of time in Images view to see various fare and help her friend pick out things to taste test (Figure 8). At the end, she said "*I felt pretty connected with her. It was neat to be able to click the map view to see where she was.*" She added, "*I really liked the pictures and being able to control what I see.*"

The friend at the market was another participant who was self-conscious about wearing the prototype, and as a result, she was more negative about the setup. She also commented on the asymmetry of the experience: "*my experience was probably really different than hers, because she is the one who is seeing everything and I'm just walking around really, I wasn't really watching her as closely on the monitor because she wasn't doing anything.*"

Remaining groups: In Group 1, two friends in attended a **Viking festival** where they walked around booths and a Nordic museum, ate some food, and watched a mock sword fight. In Group 3, a boyfriend and girlfriend went **shopping**, bought cupcakes, window shopped, and looked at shirts for him and purses for his mom. In Group 4, a husband joined his wife at an **RC airfield** where they walked around and watched a person fly a plane. In Group 9, a husband and his wife went **fly fishing** and talked about the fishing area and strategies. In Group 10, two brothers went **shopping** at a mall. Finally, in Group 12, a husband joined his wife as she took their daughter to **play at a park**.

Summary of sessions: As these session observations illustrate, people used contextual information in a variety of ways. Each contextual view was useful at least some of the time, and some views were used in specific situations. The observations also show engagement by the participants in the living room, activity input from them, and smooth negotiations about what they looked at. Next, we unpack these findings and present higher level insights about the usefulness and impact of contextual information.

4.7 Contextual Information Evaluation

Based on the observations from the sessions, each of the three kinds of contextual information was useful. We were interested to see which of them had the highest impact on connectedness and the sense of presence, and if one was more useful than the others. To this end, we analyzed the rankings and the ratings from the participants' questionnaire answers.

4.7.1 Connectedness and Sense of Presence

We found significant differences for the different types of contextual information on inside users' ratings of *connectedness*, *feeling of being there*, and *feeling part of the activity* ($p<.01$, Table 1). The pairwise differences reveal that the participants rated having the Images view in addition to a pure Skype call

significantly higher than vanilla Skype (SkypeOnly) (*connectedness: Z=-2.85 p=.004, being there: Z=-2.84 p=.004, and part of the activity: Z=-3.20 p=.002*). Moreover, they rated the Images view significantly higher than the Map view for *feeling of being there* and *feeling part of the activity* (Z=-2.81 p=.005, Z=-2.99 p=.003). These results suggest that contextual information increased connectedness and the sense of presence for the inside participant. The Images view was the most effective, while the poor quality of the video worked against the Video view.

The debrief interviews corroborated the questionnaire results. Nine of the twelve participants reported that the system helped them feel like they were at the activity with their partner. Three stated that they felt like they were there with the Images but not with the Video view, and three reported that the system did not help them feel like they were at the activity, all giving poor video quality as the reason.

Meanwhile, the outside users experienced only two conditions, which were vanilla Skype (SkypeOnly) and contextual information with Skype (SkypeAndContext). In the SkypeAndContext condition, they knew the inside user had three types of contextual information available, but they did not see what the inside user saw. Nevertheless, we also found significant differences for having and not having contextual information on outside users' ratings of *connectedness*, *feeling of partner being there*, and *feeling of partner being part of the activity* ($p<.05$, Table 1). They rated SkypeAndContext significantly higher than SkypeOnly on all three measures: (*connectedness: Z=-2.26 p=.026, partner being there: Z=-2.72 p=.006, and partner being part of the activity: Z=-2.54 p=.011*).

During the debrief interview, many of the participants commented on feeling more like their partner was with them in the SkypeAndContext condition compared to the SkypeOnly condition (see earlier comments from Groups 2 and 5). For instance, P_{7out} expressed that having Skype and contextual information was twice as good as regular Skype: "*I had face to face with her, and then she could be looking where I was seeing as well, it was literally like she was here, she had every angle, pretty much, as if she was here. It's like Skype but kind of twice as good that you can see both the person and the surroundings*".

4.7.2 Usefulness and Enjoyment

Like the inside users' ratings for connectedness and sense of presence, we found significant differences for the different contextual views on inside users' ratings of *usefulness* and *enjoyment* ($p<.01$, Table 1). Examining the pairwise differences, the inside participants rated having the Images contextual view in addition to a Skype call significantly higher than having only vanilla Skype (SkypeOnly) (Wilcoxon: *usefulness* Z=-3.11 p=.002, *enjoyment* Z=-2.83 p=.005). In addition, the Images view was rated significantly higher than the Map view for *enjoyment* (Z=-2.69 p=.007). These results suggest that including contextual information was generally beneficial for the remote attendee.

Table 1. Mean (SD) ratings of the contextual views on a 10-point scale where 1 is low and 10 is high (* p<.01; ** p<.05)

	Inside Participant					Outside Participant		
	SkypeOnly	Map	Images	Video	Friedman Tests	SkypeOnly	SkypeAndContext	Wilcoxon Tests
Connectedness	6.08 (2.11)	6.75 (1.71)	**7.75*** (1.77)	7.00 (2.22)	$\chi^2_{12,3}$=12.34, p=.006	6.67 (1.30)	**7.50**** (1.17)	Z=-2.26 p=.026
Being there	5.58 (2.35)	5.33 (2.27)	**7.08*** (2.15)	6.17 (2.73)	$\chi^2_{12,3}$=14.15, p=.003	6.75 (2.67)	**7.92**** (1.24)	Z=-2.72 p=.006
Part of activity	5.42 (2.02)	5.25 (2.01)	**7.33*** (2.15)	6.33 (2.46)	$\chi^2_{12,3}$=22.21, p<.001	6.58 (1.44)	**8.08**** (1.24)	Z=-2.54 p=.011
Usefulness	5.87 (1.95)	6.58 (1.56)	**7.83*** (1.40)	6.58 (2.28)	$\chi^2_{12,3}$=15.46, p=.001	7.5 (1.73)	8.25 (1.14)	Z=-1.27 p=.204
Enjoyment	6.08 (2.47)	6.42 (2.11)	**8.17*** (1.53)	6.83 (2.69)	$\chi^2_{12,3}$=15.25, p=.002	7.42 (1.62)	7.67 (1.97)	Z=-0.73 p=.467

They also show that a history of periodic high quality snapshots is the most useful and enjoyable form of contextual information our prototype provided.

The results for the Map view were activity dependent. In some cases, the map provided little additional information because the outside user was mostly stationary or the inside participant knew the area well. For instance, P_{12in} joined his wife and daughter for a walk that was within three blocks of their home. On the other hand, three participants ranked it as very useful for their activities.

The outside users, in general, rated their experience high on both *usefulness* and *enjoyment* for the SkypeOnly condition (median 7.0 and 7.5, respectively) and the SkypeAndContext condition (median 8.0 for both). While the ratings were higher for SkypeAndContext, the differences were not statistically significant (*usefulness:* Z=-1.27 p=.204, *enjoyment:* Z=-0.73 p=.467).

Overall, these results indicate that including contextual information did not burden the outside participants. Since they did not see any of the contextual views, it makes sense that they would not report these views personally useful or enjoyable.

4.7.3 Summary
Overall, our users found contextual information useful, enjoyable, and helpful with respect to connectedness and the sense of presence. Interestingly, the outside users reported increased connectedness and a higher sense of presence even though they could not see the contextual information. Overall, the Images view was found to be the best. The Video view suffered from poor video quality, while the Map view was useful only in certain situations. In the next section, we present the analysis of how the different views were used.

4.8 Contextual Information Use
Even though our participants rated the Images view as the best view on all measures, the Map and Video views were still used and were found to be useful. In this section, we present a closer analysis of how each of the views was used.

From the log data, we computed the number of times each view was utilized and the amount of time it was displayed (Map 15%, Images 47%, and Video 38%). Repeated measures ANOVAs with living room setup as a between subjects factor revealed a significant main effect for the amount of time each view was shown ($F_{2,20}$=6.625, p=.006), but no significant interaction effect ($F_{2,20}$=3.418, p=.053). The post-hoc pairwise comparisons revealed that the Images view was viewed significantly more than the Map view (p<.01). Usage of the Video view was in between Map and Images but not significantly different than either of them, which is consistent with the participants' ratings for the three views (Table 1).

4.8.1 Specific Uses of Contextual Views
During the sessions, we observed that there were specific instances when the inside participant looked at a particular context view.

The Map view was often used to get a sense of where the outside participant was. Sometimes these were quick glances to get a location reading. For instance, the living room participant getting a tour of China Town from his friend in Group 5 often glanced at the map to see where in China Town they were. Other times, the Map uses were longer to get a better sense of where the outside person is and where they have been. For instance, the inside

participant joining her friend at a farmers market in Group 11 used the map to check how much of the farmers market her friend had visited.

While the use of the Map view was mostly triggered by inside users' curiosity, the use of the Images view was often triggered by the outside user. Specifically, when the person outside asked the one inside "did you see that", the inside user switched to Images to review what occurred. An example of this was the teenager in Group 8 asking her friend in the living room if she saw some nearby store, which prompted the living room teenager to switch to the Images view. At times, the inside user decided to review what happened without a prompt from the outside participant. For example, the mom from Group 2 looked for the perfect shot of her son as he played with dad in the park. Finally, the Images view was used often to see details, which is not surprising given the poor quality of the video. For instance, in Group 6, the boyfriend in the living room used the Images view to see the details and price of a shirt his girlfriend held up for him at a store.

Video, on the other hand, was used mostly to see things happening live. For example, in Group 7 where two friends shared a walk along a beach, the outside participant saw paddle boarders and asked the inside participant if she could see them. The inside participant immediately switched to the Video view to see what was going on. The Video was often used in coordination with Images, with quick switches between them depending on whether the inside person was interested in things happening live or things that have already happened. Finally, we observed that the inside participant often wanted some video of the activity or of the outside partner to get some degree of live, real-time data. Hence, when the handheld phone was put away, use of the Video view increased. In the next section, we discuss this and other patterns of contextual view use that were driven by the state of the handheld phone.

4.8.2 Patterns of Contextual View Use
We discovered three patterns of contextual view use that were driven by what the outside user was doing with the handheld phone. To show these patterns, we created timelines of the free-play periods showing the contextual view that was used and the handheld phone state. One pattern mentioned already was that the participants always wanted some form of live, real-time video during the activity. For instance, participant who walked her dog in Group 8 put the phone away the entire time (Figure 9 top), which prompted the inside user to use the Video view heavily.

When the outside participant mostly used the front facing camera on the handheld phone, the living room participant hunted for views of the activity. For example, in Group 7's visit to a beach,

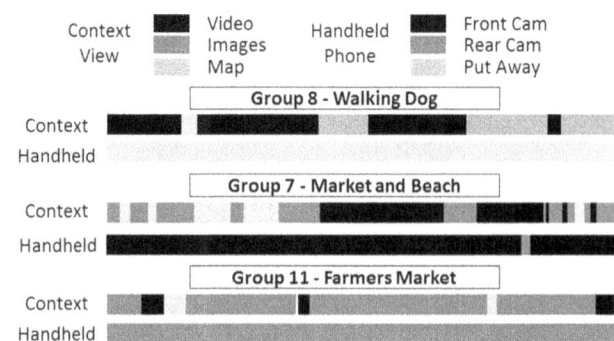

Figure 9. Timelines of context view use and handheld phone state for three different groups.

the outside user mostly used the front facing camera. As the session timeline shows (Figure 9 middle), the inside user changed views frequently as they tried to get an angle of the activity.

Finally, when the outside participant mostly used the rear facing camera, the inside user tended to use the Images more. For instance, during Group 11's visit to the farmers' market, the outside user only used the rear facing camera, which lead the inside user to mostly use Images (Figure 9 bottom). Overall, for many participants, this was reported to be the favorite combination of views – rear-facing camera video combined with Images.

4.8.3 Impact of Contextual Views

The uses of the contextual views illustrate that the living room participants were engaged and trying to get the best view of the event. They also commented that they were more engaged because they had control of the context views. For example, the mom in Group 2 who was joining playtime at a park mentioned that having some control is more fun than just watching plain video.

In addition to following the activity with contextual views, the inside participants were also able to use the views to contribute to the activity. For instance, several of the inside participants used the Map view to give directions to the outside participant. Moreover, the details afforded by the Images view let them drive the conversation by asking specific questions that were not necessarily related to what the outside person was talking about at the moment.

Interestingly, although the participants in the living room often switched among the various contextual views, none of the outside participants were able to tell which view their partner was looking at unless they explicitly told them or commented on the view. None of the outside participants expressed concern over this. In fact, many commented that they liked their partner having the freedom of choosing whatever view they wanted: "*the fact that I don't have to constantly have to switch between the two for his convenience is a blessing*" P_{10out}. Some participants, like the one on the beach in Group 7, found that the inside participant's ability to switch among the context views on their own made it feel like they were there at the activity because they could see more. At times, the outside participants were surprised at all the things the inside participants could see. For instance, the person giving the tour of China Town in Group 5 was stunned a couple of times when his friend asked him about things nearby that he did not think his friend could see.

4.8.4 Summary

In summary, each contextual view contributed uniquely to the shared experience. Moreover, the ability of the inside person to switch among the context views, together with the ability of the outside person to choose how to use the hand-held phone, resulted in smooth negotiation of what view the inside participant was looking at. Finally, the availability of the various contextual views kept the inside participants engaged in the activity and enabled them to offer activity related input back to the outside people.

4.9 Other Results

In addition to analyzing the contextual views, we were interested in privacy concerns, the experience of wearing the mobile prototype, and the how display size impact the experience in the living room.

4.9.1 Privacy

Our participants did not express any concerns about privacy during the study. As our sessions involved family, loved ones, and good friends, we did not expect such concerns, except perhaps for times when they went to the bathroom (which never happened).

However, privacy concerns were raised by people around our participants. For instance, in both of the farmers market sessions, when our participant approached booths selling art pieces, the sellers asked that no pictures of the art were taken. Meanwhile, in one of the mall shopping events, a security guard asked us to stop filming. Even though our participants informed the offended party that they were just video chatting, the concerns remained.

4.9.2 Mobile Device Form Factor

The participants liked the general hands-free nature of the wearable phone. Two participants commented on the hands-free benefit: "*When I didn't want to hold up the phone with Skype she could still see where I was*" P_{8out} and "*I could put the phone in my pocket and he could still see*" P_{12out}. This was important for participants whose hands were occupied during the activity, such as holding a child, walking the dog, or carrying parcels, and for participants who felt self-conscious about having the phone out. As P_{12out} expressed: "*I liked that I could put the regular phone in my pocket if I had to, and so the other one was still taking pictures. Or if I'm dawdling, looking somewhere else, he is still getting something.*"

The main issue with our wearable camera prototype was that it was awkward and cumbersome. Two participants felt extremely self-conscious about wearing it and explained they "*didn't like walking around with* [it]" P_{8out}, and "*looked kind of funny* [and felt] *stupid*" P_{11out}. The wearable setup was in fact one of the things least liked about the whole experience. Four participants mentioned the bulkiness of the belt to which the phone was attached. When we probed the participants on what type of wearable form factor they would prefer, they generally desired something compact, discreet, sleek, waterproof, rugged, hands-free, and voice-activated.

4.9.3 Living Room Form Factor

We were also interested in understanding how the sizes of the displays in the living room affected the experience. During the debrief interview, we asked each inside participant to compare the two living room conditions. Since each participant experienced only condition one during the study, we verbally described the other condition to them. Those who tried the Projector-TV condition commented that the video was stretched out and pixelated, and that the same quality video on a smaller display may have felt better. This belief is supported by the questionnaire results. For both *connectedness* and *feeling of being there*, Video was ranked significantly higher in the TV-Tablet setup (median=1 for both measures) than in the Projector-TV setup (median=3.5 and 3) (*connectedness*: Z=-2.19, p=.041, *being there*: Z=-2.18, p=.041). However, as these results were affected by the poor quality of 4G/LTE video, they may not hold once video quality improves.

5. DISCUSSION

Expected vs. Actual Video Quality: One of the key observations during our study was the gap between the expected quality of live video when streamed over 4G/LTE and the actual quality. All of our living room participants complained about the low video quality. Two of their expectations were at the core of the issue. First, they assumed that mobile video quality is the same on Wi-Fi as it is on 4G/LTE. Second, they thought that live streaming video should have the same quality as videos recorded on a GoPro camera. Unfortunately, because wireless bandwidth is being consumed as quickly as it becomes available, the expectations gap will impact all near future mobile shared experiences.

Types of Contextual Information: Even if the gap in the expected and actual streaming video quality on wireless networks were to be reduced, our study illustrates that video is not always the best form of contextual information. In particular, the results show that having a history of periodic images from the activity and a map of the user at the activity were also useful contextual views.

Although one reason for usefulness of Images view was their high quality, it was also useful because it enabled people to review what happened. While it is possible to review video streamed during a videoconference, Junuzovic et al. [11] found that it is difficult to do so without affecting the live conversation. This did not seem to be an issue in our study when the participants reviewed images.

The Map view helped the inside participants get a sense of bearing and enabled them to provide directions to their partners. Interestingly, Procyk et al. [16] found that having live video of what is in front of a remote partner helped with navigation tasks. Therefore, it may be useful create a system that begins to support very course-grained navigation using our Map view and then switches to a Video view as the target comes into visual range.

Cognitive Costs: Although our study shows the benefits of including the contextual information in a mobile video chat system, these benefits do not come for free. An important issue is the cognitive load forced onto the participants with additional channels of communication. In our study, neither the inside nor the outside participants complained about any stress from the contextual information being included. In fact, the cognitive load of the outside participants seemed to have been reduced as they mentioned that the activity context made them worry less about what their partners could see. Thus, it may be that cognitive load increases only for the inside participant. Since, overall, the contextual information benefited the inside participant more, perhaps this is only fair. Such fair asymmetry in the additional cognitive load is one of many [20] that future systems can leverage.

Implementation Costs: Another cost associated with contextual information is the cost of building the software and hardware needed to support it. The system infrastructure will need to be redesigned to make tradeoffs between the performances of the various views for whatever bandwidth is available. The UX of the applications will need to be redesigned in order to present the additional information in useful ways. Finally, additional sensors (e.g., wearable cameras, etc.) may be needed, and the additional hardware costs will impact both system builders and users.

Social Costs: The additional hardware also leads to social costs. Some of our participants reported that having just a smartphone out for a mobile video chat made them feel self-conscious, let alone the wearable phone. Ideally, the additional hardware should not increase the social stigma beyond that of regular mobile video chat. Therefore, its design will need to be as inconspicuous as possible.

Privacy: Related to social costs is the issue of privacy. Although our participants did not report any privacy issues, people at the activities had some concerns. These concerns did not seem to be about the people themselves being in the shot (although we believe that this can also be an issue). Instead, the concerns seemed to be copyright related and policy driven. To the artists who asked for their pictures not to be photographed, the issue was that they did not want others to digitally reproduce their art. Meanwhile, the security guard at the mall who asked for filming to stop did so because of mall policies about video recordings. Interestingly, even when our users explained that they were not actually recording anything, the artists and the security guard were still concerned. As mobile video chat becomes more pervasive, we can hope that such issues will become a thing of the past. A more proactive way to address the issue is to make it easy for people to tell when a device is recording video and when it is in a video call.

Limitations: There are several limitations with our work that are important to mention. For one, the participants used the system for only twenty minutes, so the novelty effect could have influenced our findings. Also, the quality of 4G/LTE video clearly impacted the findings. A useful question to ask is how the results would have differed with perfect video. In addition, the wearable prototype was cumbersome and awkward, which may have impacted our findings. Finally, out study had an element of artificiality because the remote participants did not join from their own living rooms.

6. CONCLUSION AND FUTURE WORK

In this paper, we explored the impact of adding contextual information to mobile shared experiences in which one person is at an activity and another joins remotely. Through a field study of events happening in the wild, we found that contextual information increased connectedness and the sense of presence for both parties. The study results also showed that contextual information is not "one size fit all." The three types of information we studied, Map, Video, and Images, all had unique positive impacts on the shared activity. Map was used for orientation and to provide directions, Video for "do you see this" moments and to maintain a sense of liveliness, and Images was used for "did you see that" moments and to see greater detail. Together the different sources of context provided additional benefits. They led to smooth view negotiation, activity input from the participant joining remotely, and high levels of engagement.

The benefits of including contextual information are not without costs. Cognitive load, social awkwardness, and privacy concerns may all increase. Thus, a careful comparison of costs and benefits is needed before adding such information to video chat systems.

In the future, we plan to build and evaluate systems that incorporate shared inking and augmented reality into mobile shared experiences. We also plan to study how stabilization of live video impacts the experience even if the video quality is poor like on current 4G/LTE networks. We will also design and evaluate new wearable form factors for these experiences.

7. REFERENCES

[1] Billinghurst, M., Kato, H., Real World Teleconferencing. *CHI EA 1999.*

[2] Bos, N., Olson, J., Gergle, D., Olson, G., Wright, Z. Effects of four computer-mediated communications channels on trust development. *CHI 2002.*

[3] Buxton, W. Mediaspace – meaningspace – meetingspace. In Harrison, S. (Ed) *Media Space 20+ Years of Mediated Life*, Springer, 2009.

[4] Dourish, P., Bellotti, V., Mackay, W., and Ma, C-Y. Information and context: lessons from a study of two shared information systems. *COOCS 1993.*

[5] Dourish, P. What we talk about when we talk about context? *PUC 2004.*

[6] Fussell, S.R., Setlock, L.D., Kraut, R.E. Effects of head-mounted and scene-oriented video systems on remote collaboration on physical tasks. *CHI 2003.*

[7] Gaver, W., Sellen, A., Heath, C., Luff, P. One is not enough: multiple views in a media space. *CHI 1993.*

[8] Inkpen, K., Taylor, B., Junuzovic, S., Tang, J.C., Venolia, G. Experiences2Go: Sharing kids' activities outside the home with remote family members. *CSCW 2013.*

[9] iPad bridesmaid attends wedding via FaceTime. http://news.cnet.com/8301-17938_105-20097249-1/ipad-bridesmaid-attends-wedding-via-facetime/.

[10] Jo, H., Hwang, S. Chili: Viewpoint Control and On-Video Drawing for Mobile Video Calls. *CHI EA 2013.*

[11] Junuzovic, S., Inkpen, K., Hegde, R., Zhang, Z., Tang, J., Brooks, C. What did I miss? In-meeting review using multimodal accelerated instant replay (AIR) conferencing. *CHI 2011.*

[12] Kuzuoka, H., Kosuge, T., Tanaka, M. GestureCam: Video communication system for sympathetic remote collaboration. *CSCW 1994.*

[13] O'Hara, K., Black, A., Lipson, M. Everyday Practices with Mobile Video Telephony. *CHI 2006.*

[14] Okada, K., Maeda, F., Ichikawaa, Y., Matsushita, Y. Multiparty videoconferencing at virtual social distance: MAJIC design. *CSCW 1994.*

[15] Olson, J.S., Olson, G.M., Meader, D.K. What mix of video and audio is useful for small groups doing remote real-time design work? *CHI 1995.*

[16] Procyk, J., Neustaedter, C., Pang, C., Tang, A., and Judge, T.K. Exploring video streaming in public settings: shared geocaching over distance using mobile video chat. *CHI 2014.*

[17] Sellen, A., Buxton, B., Arnott, J. Using spatial cues to improve videoconferencing. *CHI 1992.*

[18] Soldier watches baby born over Skype. http://www.youtube.com/watch?v=Z_w8RzYVIM4.

[19] Stafford, A., Piekarski, W., Thomas, B. Implementation of God-like interaction techniques for supporting collaboration between outdoorAR and indoor tabletop users. *ISMAR 2006.*

[20] Voida, A., Voida, S., Greenberg, S., and He, H. A. Asymmetry in media spaces. *CSCW 2008.*

Is Living With Others a Barrier to Technical Literacy?

Erika S. Poole
College of Information Sciences and Technology
The Pennsylvania State University
321E IST Building
University Park, PA 16802 USA
epoole@ist.psu.edu

ABSTRACT
Prior research describes how households coordinate to resolve technology complexity in residential settings. In this paper, we examine how social roles and routines of use can potentially hinder the development of technological literacy. Through this short paper, we aim to open a discussion about ways to increase technological literacy of the public.

Categories and Subject Descriptors
H5.m. Information interfaces and presentation (e.g., HCI): Miscellaneous.

General Terms
Design, Human Factors

Keywords
domestic computing; sociotechnical systems; technical literacy

1. INTRODUCTION
Domestic computing usage, digital housekeeping, device installation, and other forms of technical support in homes offer a variety of coordination challenges [1, 2, 4, 5, 7-10, 13-16, 18, 19]. Prior work suggests that people may rely on others within and across households for technical help, even though the providers of this help may find it a burdensome experience. This state of affairs leads to an important question, particularly as complex, interconnected technologies become part of the fabric of everyday life. *How—and how much—should technological literacy and willingness to participate in technology selection, use, and maintenance practices be encouraged?* In this short paper, we elaborate on this question via a case study of two families integrating information technologies into their homes as part of a larger research study. The differences between these families point to the importance of considering existing social norms, routines of use, and impact of life events on how technology is used and maintained in the home. Overall, their experiences in the study expose some of the "wicked problems" with technological help at home, and increasing technological literacy of the public.

2. METHODS
The data discussed in this paper is part of a larger study of technology-related practices in North American homes [12]. As part of this study, ten households set up, configured, used, and

helped their family and friends with learning more about common home electronics and information technologies that prior studies have shown to be problematic. They also installed and used a piece of custom software for collaborating and managing knowledge about their home computing environments.

We collected data via group and individual interviews, questionnaires, software logs, and written responses in log books. Households participated in a group interview and home tour at the beginning of the study. At the conclusion of this session, the household was provided a set of technology-related activities to complete over the week. Each week, the research team visited the home, conducted a short check-in interview, collected logbooks, and provided a new set of activities. At the conclusion of the study, the household members completed a questionnaire, were interviewed as a group, and were interviewed individually. Across all ten homes, we collected 35 transcribed interviews, 191 photographs, and copious field notes written after each home visit. Qualitative data were analyzed using affinity diagramming; these findings were triangulated against survey and software log data collected from each home. In this paper, we restrict our discussion to two families participating in the study, as they provide particularly salient insight into the challenges of household norms and computational literacy.

3. HOUSEHOLD 1: CONTINUITY
Steve and Janine are a couple in their mid-30s living in a suburb of a large North American city. Steve is a manager for an engineering firm, and Janine is a former teacher who now stays at home with their two children, a 4.5-year-old girl (Allie) and a 1.5-year-old boy (Billy). The home is connected to the Internet using cable Internet, and the householders exclusively use wireless connectivity for all of their computers. The family has two computers in the home, both mobile. Janine and Steve share a small notebook computer, which is used throughout the house. Janine uses it for all tasks, except when she needs to print. When she prints, she puts items on a flash drive and then uses the second computer in the home. This second computer, although a mobile device, is permanently located in a spare bedroom. This room also is home to a printer and an external hard drive that holds all of their pictures and music. Steve uses this computer for homework associated with his part-time MBA program, and the couple's daughter, Allie (4.5 years old) uses this machine to play children's video games online. The family has a digital camera, one flat screen TV in the living room, and a CRT TV in the children's playroom.

3.1 Technology Acquisition and Usage Habits
Why did the members of the household acquire these technologies? The couple's attitude toward purchasing technology appears to be reluctant at best; there are not any frivolous purchases. Everything has a purpose, and items that break are repaired such that they are usable and their flaws are hidden; for

instance, the netbook was purchased after their original laptop fell on the floor, shearing in half. To continue to have a mobile device, they purchased a new mobile computer. Steve, with the help of his technically skilled younger brother, repurposed the broken machine so that it would function as a "desktop" computer for the family to use.

A point of contention in the home with respect to appropriation of technology involves audiovisual and gaming equipment. Steve used to be an avid video gamer and AV enthusiast, but largely gave those hobbies up once he had children; his "nicer" (but more "ugly") speakers are hidden away in the children's playroom, and his video game consoles were given away to his sister. When it comes to buying new technology, Steve notes that his practices changed after having children. He notes that:

> It's more simplifying...because it's expensive to keep up with that stuff and to be you know, the first one to have things... So I don't really, I don't even research a lot. Because when you research then you want, right? [For example] it would be awful neat to have a picture on the wall that you can keep changing of all of your family photos. I could see doing that, but I just kind of try to stay away from it, because then you don't know better.

Janine considers herself to be a person who if she's "confident in how to do it then I'll do it myself." She has tackled plenty of home repairs on her own, including removing wallpaper and wiring light switches and plugs (her father, an electrician, taught her over the phone how to wire them). But computers are different. Janine says:

> I know enough about technology to get by. That would kind of sum it up.... I only need computers for what I need them for. I'm not interested in taking the time to expand myself beyond that.

What's meaningful here is that technology enters the home only for a specific purpose. We also see a coping strategy of *willful ignorance*—intentionally avoiding thinking about or examining new technologies—as they are not practical given one's current lifestyle. Rather than buying anything and everything, technology choices are much more calculated, much more by necessity.

3.2 Support Structures in the Home
Janine does not call professional tech support services because, as she states" "I have people in my family who are my tech support." Her first resource for getting assistance with technology problems is Steve, because he is the most readily available to help. Her second choice is Steve's younger brother, Phil, who lives nearby and holds the reputation of being the "technical geek" of the family. Steve and Janine will ask for technical help such as removing computer viruses in return for providing a meal or beer. Janine describes their relationship as "He's like our Geek Squad to fix our computer...I have to feed him dinner." Steve says that Phil "complains about it, but he fixes whatever it is."

Janine also gets help from her father, an electrician living in another state. Janine describes her dad as "not so much the virus kind of, cleaning it off the computer guy. He's the behind the scenes wiring guy." Her father helped them rewire the cable jacks in their home. Janine says she has a "daddy-do" list when her father visits for fixing things (technology related and otherwise). Says Steve, "She puts things on my list, and they don't get done,

so it gets transferred to his list." Despite relying heavily on others for technical assistance, Janine is well aware of the burden she places on her helpers. In the final visit at her home, she said:

> It happened this morning. My email didn't work. My email's not working today. And I don't know why, and it says, report your problem to Hotmail. I don't, I didn't do that. I would rather ask one of them [Steve or Phil] first, but I didn't want to bother them. So I turned the computer off and ignored it...I think I feel like I'm bothering people when I ask for help all the time. I feel like, nobody ever comes to me with questions. I'm always the one asking other people, so I'm never giving back.

She mentions that there are many occasions where she could ask for help, but chooses not to, because she does not want to "bother" her helpers. In summary, Janine, while not afraid to take on other sorts of technical tasks, such as rewiring electric systems in a home, does not have this attitude when it comes to computers. Although she will help her daughter and mother-in-law with very basic problems, for the most part, she is not enthusiastic about computers, nor does she want to learn more about them, or in some cases, go out of her way to ask for assistance when needed.

Since Janine has a strong commitment to purchasing and using technology only as necessary, so there are few instances to learn about new technologies. She also has a strong support structure. If technology is confusing or malfunctioning, her husband, brother-in-law, and father are all available for assistance. Although this safety net is useful to her, it is, to some extent, also a handicap. For most of her life, she has never had much opportunity to struggle with technology and realize that what she thinks are mountains of technological difficulty are merely tiny bumps in the road. Left to her own devices, Janine is not going to *want* to become more effective or confident with technology. However, Steve noted that *being in the study*, in a situation in which their normal routines were disrupted, was ultimately positive for her, because it showed her that performing some technology-related tasks were not as difficult as she initially perceived them to be.

4. HOUSEHOLD 2: DISRUPTIONS
Household 2, also located in a suburb of the same North American city, was occupied by Viola, a mother in her 50s, and her three teenage girls: Keisha, Kassandra, and Karina.

4.1 Technology Acquisition and Usage Habits
Viola is mildly interested in learning more about information technologies, but describes herself as "impatient" and "intimidated" by technology. Of the children, Karina and Keisha have their own laptops. Kassandra, the youngest, primarily uses an iPod touch and laptops owned by others in the house. Keisha and Kassandra enjoy using and learning about technology, but the oldest daughter, Karina, is largely uninterested in technology. She has a laptop for her college classes but describes herself as having little skill or interest in information technology. At first glance, the second household is technologically similar to the first. They, too, have a limited amount of technology—just enough to listen to music, browse the Internet, have the kids do homework, store photos, and print documents. The home is connected by cable Internet, and the family exclusively uses wireless connectivity. The family has a television and a stereo system, too, but nothing complicated. At the outset, the technologies in these homes are mostly interchangeable. Yet there is a distinct difference between

these families: in household two, the family had experienced a divorce.

4.2 Support structures in the home

Recent research in CSCW has focused on the impact of life disruptions on ICT use, particularly with respect to such as deaths in the family, domestic violence, unemployment, and homelessness [6, 11]. When the structure of a family changes, technology maintenance practices and resources for advice may change, too. Statistics on marriage and cohabitation show that nearly at least a quarter of all marriages in the United States end in divorce within five years; couples in second (or later) marriages, minority couples, as well as unmarried cohabiting couples are even more likely to split up [3]. When these relationships sour, it can affect technical support practices in the home. Given the frequency at which relationships dissolve, these situations may be considered—in the long term—to be both normal and worthy of consideration.

Viola, prior to her divorce, relied on her electrical engineer husband, Victor, to perform computer and electronics support. Because Victor was always available to fix problems, whether mechanical or electronic, she never had to think about these issues. When the couple divorced, however, support practices within the home shifted. Viola and her daughters had to take on the technical work that Victor had previously provided. For instance, Viola described during how she had to learn how to install speaker cable wiring on her own, because she did not have anyone else to do it. Although she had never performed the task before, and thought it was intimidating, once she actually tried it, she remarked that it was much easier than she had perceived it to be.

Her daughter, Keisha (18), took on responsibility for setting up and maintaining the wireless computing infrastructures after the divorce. Keisha was the most logical choice for this role and fell into it; when the couple was married, Keisha would follow Victor around while he was fixing things (electronics or otherwise). When she shadowed him, she would ask questions about what he was doing, and sometimes participate in the tasks as well. Thus she was the most prepared to take on these tasks once he was no longer in the home. Notably, however, is that after the divorce, Victor still served as a technical reference to the daughters. The girls would phone him for technical advice. Keisha remarked that for some of the post-divorce maintenance tasks she did, her father would coach her over the phone of how to do them. More recently, he also helped her select a new laptop for college. Viola, however, excluded herself from this resource. Her daughters served as a conduit to the father's advice, but she would not ask him for help directly.

5. DISCUSSION AND CONCLUSION

What statistics about family structure, as well as the experience of these homes suggest, is that when thinking about how to support families engaging in technical support, it is important to think about resistance to engaging in learning about technology unless there is a *transition* to a situation in which a help-provider is no longer available for whatever reason. Although events such as divorce are ultimately negative experiences, shifts in family structures may present opportunities for householders to become more confident in engaging with technical infrastructures, as they may be forced to be in situations in which they have no choice other than to learn and become proficient. These situations may

also create indirect channels through which technical information can flow.

What, then, can this vignette tell us about helping Janine? Even though she does not *want* to become a technical expert, Janine worries about being a burden to those around her when it comes to technology help. After all, help seeking is an act that requires some amount of vulnerability. Asking for help can be upsetting, uncomfortable, or embarrassing to an individual. When one asks for help, he or she potentially risks rejection or negative judgment by others; psychology literature on helping suggests that "nothing makes you feel worse than making a fool of yourself in front of others" [17]. Moreover, Janine thinks she has nothing to offer when it comes to technological advice, to even out the give-and-take of asking for help. Perhaps if she could become aware of having an audience—and get feedback that her audience finds her experiences and advice worthwhile—that may be a positive experience that could raise her confidence in her technical abilities. For instance, if Janine could see what others *do not* know, or that people are in fact taking what she has to say seriously, could that be empowering? Or would she be just as likely to hang onto the identity of being a "technically challenged" person?

Ultimately, a thorny question remains. Is Janine's technological discomfort, and limited computer literacy a problem to be solved? Should we so boldly suggest that her family experience a traumatic disruption in order to improve her technological prowess? Or do we accept the status quo? And hence, we leave an exercise for the reader: what is the minimum level of technological literacy needed for life in the 21st century?

6. ACKNOWLEDGMENTS

We thank our study participants for their time, effort, and honesty. Lawrence Jarvis and Jill Dimond assisted with data collection, and Georgia Institute of Technology provided material support for the study.

7. REFERENCES

[1] Beckmann, C., Consolvo, S. and LaMarca, A. Some Assembly Required: Supporting End-User Sensor Installation in Domestic Ubiquitous Computing Environments. In *Proc. UbiComp 2004*.

[2] Bly, S., Schilit, B., McDonald, D. W., Rosario, B. and Saint-Hilaire, Y. Broken expectations in the digital home. In *Proc. ACM CHI 2006 Extended Abstracts* Montreal, Quebec, Canada.

[3] Bramlett, M. D. and Mosher, W. D. Cohabitation, Marriage, Divorce, and Remarriage in the United States. *National Center for Health Statistics. Vital Health Stat*, 23, 22: 2002.

[4] Chetty, M., Banks, R., Harper, R., Regan, T., Sellen, A., Gkantsidis, C., Karagiannis, T. and Key, P. Who's hogging the bandwidth: the consequences of revealing the invisible in the home. In *Proc. Proceedings of the 28th international conference on Human factors in computing systems* Atlanta, Georgia, USA.

[5] Chetty, M., Sung, J.-Y. and Grinter, R. E. How smart homes learn: the evolution of the networked home and household. In *Proc. Ubicomp 2007* Innsbruck, Austria.

[6]   Dimond, J. P., Poole, E. S. and Yardi, S. The effects of life disruptions on home technology routines. In *Proc. ACM GROUP 2010* Sanibel Island, Florida, USA.

[7]   Grinter, R. E., Edwards, W. K., Chetty, M., Poole, E. S., Sung, J.-Y., Yang, J., Crabtree, A., Tolmie, P., Rodden, T., Greenhalgh, C. and Benford, S. The ins and outs of home networking: The case for useful and usable domestic networking. *ACM Trans. Comput.-Hum. Interact.*, 16, 2: 2009, 1-28.

[8]   Grinter, R. E., Edwards, W. K., Newman, M. W. and Ducheneaut, N. The work to make a home network work. In *Proc. ECSCW 2005* Paris, France.

[9]   Kiesler, S., Zdaniuk, B., Lundmark, V. and Kraut, R. Troubles with the internet: the dynamics of help at home. *Hum.-Comput. Interact.*, 15, 4: 2000, 323-351.

[10]   Kraut, R., Scherlis, W., Mukhopadhyay, T., Manning, J. and Kiesler, S. HomeNet: a field trial of residential Internet services. In *Proc. ACM CHI 1996* Vancouver, British Columbia, Canada.

[11]   Massimi, M., Dimond, J. P. and Dantec, C. A. L. Finding a new normal: the role of technology in life disruptions. In *Proc. ACM CSCW 2012* Seattle, Washington, USA.

[12]   Poole, E. S. Interacting With Infrastructure: A Case for Breaching Experiments in Home Technology Research. In *Proc. ACM CSCW 2012* Seattle, WA, USA.

[13]   Poole, E. S., Chetty, M., Grinter, R. E. and Edwards, W. K. More than meets the eye: transforming the user experience of home network management. In *Proc. ACM DIS 2008* Cape Town, South Africa.

[14]   Poole, E. S., Chetty, M., Morgan, T., Grinter, R. E. and Edwards, W. K. Computer help at home: methods and motivations for informal technical support. In *Proc. ACM CHI 2009* Boston, MA, USA.

[15]   Poole, E. S., Edwards, W. K. and Jarvis, L. The Home Network as a Socio-Technical System: Understanding the Challenges of Remote Home Network Problem Diagnosis. *Comput. Supported Coop. Work*, 18, 2-3: 2009, 277-299.

[16]   Rode, J. A. The roles that make the domestic work. In *Proc. ACM CSCW 2010* Savannah, Georgia, USA.

[17]   Shapiro, E. Embarrassment and help-seeking. *New directions in helping*, 21983, 143-163.

[18]   Tolmie, P., Crabtree, A., Egglestone, S., Humble, J., Greenhalgh, C. and Rodden, T. Digital plumbing: the mundane work of deploying UbiComp in the home. *Personal Ubiquitous Comput.*, 14, 3: 2010, 181-196.

[19]   Tolmie, P., Crabtree, A., Rodden, T., Greenhalgh, C. and Benford, S. Making the home network at home: Digital housekeeping. In *Proc. ECSCW 2007*.

Supporting Collaborative Reflection at Work: A Comparative Case Analysis

Michael Prilla
IAW, Ruhr University of Bochum
Universitätsstr. 150
44780 Bochum
michael.prilla@rub.de

Bettina Renner
Knowledge Media Research Center (KMRC)
Schleichstr. 6
72076 Tübingen
b.renner@iwm-kmrc.de

ABSTRACT

Reflection is a common activity at work. Collaborative reflection is an activity in which multiple participants add to reflection by sharing experiences, perspectives and insights together, thus transcending individual capabilities. Despite its potential for change at workplaces, there are little insights on how to support collaborative reflection with technology. To close this gap, this paper analyses four cases in which a tool to support collaborative reflection has been used at different workplaces. It uses qualitative data from app usage, an analysis of content from the tool and feedback gathered from participants to shed light on how people use support tools for collaborative reflection. The results of this wok include factors supporting and constraining reflection in tools as well as implications for tool design.

Categories and Subject Descriptors

K.3.1 [**Computer Uses in Education**]: Collaborative learning;
K.4.3 [**Organizational Impacts**]: Computer-supported collaborative work.

General Terms

Measurement, Performance, Design, Human Factors

Keywords

Reflection, Collaborative Reflection, Workplace, Learning

1. INTRODUCTION: SUPPORTING COLLABORATIVE REFLECTION

Reflection is a common activity performed by people in different work places every day: Workers ask themselves whether they can do better in certain situations, teams analyze their performance and think about improving their cooperation, and during work people question their doings and try to improve. Conceptually, reflection can be understood as returning to experiences, re-assessing them in the light of current knowledge and drawing conclusion for future work from this [3]. This refers to what Schön [23] describes as reflection-on-action in contrast to reflection-in-action which happens right while conducting a task. This process of drawing conclusions from the insights gained by reflecting on past experiences needs attention to work being done and the rationales for doing it the way it was done [32] as well as a mindset of being open to learn from current or past experiences, which needs to be established and spread to make reflection effective in organizations [30].

Despite the benefit of reflection and the awareness of people for this benefit reflection may not always be possible for workers – there might be no time and space to do this, or there may be other constraints. If it is then shifted to a certain time after the experience, fading or incomplete memories may hinder adequate reflection. In addition, relevant information to reflect on certain experiences may not be available for individuals, but only from a group of people. These and other constraints of reflection in daily practice may be diminished by tool support for reflection that helps people to keep memories of experiences, gather different perspectives on these experiences, reflect on them individually or in groups and share insights derived from reflection (see e.g., [13,15,26]).

It has been found that collaborative reflection may create insights beyond reflection outcomes that individuals can produce by combining different people's perspectives and knowledge [13,20], and that this needs specific support for the collection, coordination and combination of different contributions to the reflection process. Unfortunately, research on reflection support mainly covers individual reflection and education settings, in which constraints such as time and space occurring in many workplaces often do not play a decisive role, as reflection is part of the curriculum. Consequently, there are only a few insights on how to provide collaborative reflection support with tools (e.g., [16,26,33]). Given the potential of collaborative reflection at work there is a need to fill the resulting research gap.

2. COLLABORATIVE REFLECTION: RELATED WORK

2.1 Understanding Collaborative Reflection

Collaborative reflection differs from individual reflection, and therefore imposes additional requirements for tools: If people want to reflect together, they have to make experiences explicit, share and compare them, collaboratively gain insights and create ideas for change in future work [6,33]. This needs communication support e.g. for the exchange of similar experiences and to collaboratively understand them [4,10,33]. In work on face-to-face collaborative reflection it has been shown that structuring the process can be helpful [4], that there is need to support the articulation of issues to reflection upon [2] and the possibility to refer to each other [11].

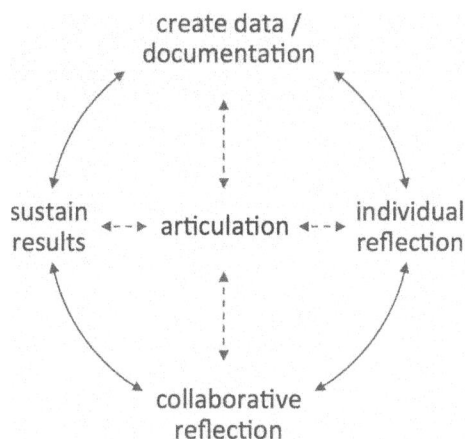

Figure 1. Collaborative reflection support blueprint [25,28].

Collaborative reflection overlaps with well-known concepts from CSCW and CSCL such as sensemaking, problem solving or group decision support (e.g., [5,24,31,36]), and this may imply that concepts from these areas may be easily transferred to collaborative reflection support. However, despite these overlaps, the discriminating aspects co-occurring in reflection – focus on past work, understanding the experience *and* planning for the future – are not present in such combination in other concepts [26]. Therefore research on collaborative reflection may draw from such concepts, but needs to explore how collaborative reflection works in practice and how people use technology to support it at their workplaces (see [26] for a detailed discussion).

Based on empirical and design work feeding into the studies presented in this paper [25,26,27] we created a model for collaborative reflection, which we use as a blueprint for the development of tools [25,28]. As shown in Figure 1 it suggests supporting collaborative reflection as interplay of reflecting in the group and leaving opportunities for individual reflection. Support includes (usually at the beginning of the process) the documentation of experiences and, if results are created from the process, possibilities to sustain these results.

2.2 Tool Support for Collaborative Reflection

An analysis on existing collaborative reflection support as part of this work revealed that this area has not been researched intensively, and that existing approaches are mainly focused on individual reflection or education settings [25,26]. This has recently also been recognized by several authors [1,19,23].

Among existing approaches on individual reflection support, a notable approach has been described by Isaacs et al [15]. In their tool, users can describe experiences, rate them according to their feelings about them and are re-prompted regularly afterwards to re-assess these rating in order to continuously reflect on them. Despite the value of this contribution, it is solely designed for individual reflection purposes. For collaborative reflection support, besides generic tools such as whiteboards also proposed for reflection purposes (e.g., [16]), Fleck and Fitzpatrick show how a series of pictures representing daily activities can trigger reflection in a social group [9], and Scott shows how learning portfolios can support collaborative reflection in education [33].

Looking at this state of the art, we can see that there is no sufficient amount of insights on tools support for collaborative work available. Our work [25,26,27] and that of a few others [19,23] aims to derive such insights and support the design of

collaborative reflection support. A decisive part of this work was the development of tools specifically tailored to collaborative reflection (see section 3.1), as there were no such apps available when we started the study.

2.3 Analyzing Reflection Support

Literature on analyzing tools to support conversations with a certain purpose among people points to the analysis of usage figures and content analysis. While the analysis of usage figures offers insights on tool adoption, activity and engagement in conversations (e.g., [8,18,35,37]), content analysis is seen as a means to look into the quality of conversations [14,37], which in our case means the quality of collaborative reflection.

Coding the content of conversations has been shown to be a key to analyzing the way these tools support people and to which extent they fulfill their goals [14,34,37]. Unfortunately, for collaborative reflection at work supported by tools there is no scheme for analyzing such content available. Existing approaches as proposed by Fleck and Fitzpatrick [9], Zhu [40] or de Groot et al. [11] stem from more general conversation analysis contexts or are related to reflection in educational settings, which differs from reflection at work. In particular, schemes from educational settings do not regard the articulation of experiences and issues in them, as the content to be reflected about is often given in such settings instead of being created by a reflection participant. In addition, these schemes are often too coarse to better understand the way people reflect. Complementing existing schemes and supporting their extension, several authors describe aspects of (collaborative) reflection that need to be considered when reflection is analyzed [3,17,21,22,29,35,39]. Among these aspects, recurring topics are

- **Returning to experiences**, including emotions and rationales for actions [3,9,21,35]
- **Probing, challenging or supporting** other contributions [11,17,29]
- **Linking** between experiences and other sources (experiences, knowledge, data) [17,22,35,40]
- **Repeating and commenting** on other contributions [22,40]
- **Sharing** perspectives and opinions [9,35,39]
- **Drawing** from experiences [3,9,11,21]
- **Transforming** insights into practice [3,21]

In combination with existing schemes for conversation analysis in related areas, these topics can be used as a foundation to develop a coding scheme for collaborative reflection.

However, such analysis may not be enough: Instead of relying solely on content coding, several authors argue for a combined approach of analyzing communication in electronic media. For example, [18] argue for using descriptive data such as communication thread length to complement content analysis. [8] propose to measure the responsiveness to others and the amount of people interacting with each other as additional information on a conversation group, and [37] describe different aspects of social network analysis to understand group activity better.

3. STUDY: COLLABORATIVE REFLECTION SUPPORT IN PRACTICE

To gain insights into how people use collaborative reflection support at work, we analyzed four groups from different workplaces and contexts using a tool we developed to support reflection on social interaction at work. The results from this analysis are based on a combination of log data analysis, social network analysis, content analysis, and qualitative data gathered from the participants of the study. Combining this data provides a

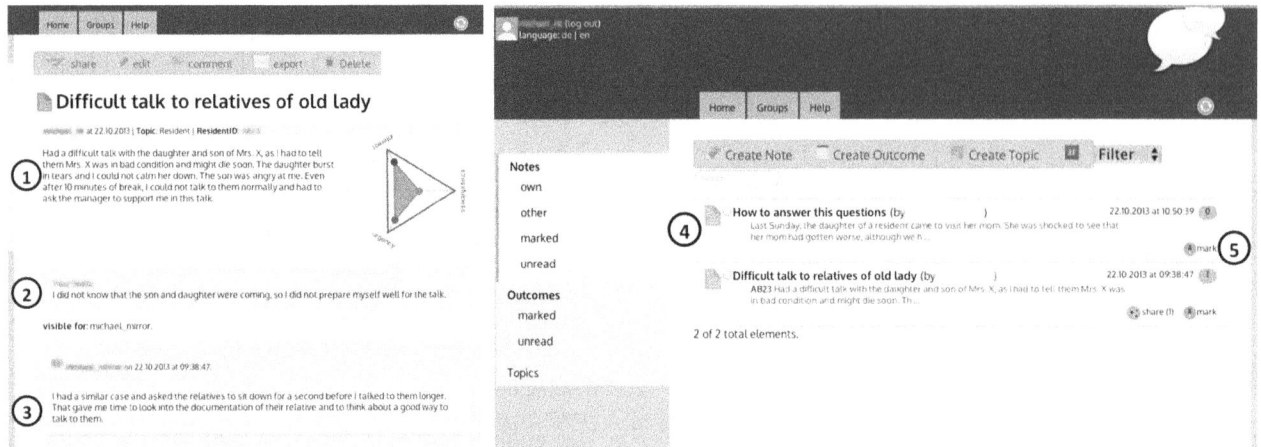

Figure 2. The TalkReflection App with an experience report commented on (left) and the list of reports created by users (right).

holistic insight into the practice of using collaborative reflection support and allows to draw conclusions both for assessing technology supported collaborative reflection groups and for designing collaborative reflection tools. The analysis of the data described in the paper was driven by three research questions:

1. How do (different groups of) people use tools supporting collaborative reflection at work?

2. Which are the factors supporting or constraining the usage of tools supporting collaborative reflection at work?

3. Which aspects of tools can support collaborative reflection at work?

This paper describes a study aiming to answer these questions, It was undertaken in four different cases, in which participants used the same tool (the 'TalkReflection App') to support collaborative reflection.

3.1 The TalkReflection App for Collaborative Reflection Support

For the analysis of collaborative reflection tool support in practice we conducted a study of different cases with different workforce, using a tool we had created from earlier studies of collaborative reflection at work [reference omitted for blind review]. The TalkReflection App supports collaborative reflection on social interaction such as conversations at work. To make sure that the study covered different situations and settings of reflection at work such as spontaneous reflection, reflection in meetings and others we did not restrict the use of the tool at the workplaces participating in the study but left usage to participants.

Based on earlier empirical work [references omitted for blind review], the TalkReflection App was built to support collaborative reflection on interactions among staff and clients, service providers and colleagues. This is a relevant topic for many organizations: In the workplaces covered by the study as examples, in medical and care domains workers have stressful interaction with patients of hospitals, residents of care homes and relatives, and in public administration people are facing difficult interactions with members of the public.

The TalkReflection App was developed to support such interactions by collaborative reflection among workers, clarifying issues in a peer group. For this, it supports the documentation of interactions and collaborative reflection on them by sharing resulting reports and commenting on them. This, in line with

related work [4,13,33,35,38], helps workers to explicate, share and reflect on experiences from conversations by supporting the steps of reflection described in the blueprint shown in Figure 1:

- Creating **experience reports:** The app supports users in documenting experiences by providing an opportunity to write them down. This includes a description of the experience and personal reflections on the report. Figure 2 (left) shows a report (no. 1) with a personal reflection comment (2). Writing down experiences can be a trigger for initial reflection [33] and provides a basis for later reflection.

- **Sharing experience reports:** Experience reports remain private to users initially, but can be shared with others. Once they are shared, other users can find them as shown in Figure 2 (right, no. 4). Sharing experiences with others can be regarded as asking them for feedback or opinions (cf. [39]).

- **Commenting on experience reports:** To engage in reflection on shared experience reports users can create comments on these reports as shown in Figure 2 (left, 3). Comments may contain similar experiences of a user, suggestions for acting in the situation described or other reflective content. Comments are core to collaborative reflection, as they enable the necessary communication for the exchange of perspectives and insights [4,10,33].

The app provides a certain structure for its users, assuming that the conduction of tasks such as creating reports of experiences, commenting on them and thinking about corresponding changes to work can create a flow of collaborative reflection.

3.2 Four Cases of Collaborative Reflection Support

The TalkReflection App was used with four different groups in three organizations, with each of the groups providing a unique context for using the app. Cases 1 and 2 were run in a public administration organization in the UK. Case 1 included the interns working in different departments of the organization, who were supposed to use the tool to learn how to interact with colleagues and members of the public professionally. Case 2 was done with participants of two departments conducting similar services, which were to be merged into one department. The aim of using the tool was to share and reflect on practices of the respective other department to support the merging process. Case 3 was done with physicians of a German hospital, who wanted to improve their abilities to talk to relatives, which is a task physicians are not prepared for well in medical school. Case 4 was conducted in a

British care home for people suffering from dementia. The aim of this study was to support care staff in improving their skills in conversations with residents, relatives and third parties.

The cases were conducted within different timeframes and with different amounts of users – the study configuration was based on the goals and resources of the different organizations. Table 1 gives an overview of time and participants for each case – it should be noted, however, that the numbers for the participants given in the table refer to the *total* amount of participants *in the beginning of the study*. In each study participants dropped after a short period of time, reducing the actual amount of users. This was especially relevant for case 1, in which six participants stopped using the tool after a couple of days of activity. As participants dropped out at similar times (some after initial usage, some after a couple of days) and given the sample size we cannot differentiate groups of users and will refer to the full number of participants for each study in this if not explicitly stated differently. Using the data of all participants is necessary because the content they put in the app during the first days cannot be removed from the rest of the content, as for example other participants commented on each the notes created by the dropouts.

Table 1. Overview for cases of using the TalkReflection App.

	Case 1	Case 2	Case 3	Case 4
Domain	Interns, public ad.	Public admin.	Hospital	Care Home
Participants	18	12	9	9
Duration (days)	51	80	42	50
Time	Sep-Oct 2013	Aug-Oct 2013	Jul-Aug 2013	Aug-Sep 2013
Dominant user	no	yes	yes	no
Process integr.	no	yes	no	no
Co-location	no	partly	yes	yes

In each case, the TalkReflection App was introduced to the participants in on-site workshops including an introduction of the app and a session of initially using of the app, asking some users to provide real experience reports and others to comment on them. It was also discussed how the app could be used in the respective workplace, including how to use it in meetings or during the day. No further instructions were given, and the groups were allowed to use the tool in a way that suited the group best.

The resulting usage of the tool, although voluntary in each case, differed in terms of organization and conduction (see Table 1): In case 1 and 4 participants used the app in a *self-directed* way to reflect in the team of workers, meaning that the organization and course of reflection was left to the participants. In contrast to that, cases 2 and 3 had *dominant users*, who took control over the reflection process: in case 2 the manager responsible for the departments took the role of driving the usage and in case 3 the head physician played this role. In cases 1, 3 and 4 the app was used in parallel to other work, while in case 2 it was integrated into the process of merging the departments, including meetings in which the participants discussed issues reported in the app. In addition, the opportunities for face-to-face communication differed, as in cases 3 and 4 users worked on the same floor, while in case 1 the interns worked at different workplaces in different buildings and in case 2 the two departments were located in different buildings as well. Table 1 summarizes this information.

3.3 Measures for Collaborative Reflection

Our work aimed at understanding the use of the TalkReflection App as a particular collaborative reflection support tool in different groups and workplaces by analyzing each group but also by comparing group behavior and output. We took into consideration specifics of each case and derived insights on the role of tools to support collaborative reflection at work.

The analysis was done with a mixture of tools to ensure a holistic view on how the participants in the studies use the TalkReflection App. For this we combined usage and content analysis with qualitative feedback from participants to also capture the subjective impact created by using app:

- **Usage analysis** was done by the amount of content created over time and analyzing the conversation structure.
- **Social network** analysis was applied to analyze the communication between participants.
- The content created by the participants was analyzed with a specially developed **content coding** scheme.
- The results from the analysis mentioned above were compared to feedback given in **interviews** and **focus groups**.

We are aware that in our analysis we are facing an observer problem: While we have detailed data on what happened in the app, we have comparably little data on reflection outside the app, that is, reflection possibly started in the app and continued in face-to-face situations without leaving traces in the app. Therefore we cannot make general assumptions on the collaborative reflection taking place in the cases from our analysis, but we can derive insights on how users reflected in the app and the impact resulting directly from using the tool for collaborative reflection. This reflects the perspectives of users reflecting in the community connected by the tool (which is not necessarily co-located as for example in cases 1 and 2), new users entering the app or users who cannot be present in certain face-to-face encounters.

3.3.1 Usage analysis: Measures
Besides content analysis, analyzing and comparing group behavior needs data describing group and individual behavior to set group activity and outcomes into context. Using a theoretical and empirical base showing that collaborative reflection relies on the sharing of experiences, articulating perspectives and opinions on such shared experiences and engaging in collaborative sensemaking and inference, we found that we also need means to describe and analyze user and group activity. Concerning descriptive data on user and group activity we use

- the **amount of experiences reports and comments** made on them (using the terminology from the description of the TalkReflection App) as information about general *activity* necessary to make reflection work in a group (creating, sharing, commenting, see [6,13,33,35]). To compare these figures among cases, they need to be *normalized*, that is set into relation to the timeframe data was collected in and the amount of users participating in the case.
- the **average length of communication threads** as proposed by [18] to provide insights on the *engagement* of users into conversations. The average length was calculated from the number of comments, not counting the experience report being the root of each thread.
- the **answer ratio** to experience reports as proposed by [8] as a measure for responsiveness of the group. This measure is also an indicator for attention to others' contributions, which is crucial for collaborative reflection [4,9,11,17]. The answer ratio was calculated as the ratio between the number of

experience reports commented on by at least one user compared to the total number of experience reports.

Adding to such descriptive data on user interaction, we use basic social network analysis as proposed by [8,37], including

- the **density of the graph** resulting from conversations as proposed by [8]. This graph is composed by directed edges between users, and an edge is added from user A to user B if user A has added a comment in a thread originating from user B's experience report. The density of the graph is then calculated as the ratio between the number of edges in the graph and the possible maximum of edges). It shows how may *different* pairs of people communicated in the group.

- the **ratio of unique edges** in the graph as a measure of diversity in group communication. The number of unique edges is calculated by counting how many edges are exactly once in the graph, and it shows how many different edges are in the graph – an edge may be in the graph more than once between two users A and B if there were multiple comments of user A to user B's reports. The unique edge *ratio* is then calculated as the ratio between the number of unique edges and the total number of edges in the graph. A high ratio thus means that many different pairs of users communicated with each other, thus indicating high diversity. A low ratio means that there were fewer pairs, implicating that there were some pairs in the group that communicated more often with each other. In contrast to the density of the graph this measure is stable against users dropping out early as it uses the actual amount of edges in the graph instead of the possible maximum amount as a basis.

Based on the suggestion to apply combined approaches for the analysis of conversations, we used the abovementioned measures to analyze collaborative reflection in the cases and to complement the content analysis described below.

3.3.2 A Coding Scheme for Collaborative Reflection Content

Besides data describing the interaction between users, the content created in the TalkReflection App provides good insights into how the tool was used in the cases. Facing the lack of existing schemes or methods to analyze collaborative reflection content in tools and drawing from the work described in section 3.3.1 on (collaborative) reflection we developed a coding scheme to analyze content of reflection support tools. It distinguishes different phases of reflection as describe din in section 3.3.1, starting from the description of an experience and ending with the description of changes in own behavior made or to be made. In particular, it includes nine phases as described in Table 2.

These phases in the scheme may build on each other. In a reflection session the description of an experience may be followed by the provision of one or more interpretation, one or more proposals for action and possibly the mentioning of learning and change. However, the choice of single codes does not depend on other codes, meaning that for example we may code 7b for solutions suggestions directly after using code 1 for a description of experiences without needing any other code in between.

Besides describing different aspects of collaborative reflection, the codes can be subsumed into three basic stages of reflection described similarly by Fleck and Fitzpatrick [9] and de Groot et al. [11]. The stages were aligned to the levels of collaborative reflection differentiated by Fleck and Fitzpatrick [9], and they include (1) the description and sharing of experiences and emotions

from them, (2) trying to understand and solve issues in experiences shared, and (3) describing learning and change.

Table 2. Coding scheme for content in collaborative reflection tools, with example from the content analyzed.

Code	Phase
1	**Description of an experience and mentioning of an issue** in an experience report or in comments, including the course of actions for the experience, e.g. "I had a very rude person on the phone. She [...]"
2	**Mentioning and describing emotions** of oneself or others to complement the description of experiences, helping the authors and others to later go back to the emotions, e.g. "this really made me angry".
3	**Interpreting or explaining behavior in the experience**, including rationales for certain own or others' behavior as well as potential reasons for issues, e.g. "It [the experience] was made worse by that fact that [...]".
4	**Linking an experience explicitly to other experiences** by mentioning or describing own or others' experiences relevant to the experience described, e.g. "I had a similar situation last week [...]".
5	**Linking an experience to knowledge** by referring to own or collective knowledge, data and other resources relevant to the experience, including advice without further explanation, e.g. "Never do [...]" or "Perhaps send an email before approaching in person".
6a	**Responding to the explanation of an experience** by **providing possible alternative perspectives** to the original interpretation, e.g. "I might have said [...]".
6b	**Responding to the explanation of an experience** by **challenging or supporting assumptions**, opinions or attributions made, e.g. "Agreed!" or "Hmmm. Is this really different from [...]?"
7a	**Contributing to work on a solution** by **providing reasons for the issue** by explicitly mentioning the background of the issue or going beyond standard solutions, e.g. "Could it be down to [...]?"
7b	**Contributing to work on a solution** by **providing solution proposals**, including reasons for the proposal or experiences linked to it, but without proposing to set them in practice; e.g. "I suggest this is escalated to your manager because [...]"
8a	**Showing insights or learning from reflection** by **describing better individual understanding** of the experience and drawing conclusions for own work, e.g. "I realized I should not be worried about ..."
8b	**Showing insights or learning from reflection** by **generalizing from reflection** by finding solutions that fit beyond the context of the current experience reflected on, e.g. "The key for us guys is definitely [...]"
9	**Describing or implementing change** such as proposing to apply practices, discussing change implementation or describing change set into practice, e.g. "Will definitely try and do [...] in the future".

Stage 1 is concerned with the basic elements of reflection such as descriptions of experiences, emotions and initial assessments, which are created by an individual.. Stage 2 comprises activities in the actual collaborative reflection process such as exchanging experiences and knowledge (codes 4 and 5) as well as critically referring to each other and contributing to solutions (codes 6 and 7). Stage 3 is focused only on outcomes as the decisive part for success of collaborative reflection. This includes the description of learning insights (codes 8a and 8b) or plans for changes (code 9). This stage needs to be separated from the reflection process conceptually, as for example in contributions tagged with codes 7a or 7b people may juggle with different thoughts and aspects, while reaching stage 3 means they have to report insights and actual change. Table 3 summarizes these stages and shows which codes belong to each stage. In our analysis we assigned a communication thread to a certain stage if at least one code of the stage applied to the session. We used these stages to analyze the success of collaborative reflection that can be perceived from using the app.

Table 3. Stages of reflection and codes related to the stages.

Stage	Description	Codes
1	**Provision and description of experience**, but no (explicitly) traces of reflection	1, 2
2	**Reflection on experiences**, including analysis and potential solutions, but no (explicit) mentioning of learning or change	3-7
3	**Learning or change** resulting from reflection explicitly mentioned	8, 9

The differentiation of these levels allows an analysis of the success of using the tool, that is, how far (in terms of results) users got in their reflection with the tool and how much these users could benefit from using the tool by becoming aware of shared perspectives on issues or learning and change happening.

3.4 Dataset for the Analysis

For the analysis of the four cases we used a dataset for each case that contains all content created in the cases within the respective timeframes shown in Table 1 as well as log data on usage of the app and qualitative data such as feedback from participants and observations made onsite in the cases.

For the analysis we reduced the resulting dataset to collaborative content, that is, content including a report describing an experience and at least one comment on that experience. This was done to ensure we only analyzed content created in interaction between people. The figures for "answer ratio" (the proportion of reports receiving at least one comment) in Table 4 show that for every case this was the vast majority of content. After coding the content, we removed non-reflective content from the dataset, that is, content in which there were no traces of reflection, indicated by no code being applicable to the conversation. Again, this was only the case for a few cases, thus not reducing the dataset drastically. Table 4 shows the resulting number of conversations analyzed for each case. These two steps reduced the dataset from 109 conversations and 176 comments to 74 conversations and 159 comments analyzed.

3.5 Participant Feedback

Additionally to the usage data and the content in the app we received different direct feedback from participants. This feedback was received on different ways in the different cases due to different possibilities to receive this feedback. Most important, while in cases

2, 3 and 4 we were able to hold focus group meetings of participants, this was not possible in case 1 due to the different workplaces of the interns. In cases 1, 2 and 3 we were able to conduct a debriefing meeting with the manager of the group, which was not possible in case 4. In case 3 we were able to conduct short interviews with participants. In all cases, we received occasional feedback via email. Given these differences the data cannot be compared to each other but still contains valuable insights on the cases.

4. RESULTS

4.1 App Usage and Group Behavior

To understand how the app was used in the different groups, we compiled the basic usage data as described above and set it into relation to the time and amount of users in each case. Table 4 shows the resulting figures describing the usage of TalkReflection in the cases. In our analysis, we differentiated between average usage per user and day to account for the different numbers of participants, and overall usage figures of activity not regarding the number of users (e.g., reports per day). While the former gives insights into the activity and motivation of each user, the latter is a measure for the impression of activity a user gets from the app.

It can be seen from Table 4 that in all cases a fairly high proportion of experience reports created were also commented on (answer ratio between 0.71 for case 2 and 0.88 for case 3). This indicates that the app has been used collaboratively and that users had an interest in reflecting together in all cases. The lower value for case 2 may be caused by scale effects, meaning that users had more choice to comment on (nearly twice as many reports) and thus stuck to the most interesting ones. Other figures show that collaboration differed in its intensity: In cases 2 and 3 the average user created 0.31 experience reports per day ("Reports/user, day"), while this was less in cases 1 and 4 – again we need to take into account that in case 1 several users stopped using the tool after a couple of days, thus lowering the respective average values for case 1. Likewise, we can see that in cases 2 and 3 the average user created more comments per day than in cases 1 and 4. Therefore we can conclude that users in cases 2 and 3 were about twice as active as users in the other cases.

Table 4. Usage figures for the four cases.

	Case 1	Case 2	Case 3	Case 4
Reports	24	45	25	15
Reports/day	**0.47**	0.56	**0.57**	0.48
Reports/user,day	**0.03**	0.05	**0.06**	0.05
Comments	47	65	39	25
Answer ratio	0.83	**0.71**	**0.88**	0.80
Comments/day	0.92	0.81	**0.93**	**0.50**
Comments/user,day	**0.05**	0.07	**0.10**	0.06
Avg. thread length	**2.35**	2.03	**1.77**	2.08

Concerning the intensity of communication, that is how many reports and comments were created per day, activity in the cases was similar, with the exception of the low number of comments per day for case 4. In case 1 there were on average more comments in communication threads than in the other cases, with case 3 showing the lowest value for average communication thread length. Thus we may conclude that case 1 showed more overall activity than the other cases (although per user and day this was different due to the dropouts), while the others trail in at least one aspect (answer ratio for case 2, thread length in case 3 and comments per day in case 4). This can only be partially attributed to the number of users in case 1, as – including the early dropouts in case 1 – case 2 had a similar number of users.

Regarding the collaborative reflection activity in the app, the answer ratio was fairly high in all cases, with case 2 trailing the others and case 3 showing the highest value. Likewise, the number of new experience reports per day is similar in all cases, while the number of new comments per day is significantly lower for case 4 than in the other cases. This means we can consider cases 1 and 3 to be most active in terms of output, while in case 2 some experience reports were not regarded by users and in case 4 users created less comments.

Besides a description of the groups and how they worked, the figures in Table 4 also provide insights into the average usage for tools supporting collaborative reflection: Averages of about 0.5 documents per day, 2.6 to 5.4 comments per user and 0.5 to 1 comment per day in all cases suggest that the usage we observed may be typical for small to medium groups using reflection tools like the TalkReflection App. Feedback from participants and our observations underpins this: Participants in different cases told us that they do not encounter critical situations every day and therefore did not use the app more often. Given that in case 1 several participants stopped using the app early (see section 3.2), we may expect the numbers to be slightly higher in practice. However, while other studies run in other settings suggest that reflection tools may be used more often (e.g., [15]), when using collaborative reflection tools in real work environments we should expect usage as described by the figures in Table 1 and Table 4.

4.2 Collaboration Network

Looking for insights into the collaboration network in the app, we applied basic social network analysis as proposed by [37,40] to the log data gathered from the cases (see section 3.3)[1]. The network graph analyzed includes the participants from the cases as *vertices* and the connection between a user commenting on another user's experience report as directed *edges* from the user commenting to the user being commented on. This means that for each graph the number of edges is the number of comments and the number of vertices is the number of users in the cases as shown in Table 4.

As Table 5 shows, graph density is lowest for case 1 and highest for case 4, with cases 2 and 3 in between. This indicates that in case 4 more users were connected to each other than in the other cases; the low density for case 1 can be explained by the several dropouts in the study as mentioned above. This is underpinned by the fact that the unique edge ratio is highest for cases 1 *and* 4, and considerably lower for cases 2 and 3. This suggests that communication in cases 1 and 4 was more diverse (more different pairs of users communicating) than in cases 2 and 3, while the low values indicate in cases 2 and 3 there might have been fewer but closer communication relationships established.

Table 5. Analysis of social network aspects in the cases.

	Case 1	Case 2	Case 3	Case 4
Graph density	**0.10**	0.17	0.19	**0.25**
Unique edge ratio	**0.62**	**0.18**	0.21	0.60

---

[1] The social network analysis was done using NodeXL, a Microsoft Excel based tool (https://nodexl.codeplex.com/).

These differences can be attributed to the different cooperation styles established or chosen in the cases: While in cases 1 and 4 participants used the tool in a self-directed manner, in cases 2 and 3 a user dominating the others was present (see section 3.2): In case 2 the manager of the participant had decided to drive the reflection in the tool, and in case 3 the senior physician had asked his staff to use the tool and promised to comment on the issues shared by them in return. This resulted in multiple communication edges between the respective manager and different other users, and (as some users were reluctant to add a comment before the dominant user had added one) fewer other edges.

4.3 Content Analysis: Collaborative Reflection Outcomes

Content coding was done independently by two coders on the level of single contributions to conversations (reports and comments). This means that a code was assigned once or not at all to an experience report or comment. The coding resulted in 597 codes assigned by the two coders.

Concerning the agreement among coders, we calculated values for Krippendorff's Alpha for each code. Results were mixed: While we found acceptable values (.75 and slightly below) for some codes (e.g., codes 4 and 5), we also found worse for others (e.g., codes 6a and 7a). Analyzing the differences between the coders we found that despite differences in some codes there was good agreement concerning the stage of reflection reached in each conversation (see Table 3 for the stages). When calculating the inter-rater agreement on these levels, we arrived at good agreement values (97% for stage 1, 96% for stage 2, 80% for stage 3). Although the level of details is lower for these stages compared to the coding scheme, the quality of the resulting data is better. Therefore we will describe results from the coding by the levels reached in the conversations. To further enhance the quality of the coding for stage 3, the coders discussed differences in using codes 8a, 8b and 9, resulting in a coding agreed upon the two coders. This data was used for the following analysis.

Table 6. Stages of collaborative reflection reached in the cases.

Stage	Case 1	Case 2	Case 3	Case 4
# Conversations	17	24	21	12
1	100 %	95.8 %	100 %	100 %
2	94.1 %	95.8 %	95.2 %	83.3 %
3	23.5 %	33.3 %	0 %	16.7 %

Analyzing the content coding and applying it to the three stages of collaborative reflection described in Table 3, we found that stages 1 and 2 were reached in most conversations throughout the cases, while there are differences in the proportion of conversations that led to outcomes on stage 3. The results for stage 1 are not surprising, because before the coding the obviously non-reflective conversations were eliminated from the sample. The conversations that did not reach this stage (only two thread in case 2, see Table 6) were initiated by the respective user with solution suggested for a certain problem and reflected upon afterwards, thus lacking the description of concrete experiences. The high proportion of conversations that reached stage 2 is a result better than we initially expected, especially for the cases with lower user numbers. The figures for stage 3 show major differences between the groups with case 2 reaching this stage for one third of all conversations and case 3 not reaching it in any thread. Table 6 gives an overview of stages reached.

Interpreting these figures, we can see that if reports on experiences received at least one comment (that is, the data set we coded) the conversation was very likely reach stage 2 and thus to be reflective – even in the worst case (case 4) 83% of the conversations reached this stage. This can be seen as a success of the tool, especially because we found in earlier studies that many conversations in which issues had been brought up were not systematically reflected on, and for the few that people reflected on there were no traces left of the corresponding conversation afterwards [reference omitted for blind review]. This shows how the TalkReflection App changed collaborative reflection in the cases: It created opportunities to reflect together asynchronously (that is, without the need to switch from other tasks or to step back immediately from work when being told about an experience) and made outcomes from reflection available after the reflection session and outside face-to-face group meetings.

In addition, we may conclude that cases 1 and 2 were more successful in terms of learning outcomes and change, and that in case 3 no learning took place. We are aware that concluding from the lack of explicit mentioning of this stage that neither learning or change resulted from using the tool is dangerous, as communication on this may have taken place outside the tool in face-to-face situations. In fact feedback from participants and our observations in workshops revealed that this was true for many cases. However, with a focus on the role of tools in collaborative reflection support, which may bring together reflection groups unable to reflect in daily face-to-face interaction, lower percentages of stage 3 reached for a group also mean that by using the tool a user gets less information on what can be learned and derived from experiences shared. The result for stage 3 is a pity especially in cases such as case 3, in which there was good effort in using the app but not even one result from reflection documented. In such cases if people are not part of meetings or other occasions in which communication on what to draw from the discussion in the tool takes place cannot take full benefit from collaborative reflection.

The high proportion of stage 2 conversations and the existence of some conversation reaching stage 3 also show the impact of using the tool: In almost all cases the tool enabled reflection among users and – especially in cases 1 and 2 – often led to explicit articulations of outcomes from reflection. Comparing this to situations we faced in earlier case studies [reference omitted for blind review], in which many experiences to be reflected as well as ideas and insights from reflection were soon forgotten, this makes reflection not only possible, but also sustainable and understandable for those not directly involved but reading through the content of a tool afterwards.

4.4 Participant Feedback

This section describes the feedback of the different sources described in section 2.5. In **case 1** participants and the manager told us that reflection with the tool helped them to cope with challenges they met as new employees in their respective jobs. We were also told that activity in the tool only lasted a short timeframe, as interns have short-time contracts and thus the user base soon became too small – new users were not added by the interns' manager.

In **case 2** participants told us that using the tool was valuable to reflect on own practices and changes on it in the upcoming merge of the departments, especially when reflection could not be done immediately. Their manager as the leading users of the tool added that in his impression the two departments had become closer to

each other as a result of reflection, and that he had liked to bring up topics and to ask his staff to reflect on them.

In **case 3** some participants told us that despite using the tool they did not see much value in it as they had known most experiences reported from face-to-face interaction before. Others mentioned that the exchange had helped them to know that others had similar problems, and to receive advice from the senior physicians, who had added this advice to nearly all reports. Overall, the perception of value added by the tools was low among the assistant physicians. The senior physician driving the usage stated that he felt the tool gave him the opportunity to train his staff.

In **case 4** participants told us that they were asked by their manager to use the tool only in breaks and in the small office of the care home, which they only used for documentation purposes. Those who had used the tool despite these constraints told us that they found it valuable to reflect on stressful cases, but were limited severely by time constraints in using the app, which was an extra effort for them. Some participants told us that they had asked for more time and to discuss some issues from the app in their meetings, which was refused by the manager.

The feedback of participants adds a flavor to the analysis that data and content analysis cannot create. In particular, is shows the attitude of participants towards the TalkReflection App, which would have been overshadowed e.g. by orders to use the app (case 3) or constraints hindering the usage (case 4).

5. DISCUSSION

The results of our studies give good insights into how participants used the TalkReflection App in each case, and also how the groups differed from each. Given the lack of insights in this area, this paper takes the support of collaborative reflection a step further. Striving to answer the research questions given above, this section analyzed these results.

5.1 Using Tools for Collaborative Reflection: Patterns in Group Activity

The results from the studies show that in each of the cases there was activity and engagement in collaborative reflection using the TalkReflection App. The results also show that there were differences in this activity and that the participants perceived the value of using the app differently. Comparing the cases reveals that there are some decisive aspects that accounted for success or low activity and perceived value.

For **case 1** we can see good values for overall collaborative reflection activity (reports and comments per day, answer ratio) and in participation (highest unique edge ratio and average thread length). Other values on activity per user would have been higher without the dropouts in the study. The case also shows a good amount of stage 3 reflection outcomes, but the number of reports is fairly low given the amount of users. Overall, case 1 can be regarded as a case in which the TalkReflection App has added value to the group. This is underpinned by the feedback we got from the interns. This may be attributed to the spatial situation of case 1, in which the interns worked at different departments and did not have the opportunity to reflect together face-to-face on problems they were facing. The TalkReflection App gave them this opportunity, resulting in good uptake and results.

For **case 2** we can see good values for reflection activity (good values for reports and comments per user and day), and low numbers for diversity (lowest unique edge ratio) and participation (lowest answer ratio). In addition, case 2 has the largest proportion of cases reaching stage 3 of reflection. Therefore, case

2 is an example in which average or low figures for participation and diversity do not predict little reflection success – on the contrary, the focus on the leading user that has caused low diversity in this case seems to also have fostered reflection outcomes. This is reflected by the feedback of users, who saw much value in using the tool.

For **case 3** we can see that despite good collaborative reflection activity (most reports and comments per day and user, highest answer ratio) the participation (low values for thread length and from social network analysis) and output (no traces of stage 3 in reports and comments, feedback indicating little impact) seems to be low. We attribute this to the organization of reflection and the dominant user in case 3: the assistant physicians had been asked to use the tool regularly, which resulted in high usage figures, but it had not been integrated into meetings and other face-to-face discussion opportunities, lowering the perceived value and outcomes. Moreover, the senior physician in case 3 acted as a dominant user giving advice in his comments how to deal with the respective situation rather than supporting reflection. This resulted in other participants waiting for him to answer and thus lowering the diversity in communication. Both of these effects may have hindered collaborative reflection to take place to an extent that resulted in traces of learning or change (stage 3).

For **case 4** we can see mediocre to low figures for activity (least reports and comments, least comments per day), high values for diversity and participation (highest graph density, high unique edge ratio) and at least some conversations that reached stage 3. Taking into account the feedback we got on the constraints of using the TalkReflection App in this case we can take it as an example in which people saw value in the tool but could not hold usage up. The resulting low usage is grounded in lacking process integration and co-location of the users.

As one conclusion from our comparison we can say that single dominant users in reflection groups can be good or bad for reflection practice. While in cases 2 and 3 activity and participation figures show engagement in reflection, the lead user led to comparably little diversity in the communication (see Table 4). This, however, led to different effects on collaborative reflection output: In case 2 it seems that the manager driving the activity in the group caused the group to be more reflective in the app, resulting in the highest number for occurrences of stage 3 reflection traces (Table 3). In case 3 the dominant user seems to have caused the opposite, as none of the communication threads contained traces of stage 3 reflection. This may be explained with the different roles these users played (see sections 3.2 and 4.4): In case 2 the manager had brought up topics and asked people to reflect on them, thus acting as an enabler and driver of collaborative reflection. In case 3 the physician had asked staff to add experience reports and – instead of driving reflection – has added his advice from the perspective of an experienced senior physician, which users may have just taken instead of continuing reflection – here the dominant user acted as an unintentional blocker of reflection activity. In both cases the focus on the dominant user may also be responsible for the low diversity in communication, as their comments may have discouraged others from commenting, resulting in edges from them other users may have dominated the respective social network.

Another conclusion from the comparison is that scale matters: the results of the different groups go along with group size and overall activity. Even if per user and day cases 3 and 4 in some respect performed equal or slightly better than cases 1 and 2, the latter cases contain more results on the outcomes stage 3 of the

content analysis. This may be caused by the fact that with more users a higher overall number of documents and comments is created, also resulting in a higher average communication thread length. In addition, for users (new or existing) of a collaboration support tool a higher amount of content available makes using the tool much more attractive, as they can see that people engage in collaborative reflection in the tool and that issues are reflected on intensively. This assumption is supported by the fact that the lower answer ratio in case 2 seems to have had no negative effect on the stages of reflection reached or any other figures – in contrast case 2 has most outcomes on stage 3 of reflection. This might be explained by the higher number of reports to choose from, which gives users the chance to decide for engagement in discussions on cases they are really interested in and which they can contribute to. Taking these observations together, we may conclude that collaborative reflection support tools such as the TalkReflection App are more beneficial to groups of 10-15 and more people than they are for small groups.

5.2 Factors supporting or constraining Reflection Support Usage

The comparison of the groups as described above points to measures and figures that help to explain why collaborative reflection works better or worse in different settings:

- **Stages of reflection:** Differentiating between the stages described in Table 3 is a good indicator of reflection success or failure; especially the differentiation between stage 2 and 3 seems to be crucial. Our results for stage 3 outcomes as shown in Table 6 go along well with the perceived value articulated in the feedback of participants, indicating that they are a measure of success in a group.
- **Thread length:** In our cases, the average length of threads was one indicator for good reflection outcomes as described above and for satisfaction of users. This seems natural, as longer threads implicate more engagement into communication in the tool, thus increasing the chances that threads will eventually lead to good outcomes.

In contrast to these measures, the analysis shows that other measures such as answer ratio or activity per user and day showed different values for the groups, but *did not predict reflection success* in any way, as cases 1 (low values per day and user) and 2 (lowest answer ratio) show. Although disregarding group size, *figures for total activity in terms of reporting and commenting worked much better*. The other way round, particularly low values for such figures such as for comments per day in case 4 indicate that reflection has not worked well. Together with thread length as a good indicator of reflection success (see above), this points to the assumption that *size and scale of reflection groups are more important* than average individual activity. A reflection group might reach a *threshold of activity* per day from which on it might be perceived more interesting to choose a relevant case and to comment on cases – further work should look into this as a success factor of tools support for collaborative reflection.

In addition to these aspects the cases also show that *some measures cannot give insights into collaborative reflection tool uptake and usage without additional context*. For example, social network analysis such as communication graph density and unique edge ratio cannot be considered predictors of collaborative reflection quality without other information given as context: In the cases, good output on stage 3 and participation co-occurred with low (case 2) *and* high (case 1) values for graph density and unique edges, and vice versa.

The aspects described above may also help the design of a socio-technical reflection setting, in which tools have to be embedded into certain circumstances and managed properly. The cases also point to decisive factors in this dimension:

- **Dominant user vs. self-directed use:** The cases show that tools support for collaborative reflection can be successful in self-directed tool usage (case 1) and directed by a dominant user (case 2) – under both circumstances it may also be less successful (cases 3 and 4). This may be a matter of scale and critical mass of users being active, as for the larger group in case 1, in which different users were active, self-directed usage worked while for the small group, in which some users did not find the time to use the app often, it did not.

- **Role of a dominant user:** Looking into cases 2 and 3 we have seen that the behavior of the dominant user was decisive for the success in these cases: A coach and driver of reflection fosters collaborative reflection activity while and advisor blocks it. We should therefore make users who might take this role aware of the impact they have on reflection. This (for some) may need a change in managers' mindset in becoming a coach rather than answering all questions, and it may need training.

- **Process integration and co-location:** The cases show that when using collaborative reflection tools in practice co-location and process integration need to be taken care of together. For the cases (partly) co-located (2, 3, 4; see Table 1) we saw that when there was no process integration (case 3 and 4) the app did not produce additional value – people used face-to-face encounters to talk about the most important issues anyway. In case 2, in which half of the users were collocated, the manager had integrated the app into meetings and made it a part of people's work. This resulted in successful reflection. We can also conclude that without process integration or good facilitation reflection support tools may provide limited value for co-located groups.

Concerning the latter finding, one may argue that this does not come at a surprise, as in co-located groups much happens in direct communication. However, we saw that with good process integration and facilitation the app provided benefit in the (partly) co-located group of case 2 and that, given different behavior of the dominant user, this might have also happened in case 3.

5.3 The Role of Tools in Collaborative Reflection

The analysis of the cases described in this paper reveals three ways in which the TalkReflection App was helpful for the participants:

- **Keeping up reflection:** For all cases our results suggest that the TalkReflection App helped participants to engage in reflection over a period of time. This is indicated by continuous usage over time, by good answer ratios to experience reports any by and overall satisfying activity in all cases. However, we can also say that keeping up reflection is not enough for reaching higher levels of reflection output and perceived value, as it was also present in the less successful cases.

- **Supporting face-to-face reflection:** Especially from case 2 we can see that reflection tools show benefit if they are used to foster reflection in face-to-face situations such as meetings. The manager in case 2 had included this usage from the beginning, which may also have motivated participants to use the tool. In other cases such as cases 3 and 4 this was not done, and consequently the app was perceived less valuable as it did

not add much to everyday communication possibilities – in case 3 participants had even asked for this support. We can therefore consider support for face-to-face reflection, for example using the content of the app in meetings like in case 2, as a way tools can become helpful for reflection.

- **Connecting reflection participants:** Case 1 and partly case 2 show that the value added by the tool lies in the connection of participants who work in different places to a (virtual) reflection group. The interns reflecting in case 1 with other interns would not have had the opportunity to reflect with peers in similar positions regularly without the tool. Therefore, given a situation in which people are not co-located or have regular meeting, connecting them to virtual reflection group is a major role tools can play in reflection support.

Besides analyzing the roles the TalkReflection App played in supporting collaborative reflection in the cases we also need to ask what improved tools for this support should be able to do. This means asking how a tool (besides using a lead user and proper processes) may support individual and groups in achieving more and better results from collaborative reflection. While our study may not provide an exhaustive list of requirements for such apps, the insights taken from the cases already point to some improvements:

- **Provoke activity:** Our analysis shows that overall activity seems to be helpful to keep up reflection and reach good results. In addition we saw that if reports received comments, the discussion was likely to become reflective. Therefore, tools supporting collaborative reflection should provoke activity among users, e.g. by reminding users of reports shared with them and prompting them to create comments.

- **Scaffold dominant user role:** We have shown that dominant users can be supportive in reflection, but that they may also drag too much attention to them and thus hinder reflection. Tools have limited power in coping with this, but may for example differentiate between user roles: If, like in case 3, it is known (and intended) in advance that more experienced users are part of the reflection group, a tool might enable them to contribute only after a certain while in order not to inhibit others from commenting from their point of view. Likewise, as tool could allow a dominant user to push reflection as a coach or driver by directly addressing others to contribute to certain discussions.

- **Point to relevant issues:** Our study indicates that more users and more cases in total may lead to better choice among experiences reports, which in turn lead to more commenting. Besides relying on such scale effects tools may support reflection even more if they recommend relevant issues to users, thus making contributions more likely.

- **Balance diversity and intensity of communication:** We have seen that diversity in communication (more links between users) and intensity (recurring links between the same users) may both be helpful to foster exchange among reflection participants and to deepen reflection. Tools may support a balance between these effects by managing the social network of reflection, e.g. showing users their existing communication partners and proposing new partners that might have similar issues at work.

Our analysis revealed differences between group activity and – from combining these differences with content analysis and qualitative feedback – insights on which differences indicate reflection success or flaws in reflection. From this we identified measures that may predict reflection success and other measures that at least point to more or less successful reflection.

In terms of *setting up technology supported collaborative reflection as socio-technical system* we can say that dominant users in the role of coaches have a positive influence in reflection tools, that process integration is decisive in small, co-located groups while connecting people is important in dislocated groups and that overall activity positively influences outcomes. In particular, our results suggest that for groups in which users are connected mainly by a tool a self-directed, non-integrated approach may be sufficient, as the surplus of being connected and able to reflect together is enough motivation for users to participate. Case 1 is a model case for this. In contrast, for small co-located groups an approach with a user driving reflection and with good integration into work such as using content from the tool in meetings seems to work, as case 2 shows. This may help to overcome flaws such as lacking time to reflect, little perceived value and others identified in cases 3 and 4.

In a way these results resemble the old-new themes of the disparity between effort invested and benefit gained [12] and added value for the individual [7], but we apply these general principles to constraints of collaborative reflection that need to be in place to make collaborative reflection work. Continuously analyzing, for example, the length of threads in a reflection tool or the overall group's activity to ensure a certain amount of activity in the tool may help to keep reflection going in a tool. However, we regard the results presented here as a start for such analysis, and we will strive to find more of such measures to allow the design of better tools to support collaborative reflection.

Our analysis also shows that results from reflection do not emerge automatically just by giving people tools. While we could see in all cases that if at least one comment was made on a report, reflection on the level of stage 2 was likely to happen. However, reflection on the level of stage 3 did not follow in the same way. Our data suggests that this stage may be reached more likely if the activity in the tool is higher and if the tool fits better to the groups, thus adding value to the setting it is used in (e.g. being used for meetings in co-located settings. Likewise, we saw that a user taking charge of the reflection process by e.g. asking others to provide stage 3 insights can foster such outcomes of collaborative reflection. Looking deeper into these results and the implications drawn from them above as well, applying them to design and orchestration of reflection tools and refining them is necessary to support collaborative reflection sufficiently.

The TalkReflection App as presented here cannot be regarded as a blueprint for collaborative reflection support tools in general, as there neither any such tools to compare it to nor a lot of insights to characterize what such tools need to do besides the support described in this paper. Therefore the results presented above cannot be generalized for all collaborative reflection support, but they can be understood as a basis to draw from for further work and research on collaborative reflection tool support. Furthermore, we expect features of other collaborative reflection support tools to overlap with the features of the TalkReflection App. In this sense, the results presented in this paper show how collaborative reflection can be done and provide insights into this currently not sufficiently researched area that can be used to build on.

6. CONCLUSION AND OUTLOOK

In this paper we have analyzed four cases of using the same reflection support tool at different workplaces. The results of the analysis shed light onto collaborative reflection support, which is an area that had not been sufficiently researched yet. From our work we could identify measures to be used when assessing collaborative

reflection, socio-technical aspects of supporting collaborative reflection and requirements for tools implementing this support. While these results are not final or generalizable, they provide good ground to start from in further research.

Besides the insights on collaborative reflection to take away from our work, we also recognized that there is need for better measures of collaborative reflection activity. We identified some measures that may help to differentiate successful from less successful reflection groups and create intervention for the later ones while learning from the former. However, these provide a rather coarse grained classification of such groups and their tool usage, which should be refined. Our future work will also look into this aspect of research on collaborative reflection. Likewise, there is a need to combine the analysis of reflection in tools better with observations of reflection practice outside tools to gain a better overview of the impact created by a tool. Combining the work presented in this paper with approaches of ethnographic work we pursued earlier on collaborative reflection [26] will thus be one direction for future work.

Our work shows that collaborative reflection support is a field worthwhile working on, as the tool used in our cases created change in terms of opportunities for collaborative reflection in each case. We also saw that there is still work to be done in order to make technology supported collaborative reflection work at workplaces and to tap from the potential that collaborative reflection has for such workplaces.

7. ACKNOWLEDGEMENTS

This work has been supported by projects MIRROR (funded by the European commission in FP7, project number 257617) and EmployID (FP7, project number 619619). We thank all members of the projects for their support and ideas on this work.

8. REFERENCES

1. Baumer, E.P., Khovanskaya, V., Matthews, M., Reynolds, L., Sosik, V.S., and Gay, G.K. Reviewing Reflection: On the Use of Reflection in Interactive System Design. Proceedings of DIS 2014, (2014).

2. Bjørn, P. and Boulus, N. Dissenting in reflective conversations: Critical components of doing action research. Action Research 9, 3 (2011), 282–302.

3. Boud, D. Reflection: Turning experience into learning. Kogan Page, London, 1985.

4. Daudelin, M.W. Learning from experience through reflection. Organizational Dynamics 24, 3 (1996), 36–48.

5. Dennis, A.R., George, J.F., Jessup, L.M., Nunamaker Jr, J.F., and Vogel, D.R. Information technology to support electronic meetings. MIS quarterly 12, 4 (1988), 591–624.

6. Dyke, M. The role of the 'Other' in reflection, knowledge formation and action in a late modernity. International Journal of Lifelong Education 25, 2 (2006), 105–123.

7. Edgington, T., Choi, B., Henson, K., Raghu, T., and Vinze, A. Adopting ontology to facilitate knowledge sharing. Communications of the ACM 47, 11 (2004), 85–90.

8. Fahy, P.J., Crawford, G., and Ally, M. Patterns of interaction in a computer conference transcript. The International Review of Research in Open and Distance Learning 2, 1 (2001).

9. Fleck, R. and Fitzpatrick, G. Reflecting on reflection: framing a design landscape. Proceedings of the 22nd Conference of the Computer-Human Interaction Special Interest Group of

Australia on Computer-Human Interaction, ACM (2010), 216–223.

10. Forneris, S.G. and Peden-McAlpine, C.J. Contextual learning: A reflective learning intervention for nursing education. International journal of nursing education scholarship 3, 1 (2006), 1–17.

11. De Groot, E., Endedijk, M.D., Jaarsma, A.D.C., Simons, P.R.-J., and van Beukelen, P. Critically reflective dialogues in learning communities of professionals. Studies in Continuing Education 0, 0 (2013), 1–23.

12. Grudin, J. Why CSCW Applications fail: Problems in the Design and Evaluation of organizational Interfaces. Proceedings of CSCW 1988, (1988), 85–93.

13. Hoyrup, S. Reflection as a core process in organisational learning. Journal of Workplace Learning 16, 8 (2004), 442–454.

14. Introne, J.E. and Drescher, M. Analyzing the flow of knowledge in computer mediated teams. Proceedings of the 2013 conference on Computer supported cooperative work, ACM (2013), 341–356.

15. Isaacs, E., Konrad, A., Walendowski, A., Lennig, T., Hollis, V., and Whittaker, S. Echoes from the past: how technology mediated reflection improves well-being. Proceedings of the SIGCHI Conference on Human Factors in Computing Systems, ACM (2013), 1071–1080.

16. Lee, S. Design and analysis of reflection-supporting tools in computer-supported collaborative learning. International Journal of Instructional Technology and Distance Learning 2, 3 (2005), 49–56.

17. Levina, N. Collaborating on multiparty information systems development projects: a collective reflection-in-action view. Information Systems Research 16, 2 (2005), 109–130.

18. Lockhorst, D., Admiraal, W., Pilot, A., and Veen, W. Analysis of electronic communication using 5 different perspectives. (2003).

19. Marcu, G., Dey, A.K., and Kiesler, S. Designing for Collaborative Reflection. Proceedings of PervasiveHealth'14, (2014).

20. Mercer, N. and Wegerif, R. Is 'exploratory talk' productive talk? Learning with computers: Analysing productive interaction, (1999), 79.

21. Moon, J.A. Reflection in learning & professional development: theory & practice. Routledge, 1999.

22. Newman, D.R., Webb, B., and Cochrane, C. A content analysis method to measure critical thinking in face-to-face and computer supported group learning. Interpersonal Computing and Technology 3, 2 (1995), 56–77.

23. Porges, Z., Yang, X., Desai, A., et al. Achieve: Evaluating the Impact of Progress Logging and Social Feedback on Goal Achievement. Proceedings of the Companion Publication of the 17th ACM Conference on Computer Supported Cooperative Work & Social Computing, ACM (2014), 221–224.

24. Power, D.J. and Sharda, R. Decision support systems. Springer handbook of automation, Springer (2009), 1539–1548.

25. Prilla, M., Degeling, M., and Herrmann, T. Collaborative Reflection at Work: Supporting Informal Learning at a Healthcare Workplace. Proceedings of the ACM International Conference on Supporting Group Work (GROUP 2012), (2012), 55–64.

26. Prilla, M., Pammer, V., and Krogstie, B. Fostering Collaborative Redesign of Work Practice: Challenges for Tools Supporting Reflection at Work. Proceedings of the European Conference on Computer Supported Cooperative Work (ECSCW 2013), (2013).

27. Prilla, M. User and Group Behavior in Computer Support for Collaborative Reflection in Practice: An Explorative Data Analysis. COOP 2014 - Proceedings of the 11th International Conference on the Design of Cooperative Systems, Springer (2014).

28. Prilla, M. Collaborative Reflection Support at Work: A Socio-Technical Design Task. Proceedings of European Conference on Information Systems (ECIS 2014), (2014).

29. Raelin, J.A. I don't have time to think!" versus the art of reflective practice. Reflections 4, 1 (2002), 66–79.

30. Reynolds, M. Critical reflection and management education: rehabilitating less hierarchical approaches. Journal of Management Education 23, 5 (1999), 537–553.

31. Roschelle, J. and Teasley, S. The construction of shared knowledge in collaborative problem solving. Computer Supported Collaborative Learning, Springer-Verlag (1995), 69–97.

32. Schön, D.A. The reflective practitioner. Basic books New York, 1983.

33. Scott, S.G. Enhancing Reflection Skills Through Learning Portfolios: An Empirical Test. Journal of Management Education 34, 3 (2010), 430–457.

34. Suchman, L.A. Plans and Situated Actions: The Problem of Human-Machine Communication. Cambridge University Press, 1987.

35. Tigelaar, D., Dolmans, D., Meijer, P., de Grave, W., and van der Vleuten, C. Teachers' Interactions and their Collaborative Reflection Processes during Peer Meetings. Advances in Health Sciences Education 13, 3 (2008), 289–308.

36. Weick, K.E. Sensemaking in organizations. Sage Publications, Inc, 1995.

37. Wever, B.D., Schellens, T., Valcke, M., and Keer, H.V. Content analysis schemes to analyze transcripts of online asynchronous discussion groups: A review. Computers & Education 46, 1 (2006), 6 – 28.

38. White, B.Y., Shimoda, T.A., and Frederiksen, J.R. Enabling students to construct theories of collaborative inquiry and reflective learning: Computer support for metacognitive development. International Journal of Artificial Intelligence in Education (IJAIED) 10, (1999), 151–182.

39. Van Woerkom, M. and Croon, M. Operationalising critically reflective work behaviour. Personnel Review 37, 3 (2008), 317–331.

40. Zhu, E. Meaning Negotiation, Knowledge Construction, and Mentoring in a Distance Learning Course. Proceedings of Selected Research and Development Presentations at the 1996 National Coventions of the Association for Education Communications and Technology, (1996).

Work Practices in Coordinating Center Enabled Networks (CCENs)

Betsy Rolland[1,2,3], Drew Paine[2], Charlotte P. Lee[2]
[1]Public Health Sciences Division, Fred Hutchinson Cancer Research Center, Seattle, WA
[2]Department of Human Centered Design & Engineering, University of Washington, Seattle, WA, USA
[3]Bloomberg School of Public Health, Johns Hopkins University, Baltimore, MD USA
{brolland, pained, cplee} @uw.edu

ABSTRACT

Coordinating Centers (CCs) are central bodies tasked with the work of coordination and operations management of a virtual organization whose purpose is to conduct multi-site research projects. We call these organizations Coordinating Center Enabled Networks (CCENs). This qualitative, interview-based study followed two CCs in the field of cancer epidemiology over seven months to answer the question: How does a CC facilitate the work of networked science in a CCEN? In order to answer the question of how CCs facilitate work, we first describe the complex ecology of CCEN work practices. We further discuss how various stakeholders engage in different work practices to facilitate scientific progress. Finally, we use the conceptual lenses of local articulation work and metawork together with the diversity of work practices to better understand what practices CCs actually coordinate.

Categories and Subject Descriptors

H.5.3 [Information Interfaces and Presentation]: Computer-supported cooperative work

General Terms: Human Factors; Design

Author Keywords: Collaboration, team science, articulation work, coordination, coordinating centers

1. INTRODUCTION

Despite recent attention in CSCW to scientific collaboration [1,3,12,20] an important form of scientific collaboration has remained understudied in CSCW: virtual organizations comprised of Coordinating Centers and multiple, associated research sites. In the field of cancer epidemiology, multi-site research projects often employ Coordinating Centers (CCs) as a tool to ease the administrative burdens of multi-site research by offloading it onto a group with substantial experience in the coordination of such projects [17]. A CC is a central body tasked with coordination and operations management of a multi-site research project.

We call the groups that the CC coordinates "Coordinating Center-Enabled Networks" (CCENs). CCENs are research networks comprised of scientists, representatives of funding agencies, and CC staff, all of whom are focused on the overarching goals of the

collaborative project, goals that can be achieved only within a network structure. In this paper we introduce and describe the CCEN as a type of organization, put forward a typology of work practices in a CCEN and then briefly show how those work practices impact the scientific outcomes of their projects. To do so we answer the question: How does a CC facilitate the work of networked science in a CCEN?

While many such virtual organizations exist, the work practices of the CC and the larger CCEN organization have been understudied. We are lacking a comprehensive model about how CCs or the projects of which they are a part function. Related work on "human infrastructure" [14] posits the necessity of multiple collaborative forms (e.g. groups, networks, organizations) operating simultaneously and dynamically coming together or apart in order to support scientific virtual organizations. This research seeks to better understand the human infrastructure of CCENS but to also understand what particular work is undertaken by different elements of the human infrastructure.

In this paper, we report on research that investigated the work of two CCs at the Fred Hutchinson Cancer Research Center as they facilitated the activities of their respective CCENs. In order to understand more thoroughly the full extent of the work of CCs and the groups they coordinate, we examined how groups in a CCEN coordinate different kinds of work practices. By developing a model of the full scope of activities in one type of CCEN, we hope to better understand the types of coordination required to sustain collaborative scientific work.

2. BACKGROUND

In recent years, biomedical research has become increasingly collaborative [10,21]. Development of information and communication technologies (ICTs) has allowed scientists to work together in larger numbers, on increasingly complex problems, over ever-greater distances. Such large collaborative projects bring together scientists from different labs, different disciplines, and different institutions, generally managing to bring all these disparate elements together into a functioning whole. Yet this collaboration comes at a cost. Coordinating large numbers of dispersed researchers working on complex questions such as global warming or early detection of cancer, across geographic and institutional boundaries requires a significant commitment of time and resources [8].

2.1 Virtual Organizations and Scientific Collaboration

Collaborative work takes many forms, including what are commonly called Virtual Organizations (VOs). A 2008 report from an NSF workshop on building effective Virtual Organizations defines VOs as "a group of individuals whose members and resources may be dispersed geographically and

GROUP'14, November 9–12, 2014, Sanibel Island, Florida, USA.
Copyright © 2014 ACM 978-1-4503-3043-5/14/11…$15.00.
http://dx.doi.org/10.1145/2660398.2660408

institutionally, yet who function as a coherent unit through the use of cyberinfrastructure (CI)" [7]. Working within such large, non-centralized organizations brings about many challenges for everyone involved, especially in the areas of coordination and facilitation. The field of CSCW has documented many of these challenges. Lawrence [13] introduces five tensions that offer a lens through which to examine collaboration, allowing us to see how collaborative research requires balancing the views and needs of many stakeholders. She notes that these tensions are not a matter of choosing one way or the other, but of balancing between the two. Ribes and Finholt [16] also address tensions inherent in collaborative research, focusing on the difficulties of sustainability and planning for cyberinfrastructure. The authors conclude by noting that their goal in this paper is to make visible the choices CI projects make on an ongoing basis, not to cast those choices as right or wrong ones. By presenting this framework, Ribes and Finholt seek to foreground the tensions inherent in CI projects that might otherwise go unremarked and unexamined.

Lee et al. [14] have described the "human infrastructure" of a CI project as "the arrangements of organizations and actors that must be brought into alignment in order for work to be accomplished." One of the main contributions of this work was their finding that the overarching organizational structure of the collaboration under study was not at all clear to most of those involved, if to anyone. In fact, most participants had very little understanding of how the collaboration was structured or how the different parts of the project functioned together, focusing instead on their own local work and the parts of the structure in which they were direct participants. Bietz et al. [2] extended the idea of human infrastructure to include what they called "synergizing," which is the "work that developers of infrastructure do to build and maintain productive relationships among people, organizations, and technologies." The authors found several strategies that CI developers use to accomplish synergy in their projects, including leveraging and aligning.

These articles make it clear that collaborative research involves great balancing acts with respect to people, goals and activities, yet they don't make clear who is responsible for balancing the various interests.

2.2 Coordinating Centers

Collaborative research is understandably difficult and can add high overhead to a scientific project, yet scientists are being pushed to do more of it with little extra support. This additional overhead can slow research down, which means wasted money, lost opportunity, and frustration for scientists. A CC is one tool that can help offload some of the administrative burden from investigators. A well-built Coordinating Center can ameliorate some of the overhead and offload some of the burden from researchers by managing the administrative aspects, facilitating collaborative activities, and empowering investigators to focus on the science. Although it is tacitly recognized that a CC affects the success of any multi-site collaborative project, very little study has been done on what makes a CC successful, why some CCs fail, or how to build a CC that meets the needs of a given project. Moreover, very little published guidance is available, as few CCs outside the clinical trial realm write about their work (see, for example, [4,5,9,15]). CC directors are, to this day, largely forced to reinvent the process through trial and error with each new collaboration.

2.3 Articulation Work

One CSCW theory that helps us think about coordination in collaborative work is Articulation Work. Articulation Work (AW) has been defined as "the work of making work go well" [11]. Strauss [19] and Corbin & Strauss [6] have similar definitions of articulation work which focus on the coordination of tasks to keep work flowing. Gerson [11] further refines the notion of AW into *local articulation work* and *metawork*. Gerson's focus is on describing the coordinative work involved in distributed organizations, using the term *reach* to refer to "the distribution of tasks across organizational, spatial, and temporal boundaries" [11]. It is within this context that Gerson defines local articulation work as "making sure all the various resources needed to accomplish something are in place and functioning where and when they're needed *in the local situation*. This means bringing together everything needed to accomplish a task at a particular time and place" [11, emphasis in the original]. Metawork is defined as "making sure that different *kinds* of activity function together well" [11, emphasis in the original].

When this work is all being done within a local organization, Gerson notes, this distinction between local articulation work and metawork is not particularly important. However, when the work is distributed across multiple organizations, it becomes more so, as the work becomes more complex and more reliant on the interrelated nature of different kinds of work. In other words, as the work becomes spread out over multiple organizations, the work of bringing it back together again into a functioning whole is increasingly important. The findings of this study help to illustrate this and offer CSCW an understudied problem space with great potential.

3. RESEARCH SITE AND METHODS

The findings presented below reflect our research on two specific CCENs, known here as the Biomarker Network (BN) and the Screening Network (SN). (The network and participant names are pseudonyms.) The CCs of these two CCENs are housed at the Fred Hutchinson Cancer Research Center (FHCRC) in Seattle, WA, and are run by a group at FHCRC that specializes in the management of multi-site research projects, the Science Facilitation Team (SFT). As such, the two CCs share many staff and Principal Investigators (PIs), making them an ideal case study in which to explore work practices as applied to two CCENs with very different scientific objectives. One of the authors of this paper is an employee of FHCRC but has not worked on either of these projects and did not receive any funding from either of them.

The BN has been in operation for approximately 12 years and has as its overarching scientific objective the discovery and validation of biomarkers for cancer diagnosis and prognosis. Biomarkers are biologic markers that can be detected in the body via biological samples such as blood or urine, and are used to detect cancer, measure its progression or monitor treatment response. The aim of this project is to prove the efficacy and reliability of such markers in order that they may be used in clinical practice.

The SN is a relatively new project, having been funded approximately four months before we began our fieldwork (Fall 2012). The SN seeks to improve cancer screening in the United States by developing a deeper understanding of the process and by searching for ways to personalize screening recommendations for patients, based on their risk profiles. Cancer screening involves routine testing (e.g., a mammogram for breast cancer or colonoscopy for colorectal cancer) to identify cancer before it is symptomatic. While general recommendations exist for how frequently and at what age someone should be screened for a given cancer, the SN hopes to develop more personalized recommendations. For example, a woman who is a heavy smoker and has a family history of breast cancer may need more frequent mammograms than a woman without those known risk factors. Yet how much more frequently and what precisely the benefits are of that increased screening remain unknown. The specific aim of the SN is the creation of a data repository of screening information across the populations at seven different research centers in order to understand the impact of screening on different populations. Three of these research centers are focused on breast cancer, three on colorectal cancer and one on cervical cancer.

These two CCENs were selected for this research because of the overlap of shared PIs and staff discussed above, as well as for their differing ages. We believed these characteristics would make for interesting comparisons between two organizations at different points in their lifecycles but with access to the same organizational knowledge and systems. Furthermore, as an employee of FHCRC, one of the authors of this paper had existing relationships with many of the CC PIs and staff, easing issues of access and trust.

For this qualitative, interview-based study, we interviewed 17 CCEN members, including nine CC staff and PIs, two funding agency representatives, three Biomarker Network PIs and three Screening Network PIs. As part of a larger study, we also conducted 95 hours of observations of meetings of the Science Facilitation Team over the course of seven months, as well as attendance at three of the larger, in-person meetings of the CCENs themselves. Interviews were semi-structured with questions focused on the work of the CCEN and the CC, questions developed based on our literature review and the first several months of meeting observations. Interviews were digitally recorded and transcribed, then coded using qualitative analysis software according to interview questions and themes.

Once transcribed, interviews were closed-coded according to questions in a first pass, then again for the themes identified in our fieldnotes. Based on the relevant literature, our research questions and knowledge of the data, we created an initial set of open codes to apply to our data. After coding the first several fieldnotes, we realized that these initial codes were too broad and were unhelpfully covering large portions of the notes instead of pinpointing areas of interest (e.g., "organizational responsibilities, leadership or tasks aka articulation work"). We refined our codes to be more specific (e.g., "meeting leadership and arrangements") and applied them to our fieldnotes and interviews. On this initial pass, some additional themes emerged and were incorporated into our coding dictionary and applied to all fieldnotes. These themes included certain actions that occurred frequently in the meeting, topics that warranted repeated discussion or interactions we noticed on more than one occasion.

Once all data were coded, conceptual memos were written for most codes, representing the first attempt to take our analysis from descriptive to analytical. Some questions were combined for memos, as the codes were most useful that way. One example of this was the questions about project success, all of which were described in one memo. Throughout the process, our analysis was used to further refine our research questions, keeping the analyses grounded in the data. Our memos allowed us to see connections among the different codes, and the analysis as seen here began to take shape. During this process, we returned to the data several times to review specific interviews or questions to support this analysis.

In this paper, data from participant interviews are noted by the participant's name in parentheses (e.g., (Rebecca)).

4. FINDINGS
In this section, we characterize what we call CCENs, the type of organization being coordinated by the CC, describing its participants and its primary responsibilities. We then put forward a typology of work practices observed in the CCEN, defining each, and describe how these work practices interact.

4.1 Coordinating Center Enabled Networks: A Definition
Coordinating Center Enabled Networks (CCENs) are research networks comprised of investigators from research centers, representatives of a funding agency, and the staff and PIs of a Coordinating Center (CC), all of whom are focused on achieving the overarching scientific goals of a collaborative research project, goals that can only be accomplished within a network structure. Seminara et al. [18] define networks in epidemiology as "*groups of scientists from multiple institutions who cooperate in research efforts involving, but not limited to, the conduct, analysis, and synthesis of information from multiple population studies.*" Such networks can be built and/or funded in a variety of ways [17]; however, in a CCEN, the research centers and the CC are funded as individual components of the network via separate Requests for Application (RFAs, the funding agency document that explains the rules under which researchers may apply to the project). The CC does not have an official pre-existing connection to any of the research centers.

As the name implies, the employment of a CC as a tool to facilitate the network's scientific objectives is a defining characteristic of a CCEN. Per the RFAs, the CC's primary responsibilities revolve around the operational and logistical coordination of the collaborative activities, and the data management and data analysis for collaborative projects. CC staff and PIs are expected to organize all network meetings, guide the collaborative activities to ensure the production of high-quality data, create systems to manage the CCEN data and perform statistical analyses on those data (BN RFA; SN RFA). The CC also plays a role in generally helping the group of diverse sites work together as a network.

The research centers are the grantees charged with performing the scientific work they proposed in their grant applications. The precise nature of the work each research center does varies, from recruiting patients to extracting data from databases, but is all done in service of the CCEN's overarching scientific objectives as defined in the RFA. In addition to their scientific work, the research center PIs are expected to participate in the collaborative activities of the CCEN. These activities include attendance at meetings, contribution to discussions about the scientific direction of the CCEN, active involvement in relevant Working Groups making decisions about scientific implementation, and participation in resource (e.g., biosample or data) sharing in compliance with CCEN policies (BN RFA; SN RFA).

The funding agency representatives in a CCEN, highly respected scientists in their own right, are there to represent the funding agency's interests in the project (Nigel). The aim of this involvement is to ensure that the work proceeds as expected by the original proponents of the project, in hopes of achieving the project's scientific goals. Funding agency representatives answer questions about the funding agency's expectations and policies, in addition to giving input on the scientific direction (Rebecca). Like the research center PIs, the funding agency scientists are expected to attend all meetings and contribute to the discussions about how to achieve the project's scientific goals (SN RFA). They also participate in working groups, as appropriate. They work very closely with the CC to track the progress of the CCEN, generally through participation in frequent conference calls between the funding agency and the CC about the work being accomplished (Tamara).

The combination of these three elements of the CCEN definition – a *scientific objective* being achieved through a *network of scientists* including a *CC as a facilitator* – together set the CCEN form of research apart from other types of research structures and other virtual organizations.

4.2 Establishing Work in a CCEN

Once the funding agency has allocated funds for a consortium to be created, the funding agency representatives write the RFA that dictates the parameters for the scientific work that they want to be done. For the BN, there were several RFAs for the different kinds of grantees; e.g., one RFA for the CC, a separate RFA for the biomarker discovery labs, etc. Likewise, the SN used two different RFAs to form the consortium, including one for the CC and one for the research centers. Applicants were required to apply as a site for research on either breast, colorectal or cervical cancer. The RFA lays out some of the responsibilities of each participant, including who participates in the Steering Committee that sets the scientific direction, as well as requirements for attendance at in-person meetings and participation in consortium projects involving multiple research centers. While some responsibilities are laid out in great detail, other aspects of participation in the consortium are left up to the participants to develop more fully.

After the RFA has been published, potential grantees write proposals in response to the RFA, laying out his/her lab's unique qualifications for completing the research the funding agency has requested in the RFA. In the proposal, the potential grantee details the work s/he will do individually at his/her research center, as well as how the lab will participate in the larger consortium activities.

Once submitted, all proposals are evaluated by peer review and the grants are made, forming the consortium. In the CCEN model, the funding agency has no way of knowing who will apply to the RFA, nor do the potential grantees know who the other participating research centers will be. As such, it is quite possible that research centers will be working with other research center PIs with whom they have no relationship or previous working experience or against whom they have been previously competing for limited research funds. After the consortium has been formed, participants start meeting as a group, either in-person or virtually, and discussing how to work together. Details of governance and operating policies need to be fleshed out, all within the structure laid out by the RFA. For example, the RFA may specify that the Steering Committee sets the scientific direction for the consortium and who sits on the Steering Committee but not the low-level details of how decisions will be made (i.e., by 50% or 2/3 majority vote). The RFA may suggest potential Working Groups but the final configuration, leadership structure and agenda are left to the group to figure out together. It is important to note here that CCENs are a *grant mechanism* (as opposed to a contract), which means that the funding agency cannot tell grantees exactly how to do their work. What this means in practice is that all decisions that affect how the consortium does its work must be made collectively and cannot be imposed from on high.

As the project progresses, all participants work together to decide how the consortium should operate and spend its resources. Participants must balance between achieving the aims they proposed in their original grant proposal and the consortium-level work like participating in working groups and committees, as well as any trans-consortium projects like the SN's screening event database or the BN's team projects. The exact consortium-level work required is dictated by the scientific objectives of the project. For example, in the case of the SN's screening event database, the consortium must decide what data points each research center will submit to the database, as well as what scientific questions the database should be designed to answer.

The Coordinating Center plays a special role in the consortium, as they are generally expected to track all of this work, as well as provide leadership to ensure that the various tasks are aligned and the consortium operates as a whole. The CC is charged with facilitating the work of the consortium, in addition to any scientific aims of their own that they proposed in their grant application. In the case of the Biomarker Network, the CC's biostatistical team works on developing novel statistical methods for the relatively new and complicated field of biomarker discovery and validation. While the RFA may describe specific tasks required of the CC, such as organizing conference calls or meetings, it also may contain responsibilities such as "facilitate other trans-[Screening Network] activities and other collaborative research" [SN RFA]. The details of how to do such work is left to the discretion of the CC PIs and staff. Additionally, as one CC PI noted, any consortium-level work that is not specifically allocated to a participant falls to the CC (Nigel).

4.3 A Typology of Work Practices in a CCEN

The work of a CCEN is varied and complex, ranging from the organization of conference calls and meetings to recruiting patients for clinical studies to running complex molecular experiments. In order to understand how the work of the CCEN is coordinated and facilitated, the overall goal of our research study, we must first understand precisely what that work entails. In this section, we present a typology of work practices of the CCEN that helps us to make sense of this complex organization.

In developing this typology, we began with the categories of CC work presented in Rolland et al. (2011), which documents the work of one specific CC and includes four types of activities: collaboration development; operations management; statistical and data management; and communications infrastructure and tool development. Our review of the literature on CC, primarily reports from individual CCs, produced a list of activities which fit into the Rolland [17] categories. We then noted that the categories of work in each CC's RFA focused on two main areas of responsibilities: facilitating network activities and work that involved data (i.e., data management, statistical analyses). Returning to our data and the types of work participants described doing, as well as the types of work we observed them doing, we developed the typology described below. We chose to fold the Rolland [17] category of "communications infrastructure and tool development" into the category of Operational Work Practices because the staff involved in both were frequently the same. Though the RFAs don't mention "collaboration work" as a responsibility of the CC, participants mentioned the work they did to negotiate the activities of the consortium frequently enough that we felt it necessitated its own category, agreeing with Rolland [17].

In their quest to achieve the CCEN's scientific goals, CCEN participants engaged in many types of work, which we subsequently classified in to five types of work practices. We observed such work practices in both the BN and SN projects through our field observations and interviews. All CCEN participants – research centers, CC, and the funding agency – may engage in work in each of these types of work practices at some time during the project, either independently or with others. The one exception to this is the lack of observed local scientific work by the funding agency representatives.

4.3.1 Structural Work Practices

Structural work practices are those activities that shape the rules of the project and dictate the organizational structure the CCEN will take, once funded and instantiated. Most of the structural work is done by the funding agency in the development of the RFA, which specifies the scientific objectives of the project, the governance structure (i.e., required committees and how the scientific direction will be set), and what the overall responsibilities of the grantees will be. While this work is predominantly in the realm of the funder, other CCEN members may need to participate in structural work if changes take place during the funding cycle.

While the majority of the structural tasks are completed before the collaboration is even formally inaugurated, sometimes changes made by the funding agency in mid-cycle require the CCEN participants to engage in structural work, such as when funding is changed (e.g., funding cuts) or scientific objectives must be modified due to new advances in knowledge. In this case, negotiations between the grantee and the funding agency may need to take place in order to determine how to adjust the grantee's deliverables. Furthermore, if a project is successfully refunded in subsequent funding cycles, the existing grantees may be asked for input on how the project should be structured in the next grant period.

Because most of this work is performed by the funding agency and does not include interaction with other CCEN entities, the majority of the structural work of the CCEN is outside the scope of this study.

4.3.2 Collaboration Work Practices (CWPs)

Collaboration Work Practices (CWPs) are the work of negotiating and deciding how to work together as a network, as well as the work of participating in those negotiations and decisions, all within the organizational structure set up by the structural work practices discussed above. A CCEN brings together researchers with differing experiences, skillsets and motivations and must work together to create a path toward achieving the project's scientific objectives. The CWPs include allocating resources when there are competing priorities, participating in committees that set the scientific direction or make decisions about how projects will get done, as well as communicating project priorities and attending meetings and conference calls. As members of the network, everyone involved in the CCEN has responsibility for some type of CWPs. These CWPs can take up a substantial amount of collaborators' time, especially if CCEN members have differing ideas of how the network should proceed toward its scientific goals.

What is not included in this category is the work of deciding specific scientific or data questions, such as creating study protocols or developing a list of requested data points, categorized as data work because it impacts the form and quality of the data. Also not included is the administrative work of scheduling committee meetings or organizing the in-person meetings, categorized as operational work. This is a fine line to draw, but is

important to make this distinction because the CWPs require different skills, different participants and different time commitments than those needed for the operational and data work practices. By separating them out, we are able to get a fuller picture of precisely how the CCEN functions.

4.3.3 Operational Work Practices (OWPs)

The Operational Work Practices (OWPs) are the administrative and technological tasks done in support of the other types of work. Their aim is to help the group's diverse and varying tasks function together as a whole, as in when the CC organizes conference calls so the group can get together and discuss how to collect data for a study or building a database that will receive appropriate data from the research centers and be used by the CC's statisticians in their statistical analyses. These activities are primarily logistical or technical in nature and, in general, require little scientific knowledge to complete them. This is not to say that those engaged in these practices have or use no scientific knowledge while performing OWPs, but, rather, that scientific knowledge is not generally required to complete these activities. Additional OWPs include such logistical tasks as organizing meetings, taking minutes, emailing collaborators for information and managing project tasks. Also included in this category are technical tasks such as building the project databases, and building and maintaining the project website. However, the design of the project database is considered a data work practice, as it requires a deep understanding of the project's data and the application of extensive relevant scientific knowledge.

4.3.4 Data Work Practices (DWPs)

The consortium's data work involves interactions around data between the CC and two or more research sites and is generally led by the CC. Data Work Practices (DWPs) are those activities whose focus is the production (i.e., the research centers generating data via lab work or extracting data from local databases) and consumption (i.e., the receipt of data for statistical analyses) of high-quality data according to protocols agreed upon by consortium participants. This data work begins with the group's efforts to agree upon protocols and common sets of data to collect, and extends through the receipt of the data and performance of statistical analyses for these collaborative, multi-site projects. Included here are such tasks as developing project protocols and study design for a consortial clinical validation study, statistical analysis, and designing scientific databases to hold data from multiple sites. Also included here are any activities done by the research centers to generate data in compliance with the agreed upon protocols, such as recruiting the correct patients or extracting agreed-upon datasets from local databases for use in collaborative projects. Not included here are the back-and-forth communications involved in managing the development of protocol and data set agreements, such as requests for comments or reminders to review the protocol, which are OWPs. Work that involves data of only one site and does not require coordination from the CC falls into the category of Local Scientific Work, described below.

4.3.5 Local Scientific Work Practices (LSWPs)

Each grantee, including the CC and the individual research centers, is a part of the consortium because the grant proposal they submitted in response to the RFA was selected by the funding agency for funding. Once the funding has been given, the grantees have committed to doing the work they proposed in their application. While this work is a part of the consortium as a whole, it is done independently of other consortium members, generally without assistance or input from the CC or the funding agency. We have named this category "local scientific work" to make clear that it is the work being done at local research centers that doesn't involve the rest of the consortium.

The aim of Local Scientific Work Practices (LSWPs) is to achieve the individual scientific objectives that a participant proposed in his or her grant application. Again, the LSWPs are scientific activities that happen in the CCEN that do not require interaction with other CCEN entities and are not guided by the collaborative protocols developed by the CCEN members. In other words, these activities are done independently by a research center or the CC; no LSWPs were observed among, or attributed to, the funding agency. As the name implies, these work practices utilize participants' extensive scientific expertise. Examples of such activities are the CC's development of novel statistical methods for biomarker science that they may later use in analyzing data from the research centers for collaborative projects, as well as assays research centers might run to discover promising new biomarkers for later consortium use. While we are aware of the existence of LSWPs performed at the research centers due to discussion of these practices in the meetings we observed and in our interviews, we did not collect extensive data on them due to our focus on the role of the CC. Thus, they are outside the scope of this study.

4.4 Coordinating Center as Facilitator

Given the complexity of the CCEN, including a diverse set of work practices, dozens of stakeholders and the uncertainty of scientific work itself, how does the CCEN manage to bring all these elements into alignment sufficiently to accomplish the group's scientific objectives? It is at this intersection of the work practices and competing interests that we see the benefits of the facilitation work done by the CC. Interviews with Biomarker Network members painted a picture of a CC whose work deeply influenced the consortium's ability to make scientific progress (e.g., Thomas). Interviews with members of the Screening Network, on the other hand, described frustration and disappointing scientific progress (e.g., Beatrice).

Again, what is particularly interesting about these two CCENs is that the Coordinating Centers are both run by the Science Facilitation Team at the Fred Hutchinson Cancer Research Center, sharing PIs, staff, systems and institutional knowledge. It would seem that applying the knowledge and systems for use in a new consortium would be straightforward. And yet, as we will see below, it was anything but.

4.4.1 Facilitating a Network

The CC had been facilitating the Biomarker Network for more than 12 years when we began our study. In interviews, research center PIs and funding agency representatives raved about the impact the CC had on the consortium's scientific progress, lamenting only that the CC's resources didn't allow them to facilitate a greater number of consortium-wide activities. In fact, Thomas, the funding agency representative, noted that the individual research center PIs frequently asked the CC for help in their local projects (Thomas).

The Screening Network was just getting started as we began our observations. As we observed biweekly funding agency-CC conference calls, attended two in-person, all-hands meetings and interviewed SN participants, it became clear that the SN was struggling to establish a scientific path. Discussions at meetings were often emotional and often didn't progress beyond

disagreements over administrative and organizational concerns. For example, instead of discussing what data elements to collect from each research center, the SN members were spending substantial amounts of time discussing how to make those decisions. Instead of discussing how the consortium could take greatest advantage of the combined dataset being compiled, research center PIs questioned which data they were absolutely required to send.

We wondered if, as some interview participants suggested, this difference in scientific progress was simply attributable to the differing ages of the two networks. However, our data suggest that this is not the case. In fact, a review of the BN annual progress reports from the first several years of the network support participants' contention that the BN made substantial progress right from the beginning (BN progress reports years 1-3). Furthermore, the conversations that the SN participants were having revolved around questions of how to work together within the structure set by the RFA and what overall scientific questions to address. Digging more deeply into the differences between the two projects, we began to notice a pattern of the SN spending a great deal of their time on collaboration work, more than we observed in the BN

4.4.2 The Impact of Structural Work on Facilitation

We attribute the differences in consortial scientific progress to the challenges the SN CC faced in facilitating the new consortium, which stemmed from the SN's relatively underdeveloped structure. This underdeveloped structure left participants unsure of the boundaries of their own work, forcing them to spend precious time clarifying those boundaries. To clarify this point, this section presents examples of how the more developed structure of the BN benefitted that group's scientific progress, followed by discussion of how the SN's less developed structure hurt that consortium.

The BN has designed an assertive evaluation process built into the yearly funding agency grantee evaluations. The goal of the evaluations is to assess how well the grantee has collaborated over the year according to agreed upon metrics. Each year, grantees must fill out an evaluation form on which they list their collaborative activities over the year, including how many meetings they attended, the number of biosamples they shared, and how many team projects they joined (Thomas, James). The result of this evaluation process is to enforce expectations of collaboration and to make the rules of engagement explicit for CCEN members.

In addition, the funding structure of the Biomarker Network developed by the funding agency representatives requires collaboration, as a portion of each research center's funds can only be spent on collaborative projects among research centers. The BN also sets aside funds from the overall BN funding pool to support larger collaborative projects. When discussing how he and his colleagues structured the BN, Thomas noted:

> From day one I wanted to emphasize, and in some cases I was very blunt to tell investigators that this is not an R01 [individual investigator grant]. Here is the need to work together. If you feel that you cannot work with others and share your findings with others towards the goal of validating biomarkers, then it's not your place to be here... I emphasized the word collaboration, collaboration, collaboration. And then I went and said that we have built the funding mechanisms within [BN] such that it not only supports collaboration but also rewards collaboration as well... Each [BN] investigator has their own grant, but almost 30% of their grant is restricted and

that restriction is lifted only when they propose a collaborative study with other members of [BN] or [with non-BN groups]… Then there is a reward system. Their reward system is that [BN] has set aside funds that are … for the use for rewarding large validation and collaborative studies" (Thomas).

The structural work in the BN set the expectation for not only the data and local scientific work but also the collaborative work that must take place in the project. By creating a structure in which collaboration is encouraged and supported, even required, by both the evaluation and funding mechanisms, the BN funding agency representatives have given shape to their idea of what the BN should look like.

In addition to the sheer amount of time spent working together, participant James, a research center PI, attributed the BN's ease of collaboration to the funding agency program staff's consistent message of the requirement to collaborate in the BN, as discussed above. He noted that only those who chose to collaborate as a way of doing science would be successful in this group.

> When we go into our [BN] meetings, everybody lifts up or opens up their books and shows everybody everything, because the ethos of the group is that if one member of the group benefits, everybody benefits. We are judged not as much by our individual institution's accomplishments. We are judged more by the group's accomplishments. So, because that ethos was instilled at the very beginning, what has happened was that program staff has really selected the membership of the [BN] based on the collaboration. The more collaborative you were, the more likely that you would be funded (James).

The structure put into place by Thomas and his funding agency colleagues has resulted in a culture of collaboration, a culture that is maintained and developed by the research center PIs themselves. As James noted in the quote above, this collaboration work also has an impact on the data and scientific work of the BN, in that "everybody lifts up or opens up their books and shows everybody everything" (James). This increased sharing changes how the science will proceed, as it changes the data and information that are available for consideration.

In summary, the BN's clarity of division of labor in the RFA, the funding mechanism and the evaluation criteria created a culture that focused on collaboration. This led to open sharing of samples and data, which resulted in more time spent on the science and greater scientific progress. This, in turn, fed back into the culture of collaboration.

In contrast, in the Screening Network the combination of a lack of clarity regarding the role of the CC in the RFA and lack of evaluation criteria led to misunderstandings among the CC, funding agency and research centers. This, in turn, led to difficulties in sharing data and resources, the outcome of which was less time being spent on the science and disappointing scientific progress.

The SN struggled with the negotiation of roles and responsibilities, especially the division of labor between the funding agency representatives and the CC. Before the CC received their funds, but after they had received word they had been selected as the CC, the funding agency branch chief responsible for the SN visited the CC at FHCRC and emphasized how important it was that they take a leadership role in "governing" the SN (Adam). Early on in Screening Network, as it became clear that the vision of the CC and funding agency representatives were not in sync, Rebecca (an funding agency

representative) asked the CC to write a list of their roles and responsibilities for their work in the SN. Tamara, a CC staff member, described how Charlie, a CC PI, used the word "leadership" in several areas of their responsibilities description. They were promptly, and in no uncertain terms, told by Rebecca to remove that word from the entire document.

> Pretty close to the beginning, we were asked by [funding agency] to create a list of roles and responsibilities for our self, [funding agency], the steering committee, and then the research centers. And so [Charlie] wrote those up and he used the term leadership in a lot of what [CC] was responsible for. You know, be a leader in the organ groups, be a leader in getting the data, and [the funding agency representatives] really balked at that. And they thought that we were overstepping our bounds in that the term 'leadership' was a poor choice of words, in their opinion.

> And I think all along we felt that we were to be the leadership of data analysis and coordinating the data, but I think [funding agency] felt that we should actually be more of a team player… You know, yes, we were the team player but we were also the folks that were responsible for the bigger picture and for, again, kind of pushing the others forward. So at first [funding agency] didn't see us in the leadership role; they felt it should be more of a collaboration. So we then started operating more as a collaborative part and [funding agency] actually came back and said you know what, you should be doing being the leadership and taking more of a lead in the steering committee, taking more of a lead in the working groups and the [research centers]. And we said well, you know, look, that's what we had intended and then you said no. And they said oh, well, I think maybe that was a mistake (Tamara).

This conflict over responsibilities between the funding agency representatives and CC had the unintended consequence of sparking a conflict between the CC and the research centers over their respective roles. When the CC was told to back off and let the research centers come forward to take more of a leadership role in selecting the data for inclusion in the SN screening event database, this change placed greater demands on the time of the research centers, who had not planned for this work. As the research center PIs were forced to spend more time on working groups and deciding on CDEs, they have had less time to spend on their individual-level projects. Combined with funding cuts in year 1 of the project, the extra demands left the research center PIs frustrated (Beatrice).

Each collaborator has only so much time that can be spent on participation in the SN. When that time is spent negotiating how best to work together, those negotiations take time and energy away from the time available to spend making scientific progress. In a new collaboration, some negotiation may be necessary or desirable, but the levels of frustration expressed by interviewees from the Coordinating Center, the research centers and the funding agency (Charlie, Adam, Tamara, Rebecca, Beatrice) indicate that the energy put into these negotiations left the participants unsatisfied with the distribution of responsibility. Had the CC been allowed to lead the data work, as it did in the BN, it is quite possible that the work would have proceeded more smoothly and these conflicts over responsibility would not have occurred.

5. DISCUSSION

The central question that has guided this research is: How does the Coordinating Center facilitate the work of networked science in a CCEN? We find the answer to this question in the CC's application of their experience and expertise to the challenges of collaborative research. The CC plays a distinct role in the CCEN, facilitating the work of the project, with the aim of making the work of the CCEN go more smoothly and generating high-quality data. This facilitation involves the application of the CC's collective and individual knowledge and experience, amassed over years of managing and supporting collaborative, multi-institutional research projects.

In service of this goal, the CC has developed systems and processes to address the challenges of networked science. When the CC is allowed to play this distinct role as a facilitator, as in the Biomarker Network, the network-level work of the CCEN moves toward the achievement of its scientific goals with little resistance. However, when the role of the CC is limited, as in the Screening Network, weaknesses and conflicts in one area of work spill over into other areas and the CC is not in a position to counteract these negative forces. As has been shown in this paper, when the BN CC was allowed to facilitate research by applying its extensive experience and expertise to the challenges of collaborative research, consortium PIs were able to spend more time on their science and make greater progress toward the achievement of the group's scientific objectives.

The five types of work practices of a CCEN described in this paper are varied and complex, but they are also intertwined in ways that are not always easy to predict or even to see without digging deeply into the work lives of CCEN participants. Understanding how a CCEN accomplishes scientific work requires that we take all the different types of work being done across the spectrum of CCEN activities into account. The lenses of local articulation work and metawork can help us to better understand the ecology of practices undertaken by the different Funding Agency, Research Centers, and Coordinating Center stakeholders.

As discussed earlier, Gerson defines local articulation work as "making sure all the various resources needed to accomplish something are in place and functioning where and when they're needed *in the local situation*. This means bringing together everything needed to accomplish a task at a particular time and place" [11]. Metawork is defined as "making sure that different *kinds* of activity function together well" [11]. In the examples above the funding agency, research centers, and CC are all engaging in local articulation work in regards to the five different work practices, with the notable exception that the funding agency does not involve itself with LSWP (local scientific work practices).

Local articulation work, in other words does not "belong" to any particular type of actor in the CCEN, nor does it "belong" to any particular kind of work practice. Rather, in a virtual organization such as a CCEN that requires constant coordination to achieve its scientific aims, local articulation work is ubiquitous. Everyone must do the work of making the work go well in these CCENs, otherwise the CCEN will not accomplish its goals.

For example, each of the many research centers engages in all or almost all of the following kinds of local articulation work:

- Structural Work Practices by contributing text and ideas to a grant proposal

- Collaboration Work Practices by attending meetings

- Operational Work Practices by sending human subjects research approval information to the CC

- Data Work Practices by entering data, researching to answer information requests from the CC about data, running previously-agreed upon assays and experiments on behalf of the CCEN

Work undertaken at a research center for a CCEN is simultaneously the "work at hand" *and* local articulation work for the CCEN. For example, a research center may look for novel biomarkers and this is at once local work for the research center but also local articulation work in service of the larger CCEN, which wants to identify which assays and experiments to run. When looking at a research center's LSWP and DWP, the work at hand and local articulation work are hardly distinguishable.

A funding agency may engage in local articulation work in the following ways:

- SWPs by writing the RFA, deciding and executing budget changes (e.g., cuts), choosing scientific objectives

- CWPs by deciding how to interpret RFA in practice (with CC), evaluating grantee progress,

- OWPs by creating agendas for meetings, scheduling site visits

- DWPs by representing interest of funding agency in protocol development, reviewing analysis results

Likewise, in the case of funding agencies, we see that the work at hand and local articulation work are interwoven. The special role of the funding agency as the funder of the CCEN gives it a measure of top-down control and responsibility that the other stakeholders do not have. The policy and scientific objective focus of the funding agency dovetail with a focus on articulation work, which is primarily about bringing together resources at a particular time and place. In fact, this is exactly the business of a funding agency when bringing together a CCEN. At the same time, we see funding agency representatives engaging in metawork, also, especially in the areas of SWP and CWPs.

Finally, a Coordinating Center may engage in local articulation work in the following way:

- SWPs by negotiating revisions to scientific objectives in case of unexpected funding changes, suggesting changes to RFAs for new funding cycles

- CWPs by deciding how to interpret the RFA in practice (with funding agency), negotiating questions of roles and responsibilities, prioritizing projects in view of limited resources

- OWPs by organizing meetings and conference calls, programming data entry systems, coordinating protocol development, managing human subjects approvals

- DWPs by distilling scientific questions to data points for collection, statistical analyses, protocol development and study design, Database design

For the CC, the work at hand is almost indistinguishable from local articulation work, and in some instances also from metawork. It is precisely this lack of distinction that simultaneously makes the role of the CC so critical to the project's progress and so challenging to do well. In our Screening Network and Biomarker Network examples above, we see some differences in terms of how the two stakeholder types (funding agency and research centers) view and interact with the CC. Some view the CC as a body that is to focus mainly on a certain type of local articulation work—the local articulation work of OWPs (organizing meetings), whereas others very much see the CC as also playing an active role in both CWPs (negotiating roles and responsibilities and prioritizing projects) and DWPs (distilling scientific questions).

In the case of the BN, we see both the funding agency taking up more intensively and directly the metawork of the CCEN and then delegating some of that metawork to the CC. While this paper studies only two cases, certainly we can see that a CC that was empowered by the funding agency to make metawork part of the CC's work at hand had a positive effect on the collaboration.

This investigation of two virtual organizations we call CCENs, reveals a very complex relationship between the actors involved and the different types of work practices. The highly interconnected way that work is necessarily done for this type of collaborative science ensures that research centers (who also have many other projects and collaborations outside these particular CCENs) must always have their eye on how their work fits in to the larger effort when they are engaged in Biomarker Network or Screening Network work. The separation between the work at hand and local articulation work breaks down.

Due to a lack of research on coordinating centers, what little is known is simply folk knowledge or personal experience reports. Consequently, research center, funding agency, and even CC stakeholders must rely heavily on what they know of previous CCs and what they think coordination in a CCEN means. For some "coordination" means setting up and organizing meetings—a narrow view that we attempt to counter with this research and a more nuanced discussion of all the different types of actors and different types of work practices that must be coordinated. Furthermore, with this discussion of different kinds of coordination, local articulation work and metawork across different stakeholders and work practices, we hope to open a larger discussion of what it means, from a scholarly perspective, to study coordination in a complex virtual organization like a CCEN. Other than works by these authors, few papers have been published on CCs over the past 30 years (see, for example [4,5,9,15]). Much more work is yet to be done.

This dearth of research has very real practical implications for CCENs. Currently, CCs and funding agencies make decisions on how to structure a consortium based primarily on previous experience and disciplinary norms. Our research provides a framework and a vocabulary for scientists and program officers to use when talking about issues of coordination. This is especially true in the area of understanding the work practices but also applies to the frequently invisible metawork and local articulation work that goes into facilitating collaborative science. Such work often falls in the gray areas between defined tasks but must be accounted for in a CCEN.

6. CONCLUSION

The participants in our study are working toward urgent goals of curing or preventing cancers, yet many of them were surprised to discover that there was a "science of design" for collaborative work and that it could be possible for someone to help them with their collaboration and coordination difficulties, problems many of them perceived as unsolvable. The field of CSCW, with its expertise on the theory and practice of collaboration and the design of sociotechnical systems to support collaboration, is well positioned to play an important role in helping networked science, especially in the area of coordinative work and the development of tools such as coordinating centers to support it.

Coordinating Centers have the potential to alleviate many of the difficulties of collaborative team science by transferring the administrative burden of collaboration from the PIs to a group of individuals with experience facilitating collaborative research. Exploring how a CC can facilitate work in a CCEN and other ways that can improve how CC, funding agency, and research centers work together have important implications for both science policy and for the creation of science infrastructure. In this study, we found that Coordinating Centers who were given the latitude to apply their expertise and experience to the CCEN were able to facilitate its work more smoothly. It is imperative that we conduct further research to determine if this holds true across more CCENs, and if so, what sorts of expertise and experience were applied to these different work practices. Building upon our current research, and the potential future work of this community, there should be important policy implications for the design of RFAs and the role that Coordinating Centers can play in emergent and evolving networked science.

In addition, CCENs are promising sites for further exploration in CSCW. The inclusion of a CC in the CCEN means that much of the coordination work that is often hidden in collaboration becomes both centralized and explicit. Furthermore, these virtual organizations offer CSCW researchers an opportunity to further develop existing notions of articulation work and metawork due to their complex organizational structure and the many work practices within. Continued theoretical development in this area may then be useful for understanding the patterns of collaboration in other types of knowledge producing organizations. This is critical as more and more work is undertaken by virtual organizations and we as CSCW scholars seek better ways of understanding how coordination is enacted and constrained.

As science tackles the most pressing questions of our time, such as improving global health and developing energy independence, interdisciplinary team science will continue to increase as the method of choice. CSCW research on interdisciplinary team science can and should play an instrumental role in improving collaborative, team science and the sociotechnical systems that support it.

7. ACKNOWLEDGMENTS

We would like to thank our participants for their generosity with their time and expertise and our anonymous reviewers for their thoughtful feedback. This work was supported by the National Cancer Institute at the National Institutes of Health (grant number R03CA150036) and by the Fred Hutchinson Cancer Research Center.

8. REFERENCES

[1] Aragon, C. R., Poon, S. S., Aldering, G. S., Thomas, R. C., & Quimby, R. Using Visual Analytics to Develop Situation Awareness in Astrophysics. Information Visualization, 8, 1 (2009), 30-41. DOI= http://dx.doi.org/10.1057/ivs.2008.30.

[2] Bietz, M. J., Baumer, E. P. S., & Lee, C. P. Synergizing in Cyberinfrastructure Development. Computer Supported Cooperative Work (CSCW), 19, 3-4 (2010), 245-281. DOI= http://dx.doi.org/10.1007/s10606-010-9114-y.

[3] Bietz, M. J., & Lee, C. P. Collaboration in metagenomics: Sequence databases and the organization of scientific work. ECSCW 2009 (2009), 243-262.

[4] Blumenstein, B. A., James, K. E., Lind, B. K., & Mitchell, H. E. Functions and organization of coordinating centers for

multicenter studies. Controlled Clinical Trials, 16, 2, Supplement (1995), 4-29. DOI= http://dx.doi.org/http://dx.doi.org/10.1016/0197-2456(95)00092-U.

[5] Collins, J. F., Martin, S., Kent, E., Liuni, C., Garg, R., et al. The use of regional coordinating centers in large clinical trials: the DIG trial. Controlled Clinical Trials, 24, 6, Supplement (2003), S298-S305. DOI= http://dx.doi.org/http://dx.doi.org/10.1016/S0197-2456(03)00101-6.

[6] Corbin, J. M., & Strauss, A. L. The Articulation of Work through Interaction. The Sociological Quarterly, 34, 1 (1993), 71-83.

[7] Cummings, J., Finholt, T., Foster, I., Kesselman, C., & Lawrence, K. A. (2008). Beyond being there: A blueprint for advancing the design, development, and evaluation of virtual organizations.

[8] Cummings, J. N., & Kiesler, S. Coordination costs and project outcomes in multi-university collaborations. Research Policy, 36 (2007), 1620-1634. DOI= http://dx.doi.org/10.1016/j.respol.2007.09.001.

[9] Curb, J. D., Ford, C., Hawkins, C. M., Smith, E. O. B., Zimbaldi, N., et al. A coordinating center in a clinical trial: The hypertension detection and followup program. Controlled Clinical Trials, 4, 1–2 (1983), 171-186. DOI= http://dx.doi.org/http://dx.doi.org/10.1016/S0197-2456(83)80023-3.

[10] Falk-Krzesinski, H. J., Contractor, N., Fiore, S. M., Hall, K. L., Kane, C., et al. Mapping a research agenda for the science of team science. Research Evaluation, 20, 2 (2011), 145-158. DOI= http://dx.doi.org/10.3152/095820211X12941371876580.

[11] Gerson, E. M. Reach, Bracket, and the Limits of Rationalized Coordination: Some Challenges for CSCW Resources, Co-Evolution and Artifacts. M. S. Ackerman & C. A. Halverson & T. Erickson & W. A. Kellogg, Eds. Springer London, 2008, 193-220. DOI= http://dx.doi.org/10.1007/978-1-84628-901-9_8.

[12] Howison, J., & Herbsleb, J. D. (2013). Incentives and integration in scientific software production, Proceedings of the 2013 conference on Computer supported cooperative work (pp. 459-470). San Antonio, Texas, USA: ACM.

[13] Lawrence, K. A. Walking the Tightrope: The Balancing Acts of a Large e-Research Project. Computer Supported Cooperative Work (CSCW), 15 (2006), 385-411. DOI= http://dx.doi.org/10.1007/s10606-006-9025-0.

[14] Lee, C. P., Dourish, P., & Mark, G. The Human Infrastructure of Cyberinfrastructure. In Proc. CSCW, ACM (2006), 483-492.

[15] Meinert, C. L., Heinz, E. C., & Forman, S. A. Role and methods of the coordinating center. Controlled Clinical Trials, 4, 4 (1983), 355-375. DOI= http://dx.doi.org/http://dx.doi.org/10.1016/0197-2456(83)90022-3.

[16] Ribes, D., & Finholt, T. Tensions across the scales: Planning infrastructure for the long term. In Proc. International ACM Conference on Supporting Group Work, ACM (2007), 229-238.

[17] Rolland, B., Smith, B. R., & Potter, J. D. Coordinating Centers in Cancer Epidemiology Research: the Asia Cohort Consortium Coordinating Center. Cancer Epidemiology Biomarkers & Prevention, 20, 10 (2011), 2115-2119. DOI= http://dx.doi.org/10.1158/1055-9965.epi-11-0391.

[18] Seminara, D., Khoury, M. J., O'Brien, T. R., Manolio, T., Gwinn, M. L., et al. The Emergence of Networks in Human Genome Epidemiology: "Challenges and Opportunities". Epidemiology, 18, 1 (2007), 1-8. DOI= http://dx.doi.org/10.2307/20486309.

[19] Strauss, A. The articulation of project work: An organizational process. The Sociological Quarterly, 29, 2 (1988), 163-178.

[20] Vertesi, J., & Dourish, P. (2011). The value of data: considering the context of production in data economies, Proceedings of the ACM 2011 conference on Computer supported cooperative work (pp. 533-542). Hangzhou, China: ACM.

[21] Wuchty, S., Jones, B. F., & Uzzi, B. The Increasing Dominance of Teams in Production of Knowledge. Science, 316, 5827 (2007), 1036-1039. DOI= http://dx.doi.org/10.2307/20036287.

Informing Digital Cognitive Aids Design for Emergency Medical Work by Understanding Paper Checklist Use

Zhan Zhang[1], Aleksandra Sarcevic[1], Maria Yala[1], Randall S. Burd[2]

[1]College of Computing and Informatics, Drexel University
3141 Chestnut Street
Philadelphia, PA 19104
{zhan.zhang, aleksarc, may36}@drexel.edu

[2]Children's National Medical Center
111 Michigan Ave NW
Washington, DC 20010
rburd@childrensnational.org

ABSTRACT

We examine the use of a paper-based checklist during 48 simulated trauma resuscitations to inform the design of digital cognitive aids for safety-critical medical teamwork. Our analysis focused on team communication and interaction behaviors as physician leaders led resuscitations and administered the checklist. We found that the checklist increased the amount of communication between the leader and the team, but did not compromise the leader's interactions with the environment. In addition, we observed several changes in team dynamics: the checklist facilitated collaborative decision making and process reflections, but it also made some team members reactive rather than proactive. As the push toward digitizing medical work continues, we expect that paper checklists will soon be replaced by their digital counterparts. Designing interactive cognitive aids for medical domains, however, poses many challenges. Our results offer directions for how these tools could be designed to support medical work in increasingly digital environments.

Categories and Subject Descriptors

H5.m. Information interfaces and presentation (e.g., HCI): Miscellaneous.

Keywords

Medical checklist; Digital cognitive aids; Communication; Team dynamics; Leadership; Emergency medicine.

1. INTRODUCTION

Medical checklists are considered valuable tools in preventing and managing errors, reducing risks, and improving patient outcomes [12]. They have become increasingly common in healthcare and are now used across different medical settings, including anesthesia [13], operating rooms (OR) [16], and intensive care units (ICU) [18]. Most medical checklists, however, are paper-based, requiring care providers to manually record the presence or absence of the checklist items. Given the intrinsic qualities of paper and values it brings to the clinical environment—as shown by seminal work in HCI and CSCW [1],[9],[14]—this persistence

of paper-based aids is not surprising. Even so, current approaches for recording clinical information are time-consuming and yield data of variable accuracy [6]. Developing more accurate medical records and more effective documentation methods are essential aspects of modernizing and improving our healthcare system.

The information captured in medical records is important for clinical decision making, care coordination, and as a source of research data, yet these functions are limited by current systems that use handwritten records or rely on manual entry into electronic health records (EHRs). Attempts to digitize paper records in trauma resuscitation began two decades ago [11] and have only recently been implemented at a few trauma centers, including Nationwide Children's Hospital [24] and the Hospital of the University of Pennsylvania [personal communication]. We believe this trend toward digitization of emergency medical care will continue, offering a range of benefits: better integration with EHRs used in other hospital units, improved data collection for quality improvement, real-time feedback on activities (e.g., alerts for skipped tasks), improved efficiency, and data display for entire teams rather than just for those who document patient encounters. Likewise, with the digitization of medical work proceeding fast, paper checklists may soon be replaced by interactive digital tools. In fact, efforts to design and develop digital checklists during crisis situations are already underway [22],[23]. Emergency medical domains, however, pose many challenges to designing interactive cognitive aids. Checklist design principles taken from the aviation industry have worked well for static, paper-based checklists [10], but may not be applicable to designing digital checklists for the dynamic and, often more chaotic, medical work. Moreover, checklist evaluation studies have mostly focused on assessing compliance and correct completion rates, with little data published on how checklist administration affects communication and interaction among members of a medical team [12],[16].

In this paper, we examine the effects of a paper-based checklist introduced to prepare for patient arrival and for use throughout patient evaluation in a trauma center of a major urban, pediatric teaching hospital. We began our inquiry by asking: How does checklist administration affect the functions of the checklist administrator—physician leader? How does it affect the leader's communication and interaction with the team? How does it affect team dynamics? Our results show how the checklist increased the amount of communication between the leader and the team, while also facilitating process reflections and joint decision making. We also show how the affordances of the checklist supported various leadership functions, led to good communication redundancy, and reinforced on-the-job training for less experienced team members. The study suggests that the practices that emerged as a result of the checklist use are important to sustain and should be considered in the design of interactive cognitive aids.

Pre-arrival Plan

Check or prepare:
- ☐ Oxygen
- ☐ Suction
- ☐ Bag and mask
- ☐ Intubation tray
- ☐ Intubation medications
- ☐ Defibrillator
- ☐ CPR board

☐ Consider ordering blood

Assign team roles:
- ☐ Airway
- ☐ IV/IO access
- ☐ Primary survey
- ☐ Team leadership

☐ Brief team on incoming patient

☐ Estimate weight: _____ kg

Primary Survey

A
- ☐ Confirm C-spine is immobilized
- ☐ Confirm airway is protected

B
- ☐ Place O_2 mask or connect existing mask to O_2

C
- ☐ Check pulses
- ☐ Establish IV/IO access
- ☐ Consider ordering blood

D
- ☐ State GCS (eyes, verbal, motor)
- ☐ State pupil size and response

E
- ☐ Completely remove patient's clothing
- ☐ Cover patient with warm blanket

RE-EVALUATE AIRWAY
- ☐ Evaluate need for intubation
- ☐ Report ET tube size and depth (if applicable)
- ☐ Confirm $ETCO_2$ color change (if applicable)

MONITOR
- ☐ Confirm heart rate is displayed
- ☐ Confirm pulse ox waveform is displayed

VITALS
State and evaluate whether WNL:
- ☐ Heart rate
- ☐ Respiratory rate
- ☐ Blood pressure
- ☐ Oxygen saturation
- ☐ Temperature

Secondary Survey

Evaluate and state findings:
- ☐ Head
- ☐ Ears
- ☐ Eyes
- ☐ Facial bones
- ☐ Nose
- ☐ Mouth
- ☐ Neck/C-spine
- ☐ Chest
- ☐ Abdomen
- ☐ Pelvis
- ☐ Upper extremities
- ☐ Lower extremities
- ☐ Log roll and back exam

Plan of Care

Determine need for:
Laboratory tests	☐ Yes	☐ No
X-rays	☐ Yes	☐ No
CT scans	☐ Yes	☐ No
OR notification	☐ Yes	☐ No
PICU notification	☐ Yes	☐ No

Departure Plan

☐ State patient destination

Prepare patient for travel:
- ☐ Equipment
- ☐ Medications
- ☐ Identify who will travel with patient

Figure 1: Trauma resuscitation checklist used in the checklist evaluation study at our research site.

We make three contributions in this work. First, we provide a detailed exploration of how the paper checklist affected leadership functions and team dynamics during emergency medical events. Second, we describe the practices that emerged as a result of the checklist use. Third, we offer design directions to support these practices as medical work becomes increasingly digital.

2. BACKGROUND & RESEARCH CONTEXT

2.1 Trauma Resuscitation Domain Overview

Trauma resuscitation is a complex, high-tempo process that requires well-coordinated effort of all team members to ensure timely patient care. The primary goal is to stabilize a critically injured patient in a short time period by identifying injuries and developing a plan for patient hospitalization. This goal is typically achieved through three stages: (1) preparation for the patient arrival (pre-arrival stage), (2) primary and secondary survey (patient evaluation stage), and (3) plan of care (departure stage).

The pre-arrival stage begins with a pager notification of an incoming trauma patient. Upon being notified, members of the trauma team rapidly gather in the resuscitation bay, a designated room in the emergency department for performing resuscitations. Teams usually have between five to 20 minutes to carry out preparatory activities and learn about the incoming patient.

Shortly after patient arrival, the team proceeds with patient evaluation following the Advanced Trauma Life Support [ATLS] protocol. The first phase (*primary survey*) is a rapid evaluation of major physiological systems, consisting of five steps ("ABCDEs"): (1) airway [**A**], (2) breathing [**B**], (3) circulation [**C**], (4) neurological status [**D**], and (5) exposure and environmental control [**E**]. These steps are then followed by a detailed head-to-toe evaluation (*secondary survey*) and diagnostic tests (e.g., x-ray examinations) to identify other injuries.

The departure stage and plans for definitive care begin after the patient has been stabilized. During this stage, the surgical team leader and emergency medicine physician work together to determine the next step in the care process.

2.2 Resuscitation Teams & the Role of the Physician Leader

The size of a resuscitation team ranges from seven to 15 providers, depending on the type and severity of injury. The team typically consists of a physician leader, an emergency medicine physician, a physician surveyor, an anesthesiologist, a respiratory therapist, bedside nurses, and a scribe nurse. Because of the *ad hoc* nature of their work, team members may not necessarily know each other. Resuscitation teams are hierarchical, with each team member having a defined role and a set of responsibilities. For example, a physician surveyor (junior surgical resident) performs hands-on patient evaluation and calls out the findings to the leader. Bedside nurses take blood pressure measurements and establish intravenous (IV) access, while the scribe documents the resuscitation process on a paper flowsheet.

The role of the physician leader is critical in ensuring that each phase of care flows in continuity. This role is usually assigned to an attending surgeon, a surgical fellow, or a senior surgical resident. The leader is responsible for supervising patient care, delegating tasks, and making decisions while being positioned at the foot of the bed for a quick overview of the patient, team and resuscitation room. Because leaders mostly rely on the findings reported by the physician surveyor, they are generally hands-off when it comes to patient evaluation. Sometimes, however, a lack of expertise in the room may require the leaders to assist with bedside tasks. Because the role of the leader is critical, it is important to understand how cognitive aids, whether paper or digital, impact the leadership functions and team dynamics.

2.3 An Opportunity for Study: Trauma Resuscitation Checklist

Despite the hierarchical nature of trauma teams, compliance with essential components of the ATLS protocol is variable, even among experienced providers and teams [7]. The performance improvement and research staff at our site have similarly observed variable compliance with the recommended steps of the protocol using video review of actual resuscitations [3]. To help teams reduce errors and delays in treatments, the Chief of Trauma introduced a checklist, the first of its kind in this medical domain (Figure 1). The checklist was designed for team leaders and was meant to serve as a compliance tool. The pre-arrival section contained items that helped teams prepare for patient arrival. The primary and secondary survey sections followed the protocol steps, including the ABCDEs, head-to-toe evaluation, and vital signs checking. The plan of care and departure items facilitated discussions about the diagnostic tests and patient disposition.

Before it was officially implemented, the checklist went through an iterative design process. Its impact on team performance was then evaluated in a simulated environment with 12 unique trauma teams participating in 12 experimental sessions representing three conditions: control, the do-list checklist scenario, and the challenge-response checklist scenario [17]. Two checklist administration methods were evaluated: a *do-list* method and a *challenge-response* method. The do-list method required the leader to call out each item and await verbal confirmation of task completion before moving onto the next item. In contrast, the challenge-response method required the leader to call for a pause at various times during the resuscitation, read aloud each item, and then wait for a team member to verbally confirm task completion. Checklist administration was assigned to the physician leader, a role least likely to be hands-on during patient evaluation. Evaluation findings showed increased team performance during scenarios using a checklist and high overall compliance with the checklist in the experimental scenarios [17].

In this paper, we use the video recordings from the checklist evaluation study [17] to understand the impact of different paper-based checklist administration methods on team dynamics and work practices in an intense medical collaboration setting. Studying the use of paper artifacts in work processes as a way of directing or inspiring the design of new technologies is a common approach in HCI and CSCW [19]. Several studies specific to healthcare have also used this approach to inform the design of EHRs and other systems [4],[25]. Similarly, the use of a paper checklist in simulated resuscitations at our research site afforded an ecologically valid and controlled environment (control and two experimental checklist conditions) for understanding checklist effects on leadership and team behaviors, as well as for deriving design requirements for interactive cognitive aids.

Trauma resuscitation differs from other medical domains in which checklists have been used or tested, providing a rich site for studying the use of this paper artifact. Most team members are performing time-critical tasks, which may prevent a pause for performing a checklist. While documentation in other clinical settings can immediately follow the patient encounter, emergency physicians and nurses often multitask and face frequent interruptions in workflow [5]. In addition, the checklist administrators—in our case, physician leaders—must actively use the checklist to ensure task completion, which may interfere with their performance. By analyzing the use of the checklist across different experimental sessions, we gained an understanding of how this artifact affected both leadership and team behaviors. The two checklist administration methods also offered insights into different checklist use styles, allowing us to broaden design implications for interactive cognitive aids in time-critical medical teamwork.

3. METHODS

3.1 Dataset: Simulated Resuscitations

Our dataset included video recordings of 48 simulated resuscitations originally performed in a pediatric trauma center in the U.S. mid-Atlantic region for the purposes of evaluating the impact of the checklist on protocol compliance. Twelve unique teams participated in a total of 12 experimental sessions, each consisting of four scenarios representing three conditions: control (two scenarios per session, no checklist), the do-list checklist scenario, and the challenge-response checklist scenario. The dataset, therefore, included 12 teams running 24 control, 12 do-list and 12 challenge-response scenarios. Presentation of the scenarios was random to reduce carry-over effects. The clinical scenarios varied by patient age, injury mechanism, and required treatments.

The simulations were performed in an actual trauma bay using high-fidelity patient mannequins with features ranging from simulated speech, a realistic airway, breath sounds, simulated ECG rhythms and capabilities of performing intravenous access. The teams were instructed to carry out each resuscitation scenario as they normally would in an actual event. Before the checklist scenarios, team leaders were first given a brief demonstration of the assigned checklist administration method and then asked to adhere to this method throughout the resuscitation.

Participants were recruited from a pool of physicians and nurses who normally participate in trauma resuscitations at the hospital. Each team had eight members, including a physician leader (emergency medicine physician or surgeon), a physician surveyor (junior surgical resident), an airway physician (anesthesiologist or critical care fellow), a respiratory therapist, two bedside nurses, a scribe nurse, and a medication nurse. Participation was tracked to ensure that each experimental session had a unique team.

Two video cameras captured each simulation, allowing us to observe a variety of team behaviors. One camera provided an overhead view and the other provided a side view of the trauma bay. The average length of controls was 13 min, ranging from 9 to 16 min; the average length of do-list scenarios was 15 min, ranging from 9 to 21 min; and the average length of challenge-response scenarios was 17 min, ranging from 11 to 22 min.

3.2 Coding Scheme Development

To identify leadership behaviors, we first developed a coding scheme. This scheme was then used during video review to mark the leaders' communication and interaction instances in 48 simulations for further analysis. One researcher reviewed six simulation videos: two do-list checklist scenarios, two challenge-response checklist scenarios, and two control scenarios. These simulations were selected after scanning the entire dataset to represent different leadership styles (active vs. passive) and team efficiencies (short vs. long resuscitations), and to include all four clinical scenarios, which differed in complexity. This mix of simulations allowed us to uncover a broad range of behaviors using an open coding technique. The initial list of behaviors (codes) was then discussed in a group session to determine which codes to keep, merge, or remove. After the list of codes was set, we created a data dictionary defining each code to standardize the coding process. Our final coding scheme contained a total of 21 codes, 13 of which represented verbal communication behaviors and 8 represented physical interaction behaviors. *Communication codes* included the following behaviors: initiate team introductions, recap pre-hospital information, assign tasks, request information, report information, acknowledge information, provide clarification, summarize process, state decision, discuss decision, brief on departure plan, plan care, and explain procedure. *Interaction codes* included behaviors such as looks at the monitor, looks at the flowsheet, looks at the checklist, writes on the checklist, checks off checklist items, evaluates patient, assists with bedside tasks, and turns to the scribe for information.

3.3 Video Review and Data Analysis

Video review was performed independently by three researchers and consisted of multiple steps. Each video was first transcribed by the first researcher to provide a linear list of the leader's behaviors. The first and second researcher then coded the transcripts, while also jotting down notes about team behaviors. Specifically, the first researcher reviewed and coded all 48 simulations, and the second researcher reviewed and coded about 30% of the videos (15 randomly selected simulations representing all scenarios). Communication and interaction codes were accompanied by the stage code (e.g., pre-arrival, primary and secondary surveys, departure plan) to identify when in the process certain behaviors occurred. We also recorded time stamps for each behavior so that we can visualize them on a timeline.

We used Cohen's Kappa coefficient to determine the inter-rater reliability by comparing the coders' scores on the 15 simulations involving 995 communication and 601 interaction instances. The resulting kappa values were analyzed using the kappa interpretation scale suggested by Landis and Koch [15]. The coders presented "Almost Perfect" agreement on the interaction codes (kappa value of 0.851), and "Substantial" agreement on the communication codes (kappa value of 0.771). Communication disagreements were mainly due to the interpretive differences attributed to 'request information' and 'assign task' codes.

To identify themes related to checklist effects on team dynamics, we asked the third researcher to review a subset of checklist scenarios (6 out of 24 randomly selected checklist sessions) and focus on team behaviors only. The notes obtained from all three researchers were discussed in a group session, compared, and then analyzed using an open coding technique by the first researcher.

Once the video review was completed, we visualized the frequency of the leaders' communication and interaction behaviors on a timeline for all 12 teams to analyze their relationship to the checklist use. Due to space limitations we show visualizations for only one team (Team 2, Figure 2). To create these visualizations, we first divided the entire resuscitation into 30-second time intervals, and then counted the instances of communication and interaction behaviors within each time interval. To further support our analysis of the checklist effects, we conducted a paired-samples t-test with 95% confidence level to compare communication and interaction behaviors among the 12 leaders for the checklist and non-checklist conditions. Finally, we created bar charts showing the frequency of leaders' activities across all 48 simulations (Figure 3).

4. FINDINGS

We report our findings in three parts. We first describe the checklist effects on leaders' verbal communication, followed by the checklist effects on leaders' interaction with the environment. We then present the checklist effects on team dynamics.

4.1 Checklist and Leaders' Communication

Leadership responsibilities are best reflected through the leader's communication with the team. For example, leaders would inquire about the patient status as they make decisions, assign tasks, or provide an overview of the process to maintain team awareness. To understand the extent to which the checklist affected these leadership tasks, we first examined the relationship between the checklist use and overall communication. We then took a closer look into different communication behaviors.

By comparing the ground truth (non-checklist) with the two checklist administration methods (do-list and challenge-response), we observed an increased amount of the leader's communication behaviors in the checklist scenarios (Figure 2); the checklist design by itself and the ways in which it was used simply made the leader communicate more frequently with the team. A closer look into the two checklist administration methods revealed that the frequency of the leader's communication and checklist use varied, with each checklist administration method shaping the nature of the leader's communication with the team. For example, the do-list method required the leader to call out each checklist item and then await verbal confirmation of task completion. This checklist use style made the leader's communication equally distributed throughout the resuscitation (Figure 2, middle chart). In contrast, the challenge-response method required the leader to call for a pause at various times during the resuscitation (usually at the end of each phase), read aloud each item, and then wait for a verbal confirmation. As a result, the leader's communication spiked towards the end of each phase, with less communication in between (Figure 2, top chart). In short, the checklist use aligned almost perfectly with leaders' communication, shaping not only team communication but also the dynamics of the resuscitation.

Among 13 communication behaviors we identified, three emerged as particularly affected by the checklist (Figure 3(a)): *request information*, *report information*, and *initiate team introductions*. We next describe each of these communication behaviors.

4.1.1 Request Information

Requests for information were the most frequent communication behaviors observed in both checklist and control scenarios, with a significant difference in the amount of requests between the two conditions, $t(11) = 8.791$, $p = 0.000$ (Figure 3(a)). This notable difference suggests that the checklist prompted leaders to request information more frequently.

In particular, our analysis showed that leaders who used the checklist inquired more frequently about three types of information: patient status (e.g., findings from patient evaluation), process status (e.g., performed procedures), and equipment and medication availability. The pattern in which this information was solicited, however, differed across conditions. For example, throughout control scenarios, patient evaluation proceeded in a standard way: physician surveyor initiated evaluation by assessing the patient's physiological systems one by one, reporting findings to the leader after each ABCD step, with the leader requesting information only if the findings raised any concerns. The pattern of information requests in challenge-response scenarios was similar to that of controls, except that requests intensified at the end of the primary and secondary surveys when the leader asked for any missing information:

> After ABCD steps were completed, the leader called for a pause and read through the primary survey items, requesting information from the physician surveyor, *"Did you check pulses? Did you state the GCS? Pupils?"* [Session 10, Challenge-response scenario]

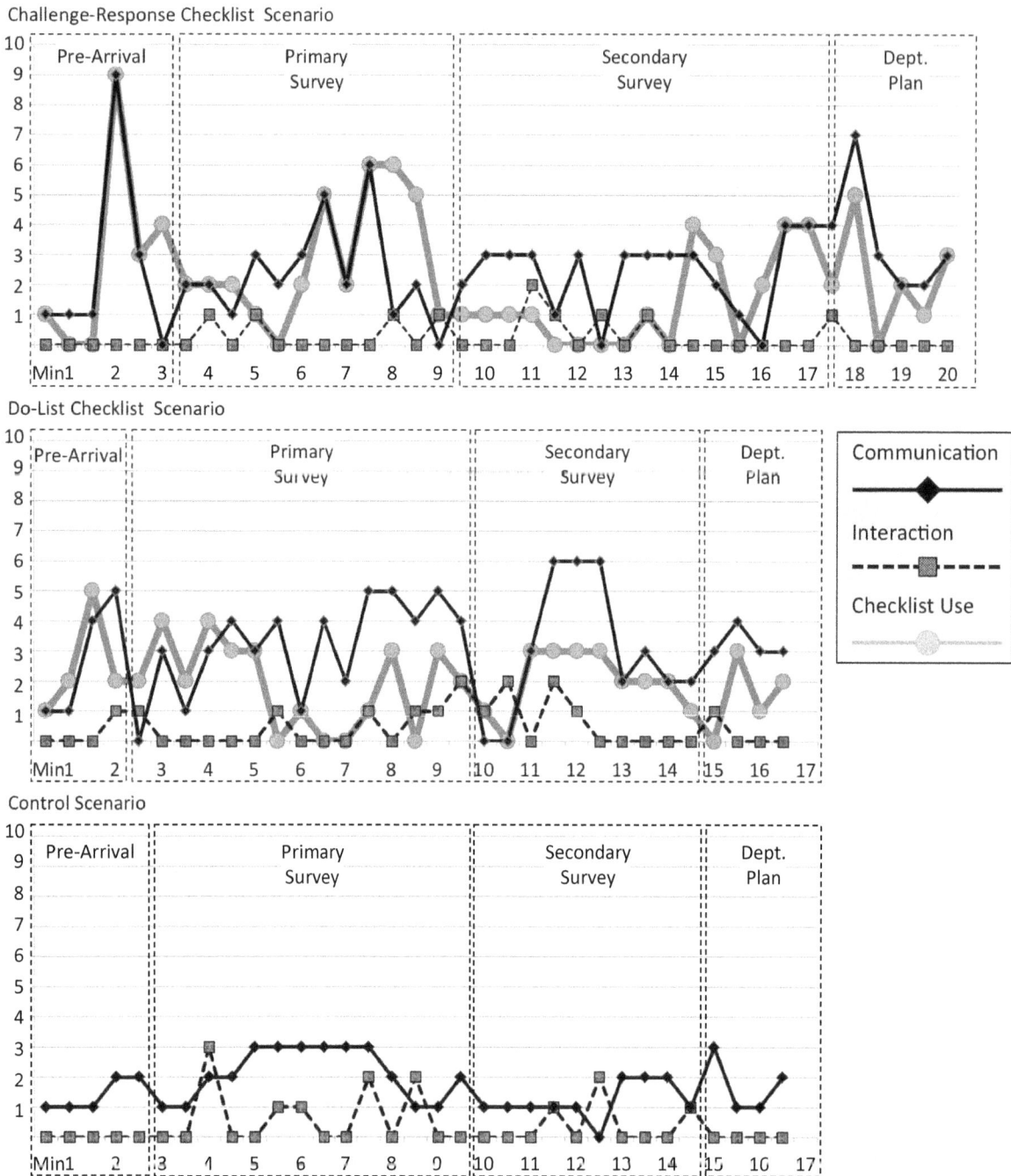

Figure 2: Relationships between the checklist use and the leader's communication and interaction behaviors, for Team 2, for three conditions (challenge-response scenario [top chart], do-list scenario [middle chart] and control scenario [bottom chart]).

In contrast, throughout the do-list scenarios, leaders requested information about findings from each evaluation step before physician surveyors started assessing the patient:

> Shortly after the patient was brought into the room, the leader looked toward the checklist and inquired, *"Protected airway?"* Hearing this prompt, the surveyor assessed the patient's airway and reported *"Yes."* [Session 6, Do-list scenario]

Requests for the overall status of the process, fluids, medications and other treatments occurred more frequently in checklist conditions, especially during the challenge-response scenarios when leaders actively used the checklist at the end of the

resuscitation phases. In contrast, the use of the checklist in the do-list scenarios followed the process steps one by one, thereby increasing awareness of the overall process status.

Inquires about the equipment and other anticipated materials (e.g., blood products, medications) usually occurred during the pre-arrival stage. We observed, however, that leaders without the checklist rarely inquired about equipment or medications prior to patient arrival. In comparison, all 12 leaders inquired about equipment readiness before patient arrival in the do-list sessions, and 10 out of 12 leaders checked for equipment and other materials in the challenge-response sessions.

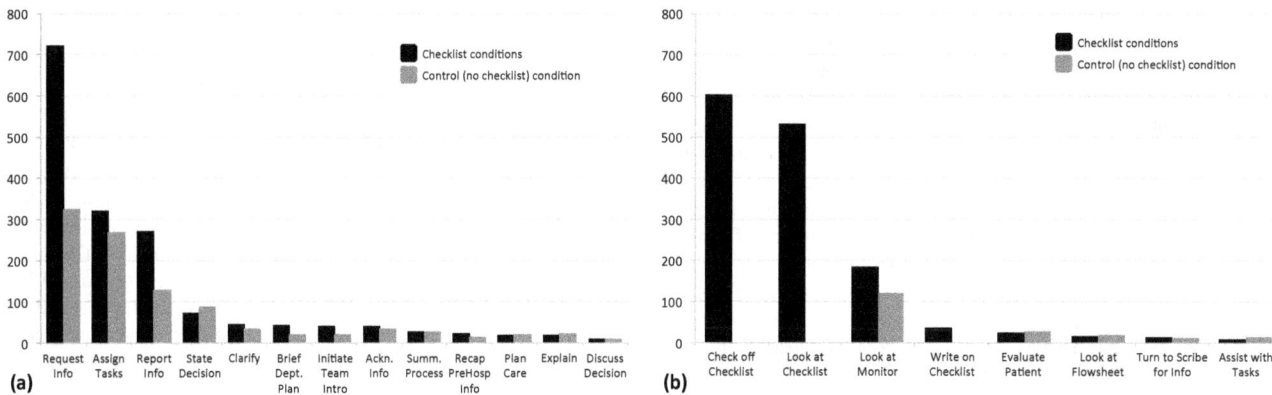

Figure 3: Aggregates of communication (a) and interaction (b) behaviors across 24 checklist (do-list and challenge-response) scenarios [black bars] and 24 control (no checklist) scenarios [gray bars].

4.1.2 Report Information

Over the course of the resuscitation, leaders would often report information back to the team about the patient or process status to help maintain overall team awareness. For example, they would restate major findings and go over current and future tasks. We found that the checklist significantly affected the leaders' reporting behavior—the amount of leaders' reports in the checklist sessions doubled compared to that of control sessions, t (10) = 3.083, p = 0.012 (Figure 3(a))—in that it prompted leaders to not only reevaluate and restate the patient's parameters and findings, but also provide their interpretations. We observed all 12 leaders frequently reporting task statuses and patient parameters in most checklist scenarios. For example:

After the team successfully stabilized the patient's airway, the leader checked off the airway item on the checklist and reported, *"We have secured the airway so we go to the next part."* [Session 12, Do-list scenario]

When the leader reached the "Vitals" section, he started looking at the vital signs monitor, reporting, *"Normal heart-rate, blood pressure is low right now, oxygen saturation is 100% and temperature is low."* [Session 4, Challenge-response scenario]

By comparison, the status of the process was reported in nine out of 24 controls and mostly referred to the current tasks (e.g., *"We have the patient intubated and everything is fine"* [Session 12]). Patient status was reported more frequently, with leaders stating vital signs and other patient data in 16 out of 24 control scenarios.

4.1.3 Initiate Team Introductions

Team introductions and role assignment during the pre-arrival stage were designed to introduce team members who did not know each other and to ensure that all team roles were covered. We found that the leaders initiated introductions in all but six simulations (five controls and one checklist). A major difference between the two conditions was that the leaders with checklists also confirmed responsibilities with particular roles, whereas leaders in controls rarely did so, t (10) = 2.571, p = 0.028. For example, in Session 2, the leader first asked other team members to introduce themselves by name. After the introductions, the leader called out each person by name and assigned roles:

"[Name] will be responsible for airway. [Name] will be responsible for IV access. [Name] for primary survey, and I will be the leader." [Session 2, Do-list scenario]

4.1.4 Other Communication Behaviors

Although no significant differences were found for other communication behaviors, we observed that the checklist played an important role during these activities. In particular, we found that *task assignments* increased only slightly in scenarios with the checklist (Figure 3(a)). We did observe, however, that leaders without the checklist failed to assign tasks during the pre-arrival and departure stages, whereas leaders in checklist scenarios regularly gave these orders. For example:

While waiting for the patient, the leader went through the pre-arrival items and issued the following orders: *"Let's make sure everything is ready... oxygen is ready, med[ication]s are ready, suction is ready... 4.5 [tube size] for intubation... get IV and bag ready."* [Session 12, Challenge-response scenario]

The *plan of care* was discussed in only half of the simulations, while the *departure plan* was discussed in 21 out of 24 checklist scenarios and in 15 out of 24 non-checklist scenarios. The discussion of plans appeared more detailed with the checklist; it included laboratory orders, transfer medications, and the patient's next destination. Plan discussions in the control sessions mostly focused on laboratory orders. We also observed fewer *decisions stated* by the leaders in the checklist scenarios, though this difference was not significant. Finally, leaders in the checklist sessions regularly briefed their teams on incoming patients, providing quick summaries of pre-hospital information, or *pre-hospital recaps*. Though no significant difference was found between the two conditions, we observed fewer leaders in the controls performing this preparatory activity (10 out of 24).

4.2 Checklist and Leaders' Interactions

In addition to leading resuscitation teams through communicative acts such as task assignments, reports or process summaries, physician leaders exhibited their leadership through interactions with the patient and environment. Although hands-off most of the time (no direct involvement in patient physical examination), leaders would sometimes approach the patient to confirm reported findings or assess the patient's breathing or pulses. Leaders would also assist with some bedside tasks, such as help remove transfer boards or pass on equipment. Assigning the checklist to leaders meant keeping their hands and eyes busy with administering the checklist. We therefore examined whether checklists affected leaders' visual attention and interactions with the environment.

When looking into the distribution of interaction behaviors (e.g., looks at the monitor, evaluates patient), we found that regardless of the condition (non-checklist, do-list and challenge-response), leaders rarely assisted with bedside tasks (Figure 2). The checklist, however, did consume leaders' attention (Figure 3(b)). Between the two checklist conditions, leaders looked at the checklist about 600 times (on average, 18 times per challenge-response scenario and 26 times per do-list scenario). The duration of each look varied depending on the scenario and leadership style, and ranged from 1 second to more than 10 seconds. The do-list administration method resulted in a higher frequency of looks than the challenge-response method because it required the leader to look at the checklist before and after each task. On the other hand, the challenge-response method required the leader to look at the checklist during time-outs, when they called a pause to ensure task completions. Checking off items on the checklist added another few seconds (sometimes even minutes) to the overall time spent on the checklist. We observed shorter but more frequent check-offs during the do-list, as opposed to the challenge-response scenarios, when check-offs clustered around time-outs. We also observed that some leaders read through the items without checking them off, suggesting that differences in frequency and durations of the checklist use were driven not only by the method but also by individual preferences.

The checklist required the leaders to write down one piece of patient information—estimated weight. Occasionally, however, the leaders used the checklist to write down other patient information or take notes as other team members reported physical findings. Content analysis of handwritten notes from 24 checklists used in the study showed that eight leaders jotted down various pieces of pre-arrival information, such as demographics, estimated arrival time, mechanism of injury, and en-route treatments. A few leaders also recorded physical findings such as pulses, neurological status, size of pupils, temperature and vitals. The recorded information served as a memory aid, allowing for more efficient information retention, especially for rapidly changing values such as vital signs.

Although using the checklist consumed some of the leaders' time, we observed that the checklist did little to distract leaders from other tasks, especially those that required their visual attention. This observation was confirmed by statistical tests showing no significant differences between interaction behaviors in the checklist and control sessions (e.g., looks at monitor: t (10) = 2.19, p = 0.051; looks at flowsheet: t (10) = -0.838, p = 0.420). Even so, we observed that the checklist played an important role during these activities. In particular, the leaders looked at the vital signs monitor more often during the checklist sessions (183 times total) than control sessions (120 times total) (Figure 3(b)). On average, they looked at the monitor 5 times in the control scenarios, 6 times in the challenge-response scenarios, and 9 times in the do-list scenarios. (The checklist contained items requiring the leader to evaluate patient vitals after primary survey, as well as to check the monitor (Figure 1)). We also observed fewer instances of looking at the flowsheet in the checklist sessions (14 times total) than in the control sessions (20 times total) (Figure 3(b)). A possible explanation is that the checklist served as a memory aid—they used it to jot down notes, as described above— thus minimizing the need for flowsheet information.

The number of instances in which the leaders approached the bed or assisted with a task was low across all simulations, t (10) = -0.461, p = 0.653 (Figure 3(b)). We did, however, observe fewer approaches to the patient bed or assistances with tasks in the checklist sessions. Most of the time, leaders approached the patient only to take a closer look at an injury, without touching the

patient. When they did engage with the patient, they either held the checklist in one hand and examined the patient with another, or they placed the checklist aside, as illustrated below:

> At about 6 minutes into the scenario, the leader asked the surveyor to prepare chest tube equipment, *"While you are preparing the chest tube, I will do the secondary survey."* The leader then approached the bed, put the checklist aside and evaluated the patient. After completing the survey, the leader stepped back, picked up the checklist, returned to her position and checked off items on the secondary survey section. When she got to the "chest" item on the list, she again approached the patient and touched the patient's chest with one hand while holding the checklist in the other. [Session 3, Do-list scenario]

4.3 Checklist and Team Dynamics

In addition to observing checklist effects on leadership behaviors, we found that the checklist altered team dynamics in three ways: (1) it introduced changes in the communication and interaction patterns between the leader and other team members; (2) it helped facilitate collaborative information seeking and decision making; and, (3) it helped facilitate process summaries during which teams reflected on the overall process status.

4.3.1 Checklist Effects on Team Communication and Interaction: Reactive vs. Proactive Team Members

Our analysis of leaders' requests for information and responses they received across three conditions suggested that by adopting the checklist, some team members became "reactive" as opposed to being "proactive"—that is, they became dependent on the leader by waiting for the leader's prompts and questions. This effect was found in 25% of the checklist scenarios, most of which followed the do-list method. Furthermore, when observed, this behavior change occurred in almost every stage of the resuscitation. For example, airway physicians and bedside nurses relied on leaders' instructions to prepare equipment, medications, blood products and other supplies for patient arrival during the pre-arrival stage, as well as for patient transfer during the departure stage. During the primary and secondary surveys in particular, the checklist affected interaction between the leader and physician surveyor. By issuing prompts during patient evaluation—that is, requesting information about physical findings for each protocol step—the leader was guiding the surveyor step-by-step through the process rather than letting him or her perform evaluation and report findings on their own:

> The surveyor performed airway, breathing and circulation steps during the primary survey following the leader's prompts. When the leader paused to delegate tasks to other team members, (e.g., get a warm blanket, establish IV access), the physician surveyor stood still and waited for the order for the next step. Near the end of the primary survey, the leader looked at the checklist and then turned to the surveyor: "T*he primary survey is completed, except for pupil size and responses, please let me know when you get it.*" The surveyor then immediately started assessing the pupils. [Session 6, Do-list scenario]

Although the checklist altered interactions between the leader and physician surveyor, we believe these effects varied based on the surveyor's experience. We observed, for example, that in some events, even when the leader delegated specific tasks to the surveyor, the surveyor responded to those orders, but then continued evaluation on their own while the leader switched to other tasks. We also observed cases when physician surveyors worked independently and did not wait for the leader's guidance, even though the leaders tried hard to guide the process using the checklist. For example:

> Most of the team was still focused on the primary survey tasks, deciding what types of fluid and medications to administer, and whether or not to intubate the patient. Without receiving specific orders to move onto the secondary survey, the surveyor started with secondary tasks immediately after completing the initial survey. The surveyor first evaluated the right side of the patient. As he was about to move to the opposite side, the leader stopped him and asked to wait until the primary survey is completed. [Session 9, Do-list scenario]

These observations suggest that team members' experience levels play a critical role in shaping their interaction with the leader. Although we did not record work experience data, we believe that surveyors with more experience are more likely to perform patient evaluation on their own. Similarly, we believe that less experienced team members are more likely to benefit from the step-by-step guidance that the checklist afforded.

4.3.2 Checklist as a Trigger for Collaborative Information Seeking and Decision Making

Our analysis showed that the checklist increased the amount of communication between the leader and others in the team. As a result, the amount of team discussion and communication increased as well. Three findings stood out.

First, we observed team members mainly responding to assignments or requests that were relevant to their roles and responsibilities. For example, airway physicians usually responded to questions about the patient's airway; physician surveyors were primarily answering questions about primary and secondary survey; and, nurses responded to questions about intravenous access and medications. In other words, team members acquired, reported and memorized information about the domain in which they specialized. Reported information was then used for decision making; if more information was needed, the team went back to observation and data collection. This consistency in role-to-task relationship was observed in all 48 simulations. What stood out in checklist conditions, however, was an emphasis on group discussions when different roles engaged in clarifying ambiguous information, as illustrated below:

> The leader was considering blood administration for the patient, but was missing information such as weight, mechanism of injury, and administered fluids. Although some data were reported initially during patient handover, the leader did not record or remember this information. She asked physician surveyor, primary nurse, and airway physician to help her retrieve the needed information and decide on the blood volume. [Session 9, Do-list scenario]

> The leader was looking at the notes he jotted down on the checklist about the patient's pre-hospital information. He noticed a discrepancy between his notes and a finding that was previously reported by the surveyor. The leader then initiated a discussion with the surveyor in an attempt to clarify this finding. [Session 2, Challenge-response scenario]

These observations suggest that the checklist served not only as a tool for improving compliance with the protocol, but it also facilitated joint information seeking and team discussions. This practice was especially common in the pre-arrival and departure stages when leaders needed input from others on particular steps.

Second, we observed fewer solo decision-making instances in checklist conditions than in non-checklist conditions (Figure 3(a)). A possible explanation is that other team members, such as physician surveyors and airway physicians engaged in decision making by suggesting interventions:

> After checking off ABCDE steps, the leader paused at the next item, announcing, "Evaluate need for intubation." The leader first asked the surveyor and physician airway about their opinion. They then discussed whether or not to intubate the patient for a minute. The airway physician also suggested what medications were needed for intubation so that the nurse can prepare them. [Session 7, Challenge-response scenario]

Finally, we observed that the checklist, by facilitating team discussions and thus increasing the amount of communication, led to some redundant communication. Two kinds of communication redundancy were common. The first refers to repeating or acknowledging information after it is reported. A typical example we heard throughout simulations was "airway, check" uttered by the leader after the surveyor reported "airway is clear." As previous work has found, this communication redundancy is intended to confirm that the reported information has been heard and received by another person [2]. The second type of redundancy refers to the leader's inquires about the information that is already reported. Because the environment was often noisy and chaotic, leaders frequently missed reports by other team members, failing to record the information on their checklists; once they realized the information was missing, they asked for it.

4.3.3 Checklist as a Mechanism for Reflection: Process Summaries

The challenge-response checklist method—when the leader called for a pause at various times during the event and then went through the checklist—took more time to administer than the do-list checklist. At times, it took the leader up to two minutes to go over the checklist items, a pause that is often a luxury in an emergency situation. In addition, the entire team had to pause their activities for the checklist to be completed. Even so, we observed one positive change these pauses brought to the team— they offered an opportunity for the entire team (and not just the leader) to get a sense of where they stand in terms of completed, pending and remaining tasks, and reflect on the current status of the patient. Specifically, the long pauses occurring after each resuscitation phase during challenge-response scenarios allowed teams to review protocol steps, discuss findings and treatments, and decide on the next steps. Team members also used this opportunity to provide their own insights into the patient status and the plan of care. As such, the pauses helped bring the entire team on the same page, ensuring that no steps have been skipped and everyone was ready for the subsequent patient care steps.

5. DISCUSSION

Our analysis of leaders' communication and interaction behaviors during checklist scenarios confirmed the benefits of using a medical checklist found in other studies [12],[13],[16],[18]. The checklist, regardless of the administration method, prompted the leaders to regularly seek patient and process information, delegate tasks to other team members, confirm task completions, and maintain overall team awareness through brief reports. As such, the checklist helped improve compliance with the protocol, as found during the initial evaluation of its impact on team performance [17]. Our results also showed that the checklist did little to distract the leaders from paying attention to the vital signs monitor or hinder their engagement with the patient or environment when needed. Finally, we observed several practices at a team level that emerged as a result of the checklist use. The checklist facilitated collaborative decision making and process reflections, and led to good communication redundancy, but it also made some team members dependent on the leader's guidance, thus reinforcing on-the-job training. These findings suggest that the checklist served not only as a tool for improving protocol compliance—as originally intended by its creators—but also as a cognitive aid that helped teams communicate, collaborate, reflect, and make decisions more efficiently. In other words, using the checklist meant more than just checking off items and ensuring each step was completed. Designers of digital cognitive aids for emergency medical work should therefore consider how to preserve these team practices while also fulfilling the primary goal of a checklist. Below we provide a few directions for how these digital aids could be designed to maintain functionality and affordances of paper checklists. The goal is to help resuscitation team members maintain awareness about the flow of work and what their colleagues are doing, while facilitating seamless communication and information sharing.

Distribute patient and process monitoring across the entire team. The resuscitation checklist was designed for the physician leader as a way of ensuring protocol compliance. As such, the checklist information was accessible only to checklist administrators, that is, leaders. While this approach aligns well with the general use of checklists [10], we saw entire teams benefiting from the checklist information. Like whiteboards, checklist can be considered as an information container that preserves information about team tasks, activities and decisions made during the resuscitation; information recorded on the checklist is expected to be persistent and visually visible all the time, much like information on the whiteboards, unless intentionally obscured [20]. Similarly, providing teams with constant visual access to the checklist information may help sustain and even encourage some of the positive changes in team dynamics, such as process reflections and joint decision making, while minimizing negative effects. For example, a system that makes the checklist information available to the entire team may make team members with less experience (especially surveyors who are still in training) proactive and less dependent on leader's instructions, as the status information will now be distributed across the entire team. Furthermore, by seeing the checklist information, other team members can collectively monitor compliance with the protocol, thereby reducing a chance for deviating from the protocol or skipping tasks. This collective monitoring for protocol compliance is also in line with general groupware design principles that recommend embedding a group process in software to provide structure to the group's activity and ensure that the process is followed [8]. Public display of the checklist information could also improve documentation by allowing the scribe nurse to compare data between the flowsheet and checklist display for accuracy and consistency.

Although administering the checklist did consume leaders' attention, we found that it did not interfere with leaders' performance, allowing them to frequently look at the vital signs monitor and engage with the patient when needed. Even so, the increased number of looks at the monitor may also be the result of a cognitive burden of using or learning how to use the checklist. For example, the leaders might have had difficulty holding the status of the patient in short term memory, so they increased their references to the monitor to be able to keep track of the patient trajectory. After all, we did observe leaders jotting down vitals information on the checklist for easier information access. While

these are just hypotheses, we believe that public display of the checklist information would help unburden the leader by distributing process monitoring across the entire team.

In short, the distributed access to checklist information among team members would allow for continuous and collective monitoring for the protocol compliance, enhanced situation awareness, and collaborative information seeking and decision making. As prior studies of time-critical, high-reliability domains have shown, increased heedful interrelating and mindful comprehension often lead to decreased errors during collective mental processes [21]. We believe that making the checklist information available to the entire team, thereby supporting the notions of collective mind and heedful interrelating, can help improve the efficiency and quality of their overall performance, as well as patient safety.

Preserve good communication redundancy. Overall, we observed that the checklist increased the amount of leaders' communication—checklist scenarios had more information requests, task assignments, and reports, than control scenarios. The checklist served as a natural script by which leaders communicated, prompting them to regularly check in with physician surveyors and other team members, and ensure task completion. These findings highlight the role of the checklist in ensuring information completeness, and facilitating team communication and collaboration. Still, we observed some communication issues that emerged as a result of the checklist use. Requests for information, for example, intensified during checklist scenarios. In fact, we can consider most of these requests as a byproduct of the checklist because they referred to the previously reported information. To be able to check off an item, the leader had to explicitly confirm a task completion. As a result, additional inquiries, triggered by the checklist, increased the amount of chatter and noise in the room while also leading to communication redundancy. Although some of this redundancy can be considered as "superfluous" and "wordy" [2], it can also benefit medical work by ensuring that all information is heard and recorded. Further study is needed to determine the extent to which these communication patterns improve teamwork as opposed to simply producing an overhead. Cabitza et al. [2] argued that technology could preserve the usefulness of redundancy and at the same time relieve actors of any additional efforts they make to ensure task completion. Public display of the checklist information could then help preserve good data redundancy while potentially reducing repetitive requests for confirming task completions. Furthermore, our findings showed that leaders who used the checklist inquired more frequently about patient status, process status, and equipment and medication availability. An implication here is that public displays, in addition to showing task completions, could also include status information about the most frequently requested items.

Augment leader-cognitive aid interaction while preserving affordances of paper. As we described above, the paper checklist allowed leaders to jot down notes and important patient data during the resuscitation. Though not widespread in the study, this practice implies that informal note taking is important because it allows for easier information retention. This simple advantage of the paper record is also one of the reasons why paper-based systems still persist [9]. It is therefore important that future cognitive aids take into account this function and allow informal data capture. An additional feature could allow the leaders to keep these informal notes hidden and then retrievable when needed. Digital cognitive aids could also allow leaders to indicate abnormal findings by using visual primitives (e.g., attention icons, circles) to draw the attention of the team and help prioritize treatments. Finally, the checklist administration method made a difference in most leadership behaviors, emphasizing the importance of the interaction mode when designing for future interactive cognitive aids. The challenge-response checklist—when the leader called for a pause at various times during the event and then went through the checklist—took more time to administer than the do-list checklist. The pauses, however, helped teams reflect on the process and get on the same page, which is a feature worth preserving. In contrast, the do-list method required more frequent looks and interactions with the checklist. Even so, the distribution of the leaders' communication behaviors during do-list scenarios was similar to that of controls (Figure 2), suggesting that the do-list administration method may fit better with the overall dynamics of emergency medical work.

6. CONCLUSION AND FUTURE WORK

In this paper, we examined the use of a paper checklist introduced to prepare for patient arrival and for use throughout patient evaluation in a regional trauma center. Our dataset comprised video recordings of 48 simulated resuscitations in which the checklist was tested for its impact on team performance. The simulations afforded an ecologically valid and controlled setting for understanding how the checklist was used and the effects it had on leadership behaviors and team dynamics. Based on these findings, we offered several directions for how interactive cognitive aids could be designed to support practices that emerged as a result of the checklist use. Our study, however, was based on observations and video review of the initial use of the checklist. To complement this data, we are planning in-depth interviews to learn about clinicians' perspectives on the checklist effects. The resuscitation checklist is now incorporated in the actual patient care and its use has been routinized, so we plan to evaluate the extent to which the first-time use of the checklist differs from an evolved, routinized use of the checklist. We also plan to conduct a longitudinal study to examine how some of the effects we observed in simulations play out in the context of patient outcomes and protocol compliance in the real-world scenarios.

7. ACKNOWLEDGMENTS

This material is based upon work supported by the National Science Foundation under Grant No. #1253285, and partially supported by the National Library of Medicine of the National Institutes of Health under Award No. R21LM011320-01A1 and Health Resources and Service Administration (HRSA) Program Emergency Medical Services for Children (EMSC) Targeted Issues under Grant No. H34-MC-19351.

8. REFERENCES

[1] Berg, M. and Bowker, G. The multiple bodies of the medical record. *The Sociological Quarterly 38*, 3 (1997), 513-537.

[2] Cabitza, F., Sarini, M., Simone, C., and Telaro, M. When once is not enough: the role of redundancy in a hospital ward setting. *Proc. Group 2005*, ACM Press (2005), 158-167.

[3] Carter, E. A., et al. Adherence to ATLS primary and secondary surveys during pediatric trauma resuscitation. *Resuscitation 84*, 1 (2012), 66-71.

[4] Chen, Y. Documenting transitional information in EMR. *Proc. CHI 2010*, ACM Press (2010), 1787-1796.

[5] Chisholm, C. D., Collison, E. K., Nelson, D. R., and Cordell, W. H. Emergency department workplace interruptions: are emergency physicians "interrupt-driven" and "multitasking?" *Academic Emergency Medicine 7*, 11 (2000), 1239-1243.

[6] Chua, R. V, Cordell, W. H, Ernsting, K. L, Bock, H. C, and Nyhuis AW. Accuracy of bar codes versus handwriting for recording trauma resuscitation events. *Annals of Emergency Medicine 22*, 10 (1993), 1545-1550.

[7] Chua, W. C., D'Amours, S. K., Sugrue, M., Caldwell, E., and Brown, K. Performance and consistency of care in admitted trauma patients. *ANZ Journal of Surgery 79*, 6 (2009), 443-448.

[8] Ellis, C. A., Gibbs, S. J., and Rein, G. L. Groupware: Some issues and experiences. *Communications of the ACM 34*, 1 (1991), 39-58.

[9] Fitzpatrick, G. Integrated care and the working record. *Health Informatics Journal 40*, 4 (2004), 291-302.

[10] Gawande, A. *The Checklist Manifesto: How to Get Things Right*. Metropolitan Books, New York, NY, USA, 2009.

[11] Gertner, A. S., Webber, B. L., and Clarke, J. R. Upholding the maxim of relevance during patient-centered activities, *Proc. ANLC 1994*, ACM Press (1994), 125-131.

[12] Hales, B., Terblanche, M., Fowler, R., and Sibbald, W. Development of medical checklists for improved quality of patient care. *International Journal for Quality in Health Care 20*, 1 (2008), 22-30.

[13] Hart, E. M. and Owen, H. Errors and omissions in anesthesia: A pilot study using a pilot's checklist. *Anesthesia & Analgesia 101*, 1 (2005), 246-250.

[14] Heath, C. and Luff, P. Documents and professional practice: "bad" organisational reasons for "good" clinical records. *Proc. CSCW 1996*, ACM Press (1996), 354-363.

[15] Landis, J. and Koch, G. G. The measurement of observer agreement for categorical data. *Biometrics 33*, (1977) 159-174.

[16] Lingard, L., et al. Getting teams to talk: Development and pilot implementation of a checklist to promote inter-professional communication in the OR. *Quality and Safety in Health Care 14*, 5 (2005), 340-346.

[17] Parsons, S., et al. Improving ATLS performance in simulated pediatric trauma resuscitation using a checklist. *Annals of Surgery 259*, 4 (2014), 807-813.

[18] Pronovost, P. J., Goeschel, C. A., Colantuoni, E., Watson, S., Lubomski, L. H., Berenholtz, S. M., and Needham, D. Sustaining reductions in catheter related bloodstream infections in Michigan intensive care units. *British Medical Journal 340*, (2010), c309.

[19] Selen, A. and Harper, R. *The Myth of the Paperless Office*. MIT Press, Cambridge, MA, USA, 2002.

[20] Tang, A., Lanir, J., Greenberg, S., and Fels, S. Supporting transitions in work: Informing large display application design by understanding whiteboard use. *Proc. GROUP 2009*, ACM Press (2009), 149-158.

[21] Weick, K. E. and Roberts, K. H. Collective mind in organizations: Heedful interrelating on flight decks. *Administrative Science Quarterly 38*, 3 (1993), 357-381.

[22] Wu, L., Cirimele, J., Card, S., Klemmer, S., Chu, L., and Harrison, K. Maintaining shared mental models in anesthesia crisis care with nurse tablet input and large-screen displays. *Adjunct Proc. UIST 2011*, ACM Press (2011), 71-72.

[23] Wu, L., Cirimele, J., Leach, K., Card, S., Chu, L., Harrison, K. T., and Klemmer, S. R. Supporting crisis response with dynamic procedure aids. *Proc. DIS 2014*, ACM Press (2014), 315-324.

[24] Wurster, L. A., Groner, J. I., and Hoffman, J. Electronic documentation of trauma resuscitations at a Level 1 pediatric trauma center. *J. of Trauma Nursing 19*, 2 (2012), 76-79.

[25] Zhou, X., Ackerman, M., and Zheng, K. Doctors and psychosocial information: Records and reuse in inpatient care. *Proc. CHI 2010*, ACM Press (2010), 1767-1776.

Verbal Equity, Cognitive Specialization, and Performance

Marcela Borge and John M. Carroll
The Pennsylvania State University
University Park, Pennsylvania 16802 USA
mborge@psu.edu, jmcarroll@psu.edu

ABSTRACT

In this paper, patterns of communication are examined in order to unpack the extent to which verbal equity is a critical factor in determining group success. A microanalysis of 20 teams working to complete a complex, information dependent, collaborative task was conducted. Interaction analysis methods were used as means to determine patterns of interaction and the sophistication of cognitive activity that teams engaged in. Findings suggest that verbal equity may not be as important as previous research indicates. A more critical variable may be cognitive specialization. The authors explain their findings by drawing on theories of cognition, thereby contributing to a better understanding of collective intelligence.

Categories and Subject Descriptors

K.4.3 [Organizational Impacts]: Computer-supported collaborative work.

General Terms

Measurement, Performance, Design, Experimentation, Security, Human Factors, Theory

Keywords

Collective cognition, macrocognition, collective intelligence, verbal equity, collaborative decision-making, cognitive specialization, collaborative problem solving, information analysis

1. INTRODUCTION

Though it is generally accepted that groups are better than individuals at solving complex, ill-structured problems, many questions regarding group processes still remain. Over the past two decades, the study of groups has evolved from the study of how individual minds and task characteristics interact with group processes towards the study of group processes themselves [8, 21]. A range of different group process variables has been examined: from knowledge building and argumentation to motivation and stress [13, 22]. More recently, researchers have examined patterns of group interaction in an attempt to understand group cognition or predict a group's likelihood of problem solving success [7, 9, 28, 30]. These studies point to the importance of key communication patterns such as equal access to information and integration of diverse perspectives. Wooley et al. [30] even indicate that there may be a collective intelligence quotient, one that is highly associated with verbal equity. Though Wooley et al.

GROUP'14, November 9–12, 2014, Sanibel Island, Florida, USA.
Copyright is held by the owner/author(s). Publication rights licensed to ACM.
ACM 978-1-4503-3043-5/14/11...$15.00.
http://dx.doi.org/10.1145/2660398.2660418

[30] shed new light on the study of group processes, with regards to turn-taking patterns and performance, they did not closely examine the content of communication and therefore could not explain why verbal equity was associated with collective intelligence.

In order to develop a better understanding of group cognition, it is necessary to examine communication patterns at a finer grain of scale than proportions of verbal contributions. We must examine the content of what is being verbalized, as this is where group cognition lives: in the verbalizations between individuals [23, 16]. It is also necessary to examine the effect of verbal equity on more complex problems than those employed in many of the studies we have cited, including the Wooley et al. study. This is why we are interested in further unpacking verbal equity by examining patterns and content of communication.

In this paper, we focus on information analysis, an important complex collaborative problem-solving domain, and elaborate on a prior study that suggested that verbal equity may not be as important as many have been led to believe [2]. We present a larger data set and a more comprehensive analysis, specifically with respect to unpacking the role of cognitive specialization in explaining the benefits of verbal equity. Our findings contribute to a deeper understanding of group cognitive processes as they pertain to verbal participation and a group's ability to perform consistently well over time.

2. PREVIOUS WORK

One of the challenges to studying group cognition is developing a task complex enough for teams to engage in knowledge building and negotiation processes, in order to create knowledge that did not exist prior to collaboration [22]. Previous studies built on the hidden profile work of Stasser and Titus [24] and designed an emergency management scenario in order to examine team communication patterns [5]. Findings from this study suggested that certain patterns of communication might be associated with a team's ability to develop common ground and may also indicate when teams are having problems building shared understanding. For example, frequency of particular speech acts can be associated with higher and lower performance [6].

Though these earlier studies produced interesting findings related to communication patterns, one of the biggest limiting factors in understanding the team's processes was the scenario itself; it was not complex enough. Participants only worked with 25 facts, and solving the problem, assuming all information was shared in simplest form, was a counting task – the option with the least cons was the answer. Furthermore, none of the teams created complex forms of *information artifacts* (i.e., emergent representations developed to help synthesize or build on information); they only made annotations on a map. More complex forms of information artifacts (i.e., charts, lists, graphical representations) could have provided more insights into the teams' processes for combining information and building on that knowledge, perhaps even helping to explain differences between high and low performing teams. Thus, their absence was problematic.

Wooley et al. [30] examined team processes and characteristics in order to determine whether there was such a thing as a group intelligence factor: a measure of a team's collective intelligence that could predict a team's performance outcomes across a variety of tasks. They conducted two studies on 192 groups as they completed a series of diverse, simple tasks and measured both individual and group characteristics. They found that a single measure, which they termed collective intelligence, or "c", significantly predicted group performance.

In trying to understand what "c" might be, they were able to rule out many variables that might be expected to predict group performance: average team intelligence, level of intelligence of the most intelligent member, motivation, group cohesion, and satisfaction. The three variables most correlated with "c" were social sensitivity, proportion of females on the team, and variance in number of speaking turns. Social sensitivity and proportion of females were strongly positively correlated, but the proportion of females was largely mediated by social sensitivity: females were significantly higher on social sensitivity than men. Variance in the number of speaking turns, a measure of verbal equity that looks at the spread between speakers in a team, was negatively correlated with performance. Teams where one person largely dominated speech turns tended to do worse on tasks than teams that were more equitable.

These findings suggest that equity of participation may be an important factor in and of its self and not because it might indicate motivation or cohesion. However, given that only turn taking was measured, but actual communication was not captured, they could not conduct qualitative studies of their participants' communication patterns to determine why verbal equity was a factor. So the question remains as to whether verbal equity is an important factor or simply a variable moderated by another variable that their methods could not measure. Understanding what types of cognitive processes might predict or improve group process is important for researchers in CSCW and CSCL, as such findings have implications for design of collaborative tools and the cognitive supports we provide. Given the limitations of the emergency management scenario and the study conducted by Wooley et al., there was a need to examine collaborative problem solving processes using a more complex task with more robust measures of communication and interaction. In this way, the relationship between verbal equity, group cognition, and performance could be further unpacked.

As part of our previous work, our research lab designed a complex information analysis and decision-making scenario that required teams to work together to solve a complex, information-based problem over a four hour time period [2]. Participants had to solve a crime that required them to understand the nature of the task, find relevant facts, make connection between facts, and connect evidence in order to make inferences about means, motive, and opportunity. Teams were also provided with a collection of materials that they could use to create shared artifacts, but they were not required to do so. Nonetheless, most teams created elaborate artifacts [4].

The information analysis and decision-making scenario allowed for closer analysis of patterns of interaction that occurred between team members [2, 4]. Early findings based on a microanalysis of ten teams, five high- and five low-performing, found a positive relationship between verbal equity and performance, but also

suggested that verbal equity might be moderated by distribution of cognitive responsibilities [2]. Carroll et al. [4] also found that higher performing teams used information artifacts in more sophisticated ways than lower performing teams. Such findings raise questions regarding importance of verbal equity in problem solving teams: is verbal equity a crucial factor in determining a team's potential or is it simply moderated by patterns of collective cognitive activity?

In this paper, we extend this work by conducting a microanalysis of 20 teams as they work on this complex problem-solving task. Our research questions are as follows: when the analysis is extended to 20 teams, (R1) to what extent do high performing teams show more verbal equity than low performing teams, (R2) to what extent do high performing teams show more cognitive specialization than low performing teams, and (R3) to what extent are patterns of cognitive specialization associated with more sophisticated forms of collective cognition?

3. STUDY DESIGN

Building on previous studies [2, 4, 5, 6, 16], we used a collaborative information analysis scenario as a means to study communication patterns during a complex, collaborative problem-solving activity. The scenario required each person on a three-person team to take on the role of specific intelligence analyst for the entire scenario. They then had to work with team members as part of a police taskforce and collectively solve an ongoing ring of computer thefts.

The team had to search, select, share, synthesize, and interpret existing intelligence in order to make complex decisions. In total, the scenario contained 222 unique pieces of data embedded into nine separate intelligence reports. These reports were distributed amongst the three intelligence analysts, each receiving entirely different, but complementary information. Each analyst received three reports total: one prior to each part of a three-part scenario. All three analysts also received a General Mission Statement containing the same information: crime descriptions, details about the reliability of information, and "rules" associated with alibis and opportunity to commit the crime.

The entire scenario took about 4 hours to complete. Participants had to use a mix of inductive and deductive reasoning in order to solve each part of the scenario accurately: (part one) narrow down a list of 26 Persons of Interest (POIs) to a list of the eight most likely suspects; (part two) identify thieves for each of four thefts, instigators or accomplices, motives, and whether there were connections among the four thefts; and (part three) predict the thief, time, and place of the next crime.

Over 70 hours of video from 20 microanalyzed teams - ten consistently high performing and ten consistently low performing - was the primary data source for the findings presented in this paper. This data is used to unpack the types of cognitive activities and process problems experienced by teams and whether patterns exist between particular cognitive processes and performance.

3.1 Participants

Participants were recruited from a large northeastern United States university. Thirty-nine teams took part in the study. Each team was comprised of three participants for a total of 117 participants. The majority of the participants were recruited from undergraduate information sciences, security and risk analysis, and psychology courses. Of these 39 teams, 20 were selected for microanalysis, based on performance. Thus, there were 60 total participants included in the microanalysis.

3.2 Protocols

Upon arrival, each participant was randomly assigned one of the three information analyst roles. The information analyst roles were, Records Specialist, Web Specialist, and Interview Specialist. Each team was also provided with a collection of materials in case they chose to create shared representations, i.e., large paper, maps, calendars, markers, pencils, notepaper, etc.

Prior to beginning part 1 of the scenario, each analyst was provided with 15 minutes to read through their first report (four to six pages, depending on role) and the General Mission Statement, (three pages). They were also asked to write down initial thoughts on potentially important information. Teams were provided with updated information between parts of the scenario and given time to reflect before beginning the next part of the scenario. The experimentor observed from a separate room and only interacted with teams in between parts of the scenario.

3.3 Assessing Task Performance

Task performance was scored based on accuracy of solutions in each part of the task: total points received/total possible points. There were eight points possible in part 1, sixteen in part two, and three points in part three. Percentages were calculated for each phase, and the average performance was used. Average performance across the three tasks ranged from 16.33% to 73%, indicating the high level of difficulty of the task.

3.4 Selection of Microanalysis Teams

Since identification of characteristics of consistently high performing teams was the primary goal, selection was based upon consistency of performance, rather than average performance, across the three parts of the scenario. Ten consistently high performing teams and ten consistently low performing teams were chosen. Cut-offs were determined by using sums of quartile rank scores across the three parts of the scenario. In cases where the sums of quartile rank scores were too similar to distinguish between cut-offs, average performance across the three parts of the scenario was used as a secondary filter.

3.5 Transcription of Video

Each of the ten selected teams' videos was transcribed following a similar format. Each new speaker utterance and/or behavior was numbered, denoting a new "turn". A "turn" ended when a different speaker introduced a new utterance. These turns were then split up into dialogue acts: separate sentences. Compound sentences were split into separate acts as well. The participants were referred to by the roles they played and were given pseudonyms in the transcript. Parentheses were used to label nonverbal gestures and events (i.e., leaving the group, making faces, creating an artifact, etc.). Brackets were used for codes, time stamps, and notes relevant to the analyses but not found in the video itself. These transcripts were utilized along with video when analyzing the artifacts and detecting common task errors.

3.6 Coding Dialogue

The coding schema used in this study was one used by previous researchers in CSCW [5, 6] and later refined to better align with literature in cognitive and educational psychology [2]. Inter-rater reliability for the coding schema is Kappa= .67, indicating substantial inter-rater reliability [15], particularly for the relatively high number of codes.

The coding schema divides dialogue into four classes of cognitive activity (in bold below) and then further breaks these down into acts. Breaking down communication to such a fine grain level allows researchers to look for patterns in different types of cognition with other variables such as problems, distribution of thought, cognitive strategies, and performance [2].

The coding schema is as follows:

Information Transfer- How new information, existing prior to collaboration, is added (i.e., information from existing documents)
(AI): Add Info- Add new information w/o prompting
(Q): Question- Prompt someone for new information
(R): Reply- Provide new information in response to a prompt

Check Understanding- How previously added info is checked, confirmed, or repaired
(CH): Check- verifying information
(CL): Clarify- clarifying or restating information
(AC): Acknowledge- signaling receipt or understanding of information

Management of Processes- How work is orchestrated
(MN) Management- discussions centered on interactions, planning how to do the work, or reflecting on what has been done
(CM) Command for action, order, or instruction that does not take others into account
(RQ) Request for action- posed as a question or indirect prompt (not a question)

Interpretation- How task information is interpreted and decisions are made
(J): Judge- Individual preference, opinion, or claim, with or without deliberation
(RA): Rationale that supports a judge (J) or alternative (AT) act
(AT): Proposing an alternative to a (J) OR (RA) act
(CO): Confirmation- Requesting agreement on a proposed decision
(AG): Agreement- Indicating agreement for prior judgment or decision

Identifying MN acts, management of process, and distinguishing between RA and AI were the most difficult aspects for coders. MN acts were hard for coders to identify, because they were often mistakenly coded as task-related activity, i.e., judgment acts, rational acts, etc. Coders had to learn to distinguish between content and process in order to distinguish this code. Also, in the process of providing rationale, participants could introduce new information about the task, making it difficult to distinguish between AI and RA acts. These difficulties were discussed and mitigated, but in order to further ensure proper coding, coders were paired, and problematic codes were collectively examined.

Over 70 hours of video was transcribed, resulting in over 34,000 dialogue acts across the 20 teams. Once dialogue was coded, the raw scores for each team were normalized. This was accomplished by calculating the percentage of specific dialogue acts to total dialogue acts. In this way, comparisons could be made across teams. Dialogue act coding was used as a means of looking for patterns of interaction as they occurred in different primary activities within the scenario.

3.7 Measuring Verbal Equity

Given that the study uses a dichotomous comparison of high and low performing teams, tests of correlation would not be appropriate. Therefore, we had to create ordinal categories that coincided with variance in speech turns. The goal was to distinguish between groups where one person dominated, two people shared authority, or all three members contributed equally. However, we wanted to be able to do this objectively and therefore used Verbal Equity Scores, a system of categorizing patterns of communication by the amount of variance between members of a team [2]. This method allowed teams to be assigned to categories mathematically. The standard deviation of talk for all participants, across all speech acts, was used as a means to determine cut-offs: SD = 0.08, or 8% talk.

There are three categories: a score of 3, or equitable verbal participation, a score of 2, or shared authority, and a score of 1, or dominance of one team member. To get a score of three, the difference in percent of total talk between the highest and lowest speaker in a team had to be less than two SDs, or 16%. To get a score of 2, the difference between highest and lowest speaker had to be more than 16%, but the difference between the two highest speakers had to be less than 8%. To get a score of 1, one of two criteria had to be met: the difference between the two highest speakers had to be more than 16% or the difference between highest and lowest speaker had to be more than 16% and the difference between the two highest speakers had to be more than 8%. Each team received a total verbal equity score, indicating the pattern of verbal equity across the entire four-hour task.

3.8 Defining Cognitive Specialization

Cognitive specialization refers to the extent to which team members distribute cognitive responsibilities. This is different than distribution of tasks in that people may verbalize similar forms of thinking even though they are working on two different tasks. Whereas distribution of cognitive responsibility requires that members focus on and verbalize different types of cognitive activity. Cognitive specialization is determined by examining two classes of cognitive activity associated with authority: (1) management of processes and (2) interpretation and decision-making activity [2]. For this reason, percent talk related to these activities was identified by team member. Based on patterns of talk, teams were then classified into one of three ordinal, cognitive specialization patterns. The lowest is a type 1, where no cognitive specialization is shown: one person controls both types of thinking processes. Type two indicates that some specialization is present, but people share rather than completely distribute cognitive responsibilities: one person controls majority of one form of thinking and shares the other with a team member. A type 3, the highest form of cognitive specialization, is defined as complete cognitive specialization, where one person controls one form of thinking and another member controls another. For example, one person might contribute 50% of all the interpretation talk, but a different person would contribute over 50% of the talk related to managing team processes.

3.9 Examining the Sophistication of Collective Cognition Through Externalized Strategies

Strategy use was utilized as a means to identify the sophistication of collective cognitive behaviors. This is because the strategies people use can provide a lens as to how people go about solving a problem [20]. We used interaction analysis as our primary method for analyzing the video data [11]. The identification of externalized collective problem-solving strategies was the result of extensive qualitative analysis headed by the first author and informed by members of the research team. Students were trained to observe and take notes on teams in order to create detailed content logs of important behaviors such as artifact use, reference to critical information, and cognitive strategies.

Content logs of video activity were developed, and notes of behaviors were stored for each of the microanalyzed teams. These logs were used to develop conceptual models of the activities the teams engaged in and were compared to student observations. Research group discussions were used as a means to verify observations and organize the primary tasks and related activities. The transcripts were also visually coded in order to indicate when certain behaviors occurred. These behaviors were then connected to speech acts. Video, transcripts, and artifacts were examined in concert in order to evaluate cognitive activity (see figure 1).

Once observed behaviors were agreed upon and connected to theory, a construct map was developed of the most common observed strategies, classified by sophistication of cognitive behavior. These were defined, assigned a code, and informed by examples of what the behavior would look like in practice. Though the first author analyzed all of the externalized cognitive strategies presented in this study, an inter-rater test was conducted in order to determine the reliability of the coding construct. As such, a senior undergraduate researcher with two years on communication analysis training used the coding construct to assess a four hour session that included 1362 speech acts and 175 speech acts associated with a cognitive artifact: Kappa = 0.71.

In order to contrast discourse content and the sophistication of cognitive behaviors on a finer grain scale of analysis, two teams were selected with similar input characteristics but different cognitive specialization and performance. Both teams included two males and one female member, showed equal levels of engagement, contained students with similar majors, and reported similar levels of psychological safety. Both teams were also extremely equitable in information transfer speech acts: verbal contributions related to members transferring information from existing documents to other team members. They also contributed similar amounts of critical information: the information that needed to be shared to solve the task. The main difference between teams was that they were on opposite spectrums of cognitive specialization and performance: one team was a high performing team with complete cognitive specialization and one team was a low performing team with no cognitive specialization.

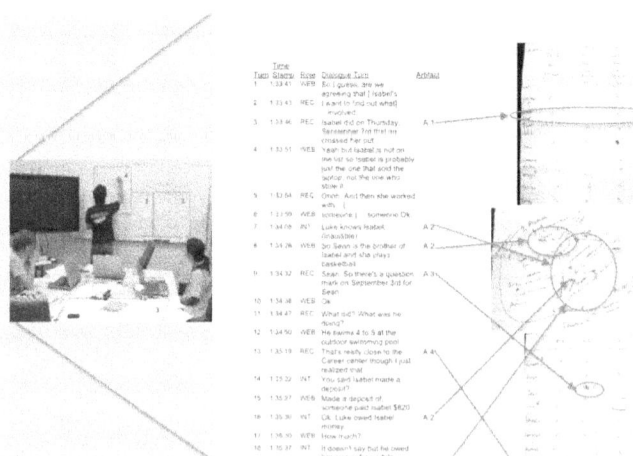

Figure 1. This picture illustrates the process that coders enacted when assessing collective problem-solving strategies and how artifacts were used. When categorizing behaviors, coders watched video while reading transcripts that identified the artifacts used and examining the artifacts referenced by the video and transcripts.

4. FINDINGS

4.1 Verbal Equity, Cognitive Specialization, and Performance

The first research question centered on examining the extent to which consistently high performing teams would show higher levels of verbal equity when compared to consistently low performing teams. Findings showed no significant differences or trends in verbal equity between consistently high and consistently low performing teams (see figure 2). The medians for verbal equity were actually higher for low performing teams than high performing teams; the medians were 3 and 1.5, respectively.

The second research question focused on examining the extent to which cognitive specialization differed between consistently high and low performing teams. Findings showed a significant difference in cognitive specialization. The median for cognitive specialization for low performing teams was 1, and for high performing teams, it was 2. The mean ranks for low and high performing teams were 8.10 and 12.90, respectively; $U = 26$, $Z = -2.068$, $p < 0.05$, $r = 0.46$. There were also no examples of low performing teams showing high levels of cognitive specialization. Eight out of the ten low performing teams had one person dominating both forms of cognitive activity. On the other hand, the majority of high performing teams (6/10) displayed some sort of cognitive specialization. Within both groups, there was also a trend for higher average scores to be associated with more cognitive specialization. Our two highest teams showed complete cognitive specialization. Thus, cognitive specialization seems to have its main effects at the extremes of our data, where scores of one are highly associated with poor performance and scores of three are only found among our highest performing teams (see figure 3).

4.2 Cognitive Specialization and Cognitive Strategies

In order to have a better understanding as to why cognitive specialization may help teams to perform consistently better over time, it is necessary to examine the content of the teams' cognitive activity and illustrate what cognitive specialization looks like in practice. For this reason, two teams were contrasted that shared similar input characteristics but differed in cognitive specialization and performance. These two extremes were compared because our findings indicate that cognitive specialization is most influential at these extremes. The major process characteristics of each team are provided first, followed by summaries and transcript examples of how the teams progressed through the activity. The two teams are team 21, a low performing team with no cognitive specialization, and team 2, a high performing team with complete cognitive specialization.

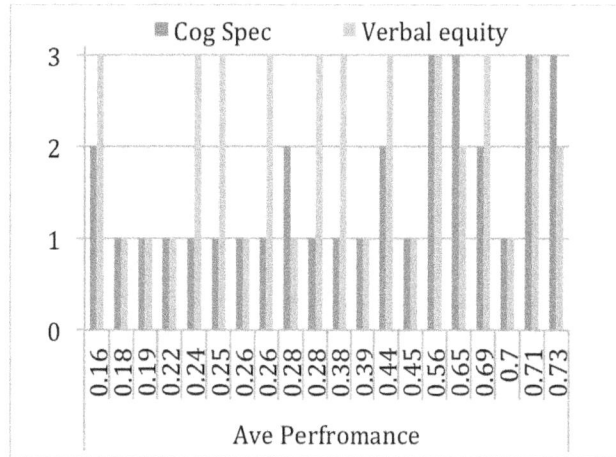

Figure 2. Cognitive specialization and verbal equity score by average performance.

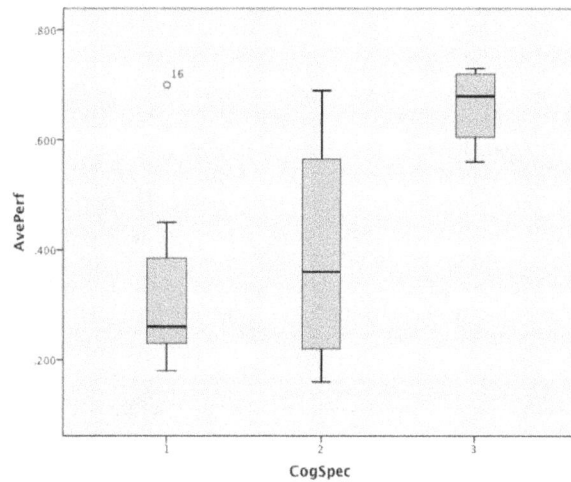

Figure 3. A box plot comparing average performance and cognitive specialization scores. Only one of the teams with the highest average performance, case 16, did not show cognitive specialization, whereas most lower performing teams showed little to no cognitive specialization.

	Total Verbal Equity	Process Management	Interpretation
Team 21 Consistently Low performing with no cognitive specialization.	30% 39% 31%	16% 32% 52%	13% 39% 48%
Team 2 Consistently high Performing with complete cognitive specialization.	37% 19% 44%	53% 41% 6%	33% 21% 46%

Figure 4: A comparison of two teams with similar input characteristics but at different extremes of cognitive specialization. Team 21 had one person contribute the majority of talk for interpretation and process management activity, whereas Team 2 had one person contribute the most talk for process management and a different person contribute the majority of talk for interpretation.

Figure 4 illustrates the process characteristics of the two teams and shows how speech acts were distributed among team members. Information transfer speech acts are not shown, since both teams were perfectly equitable in this category. This means that all members contributed equally when sharing information from their intelligence reports.

The first column in figure 4 shows the distribution of total speech acts for each team (i.e., verbal equity) across the entire scenario. The next two columns show distribution of speech acts related to different forms of thinking: process management and interpretation of content. This figure makes it possible to see visually how one member dominates process management and interpretation talk in team 21. In contrast, two different members dominate the different forms of thinking in team 2.

These differences in process characteristics and cognitive specialization can be seen in context, as the teams' progression through the activity is closely examined. Both teams faced similar challenges with cognitive load, but how this load was managed varied by team. Both teams used emergent artifacts to help reduce cognitive load, but only one team distributed cognitive responsibilities.

Both teams began part 1 of the scenario in similar fashion: they introduced themselves and the type of data they each had. Recall that the aim of part 1 was to narrow down a list of 26 persons of interest (POIs) to the eight most likely suspects by using intelligence reports to make a case for means, motive, and opportunity. Both teams proposed the same off-loading strategy about 30 minutes into part 1 of the task: create a table to go through and eliminate names as members share information about POIs. In the next few sections, differences in how this strategy was implemented and the strategies that followed are illustrated.

In team 21, the members are Interview (male), Record (male), and Web (female). Table 1, example 1, includes the transcript example, referred to in this section. Turns of speech are numbered for easy reference. Interview attempts to manage the process of sharing information by suggesting they create an elimination list by crime event (turn 1). Record steps in and suggests they also add suspects who could have done it (turn 4). Interview agrees and then Record leads the information sharing process by imposing the use of his list along with an organization strategy based on personal preference (turn 6). Record then states he will write down everyone's name on his paper and write down rationale related to potential opportunity to commit the crime. Given that this is an individual document and not immediately accessible to others, this gives Record the primary access to information necessary for decision-making. These actions inadvertently place two forms of cognitive demands on Record: (1) managing the process of information sharing and synthesis activity and (2) interpreting synthesized information.

About ten minutes in to their strategy use, they begin to show signs of cognitive overload (see table 1, team 21, example 2). Team members are sharing information about a person of interest (POI) named Jeff. Record is managing the synthesis of information and leading the decision-making process. This example demonstrates what happens when a person dominates two different forms of cognitive activity. Record is making most of the decision-making and process management speech acts. He decides when to move on to the next person (turns 1 and 11). When Record pushes to the next POI and states that he does not have any information on him in turn 1, Web states that she does (turn 2), but Record cuts her off to share irrelevant information

seemingly unaware that she has spoken (turns 3). As they share information, each takes separate notes, making it difficult to pay attention to important aspects of shared information. This may be why we see people repeating information questioningly (turns 6 and 10). Record claims that Jeff may be a suspect because they have very little information about him, and Web agrees with his claim (turns 6-7). Record then remembers that they have no

Table 1. Transcript examples for teams 21 and 2. Each episode includes time stamps above examples to indicate when in the task the example occurred. Turns are numbered for easier referencing. Team members are referred to by their task role names: interview (Int), web, and record (Rec). In team 21 (low performing), Interview proposes an initial strategy.

Team 21	
Example 1 (31:16 - 32:20)	
1 Int:	I think there's gotta be...yeah. Can we maybe go through and try and eliminate people?
2 Rec:	Or something. What is with the...what did she say to...
3 Int:	Umm...alright well why don't we start, we'll start with the first one, the August 28th one, and why don't we each go through and try and cut people out that we know were doing thing at that time or...
4 Rec:	Do you just wanna write like, okay, we do like Monday and then like write who, who's free during that time or just make a list and be like can't do it, can't do it, can't do it. Do you wanna do like that one like that one like we can use a different day, well maybe we can write each other's information.
5 Int:	Yeah, so why don't we go through and we'll, if you come across someone that was busy at 8am Friday.
6 Rec:	Okay, so 8am Friday is, it's definitely...let me see, Well I have the whole list you wanna start with Zakira. Zakira, wanna just write her name. Like I would say write everyone's name and put like a reason why. Zakira she, it wasn't her because she was a victim.
Example 2 (39:44 - 40:41))	
1 Rec:	So out. Okay then Jeff. Um...I don't have anything on him.
2 Web:	I do-
3 Rec:	- (Not awknowledging Web) Jeff used uhh (searching document)...exercise room on Friday 10/9, that's a different Friday.
4 Int:	(reading from document) All I have is that someone said Jeff was a really nice guy.
5 Web:	Jeff used the umm (searching document)..the Rec Building Thursday from 3 to 5. (looks up) That's all I have on him.
6 Rec:	(Writing on notes) Thursday? ... but that's it, so he's possible right.
7 Web:	Yeah.
8 Int:	Or Friday.
9 Rec:	(Searching notes) No wait we have no reason to steal.
10 Int:	Jeff?
11 Rec:	Yes. um..next...L-E E-L-L-E, previously interned at the same company, uhh.. Thursday 2 to 5, that's not Friday.
Team 2	
Example 1 (26:48 - 27:07)	
1 Web:	Would it be quicker if we just go through these names and eliminate all the people.
2 Rec:	Ok.
3 Int:	Yeah.
4 Web	Ok so Ariana.
5 Rec:	Ariana...
Example 2 (35:11- 36:08)	
1 Rec:	I'm getting lost in the time and the days. It's so hard to keep track. I'm going to write something. (Creation of large artifact G2_PH1_G_1.JPG; Location- Directly center on the white board)
2 Web:	What are you going to write?
3 Rec:	What's the (Inaudible). (Starts writing on big piece of paper.)
4 Web:	This is a permanent marker (tries to hand it to Record).
5 Rec:	(Record keeps using a regular marker) It's fine. What is the time of the theft? Friday 8/29, 9/3, 10/6. This is Friday.
6 Web:	Friday, Tuesday, Thursday, Friday.
7 Rec:	...Monday, Friday. What time?
8 Int:	8am ...[
9 Web:	4pm, 3pm, (Inaudible)]
10 Rec:	Ok, I'm just going to put the names down here so that then we can cross it out.
11 Int:	That last one in an AM.
12 Rec:	Oh, sorry AM. Ok.
13 Web:	You're going to put all 27 names?
14 Rec:	No whatever names we're discussing I'm going to cross them out so at least we know.
16 Web:	I guess Frank now.
17 Rec:	Ok.

motive for Jeff (turn 9). Meanwhile, Interview is unsure about whom the group is talking about (turn 10). This pattern of checking and clarifying previously shared information persists even when teammates make important claims.

Though the team displays signs of cognitive overload, they persist with the same strategy, unable to recognize that creating a shared artifact may help them with part 1 of the task. The team has 55 minutes to select the 8 most likely suspects from a list of 26 POIs, but 43 minutes into the activity, the team has only "guessed" two names. The team is unable to see that their process is flawed and that their strategy is not working. Record even states, "So far we only have like two guesses. So this is pretty good... It's working right..."

We turn now to team 2. In team 2, the members are Interview (male), Record (female), and Web (male). Similar to team 21, Team 2 (high performing) also proposes going through and eliminating names (see table 1, Team 2, Example 1). Web makes the suggestion, and Record agrees without modifying Web's strategy (turns 1-2). Web then proceeds to call for information on the first suspect by alphabetical order (turn 4). At this point, Team 2 also does not create a shared team artifact. Instead, each person takes notes.

About ten minutes into their strategy use, similar to team 21, team 2 begins to experience problems keeping track of shared information, but team 2 handles the situation differently. At this point, Record begins to take control over managing team processes. This is where overt cognitive specialization begins for Record (see table 1, Team 2, Example 2).

In this example, Record recognizes that there is too much information to keep track of it separately, so she creates a large shared artifact, a table (turn 1). Web asks what Record is creating, but before answering, Record begins to ask the team for some of the task variables and creates a matrix of POI names by crime event (turns 1-9). Record proposes using this artifact so they can enter data together and cross people out (turn 10). Web asks if Record plans to list all 26 names, but Record replies that only the names of those they discuss will be written down (turns 13-14). Record writes down the names of those the team has already discussed in alphabetical order, ending with Elle, and Web adds, "okay, I guess Frank now" (turn 16), accepting that Record will manage this process.

The team uses the table to discuss people in alphabetical order and keep track of whom they had and had not discussed. They also keep track of whether each person they discuss is available for each of the four crimes. All during information sharing and synthesis, Record manages the team's time, makes sure each member shares relevant information, and suggests they look at maps or other artifacts when necessary. At this point, interpretation activity is still fairly distributed. This changes towards the end of part 1.

Once the team finishes synthesizing all the information on the shared artifact, they realize they only selected six out of the eight suspects and are unsure how to continue. Web steps in and decides to go over the information contained on the table, making checking and clarifying statements about information contained in the table. Rec serves as a resource for clarification of the information she wrote on the table.

After this point in part 1, the primary exchanges are between Web and Rec, with Int only adding information from his documents

when necessary. Their exchanges were similar to the following example:

> Web: So Luke has criminal record and Tay has a criminal record. What else?
> Rec: What do you mean what else?
> Web: I mean who else has incentive.

This is when Web takes over responsibility of interpretation activity, pushing the team to think more deeply. Meanwhile, Record continues to manage the artifacts and time management, pushing the team to use shared data and make progress. In the end, Record asks Web to pick the final suspect for the team when they cannot decide based on the information contained in the artifact.

After both teams submitted their solutions to part 1, they were provided with the actual solutions and given time to reflect. In part 2 of the task, the teams had to take the list of eight suspects provided by the police (the solutions to part 1) and identify four thieves, accomplices, motives, and determine whether any of the thefts were related. The interaction patterns in part 2 for both teams remain the same as those they developed in part 1.

In team 21 (low performing), Record continues to dominate all forms of cognitive activity. Interview initiates creation of the shared artifact in part 2 of the task, but Record eventually takes this over. Interview creates a system of color-coding and symbols, but as Record juggles decision-making and management responsibilities, Record begins to make repeated mistakes in how the symbols and colors are applied. Record eventually starts using the artifact as a means to collect his pet theories rather than as a means to analyze shared data. Over time, Record begins to pull information from members that he sees as relevant, rather than letting team members share information they believe to be relevant. For this reason, the team uses their artifacts in fairly unsophisticated ways (see table 2). The artifacts are primarily used as a means to record shared information and pull out information as necessary.

In team 2 (high performing), Record manages most of the artifacts in part 2, creating and writing on them as the team works to deconstruct the task and synthesize information. However, when it comes time to make final decisions, Web creates a shared decision-making table and manages it for the team while Record continues to manage the other artifacts.

Over the entire three-part scenario, both teams displayed a variety of strategic behaviors associated with artifact use, but Team 2 engaged in more sophisticated strategic behaviors than team 21. Table 2 illustrates the different types of strategies displayed by both teams. Team 2 displayed sophisticated cognitive behaviors associated with deep thinking processes and abstract thinking [1, 12]. They used the inherent properties of their elimination table to organize and exclude information they included on the table and on successor artifacts. They also used multiple representations to link information across artifacts during their decision-making process. In essence, Team 2 created different artifacts to offload and organize different aspects of the task and then linked the artifacts together by pulling information from the artifacts simultaneously to look for patterns during decision-making.

It might be possible to argue that differences between the teams could have been due to motivation, but that doesn't seem to be the case. All of our participants stated greatly enjoying the task and many, including team 21, were surprised by their poor performance. Most spent considerable time after the tasks trying

Table 2. List of collective problem-solving strategies exhibited by Team 21 and Team 2 as they used shared artifacts. Team 21 had no cognitive specialization and Team 2 had complete cognitive specialization. Some of the behaviors coincide with those described by other researchers; these are cited where possible.

Types of Strategies	Behavior	Definition	Team 21	Team 2
Cognitive	Accretion [4]	Act of recording: inscribing verbalized information unto the artifact "as is" without data reduction strategy. May continue to add more information or rules to artifact.	X	X
	Fact retrieval	To refer to a piece of shared information contained in the artifact as part of an information transfer or check/clarify behavior.	X	X
	Identify needed info	To use artifact as a means to deduce what other information pieces are necessary to search for.	X	X
	Support Claims	To pull specific information piece from artifact contents to use as rationale to support claim.	X	X
	Refute Claims	To pull specific information piece from artifact content to use as evidence against a claim.		X
	Filtering/ Constraining interpretation [1, 4]	Act of filtering: To use inherent properties in the artifact to organize and exclude information from or to another artifact.		X
	Extension [1]	(Task) To make a generalization about people, events, or claims, etc. based on aggregated information contained in the artifact.		X
Sociocognitive	Confirm	To use content on artifact to ensure proper understanding of another's claim.	X	X
	Repair	To use content on artifact to identify & correct misunderstanding or missing information previously stated.	X	X
	Anchor Talk	To use information contained in the artifact to make people aware of narrowing the topic of discussion to a specific person, place, event, or location on the artifact.	X	X
	Organize Talk	To use content of artifact to organize the order in which information is shared or which topics are to be discussed.		X
Metacognitive	Task Decomposition	(Artifact) To identify and organize aspects of the artifact, such as features, symbols, and color-coding.	X	X
	Monitor	To use artifact to make a meta comment regarding amount of information shared, reliability of information, identification of missing information, or what remains to be done.	X	X
	Task Decomposition	(Task) To identify & organize variables of the task in the artifact as a means to break down the task into smaller ordered sub-tasks.		X
Cognitive Event	Cognitive Linking [12]	To use multiple representations (more than two) to link information across artifacts during decision making processes		X

to understand where they went wrong. For example, following part 1 of the scenario, Team 21 was so troubled by their poor performance that they revisited their information in attempts to figure out how they went wrong. At one point, they looked to see how they could have missed a key piece of information about one of the suspects, George. Record questions his team:

Rec: Do you have anything for George?
Web: Um let me look through it again... oh, yeah, right here! Oh, S###, it's my fault! It did say something about George having really aggressive- (reading from his intelligence documents) "I can't believe Upton f##### and vandalized my car! I saw him!".

It turned out that Web had highlighted one of George's Facebook posts as important since it referenced a victim, but Web did not share it with the team. Web accepts responsibility for the failure, but in reality it was a failure of the team, as Record controlled the sharing process. Record only asked for certain forms of information and decided when to move on to another suspect. At one point, when the team was discussing an irrelevant suspect, Web interjected that George seemed particularly violent, but Web

was ignored by the team. Web made various attempts to place George as a suspect, but Web's statements were consistently overlooked. Web asked, "George, did we do George? What was his status?" To which Record responded, "Yeah, George is out."

It is important to note that Record was not being purposefully rude and team interactions were not overtly negative. Rather, the team was simply not effectively synthesizing and negotiating ideas from all team members.

5. DISCUSSION
When it comes to complex collaborative tasks, our findings suggest that cognitive specialization may be a more critical variable than verbal equity. We found no significant differences between the verbal equity of high and low performing teams, but did find significant differences in cognitive specialization. The majority of the highest performing teams had some form of cognitive specialization. In contrast, our lowest performing teams had one member control both types of cognitive activity.

Our data further suggests that cognitive specialization may be associated with higher quality collective cognitive processes. Findings regarding the range of sophistication of cognitive behaviors and strategies used by teams indicate that when teams distribute responsibility for thinking about how to synthesize information and how to negotiate information the team as a whole engages in more sophisticated forms of thinking. Our qualitative findings illustrate that this may be due to an individual's cognitive limitations. It may be that when an individual takes on too much cognitive responsibility, they may be more prone to error and therefore act as a bottleneck to higher quality forms of team reasoning. This suggests that simply sharing cognitive responsibilities may not be helpful for a team. The goal should be to maximize cognitive power through cognitive specialization.

Existing theories of cognition and learning can help to support and explain this claim. Cognitive psychologists have long claimed that humans have a limited capacity of working memory, and this limited capacity must deal with all of the cognitive demands a person faces at any given time (for review see 14, 26). Tasks that pose high cognitive demands can overwhelm individuals [25], but researchers have theorized that cognitive optimization may be the solution to better collaborative performance [14]. This may be why groups are better able to adapt to high stress situations [3], because there are more individuals to share the cognitive load. However, as most people have experienced, the inclusion of more people on a team does not necessarily lead to better team performance. From a cognitive load perspective, one would expect better performance from teams that can utilize their members more effectively while keeping in mind the limits of individual working memory [14]. This suggests that allowing a member to specialize in one form of cognitive activity while reducing others may provide that individual with the required amount of working memory to engage in more sophisticated forms of thinking around their specialized form of cognition. Collectively, such behaviors could lead to more sophisticated levels of team reasoning.

Our findings also help shed light on previous studies that examined collective problem solving. For example, Convertino et al. [6] found the frequency of certain speech acts to be associated with performance. They found that higher amounts of check and clarify acts were negatively associated with team performance and Push acts (where members added information without prompting) were more beneficial than Pull acts (where members were asked for specific types of information). Our analysis supports and extends these findings. Team 21 (low performing) had a high frequency of check and clarify acts and our microanalysis suggests that this pattern may be indicative of cognitive overload. As such, the team displays check and clarify behaviors as a means to try to establish common ground. Thus some check and clarify acts may be helpful, but too many may be indicative of an inability to establish common ground.

Our findings may also help to explain why Push acts may be more beneficial than Pull acts. Drawing from our microanalysis of Team 21 (high performing), a high frequency of Pull acts may narrow down the scope of what is shared prematurely and may also be indicative of dominant members.

Our qualitative findings suggest there are a number of diverse cognitive deficiencies that can occur during collective problem solving. For this reason, enhancing collective intelligence may not be a simple matter of driving up one subskill or one behavior (like equity), but rather it will require a broader collection of support. Many collaborative environments focus on supporting and testing

a single skill, but our findings suggest that collaborative teams need more systemic cognitive support. Researchers have long maintained that technology must provide systemic support of cognitive, metacognitive, and social activity in order to facilitate the development of complex scientific thinking practices [21, 29]. Our findings indicate that this type of systemic support may be necessary for complex, information-dependent problem solving in general.

Studies on collective intelligence are still in their infancy and there is a need to examine collaborative processes further through the use of more complex tasks. The tasks commonly utilized in studies of collaborative problem solving tend to be less complex, as they do not require participants to engage in a range of sophisticated cognitive activities all at once. As such, these shorter, simplified tasks may not generalize well to real-world collaborative teams encumbered with solving far more complex problems.

Though our study used a more sophisticated task and examined group processes at multiple scales of analysis, it was still limited. Given our rigorous methods, we were only able to analyze a small amount of teams. Since we were looking to identify characteristics associated with performance, we also chose to do a comparison study; this limited the types of analysis we could conduct. Thus, more research in the area of collective intelligence is needed. Specifically, the field needs to look for additional variables at the process level that may impact learning and decision-making.

The results of this study are important given recent, high impact studies that indicate the importance of verbal equity [30]. Our findings provide an argument against focusing too narrowly on designing for equitable participation, a common theme in CSCW and CSCL [10, 18]. Moreover, it is important to examine interactions at the process level in order to better inform the design of collaborative technologies. For example, many researchers have focused on developing technologies to encourage verbal equity, but our findings indicate that such features may pose trade-offs that need to be considered carefully, as increasing or decreasing a specific member's amount of participation at any given time may interfere with the development of cognitive specialization.

Future research should examine the trade-offs associated with the scripting of strategies to promote cognitive specialization or technology support that enhances a team's ability to monitor and regulate information synthesis and negotiation processes. Whether or not teams can learn to engage in more sophisticated collective thinking processes and to what extent such improvement would enhance joint knowledge-building activity and collective intelligence are important questions that remain to be answered.

6. CONCLUSION

A great deal of research has focused on examining the relationship between group characteristics, processes, and group outcomes but primarily from a traditional, individualistic cognitive perspective [17], whereby the group context serves individual learning or individual characteristics affect group outcomes. Unfortunately, such studies have done little to inform our theories of collective cognition [8, 13, 26].

Current research paradigms place more importance on large, quantitative studies, but these studies have limitations when it comes to unpacking phenomenon that is dependent upon interactions between individuals, such as collective intelligence. Large quantitative studies are quite useful for detecting patterns with input and output, but are less useful in determining why these patterns exist at the process level. Understanding the collective cognitive processes that determine collective intelligence and the resulting cognitive needs of teams requires that we also carefully examine language and interactions between group members [8, 23]. This necessitates the utilization of difficult and time-consuming methods that limit the size of the population being examined. For this reason it is imperative that we as a research community do not prioritize either large quantitative or more in-depth qualitative approaches to understanding collective intelligence, but rather find ways to synthesize findings across levels of scale. In this way we can make combined progress on identifying and evaluating key variables associated with this complex phenomenon.

One of the most important contributions of this study is to push the field to recognize that "collective intelligence" needs to be theorized more broadly. At this stage of work on collective intelligence, we should be looking for more constructs to include and evaluate, and we should avoid focusing too singularly on equity or even cognitive specialization.

7. ACKNOWLEDGMENTS

We thank Craig Ganoe and Shin-I Shih for help in designing the scenario and coordinating the study. We also are grateful to all of the research assistants who worked on this project but particularly Scott Cunningham, Daniel Nussbaum, and Jennifer Stout, who spent countless hours transcribing, cleaning, and coding data. This project was partially supported by the US Office of Naval Research (N000140910303/ N000141110221), the Edward M. Frymoyer Chair Endowment, and the National Science Foundation (IIS-1319445).

8. REFERENCES

[1] Ainsworth, S. (2006). DeFT: A conceptual framework for considering learning with multiple representations. *Learning and Instruction, 16*(3), 183-198.

[2] Borge, M., Ganoe, C., Shih, S., and Carroll, J. (2012). Patterns of team processes and breakdowns in information analysis tasks. In Proceedings of the ACM 2012 conference on Computer Supported Cooperative Work. (CSCW '12). ACM, New York, New York.

[3] Brown T. , Miller, C. (2000). Communication networks in task-performing groups: effects of task complexity, time pressure, and interpersonal dominance. *Small Group Res.* 31(2):131–57

[4] Carroll, J., Borge, M., & Shih, S. (2013). Cognitive Artifacts as a Window on Design. Journal of Visual Languages and Computing (2013), http://dx.doi.org/10.1016/j.jvlc.2013.05.001i

[5] Convertino, G., Mentis, H., Bhambare, P., Ferro, C., Carroll, J. M., & Rosson, M. B. (2008). Comparing media in emergency planning. In *Proceedings of the 5th International ISCRAM Conference, Washington, DC.*

[6] Convertino, G., Mentis, H. M., Rosson, M. B., Slavkovic, A., & Carroll, J. M. (2009). Supporting content and process common ground in computer-supported teamwork. In *Proceedings of the SIGCHI Conference on Human Factors in Computing Systems* (pp. 2339-2348). ACM.

[7] Cooke, N.J., DeJoode, J.A., Pedersen, H.K., Gorman, J.C., Connor, O.O., & Kiekel, P.A. (2004). *The role of individual and team cognition in uninhabited air vechicle command-*

and-control. Technical Report for AFOSR Grant Nos. F49620-01-1-0261and F49620-03-1-00248.

[8] Dillenbourg, P., & Traum, D. (1999). *The long road from a shared screen to a shared understanding.* Paper presented at the Proceedings of the Computer Support for Collaborative Learning (CSCL) 1999 Conference, Palo Alto, California.

[9] Fiore, S., Rosen, M., Smith-Jentsch, K., & Salas, E. (2010). Toward an Understanding of Macrocognition in Teams: Predicting Processes in Complex Collaborative Contexts. *Human Factors.*

[10] Harris, A., Rick, J., Bonnett, V., Yuill, N., Fleck, R., Marshall, P., & Rogers, Y. (2009, June). Around the table: are multiple-touch surfaces better than single-touch for children's collaborative interactions?. In *Proceedings of the 9th international conference on Computer supported collaborative learning-Volume 1* (pp. 335-344). International Society of the Learning Sciences.

[11] Jordan, B., & Henderson, A. (1995). Interaction analysis: Foundations and practice. *The journal of the learning sciences, 4*(1), 39-103.

[12] Kaput, J. J. (1989). Linking representations in the symbol systems of algebra. In S. Wagner, & C. Kieran, Research issues in the learning and teaching of algebra (pp. 167±194). Hillsdale, NJ: Erlbaum.

[13] Kerr, N. L., & Tindale, R. S. (2004). Group performance and decision making. *Annu. Rev. Psychol., 55*, 623-655.

[14] Kirschner, P. A. (2002). Cognitiv load theory: Implications of cognitive load theory on the design of learning. *Learning and instruction, 12*(1), 1-10.

[15] Landis, J. R., Koch, G. G. The measurement of observer agreement for categorical data. *Biometrics* 33 (1977), 159-174.

[16] Letsky, M., & Warner, N. (2008). Macrocognition in teams. In M. Letsky, N. Warner, S. Fiore & C. Smith (Eds.), *Macrocognition in Teams: Theories and Methodologies.* Hampshire: Ashgate Publishing Limited.

[17] Norman, D. A. (1990). *Four (more) issues for cognitive science.* Department of Cognitive Science, University of California, San Diego.

[18] Marshall, P., Hornecker, E., Morris, R., Dalton, N. S., & Rogers, Y. (2008, October). When the fingers do the talking: A study of group participation with varying constraints to a tabletop interface. In *Horizontal Interactive Human Computer Systems, 2008. TABLETOP 2008. 3rd IEEE International Workshop on* (pp. 33-40). IEEE.

[19] Schafer, W.A., Ganoe, C.H. & Carroll, J.M. Supporting community emergency management through a geocollaboration software infrastructure. *Computer-Supported Cooperative Work: The Journal of Collaborative Computing, 16* (2007), 501-537.

[20] Schraw, G., Crippen, K. J., & Hartley, K. (2006). Promoting self-regulation in science education: Metacognition as part of a broader perspective on learning. *Research in Science Education, 36*(1-2), 111-139.

[21] Shimoda, T., White, B., Borge, M., & Frederiksen, J. (2013). Designing for science learning and collaborative discourse. In *Proceedings of the 12th International Conference on Interaction Design and Children* (pp. 247-256). ACM.

[22] Stahl, G. (2006). Knowledge negotiation online. In G. Stahl (Ed.), *Group Cognition* (pp. 177-189). Cambridge. MA: MIT Press.

[23] Stahl, G., Koschmann, T., & Suthers, D. (2006). Computer-supported collaborative learning: An historical perspective. In R. K. Sawyer (Ed.), Cambridge handbook of the learning sciences (pp. 409-426). Cambridge, UK: Cambridge University Press.

[24] Stasser, G., & Titus, W. (1985). Pooling of unshared information in group decision making: Biased information sampling during discussion. *Journal of personality and social psychology*, *48*(6), 1467.

[25] Sweller, J. (1994). Cognitive load theory, learning difficulty, and instructional design. *Learning and instruction*, *4*(4), 295-312.

[26] Van Merrienboer, J. J., & Sweller, J. (2005). Cognitive load theory and complex learning: Recent developments and future directions. *Educational psychology review*, *17*(2), 147-177.

[27] Warner, N., Burkman, L., & Biron, C. H. Special operations reconnaissance (SOR) scenario: Intelligence analysis and mission planning, No. NAWCADPAX/TM-2008/184, 2008.

[28] West, G. P. Collective Cognition: When Entrepreneurial Teams, Not Individuals, Make Decisions. *Entrepreneurship Theory and Practice,* 31,1 (2007), 77- 102.

[29] White, B. Y., & Frederiksen, J. R. (1998). Inquiry, modeling, and metacognition: Making science accessible to all students. *Cognition and instruction*, *16*(1), 3-118.

[30] Woolley, A., Chabris, C., Pentland, A., Hashmi, M., & Malone, T. Evidence for a collective intelligence factor in the performance of human groups. *Science, 330,* 6004 (2010), 686-688.

Supporting String-Wise Operations and Selective Undo for Peer-to-Peer Group Editing

Weihai Yu

UiT – The Arctic University of Norway

Weihai.Yu@uit.no

ABSTRACT

Real-time group editing has been envisioned as an effective manner of collaboration. For years, operational transformation (OT) has been the standard concurrency control mechanism for real-time group editing, due to its potential for high responsiveness to local editing operations. OT algorithms are generally non-trivial to be error-free and are computation intensive. Recently, commutative replicated data types (CRDT) have appeared as an alternative to OT. The state-of-the-art OT and CRDT work still lacks the basic functionality found in single-user text editors. In particular, there is no published work that supports both string-wise operations and selective undo. This paper presents an approach that combines and extends OT and CRDT strengths. It is fully decentralized and supports string-wise editing operations and selective undo. Our performance study shows that it provides sufficient responsiveness to the end-users.

Categories and Subject Descriptors

C.2.4 [**Computer-Communication Networks**]: Distributed Systems—*Distributed applications*; H.5.3 [**Information Interfaces and Presentation**]: Group and Organization Interfaces—*Collaborative computing*

General Terms

Algorithms, Performance

Keywords

Real-time collaborative editor, commutative replicated data type, operation transformation.

1. INTRODUCTION

A real-time group editor allows multiple users to simultaneously edit the same document from different places. Fully decentralized, or peer-to-peer, collaboration has generally the advantage of availability, scalability and resistance to censorship and surveillance, over collaboration via a central server.

GROUP'14, November 9–12, 2014, Sanibel Island, Florida, USA.
Copyright 2014 ACM 978-1-4503-3043-5/14/11 ...$15.00.
http://dx.doi.org/10.1145/2660398.2660401.

Operational transformation (OT) has been established as a concurrency control mechanism for real-time group editing due to its potential for high responsiveness to local operations [4, 5, 6, 7, 8, 10, 14, 15, 16, 17, 18, 19, 21]. Local operations are executed immediately at local peers and later transformed and integrated at remote peers. OT algorithms are sophisticated. Counterexamples of several published OT algorithms have been reported. Moreover, they have time complexity in the length of operation history of the document been edited, which potentially grows endlessly.

Recently, a new class of mechanisms called commutative replicated data types (CRDT) have been proposed [2, 11, 12, 13, 22, 23]. Concurrent operations of a CRDT are mutually commutative, so that a document is eventually kept consistent at all peers.

A real-time group editor should support at least the most basic functionality found in a single-user text editor. At its minimum, it should support insertion and deletion of single characters and strings of characters, as well as the undo and redo of the insertions and deletions. String-wise operations are important as they are the basis for other useful operations like copy-paste, select-delete and find-replace. Surprisingly, there is currently no published work that supports both string-wise operations and their undo.

Our work supports both string-wise operations and their undo by combining and extending existing OT and CRDT approaches.

The rest of this paper is organized as follows. Section 2 presents background and related work. Section 3 gives an overview of the approach. Section 4 presents the view-model architecture and the data structure of the model. Section 5 describes operations and updates in view and model. Section 6 describes how model and view are synchronized. Sections 7 and 8 describe how local and remote operations are integrated into the model. Section 9 shows the correctness of the approach. Section 10 presents performance results. Section 11 discusses some open issues. Section 12 concludes.

2. BACKGROUND

OT was first introduced in [4]. The basic idea is as the following. A shared document is replicated at different peers. An editing operation is first executed at a local peer and then propagated to remote peers. Suppose two peers start with "012". Peer 1 inserts "a" between "0" and "1" with $ins(1, \text{"a"})$ and Peer 2 deletes "2" with $del(2)$. The states after local executions at the two peers are "0a12" and "01". Now if the two peers execute the remote operations as is, the states at these peers become "0a2" and "0a1", which are inconsistent. With OT, the remote operations are transformed to *include* the executed concurrent operations, into $ins(1, \text{"a"})$ and $del(3)$ respectively. The two peers are in consistent state "0a1" after executing the transformed operations.

There are some challenges with this basic approach. First, a remote operation can only be transformed to include a concurrent operation that is compatible, i.e., the two operations operated on exactly the same state. To achieve this, a peer has to first transpose the history of operations to make the operations compatible, and then include the effects of compatible operations. The transposition involves the transformation of both remote operation and operations in the local history. This whole process is sometimes called operation integration. The complexity of operation transformation and integration algorithms, or OT algorithms for short, depends on factors like how operations in the operation history are ordered and whether the integration of remote operations has to follow some restricted order. OT algorithms have linear or quadratic time complexities in the length of the operation history.

Transformation functions are difficult to be made correct. Counterexamples were found for many of the published transformation functions. For instance, [5], [6], [7], [10] and [17] reported counterexamples of earlier work. [8], [10], [11], [14], [15], [16], [17] and [21] are among the few that have no counterexample reported. One source of complication is the role of deleted characters, called *landmarks* in [6] and *tombstones* in [10]. Given three peers all starting with "012". Peers 1, 2 and 3 issue concurrent operations $ins(2, "x")$, $del(1)$ and $ins(1, "a")$ respectively. Because "x" is inserted to the right of "1" and "a" to the left of "1", the final states at all peers must be "0ax2". The deleted character "1" determines the ordering of "a" and ' 'x". However, because "1" is deleted at Peer 2, the two inserted characters thus tie at Peer 2. Most counterexamples are due to failure to break the tie of this type in different combinations of concurrent operations. [20] concludes that this is the only source of puzzles, as far as normal (i.e. not undo) insertion and deletion of single characters are concerned.

Another source of complication is the undo of executed operations. Single-user editors typically support undo of operations in chronological order. In a collaborative editor, operations are not totally ordered chronologically due to concurrent operations. It is therefore necessary to support *selective undo* to undo the effect of any selected operation that has been executed. An undo operation $undo(op)$ is heavily dependent not only on the operation op it undoes, but also on the contexts in which op and $undo(op)$ are executed. Simply issuing a separate reverse operation $\overline{op}$ and transforming it as a normal operation ignore such dependencies and therefore may lead to undesirable results in certain situations, such as in the dOPT puzzle [18]. Some particular solutions are introduced to address this issue. For example, in ABTU [15], $undo(op)$ and op are associated with special attributes and are placed next to each other in the operation history. [21] concludes that operation transformation rules based solely on operation causal relations are no longer sufficient to cope with the complexity of existing OT systems, and introduces a fundamentally different *context-based* OT framework where the dependency of $\overline{op}$ on op becomes more explicit in terms of operation contexts.

Due to the inherent sophistication of OT, most published work only supports single-character insertions and deletions. GOT [19] and ABTS [14] are the only algorithms accessible in the literature that support string-wise operations. [7] identified a counterexample of GOT. Moreover, GOT seems to be superseded by the follow-up work of the same researchers in [21]. There has been no published work following [21] that supports string-wise operations. In ABTS [14], an operation history is composed of a sub-history of insertions followed with a sub-history of deletions. A string-wise deletion may be split into a set of sub-deletions during subsequent operation transformations.

Supporting selective undo or string-wise operations alone is already challenging. Supporting both can be harder. For example, ABTU [15] and ABTS [14], of the same researchers, use different (incompatible) operation history structures to support selective undo and string-wise operations. It is not obvious that ABTU and ABTS can be combined to support both selective undo and string-wise operations.

Recently, CRDT has appeared as an alternative to OT for decentralized real-time group editing. With CRDT, concurrent insertions are ordered based on the underlying data structure rather than on operation transformation, so that the time complexity may not depend on the lengths of operation histories. [2, 12, 13, 22, 23] achieve this by making use of specially designed identifiers associated with edited objects (characters, lines of characters) or operations. An identifier contains information about the relative positioning of objects [2, 12, 13, 22, 23] as well as operation causality [13]. In [2], [12] and [22], the sizes of identifiers can grow unbounded, but experiments show that the sizes stay low even in the most demanding situations. [11] takes a different approach. There, every character is uniquely identified and is associated with the previous and next characters at the time of its original insertion. This information is used for the ordering of the characters at remote peers. Experimental results [1] show that CRDT algorithms outperform OT algorithms by a factor between 25 and 1000.

As the CRDT-based approaches are still quite young, only [2] and [24] support string-wise operations and [22] supports undo. There has been no support for undo of string-wise operations.

We can think of the different approaches from a unified perspective. On the one hand, operation histories in OT approaches can be seen as abstract data types and operations that transpose and manipulate the histories exhibit certain properties similar to commutativity of CRDTs. On the other hand, CRDTs can be regarded as operation histories extended with explicit relations among operations. Based on this unified perspective, our work combines and extends the strengths of the two approaches. The data structure is basically a list of nodes (of sub-strings) that forms a total order, similar to the operation history in ABTU [15] that arranges operations in a total effects-relation order (as formally defined in [7]). In addition, the data structure materializes dependencies among operations. Dependencies among insertions are similar to [11]. To support string-wise operations, additional links connect nodes belonging to the same operations. Additional information is also provided for undo of operations.

Our earlier work on support for string-wise operations was reported in [24]. The initial ideas of this paper was first reported in a short note [25].

3. OVERVIEW OF APPROACH

A document is collaboratively edited by a number of peers at different sites. Every peer consists of a view, a model, a log of operation history and three queues (Figure 1).

A peer concurrently receives local operations from the user and remote updates from other peers. A view is mainly a string of characters. A user at a peer can insert or delete a sub-string at a position in the string, and undo an earlier executed local or remote operation. The user's operations take immediate effect in the view. Local and remote operations are first stored in queues Q_v and Q_{in} and later be integrated in the model. Integrated local operations are first stored in Q_{out} and later broadcast to other peers. When the model is rendered, the effects of integrated remote operations are shown in the view. Integrated operations are also stored in the log. A user can select an operation in the log to undo.

The model is primarily a double-linked list of nodes. Following [7] and [14, 15], we call the order in which the nodes are linked *effects-relation order*. A node contains a sub-string, together with some additional meta-data and links for the operations on the string.

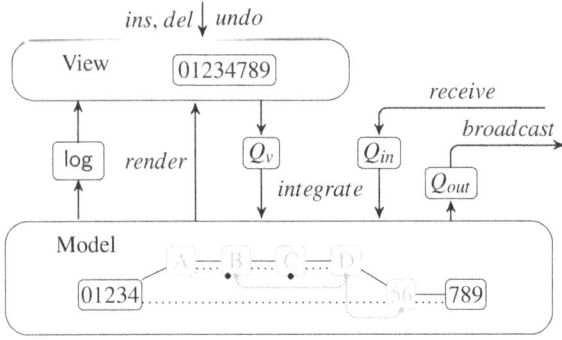

Figure 1: View, model and operations

When operations are integrated into the model, existing nodes are split at operation boundaries, and either new nodes are inserted or existing nodes are marked as deleted or undone. The list thus grows while the document is being edited.

Figure 2 illustrates a model list in different states. When string "0123456789" is first inserted, the model has only one node. Inserting "ABCD" inserts a new node and splits the existing node. Deleting a sub-string further splits existing nodes. Concurrent deletions D_1 and D_2 overlap at "B". When D_1 is undone, only sub-string "D56" is brought back in the view. "B" is still deleted, because D_2 remains in effect. In the figure, characters in gray nodes are invisible in the view. Solid lines between nodes are links maintaining the total effects-relation order among nodes. Dotted lines link nodes belonging to the same insertion. A dot at the bottom of a node indicates a deletion. Nodes of the same deletion are linked with the gray lines between the dots. A dot becomes gray when the deletion is undone. Section 4 explains the model in more detail.

4. DATA STRUCTURE

A peer has an identifier *pid* and maintains a number *pun* (peer update number). *pun* increments by one for every editing operation originated at the peer. An operation is uniquely identified with (pid, pun) at all peers.

A *character string*, or simply *string*, is a sequence of characters. A *position* in a string, represented as a non-negative integer, is a place either left to the leftmost character, between two adjacent characters, or right to the rightmost character, of the string. For string *str*, we use $str[pos]$ to denote the character right to position *pos* in *str*, or *nil* if *pos* is the rightmost position of *str*. Suppose that every character is uniquely identified. We use $pos_{str}[c]$ to indicate the position left to character *c* in *str*. For two adjacent characters c_l and c_r in a *str* and c_l is left to c_r, we have $pos_{str}[c_l] + 1 = pos_{str}[c_r]$.

A *view* is a character string currently visible to the user. The leftmost position of *view* is always 0. $curr_{view}$ is the *current position* in *view*.

A *model* consists of a set of *nodes*. A node is originated with an *ins* operation and we say that a node *belongs* to its originating *ins* operation. A node has an interoperable part and a peer-specific part. The element values of the interoperable part of nodes will be preserved at all peers. The interoperable part of a node *v* contains the following elements:

- *pid*, *pun*, the *id* of the *ins* operation which *v* belongs to.
- *str*, the character string of *v*. We also use *v.len* for *v.str.len*, the length of *v.str*.
- *offset*, the leftmost position of *v.str* with respect to the string of the *ins* operation it belongs to. When a node is originated

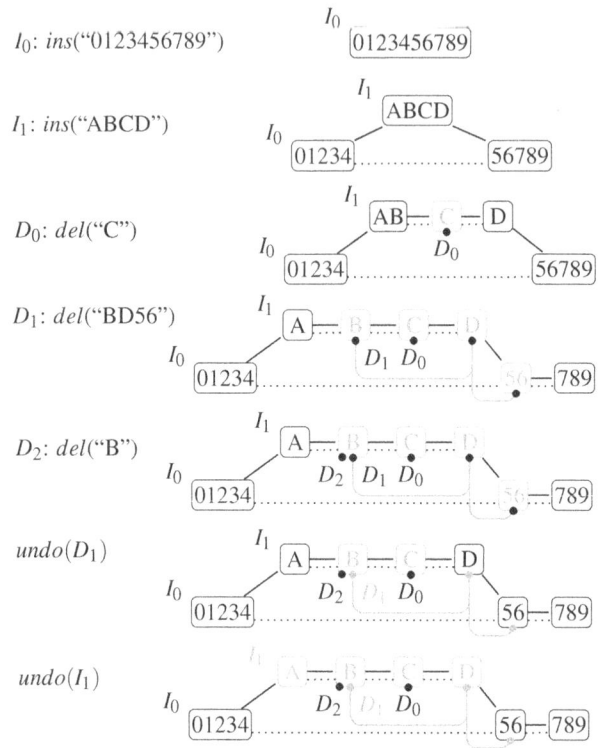

Figure 2: Examples of model updates

with an insertion, its *offset* is 0. Splitting the node at position *pos* leads to two nodes, with *offset*s 0 and *pos* respectively.

- *l*, *r*, the left and right nodes of *v* in effects-relation order. In Figure 2, the *l* and *r* links are illustrated with solid lines.
- i_l, i_r, the left and right nodes of the same *ins* operation. In Figure 2, the i_l and i_r links are illustrated with dotted lines.
- dep_l, dep_r, insert dependencies, i.e. the place of the originating insertion, represented with the right end of the left node $(pid_l, pun_l, offset_l, len_l)$ and the left end of the right node $(pid_r, pun_r, offset_r)$.
- *dels*, a set of *del* elements related to deletions of *v.str*.
- *undo*, the undo of the insertion, or *nil* if the insertion is not undone.

In a peer, a node can be directly referred to via its reference (i.e. a pointer). So the links *l*, *r* etc. refer to nodes with their references.

Node references, however, are meaningless across peer boundaries. Fortunately, a node can be uniquely identified by the *id* of the *ins(str)* operation that inserted the string *str*, together with the *offset* of the node. In Figure 2, suppose the *id* of *ins*("0123456789") is $I_0 = (1,1)$. The node with string "56" can be uniquely identified with $(1,1,5)$. We use $(pid, pun, offset)$ as the *id* of a node. Nodes are hash-indexed with their *id*s. Therefore given $(pid, pun, offset)$, a node can be obtained in near-constant time. In the worst case, if a peer cannot find a node with *id* $(pid, pun, offset)$, it can start from $(pid, pun, 0)$ and follow i_r links to find the node containing position *offset* (and then make a split there). As a convention in this paper, *offset* is specifically used to identify nodes' left ends. For positions in view or inside nodes, we use *pos* instead.

DEFINITION 1. *Node v_l is left to node v_r (or equally, v_r is right to v_l), written as $v_l \prec v_r$ or $v_r \succ v_l$, if either (a) $v_l.r = v_r$ (and*

$v_r.l = v_l$), or (b) there exist $v_1, v_2, \ldots, v_n$, such that $v_l \prec v_1 \prec v_2 \prec \cdots \prec v_n \prec v_r$.

In this paper, we use *properties* to describe invariants on data structures that are maintained by the algorithms. We use $\prec$-order for the effects-relation order among nodes.

PROPERTY 1. *The nodes in a model form a total $\prec$-order.*

An *insertion* consists of the nodes chained with the i_l and i_r links. For insertion of string *str*, if v is the leftmost node of the insertion, $v.i_l = nil \wedge v.offset = 0$; if v is the rightmost node of the insertion, $v.i_r = nil \wedge v.offset + v.len = str.len$; if v is neither the leftmost nor the rightmost node, $v.i_l \neq nil \wedge v.i_r \neq nil \wedge v.offset = v.i_l.offset + v.i_l.len$.

A *deletion* consists of the nodes containing the *del* elements of the same *del* operation. When $v.dels$ of a node contains multiple *del* elements, $v.str$ has been deleted concurrently by multiple peers.

A *del* element has the following (sub-)elements:

- *pid, pun*, the *id* of the *del* operation.
- v, the node whose *dels* contains this *del*.
- *l, r*, the left and right *del* elements of the same *del* operation.
- *undo*, undo of the deletion, or *nil*.

PROPERTY 2. *Let v_l and v_r be nodes and del_l and del_r be del elements. (a) $\prec$-order: $v_l.r = v_r \Leftrightarrow v_r.l = v_l$. (b) Insertion: $v_l.i_r = v_r \Leftrightarrow v_r.i_l = v_l$. (c) Deletion: $del_l.r = del_r \Leftrightarrow del_r.l = del_l$.*

An *undo* element consists of the following (sub-)elements:

- *pid, pun*, the *id* of the *undo* operation.
- *do*, the node, the *del* or the *undo* element this *undo* element is part of.
- *undo*, the *undo* element if this *undo* itself is undone, or *nil* otherwise.
- *ties*, a set of the *id*s of the concurrent undo operations of the same operation.

Please notice the different handling of concurrent *del*s and concurrent *undo*s. Concurrent *undo*s always refer to the same operation to be undone, and thus are regarded as a single *undo*, whereas concurrent *del*s, albeit with overlapping characters, are different operations. Therefore a node maintains a set of *del* elements (with their own sub-elements), but an *undo* element only maintains the sub-elements once for a set of concurrent counterparts.

If an undo operation itself is undone, the *undo* element refers to another *undo* element. An operation's undo elements are thus chained into a linked list.

DEFINITION 2. *An operation is* effectively undone *if it is undone an odd number of times. A node (for insertion) or an element (for deletion or undo) of an operation is* effectively undone *if the length of the undo chain of the node or element is an odd number.*

DEFINITION 3. *A node v is* visible, *written as $v.visible$, if it is not effectively undone and all $del \in v.dels$ are effectively undone.*

A node v has the following peer-specific elements:

- pos^{er}, a number indicating its relative position in the $\prec$-order of all nodes.
- *rendered, true* if the node's visibility is reflected in the view.

- *strInView, true* if the string of the node is currently shown in the view.

PROPERTY 3. $v_l \prec v_r \Leftrightarrow v_l.pos^{er} < v_r.pos^{er}$.

Note that the pos^{er} values of nodes are not globally unique. When a node is inserted between two nodes, any pos^{er} value between the pos^{er} values of the two nodes can be chosen. If there is no new value available, we can simply re-assign the pos^{er} values among a set of nodes to make sufficient interval between two adjacent values. pos^{er} is a simple implementation of a order-maintenance list [3].

PROPERTY 4. $v.rendered \Rightarrow v.visible = v.strInView$.

A node v can be split at *pos*, where $v.offset < pos < v.offset + v.len$. This results in an updated v, denoted here as v_l, and a new right-hand node v_r, such that

- $v_r.offset = pos \wedge v_l.len = pos - v.offset$ $\wedge v_l.str + v_r.str = v.str$.
- All elements of v are preserved in v_l.
- $v_l.undo$ refers to $v_r.undo$ and all other elements are deep-copied from v_l to v_r.
- v_r is inserted in all linked lists that v involves to maintain the encapsulated operations, including the *l-r* and i_l-i_r links as well as the *l-r* links of v's *del* elements.
- Property 3 is maintained.

PROPERTY 5. *The left and right ends of node v, represented with $(v.pid, v.pun, v.offset)$ and $(v.pid, v.pun, v.offset, v.len)$, can be uniquely located in a model, despite subsequent splits.*

If node v is later split into v_l and v_r, $(v.pid, v.pun, v.offset, v.len)$ can be located via $v_l.i_r$. We use $\overleftarrow{v}$ and $\overrightarrow{v}$ to denote the left and right ends of node v.

Since the left ends of all nodes are uniquely located and any character can be uniquely located relative to a node's left end, characters in a model can also be regarded as uniquely located.

PROPERTY 6. *Ordering of characters. (a) Intra-node: If $v.strInView$ and $v.offset \leq pos_l < pos_r < v.offset + v.len$, then $pos_{view}[v.str[pos_l]] < pos_{view}[v.str[pos_r]]$. (b) Inter-node: For characters $c_l \in v_l.str$, $c_r \in v_r.str$, if $v_l.strInView$, $v_r.strInView$ and $v_l \prec v_r$, then $pos_{view}[c_l] < pos_{view}[c_r]$.*

Some particular nodes are used for the synchronization between the model and the view. Node *curr* and position pos_{curr} in *curr*, define the *current position* of the model. It corresponds to the current position $curr_{view}$ of the view. $render_l$ and $render_r$ mark the range of nodes that might need be rendered to synchronize the view with the model.

PROPERTY 7. *Either (a) Empty range: $render_l = render_r = nil$ and for all v in model, $v.rendered$, or (b) Non-empty range: $render_l \neq nil \wedge render_r \neq nil \wedge render_l \preceq render_r \wedge \neg render_l.rendered \wedge \neg render_r.rendered$, and for all $v \prec render_l$ or $v \succ render_r$, $v.rendered$.*

PROPERTY 8. *Let $v_i(i = 1, \ldots, n)$ be all the nodes left to curr and $v_i.strInView$,*

$$curr_{view} = \begin{cases} \sum v_i.len + (pos_{curr} - curr.offset) & \text{if } curr.strInView \\ \sum v_i.len & \text{otherwise} \end{cases}$$

Finally, a peer maintains a *log* of operations that can be undone. A log entry has a reference to the leftmost node (for *ins*) or element (for *del* or *undo*) of the operation in the model.

5. OPERATIONS AND UPDATES

A user may execute the following (user-oriented) operations in the view:

- $ins(pos, str)$ inserts string str at position pos.
- $del(pos, len)$ deletes len characters right to position pos.
- $undo(pid, pun)$ undoes an operation identified by (pid, pun) which can be ins, del or $undo$.

After an operation is executed in the view, it is enqueued in the peer's Q_v. Consecutive operations in the queue may be merged. For example, a sequence of character operations can be merged into a string operation. These operations are turned into the following (model-oriented) operations before they are dequeued for integration in the model.

- $move(\delta)$ moves the current position a distance of δ characters. If δ is positive, move rightwards; otherwise, move leftwards.
- $ins(str)$ inserts string str at the current position.
- $del(len)$ deletes len characters right to the current position.
- $undo(pid, pun)$ is the same as the user-oriented $undo$ operation.

After a local operation is integrated in the model, a representation of the corresponding $update$ is enqueued in Q_{out} and the leftmost node or element of the operation is appended to the log.

An insertion update is represented with the id of the insertion, the inserted string str, and the dependencies dep_l and dep_r of the newly inserted node, i.e. the place of the insertion.

A deletion update is represented with the id of the deletion and a list of the ends of the nodes whose strings are deleted. We use $(v.pid, v.pun, offset_{old}, v.offset_{new}, v.len)$ to represent the two ends of node v. The leftmost node of the deletion might be the result of a split during the local integration. $offset_{old}$ and $offset_{new}$ are the $offset$s before and after the split. $offset_{old} = offset_{new}$ if the deletion happens to start at the left end of a node. A remote peers can quickly find the node before splitting with $(pid, pun, offset_{old})$ and make a new split at $offset_{new}$. The right end of v is indicated with $v.len$. For the rightmost node of the deletion, the node v_r at the remote peer is split if $v_r.len > v.len$.

An undo update is represented with the id of the $undo$, the id of the operation it undoes, and for del and $undo$, also the id of the leftmost node of the operation.

6. MODEL-VIEW SYNCHRONIZATION

A user edits the document at the view of the local peer. The executed view operations are placed in Q_v after some conversion. Meanwhile, the peer may receive in Q_{in} updates from remote peers. From time to time, the model and the view are synchronized.

Procedure $synch(fullsynch)$

---
while $op \leftarrow Q_v.dequeue()$ **do**
    $Q_{out}.enqueue(integrateLocal(op))$
if $fullsynch$ **then**
    while $update \leftarrow Q_{in}.dequeueReady()$ **do**
       $integrateRemote(update)$
$render()$

Procedure $synch$ synchronizes the view and the model. There are two options: either can a peer synchronize operations in both Q_v and Q_{in}, or can it synchronize only operations in Q_v.

Procedure $integrateLocal$ integrates a local operation. The update representations of the integrated operations are enqueued in Q_{out}, which are later broadcast to remote peers. Procedure $dequeueReady$ dequeues from Q_{in} a remote update that is ready at this peer (Definition 5). Procedure $integrateRemote$ integrates a remote update. Procedure $render$ makes the effects of integrated remote operations available in the view. Because all integrated remote operations are rendered after a synchronization, there is no concurrent update in the model when local operations are integrated.

Local $undo$ operations require immediate interaction with the model and need special handling. When a user issues an $undo$ operation, the operation is enqueued to Q_v and Procedure $synch$ is executed immediately (either full or local-only). Thus the $undo$ operation is integrated into the model after all previously enqueued local operations. After Procedure $render$ inside $synch$ is done, the effect of the $undo$ is shown in the view.

A peer may decide how often the model and the view are synchronized, with the restriction that every local $undo$ operation must involve at least a local-only synchronization. Basically, with more frequent synchronizations, the view is more responsive to remote updates, at the cost of higher run-time overhead, and the user is more frequently distracted by the concurrent remote updates. A peer may also decide how often the updates of the integrated local operations are broadcast to remote peers.

6.1 Moving a distance and going to a node

To integrate executed local operations or render integrated updates to the view, positions in the model must correspond to the respective positions in the view. This is achieved through the $move$ and $goto$ procedures. Knowing a distance (i.e. number of characters) in the view, $move$ places the current position of the model to the right position of the right node. Knowing a position of a destination node v, $goto$ finds the corresponding position in the view. Both procedures ensure that Property 8 holds.

Both the $move$ and $goto$ procedures traverse nodes via the l-r links and counts the lengths of the traversed nodes whose $strInView$ values are $true$. $goto$ compares $v.pos^{er}$ with $curr.pos^{er}$ to decide which direction to go.

6.2 Model rendering

A rendering makes the effects of integrated updates appear in the view. According to Property 7, only nodes between $render_l$ and $render_r$ (inclusive) need to be rendered. Suppose that $render_l \preceq curr \prec render_r$ and pos_{curr} is at the left end of $curr$. Procedure $renderCurrRightward$ renders $curr$ and places the current position to the left end of the node just right to $curr$. To save space and keep readability, we do not enumerate all cases of rendering a node.

Procedure $renderCurrRightward()$

---
if $\neg curr.rendered$ **then**
    if $curr.visible \wedge \neg curr.strInView$ **then**
       $view.ins(pos_{view}, curr.str)$; $curr.strInView \leftarrow true$
    if $\neg curr.visible \wedge curr.strInView$ **then**
       $view.del(pos_{view}, curr.len)$; $curr.strInView \leftarrow false$
    $curr.rendered \leftarrow true$
if $curr.strInView$ **then** $pos_{view} \leftarrow pos_{view} + curr.len$
$curr \leftarrow curr.r$; $pos_{curr} \leftarrow curr.offset$

$curr.visible$ is calculated according to Definition 3. When $curr$ is involved in many concurrent dels and $undo$s, calculating $curr.visible$ can be more costly than, say, checking $curr.strInView$. A node's visibility is only calculated while the node is being rendered.

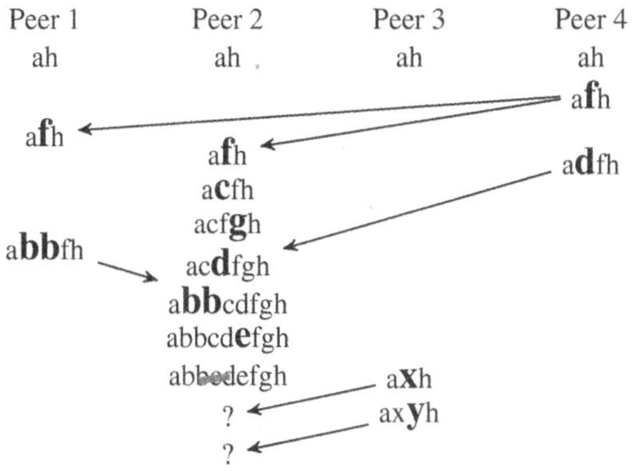

Figure 3: Example of conflicting insertions

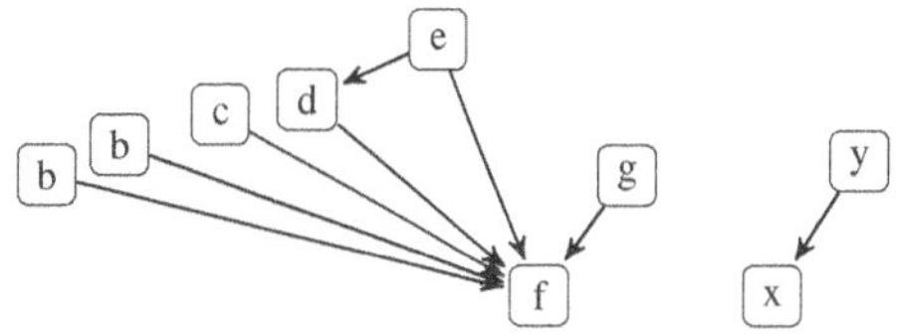

Figure 4: Insertion dependencies

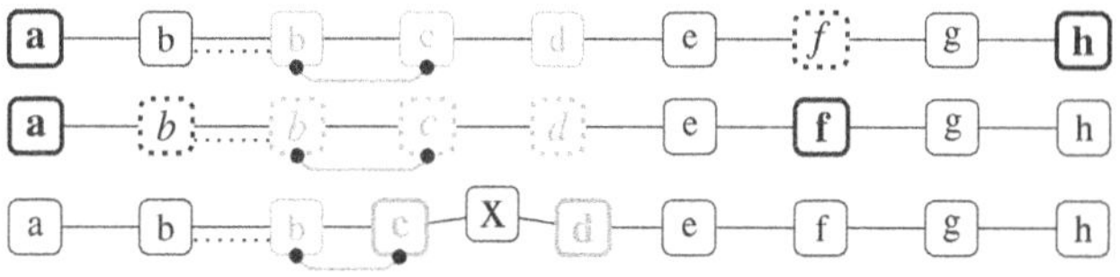

Figure 5: Ordering among conflicting insertions

7. INTEGRATING LOCAL OPERATIONS

A model integrates a local *ins* operation by inserting a new node at an empty interval of the model.

DEFINITION 4. *An* interval of a model *is a pair* $(\overrightarrow{v_l}, \overleftarrow{v_r})$ *of node ends, where* $v_l \prec v_r$. *The interval is* empty *if* $v_l.r = v_r$.

Because node ends are always uniquely located in a model (Property 5), intervals are always uniquely located as well.

If pos_{curr} is in the middle of *curr*, *curr* is split at pos_{curr} and the new node is inserted in between. Otherwise, there might be invisible nodes at the place of insertion. If this is the case, a particular order is enforced. For example, all invisible nodes are placed to the right of the new node.

The interval at which the new node is inserted is the insertion dependencies dep_l and dep_r of the new node. If this node is subsequently split, all new nodes after splitting have the same insertion dependencies. When a local insertion is integrated, there is no concurrent remote operation integrated in the model (this is enforced by Procedure *synch*). Therefore, the interval at which the new node is inserted is empty, that is, it is defined by two adjacent nodes.

A model integrates a local *del* operation by associating *del* elements to the corresponding nodes whose strings are currently in the view. Nodes at deletion boundaries may be split.

A model integrates a local *undo* by associating *undo* elements to the corresponding elements (*node* for insertion, *del* for deletion and *undo* for undo). The nodes involved in the *undo* are marked as not rendered, and the $render_l$ and $render_r$ are updated accordingly. Every local *undo* involves a synchronization between the model and the view, as described in Section 6.

8. INTEGRATING REMOTE UPDATES

A peer integrates a remote update only when the update is ready for integration at the peer. Otherwise, the update remains in Q_{in}.

DEFINITION 5. *A* remote update is ready for integration *at a peer when all its referenced node positions and elements are available in the model of the peer.*

More specifically, a remote insertion is ready when the dependent node positions are available. A deletion is ready when all node positions encoded in the deletion update are available. An undo is ready when all nodes or elements of the operation it undoes are available. The involved nodes or elements may be split due to concurrent operations. The positions and elements are regarded as available both before and after the split. The ready-for-integration condition is less strict than "ready" or "happen-before" condition in the literature (such as [7, 19]), because only the node positions and elements that the update directly depends on are required to be available.

8.1 Insertion

Concurrent insertions may conflict with one another. It is crucial that the integration algorithm enforces the same $\prec$-order at all peers. The enforcement of the total order is based on the dependencies of the insertions.

DEFINITION 6. *Let* v_α *be a node of insertion* ins_α. ins_α *insert-depends on insertion* ins_β *at interval* $(\overrightarrow{v_l}, \overleftarrow{v_r})$ *if (a) Direct dependence: there exists a node* v_β *of* ins_β *inside* $(\overrightarrow{v_l}, \overleftarrow{v_r})$, *such that* $v_\alpha.dep_l = \overrightarrow{v_\beta}$ *or* $v_\alpha.dep_r = \overleftarrow{v_\beta}$; *or (b) Indirect dependence: there is a third insertion* ins_γ *such that* ins_α *insert-depends on* ins_γ *in* $(\overrightarrow{v_l}, \overleftarrow{v_r})$ *and* ins_γ *insert-depends on* ins_β *in* $(\overrightarrow{v_l}, \overleftarrow{v_r})$.

Figure 3 shows an example of concurrent insertions. Figure 4 shows insert dependencies among these insertions at $(\overrightarrow{v_a}, \overleftarrow{v_h})$. The arrows depict direct insert dependencies. Note that *ins*("c") insert-depends on *ins*("f") at $(\overrightarrow{v_a}, \overleftarrow{v_h})$ but not at $(\overrightarrow{v_a}, \overleftarrow{v_f})$ or $(\overrightarrow{v_a}, \overleftarrow{v_d})$.

DEFINITION 7. *Two insertions* ins_α *and* ins_β *are dep-ordered, written as* $ins_\alpha \prec ins_\beta$ *if either there exists node* v *such that* $ins_\alpha.dep_r = \overleftarrow{v}$ *and* $ins_\beta.dep_l = \overrightarrow{v}$, *or there exist nodes* v_l *and* v_r *such that* $ins_\alpha.dep_r = \overleftarrow{v_l}$, $v_l \prec v_r$ *and* $ins_\beta.dep_l = \overrightarrow{v_r}$.

In Figure 4, *ins*("bb") $\prec$ *ins*("g").

DEFINITION 8. *Two insertions* ins_α *and* ins_β *conflict at interval* $(\overrightarrow{v_l}, \overleftarrow{v_r})$ *if they are not dep-ordered, both are to be inserted at* $(\overrightarrow{v_l}, \overleftarrow{v_r})$ *and none of them insert-depends on the other at* $(\overrightarrow{v_l}, \overleftarrow{v_r})$.

In Figure 4, *ins*("c") conflicts with *ins*("d") at $(\overrightarrow{v_a}, \overleftarrow{v_f})$. *ins*("e") does not conflict with *ins*("d") because *ins*("e") insert-depends on *ins*("d").

DEFINITION 9. *Two insertions* ins_α *and* ins_β *directly conflict at interval* $(\overrightarrow{v_l}, \overleftarrow{v_r})$, *if they conflict at* $(\overrightarrow{v_l}, \overleftarrow{v_r})$ *and there does not exist a third insertion* ins_γ *at* $(\overrightarrow{v_l}, \overleftarrow{v_r})$ *such that* ins_α *(or* ins_β) *insert-depends on* ins_γ.

In Figure 4, *ins*("x") conflicts with *ins*("d") at $(\overrightarrow{v_a}, \overleftarrow{v_h})$. However, *ins*("x") does not directly conflict with *ins*("d") at $(\overrightarrow{v_a}, \overleftarrow{v_h})$, because *ins*("d") insert-depends on *ins*("f").

Our algorithm enforces a $\prec$-order among directly conflicting insertions with a policy that is agreed upon at all peers. A commonly used policy is based on the *pid*s of the originating peers of the insertions. For instance, the insertion with smaller *pid* is placed to the left.

Integrating a remote insertion update is handled in iterations, as illustrated in Figure 5. To insert v_x at $(\overrightarrow{v_a}, \overleftarrow{v_h})$ at Peer 2, we first find insertions at $(\overrightarrow{v_a}, \overleftarrow{v_h})$ that directly conflict with v_x. In our example, this is the insertion of v_f. Since $ins(\text{"f"})$ has *pid* 4 and $ins(\text{"x"})$ has *pid* 3, v_x is to be inserted to the left of v_f. v_x is then to be inserted at $(\overrightarrow{v_a}, \overleftarrow{v_f})$ in the next iteration. The directly conflicting insertions are then $ins(\text{"bb"})$, $ins(\text{"c"})$ and $ins(\text{"d"})$. v_x is then inserted at $(\overrightarrow{v_c}, \overleftarrow{v_d})$ according to the *pid*s of the originating insertions. At $(\overrightarrow{v_c}, \overleftarrow{v_d})$ there is no insertion conflicting with $ins(\text{"x"})$. Therefore v_x is finally inserted between v_c and v_d.

This process is in essence the same as in [11]. Notice that deletion and node splitting have no effect with respect to the ordering of the insertions.

Procedure $insertRemote(v_{ins}, v_l, v_r)$

$v \leftarrow v_l.r$
while $v \neq v_r$ **do**
$\quad$ **if** $v.dep_l.pos^{er} \leq v_l.pos^{er} \wedge v.dep_r.pos^{er} \geq v_r.pos^{er}$ **then**
$\quad\quad$ — v directly conflicts with v_{ins}
$\quad\quad$ **if** $v_{ins}.pid < v.pid$ **then** $v_r \leftarrow v$ $\quad$ — $v_{ins} \prec v$
$\quad\quad\quad\quad\quad\quad\quad\quad\quad\quad$ **else** $v_l \leftarrow v$ $\quad$ — $v \prec v_{ins}$
$\quad\quad$ $v \leftarrow v_l.r$ $\quad$ — new iteration
$\quad$ **else** $v \leftarrow v.r$ $\quad$ — same iteration
$insertBetween(v_{ins}, v.l, v_r)$

Procedure *insertRemote* is an improvement to the process just described. It inserts v_{ins} between v_l and v_r. To integrate a remote insert update v_{ins}, we start with $v_{ins}.dep_l$ as v_l and $v_{ins}.dep_r$ as v_r. Thus v_{ins} does not insert-depend on any insertion at $(\overrightarrow{v_l}, \overleftarrow{v_r})$. The loop walks the node v through the nodes between v_l and v_r. If v does not insert-depend on any insertion at $(\overrightarrow{v_l}, \overleftarrow{v_r})$, v_{ins} and v directly conflict at $(\overrightarrow{v_l}, \overleftarrow{v_r})$. We enforce the order between v_{ins} and v according to their *pid* values and adjust v_l or v_r accordingly for the next iteration. We use the pos^{er} values to figure out whether v insert-depends on any node at $(\overrightarrow{v_l}, \overleftarrow{v_r})$. If $v.dep_l.pos^{er} > v_l.pos^{er}$ or $v.dep_r.pos^{er} < v_r.pos^{er}$, then v insert-depends on a node between v_l and v. (Without the use of pos^{er}, another loop is need for this purpose [11]). If v insert-depends on some node between v_l and v_r, v moves to the next node and the loop goes on for the same iteration.

8.2 Deletion and undo

Integrating a remote *del* or *undo* simply associates the corresponding *del* or *undo* elements in the model data structure.

A node of a deletion is represented as $(pid, pun, offset_{old}, offset_{new}, len)$ in an update message. If node $(pid, pun, offset_{old})$ has already been split by a concurrent operation at a different position, the integrating peer can use $(pid, pun, offset_{old})$, $offset_{new}$ and len to find the correct node.

When the operation that a remote *undo* undoes has already been undone by a concurrent *undo*, the corresponding element is already associated with an *undo* element. In this case, the *id* of the remote *undo* is inserted to the *ties* element of that *undo* element.

Notice that concurrent deletions of the same sub-string have an accumulative effect (i.e. the overlapping sub-string is deleted multiple times), while concurrent *undo*s have an idempotent effect. For either of them, integrating concurrent operations in different order results in the same visibility of the corresponding nodes.

9. CORRECTNESS

We consider two correctness criteria, intention preservation and convergence, as defined in [19].

9.1 Intention preservation

Intention preservation [19] requires that, for any operation op, (1) the effects of executing op at all peers are the same as the intention of op, and (2) the effect of executing op does not change the effects (i.e. intentions) of independent operations.

Intention is not formally defined in [19] and is open for different interpretations. This is one of the reasons why correctness of OT algorithms are difficult to be proven formally [7]. A commonly adopted interpretation of intention of an insertion is the effects-relation order introduced by the originating insertion [7, 11].

In our work, the *intention* of an operation is decided at the view of the originating peer. More specifically, an insertion is between two characters at the current position at the time of insertion; a deletion removes a sub-string of characters from the view; undo of an insertion removes the inserted characters from the view; undo of a deletion makes the removed characters re-appear in the view and the positions of the re-appeared characters must preserve the intentions of the corresponding insertions.

First, we verify that integrating an operation preserves its intention.

For insertion, we consider the ordering of nodes. For deletion and undo, we only consider the visibility of nodes, because they do not change the ordering of nodes.

Because splitting a node does not change the ordering among existing nodes or the visibility of nodes, it does not change the intention of any operation.

Integrating a local insertion inserts the new node between the two nodes of the visible characters at the current position. Placing the invisible nodes to the left of the newly inserted node does not change the intention. Integrating a remote insertion also inserts the new node between the two nodes of the same characters. The existence of concurrent insertions does not change the intention.

Integration of a local and remote deletion makes the same set of characters invisible in the view, thus preserving its intention.

Undo of a local or a remote insertion makes the characters of the insertion invisible. Undo of a local or remote deletion, or redo of an insertion, makes the characters that are not deleted by other deletions visible again. The intention of the original insertion is preserved after the undo or redo, because the characters are still in the same order.

Next, we verify that integration of an operation does not change the intentions of other operations.

No procedure switches the order of nodes. Therefore the intention of an insertion will never be changed by the integration of any other operation.

Undoing a deletion brings the deleted characters back in the view only when the insertions of the corresponding characters are not undone and the characters are not deleted by any concurrent overlapping deletion. Therefore undo of a deletion does not change the intention of the undo of any insertion and any other deletions. This is in contrast with all related work that defines the effect of concurrent deletions of the same character as a single deletion. Undo of one deletion thus changes the intentions of all these concurrent deletions. Two concurrent deletions, despite overlaps, are different operations. Undoing one of them should not change the intention of the other.

On the other hand, concurrent *undo*s of the same operation are considered as a single undo, because they are always defined on the same operation.

9.2 Convergence

Convergence [19] requires that, when the same set of operations have been executed at all peers, all copies of the shared document are the same.

For insertions, it is crucial to show that all peers enforce the same $\prec$-order among the characters. (Although the key idea of the algorithm was published in [11], there has not been a formal proof of its correctness.)

Due to Procedure *synch* in Section 6, there is no conflicting insertions during integration of local insertions. Therefore, we only need to verify that integrating remote insertions ensures a globally unique $\prec$-order among concurrent insertions.

To see that all peers enforce the same $\prec$-order among insertions, we verify that any peer enforces the same $\prec$-order as an ideal peer, $peer_0$, where all insertions are available. $peer_0$ integrates insertions in iterations. An iteration consists of insertions that insert-depend on insertions of earlier iterations. These insertions are separated into groups by the nodes in earlier iterations. In every group, insertions directly conflict with each other between two nodes of earlier iterations. If for node v of an insertion, $v.itr$ is the iteration in which the insertion is integrated at $peer_0$, we have $v.itr = max(v.dep_l.itr, v.dep_r.itr) + 1$. Here and in the rest of this section, $v.dep_l$ or $v.dep_r$ is used to denote the node containing that node end, when this does not cause confusion from the context.

In Figure 3, assume the insertions in Iteration 0 are {"a", "h"}, then the insertions in Iterations 1, 2, 3 are {"f", "x"}, {"bb", "c", "d", "g", "y"} and {"e"}.

LEMMA 1. *The $\prec$-order of all insertions at the ideal peer is unique.*

PROOF. We prove with induction.

At iteration 0, all conflicting insertions are directly conflicting with each other. Their $\prec$-order is decided by the *pun*s of the originating peers and therefore is unique.

Assume at iteration k the $\prec$-order of all insertions is unique. At iteration $k+1$, we show, in the following two steps, that the $\prec$-order of all insertions is also unique:

(a) Any insertion of iteration $k+1$ is uniquely placed among the nodes of iteration k or below.

(b) For all insertions of iteration $k+1$ that are to be placed at the same place among the nodes of iteration k or below, they are uniquely ordered.

To show (a), we will show that if a node v of iteration $k+1$ were inserted without the existence of any other node of the same iteration, it would have been placed immediately between nodes v_l and v_r. Then the insertion of node v' (also of iteration $k+1$) prior to v would not cause v to be placed outside of v_l and v_r. We show this with contradiction.

First, we know that either (i) $v.dep_l = v_l$, or (ii) v directly conflicts with v_l during the last iteration of Procedure *insertRemote*, because otherwise $v \prec v_l.dep_l$ or $v_l.dep_r \prec v$ and v_l would not be the immediate left neighbor of v as the final result of the procedure. Therefore, either (i) $v_l \prec v$ or (ii) $v_l.dep_l \prec v \prec v_l.dep_r$ and $v.pun > v_l.pun$.

The only possibility that the insertion of v' prior to v makes v be placed left to v_l is $v \prec v' \prec v_l$. This is impossible with case (i) above. Now consider case (ii). Because v directly conflicts with v', $v.pun < v'.pun$. However, v' is placed left to v_l either when $v' \prec v_l.dep_l$ or when v' directly conflicts with v_l and $v'.pun < v_l.pun$. In the former case, $v \prec v' \prec v_l.dep_l$ contradicts with $v_l.dep_l \prec v$. In the latter case, $v.pun < v'.pun < v_l.pun$ contradicts with $v.pun > v_l.pun$.

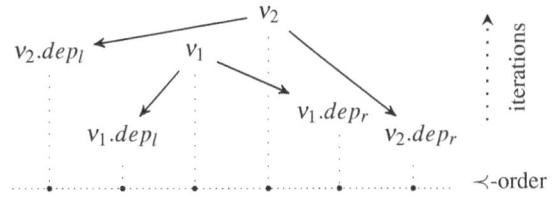

Figure 6: Resolving order between v_2 and v_1

This proves (a).

The proof of (b) is more straightforward. Because all insertions of iteration $k+1$, that are to be placed at the same place among the nodes of iteration k or below, conflict directly with each other. They are uniquely ordered according to their *pun* values. □

THEOREM 1. *When all peers have integrated the same set of insertions, the $\prec$-order of the integrated insertions are the same at all peers.*

PROOF. Assume that at a peer, a pair of insertions are integrated out of the ideal iteration order. We will show that this peer enforces the same $\prec$-order as $peer_0$. Extending this to any pair of out-of-order insertions, we can conclude that a peer enforces the same $\prec$-order as $peer_0$.

Given nodes v_1 and v_2 and $v_2.itr > v_1.itr$ (Figure 6). Assume v_1 and v_2 may be integrated out of the ideal order. Because v_1 may be integrated after v_2, v_2 does not insert-depend on v_1 (Definition 5). We show that integrating v_2 prior to v_1 enforces the same $\prec$-order as integrating v_2 after v_1.

There are only three possible cases:

1. The intervals $(v_1.dep_l, v_1.dep_r)$ and $(v_2.dep_l, v_2.dep_r)$ do not overlap, (including $v_2.dep_l = v_1.dep_r$ and $v_2.dep_r = v_1.dep_l$).

2. $(v_1.dep_l, v_1.dep_r)$ is inside $(v_2.dep_l, v_2.dep_r)$.

3. $(v_1.dep_l, v_1.dep_r)$ contains $v_2.dep_l$ and/or $v_2.dep_r$.

In case 1, either $v_1 \prec v_2$ or $v_2 \prec v_1$ (Definition 7), thus integrating v_1 (and v_2 respectively) does not involve v_2 (and v_1 respectively). Therefore integrating v_1 after v_2 results in the same $\prec$-order as integrating v_1 before v_2. In case 3, Procedure *insertRemote* in Section 8.1 first resolves $\prec$-order of v_1 against $v_2.dep_l$ and/or $v_2.dep_r$. If v_1 is placed outside $(v_2.dep_l, v_2.dep_r)$, like case 1, the rest of the procedure for integrating v_1 will never involve v_2.

Now consider that v_1 is inside $(v_2.dep_l, v_2.dep_r)$ (case 2 and the rest of case 3). If v_1 directly conflicts with v_2 at $(v_2.dep_l, v_2.dep_r)$, their ordering is decided by their *pid* values, which is independent of the temporal order of their integration.

If v_1 does not directly conflict with v_2 at $(v_2.dep_l, v_2.dep_r)$, according to Definition 9, either $v_1.dep_l$ or $v_1.dep_r$, or both, is inside $(v_2.dep_l, v_2.dep_r)$. Without loss of generality, assume that $v_1.dep_l$ is inside $(v_2.dep_l, v_2.dep_r)$. The ordering between $v_1.dep_l$ and v_2 is resolved first (when v_2 was inserted). If $v_2 \prec v_1.dep_l$, we have $v_2 \prec v_1$ and integrating v_1 does not involve v_2. If $v_1.dep_l \prec v_2$, then we consider the cases where v_1 directly conflicts with v_2 or not at $(v_1.dep_l, v_1.dep_r)$ and can similarly verify that integrating v_2 prior to v_1 enforces the same ordering as integrating v_2 after v_1.

Therefore in all three possible cases, integrating v_2 prior to v_1 enforces the same $\prec$-order as integrating v_2 after v_1. □

The convergence of deletions and *undo*s is straightforward. Because the visibility of nodes is independent on the order of operation integration, when the same set of operations are integrated at

233

all peers, every character will have the same visibility at all peers, regardless of the order in which concurrent deletions and *undo*s are integrated.

10. PERFORMANCE

Real-time collaborative editing requires high responsiveness to local user operations, since system responsiveness has clear effects on human performance. For example, [9] showed that at response time of 75ms, user performance becomes unstable, and at 225ms, user performance is degraded substantially. The effects of responsiveness to remote operations, on the other end, depends on the application and the context of the application. For instance, distributed pair programming is more demanding on responsiveness to remote user operations than collaborative writing of a technical report, particularly when the co-authors focus on different sections of the report.

The response time of local view operations is an important measure of an editor's local responsiveness. Except selective undo, all view operations are executed completely in the view. Their performance therefore are nearly the same as a single-user editor.

Local view operations are executed only when system resources (CPU, memory etc.) are available. When the system is heavily loaded, the user will experience low responsiveness even though the local view operations take very short time. Therefore responsiveness is dependent on the overall performance of the editor, including the more expensive model operations.

In this section, we first discuss time complexity of the algorithms and space overhead of the data structure, and then present experimental results.

10.1 Time complexity

Table 1 shows the time complexity of the different procedures. m is the distance of a move, i.e. the number of nodes a move traverses. r is the size of the region to be rendered, i.e. the number of nodes in the region. l is the size of an operation, i.e. the number of nodes that the operation involves. k is the number of conflicting insertions. s is the span of an operation, i.e. the number of nodes between the leftmost and rightmost nodes of the operation, including the nodes not belonging to the operation. For example, for a local insertion, s is the number of invisible nodes between two visible nodes at the place of an insertion;

Table 1: Time complexity of procedures

move	$O(m)$	*render*	$O(m+r)$
local *ins*	$O(s)$	remote *ins*	$O(k^2)$
local *del*	$O(s)$	remote *del*	$O(l)$
local *undo*	$O(m+s)$	remote *undo*	$O(l)$

It can be seen that a local *undo* can be an expensive operation, because the current position must first be moved to the node of the operation and the effect of the undo must then be rendered. For a local-only *synch*, the span of the *undo* is the size of the range for rendering. m and s can be considerably larger than l, the size of the operation to be undone.

To render the integrated remote updates, m nodes are first traversed to go to the edge of the region for rendering. This is costly when m is large. On the other hand, when m is large, the concurrent remote updates are far from the document area where the local editing is focused on. In such situation, less frequent full synchronization would reduce the overall overhead of the system.

The number of concurrent insertions k is typically small. Although in the worst case it may take up to k^2 steps to integrate a remote update, the range (v_l, v_r) in Procedure *insertRemote* typically shrinks very quickly.

In related work that do not support string-wise operations, $l = 1$, but the number of operations are much larger. This implies a larger number of invocations to the corresponding procedures, longer operation histories and larger number of network messages.

10.2 Space overhead

Materializing relations among operations incurs space overhead. The materialized relations contribute not only to the correctness of the algorithms (for example, an undo always refers to the same characters of the operation it undoes), but also to the overall performance (OT approaches, for example, derive the relations through operation transformation every time the relation is needed). This space overhead, however, may not be larger than that in related work. Notice that the space overhead is shared not only by all the characters of a node, but also by all operations associated with the node. In related work, every single operation of every single character has its own space overhead for meta-data, either in terms of state vector or operation context in OT approaches, or in terms of character identifiers in CRDT approaches. To accommodate this overhead, [22] for instance, supports line-wise, rather than character-wise, operations.

To make the analysis more specific, let us assume that for a node, the size of the fixed part (pid, pun, $offset$, $rendered$, dep_l, dep_r, pos^{er}, l, r, il, ir) is F, it represents a string of s characters, has d del elements of size D and a chain of u undo elements of size U. The total size of the node is $N = F + d \cdot D + u \cdot U$.

Here we ignore the space taken for the character string, because the same space is taken in all approaches.

Now, consider the corresponding information stored in an operations history in an OT system that only supports character operations. Assume that the size of an operation record in the history is R (a record contains information like state vector or context as well as some other meta data). The information contained in the above-mentioned node includes s single-character insertions, of each character, d deletions and u undoes. The total size of all these operation records is $R_\Sigma = s \cdot R + s \cdot d \cdot R + s \cdot u \cdot R$.

To make the comparison more straightforward, assume that $F \approx D \approx U$. The difference between the two is $N/R_\Sigma = F/(s \cdot R)$. F and R are typically comparable. When s is large, the space overhead of our approach is a small fraction of a character-wise OT approach.

10.3 Experiments

We have implemented the core algorithms in Emacs Lisp, aiming at supporting group editing in a widely used open-source editor. Our experiment for performance study is based a trace of operations for editing a program in a week's period. We then re-play the operations in different settings to measure the time of different procedures presented in Sections 6, 7 and 8. The measurement was taken under GNU Emacs 24.3.1 running in 32-bit Linux 3.10.5-ARCH on a 7-year old ThinkPad T61p (2007 model) with 2.2GHz Intel Core2 Duo CPU T7500 and 2GB RAM.

The trace first captures the editing operations in view, as presented in Section 5. The captured view operations are then aggregated and converted into model operations. There are different ways of aggregating the view operations. In the experiments, we aggregated the operations as far as possible. That is, consecutive insertions and deletions are aggregated into a single operation, until the cursor moves away from the boundary of the current inserted or deleted string. Figure 7 shows the number of model operations and their lengths (numbers of characters) obtained from the trace.

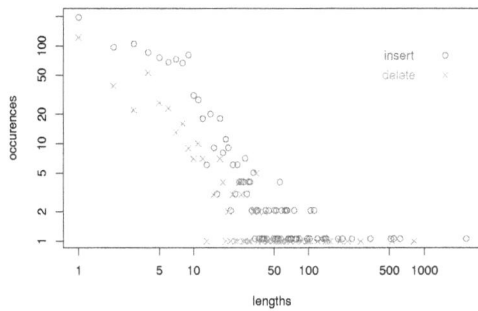

Figure 7: Occurrences of operations with different lengths

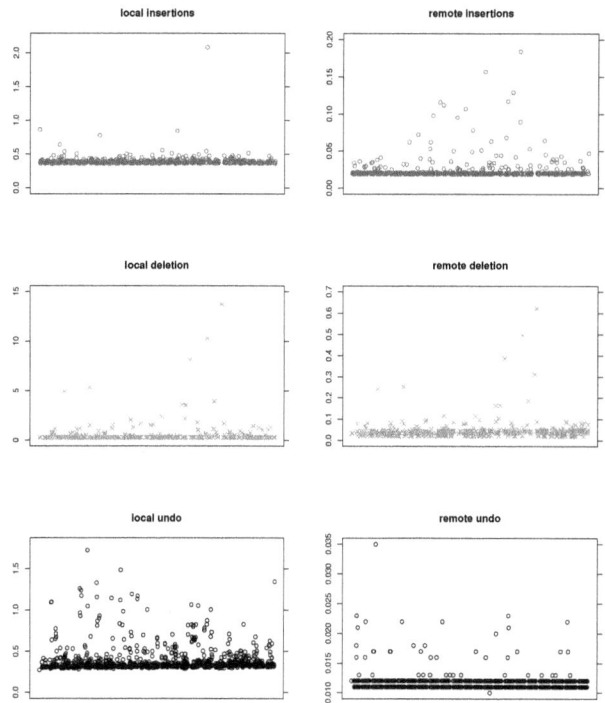

Figure 9: Time (ms) for integrating different operations

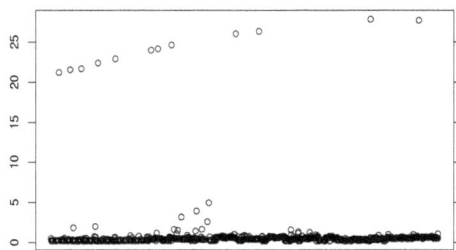

Figure 8: Time (ms) for model-view synchronization (including Emacs Lisp garbage collection)

In the first experiment, there are two peers. The first peer, the local peer, re-plays the traced operations as local operations. To measure the time for selective undo, after re-played all traced operations, the peer undoes all these operations in reverse order. The updates for the integrated operations are then sent to the second peer, the remote peer, which integrates the received remote updates.

Let us first look at Figure 8. The y-axis is the time for running Procedure *sync* at the remote peer. The x-axis is the time at which the procedure is called. Because the experiment only re-plays the traced operations, the x-axis values are of no interest and thus are not shown. For the vast majority of times, Procedure *sync* takes less than 1 ms. There are however occasions where it takes over 20 ms. It turns out, with closer investigation, that it is the garbage collection of Emacs Lisp that contributes to these long delays. In what follows, we will show the time of different procedures *without* those extra delays caused by garbage collection of Emacs Lisp.

Figure 9 shows the execution time of integrating the different operations. An overall observation is that the integration time of all operations is almost independent of the length of the operation history.

In general, integrating local operations takes longer time than integrating remote updates. One reason is that the time for integrating a local operation includes the time for encoding the update into its JSON representation, whereas the time for integration a remote update does not include the time for decoding the JSON representation, because the decoding has already been done for the testing of the *ready-for-integration* condition.

The time for integrating remote insertions seems to be more fluctuant than for integrating local insertions. In fact, if we "zoom in" with the same resolution, the time for integrating local insertions is at least as fluctuant. The fluctuation is largely due to the maintenance of Property 3, that is, to re-assign the pos^{er} values among a set of nodes, when a node is inserted between two nodes, but there is no new pos^{er} value available at the place of insertion. In addition, the numbers of invisible nodes at the places of insertion (i.e. the span s) also cause the fluctuation of the time for integrating local insertions.

Integrating a local deletion can take much longer time (up to 15 ms) than integrating a remote deletion, because the span s of a deletion could be much larger than its size l (there may be nodes that are already invisible inside the region of the deletion). Notice that the shapes of the plots indicate a strong correlation between the spans and sizes of deletions.

Integrating a local selective undo could be expensive, because it involves at least a partial model-view synchronization. As a significant part of the synchronization, the current position must go to the place of the undo. On the other hand, integrating a remote selective undo is very fast. The plot for remote undo can even show the tiny difference between the time for undoing insertions and deletions.

Figure 10 shows the time related to model-view synchronization. Procedure *move* is only called at the local peer. Procedures *goto* and *render* are called at both peers. At the local peer, they are only called during the integration of *undo* operations and their time is already shown in Figure 9. Therefore Figure 10 only includes the time for Procedures *goto*, *render* and *sync* at the remote peer. Furthermore, these three plots can be regarded as been composed of two halves: the left half for integrating remote insertions and deletions and the right half for integrating remote *undo*s.

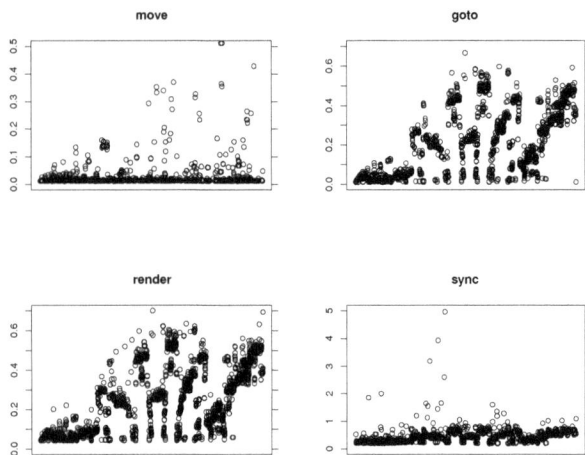

Figure 10: Time (ms) for model-view synchronization

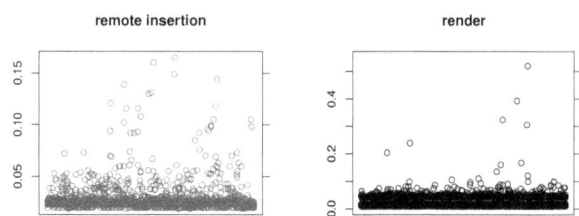

Figure 11: Execution time (ms) with conflicting insertions

For the local peer, please notice the similarity of the plot shapes between *undo* in Figure 9 and *move* in Figure 10 (flipped mirror-wise, because *undo*s are run in the reverse order of the insertions and deletions). This indicates that the overhead of integrating local *undo*s is largely determined by the distances between the current positions and the places of the *undo*s.

For the remote peer, it is obvious that the distance between the current position and the range to render is the determinant factor of the overhead of *render* and thus also *sync*. Particularly with this experiment, there is no local operation at the remote peer at all. The current position stays therefore at one end of the entire document. Consequently, the current position might have to go a long distance to get to the edge of the range for rendering, before a render is actually carried out. There are a few occasions where the *sync* takes clearly longer time, due to the integration of the remote deletions with very large spans.

To study the overhead of resolving the order of concurrent insertions, we did another experiment. Now there are three peers. Each peer re-plays the same trace of operations as in the first experiment. The updates are broadcast to all other peers to be integrated remotely. To make sure that the insertions conflict and the operations are valid (i.e. with valid positions and lengths), the peers behave as the following. For an insertion, every peer does and integrates a local insertion, receives and integrates the identical updates from the other two peers, and then undoes immediately the last identical insertions except the one originated from the first peer. For a deletion, the first peer does the local deletion and the other two peers integrate the remote update. This way of generating conflicting insertions is clearly not ideal, because all conflicting insertions follow exactly the same pattern. In fact, it is generally hard to automatically generate conflicting insertions of different patterns and with similar complexity as the example in Section 8. We tried to run experiments with different combinations of concurrent insertions, but could not find one with significant difference in execution time.

Figure 11 shows the time for integrating remote insertions and for rendering the updates. Most of the time it still takes less than 0.05 ms to integrate a remote insertion. Notice that in this experiment the number of updates are many times as in the first experiment (every insertion is done three times and undone twice), but we could not observe clear impact of the number of operations (i.e. the

length of operation history) on the performance of the procedures. It is interesting to notice that the time for rendering the updates in this experiment is actually much shorter than in the first one. The reason is that in this experiment, the current positions in all peers move hand in hand with every insertion. Therefor the overhead of moving the current position to the range for rendering is significantly reduced. The only few occasions where it takes longer than 0.1 ms to render the updates are due to deletions with large spans.

Overall, we find the experimental results consistent with the theoretical time complexity presented in Subsection 10.1. The experiments indicate that the distances of moving the current positions m and the spans of operations s (in particular, some deletions may have very large spans) are the dominant contributors to the observable (in plots, not by end-users) long delays. Local selective *undo*s are generally expensive because each of them has to involve a (partial) model-view synchronization. On the positive side, the sizes of operations l are only secondary to the overall performance. The performance is almost independent of the length of operation history (except that garbage collection of Emacs Lisp may take longer time when there are more data elements in the runtime stack). With very few exceptions (mostly deletions with very large spans), all procedures finish under one millisecond. On the other hand, the garbage collection of Emacs Lisp may take over 20 ms and still hardly any end-user ever notices the delay. This strengthens our confidence that even on an old laptop, our algorithms can provide sufficient responsiveness to end-users.

11. OPEN ISSUES

As the performance of the approach depends on the spans of operations and the number of nodes a *move* or *goto* traverses, it is desirable to suppress the model to reduce the number of nodes in the data structure. This may include discarding invisible nodes and combining adjacent visible nodes.

An invisible node plays two roles. (1) The node may become visible again when an operation associated with the node is undone. (2) The node is a landmark, i.e. another node insert-depends on it.

If we assume that (1) max L last operations originated at a peer can be undone, and (2) all updates older than L are guaranteed to have been delivered at all peers, then we can, by carefully maintaining the right visibility of nodes, discard all *del* and *undo* elements older than $p.pun - L$, where $p.pun$ is the latest known *pun* of peer p. We may also discard *str* of invisible nodes older than $p.pun - L$. We may then combine nodes of the same insertions after the discard of old elements. All this can be done locally at individual peers.

However, a peer cannot completely get rid of invisible nodes as they can be landmarks. How to effectively suppress the data structure is still a challenging issue.

Another issue is session management. When a user joins a editing session or resumes a suspended one, the latest state of the model must be established at the peer. Materialization of operation relations makes session management more complicated.

Yet another important issue, not specific to our approach, is how to practically resolve conflicts. Currently, all approaches are based on the theoretical correctness, i.e. intention preserving and convergence. However, that a solution is theoretically correct does not imply that it is also practically or semantically correct. For example, if two peers both change the word "he" to "she", the end result is "sshe", which is theoretically correct but practically wrong.

12. CONCLUSION

The work presented in this paper advances the state-of-the-art of real-time decentralized group editing by supporting both string-wise operations and selective undo. The approach combines and extends the strengths of operation transformation (OT) and commutative replicated data type (CRDT) approaches by materializing operation relations in a data structure. This contributes not only to more straightforward enforcement of correct execution, but also to better runtime performance. This, however, makes some tasks more complicated, such as session management and garbage collection. We have proved the correctness of the approach using the classical correctness criteria intention preservation and convergence. We have also analyzed the complexity of the algorithms and verified the analysis with experiments. The time complexity of the algorithms is independent of the lengths of operation histories. That is, the execution time for executing and integrating various operations does not constantly grow over time. The experimental result is consistent with the analysis and indicates that the approach provides sufficient responsiveness to end-users.

13. REFERENCES

[1] M. Ahmed-Nacer, C.-L. Ignat, G. Oster, H.-G. Roh, and P. Urso. Evaluating CRDTs for real-time document editing. In *ACM Symposium on Document Engineering*, pages 103–112, 2011.

[2] L. André, S. Martin, G. Oster, and C.-L. Ignat. Supporting adaptable granularity of changes for massive-scale collaborative editing. In *CollaborateCom*. IEEE, 2013.

[3] P. F. Dietz and D. D. Sleator. Two algorithms for maintaining order in a list. In A. V. Aho, editor, *STOC*, pages 365–372. ACM, 1987.

[4] C. A. Ellis and S. J. Gibbs. Concurrency control in groupware systems. In *SIGMOD*, pages 399–407. ACM, 1989.

[5] A. Imine, P. Molli, G. Oster, and M. Rusinowitch. Proving correctness of transformation functions functions in real-time groupware. In *ECSCW*, pages 277–293, 2003.

[6] D. Li and R. Li. Preserving operation effects relation in group editors. In J. D. Herbsleb and G. M. Olson, editors, *CSCW*, pages 457–466. ACM, 2004.

[7] D. Li and R. Li. An approach to ensuring consistency in peer-to-peer real-time group editors. *Computer Supported Cooperative Work*, 17(5-6):553–611, 2008.

[8] D. Li and R. Li. An admissibility-based operational transformation framework for collaborative editing systems. *Computer Supported Cooperative Work*, 19(1):1–43, 2010.

[9] I. S. MacKenzie and C. Ware. Lag as a determinant of human performance in interactive systems. In *Proceedings of the INTERACT '93 and CHI '93*, pages 488–493. ACM, 1993.

[10] G. Oster, P. Molli, P. Urso, and A. Imine. Tombstone transformation functions for ensuring consistency in collaborative editing systems. In *CollaborateCom*, pages 1–10. IEEE, 2006.

[11] G. Oster, P. Urso, P. Molli, and A. Imine. Data consistency for P2P collaborative editing. In *CSCW*, pages 259–268. ACM, 2006.

[12] N. M. Preguiça, J. M. Marquès, M. Shapiro, and M. Letia. A commutative replicated data type for cooperative editing. In *ICDCS*, pages 395–403. IEEE Computer Society, 2009.

[13] H.-G. Roh, M. Jeon, J. Kim, and J. Lee. Replicated abstract data types: Building blocks for collaborative applications. *J. Parallel Distrib. Comput.*, 71(3):354–368, 2011.

[14] B. Shao, D. Li, and N. Gu. ABTS: A transformation-based consistency control algorithm for wide-area collaborative applications. In *CollaborateCom*, pages 1–10. IEEE, 2009.

[15] B. Shao, D. Li, and N. Gu. An algorithm for selective undo of any operation in collaborative applications. In *GROUP*, pages 131–140. ACM, 2010.

[16] B. Shao, D. Li, and N. Gu. A sequence transformation algorithm for supporting cooperative work on mobile devices. In *CSCW*, pages 159–168. ACM, 2010.

[17] B. Shao, D. Li, T. Lu, and N. Gu. An operational transformation based synchronization protocol for web 2.0 applications. In *CSCW*, pages 563–572. ACM, 2011.

[18] C. Sun and C. Ellis. Operational transformation in real-time group editors: issues, algorithms, and achievements. In *CSCW*, pages 59–68. ACM, 1998.

[19] C. Sun, X. Jia, Y. Zhang, Y. Yang, and D. Chen. Achieving convergence, causality preservation, and intention preservation in real-time cooperative editing systems. *ACM Trans. Comput.-Hum. Interact.*, 5(1):63–108, 1998.

[20] C. Sun, Y. Xu, and Agustina. Exhaustive search of puzzles in operational transformation. In *CSCW*, pages 519–529. ACM, 2014.

[21] D. Sun and C. Sun. Context-based operational transformation in distributed collaborative editing systems. *IEEE Trans. Parallel Distrib. Syst.*, 20(10):1454–1470, 2009.

[22] S. Weiss, P. Urso, and P. Molli. Logoot-undo: Distributed collaborative editing system on P2P networks. *IEEE Trans. Parallel Distrib. Syst.*, 21(8):1162–1174, 2010.

[23] Q. Wu, C. Pu, and J. E. Ferreira. A partial persistent data structure to support consistency in real-time collaborative editing. In *ICDE*, pages 776–779. IEEE, 2010.

[24] W. Yu. Constant-time operation transformation and integration for collaborative editing. In *CollaborateCom*, pages 258–267. IEEE, 2011.

[25] W. Yu. A string-wise CRDT for group editing. In *GROUP*, pages 141–144. ACM, 2012.

A Field Trial of an Anonymous Backchannel Among Primary School Pupils

Matti Nelimarkka, Kai Kuikkaniemi
Helsinki Institute for Information Technology HIIT,
Aalto University
PO Box 19215, 00076 Aalto, Finland
matti.nelimarkka, kai.kuikkaniemi@hiit.fi

Giulio Jacucci
Department of Computer Science and HIIT,
University of Helsinki
PO Box 68, 00014 Helsingin yliopisto, Finland
giulio.jacucci@hiit.fi

ABSTRACT

Backchannels are tools that allow participants to discuss during a performance, such as lecture or presentation, without interrupting it. They are used in higher education and conferences to facilitate audience participation. This study examines backchannels in a Finnish primary school with a class of 12–13-year-old pupils. Backchannels can allow anonymous participation and this feature has been found practical in higher education. In this study, we observed that primary school pupils posted relevant messages at the same level as reported prior studies conducted in higher education. The pupils also appreciated the anonymity as it provided additional safety for self-expression.

Keywords

backchannel; anonymity; educational technology; primary education

Categories and Subject Descriptors

H.5.3 [**Information Interfaces and Presentation (e.g. HCI)**]: Group and Organization Interfaces

1. INTRODUCTION

Backchannels are computer-mediated communication (CMC) systems, which allow real-time discussion during performances such as presentations or lectures. Backchannels have been widely used in conferences [8, 12] and have been found useful: benefits of these systems include the activation of the audience to follow the performance and to contribute to it [6], the possibility to ask questions [8, 12] and the support provided to coordinate activities [12]. However, these studies rarely touch upon the design of the backchannel in use.

One interesting feature of CMC is that it can allow anonymous participation (anonymity), which can also be achieved in backchannels. Previous studies suggest that anonymous backchannels can encourage shy people to participate in classroom activities [2, 5] and provide safety when presenting feedback [9]. These studies were conducted at the university level, whereas our study examines

primary school students ($n = 22$, age 12–13 years old). This understudied group of young pupils is especially interesting, as the range of activities and level of skills increase significantly around this age [11].

Our research problem concerns the design of backchannels for primary education: what are the impact of an anonymous backchannel in this age group? To answer this questions, we conducted a one-month field trial to examine how pupils use such backchannel. During the field trial, pupils were given the opportunity to discuss in their classes using the backchannel system. We argue the anonymous mode of communication did not decrease the educational quality of the discussion: non-relevant discussions emerged at about the same level to documented backchannel studies at universities. Secondly, our findings indicate that pupils perceived anonymity positively and suggest that anonymity provided additional support.

1.1 Backchannels in education

Backchannels have been previously experimented in tertiary education, i.e. universities and colleges. Previous case studies have highlighted positive effects linked with the use of backchannels. First, group cohesion and interaction has increased [5] and students were more active participants in the classroom activities [6]. Furthermore, results have highlighted that backchannels create more balanced discussion spaces, as students who are not participating orally use the backchannel tool to express their points [7, 4]. Last, students are more comfortable asking questions and clarifications via backchannels [2].

In terms of pedagogy, backchannels can align with the constructivist approach. In this approach, the students themselves create new knowledge and peer-to-peer learning takes place. Therefore, the teacher's style of teaching impacts both the use and the utility of these systems [16]. Similarly audience response systems[1] are used to engage pupils in the teacher-driven approach and, for these purposes, often limit the interaction to voting only. So, even while both tools are part of the same ideal of a networked classroom [14], they approach it from different perspectives.

1.2 Anonymity and computer-mediated communication

Anonymity is often assumed to lead to negative outcomes in CMC. In a classic study Kilner et al. [10] studied professional online forum and reported that disabling anonymous discussion decreased the level of non-constructive comments by 89 %, even while the decrease in page views was only 10 %. Laboratory-based studies of co-located synchronous group communication do not ex-

---

[1] Research literature explores audience response systems' (ARS) utility, including anonymity (e.g. [14]). We do not engage with this literature as backchannels and ARS are different tools.

actly answer this, even though they do compare anonymous and named modes of communication. They highlight that anonymous discussion is more susceptible to the influence of priming and development of norms [13] and group polarisation [15].

This said, we need to highlight that in a co-located chat environment, anonymity – in the sense traditional CMC studies highlight it – does not exist, especially if the group is small. The participants know each others, and these groups may have existing social norms or ties in place. In this work when using the term anonymity, we mean that the system did not provide identity cues, such as an username, a pseudonymous nick or system level coding of messages. However, language characteristics etc. human factors might identify each contributor, as there was a limited group of pupils taking part into these discussions.

Furthermore, even while previous CMC studies on anonymity are more negative, for education technology anonymity is often considered beneficial. Suggested benefits are related to the lower threshold for responding or commenting [2, 3] and more critical approach to comments when needed [9]. At the same time, notes on the disadvantages have been made, such as embarrassing remarks that the anonymity allows [5]. Interviews with students have provided a mixed outcome: students are aware of the negative outcomes, but may also have a preference towards anonymity [3, 4].

2. CASE DESCRIPTION

This study was conducted as a one-month field trial with 22 pupils who were in the final grade of elementary school in the Finnish school system (i.e, 12–13 years old). The school was an ordinary Finnish elementary school located in central Finland, and the backchannel was available for the class to use freely. The topics under discussion were chosen by the teacher so that they supported the curriculum goals; the topic was indicated as a title viewed in the student display.

It was used to discuss, for instance, puberty (biology), energy consumption and renewable energy (natural sciences) and a novelist's visit (mother tongue). All these topics are related to the curriculum[2] for this age group and part of their ordinary school work. Based on students' interviews, introducing the backchannel increased amount of class discussion: traditionally they had used more exercise book-driven approach with this teacher. The teacher also noted increased activity in the classroom.

Recarding the type of anonymity, we must remind that students were co-located and the social ties in the group already existed. Therefore, when speaking of anonymity we need to acknowledge that anomymity was only partial, as explained above. However, each student had their own school desk in the classroom with space around it to allow moving. Furthermore the system was used with a smart phone, either students' own or one loaned from the research team. As these devices could be used not only for backchannel commenting, but also for other activities, one could not be identified for using the backchannel only. We therefore conclude that the use in the classroom was rather private and this way anonymity was enhanced.

The studied backchannel was developed in-house and allows participants to comment and respond to other participants' comments. Figure 1 presents the participant's view. As can be seen, the responses were visualized as conversation threads and it was possible to respond to each thread separately; also, the topic of discussion is

---

[2]In Finland generic descriptions of the curriculum are presented at the national level, but each teacher teaches the curriculum independently. Furthermore, standardised tests are not used for evaluation of either pupils or teachers.

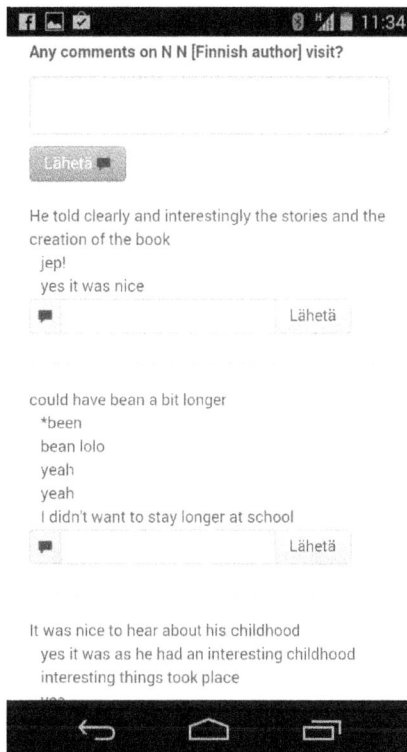

Figure 1: Pupils' user interface to the backchannel on a mobile phone

shown. There was also a public display attached to the backchannel, which can be used by the teacher to display the conversations to the class.

As discussed above, the system used full anonymity and the user-facing interaction had no names attached in it. However, for research purposes, more detailed identifiers were collected per user. Necessary parental consents were collected for all participants. No rewards were given to the pupils for participation. As said above, the pupils were allowed to either use their own smart phone or a smartphone provided by the researcher to access the backchannel. The backchannel was accessed using a web browser from a spesific URL, which started the HTML5 application. The application updated new content automatically, so no user interaction to show updates and new content. However the application needed to be open to to receive updates, i.e. the system did not send notifications to users currently not connected. Those users however saw these messages when they visited the application again, i.e. history of the currently visible discussions was always provided.

The data collected consists of the logs of the chat, a survey and interviews. The backchannel discussions took place in Finnish; they have been translated to English in this work. The survey and interviews were conducted at the end of the field trial and examined the experiences of the participants. The semi-structured interviews were circa five minutes each, focusing on the use (*How would you describe what you've done to your uncle? Did you respond to other people's comments?*), benefits and problems (*Has it been useful during the class? How could you improve the system?*) of the backchannel. Questions regarding anonymity were explicitly asked in the interview if not brought up by the interviewee (*How did you feel about the anonymity?*). These interviews were conducted individually with each pupil.

The pupils were active users of the participation system: a total of 1,205 messages were sent during the period of the pilot. The level of participation was skewed: on average, each participant sent 41.6 messages ($SD = 38.8$), ranging from 1 to 157 messages. This kind of distribution has also been observed in other studies [6].

3. RESULTS

We present the results in three sections: first by observing the message relevance and then survey results on pupils' experiences and finally interview results regarding anonymity.

3.1 Messages and relevance

Using a similar approach to the previous studies [6, 2], the messages were categorized into three categories: related content, unrelated content and duplicated content[3]. The definition of unrelated content is not obvious: messages may serve a special function even with a low informational value; for example for humour value [8] or by sharing emotions. Previous studies have defined unrelated content as irrelevant or inappropriate [6] or as messages that distracted the students from following the lecture [2].

We take a similar position and classify a message as unrelated if the message is irrelevant to the educational content and distracts from the discussion. This perspective follows the intended use of the backchannel tool to support educational interactions. To illustrate this classification, in the example below lines 6 and 5[4] are coded as unrelated, where as line 4 is duplicated content.

1 A: It's nice to be able to discuss anonymously.
2 B: Yes
3 C: Yeah
4 C: Yeah
5 C: That's what she said [message originally in English]
6 D: @@@@@@@#@@@@@@@ [... total of 145 characters]

However, short contributing responses such as those on lines 10–12 were considered relevant content. These short messages are methods used to convey emotions and responses and, therefore, vital part of the dialogue, here exploring how puberty affects the pupils. However, there was a discussion thread presenting a total of 43 emoticons. This message thread, even while serving, likely humorous value, was considered unrelated content as there was no explicit educational content in this thread.

7 E: Friends are nicer than parents
8 F: Sometimes
9 C: ĀĎĀd's
10 G: Yeah :)
11 H: true
12 E: :−D
13 I: They've always been

Lines 14–22 demonstrate a relevant discussion focused on energy forms. We can see that the thread's initial statement is followed by discussion where other participants explore the topic more and present their points of view.

14 A: well there's nothing wrong about solar panels and water power
15 but some don't like how they look
16 G: lol they are ugly
17 H: not in my oppinion

---

[3]Separating this category is sensible, as these may be due to user interface errors such as users pressing the send button several times by accident.

[4]Otherwise serving a humorous value, this same phrase was repeated in the discussions total of 15 times, therefore making it spam.

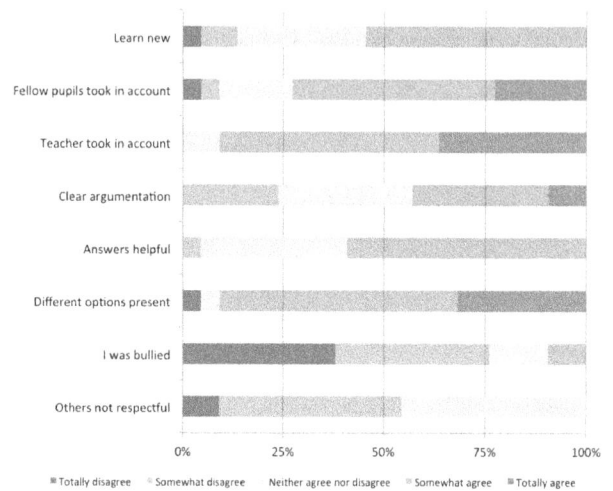

Figure 2: Experiences of the pupils

18 B: I agree
19 J: I don't know
20 A: well make them look nice. paint them with a
21 nice color or something
22 B: yeah

We observed that related content was the largest category with 70.4 % of the messages, followed by unrelated content (25.7 %) and duplicated content (3.9 %). These numbers are in similar magnitude to those observed in the previous research conducted with university students[5]. We conclude that the primary school students were able to use the backchannel tool to dicuss topics as efficiently as university students.

3.2 Pupils' experiences

We are interested not only in the observed quality of the discussion examined above but also in the subjective experience of the participants [1]. The survey examined how people perceived the backchannel and its hostility, respectfulness and utility using a 1 to 5 Likert scale. The results in Figure 2 demonstrate positive experience with the system.

First, regarding bullying and harassment, no student fully agreed with this statement and only 2 participants somewhat agreed with this statement. Second, majority agreed on the statement that other participants were respectful and the minority was neutral. These findings supports the design choice of anonymity, even for primary school students.

Furthermore, a majority (over 50 %) of the participants appreciated the comments provided and considered them beneficial for learning. They also believed that this discussion tool had an impact on both other pupils' (over 50 % agree) and teacher's actions (over 75 % agree). The following quote from the teacher supports this observation:

> Using this method, the teacher has access to the kind of information that would not be regularly expressed. Works well for the sensitive issues.

---

[5]As we discussed, the definition of unrelated content varies from study to study, and therefore the comparison between previous studies is indicator. To illustrate, [6] reported that unrelated content constituted 19 % of messages and different types of content messages 81 % of content, where as [2] reports as high as 43 % unrelated and only 57 % relevant content.

3.3 Anonymity and social support

Last, this study examines the perceived utility of anonymity via interviews with the pupils. Based on the pupils' positive reactions, anonymity was a good design choice; furthermore, they presented this opinion several times without more detailed questions on anonymity. The reasons considering anonymity positivity were that it provided an additional layer of social security when presenting ones' opinions. This includes both the fear of bullying due to opinions but also the feeling of freedom of expression, both in terms of prejudice and by forcing everyone to state their opinion. The following extracts demonstrate the pupils' experiences in detail.

The fear of being bullied due to other pupils knowing your opinions was a common topic in the interviews. It is not clear how significant problem this is in practice in this classroom: the response of Boy 3 indicates this might be a problem for the classroom, whereas Girl 1 explicitly states that this does not take place. However the explicit nature of the fear and its reasons is not the focus in this work. Rather, we are interested in the students decreased feeling of fear as a beneficial outcome in the uptake of an backchannel system.

> Boy 3: There was much larger discussion, as those who usually stay quiet started to discuss.
>
> Interviewer: But you didn't see others' names?
>
> Boy 3: No. But there were more answers.
>
> Interviewer: Why do you think that was?
>
> Boy 3: No one knew who was answering. [- -] It was easier to talk there, as I wasn't afraid that someone would comment on those responses later on [in person]
>
> Interviewer: Was it troublesome to not see people's names?
>
> Girl 1: I think it was nice. If someone had an opinion, no one would bother her later on about it.
>
> Interviewer: Well, does it happen often in your classroom that someone has an opinion and then gets laughed off for it?
>
> Girl 1: Well, not really.

However, benefits of the anonymity extend to social aspects and interactions in the classroom. Boy 6 highlights how anonymity reduced importance of ones' persona in the discussion, allowing participants to present different aspects without damage to existing social settings. This thinking was also exteded by Girl 3, who suggesst that anonymity required everyone to consider the topic, again as social support in the system was limited.

> Boy 6: It allowed us to discuss things in a different way [- -] It is easier when one doesn't need to mention names, so one can say things he would not otherwise mention. It was a different way to discuss [- -] it was closer to our age, as we are in the Internet, and you discuss similarly in there.
>
> Girl 3: It was good that when asking for an opinion, one needed to have one, not just say that "I agree with my friend'." That one needed to think through one's own perspective on the topic.

However, the anonymity was not only experienced positively, there were also a few neutral tones – no negative comments were brought up. However, pupils observed that anoymity created a trade-off with social support, as explained by Boy 5:

> Boy 5: It would be nicer if the names would be present [- -] this is not a big deal [- -] so you would know who says what.

4. DISCUSSION AND FUTURE WORK

We conducted a field deployment of a backchannel in a rather understudied group of primary school pupils. Pupils in this age group are in a pivotal developmental stage of identity forming and practices of online communications are still developing. Nevertheless, we report similar use patterns to those studies conducted in higher education, especially regarding the efficiency of use. Furthermore, the pupils and the teacher perceived the backchannel tool as a useful tool for learning. Based on these results, a free-form backchannel can be used in elementary schools.

We made an intentional choice to use an anonymous backchannel. This choice might have lead to antisocial behavior as in other studies of computer mediated communication. However pupils did not report these nor did we observe such behavior. Instead the pupils' interviews highlighted that anonymity provided an additional layer of security in the social group, and therefore enhaced the use of backchannel – a result also suggested in the previous research on backchannels [2, 5].

Based on these observations, we conclude that these results support the use of anonymous backchannels in this elementary school context. Pupils experiences however presented the nececcarly trade-off between anonymous participation and social support provided when discussing in a system with identities displayed. One of the contextual factors potentially influencing the outcome was that students knew each others already before the deployment of the system. This also highlighted the trade-off and outcomes experienced here; in other context the need for social support layer might not be as urging as those noted in these interviews.

Furthermore, contextual factors in this include the fact that pupils were co-present in the use and the use took place in an institution where a code of conduct existed and was enforced by the teacher. This is a major difference compared with the classical anonymity studies in online forums and with backchannel studies focusing on conferences or other kind of temporal settings. One challenge in understanding these contextual factors is difficulty to conduct comparative studies; for example the analysis framework used in this study is the least common nominator from existing studies and we acknowledge that more interpative framework might provide additional insight into the activities pupils engaged.

Future research can apply quasi-experimental setups to study details of different choices and draw potential differences caused by the co-located use and social interaction, which are not required by the classical computer-mediated communication. Also, questions focusing on the educational impact of backchannel tools should be further examined to support the wider uptake of these tools.

Acknowledgments

We thank the teacher and pupils for taking part in this field trial, and Screen.io for providing the technology used in this field trial. Furthermore, we thank the Finnish Funding Agency for Innovation TEKES and Learning Design - Design for Learning –project for funding this work.

5. REFERENCES

[1] Baek, Y. M., Wojcieszak, M., and Delli Carpini, M. X. Online versus face-to-face deliberation: Who? Why? What? With what effects? *New Media & Society 14*, 3 (2011), 363–383.

[2] Bergstrom, T., Harris, A., and Karahalios, K. Encouraging initiative in the classroom with anonymous feedback. In *Proceeding of INTERACT '11* (2011), 627–642.

[3] Davis, S. M., and Walk, N. Impact of Anonymity of Input in Next-Generation Classroom Networks. In *CSCL '07* (2007), 162–164.

[4] Dickey-Kurdziolek, M., Schaefer, M., Tatar, D., and Renga, I. P. Lessons from thoughtswap-ing. In *CSCW '10* (2010), 81–90.

[5] Du, H., Rosson, M. B., and Carroll, J. M. Augmenting classroom participation through public digital backchannels. In *Proceedings of GROUP '12* (2012), 155–164.

[6] Du, H., Rosson, M. B., Carroll, J. M., and Ganoe, C. I felt like a contributing member of the class. In *Proceedings of GROUP '09* (2009), 233–242.

[7] Harry, D., Gordon, E., and Schmandt, C. Setting the stage for interaction: a tablet application to augment group discussion in a seminar class.

[8] Harry, D., Green, J., and Donath, J. backchan.nl. In *Proceedings of CHI '09*, ACM Press (2009), 1361–1370.

[9] Howard, C. D., Barrett, A. F., and Frick, T. W. Anonymity to Promote Peer Feedback: Pre-Service Teachers' Comments in Asynchronous Computer-Mediated Communication. *Journal of Educational Computing Research 43*, 1 (2010), 89–112.

[10] Kilner, P. G., and Hoadley, C. M. Anonymity Options and Professional Participation in an Online Community of Practice. 272–280.

[11] Livingstone, S., Haddon, L., GÃũrzig, A., and ÃŞlafsson, K. *Risks and safety on the internet: The perspective of European children Full Findings*. LSE, London, UK, 2011.

[12] McCarthy, J. F., and danah Boyd. Digital backchannels in shared physical spaces. In *Proceedings of CHI '05* (2005), 1641–1644.

[13] Postmes, T., Spears, R., Sakhel, K., and de Groot, D. Social Influence in Computer-Mediated Communication: The Effects of Anonymity on Group Behavior. *Personality and Social Psychology Bulletin 27*, 10 (2001), 1243–1254.

[14] Roschelle, J., Penuel, W., and Abrahamson, L. The Networked Classroom. *Educational Leadership* (2004), 50–55.

[15] Sia, C.-L., Tan, B. C. Y., and Wei, K.-K. Group Polarization and Computer-Mediated Communication: Effects of Communication Cues, Social Presence, and Anonymity. *Information Systems Research 13*, 1 (2002), 70–90.

[16] Yardi, S. The role of the backchannel in collaborative learning environments. In *Proceeding of ICLS '06* (2006), 852–858.

How Do You IM When You Get Emotional?

Afarin Pirzadeh
School of Informatics
Indiana University-Indianapolis
719 Indiana Ave., U.S.E.R. Lab
Indianapolis, IN 46202 USA
apirzade@iupui.edu

Mark Pfaff
School of Informatics
Indiana University-Indianapolis
535 W Michigan, IT 476
Indianapolis, IN 46202 USA
mpfaff@iupui.edu

ABSTRACT

Nowadays instant messaging (IM) is getting very common in everyday life especially in casual contexts. Studying emotional communication in this channel is still growing. The main focus of this study is how four emotional states (relaxed, angry, happy, sad) influence the type and quantity of emotion-related cues used during informal conversations between college friends in IM. Results of the analysis revealed that the happy condition led to more use of nonverbal cues than the other three conditions, including more punctuation, vocal spellings, lexical surrogates, and minus features. Understanding how emotions affect emotional cues users apply in IM has implications for future research on emotion communication via CMC, as well as for the design of the next generation of IM tools that can facilitate communicating those emotional cues.

Categories and Subject Descriptors

H.4.3. Communications Applications: Computer conferencing, teleconferencing, and videoconferencing
J.4. Social and Behavioral Sciences: Psychology

General Terms

Experimentation, Human Factors

Keywords

Computer-Mediated Communication (CMC), Instant Messaging (IM), Emotional Cues, Lens Model

1. INTRODUCTION

Instant messaging (IM) continues to grow in everyday life. According to data from the Pew Internet and American Life project [13] over one-third of Internet users utilize instant messaging. This channel of communication has especially become popular among teens and college students [15]. Compared to an average Internet user, college students are twice as likely to use instant messaging [12]. Entertainment, affection, inclusion, and sociability are some of the main motivations for students using IM [4, 24].

Given the absence of visual and aural nonverbal behaviors as the main limitation of instant messaging communication, many theories have been developed on how this medium can influence emotional communication. A growing number of studies also

investigated how people express emotions during text-based computer-mediated communication (e.g. [10, 11, 28, 31, 32,).

To fill a gap in the text-based CMC theory with respect to emotional communication, the main purpose of this study is to test how people use text-based emotional cues in IM under four distinct emotional states. These results reveal relevant psychological factors to be taken into account for future research and design of text-based CMC systems for personal and professional applications.

2. LITERATURE REVIEW

Early research on text-based CMC compared it to other existing communication modalities and mainly characterized it as task-oriented and impersonal [28]. The lack of visual and aural nonverbal cues was given as the main cause of the impersonality of this type of communication [5, 14]. According to Mehrabian [16], in everyday communications, only 7% of the people's emotional understanding stemmed from the words spoken, whereas 38% was attributed to verbal tone and 55% was related to facial expression. However, more recent research argues that text-based CMC can be a highly interpersonal means of communication and users can compose and express their emotions if they have the time and technological affordances.

Social Information Processing (SIP) theory argues that people are indeed able to employ a variety of active and passive strategies to convey and perceive nonverbal behaviors in text-based CMC [31]. Supporting the SIP theory, Walther et al. [32] showed that likable and dislikable partners were identified in text-based CMC as accurately as face-to-face. Hancock et al. [11] suggested that individuals adapt their positive and negative emotion expression to a text-based communication environment through four strategies: degree of agreement, negative affect terms, punctuation, and verbosity. Hancock et al. [10] also showed that people in a negative mood produced fewer words and used more negative terms. Another study added further detail to these findings, by investigating the combined effects of negative and positive emotional states and situational stress on emotional communication cues [23]. The results revealed several patterns of expression associated with specific situational conditions, such as participants under stress producing significantly more negative emotion words but fewer vocal spellings (altering spelling to mimic a specific vocal inflection such as weeeell or soooo) than non-stressed participants.

Continuing on the trajectory of this prior research, the main goal of this study is to investigate the effect of users' emotional state on different emotional cues they apply in text-based IM. However, this study seeks to address some limitations of the previous studies and extends their findings in several aspects. The first aspect is the emotion elicitation strategy. In previous studies [11, 32], participants were asked to act likable or unlikable, and happy or sad. As Hancock et al. [10] explained, the role-playing nature of their emotional expression might have affected their emotional communication and made it unnatural or exaggerated. In the study reported here, short video clips were used to induce four specific moods, followed by open-ended text-based chat accompanied by memory elicitation designed to maintain those moods and encourage participants to express their emotions more naturally during chat. Therefore text-based IM communication was explored by cultivating controlled emotionally-laden situations in which participants were more likely to engage in natural emotional conversation and apply text-based emotional cues to express those emotions.

The second innovative aspect of this study is the wider range of moods studied to investigate the emotional cues in text-based IM. Compared to the previous studies [10, 11, 32], which examined a limited range of positive and negative emotions (generally happy or sad), this study investigated a range of four distinct emotions of relaxed, sad, happy, and angry. These are four major emotional states that can be expected to occur frequently in daily life. In Russell's [26] circumplex model of affect, these four different emotions occupy four separate quadrants in a two-dimensional space composed of pleasure-displeasure and degree of activation.

The third aspect of this study is the large set of text-based emotional cues selected for detection and analysis. A relatively new and novel set of verbal and nonverbal cues were extracted from Boonthanom's [2] study of asynchronous CMC (email). This set includes emotion words (e.g. happy, angry), vocal spelling (altering spelling to mimic a specific vocal inflection, e.g. weeeell or soooo), lexical surrogates (textual representations of vocal sounds that are not words, e.g. uh huh, haha), spatial arrays or emoticons (pictographs constructed from punctuation and letters, e.g. :-(for a sad face, or :-D to indicate laughing), manipulation of grammatical markers (alterations of the presentation of words, e.g. all capital letters, strings of periods or commas), and minus features (deliberate or inadvertent neglect of conventional formatting elements, e.g. abbreviation and acronyms, lack of capitalization or paragraphing). Additional cues were derived from the existing literature on the text-based CMC. Hancock et al. [11] showed that degree of agreements, verbosity, and punctuation are three strategies participants use to express positive versus negative emotion in text-based CMC. Therefore following categories were also explored in this study: assent (e.g. agree, OK, yes), negation (e.g. no, not, never), punctuation, and number of words per conversations as an indicator of verbosity.

Note that, based on Boonthanom's [2] cue taxonomy, vocal spelling, lexical surrogates, spatial arrays/emoticons, punctuation, minus features, and manipulation of grammatical markers are called nonverbal emotional cues since they mimic visual and aural nonverbal behaviors in face-to-face communication, such as facial expression, tone of voice, body gesture, or posture [2,9]. We categorized positive, negative, and swear words as verbal emotional cues.

In their study, Pirzadeh and Pfaff [23] provided empirical support for Brunswik's lens model [3] in text-based CMC, which argues that situational context and personal traits of the encoder can affect emotional communication. This approach models the process of encoding (expression), transmission, and decoding (impression) of emotional communication. Indeed, all communication, including IM, is embedded in a framework of culture, social rules, situational context, and individual differences.

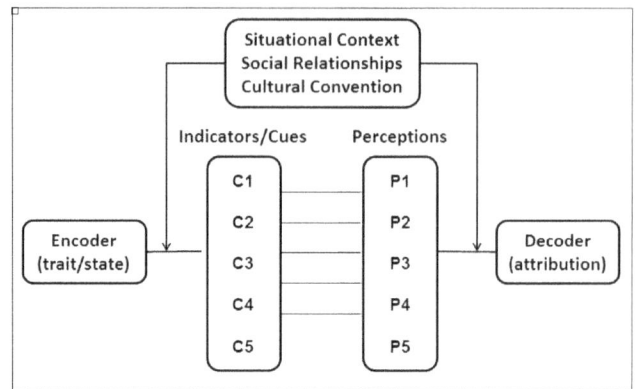

Figure 1. Modified version of Brunswik's lens model (adapted from Scherer, 2003)

Therefore, given the need for more comprehensive knowledge about emotional communication in synchronous text-based CMC, this study applied the modified version of the lens model to characterize the influences of four emotional states (relaxed, angry, happy, sad), on the proportions of different emotion-related cues used during informal IM conversations between friends in controlled emotionally-laden situations.

3. METHODS
3.1 Participants
Twenty college students in ten pairs of friends, three males and 17 females, ranging from 18 to 31 years old, received a $10 gift card for their participation in this study. We required partners to be friends who knew each other for at least six months so they were more likely to IM each other in real life, to express their emotions, and engage in natural emotional conversation [30, 20, 7, 24].

3.2 Procedure
Each pair of friends arrived at the laboratory together and were randomly assigned to separate rooms equipped with similar equipment (computer, table, and chair). After sitting at the computers, they were asked to sign a consent form and answer several demographic questions.

Participants were informed that the purpose of this study was to learn about text-based communication, with no mention of emotion. Telling participants the actual goal of the study might have increased the demand effects in which participants might not naturally achieve the desired emotional state and by either resisting or pretending to be in the mood.

The study used a within-subjects design. The experiment included two phases, repeated for each of the four emotional conditions of relaxed, angry, happy, and sad. The first phase was the mood induction. For each mood induction, a short video clip was selected to elicit the condition mood. Partners were asked to watch the video, followed by a manipulation check survey using the 28 emotion items from Russell [26]. Among different procedures to elicit emotions or induce moods, such as imagination, images, film/story, sound/music, or social interaction, the meta-analysis results by Westermann et al. [33] argued that the film/story mood induction procedure was the most effective procedure when subjects are treated individually.

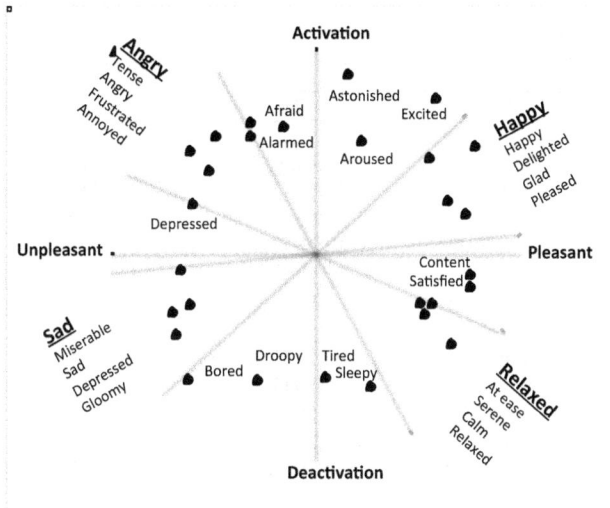

Figure 2. Emotion clusters selected from Russell's (1980) circumplex model, showing valence as the horizontal axis, and activation as the vertical axis.

The relaxed clip was treated as the baseline condition and always shown first. To avoid carryover effects, suggested by Rottenberg, Ray, and Gross [25], video clips of the same valence were shown in a blocked order. Therefore, the happy video clip was shown as the third video and anger and sad video clips were shown randomly in second and fourth position.

The second phase was informal chat via IM. The goal of this phase was to keep participants in the emotional state that was elicited using the video clip and engaging them in a chat conversation likely to include expression of their emotions. A memory elicitation technique was used to reach the goal of this phase. Participants were asked to trigger each other's memory to remember different life experiences they had related to the emotion of the film they just watched, and talk about them for ten minutes via Google Chat before watching the next movie. The memory elicitation technique is favored by several researchers since they directly trigger individual experiences of an emotion [17]. Participants were given some sample questions to use for memory elicitation (e.g. "Have you had any experiences similar to what you watched in the video?" "What makes you relaxed/happy/sad/angry?").

After watching and chatting about all four movies, participants answered a short survey on how satisfied they were expressing their emotions in chat conversation and why. They were asked to report their satisfaction in 7-point scale of 1 (totally dissatisfied) to 7 (totally satisfied). Other questions were also asked such as "Which emotion was the hardest/easiest to express through text-based chat? Why?" and "What differences do you see between expressing your emotion in IM compared to face-to-face?" At the end, participants were compensated and dismissed.

3.3 Measurements

For the manipulation check, participants reported their feelings after watching the video clip on a 5-point scale of 1 (slightly or not at all) to 5 (extremely), for each of the 28 emotion terms in Russell's circumplex model [26]. Clusters of emotions were created from the four highest-rated emotions in each condition. This created four roughly orthogonal emotion clusters, one in each quadrant of the two-dimensional circumplex model, in which the horizontal axis represents emotional valence (unpleasant on the

Table 1. Mean emotion levels by condition (SD in parentheses).

Measure	Condition			
	Relaxed	Angry	Happy	Sad
Relaxed	**2.82a** **(0.93)**	0.14a (0.28)	1.75a (0.83)	0.11ab (0.25)
Angry	0.17b (0.28)	**1.83b** **(0.73)**	0.07b (0.23)	0.84a (0.76)
Happy	1.76a (0.99)	0.00a (0.00)	**3.18a** **(0.69)**	0.00b (0.00)
Sad	0.14b (0.20)	1.01b (0.77)	0.01b (0.06)	**2.56c** **(0.92)**

Means in columns not sharing a letter are significantly different at a Bonferroni-adjusted α = .008.

left and pleasant on the right) and degree of activation on the vertical axis (Figure 2). Relaxed mood was calculated by taking mean of four emotions of *at ease, serene, calm,* and *relaxed*. The same process was done for measuring happy (*happy, glad, pleased, delighted*), angry (*annoyed, frustrated, angry, tense*), and sad (*gloomy, sad, depressed,* and *miserable*) moods. All four moods of relaxed, anger, happy, and sad were calculated for each of the four conditions.

Verbal emotional cues including positive emotion words, negative emotion words (angry, sad, anxiety), and swear words were counted using the Linguistic Inquiry and Word Count (LIWC) software [29]. LIWC was also used to count the assent and negation words, big words (words > 6 letters), fillers (blah, I mean, you know), cognitive (e.g. know, think), and perceptual (e.g. see, hear, feel). All nonverbal cues except punctuation (vocal spelling, lexical surrogates, spatial arrays/emoticons, minus features, and grammatical markers) were counted manually by the researchers. Punctuation was counted using LIWC. Since verbal cues identified by LIWC represent percentages of total words produced in each condition, we calculated nonverbal cues as percentages of total words produced in each category.

4. RESULTS

4.1 Manipulation Check

The mood manipulation was checked first to test whether the levels of each emotion (relaxed, angry, happy, and sad) were significantly higher than the other three for each of the corresponding mood inductions. Since the distribution of moods in none of the conditions was normal, the manipulation check was done by conducting Friedman's ANOVAs for all four emotions in each condition. The results were significant in all conditions at $p < .001$: relaxed (χ^2 (3) = 43.43), angry (χ^2 (3) = 45.65), happy (χ^2 (3) = 54.71), and sad (χ^2 (3) = 52.14). Results of pairwise comparisons of the means using a Bonferroni correction are in Table 1.

The results of the pairwise comparisons for each mood among four conditions showed that the desired emotional state was highest compared to the other three (noted in bold), though more in terms of valence than activation. Participants reported the negative emotion sad significantly higher than the other three emotions in the sad condition. However, in the remaining conditions, the two positive emotions were significantly different from the two negative emotions in their respective conditions, but the two same-valenced emotions were not significantly different from each other. This suggests that the manipulation was highly successful in terms of emotional valence (positive or negative),

Table 2. Mean percentages of verbal and nonverbal cues by condition (SD in parentheses)

Cue Categories	Relaxed	Angry	Happy	Sad	$\chi^2(3)$
Verbal Emotional Cues					
Affect words	8.66ab (2.68)	8.01a (2.93)	11.22b (3.02)	8.78ab (2.27)	9.60*
Positive words	7.46ab (2.17)	4.01a (1.77)	9.49b (2.71)	3.98a (1.91)	27.42***
Negative words	1.15a (0.83)	4.00b (1.99)	1.70a (0.89)	4.80b (1.47)	45.72***
Anger words	0.30a (0.44)	2.36b (1.50)	0.29a (0.33)	1.22b (1.02)	30.02***
Sad words	0.30a (0.59)	0.42a (1.12)	0.37a (0.36)	2.64b (1.49)	41.44***
Swear words	0.00a (0.00)	0.44b (0.49)	0.15ab (0.26)	.50b (0.54)	19.04***
Nonverbal Emotional Cues					
Vocal Spellings	1.24ab (1.37)	1.04a (0.93)	2.23b (1.94)	0.67a (1.03)	18.28***
Lexical Surrogates	2.34ab (1.88)	2.09ab (1.71)	2.95a (1.86)	1.38b (1.75)	9.09*
Minus Features	1.92ab (2.40)	1.26ab (1.43)	2.05a (2.83)	0.76b (0.89)	8.08*
Punctuation	16.64ab (9.14)	13.61a (7.84)	21.27b (11.30)	13.11a (8.82)	11.59**
Grammatical Markers	0.38a (0.66)	0.42a (0.82)	1.32b (1.30)	0.65ab (1.01)	17.19**
Other verbal cues					
Assent words	3.06ab (1.66)	2.78ab (1.61)	4.65a (2.67)	2.28b (1.38)	10.18*

For Friedman's ANOVA, *p < .05, **p < .01, *** p < .001.
Means in rows not sharing a letter are significantly different at a Bonferroni-adjusted α = .008.
Results for *Anxiety Words, Emoticon, Agreement, Negation Words, Big Words, Fillers, Cognitive Words*, and *Perceptual Words* were not significant.

but only partially successful in terms of activation, as only the sad condition produced an emotional response significantly less activated than the angry emotion. Alternately, the emotion clusters simply may not have included items high enough in activation to produce a significant difference. This may also be due to an emotional ceiling effect. Participants generally arrive in the laboratory in a positive mood, causing negative mood manipulations to have a much stronger effect than positive mood manipulations. However, even without a neat and mutually exclusive division of the four emotional responses, the four mood conditions successfully produced four clearly distinguishable and appropriate mood profiles, which was the goal of the manipulation.

4.2 Emotional Cues

Table 2 shows the results of Friedman repeated-measures ANOVAs for each of the cues categories. There were significant differences among all categories, except big words (words > 6 letters), filler (blah, I mean, you know), emoticons, anxiety, cognitive, perceptual, and negation words in the four conditions. Follow-up pairwise comparisons were conducted for each condition using a Bonferroni corrected level of significance (.008).

4.3 Survey

Overall, participants were satisfied (average response: 5.9/7) with emotion expression to their friends via IM communication. The main reason of their satisfaction was reported as comfortable conversations they had with friends that have known them for a long time. For example, "It helps to know the person you're chatting with in the first place. If it was with a stranger it would be harder but I found it easy because of the way we communicate already and then we just transferred that to this chat room" "I feel very comfortable talking to (friend's name). It almost felt as though we were chatting at home." "I feel like (friend's name) knows me well enough to understand what tone I am using when I use text-based chat".

More than half of the participants (14/20) reported happiness as the easiest emotion to express, since they can apply different strategies such as emoticons, lol, haha, and punctuations to show

their emotions. They also reported that they tend to IM with their friends more when they are happy, so they know how to express happiness and joy to their friends. For example, "it is very easy to joke around, use a 'haha' or 'lol' or emoticons to express happiness while chatting", "BECAUSE YOU CAN DO THISSSS! :D HAPPPPINNNNESSSSSS", or "the use of smiley faces, "lol", and "hahah" helps to easily show joy and ease. Also, usually when I talk to (friend's name) I'm happy so I knew how to tell her I was happy". The rest of participants (6/20) reported anger as the easiest emotion to express in their conversations. They reported emotion words, emoticons, and upper case letters as the main cues that make it easy for them to express anger. For example, "it's very easy to portray when you're angry and type angry, using different words, visual cues and using all caps."

The answers to the most difficult emotion to express, however, were more diverse. Nine out of twenty participants reported sadness as the hardest emotion to express. Lack of emoticons was one of the reasons they reported. They also reported that sadness is a deep emotion and they usually communicate it through subtle facial cues such as eye expression, which are missing in IM. "For me, sadness is displayed in my face and my eyes. When I'm sad, I don't want to talk about it. So when the only way of communicating my sadness is through message, that makes it difficult to do.", "sadness is a very personal emotion so you have to be around people to feel it", or "I think sadness is the hardest because, the only way (friend's name) would know I was sad is if I put a sad face (:(:\ )". Seven out of twenty participants reported contentment/relaxed as the hardest emotion to express, since they were in a neutral state and had no extreme emotion to express. The rest of participants, four out of twenty, reported anger as a hard emotion to express. Some of their answers were: "when it comes to deeper emotions like sadness or anger I tend to use a lot of gestures, facial expressions and I seek them in the respondent. Not being able to utilize those aspects of conversation was frustrating", "I like to focus on why I'm angry before expressing my anger", " or "I like to vent anger physically, through sports and lifting weights rather than emotionally".

5. DISCUSSION

Overall, the results of this study provide empirical support for Brunswik's lens model [3] in synchronous text-based CMC, demonstrating that emotional state of encoder can affect emotional communication and the usage of text-based cues in IM.

5.1 Verbosity

The first interesting point was the number of words per conversation and words per minute participants used among four conditions. Similar to Hancock [11] participants in all four conditions produced words at approximately the same rate. However, inconsistent with their results that showed participants in negative mood used fewer words compared to a positive mood, we found no significant differences in the number of words per conversation among four conditions. A possible explanation could be the substantially different informal context of our experiment and using participants that knew each other for a quite some time that could talk about positive and negative emotions. Since the number of words per conversation was consistent across conditions, this increased our interest in exploring the relative proportions of the number of cues that were used in different conditions.

5.2 Verbal Emotional Cues

As expected, in the happy condition, participants used more positive emotion words compare to the other three conditions. Similarly, in the angry condition participants used more angry words compared to the other three conditions, and likewise for the sad mood. Of course, this is partially influenced by the topics of their conversations in those conditions, which were life experiences specifically portraying events that would be described with those words. These results demonstrated that memory elicitation in the second phase of the experiment could maintain users in the emotional states we required.

5.3 Nonverbal Emotional Cues

Consistent with the Hancock [11] study, participants used more punctuation in the happy condition than the sad and angry conditions. Participants also used a significantly higher number of vocal spellings (e.g. sooo, weeell) in the happy condition compared to the sad and angry conditions. This result from informal chat aligns with a previous task-based study [23] in which participants used less vocal spelling during time-pressured conditions that were designed to frustrate participants through frequent task switching. The proportion of manipulations of grammatical markers (alterations of the presentation of words, e.g. all capital letters, strings of periods or commas) were higher in the happy condition than the angry and relaxed condition, but not the sad condition. The proportion of lexical surrogates (e.g. uh huh, haha) and minus features (abbreviations and acronyms) were used significantly higher in happy than sad condition.

Cue categories such as punctuation, vocal spelling, lexical surrogates, and manipulation of grammatical markers are noteworthy in how they attempt to mimic real speech [9]. Participants seem to apply these types of emotional cues to adapt the prosody of face-to-face communication to text-based CMC, especially when they are in a happy mood more than the other three moods of relaxed, angry, and sad. As such, these results extend to CMC the face-to-face findings of Scherer [27] and Ekman [8], which showed prosody (e.g. tone of voice, frequency, pitch) is one of the main cues to emotional expression and is exhibited differently across various emotions. These results may have implications for the automatic detection of positive mood, as

these groups of emotional cues are relatively easy to capture in real time during a chat conversation.

Another interesting result is the usage of emoticons. Emoticons were defined as symbols that resemble facial expression and body movements and are used very often especially in instant messaging [7]. Derks et al. [6] showed that participants used more emoticons in positive than negative emotional states. The results of this study, however, showed no significant difference in the number of emoticons participants used in four conditions. One possible explanation of this result may be the diversity of emoticons (both positive and negative) we had in our experiment, since in their study [6] a limited number of emoticons for negative emotional expression was provided.

Overall, the happy condition led to more use of nonverbal cues than the two negatively-valenced conditions of sad and angry. The manipulation check after watching the video clips confirmed that participants were in the desired mood at the beginning of the chat conversation and it persisted throughout each chat session as shown by the use of significantly different numbers of positive, angry, and sad words. Yet the main nonverbal manifestation of the negative moods (angry and sad) in the chat logs was simply a reduction in the number of nonverbal cues used compared to the happy condition. It suggests that a happy mood promotes an overall increase in nonverbal emotional expressivity in IM, which could be a possible explanation of why most of the participants reported happiness as the easiest emotion to express. This increase in nonverbal emotional expressivity has three potential explanations.

The first is that IM, as it is currently implemented in common desktop and web-based applications such as Google Chat, may not support negative expressivity sufficiently. It may be that letters, numbers, punctuation, and even emoticons are ill-suited to express negative emotions. This explanation is in line with the survey results, in which some of the participants reported that sadness and anger are difficult to express in IM because of the lack of cues to communicate facial expression in this medium. This explanation also put SIP theory in a new perspective with respect to the negative emotions, since the results showed that users were not able to find any strategies to convey nonverbal behaviors to express their negative emotions. The second explanation is that participants expressed negative emotions using cues not among those captured in this analysis. Lastly, the third explanation is that perhaps sad and angry partners chatting informally turn their focus inward and become less expressive overall. This explanation is in line with the survey results, in which some participants reported they want to focus more on the reason that made them angry before expressing their anger. This is also in line with the results of Pfaff's [22] study showing an increased inward focus of participants in a negative mood in the NeoCITIES simulation, a six-person team decision-making task. This behavior manifested as reduced attentiveness to their partners.

5.4 Assent words

Participants used a significantly higher number of assent words (e.g. agree, OK, yes) in the happy condition than the sad condition. Hancock [11] also showed the degree of agreement as one of the main strategies that participants used to express their positive emotion compared to negative emotions in CMC. However, their data showed that it is the frequency of negation words (e.g. not, no, never), rather than the frequency of assent words, which differentiates positive emotion from negative. Our data showed no significant difference in the frequency of negation words in different conditions. A possible explanation for not having significant difference among negation words can be explained by the conversation context of this study. Participants mainly talked about their personal experiences and they might have not had many opportunities to express disagreement, compared to the task-based context in Hancock [11] study.

6. CONCLUSION AND FUTURE WORK

This study specifically investigated how different emotional states influence cues individuals apply in instant messaging. The results of this study provide empirical support for Brunswik's lens model [3] in synchronous text-based CMC, demonstrating that emotional state of encoder can affect emotional communication in IM. This model can be used as a framework for future studies to explore how unique patterns of emotional cues in addition to other factors (such as personal traits, culture, or social relationships) can characterize different emotional states in IM. Understanding the usage patterns of nonverbal emotional cues has implications for future research on emotion communication via CMC, as well as for the design of the next generation of IM tools that can facilitate a wider range of emotional expression. Results of this study also contribute toward sentiment analysis and automatic extraction of opinions and emotions from text. Detection of emotional cues applied in text-based CMC can inform different models which are employed in text analysis [1,19].

The relatively small sample size (ten couples) was one limitation of this study, though the within-subjects design across four conditions produced forty conversations total, an ample amount of data. Significant results found in this sample shows that this topic merits further consideration and future studies need to re-examine these findings with chat data from a bigger sample. The higher number of female compared to male participants is another limitation of this study. Although Hancock et al. [10,11] found no gender affect on emotion expression and detection in instant messaging, future studies should reexamine the results of this study in a more diverse participant pool (in terms of gender, age, and ethnicity) than this overwhelmingly young female sample.

The main goal of this study was, through a quantitative approach, to see whether pre-defined cues, such as those provided by Boonthanom [2], would appear in different proportions under different emotional conditions. The advantage of the quantitative approach was the speed and efficiency to mine large data sets, though they only capture content, not context. Therefore studies are planned that take a qualitative approach and apply conversation analysis to preserve the complexity and richness of the content. These studies will focus more intently on the emotional cues participants used and the reasons behind using those cues in different emotional states and specifically explore why IM supports happy emotion more richly than negative emotions of sadness and anger. Further analysis of the content of statements can also provide a strong research foundation for designers to develop solutions to support different emotional cues in emotional communication in IM.

Overcoming the limitations of prior work on emotion expression in text-based CMC [11, 32] that used role-playing to make users express their emotions, this study explored the topic by cultivating emotionally-laden situations, in which participants were more likely to engage in natural emotional conversation, by using video clips and memory elicitation techniques. Future studies need to apply other creative techniques to increase the emotion expression in natural conversation among friends. An alternate approach is to acquire a large natural corpus of IM data and use content analysis to classify conversations into appropriate emotional categories to then be analyzed for verbal and nonverbal cues.

Continuing with the need to better understand IM users, prior work demonstrates the importance of considering individual personality traits when assessing communication behaviors [34]. Extraversion [27] and Emotional Intelligence [21] are the most likely factors to explain some of the variation between individuals in their use of verbal and non-verbal cues to express emotion in IM, and should be considered in future research in this area.

Future studies also need to consider that emotional or social cueing (verbal and nonverbal) is not the only mechanism that connects people together in text-based CMC. Whittaker [34] explains different cognitive cues such as turn taking, availability, shared attention, and interactivity are additional types of cues that facilitate expressive communication. Nardi [18] goes beyond cognitive and social cueing to discuss social connection and different categories of activities for social bonding (affinity, commitment, and attention) that need to be considered in any type of communication, including text-based CMC in the absence of traditional nonverbal cues. Longer-term goals are to study text-based CMC beyond emotional expression to explore different categories of cues and activities that individuals use to connect and develop social bonds. Applying the knowledge of the different cues individuals apply in text-based CMC with a participatory design process will help to develop different technological strategies that facilitate effective and transparent emotion expression in text-based CMC.

7. REFERENCES

[1] Alm, C. O., Roth, D., and Sproat, R. 2005. Emotions from text: machine learning for text-based emotion prediction. In *Proceedings of the conference on Human Language Technology and Empirical Methods in Natural Language Processing*, 579-586.

[2] Boonthanom, R. 2004. *Computer-mediated communication of emotions: a lens model approach.* Unpublished Ph.D. Dissertation. Florida State University.

[3] Brunswik, E. 1956. *Perception and the Representative Design of Psychological Experiments.* Berkeley, CA: University of California Press.

[4] Chung, D., and Nam C. 2007. An analysis of the variables predicting instant messenger use. *New Media & Society.* 9, 2 (2007), 212-234.

[5] Culnan, M. J. and M. L. Markus 1987. Information Technologies. In F. M. Jablin, L. L. Putnam, K. H. Roberts and L. W. Porter (Eds.), *Handbook of Organizational Communication: An Interdisciplinary Perspective* (pp. 421-443). Newbury Park, CA: Sage Publications.

[6] Derks, D., Bos, A. R., and von Grumbkow, J. 2008. Emoticons in Computer-Mediated Communication: Social Motives and Social Context. *Cyberpsychology & Behavior*, 11, 1 (2008), 99-101. DOI=10.1089/cpb.2007.9926

[7] Derks, D., Fischer, A. H., and Bos, A. E. R. 2008. The role of emotion in computer-mediated communication: A review. *Computers in Human Behavior, 24*, 3 (2008), 766-785. DOI= http://dx.doi.org/10.1016/j.chb.2007.04.004

[8] Ekman, P. 1982. *Emotion in the human face.* Cambridge University Press.

[9] Hancock, J.T. 2004. Verbal irony use in computer-mediated and face-to-face conversations. *Journal of Language and Social Psychology*, 23, 447-463.

[10] Hancock, J. T., Gee, K., Ciaccio, K., and Lin, J. M. H. 2008. I'm sad you're sad: Emotional contagion in CMC. In *Proceedings of CSCW '08: ACM Conference on Computer Supported Cooperative Work,* 295-298.

[11] Hancock, J. T., Landrigan, C., and Silver, C. 2007. Expressing emotion in text-based communication. In *Proceedings of SIGCHI' 07: ACM Conference on Human factors in computing systems,* 929-932.

[12] Jones, S. 2002. *The Internet goes to college: How students are living in the future with today's technology.* [Online]. Washington, D. C.: Pew Internet & American Life Project.

[13] Jones, S., and Fox, S. 2009. *Generations online in 2009. Pew Internet and American Life Project.* http://www.pewinternet.org/Reports/2009/Generations-Online-2009.aspx. Accessed March 18, 2012.

[14] Kiesler, S., Siegel, J., and McGuire, T. 1984. Social psychological aspects of computer-mediated communication. *American Psychologist. 39,* 1123–1134.

[15] Leung, L. 2001. College student motives for chatting on ICQ. *New Media & Society.* 3, 4 (2001), 483–500.

[16] Mehrabian, A. 1972. *Nonverbal commmunication.* Chicago: Aldine-Atherton.

[17] Morris, W. N. 1989. *Mood: The Frame of Mind.* New York: Springer-Verlag.

[18] Nardi, B. 2005. Beyond bandwidth: Dimensions of connection in interpersonal communication. *Computer Supported Cooperative Work, 14, 2(2005),* 91-130.

[19] Pang, B., and Lee, L. 2008. *Opinion Mining and Sentiment Analysis.* Now Publishers Inc.

[20] Parkinson B, Fischer AH, and Manstead ASR. 2005. *Emotions in social relations: cultural, group and interpersonal processes.* New York: Psychology Press.

[21] Petrides, K., Pita, R., & Kokkinaki, F. 2007. The location of trait emotional intelligence in personality factor space. *British Journal of Psychology.* 98, 273-289.

[22] Pfaff, M. S. 2012. Negative affect reduces team awareness: The effects of mood and stress on computer-mediated team communication. *Human Factors.* 54, 4 (2012), 560-571.

[23] Pirzadeh, A., and Pfaff, M. S. 2012. Emotion expression under stress in instant messaging. *Proceedings of the Human Factors and Ergonomics Society.* 493-497.

[24] Ramirez, A., and Broneck, K. 2009. 'IM me': Instant messaging as relational maintenance and everyday communication. *Journal of Social and Personal Relationships.* 26, 291-314.

[25] Rottenberg, J., and Ray, R. D., & Gross, J. J. 2007. *Emotion elicitation using films.* In J. A. Coan & J. J. B. Allen (Eds.), *The handbook of emotion elicitation and assessment.* London: Oxford University Press.

[26] Russell, J. A. 1980. A circumplex model of affect. *Journal of Personality and Social Psychology.* 39, 1161–1178.

[27] Scherer, K.R. 1978. Personality inference from voice quality: The loud voice of extroversion. *European Journal of Social Psychology.* 8, 467–487.

[28] Short, J, Williams E, and Christie, B. 1976. *The social psychology of telecommunications.* London: Wiley Press.

[29] Tausczik, Y. R., and Pennebaker, J. W. 2010. The psychological meaning of words: LIWC and computerized text analysis methods. *Journal of Language and Social Psychology. 29, 1 (2010),* 24–54.

[30] Wagner, H. L., and Smith, J. 1991. Facial expression in the presence of friends and strangers. *Journal of Nonverbal Behavior.* 15, 201–214.

[31] Walther, J.B. 1992. Interpersonal effects in computer-mediated interaction: A relational perspective. *Communication Research.* 19, 52-60.

[32] Walther , J.B., Loh, T., and Granka, L. 2005. Let me count the ways: The interchange of verbal and nonverbal cues in computer mediated and face-to-face affinity. *Journal of Language and Social Psychology.* 24, 36-65.

[33] Westermann R, Spies K, Stahl G, Hesse FW. 1996. Relative effectiveness and validity of mood induction procedures: a meta- analysis. *Eur. J. Soc. Psychol.* 26, 557–580

[34] Whittaker, S. 2003. Theories and Methods in Mediated Communication. In A. Graesser (ed.): The *Handbook of Discourse Processes.* Cambridge: Hillsdale NJ: Lawrence Erlbaum.

Citizen Adoption of Technology Mediated Social Participation Systems

Fahad Alayed

University of Maryland Baltimore County [UMBC]
1000 Hilltop Cir, ITE-404
Baltimore, MD 21250
f.alayed@umbc.edu

ABSTRACT

I study technologies developed to encourage the public to contribute to the public good. However, few of these systems are well accepted and adopted by public. Using a mixed methods approach grounded on technology acceptance theoretical frameworks , my dissertation explores why people are motivated to take participatory actions to be more involved and engaged within their communities? By using an example of Balagh Tejary, a public participation mobile application used to report merchant violations with the Ministry of Commerce in Saudi Arabia I aim to explore the motivational factors underpinning the acceptance of public participation systems in public good domain.

General Terms: Management, Human Factors, Theory

Keywords: Community; Technology Mediated Social Participation ; Technology Acceptance; Motivations; Public Good

1. RESEARCH CONTEXT AND MOTIVATION

Despite the familiar concept of public participation, the reality of attracting sustained public participation is difficult. Technology is often seen as part of the solution. However, technology itself may in fact exacerbate the issue. In my dissertation, I focus on the Technology Mediated Social Participation (TMSP) systems. I aim to study the technologies that facilitate public and social collaborative participation. Specifically, the user acceptance and adoption of these technologies.

The success of TMSP systems relies on the volume of participation activities. They have to have a large number of collaborators and contributors or what Computer Supported Cooperative Work (CSCW) researchers have called "Critical Mass". The lack of critical mass may be the primary reason of any public participation initiative failure; regardless of how extensive an investment has been made.

The public first needs to accept the technology before it can adopt and use it. Hence, there is the problem of how to make TMSP systems socially usable and acceptable. How can we motivate people to use these applications to contribute knowledge for the public good? We may need to focus not only on how to motivate the public to participate, but also on how to make the participation technology channels acceptable. Traditional system usability has focused on creating efficient interfaces and systems that are simple. Although this is very important for design space, just because a system is easy to use, does not mean it will engage users or attract them to use it.

Another problem in the TMSP research area, is that researchers have done many studies on the technical side of the TMSP spectrum while downplaying the social side. Developing applications that are very usable will not guarantee success for these systems. TMSP system designers should pay attention to social needs and a wider set of factors that would attract critical mass to use them.

As Ben Shneiderman notes, "understanding how to increase the motivations for participation is a deep science question that will occupy researchers for many decades." [6] The fundamental activity of users in TMSP is participation; which begins with motivation and the adoption of technology. Despite the fact, that most of TMSP systems fail due to the lack of critical mass , the exponential growth of participatory systems is obvious; less obvious are the concrete factors which lead individuals to adopt and continue using a given technical system that allows users to participate with each other especially in non Western countries.

By using an example of Balagh Tejary, a public participation mobile application used to report merchant violations with the Ministry of Commerce in Saudi Arabia, I aim to explore the motivational factors underpinning the public participation.

2. RELATED LITERATURE

Public participation for the public good can be demonstrated in several instances such as community policing and crime prevention [1] and neighborhood maintenance [2]. Public engagement and participation is still an evolving field of research which can be difficult to classify. While there are many digital government initiatives to engage citizenry, most research on the topic has been done with citizen science which is a very different kind of public participation. Several researchers have investigated the motivations behind public participation in different domains such as online communities [4] and citizen science[5], but motivation behaviors are complex and not always obvious. Participation for public good is at the heart of community engagement, so it is crucial to understand how can we promote public to take part in such activities? What are the barriers of public of engagement systems by understanding the drivers for involvement? Most importantly is to understand the factors that affect the acceptance of the participation systems.

3. RESEARCH QUESTIONS

The general research question of interest is: Why people are motivated (or not motivated) to take participatory actions to be more

GROUP'14, November 9–12, 2014, Sanibel Island, Florida, USA.
ACM 978-1-4503-3043-5/14/11.
http://dx.doi.org/10.1145/2660398.2660431

involved and engaged within their communities? This general question has three sub research questions as follow :

RQ 1: What are the key factors that influence the acceptance and use of TMSP systems?

RQ 2 : How are different motivational factors associated with the intention of using the TMSP systems?

RQ 3:Given the factors identified in answering the first two research questions, what are the design guidelines for TMSP systems to motivate user acceptance?

4. RESEARCH APPROACH AND METHODS

The research design will be a two-phase, mixed methods design that utilize a case study approach. The design is adapted from the "sequential exploratory design" described by Creswell[7] (collection and analysis of qualitative data followed by the collection and analysis of quantitative data) (see Figure 1) as follows:

Initially we conducted a pilot study using focus groups in the USA to collect initial qualitative data.

The first phase explores motivational factors through conducting individual and/or group interviews about public perceptions, attitudes, and opinions regarding TMSP systems. This is to identify motivational factors that may affect acceptance. These factors will be compared to the list of factors identified from the literature.

The second phase of this is study explores the relationships between the factors and public's intention and/or action by using a survey to gather data about their motivations for use (or non use) of TMSP systems in addition to their perceptions of engagement for public good and their demographic information. This survey instrument will be designed based on the results acquired from phase one.

The interview guide will include three major sets of questions: a) general questions about the people's background, b) questions about the adoption of various participation and engagement tools, and c) specific questions about the motivation and barriers of participation tools that exist in Saudi Arabia. The questions are based mainly on the themes grounded in the literature, theoretical foundations, and models of technology acceptance. The analysis will also take an analytic induction approach to uncover new themes that emerge from the data that have not been previously developed in the literature.

5. RESEARCH CURRENT STATUS AND RESULTS

I have already completed the pilot study and half of the phase one research activities. By conducting four focus groups in the US and Saudi Arabia, I collected qualitative data which will inform the design of my survey instrument. (I am scheduled to defend my dissertation proposal in the Fall of 2014.)

The initial results have already successfully identified interesting themes and motivation factors for TMSP systems acceptance. For example, beside the well identified factors of technology acceptance model (Usefulness and Ease of Use) I found that applying Expectancy Theory concepts to public participation technologies may increase the acceptance of the TMSP systems as the public would be more eager to participate when they expect a positive outcome from their engagement. Data collected indicated that the public are more willing to accept these systems if they are equipped

with a tracking functionality that allow participants to follow the progress of a submitted report. Moreover, the data showed some factors related to Community Sense theory as participants reported welling to accept these systems and sustain use them for reasons such as community membership and having influence on someone's own community. Although this initial data analysis is still undergoing, it seems that our model will consist of three core categories of factors: Technical, Social-Contextual and Organizational.

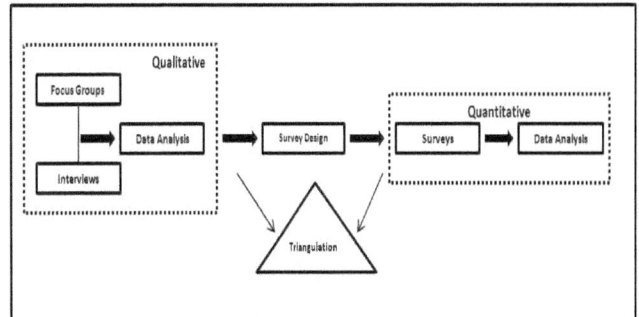

Figure 1. Study Design : mixed method approach

6. EXPECTED CONTRIBUTION

My dissertation's findings should have theoretical and practical contributions. A theoretical basis for TMSP can explain why some systems succeed and others fail, provide a basis for simulating activity in existing TMSP systems, and aid in predicting whether a new TMSP system will succeed [3]. I expect to construct a model for TMSP systems acceptance for public good. I also anticipate that my dissertation will provide a guideline for TMSP systems designers to implement features that encourage the acceptance of these systems.

7. REFERENCES

[1] Brush, A.J.B., Jung, J., Mahajan, R., and Martinez, F. Digital Neighborhood Watch: Investigating the Sharing of Camera Data Amongst Neighbors. *Proceedings of the 2013 Conference on Computer Supported Cooperative Work*, ACM (2013), 693–700.

[2] King, S.F. and Brown, P. Fix My Street or else: Using the Internet to Voice Local Public Service Concerns. *Proceedings of the 1st International Conference on Theory and Practice of Electronic Governance*, ACM (2007), 72–80.

[3] Kraut, R., Maher, M.L., Olson, J., Malone, T.W., Pirolli, P., and Thomas, J.C. Scientific Foundations: A Case for Technology- Mediated Social- Participation Theory. *Computer 43*, 11 (2010), 22–28.

[4] Kuznetsov, S. Motivations of Contributors to Wikipedia. *SIGCAS Comput. Soc. 36*, 2 (2006).

[5] Rotman, D., Preece, J., Hammock, J., et al. Dynamic Changes in Motivation in Collaborative Citizen-science Projects. *Proceedings of the ACM 2012 Conference on Computer Supported Cooperative Work*, ACM (2012), 217–226.

[6] Shneiderman, B. Technology-Mediated Social Participation: Deep Science and Extreme Technology. *In A. An, P. Lingras, S. Petty and R. Huang, eds., Active Media Technology. Springer Berlin Heidelberg,* (2010), 1–4.

[7] Tashakkori, A. and Teddlie, C. Handbook of mixed methods in social & behavioral research. *SAGE Publications, Thousand Oaks,*(2003)

Networked Handhelds for Collaborative Sense-Making in Undergraduate Physics

Lisa Hardy
University of California, Davis
School of Education
One Shields Ave, Davis, CA 95616
lahardy@ucdavis.edu

ABSTRACT

Classroom networks of handheld devices have the potential to support a new genre of collaborative learning activities, enabling complex small group tasks that encourage and support the simultaneous engagement of all students. At the same time, one-to-one personal computing with intuitive touchscreen interfaces offers engaging simulations and visualization aids to individual learners. However, it is not well understood how to design effective simulations to be used by and to engage *groups* of students in a collaborative setting. My dissertation work is an exploration of the collaborative physics activity design space opened up by networked handheld devices. Specifically, I study the design of networked simulations with the aim of engaging students in high-level discourse about physics concepts.

Categories and Subject Descriptors

K.3.1 [**Computer Uses in Education**]: Collaborative learning

Keywords

Small group collaboration; simulations; physics education; handhelds; mechanical waves

1. INTRODUCTION

A reform movement within university physics has tasked course developers with designing engaging collaborative activities [1]. My dissertation research involves an exploration of the activity design space opened up by networked handheld devices. This work is located relative to two distinct axes of prior research and activity design. Research in collaborative learning indicates that tasks are likely to be most effective when they are sufficiently open-ended and complex to necessitate contributions from each member [2], and when participants engage the task and one another in ways that sustain that variety of contributions [3]. Along this line of work, networked handhelds can facilitate greater communication, coordination and negotiation among peers [4], and expand and enrich avenues for active participation in joint problem-solving activity [5]. At the same time, simulations and interactive multimedia can engage students and assist in complex visualization [6]. One aim of this research is to design

GROUP'14, November 9–12, 2014, Sanibel Island, Florida, USA.
ACM 978-1-4503-3043-5/14/11.
http://dx.doi.org/10.1145/2660398.2660432

technology-supported activities that synergistically draw on both the individual and collaborative offerings of networked handhelds. Thus, my research draws on literature related to the use of simulations and interactive media in physics, as well as collaborative learning and computer-supported collaborative learning. My research will contribute to the bridging of these areas, by deepening our understanding of group sense-making as mediated by collaborative physics activities and simulations.

2. CONTEXT

The Physics 7 series at University of California, Davis is a three-quarter introductory Physics sequence for biological science majors. The sequence is unusual in that Physics 7 students spend 5 hours per week in a hybrid Discussion/Laboratory, and only about an hour per week in a traditional lecture. The goal of these Discussion/Laboratory sections is for students to engage in high-level conceptual reasoning about physics concepts, in what the course designers call "active sense-making." [7] Two main instructional strategies serve that goal: small group collaboration, and a focus on a small number of conceptual models. Nearly all class work is done in a face-to-face setting in groups of five. Additionally, the course content is structured around a relatively small set of physics models designed to focus the students' attention on the "big ideas" of Physics. In these Discussion/Lab sections students work through problems, discuss, argue, explain and make sense of physics problems.

The PHoTOnICs project is a joint effort by researchers in the UC Davis School of Education and the Physics Department to develop and investigate the use of handheld devices (specifically iPads) in physics classrooms. As part of this project, my dissertation research aims to investigate the technological support of group sense-making in Physics 7. Through successive cycles of design based research, my research will involve the development of technology designs and activities with the dual aims of augmenting the existing class configuration, and contributing to basic understanding of group learning about physics as supported by those designs.

3. RESEARCH QUESTIONS

My dissertation research will be guided by the following primary research questions.

1. In what ways and to what extent do our collaborative technology and activity designs mediate or support student learning about, and participation in interactions around, physics models and their applications?

2. Does the tablet-based approach to physics 7 improve on the existing D/L model, in terms of student learning outcomes or observations of group interactions?.

4. APPROACH AND METHODS

My dissertation work will be methodologically grounded in design-based research. Over the course of several design cycles, I will implement a design, collect data on its use in a classroom, and use findings from an analysis of that data in the context of my primary and emerging research questions to guide the next redesign. As my research questions ask about both collaborative processes and learning outcomes, I will take a mixed-methods approach to data collection and analysis. In investigating collaborative processes—interactions and participation-- my primary data sources will be audio and video recordings of group work during Physics 7 Discussion/Laboratory sections and log file entries that allow me to reconstruct student interactions with the technology during those sessions. To look at learning outcomes, I will collect samples of student work, both as part of their regular weekly written quizzes, and on assessments designed specifically to target the learning objectives of the activity. I will analyze the video data qualitatively, for example using discourse and gesture analysis, to identify participatory processes and group interactions associated with participation in our designed activities. Ultimately I will seek to correlate identified collaborative processes with assessment outcomes.

5. RESULTS

The first activity design was informed by preliminary classroom observations of two groups as they worked through activities focused on models of simple harmonic motion and mechanical waves. We chose to target waves in the initial design for two reasons: reasoning about waves requires visualization that is both difficult for students and amenable to simulation, and the coordinated nature of wave motion lends itself well to a collaborative activity design. As such, wave motion represented a good candidate for investigating the affordances of networked handhelds for both the individual and group levels. Much of the observed small group and whole-class discussion revolved around the concept and graphical representation of mechanical waves as sinusoidal variations, both *in time* and *in space*. Students had difficulties visualizing the motion of a single point along the wave. At the group level, we noted several instances in which the students appeared to have difficulties communicating about the dynamic phenomena involved, while only having static media at hand. For example, students would turn their backs to one another to gesture at, in an attempt to 'animate,' a drawing on a shared chalkboard. Based on these observations, one aim of our design is to equip students with interactive visualizations and shared, dynamic objects that will allow them to more readily reason and communicate about these complex phenomena.

Making Waves: First Design Iteration Our first design is an interactive simulation of a mechanical wave made by many independent oscillators lined up along the x-axis. The initial position and direction of each oscillator can be observed and controlled using a "unit circle tool" (Figure 1). When used in the collaborative mode by a group of students, each student has control over the phases of a subset of the oscillators. When a student changes the phase of an oscillator, the app connects to a local server that communicates the change to the rest of the group. The students are given worksheets asking them to build a wave

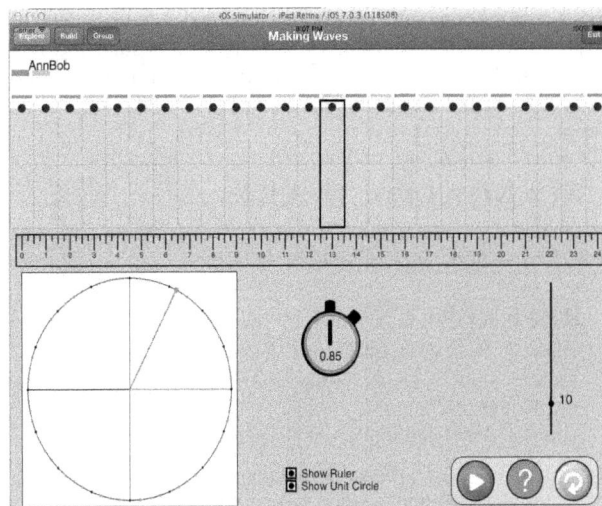

Figure 1. A screenshot of the Waves app, showing the series of individual oscillators, and the unit circle tool

with a given wavelength and direction, and to explain how their strategy works. To successfully build a wave with the correct wavelength, the group must coordinate the phases of their individual oscillators. In asking students to perform this coordination, we intend to occasion meaningful interactions around the concepts of phase, relative phase, position and direction, phase intervals, and phase as a function of both position and time. At the same time, we intend for our design to provide students with dynamic interactive visualizations to scaffold those interactions.

Classroom Intervention Using these tools, students constructed a wave, along with an explanation of a strategy to change the wave's direction using their "unit circle tools." A discourse and gestural analysis of this episode has suggested that the form of students' explanations is strongly tied to the salient features of the interface. That is, the explanation created by the groups linked together the behaviors of elements of the simulation (and nothing else): the unit circle, the individual oscillator, and the wave profile each were referenced in the explanation, primarily through gestures that mimicked the motions of these elements. In this sense, these elements of the design supported the students' sense-making— students relied on gesture to refer to the behavior in their explanations, rather than on complex verbal descriptions.

Other phenomena such as the *relative* motion of two oscillators, which was not directly represented on the screen, were not invoked as a part of the group's explanation of their strategy. My current interpretation of this is that the interface does not effectively scaffold talk about the *relative* motion of oscillators. This may be because this concept is not made salient by a particular onscreen object, or because the lack of such an object to reference in talk makes it too difficult for the students to talk about it. So in the next design iteration, I will add a "comparison" tool to the interface that will allow students to observe the relative phase between two selected oscillators. I suspect that this tool may be taken up in the group discussion and used in the subsequent explanation of wave direction.

6. CURRENT STATUS

Designs, data collection, analyses and redesigns are ongoing. As of Spring 2014, I have collected a round of data on the Waves app, am furthering the analysis described above, and am beginning the redesign of the Waves app to include the new "comparison" tool to be used in a second round of data collection this Fall. A second design targeting Circuits will be piloted in the Spring.

7. ACKNOWLEDGEMENTS

This material is based upon work supported by the National Science Foundation under Grant No. 1252508.

8. REFERENCES

[1] Hake, R. R. (1998). Interactive-engagement versus traditional methods: A six-thousand-student survey of mechanics test data for introductory physics courses. American journal of Physics, 66, 64.

[2] Cohen, E. (1994). Restructuring the classroom: Conditions for productive small groups. Review of Educational Research, 64(1), 1-35.

[3] Barron, B. (2003). When smart groups fail. Journal of the Learning Sciences, 12, 307-359.

[4] Zurita, G., & Nussbaum, M. (2004). Computer supported collaborative learning using wirelessly interconnected handheld computers. Computers & education, 42(3), 289-314.

[5] White, T., & Pea, R. (2011). Distributed by design: On the promises and pitfalls of collaborative learning with multiple representations. Journal of the Learning Sciences, 20(3), 489-547.

[6] Adams, W. K., Reid, S., LeMaster, R., McKagan, S. B., Perkins, K. K., Dubson, M., & Wieman, C. E. (2008). A Study of Educational Simulations Part I-Engagement and Learning. Journal of Interactive Learning Research, 19(3), 397-419.

[7] Potter, W., Webb, D., West, E., Paul, C., Bowen, M., Weiss, B. & De Leone, C. (2012). Sixteen years of Collaborative Learning through Active Sense-making in Physics (CLASP) at UC Davis. American Journal of Physics, 82, 153-163 (2014), DOI:http://dx.doi.org/10.1119/1.4857435

Using Technology to Increase Meaningful Engagement in a Memory Care Unit

Amanda Lazar
University of Washington
Box 358047
Seattle, WA 98109
alaz@uw.edu

ABSTRACT
Dementia is affecting an increasing number of people due to the global aging of the population. People with dementia living in memory care units (MCUs) often lack access to meaningful activities and social interactions. Information and communication technologies (ICT) have a tremendous potential to increase activity opportunities for people in MCUs. In two longitudinal studies, I used observations, interviews, and repeated quantitative measures to evaluate the use of a commercially available multi-functional technology system with people with dementia, staff, and family members. Next steps include data analysis and generating recommendations for system designers.

Categories and Subject Descriptors
J.3. Life and Medical Sciences (Health)

General Terms
Human Factors

Keywords
dementia; accessibility; multimedia; ICT

1. INTRODUCTION
14.7% of Americans over the age of 70 were affected by dementia in 2010 [1]. As the older adult population grows, the number of individuals with dementia will increase proportionally. Cost of health and long-term care for people with dementia is estimated to rise from $200 billion spent in 2012 to $1.1 trillion spent in 2050 [2]. A significant cost of care with people with dementia are housing costs, as 30-40% of people with dementia live in nursing or assisted living facilities and memory care units, compared to only 2% of older adults without dementia [2]. With dementia care already prohibitively expensive and a shortage of paid staff, recreational and leisurely activities may be overlooked.

1.1 The Importance of Activities for People with Dementia
Structured activities are extremely important for people with dementia. Unlike pharmacological treatments (which certainly

Permission to make digital or hard copies of part or all of this work for personal or classroom use is granted without fee provided that copies are not made or distributed for profit or commercial advantage, and that copies bear this notice and the full citation on the first page. Copyrights for third-party components of this work must be honored. For all other uses, contact the owner/author(s). Copyright is held by the author/owner(s).
GROUP'14, November 9–12, 2014, Sanibel Island, Florida, USA.
ACM 978-1-4503-3043-5/14/11.
http://dx.doi.org/10.1145/2660398.2660433

have benefits), activity interventions may address loneliness, sensory deprivation, and boredom, which are often at the root of problematic behaviors [3]. People with dementia experience benefits such as greater well being during activities [4], reduced agitation [5], and delayed progression of cognitive impairments [6]. Despite the benefits, people living in MCUs may not have opportunities for sustained social interactions and stimulating activities [7]. There is a clear unmet need for stimulating activities that don't place an additional burdens on staff, the MCU or the healthcare system.

2. Related Work
2.1 ICT and Dementia
ICT has the potential to support cost-effective activities in a way that reduces staff burden. Marshall described nine uses of technology for people with dementia, including compensation, stimulation and relaxation [8]. Topo added communication to this list [9].

Many projects explored ICT interventions for people with dementia for single purposes, such as communication [10] and musical stimulation [11].

2.2 Multifunctional Technology Systems
Single-purpose ICT interventions may be problematic for several reasons, including cost, setup time, technical expertise, and learning time. Additionally, space may be quite limited in MCUs. Multi-functional systems can alleviate some of these issues. I conducted a systematic literature review of multi-functional technology tools designed for or used with people with dementia on five databases including Compendex and Inspec. I found 14 systems which met the criteria of containing at least one application in at least two areas: cognitive, psychosocial, sensory, and movement (these categories are from [12]). The retrieved related work was limited in that systems were often designed and used only with people with mild dementia, were not commercially available or accessible to the general population, and were quite limited in terms of the number and range of applications supported. Later I describe the technology system that I used for my study, which addresses each of these issues.

3. Research Questions
My research questions are the following:

1. How is a multi-functional interactive technology system designed to facilitate engagement in activities in people with dementia perceived by staff, residents, and family members?

2. How does the system facilitate and support interactions between people with dementia, a researcher, family members, and staff?

3. What recommendations for designers of a system to improve access and support of activities for people with dementia can be generated from data gathered throughout the evaluations?

Figure 1: **The computer system used for this study**

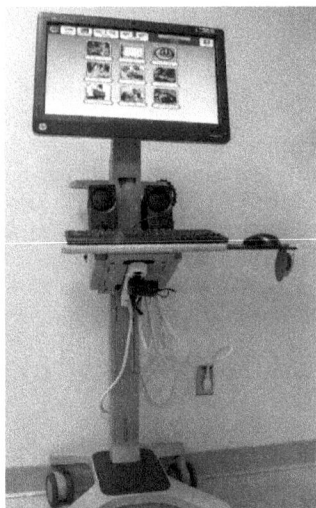

Figure 2: **Organization of applications on home screen**

4. Methods

My project is composed of three parts: 1) an evaluation of a commercially available multi-functional technology system in a memory care unit, 2) an evaluation of the system in a memory care group, and 3) the creation of recommendations for designers of technology for this population.

4.1 Technology System Used for this Study

The technology system that was evaluated is depicted in Figure 1. The version I used for this study has a prototype version of an interface designed for people with dementia. The system is intended to provide opportunities for social involvement (e.g. video calling, email-access, and Facebook), recreation (e.g. games, puzzles, exercise videos, movies, and music) and cognitive training (e.g. memory games). Applications are organized into categories as shown in Figure 2. It is also possible to create custom grouping of applications and place them under icons for a specific resident or staff member. The unit can be wheeled from room to room and has a webcam, microphone, and speakers. It also comes with a video camera, bike pedal, joystick, and headset. The touch-screen monitor can be plugged into an external monitor. The height can be adjusted to be used by people seated or standing.

4.2 Evaluation in a MCU

Residents of a local MCU were enrolled for six months with a family member whenever possible. Five residents, four family members, and seven staff were enrolled in the study. I conducted weekly sessions with the residents, taking handwritten notes, and administered standardized instruments on measures such as quality of life and resource utilization at three time-points. I interviewed staff monthly and family members at three time points.

4.3 Evaluation in a Memory Care Group

Residents of the facility in which the MCU from the previous study was located were enrolled for three months in this second study. The memory care group is a service provided by the facility for people showing signs of memory impairment but deemed able to engage in stimulating group activities. Three residents and two staff members were involved in this study. I observed the use of the system twice a week for two hours and took notes, including rating factors such as whether residents interacted with staff, each other and the system. I also interviewed staff monthly, and interviewed and administered standardized instruments to residents at baseline and exit.

4.4 Recommendations

I will generate recommendations for designers of activity systems for people with dementia using a secondary analysis of the data from parts one and two and validate them with a panel of experts, including experts from HCI and gerontology.

5. Current Status and Next Steps

Based on preliminary analysis, findings include that staff and family members found benefit in using the system such as providing residents with something to do, giving residents a sense of accomplishment, and enabling conversations about new topics. Different applications were found appropriate for group use versus individual use, and individual use was seen as more beneficial but also less likely to occur due to time and staff shortages. People with dementia were able to use and benefit from the system with the assistance of a member of the research team or staff, but not independently.

Next steps include a systematic analysis of the data through open coding and the generation of recommendations.

6. Expected Contributions

This work has several areas of potential contribution towards the fields of HCI and CSCW, including understanding and exploring:

- The impact of the introduction and utilization of technology on relationships between people with dementia, staff, family members, and researchers.

- How organizational factors, such as different group sharing a system and the system being located in a communal space, impact the use of the system.

- How the system impacts staff workflow and roles in the care of people with dementia.

7. ACKNOWLEDGEMENTS

This work was supported by the National Science Foundation Graduate Research Fellowship [Grant Number DGE-0718124] and the National Library of Medicine Biomedical and Health Informatics Training Grant Program [Grant Number 2T15LM007442-11].

8. References

[1] Hurd, MD, Martorelli, P, Delavande, A, Mullen, KJ, Langa, KM. Monetary Costs of Dementia in the United States. *NEJM 368,* 14 (2013), 1326-1334.

[2] Alzheimer's Association. Alzheimer's disease facts and figures. *Alz & Dem 8,* 2 (2012), 131-168.

[3] Cohen-Mansfield, J. Nonpharmacologic Interventions for Inappropriate Behaviors in Dementia. *Am J Geriatr Psychiatry 9,* 4 (2001), 361-381.

[4] Brooker, D, Duce, L. Wellbeing and activity in dementia: a comparison of group reminiscence therapy, structured goal-directed group activity and unstructured time. *Aging & Mental Health 4,* 4 (2000), 354-358.

[5] Buettner, LL, Lundegren, H, Lago, D, Farrell, P, Smith, R. Therapeutic recreation as an intervention for persons with dementia and agitation: an efficacy study. *Am J of Alz Dis & Other Dem 11,* 2 (1996), 4-12.

[6] Cheng, ST, Chow, P, Song, YQ, Yu, ECS, Chan, ACM, Lee, TMC, Lam, JHM. Mental and Physical Activities Delay Cognitive Decline in Older Persons with Dementia. *Am J Geriatr Psychiatry 22,* 1 (2014), 63-74.

[7] Hancock, GA, Woods, B, Challis, D, Orrell, M. The needs of older people with dementia in residential care. *Int J Geriatr Psychiatry 21,* 1 (2006), 43-49.

[8] Marshall, M. Dementia and technology: some ethical considerations. In *Elderly people in industrialised societies.* (1996), 207-215.

[9] Topo, P. Technology Studies to Meet the Needs of People with Dementia and their Caregivers: a Literature Review. *J of Applied Gerontology 28,* 1 (2008), 5-37.

[10] Astell, AJ, Ellis, MP, Bernardi, L, Alm, N, Dye, R, Gowans, G, Campbell, J. Using a touch screen computer to support relationships between people with dementia and caregivers. *Interacting with Computers 22,* 4 (2010) 267-275.

[11] Topo, P. Assessment of a Music-Based Multimedia Program for People with Dementia. *Dementia 3,* 3 (2004) 5-37.

[12] Gardette, V, Coley, N, Andrieu, S. Non-pharmacologic Therapies: A Different Approach to AD. *Can Rev of Alz Dis & Other Dem 13,* 3 (2010) 13-22

Designing Communication Technologies
for Children with a Chronic Illness

Leslie S. Liu
Biomedical & Health Informatics
University of Washington
lsliu@uw.edu

ABSTRACT

Children with a chronic illness who must frequent the hospital for various treatments and procedures are removed from familiar environments, such as their home or school, to stay close to the hospital. Their temporary removal from familiarity can cause feelings of isolation. Social connectedness with their friends and classmates may help alleviate their feelings of isolation and help make them feel more "normal" like their healthy counterparts. However, current communication technologies are not designed specifically for chronically ill patients. By understanding how patients use current technologies to stay connected with their friends, I propose to develop and carry out a participatory design methodology to produce technologies that assist the chronically ill pediatric population.

Categories and Subject Descriptors

J.3 Life and Medical Sciences (Health)

General Terms

Human Factors.

Keywords

Children; chronic illness; participatory design; communication technologies.

1. INTRODUCTION

For children diagnosed with a chronic illness, growing up can be harder than their healthy peers. These patients face challenges in staying connected with their social circle. They may feel isolated because of their temporary removal from familiarity. Patients may also feel as if they are no longer who they use to be because of the changes in their physical appearance. Nowadays, patients, particularly teenagers, are likely to use some communication technology to keep in touch with friends while they are in the hospital or at home. Studies have focused on healthy children and the ways they communicate such as teenagers and video chat [2]. Few studies have examined how younger children with chronic illnesses communicate with healthy peers.

GROUP'14, November 9–12, 2014, Sanibel Island, Florida, USA.
ACM 978-1-4503-3043-5/14/11.
http://dx.doi.org/10.1145/2660398.2660434

My research aims to not only inform the actual design of communication technologies for children with a chronic illness, but also to inform potential *design methodologies* specific to such children.

2. RELATED WORK

Children with a chronic illness may not be able to attend school or certain events due to procedures or a compromised immune system. Cancer survivors feel greater isolation [9], play less than healthy peers [10], and are teased [11]. However, being seen as "normal" by peers was helpful for patients [13].

Social support from peers may help alleviate their feelings of isolation and increase their social connectedness. Increasing positive peer relationships is associated with prosocial behavior, academic achievement, and also the ability to withstand stress [12]. Support from peers was found to be important [6] for reminding patients to stay optimistic [13].

Work on children and HCI has mostly focused on communication technologies for healthy children [1, 4]. Studies that have examined how to design for and with children with health conditions tend to emphasize solutions that allow children to communicate their needs to specialists [8] rather than friends.

3. STUDY DESIGN

To understand how to design communication technologies for chronically ill pediatric patients, I have broken my research into two steps: (1) understanding current communication practices of how patients stay connected with their friends; (2) informing the design of technologies and design methodologies through participatory design sessions.

3.1 Communication Practices and Challenges for Patients

To understand how to design communication technologies for chronically ill pediatric patients, I first examined how patients remain connected to their peers [5]. I conducted semi-structured interviews with 22 participants. Fifteen participants were healthcare professionals (e.g., physicians, social workers) working at a large children's hospitals. Six were parents of children with cancer and one had a child with a blood disorder. Patients ranged from 5 to 17 years old.

I coded transcribed interviews looking for emergent themes using a grounded theory approach [10]. I interviewed healthcare professionals because they interact daily with a large number of patients and can give a broad perspective across many patients. I interviewed parents because they are able to reflect upon their child's experiences more easily than young children. Due to the sensitive nature of these illnesses, I felt it was important to gain an understanding of the key issues before interacting directly with the children.

My findings revealed that a major concern of pediatric patients was that their illness affected their feelings of normalcy. Due to this life-changing disruption, patients used various technologies to try and maintain normalcy in their lives. While striving for normalcy, patients knew that they could not continue to have the same lives as their healthy peers. Patients used various methods to "create a new normal", such as using Facebook postings to mediate classmates' reactions to their different appearance (e.g., baldness).

3.2 Design by Play

Based off of my previous study, the next step is to understand how the design of technologies can support normalcy and how to help patients stay connected to friends. Design by play is a potential design methodology for these sensitive populations.

Inspired by Druin's approach to participatory design (PD) from her cooperative inquiry framework [3], I plan to hold weekly PD sessions over 3 months. PD studies involve the end-user in activities that lead to design and products [7]. My PD sessions will be held at the Seattle Children's Hospital near outpatient clinics. Long-term PD sessions can foster community building within Seattle Children's Hospital.

I will target patients who are between the ages of 7-12 years old. The benefits are threefold. First, Druin [3] suggests that children between the ages of 7-10 can often make good design partners because they are able to discuss what they are thinking but are not influenced by pre-conceived notions. Second, many technologies such as Facebook and Twitter require users to be at least 13 years old. Therefore, pre-teen patients may not have as many resources to stay in touch with friends. Third, children have been found to be able to lead co-design sessions [14].

Because patients often come in and out of the hospital, the PD sessions will be designed to not require prior knowledge or involvement in order to participate. Each PD session will follow the below structure [14]:

1. **Hangout Time.** After introducing themselves and how many times they've participated in the sessions, patients will get to know each other without pressure to conduct design activities.

2. **Play Design Activity.** Activities will vary weekly to ensure that patients who have participated previously will still be engaged. Activities informed by my first study will revolve around a "Story of the Week" (e.g., Jo isn't able to play or see her friend, Bob, for a few weeks. Can we think of ways to help Jo play with Bob?). Using low-fidelity materials (e.g., Play-Doh, Legos, markers) [3] in small teams, I will ask patients to come up with ideas on how to answer the Story of the Week.

3. **Sharing Time.** Teams will then share what they have come up with other teams.

4. CHALLENGES

PD literature on healthy children do not address the challenges of having pediatric patients as participants. Patients may feel more comfortable having siblings, friends, or parents with them, but they may become too overprotective of the patient and hinder the patient's participation. Patients may also have varying levels of physical and cognitive limitations. When using different low-fidelity design materials, I will need to consider all levels of limitations to ensure that patients are not isolated from participation.

5. CONCLUSION

Children with a chronic illness lead very different lives than their healthy friends. Communication technologies can support patients in feeling connected with peers. However, many current communication technologies are not designed for younger children who are not well. My research will provide a deep understanding of how patients currently use technologies to stay in touch with friends as well as the design of these technologies. I also expect to contribute design methodologies specifically for children with chronic health conditions.

6. ACKNOWLEDGMENTS
Our thanks to ACM SIGCHI for allowing us to modify templates they had developed.

7. REFERENCES
[1] Benford, S., Bederson, B. B., Akesson, K., Bayon, V., Druin, A., Hansson, P., Hourcade, J. P., Ingram, R., Neale, H., O'Malley, C., Simsarian, K., Stanton, D., Sundblad, Y., and Taxén, G. Designing Storytelling Technologies to Encourage Collaboration Between Young Children. In Proc. CHI'00, 556- 563.

[2] Buhler, T., Neustaedter, C., and Hillman, S. How and why teenagers use video chat. In Proc. CSCW'13, 759- 768.

[3] Druin, A. Cooperative inquiry: Developing new technologies for children with children. In Proc. CHI'99, 223–230.

[4] Inkpen, K., Du, H., Roseway, A., Hoff, A., and Johns, P. Video Kids: Augmenting close friendships with asynchronous video conversations in VideoPal. In Proc. CSCW'12, 2387-2396.

[5] Liu, L.S., Inkpen, K., and Pratt, W. "I'm Not Like My Friends": Understanding How Children with a Chronic Illness Use Technology to Maintain Normalcy. To Appear in Proc. CSCW'15.

[6] Mitchell, W., Clarke, S., and Sloper, P. Care and support needs of children and young people with cancer and their parents. Journal of Psychooncology 15, 9 (2006), 805-816.

[7] Muller, M.J. Participatory design: the third space in HCI. The Human-Computer Interaction Handbook, (2002), 1051- 1068.

[8] Ruland, C., Starren, J., and Vatne, T.M. Participatory design with children in the development of a support system for patient-centered care in pediatric oncology. JBI 41, 4 (2008), 624-635.

[9] Spirito, A., Stark, L.J., Cobiella, C., Drigan R., Androkites, A., and Hewett, K. Social adjustment of children successfully treated for cancer. Journal of Pediatric Psychology 15, 3 (1990), 359-371.

[10] Strauss, A. and Corbin, J. Grounded theory methodology: An overview. Handbook of Qualitative Research. Sage, Thousand Oaks, CA, 1994.

[11] Wasserman, A.L., Thompson, E.I., Wilimas, J.A., and Fairclough, D.L. The psychological status of survivors of childhood/adolescent Hodgkin's disease. Am. J. of Diseases of Children 141, 6 (1987), 626-631.

[12] Weiss, P.L., Whiteley, C.P., Treviranus, J., and Fels, D.I. PEBBLES: A personal technology for meeting educational, social and emotional needs of hospitalised children. Journal of PUC 5, 3 (2001), 157-168.

[13] Woodgate, R.L. (1999). Social support in children with cancer: a review of the literature. Journal of Pediatric Oncology Nursing 16, 4 (1999), 202-213.

[14] Yip, J.C., Foss, E., Bonsignore, E., Guha, M.L., Norooz, L., Rhodes, E., McNally, B., Papadatos, P., Golub, E., and Druin, A. Children Initiating and Leading Cooperative Inquiry Sessions. In Proc. IDC'13, 293-296.

Distributed Leadership in OSS

Nora McDonald
Drexel University
2100 Delancey Pl
+16102569632
norakmcdonald@gmail.com

ABSTRACT

Open-source software (OSS) is software whose source code is available to view, change, and distribute without cost, and is typically developed in a collaborative manner that has captured the imagination of those who view the web as enabling more "democratic" models of governance. Researchers have, for years, debated the social structure of OSS projects – in particular, the extent to which they represent decentralized forms of organization. Many have argued that the significant concentration of code development responsibility raises doubts about whether the level of power-sharing truly qualifies as "distributed" in the way early observers predicted. This research will investigate how changes in the technology that supports these projects – specifically the greater visibility that characterizes the GitHub workspace may lead to a more broadly and quantifiably distributed leadership. Over the course of several studies employing several methodologies, it will examine leadership in OSS projects when visibility is a feature of the workspace.

Categories and Subject Descriptors

H.5.3 [**Information Interfaces and Presentation**]: Group and Organization Interfaces --- *collaborative computing; computer-supported cooperative work; theory and models; web-based interaction.*

General Terms

Management, Human Factors

Keywords

Open-source software; distributed leadership; social computing

1. INTRODUCTION

OSS has received considerable research attention, with leadership typically measured in terms of contribution of code and contribution of talk. The collaborative and open manner in which OSS is developed invites observers to view and describe those communities as "meritocracies" where the best contributions prevail in a broadly participatory marketplace of ideas. However, analysis of code and talk contributions often reveals something

GROUP'14, November 9–12, 2014, Sanibel Island, Florida, USA.
ACM 978-1-4503-3043-5/14/11.
http://dx.doi.org/10.1145/2660398.2660435

closer to an "eight-twenty rule," in which a relatively small number of participants shoulder most of the weight. Some OSS projects, like Linus Torvalds' well-known Linux project, are depicted as something closer to a "benevolent dictatorship" – permissive but fundamentally centralized – potentially establishing a pattern widely adopted by other OSS communities that followed. But as infrastructures that support and house OSS development become more transparent, flexible, and informal, new opportunities for more distributed forms of leadership emerge. That evolution in structure, and the potential changes in behavior that may result, invite new ways of measuring leadership in these communities which can take account of new patterns of distributed interactions.

One such infrastructure is, arguably, GitHub, a code-hosting repository that uses Git version control system and makes the level of participation on OSS projects readily visible. With the introduction of GitHub, the level of participation on OSS platforms is also broader. Perspectives on GitHub's more transparent and collaborative interface, and its potential to transform collaboration, were first introduced to the literature by Dabbish, Stuart, Tsay and Herbsleb [1]. The focus of their research has been on individual user processes and motivations, rather than project-level participation or success, and they have demonstrated the relationship between transparency and collaboration. The implications of *transparency* for leadership structure are equally important. Transparency not only enables participants to co-create work-product; it also supports development of new leadership behaviors such as monitoring, planning, and ad hoc coordination – leadership behaviors that are distinct from code and talk, and not necessarily measured by it.

2. RESEARCH GOALS

Our current understanding of leadership in the context of OSS communities is limited in at least two ways. First, leadership theories tend to conceive of leadership as emanating from a notional top, or as a set of qualities possessed by a single or a set of individuals – not something that is shared collectively. In a virtual "community" defined entirely by shared focus on tasks and goal-related outcomes, with no explicit leadership structure, qualities traditionally associated with leadership (e.g., charisma, influence, persuasion) are not present or take different forms. The second limitation flows naturally from this first – the inevitable tendency to measure what we can readily see. Thus, the metrics traditionally used to measure leadership in OSS communities are actually better suited to measuring productivity, which is clearly a different idea, than they are to measuring leadership. When there is no established "oversight" or known leadership structure, one is tempted to use as a proxy for influence the available measures of activity. Leadership, however, is a qualitative idea, and quantity of behavior does not necessarily do it justice.

In order to understand how platform visibility can influence patterns of leadership, it is necessary to employ a broader set of metrics that can produce a more nuanced understanding of leadership and community member interactions. The goal of this dissertation research is to answer the question, *How does technology support and transform leadership in OSS? by focusing specifically on leadership in communities on the GitHub platform, using metrics and methods that allow for a broader conception of leadership than has previously been employed.*

3. THEORETICAL FRAMEWORK

Distributed Leadership (DL) [2] offers a theoretical lens through which to think about the dispersion of leadership. DL is a theory that suggests leadership is shared among members of an organization; it argues that members of a community who do not occupy any formal leadership role can and do perform leadership activities or behaviors. It also attempts to understand how, why, and when participants demonstrate leadership behaviors, and the relationship between different forms of distributed leadership and community effectiveness. This more fluid, ad hoc conception of leadership lends itself well to technology-based *sui generis* communities that have no established leadership structure, although it has not traditionally been propagated or analyzed in a technology context.

Distributed Cognition (DCog) is another theory that may help fill in the gaps left by DL. DCog advances the view that knowledge resides not only with individuals, but also with the social and physical environment. The theory, along with actor-network theory (ANT), considers non-human objects to perform social roles, setting the stage for assignment of leadership behaviors to both people and technology objects.

4. RESEARCH APPROACHES

GitHub, a successful code-hosting repository, provides a fertile ground for an investigation of technology platform and leadership because its features expose the activities of community members to one another. My research encompasses qualitative interviewing, conversation analysis, observation, study of electronic archival data, and finally, a series of quantitative surveys.

Figure 1. Communication networks of prominent projects on GitHuh

First, Exploratory research, including conversation analysis of pull request communications (Figure 1), walk-throughs, analysis of IRC channels, was conducted to support hypothesis development and study design. Next, 28 semi-structured interviews were conducted with respondents from eight different

communities. In addition to asking respondents to describe how their roles and responsibilities had evolved throughout the course of their participation, interviews explored how the *project* had evolved on the platform; how the respondent/community uses its features and coordinates work; and how participants measure project "success." Preliminary findings from this research were published [3]. Based on these analyses, I developed a set of metrics for use in making systematic project comparisons between projects on GitHub. A survey instrument for measuring success was also fielded to contributors on five OSS projects.

Results of an early pilot study focused on exploring ways to operationalize distributed leadership behaviors as an increase in awareness and monitoring of others using GitHub features. An example from this early study is shown in Figure 2, in which participants were asked to consider their awareness of what others are doing on GitHub versus other code hosting platforms.

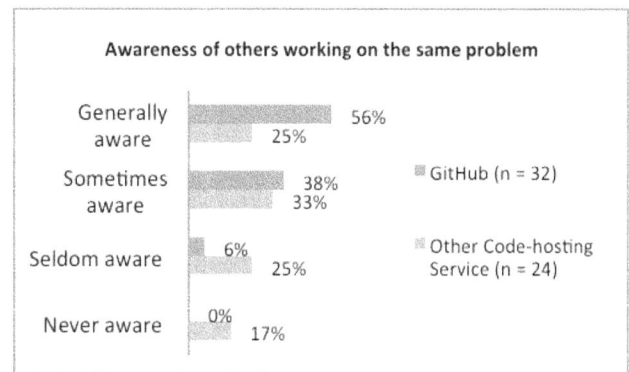

Figure 1. Example of survey results from pilot study

5. CONTRIBUTION

Findings from this dissertation will demonstrate both the relevance of transparency to the emergence of leadership behaviors and potentially broaden our conception of how leadership is appropriately defined in virtual collaborative workspaces.

6. REFERENCES

[1] Dabbish, L., Stuart, C., Tsay, J. and Herbsleb, J. 2012. Social coding in GitHub: transparency and collaboration in an open software repository. *Proceedings of the ACM 2012 conference on Computer Supported Cooperative Work* (New York, NY, USA, 2012), 1277–1286.

[2] Gronn, P. 2002. Distributed leadership. *Second International Handbook of Educational Leadership and Administration.* Dordrecht: Kluwer. 653–696.

[3] McDonald, N. and Goggins, S. 2013. Performance and Participation in Open Source Software on GitHub. *CHI '13 Extended Abstracts on Human Factors in Computing Systems* (New York, NY, USA, 2013), 139–144.

The Collaborative Management of Information Problems in Hospitals

Alison R. Murphy
The Pennsylvania State University
College of Information Sciences and Technology
323 IST Building
University Park, PA 16802
arm193@psu.edu

ABSTRACT

With the rapid emergence of health information technologies (HIT) in hospitals, it is important to understand how the design of these systems affects the communication of patient information and the collaboration of hospital teams. HIT systems can provide benefits to the patient-care process [2,4,5], but they do not always address serious information problems. In some cases, the design and use of HIT systems can cause additional information problems [2,4]. Therefore, this qualitative study seeks to understand how hospital teams identify and manage these information problems, and how information problems impact the collaborative activities of the hospital team.

Categories and Subject Descriptors

H.5.3. Group and organization interfaces: Computer supported cooperative work; J.3. Life and medical sciences: Medical information systems.

General Terms

Design, Human Factors.

Keywords

Health information technology; information problems; computer-supported cooperative work; collaboration; system design.

1. INTRODUCTION

Hospitals are highly collaborative, information-rich environments where hospital staff rely on the availability, accuracy, and completeness of information in order to make well-informed decisions about patient care. However, hospital staff frequently encounter information problems. These information problems include wrong, outdated, conflicting, incomplete, or missing information that may interfere with the ability of the hospital staff to do their work. Although these information problems have existed for some time in paper-based patient records [2], there is an increasing need to focus on information problems in electronic records. This is because of the tremendous growth of health information technologies (HIT) in U.S. hospitals due to recent government incentives [8]. Researchers describe how HIT can provide various benefits to users [2,4,5]. However, the use of HIT also changes how hospital teams document, share, and retrieve patient information [2]. In some cases, the design and use of HIT systems can actually introduce new information problems [2,4]. If these information problems are not appropriately identified and managed, they can pose a risk to the patient-care process and to the patients themselves [2].

Although researchers have identified some of the information issues associated with HIT [1,2,4-7,9], this research is still limited because it focuses on the individual users of the system and does not always consider the collaborative nature of hospital teams. Therefore, my study seeks to address this limitation by describing how the identification and management of information problems affects the collaborative work of the hospital teams. This research is relevant to the GROUP community because it can improve the understanding of how collaboration and system design impact the identification and management of information problems. This can then help to inform the design and use of HIT systems within hospitals.

2. BACKGROUND

Current research primarily focuses on the causes of information problems. Researchers discuss the challenge of designing HIT for the information-rich and fast-paced environment of hospitals. Studies show that HIT systems tend to be overly structured with rigid rules that encourage data standardization, which can result in information problems caused by the HIT design [2]. Information fragmentation is one HIT design issue that leaves the user with incomplete patient information and the loss of a cohesive overview of the patient's record [2,5]. Current HIT system design has also led to a variety of data entry issues including difficulty entering non-standard data, unintentional selection of default values, and data truncation [1,5]. Additionally, ineffective HIT design can also prevent the entry of important descriptive information by forcing the use of standardized drop-down values [1] and result in the loss of psycho-social information that is said to provide, "*continuity of patient care...[and] a richer picture of the patient's situation*" [9:2065].

Additionally, information problems are also caused by the users themselves. For instance, users tend to copy-and-paste information from prior notes. This can lead to outdated or incorrect information being carried throughout the system [4] and it can result in "*reducing the credibility of the recorded findings, clouding clinical thinking, limiting proper coding, and robbing*

GROUP'14, November 9–12, 2014, Sanibel Island, Florida, USA.
ACM 978-1-4503-3043-5/14/11.
http://dx.doi.org/10.1145/2660398.2660436.

the chart of its narrative flow and function" [7:495]. Delayed information entry can also result when clinicians are too busy or tightly scheduled to enter patient data into the HIT directly after seeing a patient, which can cause information in the system to be outdated or incomplete for extended periods of time [6]. This negatively affects other team members who need access to up-to-date, accurate records [2]. Therefore, this study seeks to extend this research by, not only identifying how information problems are identified and managed by hospital teams, but also understanding the impact that information problems have on the collaborative work of hospital teams.

3. RESEARCH QUESTIONS
The three main research questions of this study are:

RQ1: How do collaborative hospital teams identify information problems?

- *How does technology help or hinder the identification of information problems?*
- *How do work practices help or hinder the identification of information problems?*

RQ2: How do collaborative hospital teams manage information problems?

- *How does technology help or hinder the management of information problems?*
- *How do work practices help or hinder the management of information problems?*

RQ3: How does collaboration within hospital teams play a role in identifying and managing information issues?

- *How do hospital teams make each other aware of information issues?*
- *How do hospital teams determine accountability for managing or fixing the information issues?*

4. RESEARCH METHODOLOGY
This study will use qualitative methods, including direct observations and semi-structured interviews. This methodological approach is appropriate for this study because qualitative research can provide rich, detailed descriptions of the participants' behaviors and perceptions, and other HIT researchers have used it for this similar purpose [2,6,9]. The field study will be conducted in the in-patient area of a large teaching hospital in northeastern United States. I will shadow members of a hospital team (e.g., physicians, residents, nurses, social workers, care coordinators) and take field notes on their communication activities (e.g., spoken discussions, formal paper or electronic documentation, informal transitional documentation). In addition, I will observe activities that involve the collaborative review of patient records, such as hand-off and discharge planning discussions. The field notes will be transcribed and reviewed in a continuous, systematic way in order to ensure that I am capturing rich, descriptive data that address the study's research questions. The observations will provide an understanding of the general workflow and local terminology, and provide specific examples of information problems that arise for the participants. The observations will also help to inform the interview protocol.

After I have gained a sufficient understanding of the workflow and information problems, I will conduct semi-structured interviews with the participants. The interview protocol will provide an opportunity to gather the participants' perceptions of information problems, how HIT helps or hinders their ability to manage information problems, and how information problems impact their collaborative work activities. The interviews will be audio-recorded, and then transcribed for data analysis purposes. The data will then be analyzed using Braun & Clarke's six-phase thematic analysis approach [3]. This approach facilitates the process of becoming familiar with the data, systematically identifying codes and themes, and defining the common themes found across the data.

5. PRELIMINARY FINDINGS
I conducted a 3-month preliminary field study to understand hospital staff's collaboration and use of HIT in an emergency department. Findings from this preliminary study showed that information problems frequently occur in hospitals. The various types of information problems identified by the participants included wrong, outdated, conflicting, incomplete, or missing information in the HIT, which are similar to information issues summarized in prior literature [1,2,4-7,9]. The study also identified issues encountered when trying to manage the information problems within a collaborative healthcare team where multiple people are responsible for co-managing the information. Some participants described their lack of editing rights when trying to fix information issues, as well as the conflicting and ambiguous perceptions of who is responsible for fixing the problems. For example, a social worker recalled a time when trying to fix inaccurate patient information in the system: "*Since I cannot update it as a social worker, I try to call others to update it. But they sometimes say that it's someone else's responsibility. I talk to registration, but they say that it's the nurse's responsibility, but when I talk to the nurse, they say it's not their responsibility.*" When asked if there was an unclear understanding of responsibility for this situation, the participant responded: "*Well, it's clear to them that it's not their responsibility [laughs]! But it's not clear whose responsibility it is.*" The findings also describe how managing information problems can lead to user frustration, workflow disruptions, and the use of workarounds.

Therefore, the research study summarized in this paper seeks to extend these preliminary findings in order to better understand the information problems that hospital teams face. In addition, this study also plans to explore the role that collaboration plays in identifying and managing these information problems. This includes addressing accountability issues, such as those described by the social worker in the preliminary data.

6. CURRENT STATUS AND NEXT STEPS
I passed my dissertation proposal in January 2014 and will collect my field study data from May through September 2014. I will then analyze data and perform any follow-up data collection during Fall 2014 and Spring 2015. I anticipate defending my dissertation in Summer 2015.

7. EXPECTED CONTRIBUTIONS
This research will provide a better understanding of how information problems are identified and managed by hospital teams, as well as how information problems impact the collaborative activities of the team. It will also offer socio-technical design implications for how HIT systems can be more

effectively designed to help collaborative teams identify and manage these information problems. This work is supported by the U.S. National Science Foundation under grant IIS-1017247.

8. REFERENCES

[1] Abramson, E.L., Patel, V., Malhotra, S., Pfoh, E.R., Osorio, S.N., Cheriff, A., Cole, C.L., Bunce, A., Ash, J., Kaushal, R. (2012). Physician experiences transitioning between an older versus newer electronic health record for electronic prescribing. *International Journal of Medical Informatics, 81*, 539-548.

[2] Ash, J.S., Berg, M., Coiera, E. (2004). Some unintended consequences of information technology in health care: The nature of patient care information systems-related errors. *Journal of the American Medical Informatics Association, 11*(2), 104-112.

[3] Braun, V. & Clarke, V. (2006). Using thematic analysis in psychology. *Qualitative Research in Psychology, 3*(2), 77-101.

[4] Embi, P.J., Yackel, T.R., Logan, J.R., Bowen, J.L., Cooney, T.G., Gorman, P.N. (2004). Impacts of computerized physician documentation in a teaching hospital. Perceptions of faculty and resident physicians. *Journal of the American Medical Informatics Association, 11*(4), 300-310.

[5] Koppel, R., Metlay, J.P., Cohen, A., Abaluck, B., Localio, A. R., Kimmel, S.E., Strom, B.L. (2005). Role of computerized physician order entry systems in facilitating medication errors. *Journal of the American Medical Informatics Association, 293*(10), 1197-1203.

[6] Park, S.Y., Lee, S.Y., & Chen, Y. (2012). The effects of EMR deployment on doctors' work practices: A qualitative study in the emergency department of a teaching hospital. *International Journal of Medical Informatics, 81*, 204-217.

[7] Siegler, E.L. & Adelman, R. (2009). Copy and paste: A remediable hazard of electronic health records. *American Journal of Medicine, 122*(6), 495-496.

[8] U.S. Department of Health & Human Services – HealthIT.gov. "Benefits of EHRs." Retrieved from: http://www.healthit.gov/providers-professionals/benefits-electronic-health-records-ehrs.

[9] Zhou, X., Ackerman, M. S., & Zheng, K. (2009). I just don't know why it's gone: maintaining informal information use in inpatient care. In *Proceedings of the SIGCHI Conference on Human Factors in Computing Systems*, 2061-2070.

The Potential of VMC Systems to Support Social Capital

Katja Neureiter
ICT&S Center, University of Salzburg
Sigmund Haffner Gasse 18
5020 Salzburg, Austria
Katja.Neureiter@sbg.ac.at

ABSTRACT

Video-mediated communication systems allow to communicate over distance and offer possibilities to build up or maintain social relationships. Such systems convey a variety of non-verbal cues (e.g., gestures or facial expressions), which support mutual understanding and can evoke the feeling of being close to the remote communication partner. The aim of my thesis is to investigate the potential of video-mediated communication systems to increase cohesion and identity of small groups and develop a sense of belongingness, i.e., support bonding forms of social capital. This will be done by investigating the interrelation between social presence and social capital in video-mediated communication.

Categories and Subject Descriptors

H.5.m [**Information interfaces and presentation (e.g., HCI)**]: Miscellaneous.

Keywords

Social Capital; Social Connectedness; Social Presence

1. MOTIVATION AND CONTEXT

Video-mediated communication (VMC) systems have become an integral part of everyday life for many people. For example, Skype or Face-time, allow to communicate over distance at almost every time and place and hold potential to build up and maintain social relationships. These relationships imply actual or potential resources, i.e., social capital [2]. In research there is a growing interest in social capital theory, but it has so far mainly been investigated in the context of social network sites (e.g., [3, 4, 6]).

According to Putnam [10], it can be distinguished between bonding and bridging forms of social capital. Whereas bridging capital facilitates the access to external resources, e.g., providing aid for career moves [5], bonding forms increase cohesion and identity of small groups. Members of such groups share a strong sense of belongingness, which is mainly based on common norms and attitudes.

In my thesis, I will explore in what way VMC systems hold potential to build up and/or maintain social relationships that increase cohesion and identity of small groups, i.e., how bonding forms of social capital can be supported. VMCs allow to convey a variety of non-verbal cues, which are important in human communication [7] and allow to experience being close to the communication partner (i.e., social presence).

The concept of social presence, helps to understand a user's experience when communicating over distance and provides insights how natural communication can be supported. Social presence can be defined as the sense of being with another person, *'the moment-to-moment awareness of co-presence [...] the sense of accessibility of the other being's psychological, emotional, and intentional states'* [1] (p.10) or as Short et al. [11] would define the *'degree of salience of the other person in a mediated communication and the consequent salience of their interpersonal interactions'* (p.65).

To support social presence, a system needs to be designed to allow, for example, interactivity and immediacy [12]. Interactivity is considered as engagement and is illustrated by activities users perform and the feedback they receive. It might be comparable to what Biocca and Harms [1] define as mutual understanding or psychological involvement that is influenced by a temporal component: immediacy. Immediacy influences interactivity through straightforward reactions of communication partners. This in turn might have a positive impact on social presence [12] and can support natural communication. VMC systems enable the transportation of non-verbal cues (e.g., facial expressions) and allow to convey unspoken information, which are important in human communication [7]. However, a VMC system that enables natural communication does not necessarily increase cohesion or a sense of belongingness.

2. RESEARCH QUESTIONS

To understand in what way VMC systems that enable social presence actually hold potential to support bonding forms of social capital, a theoretical understanding of the dimensions and constituting factors of social presence in VMC, and a profound understanding about the interrelation between social capital theory and social presence is required. Accordingly the following research questions were defined:

RQ1 What are dimensions and constituting factors of social presence in VMC?

GROUP'14, November 9–12, 2014, Sanibel Island, Florida, USA.
ACM 978-1-4503-3043-5/14/11.
http://dx.doi.org/10.1145/2660398.2660437 .

RQ2 In what way do VMC systems that support social presence hold potential for social capital?

Based on these insights implications for the design of VMC systems will be derived. This leads to my third research question:

RQ3 How do VMC systems need to be designed to support bonding forms of social capital?

3. WORK IN PROGRESS AND RESULTS TO DATE

The first steps towards answering RQ1 were a literature analysis on the concept of social presence and user studies in the lab, in order to investigate different dimensions of social presence that are important in VMC. So far, two studies have been carried out, using a VMC system that consists of two screens and two cameras. It illustrates the communication partner almost life-sized and conveys a variety of non-verbal cues (see Figure 1).

Figure 1: The VMC System

The first study aimed at investigating interdependencies of eye contact, gaze behavior, and gestures with respect to social presence. This work has already been published as work-in-progress at CHI 2013 [9]. For the study a between subject design with two experimental conditions (eye contact/no eye contact during a VMC) was applied. The results indicate that the perception of non-verbal cues (e.g., gestures) is highly depending on whether eye contact is possible or not.

Based on the first study that provided initial insights on the importance of eye contact on social presence a follow-up study was done in summer 2013 to further investigate the interrelation between non-verbal cues in VMC and social presence. A within subject design with the same experimental conditions was applied to reduce error variance, associated with individual differences of the users. The results of the second study show that a user's awareness of having eye contact positively influences social presence, indicating the importance of the subjective perception of a user within a mediated communication [1].

The process of answering RQ2 has just begun and started with investigating the interrelation between social capital theory and social presence. First results of this work have been published at ISPR 2014 [8]. To gain insights in what way a VMC system allows to build up relationships and supports a feeling of connectedness an explorative field study, carried out in spring 2013, was analyzed using social capital theory. The work was inspired by and related to a three year's project that aimed at developing a VMC system for older adults, who are hardly able to meet their family and friends face-to-face due to age-related disabilities [2].

Older adults, who did not know each other before, used the aforementioned VMC system over a period of six weeks to be in contact with each other. It was investigated in what way participants experienced social presence, and if their perceived feeling of being connected to other users (perceived bonding capital) changed over time. For data assessment a multi-method approach was chosen, including qualitative and quantitative methods (e.g., interviews, questionnaires). The data was interpreted based on social capital theory and allowed to explore the interrelationship between social presence and social capital. The results indicate, that social presence in terms of co-presence and mutual understanding is a core factor to establish trustworthy relationships and to enhance reciprocity, which in turn are important dimensions of bonding forms of social capital.

In a next step it is planned to further investigate the different dimensions of social presence that might be relevant for social capital, using VMC systems such as Skype or FaceTime. A user study in the field is planned, applying qualitative and quantitative methods to assess participants' perceived bonding capital (e.g., [4]). In parallel, in order to answer RQ3, first implications for the design of VMC systems are developed.

4. EXPECTED CONTRIBUTION

This research work is expected to result in a more holistic understanding in what way VMC systems support the development of bonding forms of social capital. By exploring different dimensions of social presence and investigating the interrelationship with social capital it is intended to elaborate a concept that allows to identify relevant aspects for the design of VMC systems. This should support the establishment and maintenance of valuable social relationships that increase cohesion and identity and support a sense of belongingness.

5. ACKNOWLEDGMENTS

This research was enabled by the Connected Vitality project and was supported by PresenceDisplays who provided the system. The financial support by the AAL JP is gratefully acknowledged.

6. REFERENCES

[1] F. Biocca and C. Harms. Defining and Measuring Social Presence: Contribution to the Networked Minds Theory and Measure. *In Proc. of PRESENCE*, 2002:1–36, 2002.

[2] P. Bourdieu. *The Forms of Capital. Handbook of Theory and Research for the Sociology and Education, red. JG Richardson*. Greenwood, New York, 1986.

[3] M. Burke and R. Kraut. Using facebook after losing a job: differential benefits of strong and weak ties. In *Proc. CSCW'13*, pages 1419–1430. ACM, 2013.

---

[1] the study has not been published yet

[2] http://www.connectedvitality.eu

[4] N. B. Ellison, C. Steinfield, and C. Lampe. The benefits of Facebook "friends:" Social capital and college students' use of online social network sites. *Journal of Computer-Mediated Communication*, 12(4):1143–1168, 2007.

[5] M. Huysman and V. Wulf. Social capital and information technology: Current debates and research. *Social capital and information technology*, pages 1–15, 2004.

[6] C. Lampe, J. Vitak, and N. Ellison. Users and Nonusers: Interactions between Levels of Adoption and Social Capital. In *Proc. CSCW'13*, pages 809–820. ACM, 2013.

[7] S. Mukai, D. Murayama, K. Kimura, T. Hosaka, T. Hamamoto, N. Shibuhisa, S. Tanaka, S. Sato, and S. Saito. Arbitrary view generation for eye-contact communication using projective transformations. In *Proc. VRCAI'09*, pages 305–306. ACM, 2009.

[8] K. Neureiter, C. Moser, and M. Tscheligi. Presence as influencing factor for social capital. In *Proc. of the 15th International Conference on Presence*, pages 57–64, 2014.

[9] K. Neureiter, M. Murer, V. Fuchsberger, and M. Tscheligi. Hand and Eyes: How Eye Contact is Linked to Gestures in Video Conferencing. In *Proc. CHI EA'13*, pages 127–132. ACM, 2013.

[10] R. D. Putnam. *Bowling Alone: The Collapse and Revival of American Democracy*. Simon and Schuster New York, 2000.

[11] J. W. Short and B. Christie. *The Social Psychology of Telecommunications*. JWA, 1976.

[12] C.-H. Tu and M. McIsaac. The Relationship of Social Presence and Interaction in Online Classes. *The American journal of distance education*, 16(3):131–150, 2002.

Pregnancy Ecologies as Teachable Moments for the Lifecourse: Changing the mHealth Design Paradigm

Tamara Peyton
College of Information Sciences and Technology
Pennsylvania State University
University Park, PA 16802
tspeyton@ist.psu.edu

Abstract

I investigate the potential for mobile health communication and social collaboration technologies (mHealth) to have a positive impact on pregnancy for lower-income American women. Recognizing that pregnancy is more than medical health, I set out to understand what pregnancy is for this population and how the embodied experience of pregnancy impacts women's lives. I have initiated a mixed methods study, which uses focus groups, interviews, information landscape analysis and social media discourse analysis. From the preliminary focus group and interview data, I have created a structuring health concept that I call the pregnancy ecology, accounting for the multi-faceted experience of pregnancy as a transformational event. The future work will incorporate all of the data into a holistic health ecology concept for pregnancy. Using this concept, I intend to design and build a mHealth app that treats pregnancy as a teachable moment for health, wellness and social support throughout the lifecourse.

Author Keywords

mHealth; pregnancy; design paradigms; life course management; health and wellness; mixed methods

ACM Classification Keywords

H.5.m. Miscellaneous

INTRODUCTION

Appropriate pregnancy management for lower income women in developed nations is part of the Millennium Goals for Maternal and Child Health [1] from the World Health Organization (WHO). Recognizing that maternal health impacts mother and child, the WHO suggests that a way to address healthy pregnancy is to treat it as a social issue. They further suggest that this issue is addressable through the design of appropriate health information and health social support networks, delivered via mobile devices [5].

In order to design appropriate mHealth interventions for this period of life, the WHO suggests the use of approaches that account for the network of people, health issues, informational needs and social support required for a women to have healthy pregnancies and produce healthy offspring. Healthier pregnancies mean less risk of pregnancy-related health complications (e.g.: gestational diabetes, pregnancy-induced hypertension, caesarean delivery, post-partum obesity) and lower fetal and infant mortality rates [10].

GROUP'14, November 9–12, 2014, Sanibel Island, Florida, USA.
ACM 978-1-4503-3043-5/14/11.
http://dx.doi.org/10.1145/2660398.2660438

Despite the multiple touchpoints, influencers and forces that impact a woman's pregnancy management practices, pregnancy in the United States is often treated as a medical issue, stemming from the way the period of pregnancy is dominated by medical care. Women and their partners are expected to turn to medical practitioners for advice and information. Consequently, the care and treatment given to pregnant women focuses narrowly on health activities like diet, exercise and medical planning. But a gap in care exists. In American medicine, care for pregnancy often does not begin until the end of the first trimester, particularly among the lower income demographic [8,12]. Yet women often want information immediately upon finding out they are pregnancy, and like many current health consumers, women turn to the Internet for information, using mobile devices [4]. The structural gap in care results in women turning to their social networks, to the Internet, and to 'for profit' mobile apps for pregnancy advice and information.

Following the WHO recommendations, I am working to address the reality of pregnancy for lower income women within a new paradigm for mobile health application design and information provision. This is intended to provide more appropriate pregnancy management interventions, through technology as well as through clinical care. To approach pregnancy from this perspective, my methods and design guidelines were directed by three research questions:

1. What does pregnancy look like and act like for lower-income American women, when I consider pregnancy to be a major transition within the life course of a woman and her family?

2. What happens to design planning if I shift the understanding of pregnancy, away from the strict medical realm of knowledge and intervention, towards a more holistic and ecological account of pregnancy as a life event?

3. What does an ecological approach to pregnancy do to change the design paradigms of mHealth initiatives for my target group?

APPROACH & METHODS

To direct my research and design activities, I am working with two medical doctors specializing in women's health, and two other HCI researchers, all four of whom are faculty members at my university. Because we understand that health interventions and mobile UX design efficacy are both shaped and determined by users' subjective experiences, we have designed a mixed methods approach to understanding the pregnancy ecology of our target population of lower-income pregnant women. We started with a qualitative study of lower-income women served by Women and Infant Care (WIC) federal assistance clinics in Pennsylvania. We conducted four focus groups of 4-6 women each. Drawing on what we learned in those focus group interactions (Figure 2), we recruited 6 additional women for design-directed interviews. In those interviews, I met with 6 pregnant women in their homes, with their husbands or partners where possible. I led them in a series of exercises around current app and website use. I solicited their feedback on GUIs, information paradigms and appropriateness of existing systems for their informational and support needs.

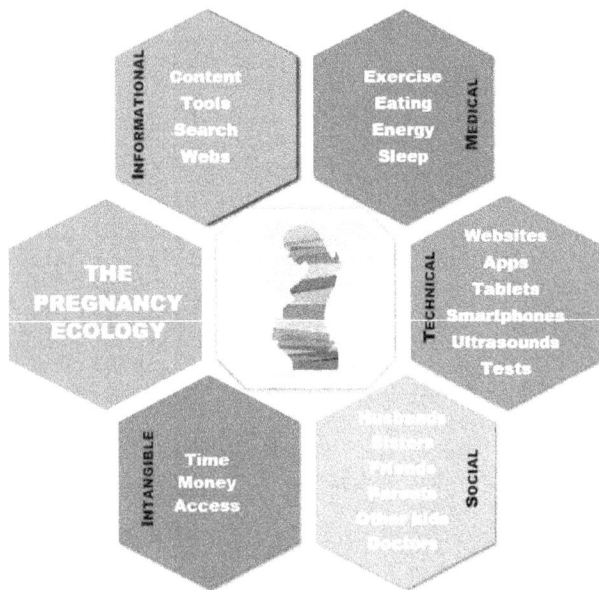

Figure 1: Facets of the Pregnancy Ecology concept

FINDINGS

There are four preliminary findings from the initial research activities, which shape what I have called the 'pregnancy ecology' (Figure 1):

1. Women reject medical guidelines for pregnancy, seeing them as too broad and not specific enough because "every pregnancy is different".
2. Women's bodies rule them during pregnancy, as a result of waning energy levels, food aversions and cravings, hormone spikes, and a variety of unanticipated discomforts.
3. Women turn to "Dr. Google" for advice, because medical advice is not available immediately, family members live too far away, and work and family schedules leave little time for socializing with other women; but Dr. Google confused and scared them with misleading stories of potential serious issues.
4. "Husbands" are key drivers to healthy sane pregnancies, rather than physicians or online social media networks (e.g. Facebook).

As a concept, the pregnancy ecology is influenced by a fusion of social science [12,13], information science [7] and HCI [3]. The concept accounts for the forces, influences and events that shape the experience and health of pregnant lower-income American woman. Based in our participants' stories, the pregnancy ecology has five major facets: medical; social; informational; technical; and intangibles; each with corresponding actors. Each of the ecology facets acts as influences on a woman's subjective experience of pregnancy, as a health event, as a social event and as a life event. The stories we heard from participants about the multi-faceted experience of pregnancy (see Figure 2 for examples) underscores for

me that pregnancy should be understood by mHealth designers as a bounded experience within the life course of a woman and her family, as opposed to a medical health issue.

Shifting the focus away from medicine and towards health and wellness suggests that the informational triggers in existing mHealth initiatives may be flawed and short sighted. The existing paradigms work on risk reduction paradigms, such as diet and exercise tracking diaries, or fetal growth charts. Instead, I believe that the transition period of pregnancy can be treated as a 'teachable moment' for encouraging healthy life management techniques for stress, diet, time and other concerns for the pregnant woman and her core supporters, and that this approach can be supported through a corresponding mHealth design. An ecological approach to mHealth design should continue to incorporate diet and exercise recommendations, but should also include informational triggers for holistic health, social and overall life support, rather than merely reinforcing medical guidelines for health.

DESIGN IMPLICATIONS

This means that an ecologically-aware pregnancy mHealth design should incorporate, for example:

1. information and support on strategies for improving sleep;
2. maintaining healthy relationships in times of stress and transition;
3. downplaying the negative effects of food aversions and cravings through appropriate exercise; and
4. supporting healthy emotional and social states despite hormonal changes.

All of these aspects of life are variable during pregnancy, and women and their significant others have a vested interest in appropriately managing the life variability.

The social support aspect of pregnancy is recognized in prior HCI work as a core part of health management [6,9,11], yet often in design work about pregnancy and early parenting, the father is curiously invisible. Because women expressed a decided interest in enabling their spouses to be fully involved in pregnancy management, as well as solicit assistance and share key milestones in an effective manner to a trusted group of close confidantes, a pregnancy app should enable appropriate social support, so that the social cohesion of a woman's life is respected during the period of change that is pregnancy.

FUTURE WORK

Ongoing research work includes a landscape analysis of the existing information and social support apps, websites and literature for pregnancy, alongside an investigation into pregnancy talk on Twitter.

For my future work, I intend to create a design prototype for a pregnancy mHealth system for lower-income American women. To do so, guided by value-based design principles from Action Research and Participatory Design, I foresee conducting design workshops with pregnant women and their spouses. I anticipate that the app would incorporate aspects of the pregnancy ecology. I forsee the app presenting health information, providing behavioural 'nudges' [2] and offering social support avenues for pregnancy. The meta-goal of the app would be to frame a woman's pregnancy as a 'teachable moment' that scaffolds better life-long adaptation to embodied health, social and emotional support, and improved feelings of wellness capacity.

Figure 2: Participants talk about pregnancy support from doctors and spouses

---

Participants talk about: *Doctor versus Dr. Google*

" Like, my ... my doctor didn't tell me about round ligament pain, until ... gosh! Maybe four weeks ago... but I was having it from you know, like, 13 weeks on...so I was having this severe cramping, and like, there is something wrong! What's going on? I am freaking out..."

"Two weeks ago, I was having pain around my belly button then I started to spot. Well I googled it... it asked if I was showing signs of ectopic pregnancy, and all that, so that's where sometimes googling is not a good thing."

Participants talk about: *Importance of spouses*

"Cause my husband, like, for example, he comes off work and...he goes off to do something with the kids and leaves me by myself. That helps me because if he didn't do that, I will be sitting in the kitchen, eating ... bingeing and just being so mad! He just gives me time."

"I was trying to make pancakes, using a new recipe. And they weren't turning out right. My pan was burning them... And so I was getting mad and ... the kids are getting yelled at, and all of a sudden my husband disappears... and then I ask... 'Where is your dad?'... 'He went out in the car'... 'ohhh well he's really going to get it!'... But he comes in, with a brand new griddle! He went out and bought me a griddle! And I just started bawling! I plugged in the griddle and the pancakes are saved... like, he saw what the real issue was, was all my pancakes were burning, so he went out and took care of it...you just get in a really bad mood about stuff and that totally defused it. So that's the best thing he could have done, when he bought me a griddle."

CONTRIBUTION

I expect to realize the overall goal of my dissertation project through the design of a mobile-enabled health and wellness approach to pregnancy management support skills. This approach would move pregnancy mHealth design away from medical information, diet and exercise tracking, and risk discourses, toward the use of pregnancy as a teachable moment in encouraging healthy life management practices generally.

REFERENCES

1. Beaglehole, R. and Irwin, A. The World Health Report 2003: Shaping the future. World Health Organization, Geneva, Switzerland, 2003.

2. Choe, E.K., Lee, B., Munson, S., Pratt, W., and Kientz, J.A. Persuasive performance feedback: The effect of framing on self-efficacy. AMIA Annual Symposium Proceedings 2013, (2013), 825–833.

3. Crabtree, A. and Rodden, T. Hybrid ecologies: understanding cooperative interaction in emerging physical-digital environments. Personal and Ubiquitous Computing 12, 7 (2008), 481–493.

4. Fox, S. and Duggan, M. Mobile health 2012. Pew Research Center, 2012.

5. Kay, M., Santos, J., and Takane, M. mHealth: New horizons for health through mobile technologies. World Health Organization, Geneva, Switzerland, 2011.

6. Morris, M.R. Social networking site use by mothers of young children. Proceedings of the 17th ACM Conference on Computer Supported Cooperative Work & Social Computing, ACM (2014), 1272–1282.

7. Nardi, B.A. and O'Day, V. Information Ecologies: Using Technology with Heart. MIT Press, 1999.

8. Peyton, T., Poole, E., Reddy, M., Kraschnewski, J.L., and Chuang, C.H. "Every pregnancy is different': Designing mHealth for the pregnancy ecology. Proceedings of the ACM SIGCHI Conference: Designing for Interactive Systems 2014, ACM (2014).

9. Poole, E.S. HCI and mobile health interventions. Translational Behavioral Medicine, (2013), 1–4.

10. Rasmussen, K.M. and Yaktine, A.L., eds. Weight Gain During Pregnancy: Reexamining the Guidelines.

11. Schoenebeck, S.Y. The Secret Life of Online Moms: Anonymity and Disinhibition on YouBeMom.com. ICWSM 2013, (2013).

12. Stengel, M.R., Kraschnewski, J.L., Hwang, S.W., Kjerulff, K.H., and Chuang, C.H. "What My Doctor Didn't Tell Me": Examining Health Care Provider Advice to Overweight and Obese Pregnant Women on Gestational Weight Gain and Physical Activity. Women's Health Issues 22, 6 (2012), e535–e540.

13. Szwajcer, E.M., Hiddink, G.J., Maas, L., Koelen, M.A., and van Woerkum, C.M.J. Nutrition-related information-seeking behaviours of women trying to conceive and pregnant women: evidence for the life course perspective. Family practice 25 Suppl 1, (2008), i99–104.

Emotional Communication in Instant Messaging

Afarin Pirzadeh
School of Informatics and Computing
Indiana University-Indianapolis
535 W Michigan, IT 476
Indianapolis, IN 46202 US
apirzade@iupui.edu

ABSTRACT

In spite of rapid growth of text-based instant messaging (IM) in diverse settings, emotion communication in IM has received limited empirical scrutiny, especially inside casual settings. The main goal of my dissertation project is to, through design research, critically examine how users communicate their emotions in IM and to establish user-centered design solutions to comprehensively support emotional communication via this medium.

Categories and Subject Descriptors

H.5.2. Information Interfaces and Presentation: User Interfaces

Keywords

Instant messaging (IM); text-based CMC; Design research; emotional communication

1. PROJECT OVERVIEW

Technology has revolutionized the way people communicate. People use a variety of media to enhance and extend interpersonal communication depending on social, security, or efficiency factors. Communications media, however, affects the quantity and quality of the messages and can change senders' and receivers' behavior and attitudes [1]. Instant messaging (IM), as one type of synchronous text-based computer-mediated communication (CMC), is not an exception. Despite the advantages of IM communication (e.g. convenience, mobility, and control) over face-to-face, the absence of visual and aural nonverbal behaviors affects communication. There are two lines of research that have studied the effect of IM technology on interpersonal communication.

One line of research showed that the lack of visual and aural nonverbal cues causes some limitations on users' emotional communication in IM [12]. IM users sometimes have difficulties expressing their emotions accurately and fail to accurately understand the actual emotion coming from their partners due to the absence of visual and aural nonverbal behaviors. According to Mehrabian [6], in everyday communications only 7% of peoples' emotional communication stemmed from the words spoken, whereas 38% was attributed to verbal tone and 55% was related to facial expression. Aligned with this line of research, the absence of visual and aural nonverbal cues in IM and its limits on

emotional communication presents a variety of new challenges and opportunities for researchers in the area of HCI and design. A growing number of features, mostly technology focused, such as emoticons, avatars, haptics, and dynamic typography, have been integrated with existing IM systems to support emotional communication [5]. This technological-focus leads to developing systems that are novel, but not always able to satisfy user needs in emotional communication via text-based IM.

Another line of research, however, showed that as IM began growing in everyday life, especially among teenagers and college students [10], despite the absence of visual and aural nonverbal behaviors, communicators discovered new ways to adjust emotional communication to IM. One of the main theories representing this perspective is Social Information Processing (SIP) [11]. SIP argues that people are able to employ different active and passive strategies to convey visual and aural nonverbal behaviors in text-based CMC. Supporting SIP, a growing number of studies have identified different strategies (e.g. verbosity, speed of response, or degree of agreement) and diverse text-based emotional cues (e.g. lexical surrogates such as haha, and aha, vocal spelling such as sooo, and weeell) users apply to express their emotions in IM [3,4,9].

User-centered design research [13] is needed to connect these bodies of literature, first to explore how IM users communicate emotions, and second to establish creative solutions to support emotional communication through this medium. Therefore, the main goal of this project is to, through design research, critically examine how users communicate their emotions in IM and to establish user-centered design solutions to comprehensively support emotional communication via this medium. With a more complete understanding of users' emotional communication in IM, the design issues and corresponding design solutions involved will identify gaps in theories and models of emotional communication. They will also provide a solid, long-term intellectual basis for the creation of substantially improved text-based CMC applications. Such applications will support emotional communication and minimize emotional miscommunication that may occur due to the absence of visual and aural nonverbal behaviors in IM. To achieve the main goal of the project a mixed-methodology approach will be taken through following three specific aims:

Aim #1: *Investigating which emotions are most challenging for users to express in IM communication, to narrow the design focus.* To reach this aim of the project, a quantitative approach will be taken to investigate to what extent different emotional states (contentment, angry, happy, and sad) influence the type and proportions of emotional cues individuals apply to express their emotions in the actual context of informal IM conversations. The type and quantity of emotional cues users apply to express different emotions could be a possible indicator of how challenging those emotions are communicated in IM. Participants will be involved in informal emotional conversations with their friends in IM and their conversations will be quantitatively analyzed to identify how emotional states affect the type and proportion of text-based cues users applied to communicate their emotions. Several open-ended questions will also be asked about what emotions participants consider the most challenging to communicate in IM. Accomplishing this aim provides initial results to narrow the design focus for the following aims and refine the problem space.

Aim #2: *Critically examining how people communicate the emotions identified in Aim #1 in IM.* To reach this aim of the project, a qualitative approach will be taken to examine how users communicate the emotions identified in Aim #1 in IM conversations. Parts of IM conversations related to those specific emotions from Aim #1 will be analyzed through conversation analysis to investigate how emotions are expressed, responded to, and developed in IM conversations. Accomplishing this aim provides a framework for emotional communication in the context of informal IM conversations and will detail the different strategies and emotional cues users apply to communicate the emotions identified in Aim #1 in IM. Aim #1 and #2 will provide an upfront research foundation for Aim #3.

Aim #3: *Establishing and evaluating innovative non-text based design solutions to support communication of the emotions identified in Aim #1 in IM, based on the findings identified in Aim #2.* To reach this aim of the project, based on the strong foundation gained through Aim #1 and #2, design ideation brainstorming and participatory design sessions will be conducted to gain insights and establish and evaluate non-text based design solutions to support communication of the emotions identified in Aim #1 in IM. Through an active process of ideating, iterating, and critiquing potential design solutions, the output of this aim will be 1) a concrete problem framing of communication of the emotions identified in Aim #1 in IM, 2) articulation of the preferred styles of the communication of those emotions in IM, 3) a set of non-text-based design solutions to support communication of those emotions in IM, and 4) challenges encountered in this design process and insight for future studies.

2. SIGNIFICANT OF THE STUDY

Emotional communication is fundamental to everyday interaction. How well emotions are communicated is crucial to interpersonal relationships and individual well-being [2]. Emotional communication in IM can be challenging sometimes because of the absence of visual and aural nonverbal behaviors in IM. Despite the growing number of technologically-focused solutions for supporting emotional communication in IM, limited design research has been done to study the actual users' behaviors in communicating their emotion in IM and strategies they use to adapt emotional communication to this medium, with the purpose of establishing design solutions to support emotional communication in IM.

3. MOTIVATION AND STUDY PURPOSE

This project was started three years ago with the ultimate goal of developing solutions to support IM users communicating their emotions in IM. The idea for this study developed out of a combination of the candidate's personal experiences and academic interests. It started, on the personal level, with experiencing and witnessing difficulties IM users have in communicating their emotion in IM and how they overcome this

challenge. Additionally, the candidate's academic interests have driven her to pursue design research, prototyping, and developing tools to support individuals and improve the quality of their lives.

The candidate's first study (Preliminary Study I) was conducted as an exploratory study on a preexisting set of 168 chat logs from a previously conducted study on the effects of mood and stress on group communication and performance in NeoCITIES, a multi-player emergency response simulation [7]. The main purpose of this study was to investigate whether two psychological states (mood and stress) affect the type and quantity of emotional cues users apply in task-focused IM communication. The results of this study offered evidence that studying text-based emotional cues in IM merited further study. This study was published and presented as extended abstract at CSCW12 [8] and full paper at HFES2012 [9]. The candidate also conducted another study (Preliminary Study II) to explore the potential of gestures to support emotional expression in IM. Preliminary Study II was presented and published as a work-in-progress at CHI14.

The findings of preliminary studies I and II offered evidence that emotional communication in IM merited further attention in all areas of HCI, design, and communication. These studies also provided insights to define three main aims of the study. Aim #1 has already been accomplished and the results were reported as a full paper, which has been accepted by GROUP14. The findings of the Aim #1 study specifically helped to refine the problem space and narrow the design focus on communicating sadness and anger in IM. Based on the results of this study, angry and sad emotions were identified as the most challenging emotions among four emotions of happy, sad, anger, and contentment. Data gathered in this aim of the study also provided a rich data set for conversation analysis during Aim #2.

4. REFERENCES

[1] Cathcart R, Gumpert G. (1983). Mediated interpersonal communication: toward a new typology. Q. J. Speech 69:267–77

[2] Fussell, S. R. (2002). The verbal communication of emotion: Interdisciplinary perspectives: Introduction and overview. In S. R. Fussell, (Ed.) The verbal communication of emotion: Interdisciplinary perspectives. Mahwah, NJ: Lawrence Erlbaum Associates. Download Preprint (PDF)

[3] Hancock, J. T., Gee, K., Ciaccio, K., & Lin, J. M. H. (2008). I'm sad you're sad: Emotional contagion in CMC. Proceedings of CSCW '08: ACM Conference on *Computer Supported Cooperative Work*, 295-298. 13.

[4] Hancock, J. T., Landrigan, C., & Silver, C. (2007). Expressing emotion in text-based communication. *Proceedings of SIGCHI' 07: ACM Conference on Human* factors in computing systems, 929-932.

[5] Lo, O. (2006). The roles of gratification opportunities, gratifications-obtained, and demographics in determining usage preference of instant messaging and e-mail among college students. Unpublished thesis, School of Journalism & Communication, The Chinese University of Hong Kong.

[6] Mehrabian, A. (1972), *Nonverbal commmunication.* Chicago: Aldine-Atherton.

[7] Pfaff, M. S. (2012). Negative affect reduces team awareness: The effects of mood and stress on computer-mediated team communication. *Human Factors, 54(4),* 560-571.

[8] Pirzadeh, A., & Pfaff, M. S. (2012), "Expression of Emotion in Instant Messaging", In Proc. CSCW2012.

[9] Pirzadeh, A., & Pfaff, M. S. (2012). Emotion expression under stress in instant messaging. *Proceedings of the Human Factors and Ergonomics Society,* 493-497.

[10] Ramirez, A., & Broneck, K. (2009). 'IM me': Instant messaging as relational maintenance and everyday communication. Journal of Social and Personal Relationships, 26, 291-314.

[11] Walther, J. B. (1992). Interpersonal effects in computer mediated interaction – A relational perspective. *Communication Research, 9(1),* 52-90.

[12] Walther, J.B., Loh, T., & Granka, L. (2005) Let me count the ways: The interchange of verbal and nonverbal cues in computermediated and face-to-face affinity. *Journal of Language and Social Psychology, 24*, 36-65.

[13] Zimmerman, J., Forlizzi, J., & Evenson, S. (2007). Research through design as a method for interaction design research in HCI. In Proc. CHI '07 , 493-502

Collaboratively Designed Information Structures in Wikipedia

Katherine Thornton
University of Washington
Information School
Box 352840 - Mary Gates Hall
Seattle, WA 98195-2840
thornt@uw.edu

1. INTRODUCTION

The experience of browsing Wikipedia can be so all-consuming that people colloquially invoke the trope of Alice's fall down into the rabbit hole when they recount a session of Wikipedia surfing. They tell of sessions that could have started with a question about the USS North Carolina and ended several hours later on the page for phylum Echinodermata. In addition to the search function of Wikipedia, and the network of hyperlinks between articles, the Wikipedia community has created several information structures that support navigation. Framed against the backdrop of the theories of classification, and the discipline of information organization, this dissertation will investigate the spectrum of types of information structures that are used for information organization, and will seek to identify the design criteria and evaluative criteria that will best inform the creation and justification of these structures.

The question of whether search can replace classification has been pulled into mainstream discussions by Shirky (2005) and Weinberger (2007). It is striking that despite the fact that search works so well in Wikipedia, and that Wikipedia is so well-indexed by Google (and other search engines), that the community places importance on creating human-built information structures to support information organization in Wikipedia.

Hjorland recently argued that classification cannot be replaced entirely by search (2012: 311). Toward a definition of classification as a behavior, he argued: "To sum up, to classify is to define the "kind" which a given "thing" is, and how that kind is related to other kinds. This is a fundamental process that all human beings carry out many times each day" (2012: 307). Perhaps this definitional activity is one of the forces that compels Wikipedians to maintain a category system.

As early as 1997 researchers were exploring attempts to combine information retrieval and human-curated metadata in order to improve information seeking. (Efthimiadis and Carlyle 1997: 5). The fact that multiple structures have been created by the community to organize information in Wikipedia, offers us an opportunity to compare and contrast the goals the community had

for these various structures and to provide evaluative criteria that could be used to assess their success as structures for the organization of information.

Mai reminds us of the recommendations of Svenonius 1986, Fidel 1991 and Rowley 1994, each of whom argues that the combination of using both search and classified directories in conjunction help users in information seeking (2004: 92). Mai tells us that "When searching for information that can be expressed in multiple ways it is more effective to use classified Web directories". This could be one reason that the Wikipedia community has invested so much effort in the creation and maintenance of information structures like the category system, the portal system, and navigation boxes despite the fact that the search options in Wikipedia are so effective on their own.

Williamson reminds us that: "In any event, while information systems may change to achieve greater success, they must continue to meet two fundamental requirements of information seekers: to permit users to locate information on a subject directly and to allow them to browse so as to familiarize themselves with a domain or to refine a request" (2007: 330). I will use the theory from information organization and information science to explore the large-scale, collaboratively-built systems of information organization: the category system, the information boxes and the Wikidata project within Wikipedia. This work forces us to reconsider the current conceptualizations and definitions of such structures in information organization, many of which date to the period when information organization systems were designed primarily for the control of physical items rather than digital content.

2. CATEGORY SYSTEM

Wikipedia is an online encyclopedia created entirely of user-generated content. Roughly two years after Wikipedia began, the community decided to create a category system to organize and tag the content of the site (Voss 2006). The category system has changed over time, as have conceptualizations of what role it should serve in Wikipedia. The category system was proposed, designed and implemented entirely by members of the Wikipedia community. The Wikipedia community includes anyone who edits Wikipedia. Anyone with access to the internet can edit Wikipedia. Any Wikipedia editor has the ability to apply category labels to pages, to remove category labels to pages, to create new categories, and to suggest categories to be considered by the group for deletion.[1]

Group'14, November 9–12, 2014, Sanibel Island, Florida, USA.
ACM 978-1-4503-1051-2/12/02.
http://dx.doi.org/10.1145/2660398.2660440

---

[1] http://en.wikipedia.org/wiki/Wikipedia:Categorization Accessed June 29, 2012.

Discussion of the category system takes place on the talk page for 'Categorization'.[2] Talk pages in Wikipedia are pages, associated with other pages, where editors can leave comments that are publicly visible in order to discuss issues related to the original page.[3] Each article in Wikipedia, for example, has an associated talk page where editors discuss content, propose changes, explain decisions they have made about how the page should look or what the page should contain, etc. The fact that discussion about the design and implementation of the category system has been archived within the Wikipedia site presents an opportunity to read the comments editors made throughout this process, and to understand how the category system came to be in its current form.

3. STRUCTURED INFORMATION IN WIKIPEDIA

There are several types of information structures in Wikipedia which support information seeking: see also links, information boxes, navigation boxes, the portal system and the category system. Of these, the category system has the longest history in Wikipedia. The primary focus of this work will be the category system, information boxes and Wikidata. The Wikipedia community has explicit goals related to supporting navigation for each of these structures. For the category system they state: "The central goal of the category system is to provide navigational links to all Wikipedia pages in a hierarchy of categories which readers, knowing essential - defining - characteristics of a topic, can browse and quickly find sets of pages on topics that are defined by those characteristics".[4] For infoboxes the community says that they are a type of "fixed-format table designed to be added to the top right-hand corner of articles to consistently present a summary of some unifying aspect that the articles share and sometimes to improve navigation to other interrelated articles".[5] For navigation boxes the community states: "a grouping of links used in multiple related articles to facilitate navigation between those articles".[6]

Categories are displayed at the bottom of Wikipedia pages. Each category into which the page has been grouped is listed as a hyperlink. Clicking on the links takes you to the page for that category.

Structured information is frequently mined from Wikipedia to populate artificial intelligence applications or repositories of structured data that other programs utilize. This information is then propagated to many other applications and programs. The importance of researching the structured information in Wikipedia lies in the frequency with which it is reused. As Bao et al. highlight, many information retrieval (IR), natural language processing (NLP), and artificial intelligence-based systems use data mined from Wikipedia. While research into the optimization

of these systems and their underlying algorithms is being conducted, (Wu and Weld 2008, Bao et al. 2012, Yu et al. 2007, Lange et al. 2010, Kohncke and Balke 2010), evaluative research into the best design for the information structures themselves is not currently being pursued. Rather than taking the current set of structured data available in Wikipedia as a given, the research I propose in this dissertation will provide us with a framework for discovering what the optimal design of the information structures would be, allowing us to extract an even-more-complete set of structured data from the Wikipedia system.

Infoboxes are graphical information resources that can be placed on the upper right-hand corner of an article in Wikipedia. The community uses them to provide a summary of the content on the page and to provide links to related content. They are the source of a large amount of the structured data currently extracted from Wikipedia.

While the Wikidata project is in the early stages of implementation, it will serve as the repository of all structured data for Wikipedia and the other Wikimedia projects.

Looking at the category system, the information boxes and the Wikidata project within Wikipedia will allow us to explore three case studies of how information is structured in Wikipedia and how these information structures are collaboratively designed.

4. REFERENCES

[1] Shirky, Clay. (2005). Ontology is overrated: categories, links, tags.
(http://shirky.com/writings/ontology_overrated.html)
Accessed October 23, 2012.

[2] Weinberger, D. (2007). Everything is miscellaneous: The power of the new digital disorder. New York: Times Books.

[3] Hjørland, B. (2012) "Is classification necessary after Google?", Journal of Documentation, Vol. 68 Iss: 3, pp.299 – 317.

[4] Efthimiadis, E.N., and Carlyle, A. (1997). Organizing Internet resources: metadata and the Web. Bulletin of the American Society for Information Science, 24, 4–5.

[5] Mai, J-E. (2004). "Classification of the Web: Challenges and Inquiries", Knowledge Organization, 31 (2): 92-97.Schwartz, M. Guidelines for Bias-Free Writing. Indiana University Press, Bloomington, IN, USA, 1995.

[6] Svenonius, E. (1986). Unanswered Questions in the Design of Controlled Vocabularies. Journal of the American Society for Information Science, 37(5), 331-340.

[7] Fidel, Raya. 1991. Searchers' Selection of Search Keys: II. Controlled Vocabularies or Free-Text Searching. Journal of the American Society for Information Science. 42 (7): 501-514.

[8] Rowley, Jennifer. 1994. The Controlled Versus Natural Indexing Languages Debate Revisited: a Perspective on Information Retrieval Practice and Research. Journal of Information Science. 20 (2): 108-119.

[9] Weld, D., Hoffmann, R., Wu, F. 2008. Using Wikipedia to bootstrap open information extraction. SIGMOD Record, 37(4): 62–68.

[10] Wu, F., Weld, D. 2008. Automatically refining the Wikipedia infobox ontology. In: Proceedings of the 17th International World Wide Web Conference, pages 635–644.

---

[2] https://en.wikipedia.org/wiki/Wikipedia_talk:Categorization Accessed May 8, 2012.

[3] https://en.wikipedia.org/wiki/Help:Using_talk_pages Accessed May 8, 2012.

[4] http://en.wikipedia.org/wiki/Wikipedia:Categorization Accessed November 13, 2012.

[5] http://en.wikipedia.org/wiki/Help:Infobox Accessed July 11, 2012.

[6] http://en.wikipedia.org/wiki/Wikipedia:Navigation_templates Accessed July 11, 2012.

[11] Yu, J., Thom, J. A., & Tam, A. (2007). Ontology evaluation using wikipedia categories for browsing. (M. J. Silva, A. H. F. Laender, R. A. Baeza-Yates, D. L. McGuinness, B. Olstad, Ø. H. Olsen, & A. O. Falcão, Eds.)Proceedings of the sixteenth ACM conference on Conference on information and knowledge management CIKM 07, 223.

[12] Bao, P., Hecht, B., Carton, S., Quaderi, M., Horn, M. and Gergle, D. (2012). Omnipedia: Bridging the Wikipedia Language Gap. In: Proceedings of the ACM Conference on Human Factors in Computing Systems (CHI 2012). New York: ACM Press.

[13] Köhncke, B. and Balke, W. (2010). Using Wikipedia categories for compact representations of chemical documents. In: Proceedings of the 19th ACM international conference on Information and knowledge management (CIKM '10).

[14] Lange, D. Böhm, C. and Naumann, F. (2010). Extracting structured information from Wikipedia articles to populate infoboxes. In Proceedings of the 19th ACM international conference on Information and knowledge management (CIKM '10). ACM, New York, NY, USA, 1661-1664.

Supporting the Information Management Needs of People Helping Animals in Disasters

Joanne I. White
Project EPIC
University of Colorado Boulder
joanne.white@colorado.edu

ABSTRACT

Many things influence human decision-making in disasters. This work considers the information management needs and collaborative work of those focused on animal care and evacuation in disasters. Empirical ethnographic work on-site at two animal evacuation locations, as well as fieldwork responding to large animal needs, and ongoing participant observer fieldwork between events has led to both academic and practical contributions aimed at improving the ways animal advocates, animal owners and emergency responders are able to communicate and attend to the needs of animals and their owners in a disaster.

Categories and Subject Descriptors

H.5.3. Groups & Organization Interfaces—collaborative computing, computer-supported cooperative work; K.4.2. Social Issues

General Terms

Design, Human Factors.

Keywords

Animals, computer-supported cooperative work, crisis informatics, disaster, emergency, social computing.

1. INTRODUCTION

There are myriad problems associated with animals in disasters. In a disaster, people may make decisions about whether to evacuate or stay based on their ability to take their animals. People re-enter disaster zones to retrieve pets before officials deem it to be safe. If pets are left to perish, it impedes recovery for owners, particularly for the most vulnerable in society–the elderly and children. [2,7,3]

Following 2005's Hurricane Katrina, when tens of thousands of pets and service animals were left to perish, the US Government passed The Pets Evacuation and Transportation Standards Act (2006), known as the PETS Act [8]. The Act serves to provide financial support to responders who evacuate service and companion animals alongside their owners. While effective, there are still huge challenges for people who are concerned with animals in disasters. For example, the Act does not provide

assistance or direction for displaced pets, and it does not address the needs of people who own livestock.

2. RESEARCH QUESTIONS

Understanding and addressing the needs of people concerned with animals in disasters presents multiple opportunities for exploration.

First, what motivations do people have in decision-making about preparation and evacuating when they own animals? What motivates responding volunteers in attending to the needs of animals in disasters? What role does information communication technology play in the ways motivated people attend to the needs of animals in disaster? Understanding motivation will demonstrate what kind of support is needed, and how best to provide it.

Second, in what ways do information, expertise and knowledge intersect in this domain? What roles do each of these elements play in the materiality of response work focused on animals? How do we leverage the implicit knowledge of specialist animal experts in identifying the best ways to respond and in the coordination of that response?

Finally, how might we build relationships between people interested in animal advocacy and emergency responders, to assist both groups in their efforts to attend to the needs of animals in disasters?

3. METHODS

I have used ethnographic methods to investigate the above research questions. These methods were used as follows.

I observed the Hurricane Sandy Lost and Found Pets Facebook Page for a seven-month period, beginning in the first days following Hurricane Sandy in October 2012 through to May 2013. I took extensive field notes about the behaviors and content shared and organized on the Page, digitally capturing user and administrator engagements. I conducted email interviews with 12 people who had been particularly active on the Page using open-ended questions aimed at exploring their beliefs about pet advocacy and their backgrounds in disaster response.

I was a participant observer at two animal evacuation sites during the Black Forest Fire in Colorado, in June 2013. I worked at the Kiowa Fairgrounds and the El Paso County Fairgrounds assisting with animal care, intake and release. I conducted depth interviews with volunteers and evacuees, wrote extensive daily field notes and took over 200 photographs.

Following the Colorado flash floods in September 2013, I assisted during an independently organized evacuation of 38 horses from a ranch located in a remote area of the mountainous Colorado Front Range. Conducting a multi-sited ethnography, I shadowed the ranch owner throughout the evacuation, audio recording conversations between her and the responding volunteer horsepeople. I took nearly 200 photographs and interviewed seven volunteers who had been active in the evacuation, two officials, the Ranch owners and employees, using the photographs as probes. I also reviewed personal email correspondence and social media posts related to the evacuation.

4. WORK TO DATE

Ethnographic fieldwork forms the centerpiece of my dissertation. Its analysis provides the theoretical orientation that has informed my creative work in design and development of tools aimed at supporting the information needs of those concerned with animals in disasters.

The work I have produced has been informed by continuing engagement with these responding communities. I have completed numerous FEMA training modules, and am a recognized volunteer member of the Douglas/Elbert County Community Animal Response Team, and a credentialed member of the Colorado Veterinary Medical Reserve Corps.

My experience, training and data collection have informed the following studies.

4.1 Emergency PetMatcher

In 2012, I worked with two colleagues at Project EPIC to design a tool focused on reuniting animals with owners after a disaster, called Emergency PetMatcher (EPM). The application design was intended to support crowdwork in recommending matches between lost and found pets displaced in disasters. We conducted user tests, and iterated the design. The design received 4th place in the CHI2012 Student Design Competition. EPM is being readied for deployment in Fall 2014's hurricane season.

4.2 Hurricane Sandy Lost and Found Pets

The data collection on the Hurricane Sandy Lost and Found Pets page led to the CSCW2014 paper, "Digital Mobilization in Disaster Response: The Work and Self-Organization of On-Line Pet Advocates in Response to Hurricane Sandy" [10]. The paper's contributions built upon previously seen online digital volunteer behavior [eg, 9] and activism [eg, 6], and provided insight to motivations of volunteers concerned with animals. We observed animal advocates pivot their usual foci on a range of pet issues to the needs of animals that were a direct result of the disaster. Admins of the Page used the albums feature of the Facebook Page as a content management system where animal flyers could be organized according to species, lost and found, and location. Users were able to use the comment thread attached to each photograph to suggest matches between lost and found pets displaced by the disaster. The aim of the Page was to reunite as many pets as possible, and rehome those pets who had to be relinquished due to the devastating effect of the hurricane on families.

4.3 Community Mapping of Evacuation Sites

My experiences and data collection at two animal evacuation sites during the 2013 Black Forest Fire informed an opportunity to conduct a participatory design exercise. Most counties in Colorado have agreements with local Fairgrounds and other animal-focused centers that state in the event of a disaster, animals being evacuated may be sheltered there. While the public may be familiar with these locations in non-disaster times, there

was a need to create maps to direct people with animals via specific routes to gain access to the fairgrounds in an evacuation.

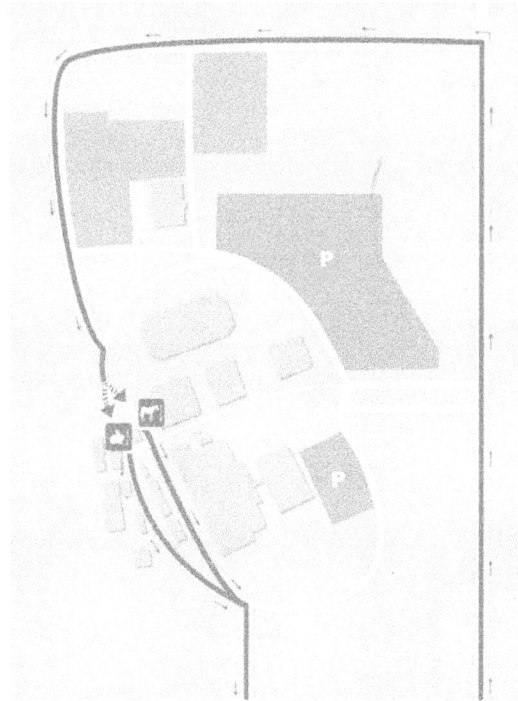

Figure 1: Elbert County fairgrounds base map.

I directed 12 senior computer science students (BS/MS) in a five-week participatory design project, during which the students collaborated with official representatives of Douglas/Elbert County and Jefferson County. We used Open Street Map to create a base layer map of each site. We then met with county, volunteer and fairground representatives onsite to collaboratively identify what they needed on a map to support their work, specifically the infrastructure, resources and traffic flows they wanted the public to know in an evacuation. We walked the fairground sites and identified these locations on walking papers. The teams developed designs for the maps, as shown in Figure 1. We gathered feedback from the stakeholders and iterated the designs to final versions. The final maps were provided to the respective county and state officials, who have said they will use them in their next animal evacuation.

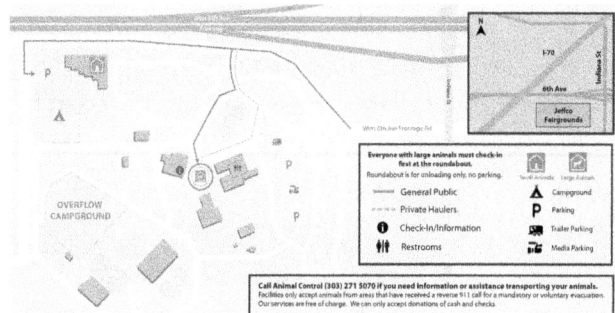

Figure 2: Final Jefferson County map.

Jefferson County has already placed one map on its preparedness website for owners of equines, so they can be ready to converge onto the Fairgrounds location in a directed way (see Figure 2).

These maps will help prevent gridlock of horse trailers and other vehicles as they converge onto the Fairgrounds sites.

Additionally, Colorado State officials are interested in replicating this work to other county fairgrounds. This work included the creation of standardized map symbols specific to animal evacuations. We noted there are no standardized symbols relevant to animal evacuation centers, so these were also iterated upon, and have been submitted to The Noun Project and ReliefWeb for open access use in other humanitarian mapping endeavors.

I continue to be a trained responder on the ground in the event of an animal evacuation, and in a local event will gather data on the application of the maps we have produced.

5. FUTURE WORK

I have begun working on a high-fidelity prototype of an animal evacuation CMS and mobile phone app that will assist with the intake, shelter care and release of animals at an evacuation site (Figure 3).

Animals brought to a site are identified via paperwork, which may be destroyed over the course of an evacuation. The Animal Evacuation Management Tool will make it easy to link an animal

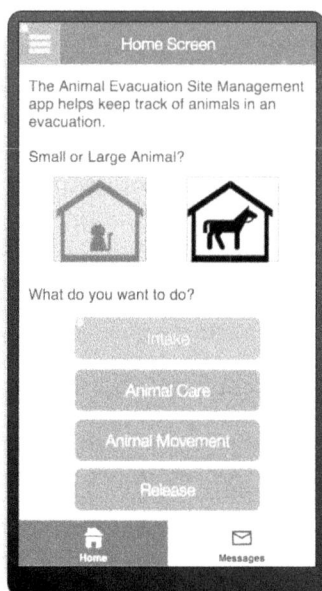

Figure 3: Animal evacuation management tool prototype.

with its paperwork, without needing to keep paper at the stall.

It will also provide realtime monitoring of animals while they are on site and is designed to leverage additional functions such as realtime reporting on collected data to provide the Emergency Operations Center with information about all the animals at each evacuation site, without state and federal officials having to call to check with barn managers. The tool will complement the paper-based systems already in use at animal evacuation centers, and provide a robust information architecture to support the needs of workers and owners during an evacuation event.

6. ACKNOWLEDGMENTS

I am grateful for the support of Project EPIC for this work particularly its director Dr Leysia Palen, officials, volunteers and owners concerned with animals for their collaborations and input, and to colleagues at CU. This work has been supported by US National Science Foundation grant IIS-0910586.

7. REFERENCES

[1] Barrenechea, M., Barron, J., and White, J. (2012). No Place Like Home: Pet-to-Family Reunification after Disaster. In Ext. Abs. of CHI2012, 1237-1242.

[2] Glassey, S., & Wilson, T. M. (2011). Animal Welfare Impact Following the 4 September 2010 Canterbury (Darfield) Earthquake. Australasian Journal of Disaster and Trauma Studies, 2011-2 (Special Issue: A Focus on the Canterbury Earthquake), 49-59.

[3] Irvine, L. (2007). Ready or Not: Evacuating an Animal Shelter during a Mock Emergency. Anthrozoos, 20(4), 355-364.

[4] Irvine, L. (2009). Filling the Ark: Animal Welfare in Disasters (Animals and Ethics). Temple University Press: Philadelphia, PA, USA.

[5] Kilijanek, T. and Drabek, T. (1979). Assessing Long-Term Impacts of a Natural Disaster: A Focus on the Elderly. The Gerontologist, 19, 555-556.

[6] Lee, Y-H and Hsieh, G. (2013). Does Slacktivism Hurt Activism?: The Effects of Moral Balancing and Consistency in Online Activism. In Proc. of CHI 2013, 811-820.

[7] Lowe, S., Rhodes, J., Zwiebach, L., and Chan, C. (2009). The Impact of Pet Loss on the Perceived Social Support and Psychological Distress of Hurricane Survivors. Journal of Traumatic Stress, 22(3), 244-247.

[8] Mike, M., Mike, R., Lee, C. (2011). Katrina's Animal Legacy: The PETS Act. Journal of Animal Law and Ethics, 4(1), 133-160.

[9] Starbird, K., & Palen, L. (2011, May). Voluntweeters: Self-organizing by Digital Volunteers in Times of Crisis. In Proceedings of the SIGCHI Conference on Human Factors in Computing Systems, 1071-1080.

[10] White, J.I., Palen, L., & Anderson, K. (2014). Digital Mobilization in Disaster Response: The Work & Self-Organization of On-Line Pet Advocates in Response to Hurricane Sandy. In Proc. Of CSCW 2014, 866-876.

[11] Zotarelli, L.K. (2010) Broken Bond: An Exploration of Human Factors Associated with Companion Animal Loss During Hurricane Katrina. Sociological Forum. (25), 110-122.

The Collaborative Agile Knowledge Engine CAKE

Ralph Bergmann
University of Trier
Business Information Systems
54286 Trier, Germany
bergmann@uni-trier.de

Sarah Gessinger
University of Trier
Business Information Systems
54286 Trier, Germany
gessinge@uni-trier.de

Sebastian Görg
University of Trier
Business Information Systems
54286 Trier, Germany
goergs@uni-trier.de

Gilbert Müller
University of Trier
Business Information Systems
54286 Trier, Germany
gilbert.mueller@uni-trier.de

ABSTRACT

The Collaborative Agile Knowledge Engine (CAKE) is a prototypical generic software system for integrated process and knowledge management. CAKE integrates recent research results on agile workflows, process-oriented case-based reasoning, and web technologies into a common platform that can be configured to different application domains and needs. We describe the main concepts and the architecture of CAKE and sketch three example applications.

1. INTRODUCTION

One of the biggest challenges today arises from the fact that many companies and organizations must be able to more quickly adapt their business according to newly arising market opportunities and demands from customers. Also in private life, changes are more frequent today (e.g. switching jobs, places to live, houses, etc.) and managing those change requires a substantial amount of specific knowledge of how to best act in a certain environment. The increased agility of business and private life asks for new tools for dealing with "procedural knowledge" that support groups of people in finding or defining the right procedure to execute for a certain purpose and that support their collaborative execution.

Workflow management is an established area that aims at the automation of a business process according to a set of procedural rules, which has expanded in the recent years from business use towards new areas. For example, in e-science *scientific workflows* are executable descriptions of automatable scientific processes such as computational science simulations and data analyses [18]. In medical health-care, workflows can be used to support the execution of *medical guidelines* [10]. In cookery, workflows can be used as a means to represent the cooking instructions within a recipe [11] in order to provide step-by-step guidance during cooking. Recently, social workflows are proposed as an executable process representation, serving private people and groups of people to fulfill their objectives by providing means to store, create, and link personal activities and data objects according to procedural rules [6]. Such new applications of workflows typically deal with a number of new difficulties, particularly due to

- an increasing number and increasing complexity of specific workflows potentially relevant in a domain,

- an increased demand for more flexibility, resulting in *agile workflows*, and

- the need to enable non-IT staff (e.g. private persons) to create workflows and to control their execution.

These new challenges ask for new methods and tools that tightly integrate knowledge and process management. In our work during the past couple of years, we focus on the combination of case-based reasoning (CBR) [1], which is a technology for experience-based problem solving [2], agile workflows [15, 16, 19] enabling flexible and adaptive business processes, and Web technologies providing standards to link with people, data sources, and services on the web. We developed new methods for workflow agility interweaving collaborative workflow modeling and execution [14, 15], we developed new methods for process-oriented CBR (POCBR) enabling workflow retrieval and adaptation [13, 3, 11], and we developed new concepts to implement workflow support as a software as a service (SaaS) to be used by a group of users or a social network [9, 7, 6]. To demonstrate our research, the CAKE[1] (Collaborative Agile Knowledge Engine) framework has been developed. It is a generic software system for integrated process and knowledge management, which can be configured to different application domains and needs. In this paper, we describe the main concepts and the

---

[1]See http://cake.wi2.uni-trier.de

architecture of CAKE and sketch three example applications to be demonstrated.

2. THE CAKE ARCHITECTURE

The CAKE architecture is illustrated in Figure 1. The server component consists of a storage layer which handles persistency of all workflow-related data objects, an interface layer for the communication with web applications and two central engines, i.e., the agile workflow engine and the knowledge engine working together on the same data items accessed via the storage layer.

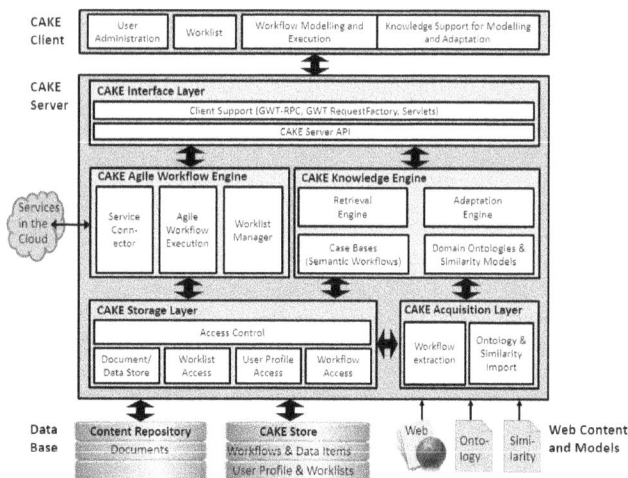

Figure 1: CAKE System Architecture.

2.1 Agile Workflow Engine

The agile workflow engine is used for the enactment of agile workflows and supports their collaborative modeling and adaptation in a consistent manner. Agile means that workflows can be modeled and changed on demand at any time by any user who is granted the respective access right. Workflow instances already running can be paused, not already executed parts of the workflow instance can be adapted, and the workflow execution can then continue while consistently considering the changes just made. The internal structure of this workflow engine is strongly tied to the reference architecture of the Workflow Management Coalition (WfMC) [4]. Thus, the workflow engine provides interfaces for modeling and execution of workflows, for invoking applications (service connector), and an interface for the delegation of tasks to humans (worklist manager). During workflow enactment, certain tasks may have to be executed by services (e.g. to check the weather conditions) while other tasks may require an activity of a human workflow participants. For the synchronization of collaborative modelling and execution of workflows CAKE has a real-time push-event system and an internal synchronization that ensures workflow consistency [8]. The workflow engine is based on a block-oriented workflow language which supports sequential, parallel, and conditional execution of tasks. It also supports loops and the execution of sub-workflows. Further, the exchange of products (e.g. data items) can be modeled. For workflow modeling, we developed a graphical workflow modeling language we call 'CAKE Flow Cloud Notation' (CFCN) which

is derived from UML activity diagrams [9]. As a specific instrument for implementing agility, we introduced a stop sign icon (i.e., a kind of break point) that can be placed into the control flow of a running workflow to pause workflow execution in case the stop sign is reached [14]. Placing the stop sign enables the adaptation of the subsequent sub-workflow.

2.2 Knowledge Engine

Workflow modeling usually requires significant skills and experience in the respective domain. The purpose of the knowledge engine is thus to support users in finding, defining, and adapting workflows according to their current needs. Therefore, the knowledge engine implements a specialized case-based reasoning (CBR) method. CBR is an established Artificial Intelligence methodology to problem solving based on the assumption that similar problems have similar solutions [1, 2]. Experience items (called cases) capture solutions to previous problems and are collected and stored in a case base, i.e., a repository of successful problem solving episodes. When a new problem must be solved, cases addressing similar problems are retrieved from the case base and their solution is adapted to become a solution of the new problem. Thus, problem solving from scratch is avoided. General problem solving knowledge is replaced by a collection of concrete cases, which will grow over time and thereby continuously improve problem solving performance.

Process-oriented CBR (POCBR) particularly addresses experienced-based problem solving for procedural experience represented as processes or workflows [13]. Thereby a community of users is supported in collecting their workflows in a repository. This repository is the collective experiential workflow knowledge of this user community. The content of this repository can be shared among the users and the POCBR methods support the reuse of workflows from the repository by retrieval and adaptation. The POCBR approach implemented in CAKE enables the retrieval of semantically annotated workflows [3] based on a ranking of the similarity of workflow sub-graphs. In addition to a repository of workflows, also a repository of workflow adaptation episodes can be collected. CAKE supports the transfer of previous successful adaptations to the context of a new workflow in order to adapt it to changed requirements [11].

2.3 Storage Layer

Workflow sharing requires that users are enabled to actively control the access rights to their workflows. In CAKE, all resources can be managed and controlled by their users. The resource model implemented in the storage layer [7] ensures that any stored resource (a workflow, a task, a document, and any further workflow related resources) is accessible and possesses a clear ownership. The access control mechanism is a decentralized discretionary access control with subject-object relationships specified in access control lists. In this context decentralized means that a user can transfer access rights to another subject or a group of subjects. The basic idea is that every resource (a workflow, a task, a document, and any further resources) in the system has a dedicated owner who is allowed to manage the access rights for the resource (read, write and execute). This way, workflows can be shared and reused among an online community. The access control mechanism of CAKE is a workflow specific concept.

2.4 Interface Layer and Clients

The overall CAKE software is implemented in JAVA as Web-based system running as a SaaS. The client user interfaces are implemented using the Google Web Toolkit (GWT)[2], enabling access to all workflow related functions such as workflow modeling, execution, similarity-based retrieval, and adaptation using a standard browser (see Fig. 2). Further, the CAKE Server API also allows mobile applications to directly connect to CAKE, e.g., to support the mobile execution of tasks on an Android-based device.

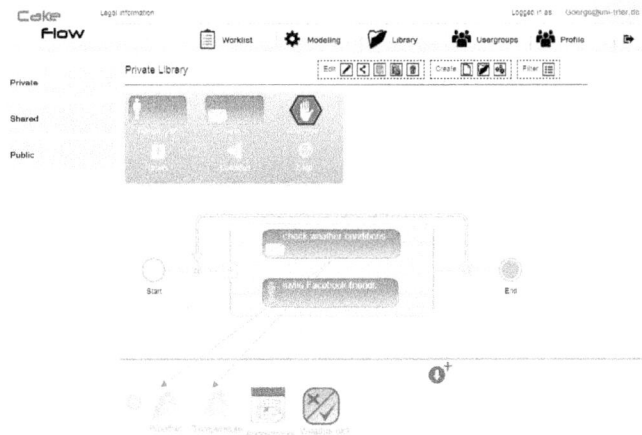

Figure 2: Browser-Based Access to CAKE.

A running live demonstrator of CAKE will be shortly accessable via the CAKE website. Further, the CAKE software will become publicly available under the AGPL V3 Open Source Licence.

3. EXAMPLE APPLICATIONS

Several applications domains for CAKE have been explored recently, some of which are now briefly described.

3.1 Deficiency Management in Construction

Construction industry is characterized by complex processes, a variety of involved parties, as well as a high degree of agility. Changes to already planned processes and reassignments of activities are daily business. We assume that integrated process and knowledge management as provided by CAKE can lead to significant productivity benefits in this domain. It can support the inherent agility of the processes by enabling changes to already running construction workflows as they are required. It can support their execution and provides up to date information about their current status. Repositories of collected best-practice workflows (e.g. representing procedures for specific or novel crafting activities) can be used as a basis for defining a good workflow to follow.

We are particularly investigating the subfield of deficiency management in construction, which is very important and challenging due to the high degree of agility [5]. For instance, a construction company receives an email from a customer notifying a certain facade crack and requesting remedy under warranty. An employee records the reported deficiency by extracting the customer data from the email, determining the type of the crack. Based on this information, the employee searches the workflow repository managed by CAKE and selects a workflow appropriate for processing deficiencies. The first step of the workflow invokes the approval of whether the notified deficiency is formally eligible for remedy under warranty. An employee qualified to take this decision is assigned and she receives the approval request on her task list, together with the relevant information to take the decision. After approval, the customer is informed by an automatically generated email, triggered by a subsequent workflow task. In parallel, a construction manager who is just at another construction site receives a work order asking him to perform a visual inspection of the facade crack. The construction manager uses the mobile CAKE app running on his mobil phone[3]. He makes a brief detour to investigate the facade crack and documents it by photos captured and semantically annotated by the mobile CAKE app. Supported by the CAKE knowledge engine, he selects a workflow appropriate for repairing the specific kind of crack and starts this new workflow. The office employee responsible for the coordination of all employees recognizes the new workflow and assigns the first task to a plasterer who is currently working near by. The plasterer receives the work order on his mobile CAKE app. He fixes the crack according to the procedure described. With a short report and a photo he documents the deficiency repair via the app.

3.2 Social Workflows

Social Workflows are a new research area [9, 6] which deals with the utilization of workflow technology to provide benefit to private persons. The idea is based on the fact that more and more online services arise in the Internet and are used by people for their private purposes. Today, people are used to install new apps on their mobile phones or tablets and thereby rely on connected online services to solve real-world tasks. Actually, there is no possibility to link such services to form a flow of activities, although the complex goals of private persons require a detailed planning of several tasks to be done, involving different people such as friends or professionals. With CAKE we investigate the idea of transferring the workflow concept to address this issue.

An example scenario that mostly everyone has faced already is moving to a new city. It requires searching available apartments first, then selecting potentially appropriate ones, making appointments with the landlord, visiting the apartment, and taking a decision. Meanwhile, information about the quality of the city district are collected, appointments must be scheduled, and information about the local infrastructure are regarded. These additional steps can be done with an online enquiry about the city district, a calendar tool, and an online map service showing near-by supermarkets, bus lines, or restaurants. A social workflow integrates these online services and provides apartment listings of local newspapers and magazines in an aggregated form. CAKE enables the execution of social workflows by invoking online services and integrating private persons by the inclusion of Facebook users. This way experts, friends, or volunteers can be included in the execution of a social workflow and people can conjointly solve problems or reach goals. Regarding this collaboration, the ability of CAKE to share, discover, and

---

[2]http://www.gwtproject.org/

[3]A short demo video of the CAKE mobil app is available at https://www.youtube.com/watch?v=iLEAOkitodY.

reuse workflows is especially meaningful for the creation of an online community.

3.3 Cooking Instructions

The third application example is from the of cooking. In this domain a cooking recipe is represented as a workflow describing the instructions for cooking a particular dish. Today, cooking recipes are widely available in Internet communities. In CAKE, we developed a specific information extraction approach to automatically transform textual cooking recipes into formal workflow representations [17]. These workflows are enriched by semantic annotations referencing to ontological knowledge of ingredients and cooking steps. CAKE can provide a step-by-step approach to cooking, but more interestingly we focus on the selection and adaptation of cooking workflows based on user preferences as well as specific requirements and restrictions.

In this context, the POCBR knowledge engine of CAKE is essential as it provides methods to retrieve and to adapt workflows. While traditional recipe repositories solely regard ingredients, categories or recipe names during recipe search, CAKE is able to consider additional knowledge such as required cooking tasks, difficulty level, costs, resource consumption, available tools, and diaries. Regarding this knowledge, CAKE retrieves the most suitable recipe workflow. However, as users have different preferences, the adaptation of the workflow from the repository might be required, e.g. by adding an additional ingredient or modify tasks due to limited preparation tools available [12]. CAKE supports this process by automatically adapting workflows to the users' needs, which particularly supports inexperienced cooks to prepare personally optimized dishes.

4. ACKNOWLEDGMENTS

The presented work is partially funded by Stiftung Rheinland-Pfalz für Innovation under grant 974 and by the German Research Foundation (DFG) under grant BE1373/3-1.

5. REFERENCES

[1] A. Aamodt and E. Plaza. Case-Based Reasoning: Foundational Issues, Methodological Variations, and System Approaches. *AI Commun*, 7(1):39–59, 1994.

[2] R. Bergmann. *Experience Management: Foundations, Development Methodology, and Internet-Based Applications*, volume 2432 of *LNAI*. Springer, 2002.

[3] R. Bergmann and Y. Gil. Similarity assessment and efficient retrieval of semantic workflows. *Information Systems*, 40(0):115 – 127, 2014.

[4] David Hollingsworth. The workflow reference model, 1995.

[5] S. Gessinger and R. Bergmann. Potentialanalyse des prozessorientierten Wissensmanagement für die Baubranche. In H.-C. Sperker and A. Henrich, editors, *LWA 2013 Lernen - Wissen - Adaption, 7.-9.10.2013 in Bamberg*, pages 212–219. Otto-Friedrich-Universität Bamberg, 2013.

[6] S. Görg and R. Bergmann. Social workflows: Vision and potential study. *Submitted for publication*.

[7] S. Görg, R. Bergmann, S. Gessinger, and M. Minor. A Resource Model for Cloud-Based Workflow Management Systems - Enabling Access Control, Collaboration and Reuse. In *Proceedings of the 3rd International Conference on Cloud Computing and Services Science, Aachen, Germany, 2013*. SciTePress 2013, 2013.

[8] S. Görg, R. Bergmann, S. Gessinger, and M. Minor. Real-time collaboration and experience reuse for cloud-based workflow management systems. In *CBI*, pages 391–398. IEEE, 2013.

[9] S. Görg, R. Bergmann, M. Minor, S. Gessinger, and S. Islam. Collecting, reusing and executing private workflows on social network platforms. In A. Mille, F. L. Gandon, J. Misselis, M. Rabinovich, and S. Staab, editors, *WWW (Companion Volume)*, pages 747–750. ACM, 2012.

[10] K. Maximini and M. Schaaf. The PROGEMM approach for managing clinical processes. In *International Workshops on Enabling Technologies: Infrastructure for Collaborative Enterprises (WETICE'03)*, pages 332–337. IEEE, 2003.

[11] M. Minor, R. Bergmann, and S. Görg. Case-based adaptation of workflows. *Information Systems*, 40(0):142 – 152, 2014.

[12] M. Minor, R. Bergmann, S. Görg, and K. Walter. Adaptation of cooking instructions following the workflow paradigm. In C. Marling, editor, *ICCBR 2010 Workshop Proceedings*, pages 199—208, 2010.

[13] M. Minor, S. Montani, and J. A. Recio-Garcia. Process-oriented case-based reasoning. *Information Systems*, 40(0):103 – 105, 2014.

[14] M. Minor, D. Schmalen, A. Koldehoff, and R. Bergmann. Structural adaptation of workflows supported by a suspension mechanism stand by case-based reasoning. In *Enabling Technologies: Infrastructure for Collaborative Enterprises, 2007. WETICE 2007. 16th IEEE International Workshops on*, pages 370–375, 2007.

[15] M. Minor, A. Tartakovski, D. Schmalen, and R. Bergmann. Agile Workflow Technology and Case-Based Change Reuse for Long-Term Processes. *IJIIT*, 4(1):80–98, 2008.

[16] M. Reichert and P. Dadam. ADEPT-Supporting Dynamic Changes of Workflows Without Losing Control. In *Journal of Intelligent Information Systems*, pages 93–129, 1998.

[17] P. Schumacher, M. Minor, K. Walter, and R. Bergmann. Extraction of procedural knowledge from the web. In *WWW'12 Workshop Proceedings*. ACM, 2012.

[18] I. J. Taylor, E. Deelman, and D. B. Gannon. *Workflows for e-Science*. Springer, 2007.

[19] B. Weber and W. Wild. An Agile Approach to Workflow Management. In Bernhard Rumpe and Wolfgang Hesse, editors, *Modellierung 2004*, volume 45 of *LNI*, pages 187–201. GI, 2004.

BIG Science: A Collaborative Framework for Large Scale Research

Samuel J. Hill
Furman University
3300 Poinsett Hwy.
Greenville, SC 29613
00+1+804-349-8808
sam.hill2@furman.edu

Kyle A. Brown
Furman University
3300 Poinsett Hwy.
Greenville, SC 29613
kyle.brown3@furman.edu

Andreea I. Cirstea
Furman University
3300 Poinsett Hwy.
Greenville, SC 29613
andreea.cirstea@furman.edu

Alexandra R. Morgan
Furman University
3300 Poinsett Hwy.
Greenville, SC 29613
alex.morgan2569@furman.edu

Ahmed Mustafa
Furman University
3300 Poinsett Hwy.
Greenville, SC 29613
ahmed.mustafa@furman.edu

Andrea Tartaro
Furman University
3300 Poinsett Hwy.
Greenville, SC 29613
00+1+864-294-2932
andrea.tartaro@furman.edu

ABSTRACT

Large-scale research projects that involve multiple investigators from many disciplines and many universities face challenges that affect collaboration and cohesion of the project. In this poster, we propose a "Big Science" collaboration system that uses Human Computer Interaction, Artificial Intelligence and Big Data methods to identify project cohesion and create effective collaborative connections.

Categories and Subject Descriptors

H. Information Systems
  H.5 INFORMATION INTERFACES AND PRESENTATION (I.7)
    H.5.3 Group and Organization Interfaces
      Subjects: Computer-supported cooperative work

General Terms

Design

Keywords

large-scale research; big data; recommendation systems.

1. INTRODUCTION

Large-scale, collaborative research projects that involve multiple investigators from many disciplines and many universities face challenges that affect collaboration and cohesion of the project. Various technologies, such as video conferencing and wikis, support communication across these "Big Science" projects, but few tools exist for creating, promoting, and evaluating collaboration on such a large scale. Our goal is to develop tools

and technology aimed at cohesive collaboration. This poster proposes a Big Science collaboration system.

2. BACKGROUND

Several existing technologies and tools aid Big Science projects in communication (e.g. email, Skype [1], or SMS), knowledge transfer (e.g. CiteSeer [2], or Web of Science [3]), or access to funding through institutions such as the National Science Foundation (NSF). Websites such as the Interactive Autism Network (IAN) [4], link researchers and community members for sharing information and data. Current research on large scale collaborative projects focus on topics such as server architecture for supporting collaborative work (e.g., [5]), data sharing (e.g., [6]), and supporting creativity in distributed scientific communities (e.g., [7]). Although these approaches enable constant access to data, information or colleagues, they are not specifically designed to identify cohesion in research projects and potential collaborations. This role usually falls to people. Spencer et al. argue that successful projects depend on social interactions, and project managers play a key role in managing relationships [8]. In a review of research on informal information systems, Holland identifies people called "special communicators" as a key source of information [9]. "Special communicators" are identifiable individuals with high "information potential (IP)," that is, they possess a high quantity of quality information that they make accessible to colleagues [9]. Holland describes a number of characteristics of special communicators, in particular they are "catalysts" of information: they make connections between ideas, and refer colleagues to each other. Our goal is to develop a system modeled after the "special communicator" that automatically identifies cohesion across large projects. The system will support both reporting, i.e., to agencies funding large projects, and identifying opportunities for collaborations.

3. PROPOSED SYSTEM

We propose a Big Science collaboration system that will use Human Computer Interaction (HCI), Artificial Intelligence (AI), and Big Data methods to identify project cohesion and create effective collaborative connections. This system will create links between papers with information automatically extracted from the text and bibliography, and group papers to identify places of cohesion and potential collaboration, as illustrated in Figure 1 and described below.

3.1 DATABASE

The database will include papers submitted by scientists that will then be linked to other papers in the database. To minimize the efforts of the scientists involved, we will generate most of the information in the database automatically from a simple pdf submission of the text.

3.1.1 Text

To determine which papers have similar topics we will need to look at the text of each paper. This could be as simple as automatically extracting a list of keywords from the text, or could be more complex and use Natural Language Parsing (NLP) techniques such as Part of Speech (POS) parsing and Text Classification. The NLP techniques will parse the documents for their meaning.

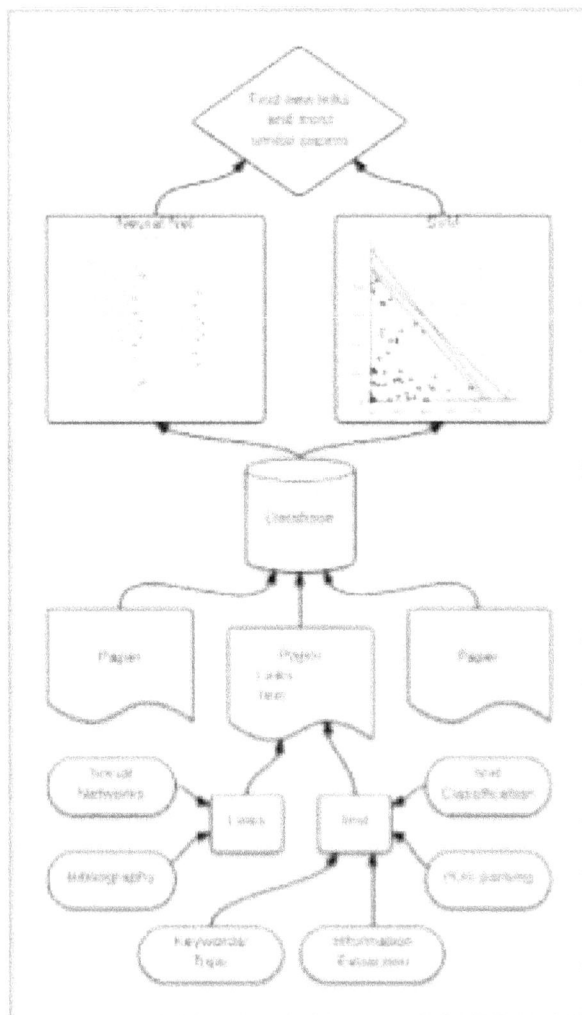

Figure 1: A basic diagram of our learning system

3.1.2 Other Links

In addition to processing text to find similar topics between papers, we will also use bibliographies to link papers based on common citations. These links will be supplemented with information from social networks such as LinkedIn, Twitter or Facebook. While the bibliographies let us know where researchers

are finding their information, the social media links could tell us which researchers are talking to each other.

3.2 LEARNING

After we have compiled our database, we will analyze the data and use machine learning to develop a function for good collaboration. We will introduce training sets of data to our system to teach it where matches are typically found and which matches are most helpful. Using the links between papers described above, the system will develop its own theories about matching papers via neural networks and support vector machines. This process will be guided by a user-driven recommendation system, which provides heuristic values for variables such as reference quality.

3.2.1 Neural Networks

Neural networks are networks of individual functions that act similarly to neurons in a central nervous system. Each input is run through the network which weights and transforms the value to assign an output value [10]. Using our training data, the system will develop a function to weight the importance of each variable for determining similarity, e.g. text classification, keywords, similar links, etc. It will apply the function to the papers to find those most related.

3.2.2 Support Vector Machines (SVMs)

SVMs use algorithms to separate sets of data based on what is most similar. Our system will plot each paper onto a field such that similar papers are closer together, and divide up the papers into groups that are most similar [10]. From there we will identify links between groups, which may suggest that a paper in one group has a higher probability of being related to a paper from the other group than other papers.

3.2.3 Recommendation Systems

To further support these learning algorithms, we will provide an interface that enables users to provide feedback to the system. Similar to sites like Pandora [11] and Spotify [12] that recommend music based on user preferences, the system will use this feedback to recommend other papers, while continuously training itself by creating new links between papers researchers have "liked."

4. CONCLUSION

This research aims to support Big Science projects by supporting project cohesion. We propose a system that will identify cohesion in the project by analyzing papers and researchers' social networks. The system will automatically create links between papers by extracting information from text and bibliographies. It will use machine learning algorithms to develop functions to identify related papers, and recommend opportunities for collaboration to researchers.

5. ACKNOWLEDGMENTS

Material on this site is based upon work supported by the National Science Foundation-EPSCoR program under Grant Number EPS-0903795. Any opinions, findings, conclusions, or recommendations expressed in this material are those of the South Carolina EPSCoR/IDeA Program and do not necessarily reflect the views of the National Science Foundation.

6. REFERENCES

[1] Skype; http://www.skype.com/en/

[2] CiteSeerX; http://citeseerx.ist.psu.edu/

[3] Web of Science: http://wokinfo.com/

[4] IAN; https://www.ianresearch.org/

[5] Shengwen Yang; Jinlei Jiang; Meilin Shi, "A Scalable Framework for Large-Scale Distributed Collaboration," Computer Supported Cooperative Work in Design, 2006. CSCWD '06. 10th International Conference on , vol., no., pp.1,6, 3-5 May 2006 doi: 10.1109/CSCWD.2006.253070.

[6] Birnholtz, Jeremy and Matthew Bietz, Data at Work: Supporting Sharing in Science and Engineering. Conference on Supporting Group Work. (2003) 339-348.

[7] Umer Farooq, John M. Carroll, and Craig H. Ganoe, "Supporting Creativity in Distributed Scientific Communities" Proceeding from GROUP '05, Proceedings of the 2005 international ACM SIGGROUP conference on supporting group work, Pages 217 - 226.

[8] Spencer, Dimitrina; Zimmerman, Ann; Abramson, David; "Special Theme: Project Management in E-Science: Challenges and Opportunities", Computer Supported Cooperative Work (CSCW), vol. 20, num. 3, Pages 155-163, Springer Netherlands: 2011-06-01 10.1007/s10606-011-9140-4

[9] Spector, A. Z. 1989. Achieving application requirements. In *Distributed Systems*, S. Mullender, Ed. ACM Press Frontier Series. ACM, New York, NY, 19-33. DOI= http://doi.acm.org/10.1145/90417.90738.

[10] Holland, W.E., "The special communicator and his behavior in research orpanizations: A key to the management of informal technical information flow," Professional Communication, IEEE Transactions on , vol. PC-17, no.3-4, pp.48,53, Sept.-Dec. 1974 doi: 10.1109/TPC.1974.6591308

[11] Pandora; http://www.pandora.com/

[12] Spotify; https://www.spotify.com/us/

Support for Collaboration Between Large and Small & Medium Enterprises

Wolfgang Gräther
Fraunhofer FIT
Schloss Birlinghoven
53754 Sankt Augustin, Germany
+49 -2241 -14 -2093
graether@fit.fraunhofer.de

Michal Laclavik
Institute of Informatics
Slovak Academy of Sciences
Bratislava, Slovakia
+421-2-5941 1256
michal.laclavik@savba.sk

Martin Tomasek
InterSoft, a.s.
Florianska 19
Kosice, Slovakia

martin.tomasek@intersoft.sk

ABSTRACT
Collaboration between large and small & medium enterprises is still not adequately supported by current groupware solutions. In this paper, we present the VENIS approach for lightweight collaboration that addresses the challenges of inter-enterprise collaboration. Key elements of our approach are interoperability to legacy applications, basic services for sharing and management of shared collaboration spaces, use of email for collaboration on the SME's side and the application of lightweight semantic technologies to enable semantic search in inter-enterprise collaborations. We tested the approach on a use case from software development and describe the results.

Categories and Subject Descriptors
H.5.3 [**Group and Organization Interfaces**]: Collaborative computing, computer-supported cooperative work.

General Terms
Design, Human Factors.

Keywords
Groupware, interoperability, lightweight semantics.

1. INTRODUCTION
Collaboration between large enterprises (LE) and small and medium enterprises (SME) is often solely based on the exchange of documents via email, which, for example, leads to high barriers for newcomers in collaboration processes or to divergent document versions. This situation is attributable to some reasons:

- large enterprises do not allow use of and access to their collaboration solution in the enterprise, especially for temporary partnerships;

- SMEs do not have the resources, either financially or with respect to personnel, to install and use all the different collaboration systems of their LE partners;

- the cooperating enterprises compliance rules do not allow to use services in the cloud such as Doodle for scheduling or Dropbox for sharing;

- the cooperating enterprises are using different collaboration systems that are not interoperable.

There are in principle two basic models to achieve inter-operability of collaboration systems. The first model connects the enterprises collaboration systems to each other, i.e. each collaboration system provides the selected features. For shared workspaces, for example, the features could be create and delete shared workspaces, invite or un-invite members, assign roles to members, add, remove, lock, version and revise documents, notify members about activities, etc. This model has the advantage that no coordination instance is necessary. On the other side, the enterprise collaboration system has to be adapted and the number of different collaboration systems in the involved enterprises determines the necessary effort for this approach.

The second model connects the enterprises collaboration systems via a common collaboration system that is selected by the involved enterprises, i.e. the common collaboration system implements and provides the selected collaboration features that ensure the collaboration between the enterprises. The common collaboration system does not necessarily have to be a single system, but could also be a mash-up of different interconnected modules or services. This model has the advantage that the enterprise collaboration system has to be adapted only once to the set of collaboration features provided by the common collaboration system. Yet the common collaboration system has to be bought or leased, hosted and managed, and could be a bottleneck with regard to overall performance.

A reference architecture that supports collaborative work environment interoperability based on the first model as well as experiences with concrete implementations can be found in in [7] and in [6]. An interesting approach that suggests collaborative sharing with email is described in [5].

2. THE VENIS APPROACH
The VENIS approach to interoperable collaboration is based on the second model and the VENIS services for enterprise interoperability (VSI) serve as common collaboration system that integrates also usage of email. Adapters connect to the legacy systems of the collaborating enterprise, i.e. the legacy systems have not to be changed and the way of working remains almost unmodified, see Figure 1.

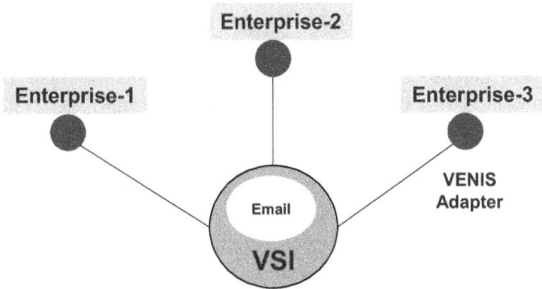

Figure 1: VENIS approach to interoperable collaboration.

Figure 2 presents a schematic overview of inter-enterprise collaboration and shows in the left-hand part the usual situation when a large enterprise collaborates with a small enterprise. That is a member of the large enterprise prepares data and documents, required by the small enterprise to fulfill the contract, using legacy applications such as groupware, systems for enterprise resource planning, customer relationship management, content management or databases etc. Then this compiled information is put into an email, the documents are attached and the email is sent to the corresponding member of the small enterprise. The small enterprise does the required work and sends back information and documents using email. Then in the large enterprise the information and documents are extracted from the received email and used to update the corresponding information and documents in the legacy application.

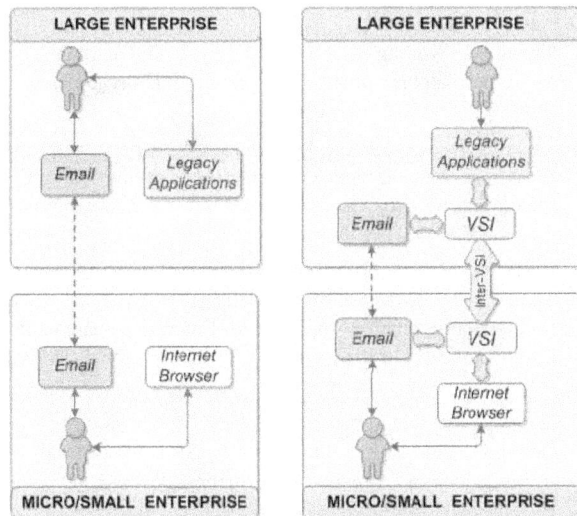

Figure 2. Collaboration of LE and SME. Left: today's practice, right: using VSI.

The right-hand part of Figure 2 shows the improved situation where both enterprises are using the VSI infrastructure that adapts to legacy applications, supports sharing and versioning of documents and notifies about activities of the co-workers. That is, for the simple process described above, the member of the large enterprise gives access to the information in the legacy application and the member of the small enterprise can directly update the corresponding business documents, for example a confirmation of order or a process sheet, and has basic groupware features available.

2.1 The VENIS Platform

The VENIS approach is based on REST/SOAP Web services that allow easy integration with legacy systems as well as user interfaces. Figure 3 shows the various modules of the VSI.

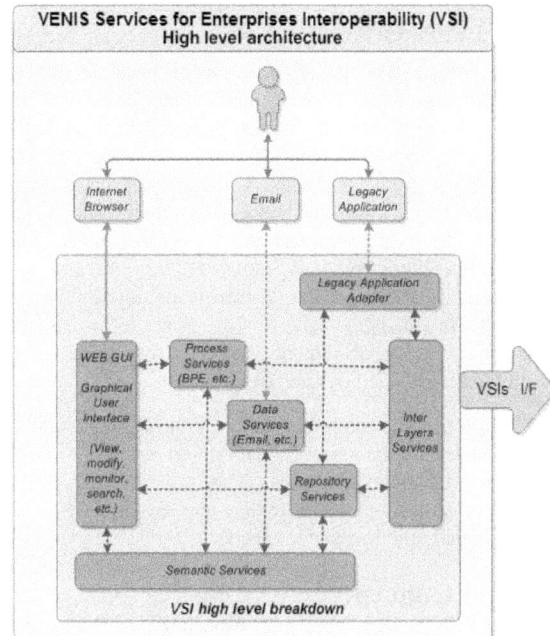

Figure 3. VSI architecture and interfaces with enterprise applications.

The basic modules of VSI are the repository services and the data services. Both services benefit from the semantic services and are connected to the inter-layer services which support distribution of events to notify users, for example. The basic services and the semantic services provide the necessary user-related features as services for the Web browser GUI and the integration into email client interface. The process services are currently under development and not further presented in this paper.

The repository services support upload, download and versioning of documents. In addition, the repository services provide a token-based access to shared artifacts. Legacy application adapters connect the repository services to legacy applications and enable either retrieval of documents in groupware or document management systems or create human readable documents from information stored in legacy systems such as ERP, CRM or database systems. Update of documents is also supported.

The data services support the creation and management of collaboration spaces, i.e. containers for a set of documents accessible by a group of users. Email attachment stripping is a service designed especially for the interaction with SMEs. This service strips attachments from emails, create a collaboration space if necessary, upload the attachments into the repository and replaces the attachments in the email by the corresponding links that allow token-based access. The data services comprise an indexing service to support full-text search in the documents and emails of the collaborations.

The semantic services are a further key feature of the VENIS approach. They support automatic extraction of tags and annotations in the artifacts of collaborations and offer semantic search, see next section on lightweight semantics and search.

2.2 Lightweight Semantics and Search

Lightweight semantics based on tags and annotations are used in many social media systems such as Wikipedia, Twitter or Facebook and seem adequate for LE-SME collaborations because no complex ontology has to be set up and no inference techniques with exponential complexity have to be used.

The semantic information is extracted from human-readable documents and communications (email) that are used in collaborations. The semantic information is stored in a semantic network as a free collection of types. In earlier research work [4] default annotation types for business documents have been identified: organization, person, address, product, document, inventory, etc. The type organization, for example, is sub-structured into attributes such as name, registration and tax registration number. The type of a document could be invoice, order, contract, or change request. For example, a set of annotations for an invoice document could be {[org.name: abc], [doc.type: invoice], [id: 4711], [date: 2014-08-01]}.

The extracted semantic information enable rich semantic search over communication (emails) and collaboration artifacts [1] [2] and can trigger business processes. The semantic search is envisioned to substitute to certain extend the missing CRM or ERP system in small and medium enterprises.

2.3 Proof of Concept

The ongoing VENIS developments, especially the semantic search, have been tested with the use case and data from the project partner InterSoft [3]. In this use case a customer asks a large provider of software solutions to fulfill a complex project. The provider does not have all the required resources available and therefore searches for suitable subcontractors. The management of such collaborations is usually achieved by email communication including exchange of documents.

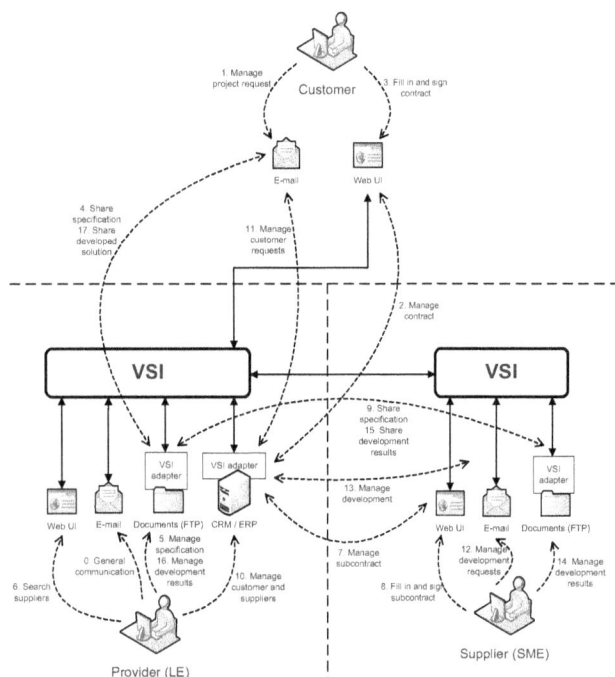

Figure 4. Data flow, actors and services. Use case: software development supply chain.

The VENIS platform supports this use case with various features. For example, the email conversation between customer and provider is automatically stored in a collaboration space and information extraction methods create semantic information of the content of the emails. An adapter for the provider's CRM/ERP system allows the customer to fill in and sign the contract via a Web form. On the provider's side the search for adequate subcontractors is supported by semantic search in earlier collaborations. Sharing of specifications, development results and other documents between the provider and supplier is supported by the corresponding adapters of the respective FTP servers. The cooperating partners are notified by email about changes in shared documents.

3. FUTURE WORK

Currently the process services that support modeling, configuration and execution of business procedures are further developed. When all VSI modules are available, tested and integrated, then a broader use of the VENIS platform will take place and an evaluation and feedback cycle will follow.

4. ACKNOWLEDGMENTS

Our thanks are due to all partners of the VENIS (Virtual Enterprises by Networked Interoperability Services) project that is partially funded by the EU under grant number 284984. Special thanks go to Bruno Casali who created Figure 2 and Figure 3.

5. REFERENCES

[1] Ciglan, M., Norvag, K., Hluchy, L. 2012. The SemSets Model for Adhoc Semantic List search. In *Proceedings of WWW 2012*. ACM, 131-140.

[2] Laclavik, M., Ciglan, M., Dlugolinsky, S., Seleng, and Hluchy, L. 2012. Emails as Graph: Relation Discovery in Email Archive. In *Proceedings of WWW 2012 companion*. ACM, 841-846.

[3] Laclavik, M., Dlugolinsky, S., Seleng, M., Ciglan, M., Tomasek, M., Kvassay, M., and Hluchy, L. 2012. Lightweight Semantic Approach for Enterprise Search and Interoperability. In *Proceedings of the 5th Interop-Vlab.IT Workshop*.

[4] Laclavik, M., Dlugolinsky, S., Seleng, M., Kvassay, M., Gatial, E., Balogh, Z., and Hluchy, L. 2011. Email Analysis and Information Extraction for Enterprise Benefit. *Computing and informatics*, 3(1), 57-87.

[5] Mahmud, L., Matthews, T., Whittaker, S., Moran, T. P., and Lau, T. 2011. Topika: Integrating Collaborative Sharing with Email. In *Proceedings of the SIGCHI Conference on Human Factors in Computing Systems*. CHI 2011, ACM, New York, NY, 3161-3164.

[6] Peristeras, V., Fradinho, M., Lee, D., Prinz, W., Ruland, R., Iqbal, K., and Decker, S. 2009. CERA: A collaborative environment reference architecture for interoperable CWE systems. *Service Oriented Computing and Applications* 3(1), 3–23.

[7] Prinz, W., Löh, H., Pallot, M., Schaffers, H., Skarmeta, A., and Decker, S. 2006. ECOSPACE - Towards an Integrated Collaboration Space for eProfessionals. In *Proceedings of CollaborateCom 2006*. IEEE press.

"I Am Not a Lawyer":
Copyright Q&A in Online Creative Communities

Casey Fiesler
GVU Center
Georgia Institute of Technology
85 5th St. NW Atlanta, GA 30332
casey.fiesler@gatech.edu

Jessica Feuston
GVU Center
Georgia Institute of Technology
85 5th St. NW Atlanta, GA 30332
jfeuston@gatech.edu

Amy S. Bruckman
GVU Center
Georgia Institute of Technology
85 5th St. NW Atlanta, GA 30332
asb@cc.gatech.edu

ABSTRACT

Once referred to by the Supreme Court as the "metaphysics" of law, many parts of copyright policy are historically confusing. Therefore, it isn't surprising that in communities where amateur content creators work within a legal gray area, copyright is a frequent topic of conversation. Here, people with often little knowledge of the letter of the law are asking and answering complex legal questions in the context of their creative activities. Working from a content analysis of public forum conversations in eight different online communities, we have examined these questions and answers more closely. By studying these interactions, what can we learn about how people engage with the law and how non-expert advice affects behavior and knowledge?

Categories and Subject Descriptors

K.4.1 [**Computers and Society**]: Public Policy Issues ---
Intellectual property rights

General Terms

Legal Aspects

Keywords

Copyright; Creativity; Expertise; Intellectual property; Law; Online communities; Policy; Social Q&A; User-generated content

1. INTRODUCTION

The phrase "I am not a lawyer" is so common in online discussions that it comes with a commonly used acronym: IANAL. Typically followed by a "but..." this disclaimer goes hand-in-hand with frequently offered amateur legal advice in a variety of contexts all over the Internet. One common topic is that of copyright, which though once mostly relevant to professional artists and big corporations now touches ordinary Internet users on a daily basis. Thanks to the ease of digitization and wide dissemination of content, anyone with an Internet connection and a "share" button is engaging with copyright.

However, more people engaging with this aspect of the law does not make it less complex. On the contrary, technological advances only exacerbate existing confusions in the law. Consider, for example, how easy and common it is now to appropriate existing copyrighted work—from popular YouTube remix videos to viral image memes to *Star Trek* fan fiction. Whereas the average Internet user might know that it is illegal to download a copyrighted song, whether that song can be used as part of a remix is a more difficult question. In a seminal case about remix prior to widespread use of the Internet, the Supreme Court in *Campbell vs. Acuff-Rose* (1992) referred to issues of appropriation as the "most troublesome" part of all of copyright law.

Most online sites where people share creative work include some way for users to interact beyond simply commenting on one another's work. In these spaces where intellectual property matters come up frequently, much of this discussion focuses on questions and answers. In the same online communities where users are posting digital art, fan fiction, remix videos, and music remix, they are asking each other questions like "How does the law apply to my work?", "Is this illegal?", and "Why did I get in trouble?" This is a rich example of an online question-and-answer space in which non-experts are relying on one another's (often imperfect) knowledge and advice in order to make decisions.

As part of a broader study on copyright knowledge and norms in online creative communities [6,7], we conducted a content analysis of public forum conversations about copyright in eight different online communities. In looking specifically at how users are asking and answering questions, we have begun to see some patterns in social question asking (Q&A) taking place among strangers with a shared creative interest.

2. BACKGROUND

Our prior work began with the problem of gray areas in the parts of copyright law relevant to online content creators. Judging from previous research, including studies of documentary filmmakers [10], remix video creators [2], and knitters [9], we expected to see misunderstandings of the law among remixers. However, a more surprising finding was how similar their ideas were. Focusing on fair use,[1] the legal doctrine that allows for some uses of copyrighted content, we found both nuances of understanding and patterns of misconceptions [6]. Many of these patterns seemed tied to social norms, which suggests that they form within the

---

[1] Fair use in U.S. law (though there are similar concepts for other countries) is a codified exception to copyright law. It covers, for example, parody, news reporting, and creative re-uses such as remix. Determinations are made by a judge on a case-by-case basis.

community itself. This includes not only misconceptions but also social constructions of the law. One hypothesis is that these constructions could be formed by learning within the community, including information seeking behavior.

Though there is little work in the area of Q&A specifically related to intellectual property, Humphries' study of Ravelry, an online community of knitters, examined copyright discussions in the site's online forum [9]. The conclusion was that the community seemed to have very little consensus over what constituted legal or ethical behavior. As the author pointed out, if a simple request for information resulted in a thread with over 80 posts that culminates in a suggestion that the poster consult an attorney, there is likely a problem with both legal literacy and uncertainty. Humphries also suggested that these Q&A sessions result only in frustration rather than encouraging people to learn more.

Of course, it is not unusual for people to seek answers to their questions online, and from a number of different sources. Research in this area has explored formal Q&A sites such as Quora and Yahoo! Answers [1,13] where most of the interaction is between strangers, as well as the use of personal social networks [8,12] (such as Twitter and Facebook) for information-seeking. We know some reasons why someone might choose to ask a question on Facebook, for example, as opposed to seeking out a specific expert, such as personal context and trust [12]. Choi et al. have proposed four models of Q&A sites: community, collaborative, expert-based, and social [4]. One might consider an online affinity space, in which people come together because of a shared interest or common activity (rather than simply Q&A) to be somewhere in between a social and community model.

In these spaces, when someone asks a question and the answer comes from a stranger, they know something about them—that they are likely also an artist, or a writer, or a knitter. They share a common experience, and common problems related to the question—in this case, the struggle to understand the boundaries of copyright law in the context of their creative work. Trust and context are still benefits, but information seekers also have to make decisions about authority and expertise—which we know from credibility research can be difficult to judge [5,13]. Additionally, the legal context makes the questions potentially high risk—could trusting a wrong answer lead to legal trouble? In this way, the environment is similar to health information seeking, where source credibility is an important factor in Q&A [5].

3. METHODS

As part of a broader research project [7], we are focusing on creative activities often burdened with unclear copyright issues—i.e., remix and appropriation. Therefore, our data set comes from online communities for which creative appropriation is common. We identified eight popular online communities representing four common remix media types: art, music, writing, and video (see Table 1). Each site features user-generated content and has a public forum with posts primarily in English.

Our data set comes from public (publicly viewable to anyone on the web without account creation) forum posts scraped from these websites in the spring of 2013 [7]. We used an inter-rater reliability measure to validate a keywords used to identify posts about copyright from this set of posts, and then created a random sample with a maximum of 50 posts from each site. In sum, we began with a set of millions of forum posts across these eight different online communities, narrowed down this data set to

posts that were likely about copyright, and then narrowed this down to a tractable number of posts about copyright based on a random sample (see Table 1). The final data set consists of 339 posts. Table 1 also shows an estimate of the percentage of copyright-related posts in each forum generally, based on analysis of an additional random sample. Though these numbers might seem small, for DeviantArt's 15 million posts, for example, three percent still represents hundreds of thousands of conversations.

For data analysis, we looked to grounded theory, which provided us with a systematic process for analysis while maintaining flexibility to fit this unique data [2]. We began with inductive, open coding, and coded the data for emergent phenomena. Two independent coders met to periodically discuss codes and then synthesized them into a final set. One coder was the first author, who is a law school graduate and copyright expert. Once the categories were finalized we coded the data again and used an overlapping set of 10% to calculate inter-rater reliability with a percent agreement of 94% and Cohen's Kappa of .77 [6].

4. FINDINGS

In our analysis of the resulting data set, we grouped our codes into eight higher level categories: type of post, legal concepts, policies and enforcement, ethics, attitudes, media, problems, and Q&A. For more detail on methods and additional findings, see [7]. For the current discussion, we are focusing on our initial findings about Q&A based on this analysis.

The general types of copyright-related conversations we identified in this data set were: Q&A, requests for action, policy commentary, complaints, discussion of a specific case, and other (veering off-topic to copyright). In categorizing the posts by type, we found that the most common by far was Q&A. In the two largest sites that we studied, DeviantArt and YouTube, Q&A posts made up more than half of those posts in our data set.

Essentially, the majority of the copyright-related conversation taking places in these communities stems from someone asking a question. We also categorized the most common questions that posters asked:

- Is this okay?

- How can I avoid getting into trouble?

- Why did I get into trouble?

- How can I protect my work?

- I don't understand this rule; can someone explain it to me?

A great many of these questions boil down to requests for amateur legal advice. "Is this okay?" is the most common, with a poster expressing concern about some creative activity and whether it might be illegal or against site policies. What complicates matters is that rarely are there black-and-white answers to these questions, but instead they can be legally complex. For example, one poster on Overclocked, a music remix site, asked whether it is legal to use extracted vocals in a remix of a commercial song. Another asked if it was legal to use chiptune effects on an album intended to generate revenue for a religious entity. The answers to both of these questions depend upon a fairly complex fair use analysis.

	Description	~ Total Posts	~ Posts Scraped	Posts in Data Set	Estimated Copyright Percentage
DeviantArt Art c. 2000 forum.deviantart.com	One of the largest social networks on the web, a popular space for artists both amateur and professional to showcase their work	15,800,000	49,464	50	3%
Fanart Central Art c. 2004 forums.fanart-central.net	An online art gallery that hosts primarily fandom-based art and fiction, but also allows original submissions	278,000	20,875	50	11%
Remix64 Music c. 2002 remix64.com/board	A Commodore 64 and Amiga music remix community, containing news and reviews as well as a place for users to upload their work	73,000	1,099	50	5%
OverClocked Remix Music c. 2003 ocremix.org/forums	A video game music community featuring fan-made remixes and information	636, 000	7,642	50	5%
YouTube Video c. 2005 productforums.google.com/ forum/#!forum/youtube	The largest user-generated content video site on the web; though it does not have a general forum for discussion, it does have a very large help forum in a Google Group	500 per day	17,546	50	13%
MMORPG Forum Video c. 1999 mmorpgforum.com	A site for discussion of massively multiplayer online roleplaying games; the largest sub-forums are dedicated to machinima, Warcraft movies and Warhammer movies	113,000	364	23	3%
HarryPotterFanFiction.com Writing c. 2009 harrypotterfanfiction.com/forums	The oldest fan fiction site on the web dedicated to the *Harry Potter* novels, housing over 78,000 stories	70,000	1,211	16	2%
Twisting the Hellmouth Writing c. 2008 forum.tthfanfic.org	A fan fiction archive with over 15,000 stories based on the *Buffy the Vampire Slayer* and *Angel* television shows	54,000	1,590	50	7%

Table 1: Website information and statistics

Nearly every question in our data set was answered by at least one person—sometimes by several people, with conflicting answers. The question above about chiptunes and religious entities generated four pages of discussion, including one complex (and fairly accurate) fair use analysis, some blatant misinformation, and advice to consult a lawyer. One later commentator pointed out the humor in the conflicting advice, writing that the comments either boiled down to "Don't do it or you could go to jail" or "Come on, just do it, nobody will notice." Another poster pointed out that the Internet is a poor substitute for legal advice, and yet another praised the thread for helping them to learn about copyright law.

Though that particular thread benefited from participants who had some understanding of law, many do not. Some answers to questions express basic misunderstandings about copyright, such as telling a poster that they have to register with the copyright office in order to have a copyright in their work, that any image found online is public domain and thus available to use, or that writing "no copyright infringement" as a disclaimer carries legal weight (all of which are incorrect). Misinformation also comes in the form of too strictly construing copyright law. One respondent incorrectly stated that remixing anything without a license in writing constitutes criminal activity. When one YouTube poster questioned whether their video taken down for a copyright violation may have been fair use, one commenter answered that there is no such thing as fair use. In our data set, nearly a quarter of the posts contained some incorrect legal information.

Even when incorrect, more often than not, answers are presented as fact rather than opinion. We coded for degree of confidence, and absolute confidence was far more common than "I'm not sure, but…" or IANAL disclaimers. However, it was also rare for answers to provide either citations or indications of expertise (occurring in less than 5% of the posts). Occasionally a poster would link to an external resource, such as a Wikipedia page or even to the actual legal code, but this was unusual. Even more unusual—seen only once in our entire data set—did someone express personal expertise. Here, we saw the opposite of IANAL: "I *am* a lawyer, but this is not legal advice" (a necessary disclaimer for attorneys to avoid creating attorney-client relationships strangers on the Internet).

Based on this data alone it is difficult to speculate about the outcomes of questions being answered. However, we can infer that posters take the advice offered at least some of the time. In cases of incorrect information, this could be potentially troubling. Though interestingly, what we see *less* often is advice that might get the original poster into legal trouble (telling them that something is okay when it isn't). Instead, the more common problem would be advice that might stifle the poster's creativity (telling them that something *isn't* okay when it might be). In legal terms, not doing something that you should be able to do because you fear legal consequences is a *chilling effect*. Erroneously telling a creator that their work is illegal could result in that creator choosing not to share their work.

Throughout the entirety of our data set, an overarching theme was that of incomplete information: information seeking, expressions of confusion about the law, misleading or contradictory answers. However, also among incorrect information is *correct* information, and the occasional nuanced discussion that goes beyond typical copyright knowledge. Within our data, we saw examples of posters going out of their way to answer questions in their communities. These individuals tended to have more legal knowledge than those providing quick, one-off answers. Another side effect of these discussions is that community members sometimes do legal research and learn about things that they wouldn't otherwise. Copyright Q&A sessions therefore are in a position to both contribute to knowledge and spread misinformation. As in other potentially high-stakes contexts such as health information, this position can be precarious.

5. DISCUSSION & FUTURE WORK

Social media Q&A research has been exploring important issues of how people seek information online from varying sources. Much of this research has focused on either answering questions from strangers (e.g., Yahoo! Answers) or from their social networks (e.g., Facebook). The domain of copyright conversations among online content creators offers some potentially unique questions and problems in this space. Here we see information-seeking behavior towards people who are neither trusted friends nor strangers nor experts—but rather, people with a shared experience. However, similar to health information seeking behavior, legal advice could have potentially high stakes.

Our work so far begins to describe these communities as a Q&A space, examining the type of questions being asked, and the answers provided. We see that questions are almost always answered with a high degree of confidence and with few citations. This coupled with a high degree of incorrect information is potentially problematic.

Future work includes an examination of how judgments of expertise are actually happening within these communities. How are question askers deciding whom to trust? What are the outcomes of these interactions? Are there times when Q&A is more harmful than helpful if misinformation is disseminated? Are the interactions more similar to those with expert-strangers or non-expert-friends?

Moreover, there is a potential design space here. How can the designers of these communities better support more productive and useful conversations about copyright? All of this conversation is taking place despite none of these communities providing dedicated spaces for legal discussions or Q&A. Encouraging better understandings of copyright could both discourage chilling effects on creativity and help mitigate the air of legal uncertainty in these communities.

6. ACKNOWLEDGMENTS

This work is supported by NSF IIS-1216347.

7. REFERENCES

1. Adamic, L.A., Zhang, J., Bakshy, E., Ackerman, M.S. and Arbor, A. Knowledge Sharing and Yahoo Answers: Everyone Knows Something. In *Proceedings of the 17th International Conference on World Wide Web*, (2008).

2. Aufderheide, P., Jaszi, P., and Brown, E.N. The Good, The Bad, and The Confusing: User-Generated Video Creators on Copyright. *American University Center for Social Media*, 2007.

3. Charmaz, K. *Constructing Grounded Theory: A Practical Guide Through Qualitative Analysis*. SAGE Publications, London, UK, 2006.

4. Choi, E., Kitzie, V. and Shah, C. Developing a Typology of Online Q&A Models and Recommending the Right Model for Each Question Type. *Proceedings of the American Society for Information Science and Technology*, (2012).

5. Eastin, M.S. Credibility Assessments of Online Health Information: The Effects of Source Expertise and Knowledge Content. *Journal of Computer Mediated Communciation*, 6(4), (2001).

6. Fiesler, C. and Bruckman, A.S. Remixers' Understandings of Fair Use Online. *Proceedings of the 17th ACM Conference on Computer Supported Cooperative Work & Social Computing*, (2014).

7. Fiesler, C., Feuston, J. and Bruckman, A.S. Understandings of Copyright in Online Creative Communities. *Proceedings of the 18th ACM Conference on Computer Supported Cooperative Work & Social Computing*, (2015, in press).

8. Gray, R., Ellison, N.B., Vitak, J. and Lampe, C. Who Wants to Know? Question-Asking and Answering Practices Among Facebook Users. *Proceedings of the 2013 Conference on Computer Supported Cooperative Work*, (2013).

9. Humphreys, S. The Challenges of Intellectual Property for Users of Social Networking Sites: A Case Study of Ravelry. *MindTrek '08: Proceedings of the 12th International Conference on Entertainment and Media in the Ubiquitous Era*, (2008).

10. Larsen, L.O. and Nærland, T.U. Documentary in a Culture of Clearance: A Study of Knowledge of and Attitudes Toward Copyright and Fair Use Among Norwegian Documentary Makers. *Popular Communication 8*, 1 (2010), 46–60.

11. Lombard, M., Snyder-Duch, J., and Bracken, C.C. Content Analysis in Mass Communication: Assessment and Reporting of Intercoder Reliability. *Human Communication Research 28*, 4 (2002), 587–604.

12. Morris, M.R., Teevan, J., and Panovich, K. What Do People Ask Their Social Networks, and Why? A Survey Study of Status Message Q&A Behavior. In *Proceedings of the SIGCHI Conference on Human Factors in Computing Systems,* (2010).

13. Paul, S.A., Hong, L., and Chi, E.H. Who is Authoritative? Understanding Reputation Mechanisms in Quora. In *Proceedings of Collective Intelligence,* (2012).

Presenting the Kludd – A Shared Workspace for Collaboration

Stefan Nilsson
University West
Gustava Melins Gata 2
461 32 Trollhättan
+46 520-22 35 26
stefan.nilsson@hv.se

Lars Svensson
University West
Gustava Melins Gata 2
461 32 Trollhättan
+46 520-22 35 64
lars.svensson@hv.se

ABSTRACT

In this poster, we would like to present the current state of the Kludd system. Kludd is a web-based collaboration tool, enabling users to collaborate around various media objects like images, videos, texts and audio in a shared workspace. The design metaphor is an online whiteboard, where multiple actors can add, manipulate and remove objects, all while everyone sees the same view. The system is made with standard components like HTML5, CSS3 and a number of open-source javascript libraries enabling real-time collaboration in a browser. Utilizing a Design Science Research methodology, the initial design was based on 9 design requirements. In this poster, a further four requirements are presented as a result of the analysis of the first phase, and an initial design of the second phase of the project is presented.

Categories and Subject Descriptors

H.5.3 [**INFORMATION INTERFACES AND PRESENTATION (e.g., HCI)**]: Group and Organization Interfaces – *Collaborative computing, Synchronous interaction, Web-based interaction*

General Terms

Design.

Keywords

Shared workspace, collaboration, real-time, HTML5

1. INTRODUCTION

In this text, we would like to present the current state of development of the Kludd system. Kludd is a shared workspace in the browser, where users can interact and collaborate around various media objects such as video, sound, images and texts. Developed using standardized technologies such as HTML5 and CSS3, the system is enhanced with a number of open-source javascript libraries and frameworks that for example enable real-time visualization of co-present users, simplified upload of different types of media and manipulation of that media directly in the browser.

As such, we are faced with a number of interesting challenges, both technical challenges as well as challenges regarding the interaction design. While the design of traditional web-based interfaces has seen extensive coverage in both the academia as well as in the web industry, design of web based shared real-time workspaces has seen less attention. We believe there is a need to explore these types of systems to further the knowledge of how to design collaborative systems in general and real-time shared workspaces in particular.

The Kludd system is developed using a design science research (DSR) methodology (see for example [1], [2]), and at the time of writing the system is entering the second cycle of the process. In this cycle, the evaluation from the initial phase has led to a number of new requirements and, subsequently, changes to the functionality, user interface and interaction model.

This poster will briefly outline the work done on the first phase leading up to the first set of design requirements, and elaborate on the design changes to be implemented in the second phase of the research project.

2. THEORETICAL FOUNDATIONS

As we are utilizing a DSR approach, kernel theories guiding the initial development is of great importance. The two main conceptual models for the system is "Social Translucence", a concept introduced by Erickson & Kellogg [3]. Here, visibility, awareness and accountability are key factors in creating a social system. By visualizing users presence and activities, an awareness of each other is created. And with awareness, the concept of accountability is enabled. The idea is that "I know you are there, I know what you are doing and I can hold you accountable for your actions in this shared environment". And on the flip side, "I know that you know I am here, what I am doing and others can hold me accountable for my actions". We believe this process is essential in a collaboration process, online and otherwise.

The second main kernel theory derives from the concept of calm technology [4], where the user interface is designed to be as unobtrusive as possible, making itself visible when needed or requested.

The features of the system also come from a longitudinal study into awareness and its role in collaborative computing (see Nilsson et al. [5] for more on the longitudinal study). Together with two observation studies and focus groups, the final design requirements for the first phase of the DSR was assembled.

The observation studies were conducted on the teacher's end of an online tutoring session in a higher education setting. The researchers followed the teachers where they set up the sessions using a variety of tools and technologies available to them, such as voice communication, screen sharing applications and e-mail. The audio from the session was recorded and notes were taken at the time and the material was subsequently analyzed revealing areas where the interaction between tutor and student was sub-optimal.

The focus group sessions involved teachers experienced in web-based education. All had been involved in online tutoring and net-based collaboration, and the sessions focused on what type of requirements a tool for collaboration would benefit from.

The next section discusses the outcome of this methodological approach and provides a rationale for the subsequent design requirements.

3. DESIGNING THE KLUDD SYSTEM

A key factor in creating a social system is ability of the system to support the creation, recreation and reinforcement of social norms within the system [5]. An important factor in this ongoing process is to visualize co-present users and their actions. This is also supported by Ericson & Kellogg [3] that suggests that a social system must be able to support the notion of awareness of others through visualization of their activities. Findings from the longitudinal study [5] show that we not only need current visualization, but also a historical insight into what has happened before.

At the same time as there is a need to visualize the actions of other users in the system, both current and historical, there is also a need to enable both real-time and historical conversations between users. Norms are developed and upheld by both words and actions [5].

With the Internet being such a diverse place with computers, tablets and phones used to connect to it, it is important to keep the system as open, platform independent and lightweight as possible to enable as many users as possible to access the system. To further the ease of access, the system should not require a local installation of files. At the observation study, these issues became apparent, with users having trouble running proprietary software due to restrictions to install applications locally on the computer. Such restrictions are common in for example educational institutions, libraries and other public spaces as well as In some workplaces.

Along the same line, storing files in the cloud, thus removing the need for local storage of files that are collaborated around, and linking in resources like for example video from external services into the collaboration system would be beneficial to the system design.

The observation study also revealed a need to easily share documents with each other, preferably with document history. Issues that were prominent in the tutoring session revolved around what had been said at the previous tutoring session and what state the project was in back then.

From the kernel theory of calm technology, we derive the design notion that the system should be unobtrusive, only revealing its user interface when needed. The objects in the system and the awareness of co-present users should be the focus of attention, not the system itself.

The requirements of the system are thus;

1. It should be open and platform independent
2. Not requiring installation
3. Lightweight, or scalable for slower computers
4. Provide historic visualization
5. Enable document sharing
6. Provide real-time awareness visualization
7. Incorporate external connections
8. Provide a platform for discussion
9. Have an unobtrusive interface

The next section will outline the technologies used to develop the system based on these requirements.

3.1 Implementation

As described in the introduction, the Kludd system is developed using standards such as HTML5, and CSS3 and together with advanced javascript libraries and frameworks enables real-time shared workspaces in a browser. The HTML5 specifications enable incorporation of video and sound, and together with CSS3 developers are enabled to create powerful applications run in a modern browser. The HTML5 specifications are not finalized yet, and new features added and old ones altered, making the development of applications using these technologies somewhat cumbersome. To add to the uncertainty of web development with HTML5 and CSS3, modern web browsers such as Google Chrome, Mozilla Firefox, Opera and Microsoft Explorer have different levels of adherence to the current specifications of HTML5. As such, some parts of a web application might work better or worse in some browsers, while some functionality might not work at al in some browsers. As a developer, you must be prepared to handle all variations of browser's specifications.

One of the key features of HTML5 used by the Kludd system is the websocket. Unlike the older uni-directional webserver connection where the server sends the client browser data, the websocket connection is bi-directional enabling real-time communication between the webserver and client browser. In non-technical terms, this means that an action from a user can be sent to the web server, which then propagates this action to all other valid users. The websocket communication is central in the Kludd system, as it forms the foundation of the shared workspace, transferring the real-time data between users in the system.

The next section will provide a description of how the interaction in the Kludd system is modeled.

3.2 Usage description

Upon entering a Kludd (see Figure 1 – note that the system in the first phase was named "CloudBoard"), a user is presented with the objects that users belonging to the Kludd have added or created (or, if the Kludd is new, an empty space). Objects are added by dragging an object to the browser window containing the Kludd and drop it anywhere. This can be any type of file, for example images, PDF files, Microsoft Office documents or video files. Objects can also be added entering a link to an object from the Internet. This can be links to a Vimeo or YouTube video, or an image from Dropbox. Twitter feeds and Instagram links can be added the same way. When an object is added, all other user of the Kludd can see the object being added and can begin to collaborate around it. Different filetypes are visualized in the system in various ways. For example, where an image is shown as is, a video is usually displayed with controls for playing and pausing while a more unusual file type could be displayed with a generic icon symbolizing the file.

An object can be moved, resized and manipulated in various ways (depending on the objects nature) or hidden by any user. Users can also annotate objects with comments. While using the system, other users pointers are visible, so every move a user makes is visible to others. Other users pointers have their respective names attached, so one knows what pointer belongs to whom. Obviously, this is only applicable to users utilizing a computer to access the Kludd. Using a phone or tablet with touch input, a pointer is not visible until the user starts to manipulate an object or tap somewhere in the Kludd.

While the Kludd is mostly a real-time system visualizing current activities, it also incorporates an historical view. Using a slider, users can reverse the Kludd, and see how it looked at any time in the past. Users can follow the build-up of texts, different placements of images etc. In this view, users are also allowed to revive hidden objects on the Kludd, thus making them usable in the real-time view.

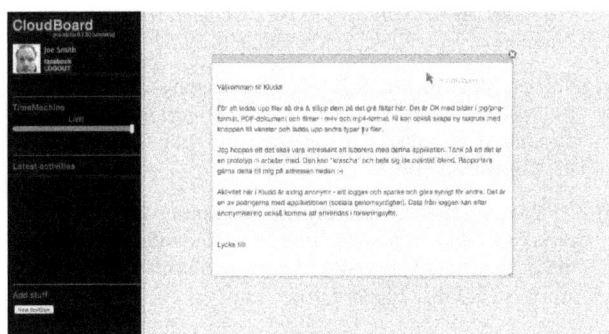

Figure 1. The Kludd System, first phase

3.3 Evaluation

The Kludd system was evaluated using students in an online university course. The students evaluated the system and wrote a report on their experiences using the system in small groups. Each group was given a separate Kludd space to evaluate. The student's reports were used to evaluate the Kludd together with the logs that the system was automatically creating as the students used the system.

The reports were analyzed with the aim to identify different types of problems or errors in the system. The reports and the logs revealed four main issues with the system.

First, as the system used new ways of interaction not familiar to the students, the student's preconceived mental models of how to interact with more traditional functions on a website became an issue. As an example, a text field where users could annotate objects in the Kludd was perceived as a "chat", and evaluated as such. We believe that it is important in the next phase to create a better visual distance between traditional designs of interaction and interaction in a collaborative web system.

Secondly, users expected a multi-modal experience. They stated that seeing the pointers of others moving around while not hearing anyone speak or seeing them was eerie. We believe there is a point in enabling a more rich experience, giving the users an option to enable both sound of others as well as video of each other in the system.

The third aspect involved a hesitation to use the system and skepticism as to the functionality. For example, as users uploaded objects to the Kludd, it was often followed by a text saying, "can you see the image I just uploaded". As the users just see their view in a shared workspace, it would perhaps be a good idea to in some ways notify uploaders that others can see their image.

The fourth issue was with the awareness system itself – users were often not aware of who was logged in and who was doing what. The system was inadequate in making users feel aware of each other and everyone's actions, juxtaposing the actual purpose of the system. This is a main issue that will be addressed in the second phase of DSR process.

As the evaluation of the first phase of the design cycle concluded, it became apparent that the system had to incorporate further design requirements to be sufficient as a real-time shared workspace collaboration tool. The following section will outline the work currently undertaken to formalize the evaluation into design requirements, and the practical work of realizing the new design

4. CONCLUSION

The following additional design requirements can be derived from the evaluation of the first phase of the DSR.

10. Provide visual distance from old interaction models
11. Provide the opportunity to hear and see each other
12. Feedback and confirmation of own actions and what others are seeing in the system
13. Provide a clear, simple awareness visualization

These four requirements together with the original nine, will provide the basis of the Kludd system being built in the second phase of the design science research project. We believe that this project has a potential to add to the body of knowledge on collaborative systems, and more specifically on real-time, shared workspace systems.

4.1 Further work

As the second phase of the project has started at the time of writing, we have begun work on incorporating these new requirements by tweaking the user interface and interaction model. The main focus lies in providing a better way of creating an awareness of the presence and actions of other users, as this is cornerstone in a collaborative system.

We are increasing the visibility of the pointers of co-present users, making their actions more prominent. We also work on better visualizing users entering and leaving the system, making a list of who is present clearer. We are also focus on removing all graphical elements of the system not immediately necessary, thus putting more focus on the objects in the system and the visualization of others' activities. To further the awareness of others, we are including a video conferencing function, where users can engage in more natural conversations alongside visualization of actions within the system. We believe this is going to heighten the feeling of awareness of others in the system, as well as removing the eerie feeling described in the reports.

Further, we are going to work on distancing the interaction models of the Kludd system from traditional interaction models for web based systems. Exploring an interaction design of for example a real-time collaborative text-editing module is a challenge we are facing in this second phase.

Creating a loopback function, where we are going to provide feedback to users that their own actions are visible to others in the shared workspace is going to be a challenge.

Figure 2 shows an early version of the reworked Kludd, though being an interactive system, an image will not make it justice. Here, we have removed much of the interface to the left of the screen, making the controls "on demand", when the users are requesting it.

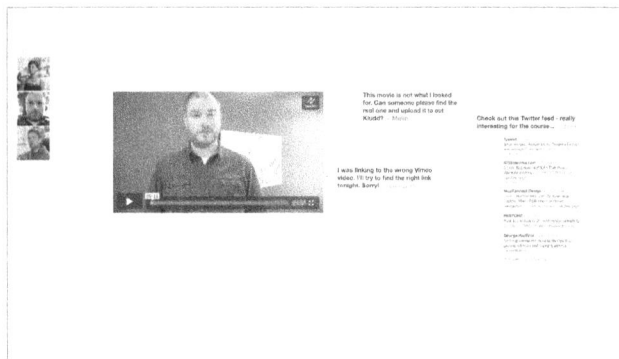

Figure 2. The second phase Kludd

As new users are entering a Kludd, their image is shown for a brief period of time to signal to other users that a new person has joined the Kludd. Further, when a person leaves the system, their image is shown and slowly faded away to symbolize their departure. The faces of those present at the moment are available on demand, so anyone can check to see who is present.

With the second phase of this research project, we hope to be able to shed further light on the aim of this research; to add to the body of knowledge of how to design real-time shared workspaces.

5. REFERENCES

[1] Peffers, K., Tuunanen, T., Rothenberger, M., & Chatterje, S. (2007). A Design Science Research Methodology for Information Systems Research, *Journal of Management Information Systems*, 24(3), 2007, pp. 45-77.

[2] Winter, R. 2008. "Design science research in Europe," *European Journal of Information Systems*, 17, 2008, pp.470–475.

[3] Erickson, T & Kellogg, W. A. 2000. Social translucence: An approach to Designing Systems that Support Social Processes. *ACM Transactions on Computer-Human Interaction*, Vol. 7, No. 1, March 2000, 59-83.

[4] Weiser, M. & Brown, S.J. 1997. The coming age of calm technology, *In Beyond Calculation: The next fifty years of computing*, Denning, P.J. and Metcalfe, R.M. (Eds.), pp. 77-85, Copernicus, 1997.

[5] Nilsson, S. (2010). *Exploring the relationship between awareness information and user activities online*. Licentiate thesis, Goteborg University. Papers in Informatics, Paper 13, April 2010, ISSN 1400-7428

Sound Planet: An Interactive Sound Visualization on the Spherical Display for Group Work

Seong-Hoon Ban
Graduate School of Culture Technology, KAIST
Daejeon, South Korea
bahn@kaist.ac.kr

Kwangyun Wohn
Graduate School of Culture Technology, KAIST
Daejeon, South Korea
wohn@kaist.ac.kr

Figure 1. *Sound Planet* at the DDP(DongDaeMun Design Plaza), Seoul, Korea.

ABSTRACT

Sound Planet is a spherically-shaped interactive installation with the group interaction and the real-time visualization against audiences' voice and singing. The audience approaches the sleeping planet, wakes it up, creates some artifacts such as soil, water, and atmosphere, and then populates it with the life forms, thereby creating a living planet of their own. Its compelling storyline reinforces the audience's experience while the audience - mostly young children - establishes an emotional engagement with the fictitious planet. The installation whose primary purpose is to provide the synesthetic experience to young children has been operational since April 2014, serving about one hundred children and their family per day.

Categories and Subject Descriptors

H.5.3 [**Group and Organization Interface**]: Computer-supported cooperative work

General Terms

Design; Human Factors

Keywords

Sound visualization; Interactive art; Spherical display; Interactive storytelling; Group interaction

1. INTRODUCTION

Sound Planet is an artistic audio/visual installation based on the sound visualization onto a spherical display. It was installed at DDP (DongDaeMun Design Plaza), a new landmark designed by the world-famous architect Zaha Hadid, in Seoul, South Korea.

The installation aims at providing the synesthetic experience to young children, who will design and create a new 'planet' through their voice as the input interface, roughly following the 5-minutes story line [2][4]. The primary reason that *Sound Planet* was designed with sound interaction has to do with the concern on the level of difficulty. The interaction should be designed without high difficulty because the target age of exhibition is young children who cannot understand any sophisticated interaction. The story line consists of singing and voicing so that any audience can easily participate and see the artistic result on the fly [3].

We have studied various technologies for creating interactive multimedia contents on various display systems such as media façade, titled LCD's, and spherical displays. *Sound Planet* is one of our latest attempts where a multitude of audience members interact, collaborate, and most of all, enjoy themselves through the multimedia visualization.

2. SOUND PLANET

2.1 Spherical Display System

The spherical display system has the following advantages over the conventional flat display:

1. **Symmetrical experience:** Each and every participant is treated fairly in the sense that he/she is positioned equally against the installation. In a typical two-dimensional flat display setting, the audience, depending on which part of the display he/she stands at, may exercise different experiences. However, when the audience surrounds the spherical display, any experiential variation by location becomes negligible.

2. **Focused experience:** Participants can easily recognize the object of their own control. Due to the structural characteristics of the spherical screen, the audience perceives images larger and clear at the right angle than on the other side, thereby creating more vivid and engaging experience.

Sound Planet was implemented based on the external projection system with four projectors. Since 2004, we have developed numerous contents for the spherical display [1]. The external Projection system is more complex than the internal projection system, but it can produce brighter and clearer images on the surface [6].

The configuration of the display system consists of one spherical screen, one computer, and four projectors. The diameter of the screen is two meters, and the reflection gain of the surface is close to 1.0. The screen was made of molded two hemispherical screens by welding, and the weight is about 200Kg. The display is installed 40cm above the floor using a horizontal cylinder bar of 76mm in diameter.

Each projector is placed in a position based on a 90-degree angle near the projector and 2.3m, 2.1m, 2.3m, and 3.3m away from the screen. The distance from the ground is 2.1m, so that shadow made by the audience can be minimized. All the projectors are controlled by one computer that four channel displays throughout two graphic cards (GTX760).

The software for *Sound Planet* was coded in Processing[1], which is one of the visual art tools based on Java language. The program makes virtual spherical objects in a three-dimensional virtual space, and four virtual cameras shoot the spherical object at the projector's locations. The images generated from the computer are transmitted to the projectors so that a real spherical displaying is realized.

2.2 Sound Visualization

Although precise and accurate interactions based on the voice/speech recognition may not be realizable, simple and natural interactions based on sound and voice may be appropriate for the spontaneous, multi-user environment [5]. In *Sound Planet*, the pitch detection technique based on FFT (Fast Fourier Transform) and the loudness of voice are used to reflect the audience's intention. *Sound Planet* processes and visualizes the audience's voicing in real-time through the multi-channel audio processing. MAX/MSP[2], simple music software and the OCTA-CAPTULE by ROLAND, an external audio interface are used to handle multi-channels audio signals from the microphone.

The two primary roles of sound are the landscape design and the creature design. *Sound Planet* first paints the landscape with various colors, and then at the following stage, creates four different life forms, all depending on the pitch and loudness.

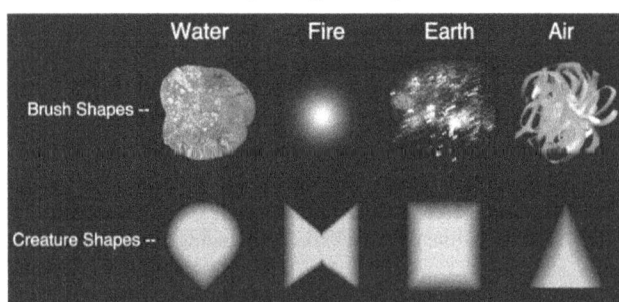

Figure 2. Four-elements metaphor on the *Sound Planet* story line. There are four creatures – fishes, bugs, mammals, and birds, respectively

We borrowed the classical four-element metaphors for the basic story line. The concept of four elements is suitable for the subject

---

[1] Processing - http://www.processing.org

[2] Cycling 74 MAX/MSP - http://cycling74.com/products /max

on how to design a planet. Furthermore, the distinction of the concept is useful to help the audience recognize their interaction feedback with the minimal cognitive load. The concepts of 'water, fire, earth, and air' represent the different shapes of brush in the level of 'Nature of Sound Planet', and it also affects the shapes of artificial creatures (See Figure 2).

3. STORY DESIGN

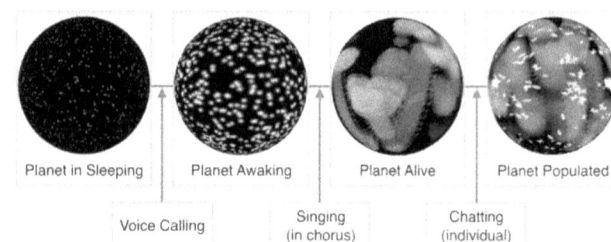

Figure 3. The structure of interactive storytelling.

In numerous literatures, it has been argued that compelling stories reinforce the quality of experiences, especially group experiences. In our *Sound Planet*, the three main points was taken into account. First, the story should enable the audience to participate actively, getting out of the passive participation. The active experience is mainly correlated with physical presence like 'hear sound', 'look at image'. Second consideration point is the nature of the group interaction - either collaboration or competition. For group interaction with the audience of over ten people, it is known that collaboration task is more appropriate. Therefore, the group interaction mainly consists of collaboration task and contains some competition task as well. Last consideration point is functionality. The exhibit should be able to provide fun and learning through the designed story line.

The following interaction techniques were used to express above considerations:

1. Story in steps: The *Sound Planet* responds only to the voices of audience throughout the story run, and it proceeds to next step only when participation is achieved.

2. Visual feedback: In order to express the reaction of a voice effectively, Sound Planet provides visual feedback. It also supports the function of fun and education with artistic visualization using various combination of color.

3. Audio feedback: Appropriate sound effects are provided to induce the audience's action depending on situation.

4. Rotation: affecting range is unavoidably limited because the audience cannot see the whole screen at a time. Therefore, visual components are rotated to enable effective cooperation experience.

5. Characterized agent: Creating characterized agent depending on each participant arouses the competition between the audiences.

The story line of *Sound Planet* incorporates the universal notion of 'Creation of Life'. The story consist of following four steps:

1. **Sleeping Sound Planet:** The Planet looks like a colorless, desolate planet in the beginning. When the audience is gathered and begins to give voices, the Planet begins to react for a little bit of shine. When the participants gathered their voice cooperatively, the story goes to the next step.

2. **Nature of Sound Planet:** After the wake, *Sound Planet* begins to formulate landscape with various colors. The audience controls the different kinds of elements (water, fire, soil, air) depending on the location of the microphone. Because of this difference, the participants should cooperate for making well-decorated *Sound Planet*.

3. **Living Life of Sound Planet:** Having completed the colorful landscape, the living creatures start getting populated. Similarly to the preceding steps, the audience controls the four different creatures depending on the location of the microphone. The participants' singing and voicing can help the creature's liveliness. When the participant makes his voice louder, the bigger creature is created. If the audiences actively participate in the competition, the population of Sound Planet has reached its maximum.

4. **Revived Sound Planet:** In the case where the audience is actively involved, *Sound Planet* expresses its appreciation to the audience with the farewell messages.

Figure 4. Views of the exhibition, proceeding from a) to d).

4. CONCLUSION

From the technical point of view, *Sound Planet* is a novel platform to investigate some of the critical research issues such as information visualization, ubiquitous display systems, natural user interface and multi-user interaction. At the same time, it is a multimedia installation that serves both educational and entertainment purposes. Some of the future work is as follow:

1. Incorporating other voice/music parameters for richer interactions, such as tonality, beat, and voice color.

2. Incorporating other input modalities for richer interaction, such as audience's position and gesture.

3. Incorporating other auxiliary displays such as wall display and mobile displays for richer and more immersive surrounding.

5. ACKNOWLEDGEMENT

This work is partially supported by the NRF and by the BK21 Plus Postgraduate Organization for Content Science.

6. REFERENCES

[1] J. Jin, K. Wohn. 2007. High quality spherical screen projection for space experience, *8th RTT Conference, RTT Emerging Technology Contest*.

[2] K. L. Ma, I. Liao, J. Frazier, H. Hauser, and H. N. Kostis. 2012. Scientific storytelling using visualization, *IEEE Computer Graphics and Applications*, vol.32, pp. 12-19.

[3] T. Hall, L. Bannon. 2005. Designing ubiquitous computing to enhance children's interaction in museum, IDC'05, Proceedings of the 2005 conference on interaction design and children page 62-69.

[4] N. Gershon, W. Page. 2001. What storytelling can do for information visualization, *Communications of the ACM*, v.44 n.8, p.31-37, Aug.

[5] P. Kortum. 2008. HCI beyond the GUI: design for haptic, speech, olfactory and other nontraditional interfaces, *Morgan Kaufmann*.

[6] T. R. Ligon. 2002. Spherical image projection system using a convex reflecting image dispersing element, Google Patents.

[7] P. Dewan, R. Choudhary. 1992. A High-Level and Flexible Framework for Implementing Multiuser Interfaces, ACM Transactions on Information Systems, Vol. 10, No.4m October 1992, Pages 345-380.

Evaluating Mobile Remote Presence (MRP) Robots

Tristan Lewis
The MITRE Corporation
202 Burlington Rd
Bedford, MA 01730
+1 (781) 271-5380
tmlewis@mitre.org

Jill L. Drury
The MITRE Corporation
202 Burlington Rd
Bedford, MA 01730
+1 (781) 271-2034
jldrury@mitre.org

Brandon Beltz
The MITRE Corporation
7515 Colshire Drive
McLean, VA 22102
+1 (703) 983-4997
bbeltz@mitre.org

ABSTRACT

Video teleconferencing systems (VTCs) have enhanced remote meetings because their ability to convey nonverbal or social cues can make them simulate in-person interaction more closely than telephone conversations. Yet many people feel that something is still lacking, most likely because VTCs require all interaction to take place in a pre-defined set of rooms and/or from a single viewpoint. In contrast, mobile remote presence (MRP) robots, sometimes called telepresence robots, enable participants to move their focus from their colleagues' faces to a screen at the front of the room, to artifacts on a table, to posters or sticky notes on the room's walls, etc. Consumers now have a choice of several commercially available MRP systems, but there are few evaluation methods tailored for this type of system. In this paper we present a proposed set of heuristics for evaluating the user experience of a MRP robot. Further, we describe the process we used to develop these heuristics.

Categories and Subject Descriptors

H.5.3 [**Group and Organization Interfaces**]: Computer-supported cooperative work

General Terms

Human Factors, Experimentation

Keywords

Human Robot Interaction, Heuristics, MRP, Telepresence, Robotics, Usability, Robot.

1. INTRODUCTION

VTCs can be thought of as telepresence (stationary remote presence) systems. Sheridan described telepresence as a remote human operator receiving "sufficient information about the teleoperator and the task environment, displayed in a sufficiently natural way, that the operator feels physically present at the remote site." [10, pg. 6] Rosenberg defined telepresence as "a human-computer interface which allows a user to take advantage of natural human abilities when interacting with an environment other than the direct surroundings" [8]: in other words, a system that can enable users to interact naturally with a remote environment. Steuer defined telepresence as "the experience of presence in an environment by means of a communication medium" [9, pg. 74] the feeling of "being there." [9, pg. 76]

Mobile telepresence robots (that is, mobile remote presence, or MRP, robots) can provide a more flexible telepresence experience than VTCs by allowing participants to have some degree of mobility in the remote environment. MRP robots are typically a mobile platform with some form of audio/video system installed on them. The increased mobility allows remote participants a greater degree of agency, as opposed to a fixed-place video camera and screen.

Due to a number of technical achievements in the past ten years, there has been an increase in the number and variety of MRP robotic products available. Often they are specialized to a specific environment such as elder care (e.g., Giraff, manufactured by Giraff Technologies AB), health care (e.g., RP-7 by InTouch Health), or as an office product (e.g., the MantaroBot TeleMe by Mantaro). Currently there are robots with a wide variety of capabilities and price ranges on the market [4]. There has been an increased interest in the use of MRP robots by geographically diverse companies as a way to facilitate remote employees' collaboration, as well as to reduce travel expenses. With the increasing cost of travel, it often does not take long to recoup the investment in a MRP system.

Our company owns several VGo robots, which we have been using to study the social aspects of MRPs in office settings. Over the course of several years of using this robot, we have established an understanding of the capabilities and challenges associated with this particular model. We also developed a base of users who are familiar with its operation.

Thanks to iRobot's generosity in lending us their new MRP robot, the iRobot Ava 500, recently we had a chance to evaluate this robot in our corporate environment. The Ava is a very different robot from the VGo, as can be seen by comparing their characteristics in Table 1. It is pictured in Figure 1.

We wished to learn as much as possible about the Ava, but did not have the luxury of evaluating the system in multiple ways over a period of years as we had done with the VGo. In fact, we only had two days with the Ava, and the first day needed to be devoted to the technical integration of the system into our VTC network. Thus we were faced with the challenge of performing an evaluation very quickly that would yield insights into how well the robot would be likely to fit our collaboration needs and work environment.

Permission to make digital or hard copies of all or part of this work for personal or classroom use is granted without fee provided that copies are not made or distributed for profit or commercial advantage and that copies bear this notice and the full citation on the first page. Copyrights for components of this work owned by others than ACM must be honored. Abstracting with credit is permitted. To copy otherwise, or republish, to post on servers or to redistribute to lists, requires prior specific permission and/or a fee. Request permissions from permissions@acm.org.

GROUP'14, November 9–12, 2014, Sanibel Island, Florida, USA.

Copyright © 2014 ACM 978-1-4503-3043-5/14/11…$15.00.

http://dx.doi.org/10.1145/2660398.2663777

2. METHODOLOGY

When usability engineers need to evaluate a system quickly, they often turn to heuristic evaluation [6] because this method has been shown to uncover a large fraction of the system's potential interaction problems within a short period of time [7]. While we know of a specialized heuristic evaluation method for assistive robotics, which encompasses some forms of MRP robots [11], we have not seen a heuristic evaluation technique aimed specifically at MRP robots. We thought it would be useful to create such a set of heuristics for MRP robots. Since a number of different types of MRP robots are becoming more widely available, we felt that others may also find such a method to be useful.

Table 1. Characteristics of Two MRP Systems

Characteristic	VGo	Ava 500
Manufacturer	VGo Communications, Inc.	iRobot
Cost	Approx. $6,000	Approx. $70,000
Integration with existing Video teleconferencing systems	No	Yes
Obstacle detection	Yes, but limited to a range of inches	Yes, with a range of several feet
Obstacle avoidance	No	Yes
Weight	19 lbs.	170 lbs.
Camera resolution	640x480	1080p
Screen size	6"	21.5"
Screen resolution	640x480	1080p
Height	48"	Adjustable from 52.5" to 64.5"
Adjustable camera angle	Yes	Yes
Autonomous navigation	No	Yes
Requires mapping of area before use	No	Yes
Self docking	Yes, within feet	Yes, from anywhere

Coincidentally, some of our research group members have been investigating the state-of-the-art of specialized heuristics: those heuristics that are aimed at a class of systems or interfaces instead of being a general-purpose set that can be used to evaluate almost any type of computer-based application (such as Nielsen's heuristics [7]). As part of our investigations, we have been examining best practices for developing these sets of heuristics. We saw an opportunity to exercise these best practices to create a set of heuristics suitable for evaluating MRP robot systems.

After examining 60 specialized heuristic sets, we saw some commonalities in how they were developed. Some developers relied heavily upon Nielsen's heuristics [7], some incorporated theoretical- or empirical-based literature, and some used empirical evaluation methods such as field observation or previously

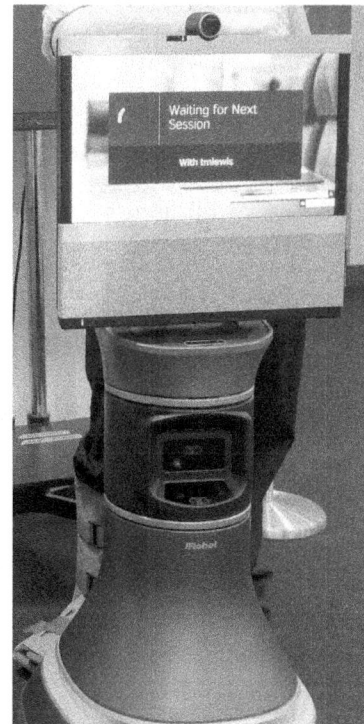

Figure 1. Ava 500 robot is preparing to connect to a remote operator. It is shown in the lower height position.

submitted usability issue reports to create categories of usability problems which were then turned into heuristics. Because there are strengths associated with each approach, we believe it is a best practice to combine all three.

Accordingly, we examined the literature for principles that, if followed, could lead to MRP designs that avoid problems observed in empirical investigations. For example, Lee and Takayama used a combination of critical incident interviews, surveys, and observations to identify problems with MRP systems and develop principles to avoid them [5].

To begin gathering empirical data, we reached out to our MRP user community to solicit comments on their experiences. We asked them questions aimed at eliciting both the positive and negative aspects of using an MRP in an office environment. These operators often used the VGo in meetings that emphasized information sharing and information building. We also gathered observations based on seeing VGo robots used for department meetings and corporate-sponsored social events.

Ideally, we wished to have a set of heuristics prior to the period in which we could use the Ava robot, so that we could use them to evaluate the Ava. This approach would imply that the empirical information used to develop the heuristics would be confined to VGo-related data. Yet we knew we would have a richer set of data if we could gather at least some from using the Ava. Consequently we decided to use our brief time with the Ava to gather empirical data that could inform heuristic development.

During the loan period, we had a chance to use the Ava for a large meeting with breakout sessions in the main conference room and several remote participants. This was a "real" meeting in the sense that it was not a contrived event whose purpose was to evaluate the Ava. The primary purposes of this meeting were to share information and brainstorm ideas. We recruited one of the remote participants to use the Ava. We arranged to interview that participant after the event using a set of questions developed based on our knowledge of the VGo.

We used the grounded theory qualitative analysis method [3] to analyze the observation data from both robots to surface positive and negative experiences. When analyzing the data, we remained alert for issues that are especially pertinent to MRP robotics in contrast with general-purpose software or computer-supported cooperative systems hosted on conventional (that is, non-mobile) computer systems. For example, we envisioned that collaborators' and bystanders' safety would be a concern in MRP robotics.

Grounded theory results in groupings of data based on similarities of the data within a group in a relevant dimension. We compiled a list of comments and impressions from our MRP users of both Ava and VGo. We then looked for common themes in these comments, which resulted in thematic groupings. These groupings evolved into heuristics.

3. HEURISTICS AND SUPPORTING OBSERVATIONS

3.1 Minimize driving costs
We have seen two approaches for navigating a MRP to a specific location. These two options depend on the level of autonomy of the particular MRP. The first is for the MRP to be driven directly to specific location by the operator. This can be a tedious task, often requiring several minutes of navigating down long hallways. The VGo robot is an example of this type of MRP. The second option requires a much higher degree of autonomy. The operator selects a location, and the MRP autonomously navigates to the location. Once there, it alerts the operator of its location and availability. The Ava is an example of this type of MRP.

The remote user of the VGo presses the arrow keys on the preconfigured laptop in the direction they want the robot to travel. Alternatively, operators can use a mouse on a half circle on the UI. This half circle represents the amount of forward translation and rotation commands that could be issued to the robot. The robot will not move without these commands being issued by a user.

Prior to normal use, the Ava requires a pre-mapped area of operations to show it the physical limitations of the room. Additionally, the Ava has multiple sensors that fuse information for advanced obstacle detection and avoidance capacities. This approach allows the Ava to autonomously navigate to a given location without any input from the user other than the initial command to move to a specific point. Once the robot has autonomously reached its location, it alerts the user and establishes a video teleconference between the two end points. Essentially it is possible for operators to point on a map to where they want the robot to be located and the robot will autonomously drive to that location.

This autonomous approach resolves an issue noted by Lee and Takayama, who found "The most frequently mentioned downside was the burden of driving. Pilots reported that the hassle of driving the MRP to go to a meeting room made the MRP system less useful and efficient" [5, pg 38]. Long stretches of driving without useful interaction are clearly burdensome to the operator.

3.2 Allow flexible use
The "M" (mobility) in MRP allows for certain freedoms and benefits in addition to those offered by traditional VTC telepresence. Benefits include being able to travel to a remote individual's office, participating in side conversations, moving between break-out sessions, dynamically switching viewpoints between different areas and artifacts, and taking part in group discussions while being able to make greater use of body language. We saw these benefits manifested in the Ava's travels among breakout tables, which could not occur using a traditional VTC.

A similar heuristic is included in Nielsen's heuristic set [7] and is also discussed in Lee and Takayama [5].

3.3 Design the MRP to elicit the appropriate amount of interaction from humans collocated with the robot
One common thread among the users was the lack of courtesy of other people regarding the robot as a stand-in for another person. Often they found that people would walk in front of the robot and block it in seemingly unintentional ways. We observed one person interject themselves into a conversation between the Ava and another person. This interjecting person then maneuvered his body to block the view of the robot. We believe that people did not always see the robot as a full avatar for its remote user, since the robot was not accorded the same spatial considerations as another person. The Ava operator explicitly commented about it being difficult to start a conversation with remote colleagues because of this effect.

3.4 Ensure safety
One comment received from the co-present meeting participants is that the Ava robot moves at a fast pace when it is autonomously navigating. While the sensors prevent it form running into objects or people, the robot startled several meeting participants, who feared it might run into them. This heuristic is also included in Tsui [11].

Safety is obviously an important feature; it would be unfortunate to have the robot cause injuries to other meeting participants. One study showed that if the robot operator is engaged in a secondary task as cognitively simple as pushing a correct button, their ability to safely operate the robot was drastically reduced [2]. A co-occurring task with a higher cognitive load, such as having a technical discussion, could obviously distract the operator more, thus increasing the risk of creating damage due to a driving error. It is for these reasons we included safety as a key design focus.

3.5 Provide operators with awareness of the rationale for the robot's autonomy-influenced behaviors
Ava's operator was frustrated when the robot's autonomous algorithms prevented it from getting as close to the table as the operator desired. (Note that the operator had not had a chance to be trained on the "push" mode that would have enabled him to place the robot in contact with the table.) In this case, the operator did not know that the autonomy "safety" algorithm was keeping the robot from driving very close to the table.

This same safety algorithm caused the robot to drive around obstacles the operator could not see, thus surprising the operator when the robot did not travel in a straight line.

3.6 Provide feedback regarding system state

The system state includes the status of the MRP, the operator interfaces, and their connection to each other.

Often VGo users encountered problems with obstacles, which stopped the VGo from moving. The operator was not alerted that the MRP was unable to move. This left the operator unsure if the commands were received, the motor was not working, or if the MRP was in an unmovable state.

The Ava operator commented about the controls for operating the robot being overlaid on the map, so he was unable to use both the controls and the map at the same time. This design decision may have been a tradeoff due the limited screen size of the user interaction device, an iPad mini.

Note that this heuristic is similar to one in Nielsen's heuristic set [7].

3.7 Provide for an immersive operator experience

Robots represent their operators, and thus through the robots the operators should be able to experience as many sights and sounds as they would if they were co-located with other participants. This sense of immersion is based on having sufficient sensory experiences to enable operators to feel as though they are "being there." Lee and Takayama [5] describe the importance of achieving a feeling of immersion.

In the case of our observations, operators of both the VGo and Ava robots wished that they had a zoom feature to view artifacts as though they were physically picking them up and examining them closely. We also found that users of both robots experienced difficulty with visual light balance problems. Whenever users looked at a screen or a projection they were effectively blinded: the light from a projector or screen was too bright and users could neither see what was being presented, nor the rest of the meeting participants—effectively ruining any feeling of immersion.

One common comment of the VGo users was that the field of view was not wide enough to see two other people sitting at a medium sized table, again eliminating a feeling of immersion. Further, VGo users commented that the camera did not have a high enough resolution to read what was written on the white board in the room. In contrast, the Ava user appreciated the full HD video and thought it contributed very positively to his interactions.

4. FUTURE WORK

MRP robots in a corporate work environment have seen a lot of growth and development in the past few years. It is an area that we expect to see both technological advancement and new social mores develop in the future. Based on the Ava and VGo observations, many employees are not used to seeing a robot in the workplace, which means that there is the opportunity to study the social interactions as they evolve with increased familiarity.

Future work will focus on validating these heuristics. We plan to use these heuristics to assess additional MRP systems in the workplace, and compare the results to those obtained by performing both an evaluation using Nielsen's heuristics and a formal usability test.

In addition, it may be fruitful to investigate the potential relationship between the heuristics proposed here and the heuristics that have been proposed specifically for collaborative systems, such as Baker et al.'s [1] heuristics for groupware based on the mechanics of collaboration.

5. ACKNOWLEDGMENTS

We would like to thank iRobot for lending us their robot. We would like to thank Amanda Anganes for consultation regarding specialized heuristic evaluation, and others of the MITRE Corporation who participated in the evaluation. This work was funded by the Collaboration and Social Computing Department. All product names, trademarks, and registered trademarks are the property of their respective holders. Photo by Julia McHugh of The MITRE Corporation. © 2014 The MITRE Corporation. All Rights Reserved. Approved for Public Release; distribution unlimited; case #14-2538.

6. REFERENCES

[1] Baker, K., Greenberg, S., and Gutwin, C. 2001. Heuristic evaluation of groupware based on the mechanics of collaboration. *Proceedings of the 8th IFIP Working Conference on Engineering for Human-Computer Interaction (EHCI'01)*, Toronto, Canada, May.

[2] Carlson, T. and Demiris, Y. 2010. Increasing robotic wheelchair safety with collaborative control: Evidence from secondary task experiments. *Robotics and Automation (ICRA), 2010 IEEE International Conference* Anchorage, Alaska, *(ICRA), 2010 IEEE International Conference* 5582-5587

[3] Glaser, B. and Strauss, A. L. 1967. *The discovery of Grounded Theory: Strategies for qualitative research.* Aldine Publishing Co., Chicago, IL.

[4] Kristoffersson, A., Coradeschi, S., and Loutfi, A. 2013. A review of mobile robotic telepresence. *Adv. in Hum.-Comp. Int.* 2013, Article 3 (January 2013).

[5] Lee, M.K. and Takayama, L. 2011. "Now, I have a body": uses and social norms for mobile remote presence in the workplace. In *Proceedings of the SIGCHI Conference on Human Factors in Computing Systems* (CHI '11). ACM, New York, NY, USA, 33-42.

[6] Molich, R. and Nielsen, J. 1990. Improving a human-computer dialog. *Communications of the ACM*, 33(3), 338 – 348, March.

[7] Nielsen, J. 1994. Enhancing the explanatory power of usability heuristics. In *Proceedings of the SIGCHI Conference on Human Factors in Computing Systems* (CHI '94), Beth Adelson, Susan Dumais, and Judith Olson (Eds.). ACM, New York, NY, USA, 152-158.

[8] Rosenberg, L. 1994. Virtual haptic overlays enhance performance in telepresence tasks. In *Proc. SPIE 2351, Telemanipulator and Telepresence Technologies*, Boston, MA, October 31, 1994.

[9] Steuer, J. 1992. Defining Virtual Reality: Dimensions Determining Telepresence. *Journal of Communication*, 42, 4, 73-93.

[10] Sheridan, T. B. 1992. Musings on telepresence and virtual presence. *Presence: Teleoper. Virtual Environ.* 1, 1 (January 1992), 120-126.

[11] Tsui, K.M., Abu-Zahra, K. Renato, C., M'Sadoques, J., and Drury, J. 2010. Developing heuristics for assistive robotics. In *Proceedings of the 5th ACM/IEEE International Conference on Human-robot Interaction* (HRI '10). IEEE Press, Piscataway, NJ, USA, 193-194.

Designing Meaningful Participation: Analyzing Contribution Patterns in an Alternate Reality Game

Nassim JafariNaimi
School of Literature, Media and Communication
Georgia Institute of Technology
TSRB 320, 85 5th ST NW, Atlanta, GA nassim@gatech.edu

Eric M. Meyers
The iSchool@UBC
University of British Columbia
1961 East Mall, Vancouver, BC
eric.meyers@ubc.ca

Allison Trumble
The iSchool@UBC
University of British Columbia
1961 East Mall, Vancouver, BC
a.trumble@alumni.ubc.ca

ABSTRACT

This article presents an analysis of participation patterns of an Alternate Reality game World Without Oil. This game aims to bring people together in an online environment to reflect and share insights about oil dependence. We present a series of participation profiles based on a quantitative analysis of 1554 contributions to the game narrative made by 322 players. We build on these profiles to suggest a preliminary outline of design challenges for building effective interactive learning environments that foster meaningful participation.

Author Keywords
Alternate Reality Games; ARGs; Participation; Learning

ACM Classification Keywords
H.5.m. Information interfaces and presentation (e.g., HCI): Miscellaneous.

INTRODUCTION

The idea of using games for learning is commonplace in discourse on education today [e.g., 3, 12]. Alternate Reality games (ARGs) are a specific set of games that are based on collaborative problem solving and storytelling. These games have been part of the gaming landscape since around 2001 as transmedia entertainment or promotional pieces for product launches [5, 7, 8]. Recently, a second wave of ARGs seeks to address societal issues (e.g., poverty and hunger) through widespread collaboration. These simulations function as "public pedagogies" that engage a wide range of audiences. It's been further argued that such environments are a powerful means of engaging participants in awareness-building, collective intelligence, and participatory forms of learning [6, 9, 10]

However, much of the current literature on the success of ARGs as educational environments relies heavily on the

observations of ARG designers and developers [e.g., 1] as opposed to empirical evidence of the learning outcomes (with few exceptions such as [2]). If we are to take the claims of ARG proponents seriously, we need to address key questions, among them: what are the kinds of engagement fostered in these environments?; and do those engagements support the learning objectives sought by their designers?

This paper presents a preliminary study of one ARG, called World Without Oil (WWO) to address the above questions [13]. Based on quantitative analysis of player responses, we put forward a set of participation profiles that characterize different levels of engagement. We draw on these participation profiles to outline a set of challenges for designing ARGs that foster sustained engagement and desirable learning outcomes.

BACKGROUND AND PREVIOUS WORK

ARGs are multi-player narratives that involve online and offline participation using a variety of tasks, challenges, puzzles, and prompts to engage players in co-constructing a fictional scenario. One or more "puppet masters" guide the narrative and serve as architects of user participation by drawing on player engagement to alter the narrative flow, encouraging specific forms of participation, or redirecting player efforts. As an emergent, interactive problem-based story, the ARG genre combines elements from live action role-play, transmedia storytelling, and cooperative games.

One of the key characteristics of ARGs is the requirement for players to perform tasks or act in the world and then document and report these actions as part of their participation in the game. The online and offline components constitute different kinds of engagement that may be considered a kind of "move". Some moves are public, as when a player documents or responds to the game through social media, a blog post, or a public action at the prompt of other players or the puppet masters. Some of these moves may be private, as when a player changes his awareness, behavior, or attitude concerning the topic of game play. The moves, in aggregate, constitute the narrative of the game. One can argue that multiple narratives are created in this process: the personal or private narrative, comprised of the individual's self-constructed "story" of the game and their part in it, and the social or public narrative, which is the combined effort of all the players including the puppet masters.

The interplay between these public and private narratives is where ARGs have the potential to be rich spaces for learning and knowledge construction. As players engage in reflection on their own moves and the moves of others, they are experiencing a form of learning through individual and collective storytelling and listening [4]. The quality of this learning depends on the level and quality of the participatory opportunities offered by the game narrative, and the extent to which players engage with the narrative and each other [11]. Thus, analyzing participation patterns in these collaborative narratives is an important aspect of understanding how ARGs work as informal learning environments.

WORLD WITHOUT OIL

World Without Oil (WWO) is a massively collaborative imagining of the first 32 weeks of a global oil crisis. Designed by Ken Eklund (Creative Director) and Jane McGonigal (Participation Architect), the game aims to bring people together around a shared concern, namely getting them to reflect and share insights about oil dependence with the aim of devising plausible and effective courses of action in response to it. The design team sought to elicit this response by posting the news of an imaginary oil crisis on their website for the period of 32 days starting April 30, 2007. Each day represented a week of the crisis. Players engaged with the game by imagining how such news might change their life and local environment as well as the steps they were taking to respond to this imaginary crisis. WWO is a learning environment based on two central concepts that are highlighted by the designers: positive behavior change and collective intelligence.

Positive Behavior Change
The first concept central to the design of WWO is that individuals are creative and capable of initiating change, yet in real life they lack the motivation to change or take action. As a result, the game aims to provide motivation and remove the negative pressures associated with making changes in real life. According to McGonigal, real life can be "fixed" by creating scenarios and reward systems that motivate people to act in more positive ways. These scenarios can be applied to a range of tasks and activities ranging from household chores to "saving the world" [9].

Collective Intelligence
The second concept that is central to the design of WWO is the ability of a diverse group of people with different life experiences to devise innovative solutions to complex problems. Being experts in their own needs, it is individuals who can best imagine how their everyday practices might change in a hypothetical situation such as an oil crisis. By engaging in realistic scenarios and stories, players are contributing to a collective intelligence on the issue of oil dependence. Through their participation, players learn by heightening their awareness of environmental issues and changing their behavior in ways that lessen their dependence on oil. At the same time, the entire community can learn from the players' responses because they present a diversity of ways that one might prepare for and/or survive in a world without oil. These two kinds of learning depend on active participation by players. In what follows we analyze and reflect on this participation.

METHOD
According to the WWO website, over 1900 people signed up as players and submitted over 1500 stories with over 60,000 active observers [13]. However, these numbers tell us very little about the character of participation, and how individual contributors shaped the game narrative. To better understand participation patterns at a granular level, we constructed a database of participant contributions – an aggregate record of the game narrative – that we could explore both quantitatively and qualitatively.

Basic metadata about participation in the game is hosted in two places: on the archived WWO site itself and in an offsite archive set up by the game designers in partnership with the Internet Archive's Wayback Machine. While the WWO site still exists, many of the links to the original posts are no longer valid. The game archive captured 94% of the content from the posts made during the game's duration of 32 days (with some gaps most likely related to participants deleting their own posts prior to the construction of the archive). Our database includes 86 audio files, 1274 blog entries, 116 images, and 75 videos.

FINDINGS
It has been noted that World Without Oil attracted 60,000 unique views and over 1600 contributions from players across several continents [13]. At face value, these seem like impressive numbers. However, when exploring in detail we see that engaged participation was not as broad as these numbers might suggest. Furthermore, our analysis reveals high attrition rates among participants early in the simulation, and a small number of contributors authoring the majority of the narrative.

Participation Patterns
The overall participation trend shows a sharp decline at the beginning, with the first day being the highest participation date, strong declines over the first five days, and then steady decline in posting with a brief uptick at the end (Figure 1).

If we use participation in the game narrative as one measure of engagement, we can break participation into three groups: limited, moderate and high engagement. We considered limited engagement 4 or fewer posts (an average of once per week of the simulation or less); 227 of the 308 participants (excluding designers) fall into this category, accounting for 367 posts. Moderate engagement was set at 5–9 contributions to the game; 38 participants engaged at this level, accounting

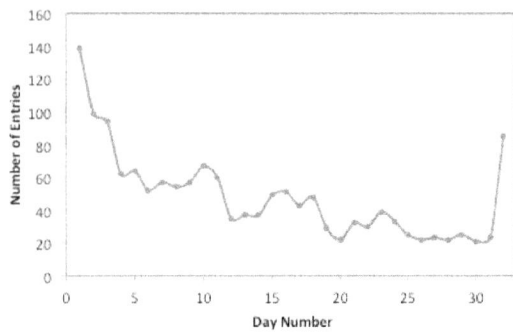

Figure 1: Total number of entries per day versus days passed

for 244 posts. There were 43 high-engagement players, those who submitted 10 or more posts accounting for 827 posts.

With an open game narrative like WWO, one would expect there to be more persons interested in observing the simulation than active players constructing the narrative. However, we see the ratio of engaged participants to lurkers even smaller than expected. The 30 most frequent participants (top 10% by number of posts) accounted for roughly 50% of contributions. The 60 most frequent participants (top 20%) accounted for roughly 67% of contributions. These ratios are slightly better than the 80-20 rule, a marketing maxim which suggests that 20% of customers produce 80% of sales. However, the number of unique hits on the site during the 32 days of the simulation numbered over 60,000. The number of contributors, then, is less than 1% of all those who expressed interest in the simulation itself. Furthermore, we see that the ratio of highly engaged participants to all participants is exceptionally small, with only a few dozen contributors accounting for most of the narrative, and over 50% attrition of active contributors at the midway point of the simulation.

Player Participation Profiles
Game participation patterns, when examined at the level of the individual contributor, reveal a number of "profiles" or clusters of participant behavior:

Toe-Dippers – These players posted a single contribution, or in 13 cases contributed two times on the same day, but thereafter did not contribute again. We identified 150 players as Toe-Dippers, 46.6% of active contributors. The majority of Toe-Dippers contributed early in the game; 57% contributed in the first five days and 87% in the first 16.

Lurkers – These players also posted a single contribution to the game narrative, but on the final day of the simulation and with some evidence in the post that they had been reading and engaging with the WWO story. We identified 18 Lurkers, comprising 5.6% of contributors. We call out this group as they demonstrate the kind of summative reflection that may be overlooked by exploring the player profiles strictly algorithmically.

Drop-Outs – These players posted frequently in the early days of the simulation then fell away by the middle, with no posts past the mid-way point of the game. We labeled 65

players as Drop-Outs, 20.2% of players. Of these, 24 players posted 3 or more times in the first five days, but were not heard from again, suggesting initial excitement that did not lead to continued engagement.

Late-Comers – Late-Comers were players who joined the game in the second half of the simulation, contributing regularly between days 20 and 32. Some of this later interest may have been driven by documentation of WWO on public radio, which partially funded the development of the game. The Late-Comers account for 15 players, only 4.7% of active contributors. This includes some participants who did not actively contribute to the game narrative until the final week.

Regulars – Only 39 players (12.1% of active contributors) participated steadily throughout the game, posting 5 or more times (greater than once per week) including posts in the final days of the simulation. We used standard deviation to account for post spread to eliminate players who may have posted a flurry of contributions in the final week (distinguishing Late-Comers from Regulars). The Hyper-Engaged, a subset of this group, totaled 9 players, posting more than 25 times apiece. Although they comprised 1/8 of the players, this group – along with the game designers – submitted nearly half the narrative content.

DISCUSSION
In this section, we go back to our research questions and discuss how this initial overview of participation begins to answer them. *What are the kinds of engagement fostered in these environments and do those engagements support the learning objectives sought by the game designers?*

At the most basic level we see a high drop in participation after the first few days, raising the question of how varied mechanisms such as diverse storylines, feedback, or varied kinds of content may be used to sustain participation. For example, an important element in maintaining player interest in games is feedback. Ipsatic feedback (how you are doing relative to your own prior play) and normative feedback (how you are doing relative to all players) permit participants a richer understanding of the game and how their contributions construct the game narrative. Real-time feedback during the game – such as personalized reminders, return prompts, or other tools commonly employed by commercial sites and social networks to increase and sustain user engagement – may also be used productively to sustain interest and engagement in the game.

The participation profiles outlined in the previous section enable a more detailed assessment of participation in WWO than has previously been possible. They also serve as an analytical tool to guide thinking about meaningful engagements in such environments. For example, we might consider the presence and contribution of "Toe-Dippers" and "Drop-Outs" in the overall success of the game as a learning environment. These players are able to enter the space because of the low barrier to participation and no commitment requirements. Ease of entry to the game is arguably important for inviting people to try a novel experience; furthermore it helps create the excitement and sense of collective mission that is key to building momentum. At the same time, these players may misguide more committed players and masters regarding the game's initial success.

The Hyper-Engaged players pose a different but related challenge. These players' engagement and participation is important to the success of the game, as their frequent contributions keep the narrative fresh and moving. At the same time the intensity of their participation might dominate the flow and direction of the narrative at the expense of marginal voices. This goes against one of the central concepts of ARGs: their ability to bring together players with diverse backgrounds and experiences, thus enabling the entire player community to learn.

Future ARGs might employ the profiles developed from this exploration to balance the number of "Toe-Dippers" and "Drop-Outs", increasing long-term engagement and improving the likelihood of fostering learning and change from the game experience. While the algorithmic nature of the profiles may change to suit a particular game experience, the five profiles we propose can serve as patterns off of which participation designers can craft better game mechanics.

FUTURE WORK
The construction of a database to analyze participation patterns has permitted us a unique view of WWO. This view stands in contrast to the mainstream discussions of ARGs that rely heavily on overall participation statistics and anecdotal evidence from designers or a small set of players. Our preliminary analysis shows that participation is varied across players in ways that may inhibit some of the stated learning objectives. Our next step in this direction is qualitative analysis of the content generated by players to gain a better understanding of how participants develop their personal story in the game, how the collective narrative of the game unfolds, and whether and how these narratives indicate individual or collective learning by the participants.

CONCLUSION
Extended multi-player game experiences have a variety of players and participation levels. A balance of player types and commitments is required for an environment to support learning. We suggest that cultivating effective play, particularly that which leads to learning and change, demands cultivating commitment from more than a handful of devoted contributors. Understanding, predicting, and designing for player participation will likely result in more powerful game experiences. Our future analysis will complement this initial work by enabling more nuanced and comprehensive understandings of ARG play with implications for the design of other interactive learning environments.

REFERENCES
1. Bonsignore, B. 2012. Designing alternate reality games. In *CHI '12 Extended Abstracts on Human Factors in Computing Systems* (CHI EA '12). ACM, New York, NY, USA, 911–914.

2. Boskic, N., Dobson, T., and Rusnak, P. 2008. Play it seriously: Juxtaposing AR and RW crises. In *Proceedings of the 2nd European Conference on Games Based Learning*. Barcelona, Spain.

3. Gee, J. P. 2004. *What video games have to teach us about learning and literacy*. New York: Palgrave Macmillan

4. Greeno, J. G., Collins, A., and Resnick, L. B. 1996. Cognition and learning. In (D. Berliner and R. Calfee, eds.) *Handbook of Educational Psychology*. Macmillan: New York, NY, USA, 15 – 46.

5. Gurzick, D., White, K. F., Lutters, W. J, Landry, B. M., Dombrowski, C, and Kim, J. Y. 2011. Designing the future of collaborative workplace systems: lessons learned from a comparison with alternate reality games. In *Proceedings of the 2011 iConference* (iConference '11). ACM, New York, NY, USA, 174 –180.

6. Hayes, E. and Gee, J. P. 2011. Public pedagogy through video games. In (J. Sandlin, B. Schultz and J. Burdick, eds.) *Handbook of public pedagogy: Education and learning beyond schooling*. New York: Routledge.

7. Jenkins, J. 2006. *Convergence culture: Where old and new media collide*. New York: NYU Press.

8. Kim, J., Allen, J. P., and Lee, E. 2008. Alternate reality gaming. *Comm. of the ACM*, 51 (2), 36

9. McGonigal, J. 2011. *Reality is broken: Why games make us better and how they can change the world*. NY: Penguin.

10. McGonigal, J. 2008. Why I Love Bees: A case study in collective intelligence gaming. In (Katie Salen, ed.) *The Ecology of Games: Connecting Youth, Games and Learning*, pp 199 – 228. Cambridge, MA: MIT Press.

11. Pelletier, C. 2009 Games and learning: What's the connection? *International J. of Learning and Media* 1, 1, 83 – 101.

12. Salen, K. 2008. *The Ecology of Games: Connecting Youth, Games, and Learning*. The John D. and Catherine T. Macarthur Foundation Series on Digital Media and Learning. Cambridge, MA: MIT Press.

13. World Without Oil, http://worldwithoutoil.org

Human-Robot Interaction in Groups:
Theory, Method, and Design for Robots in Groups

Lionel P. Robert Jr.
University of Michigan
Ann Arbor, MI, USA
+1-734-764-5296
lprobert@umich.edu

Sangseok You
University of Michigan
Ann Arbor, MI, USA
+1-734-730-4124
sangyou@umich.edu

ABSTRACT

For the last decade, robots have been adopted into group work ranging from corporate offices to military operations. While robotic technology has matured enough to allow robots to act as team members, our understanding of how this alters group work is limited. In particular, little work has examined how the adoption of robots might alter group processes and outcomes. The purpose of this workshop is to bring together researchers investigating issues related to the theoretical frameworks and methodological approaches to studying human robot interactions within groups. We expect the workshop will contribute to our understanding of how to better design robots for group interactions.

Categories and Subject Descriptors

H.5.0 Information Interfaces and Presentation (e.g., HCI): General

General Terms

Design, Human Factors, Theory

Keywords

human-robot interaction, groups, teams, computer-supported cooperative work

1. INTRODUCTION

Organizations are increasingly relying on the use of work groups [3-5, 12, 16, 17]. Communication and information technologies have changed the way groups operate [1, 15, 20, 21]. The explosion of robot adoption in groups for the last decade has been reshaping how groups work in practice. As other technologies did, robots in groups can evoke new socio-technical issues between workers and technology. These issues are likely to have major implications for group processes and outcomes [7, 11, 19]. Yet, little is known about this emerging area of study.

Robots have been adopted in many contexts and domains of group work. For example, telepresence robots enable geographically dispersed teams to communicate more effectively [23]. By using robots to represent dispersed group members, these members can have a greater sense of social presence during group discussions, which facilitates social interactions between members in different

Group 2014, November 9–12, 2014, Sundial Island, FL, USA.
ACM 978-1-4503-3043-5/14/11.
http://dx.doi.org/10.1145/2660398.2660426

locations [15]. Furthermore, some scholars believe that the use of robots to represent dispersed team members will only increase [24].

In addition, government and private businesses have adopted robots as group members [8, 25]. Extreme work groups, such as SWAT teams, use multiple robots in tactical field operations [7]. Construction companies have started to utilize autonomous robots for dangerous construction tasks to avoid loss of human life [25, 26]. Robots are also being used for non-task-related activities. Service robots such as Snackbots provide refreshments to employees throughout the work day [10, 13].

Human–robot interactions can also lead individuals to develop strong emotional attachments to robots. Evidence of this is often seen when individuals put clothes and accessories on their robots, treating them as if they were human [10]. Furthermore, research has shown that these emotional attachments can elicit in-group behaviors by which humans feel that the robot belongs to them or their group rather than the whole organization [19].

The inclusion of robots as team members can lead to new insights about how groups work, which we believe is fundamentally different from what we know of all-human groups. For example, how does the inclusion of robots help or hurt team coordination or cooperation? Does the inclusion of robots facilitate or impede the development of team trust? Despite these new and interesting questions, we know very little about this area [14, 22, 24].

2. Goals

This workshop is designed to stimulate interest in human–robot interactions within groups by assembling researchers who share a common interest in this area. Another goal is to promote the use of a diverse set of theoretical frameworks and methodological approaches to studying human–robot interactions within groups. We also expect that the workshop will inform design by providing insights into how the design of robots can facilitate or hinder group interactions. As such, the goals of this workshop are as follows:

- To bring together and establish a community of researchers and designers who are interested in human–robot interactions within groups.

- To present and discuss theoretical frameworks that differentiate research on human–robot interaction in groups from previous work that focuses mainly on individuals.

- To brainstorm and develop reliable and valid methodologies for studying human-robot interactions in groups.

- To identify and form suggestions and implications for designing robots to better support group work.

3. Themes

To achieve the workshop goals stated above, we suggest some potential themes that should allow a variety of perspectives to emerge. The suggested themes include but are not limited to the following:

- Theories that can be applied to or developed for human–robot interaction in groups.

- Research methods for studying social dynamics and group outcomes in groups using robots.

- Development of affordable and accessible robots for studying human–robot interaction in groups.

- Design suggestions and prototypes for robots in group contexts.

- Socio-technical issues in collaboration among humans using robots.

- Examination of the gap between social requirements and technical feasibility in human–robot collaboration [2].

- Social psychological principles for human–robot or human–human behaviors in groups using robots.

- Collaboration with autonomous, intelligent robots for knowledge-based works.

- Coordination and communication issues involving multiple humans and multiple robots.

- Development of experimental tasks for studying human–robot interaction within groups in various contexts.

- Opportunities and challenges that arise from bringing robots into group processes.

- Use of autonomous intelligent robots in groups.

- Testing team process variables such as cohesion and trust by adopting robots in collaboration.

- Group performance measures in groups using robots.

- Use of telepresence robots, which involves multiple people.

4. Workshop Structure

This is a full-day workshop that consists of four main sessions: 1) short presentations of workshop papers, 2) open discussions on topics, in general, 3) group activities in the afternoon, and 4) a reflective discussion on what was learned. However, the workshop is loosely structured so that the following arrangement can be spontaneously run on the day of workshop.

The workshop will begin with introductions to the topics by the organizers followed by a presentation of the day's agenda. Participants will each give a short presentation (10–15 minutes) on their paper. Participants are encouraged to provide demonstrations of human–robot interactions within groups by using actual robots, video and/or other materials. After all presentations, participants will engage in a discussion about the papers presented. Although there will be preplanned discussion topics there will be time set aside for emergent topics that come out of workshop discussions.

The afternoon session will be filled with small-group discussions. The small groups will be formed based on the final themes derived from the workshop discussions in the morning session. Based on the number of participants and themes, the participants will be divided into 3–4 groups. Each group will be encouraged to produce a slide show summarizing the outcome of their discussions. In the final session, the slides will be shared and discussed with all participants. The workshop will be concluded with a reflective discussion followed up with a summarization of the insights that emerged during the workshop. Participants will also be encouraged to provide feedback about the workshop and provide any future suggestions for other workshop participants.

5. Call for Participation

Potential participants should submit a two-page position paper to the organizer before the workshop. Authors can refer to the suggested workshop themes but are encouraged to bring up new perspectives that our themes do not cover. Along with the position paper, authors should also bring a 10- to 15-minute slide presentation. Please use the ACM standard format for submissions. Audio/visual equipment is highly encouraged but not required. The maximum number of participants is 15 but is subject to change based on the number of workshop submissions.

6. Organizers

Dr. Lionel P. Robert, Jr., is an assistant professor of information at the University of Michigan School of Information, Ann Arbor. His research focuses on team collaboration through virtual communication environments. Dr. Robert was a BAT doctoral fellow and KPMG scholar at Indiana University, where he completed his Ph.D. in Information Systems and minored in Social Informatics through the Center for Social Informatics.

Sangseok You is a doctoral student at the School of Information at the University of Michigan. His research focuses on technologically enabled small-group collaborations including use of intelligent robots. His recent work explores examination of team process and perception toward robots in physical human–robot collaboration such as construction sites; coordination and communication issues in collaboration in teams with multiple humans and multiple robots; and information seeking and sharing using robots in groups.

7. REFERENCES

[1] Ackerman, M. S., & McDonald, D. W. (1996, November). Answer Garden 2: merging organizational memory with collaborative help. In Proceedings of the 1996 ACM conference on Computer supported cooperative work (pp. 97-105). ACM.

[2] Ackerman, M. S. (2000). The intellectual challenge of CSCW: the gap between social requirements and technical feasibility. Human–Computer Interaction, 15(2-3), 179-203.

[3] Alnuaimi, O. Maruping, L.M. Robert, L.P. Social Loafing in Brainstorming CMC Teams: The Role of Moral Disengagement. In Proc. HICSS 2009, IEEE Press (2009), 1-9.

[4] Dennis, A.R., Robert, L.P., Curtis, A.M., Kowalczyk, S.T., and Hasty, B.K. Trust is in the Eye of the Beholder: A Vignette Study of Postevent Behavioral Controls' Effects on Individual Trust in Virtual Teams. Information Systems Research. 23, 2, (2012), 546-558.

[5] Goyal, S., Maruping, L, Robert, L. Diversity and conflict in teams: A faultline model perspective, in Proc. Acad. Manage. Conf., 2008, pp. 1–6

[6] Green, S. A., Billinghurst, M., Chen, X., & Chase, J. G. (2008). Human-robot collaboration: A literature review and

augmented reality approach in design. International Journal of Advanced Robotic Systems, 5, 1–18.

[7] Hinds, P. J., Roberts, T. L., & Jones, H. (2004). Whose job is it anyway? A study of human-robot interaction in a collaborative task. Human-Computer Interaction, 19(1), 151–181.

[8] Jones, H., & Hinds, P. (2002, November). Extreme work teams: using SWAT teams as a model for coordinating distributed robots. In Proceedings of the 2002 ACM conference on Computer supported cooperative work (pp. 372-381). ACM.

[9] Kumar, T. S., Jung, S., & Koenig, S. (2014). A Tree-Based Algorithm for Construction Robots.

[10] Lee, M. K., Kiesler, S., Forlizzi, J., & Rybski, P. (2012, May). Ripple effects of an embedded social agent: a field study of a social robot in the workplace. In Proceedings of the SIGCHI Conference on Human Factors in Computing Systems (pp. 695-704). ACM.

[11] Ljungblad, S., Kotrbova, J., Jacobsson, M., Cramer, H., & Niechwiadowicz, K. (2012, February). Hospital robot at work: something alien or an intelligent colleague?. In Proceedings of the ACM 2012 conference on Computer Supported Cooperative Work (pp. 177-186). ACM.

[12] Munson, S. A., Kervin, K., Robert, L.P., 2014. Monitoring email to indicate project team performance and mutual attraction. In Proceedings of the 17th ACM conference on Computer supported cooperative work & social computing (CSCW '14). ACM, New York, NY, USA, 542-549.

[13] Mutlu, B. & Forlizzi, J. (2008). Robots in organizations: The role of workflow, social, and environmental factors in human-robot interaction. Proc. of HRI'08, 239-248.

[14] Mutlu, B., Osman, S., Forlizzi, J., Hodgins, J., & Kiesler, S. (2006). Perceptions of ASIMO: an exploration on co-operation and competition with humans and humanoid robots, 351–352.

[15] Nakanishi, H., Kato, K., and Ishiguro, H. Zoom cameras and movable displays enhance social telepresence. In Proc CHI '11, ACM (2011), 63–72.

[16] Newell, J., Maruping, L.M., Riemenschneider, C. and Robert, L.P. Leveraging E-Identities: The Impact of Perceived Diversity on Team Social Integration and Performance. In Proc. ICIS 2008.

[17] Newell, J. Robert, L.P., Riemenschneider, C. Maruping, L.M. Influencing Individual Perceptions of Deep Level Diversity in Virtual Learning Teams (VLT), In Proc. HICSS 2009, IEEE Press (2009).

[18] Orlikowski, W. J. (1992). Learning from Notes: organizational issues in groupware implementation, 362–369.

[19] Rae, I., Takayama, L., & Mutlu, B. (2012, May). One of the gang: supporting in-group behavior for embodied mediated communication. In Proceedings of the SIGCHI Conference on Human Factors in Computing Systems (pp. 3091-3100). ACM.

[20] Robert, L. P. (2013, February). A multi-level analysis of the impact of shared leadership in diverse virtual teams. In Proceedings of the 2013 conference on Computer supported cooperative work (pp. 363-374). ACM.

[21] Robert, L. P., Andoh-Baidoo, F. K., & You, S. (2013). Perceived Differences, Team Empowerment and Shared Leadership in Virtual Teams. In Academy of Management Proceedings (Vol. 2013, No. 1, p. 17336). Academy of Management.

[22] Sung, J. Y., Guo, L., Grinter, R. E., & Christensen, H. I. (2007). "My Roomba Is Rambo": Intimate Home Appliances. In UbiComp 2007: Ubiquitous Computing (pp. 145-162). Springer Berlin Heidelberg.

[23] Takayama, L., & Harris, H. (2013). Presentation of (telepresent) self: on the double-edged effects of mirrors. Presented at the HRI '13: Proceedings of the 8th ACM/IEEE international conference on Human-robot interaction, IEEE Press.

[24] Tannenbaum, S. I., Mathieu, J. E., Salas, E., & Cohen, D. (2012). Teams are changing: are research and practice evolving fast enough?. Industrial and Organizational Psychology, 5(1), 2-24.

[25] Vähä, P., Heikkilä, T., Kilpeläinen, P., Järviluoma, M., & Gambao, E. (2013). Extending automation of building construction—Survey on potential sensor technologies and robotic applications. Automation in Construction, 36, 168-178.

[26] Wang, W., Dong, W., Su, Y., Wu, D., & Du, Z. (2014). Development of Search□and□rescue Robots for Underground Coal Mine Applications. Journal of Field Robotics, 31(3), 386-407.

Potentials of the 'Unexpected': Technology Appropriation Practices and Communication Needs

Manfred Tscheligi[1], Alina Krischkowsky[1], Katja Neureiter[1], Kori Inkpen[2],
Michael Muller[3], Gunnar Stevens[4]

(1) Christian Doppler Laboratory
for Contextual Interfaces,
ICT&S Center,
University of Salzburg,
Salzburg, Austria
{firstname.lastname}
@sbg.ac.at

(2) Microsoft Research,
One Microsoft Way,
Redmond, WA, USA
kori@microsoft.com

(3) IBM Research,
One Rogers Street,
Cambridge, MA, USA
michael_muller@us.ibm.com

(4) University of Siegen,
Hölderlinstr. 3,
Siegen, Germany
gunnar.stevens@uni-siegen.de

ABSTRACT

Whether in private or professional life, individuals frequently adapt the technology around them and work with what they have at hand to accomplish a certain task. In this one-day workshop, we will discuss how this form of technology appropriation is used to satisfy communication needs. Thereby, we specifically focus on technology that was not intended to facilitate communication, but which led to appropriation driven by individuals' communication needs. Our aim is to identify 'unexpected' communication needs, to better address these in the design of interactive systems. We focus on a variety of different contexts, ranging from not restricted contexts to environments that are characterized by strict regulations (e.g., production lines with 24/7 shift production cycles). Consequently, this workshop aims at better understanding how users adapt technology to match their individual communication purposes and how these appropriation practices interrelate with and support organizational cooperation.

Categories and Subject Descriptors

H.5.m. Information interfaces and presentation (e.g., HCI): Miscellaneous.

General Terms: Human Factors

Keywords: Technology appropriation; 'unexpected' communication needs; special contexts.

1. Workshop Theme

Conclusions from various user studies, in particular within Computer-Supported Cooperative Work (CSCW) and Information Systems (IS) research, propose to investigate appropriation processes within practice, from theoretical (e.g., [6], [9]) but also bottom-up observational perspectives (e.g., [22], [23]). Such field-driven, observational user studies, many of those published within CHI and CSCW conferences, have drawn attention to particular

GROUP'14, November 9–12, 2014, Sanibel Island, Florida, USA.
ACM 978-1-4503-3043-5/14/11.
http://dx.doi.org/10.1145/2660398.2660427

cases in which individuals *"complete the design through their actions"* [12], as they adapt the technologies around them in ways that have not initially been intended by the designers [1]. These investigations range from everyday appropriation practices in private (e.g., [4], [11]) and business settings (e.g., [5], [16], [17]) to highly challenging and specific contexts that go beyond traditional work/office environments (e.g., [2], [6], [7]). However, understanding and conceptualizing these application contexts and domains [5], and in particular reflecting upon experiences regarding appropriation practices within these respective contexts is critical when it comes to the abstraction of knowledge to provide an informed basis [3], of how to design for the 'unexpected'.

Our proposed workshop aims at extracting and consolidating 'successful' and 'unsuccessful' technology appropriation experiences from a wide range of application contexts. Interrelating these technology appropriation experiences with the context of use is of particular importance in order to actually understand the situated nature of interaction [14]. Therefore, we consider highly specific contexts (e.g., production lines with 24/7 shift production cycles or safety critical contexts such as cars) particularly interesting, as they are frequently characterized by strict regulations that are defined to avoid appropriation practices. However, throughout our own research activities, we came to understand that even in these restricted environments, technology appropriation happens for various reasons, and one of these is the need for communication. Some research draws particular attention to the importance of the *social* context and the conditions in which appropriation is actually happening (e.g., [19], [21]). Following Draxler et al. ([21], p. 2835) appropriation can be considered *"as being highly cooperative, situated, socially embedded, and often connected to particular work situations"*. Here, appropriation itself is seen as a highly social activity, which is embedded in very specific context-related situations wherein the technology adaption is mostly performed between peers or colleagues [21]. Accordingly, appropriation should be understood as a phenomenon that is characterized by many creative and collaborative activities [10].

Whereas appropriation may be regarded as a *social* phenomenon itself, *our workshop in particular strives to investigate technology appropriation for* MEETING SOCIAL PURPOSES, i.e., communication and cooperation. Therefore, 'unexpected' communication requirements need to be identified and consolidated through looking at users' appropriation behavior. Here, communication needs that were satisfied through appropriating the technology may be considered as 'successful'; however, also 'unsuccessful', i.e., appropriation that aimed, but did not result in, satisfied communication needs, are of relevance. Thereby, not only experiences with unanticipated use, but also unanticipated users (e.g., [8], [17] [18]) may be discussed in the workshop, which might provide a further understanding of appropriation in specific contexts. Dix [1] and Carroll [12] highlight that *"design can never be complete"* as it is impossible to design for the 'unexpected', but that *"you can design to allow the unexpected"*. These appropriation practices then constitute the basis for the design and implementation of technology innovations [12]. Consequently, they may be considered an essential and positive phenomenon ([1], [12], [14], [20]). In line with this perspective, our proposed workshop is not aiming to derive concrete design implications, but to reflect on experiences with such 'unexpected' communication requirements identified through technology appropriation to provide an informed basis for research and design.

Previous related workshops within the CHI and CSCW community have mainly concentrated on CSCW- and IS- oriented theories and topics. Those workshops aimed at finding systematic approaches to map existing research in order to strive for future research agendas [25], identifying approaches of community appropriation through involving participants in a process of design and appropriation as a tool for reflection [24], but also supporting strategies of sustainability through reuse [13]. Another workshop at CHI aimed at bridging the persisting gap between users, researchers and designers within appropriations research, in order to unite observations and theoretical viewpoints with practical design efforts [3].

In contrast to these workshops, we explicitly attempt to consolidate and extract experiences that particularly focus on individuals' communication needs and how these potentially 'unexpected' needs have been satisfied through the users adaption of the technology at hand. Our focus in the proposed workshop furthermore includes contexts with specific characteristics, such as restricted production industries, as exploring the context of use is necessary to actually understand the situated nature of interaction [14]. In an earlier workshop at CSCW [15], we have discussed collaboration activities in challenging environments. While one might argue that restricted contexts do not allow appropriation, as for instance, users are strongly urged to follow the rules, we found in our own research that there is nevertheless a variety of appropriation behavior to facilitate communication, which indicates unfulfilled needs.

2. Workshop Objective
This one-day workshop aims to bring together researchers and practitioners with a variety of backgrounds (e.g., Social Sciences, design of collaborative systems, etc.), who share an interest in understanding technology appropriation to satisfy communication needs. The workshop addresses the following goals and questions:

Identifying appropriation practices:
- What appropriation practices may be identified that aim to satisfy communication needs?

Relating appropriation practices to communication needs:
- In what way has the technology been appropriated to fit certain communication needs?
- What 'unexpected' communication needs may be derived from these examples? How are these characterized?

Embedding practices and needs into the context:

- How have technologies been 'domesticated' in various contexts?
- How do specific contexts with their inherent characteristics imply certain communication channels that lead to these particular technology appropriations?

Deriving an informed basis for research & design:
- What potentials do these experiences have to inform the design of such technologies?
- What can research and design learn from these appropriation strategies?

In order to discuss these questions, we invite position papers to the following topics (but are not limited to):

- Examples of successful or unsuccessful technology appropriation for communication needs in various contexts with specific characteristics, as well as examples of technology appropriation by unanticipated users (addressing either expected or unexpected communication needs)

- Methodological approaches to investigate technology appropriation for communication

- Theoretical backgrounds to technology appropriation for communication

- Design of collaborative systems that address expected or unexpected communication needs as a response to technology appropriation practices

The goal of the workshop is to share and discuss experiences around the above-mentioned topics, as well as to explore future potentials of addressing expected and unexpected communication needs in varying contexts.

3. Workshop Description
This is a one-day workshop with break-out sessions, alternated with moderated group discussions. After a short introduction to the workshop topic by the organizers, the workshop will mainly focus on the participants' experiences about the topic. Participants will briefly present themselves and their stance on the workshop topic. In this part, the organizers will also outline their own observational experiences and reflections on the topic (e.g., within a production context employees have appropriated technology for their own communication purposes, thereby revealing 'unexpected' communication needs).

In a break-out session the participants will then try to identify technology appropriations and their relating 'unexpected' communication needs. The workshop organizers will provide guiding questions to be answered within the break-out sessions to stimulate the participants thinking about this topic. In the afternoon the break-out session will continue, asking the participants to reflect upon successful work-arounds for enabling and supporting communication and in particular how these technology appropriations can be characterized. Throughout this identification and characterization process, the participants are also asked to reflect upon the potentials for design, and in particular what researchers and practitioners can learn from these appropriation strategies.

The workshop organizers will actively take part in the break-out sessions to stimulate discussion and bring together the participants' experiences. The outcome of the break-out sessions' will then briefly be presented.

Finally, a plenary discussion will be held to critically reflect on challenges and potentials. The goal is to provide an abstracted knowledge basis for future support of communication needs through technology.

4. After the Workshop

The workshop organizers will consider the publication of revised versions of accepted papers as part of a special issue in a CSCW related journal. In order to be considered for publication in this special issue, papers will have to be resubmitted and undergo a reviewing process with external reviews.

5. Intended Audience

We encourage the participation of researchers and practitioners from different communities and with various backgrounds in order to foster interdisciplinary discussions. These include academics, industrial researchers and designers but also other practitioners that have any kind of experience in technology appropriation to satisfy communication needs. In order to encourage exchange and interaction between all participants the maximum group size is set between 15 to 20 participants. Submissions will be reviewed by the workshop organizers with support of other researchers forming a dedicated program committee. The submissions will be selected according to their significance and their potential to stimulate discussion. A mixture of academic and industrial participants is anticipated and will be ensured by the organizers background and networks. The workshop organizers have previous experience in setting up related events at conferences such as CHI, NordiCHI, CSCW, MobileHCI, and IDC.

6. Resources

For conducting the workshop we will require a projector, flip charts, power strips and associated electricity, and Internet connectivity.

7. Organizers

Manfred Tscheligi is professor for HCI & Usability at the University of Salzburg, directing the ICT&S Center. He is also Head of the Business Unit Technology Experience at the Austrian Institute of Technology (AIT). He was involved in a range of conference activities (e.g., co-chairing CHI2004 in Vienna, ACE 2007 and AUI 2011 in Salzburg) and co-organized several workshops and SIGs (e.g. CHI, MobileHCI, CSCW, Interact, AutomotiveUI, recently MobileHCI2013).

Alina Krischkowsky is research fellow at the ICT&S Center of the University of Salzburg. She has done her master degree in Sociology and has been engaged in various contexts, such as Ambient Assisted Living, social media, factories, and cars. She is currently working on her PhD thesis regarding the use of social roles as analytical tool to investigate, understand and conceptualize social context aspects in general but particularly collaborative processes.

Katja Neureiter is research fellow at the ICT&S Center of the University of Salzburg. She has done her master degree in Sociology and focuses in her PhD on the interrelationship between Social Presence and Social Capital, e.g., how to foster social connectedness through Social Presence via ICTs, i.e. video mediated communication systems. Moreover, she is engaged in various projects in the area of Ambient Assisted Living.

Kori Inkpen is a Principal Research / Research Manager in the neXus group at Microsoft Research. The neXus team combines research in Social Computing, Computer Supported Collaborative Work, and Information Visualization to support rich collaboration across a variety of domains. She has been on the organizing committee of many conferences including Technical Program chair for CHI 2015, conference Chair for CSCW 2011, and conference Chair for Group 2007. Prior to joining Microsoft Research she was a Professor of Computer Science at Dalhousie University (2001-2007) and Simon Fraser University (1998-2001).

Michael Muller works as a research staff member at IBM Research, Cambridge MA US. His research has included studying how employees appropriate enterprise software. He has co-organized several workshops at CHI and CSCW, and has chaired subcommittees for the CHI and DIS conferences, and co-chaired the 2012 HCIC program on social media.

Gunnar Stevens is an associate professor of human-computer interaction at the University of Siegen. He co-organized several workshops (e.g. on DIS, CSCW, M&C) and involved in several conference organizations (e.g. IS EUD, COOP, EuroITV). His research on technology appropriation has been published in several journal and conferences (e.g. CHI, COOP, JCSCW, ToCHI, JEUC) and got different awards (e.g. IBM Eclipse Innovation Award, Siegen-Wittgenstein PhD Award).

8. ACKNOWLEDGMENTS

The financial support by the Austrian Federal Ministry of Science, Research and Economy and the National Foundation for Research, Technology and Development is gratefully acknowledged (Christian Doppler Laboratory for "Contextual Interfaces").

9. REFERENCES

[1] Alan Dix. 2007. Designing for appropriation. In Proceedings of the 21st British HCI Group Annual Conference on People and Computers: HCI...but not as we know it - Volume 2 (BCS-HCI '07), Vol. 2. British Computer Society, Swinton, UK, UK, 27-30.

[2] Amaya L. Becvar, James D. Hollan. 2007. Transparency and technology appropriation: social impacts of a video blogging system in dental hygiene clinical construction. In *Proceedings of the 2007 international ACM conference on Supporting group work* (GROUP'07). ACM, New York, NY, USA, 311-320.

[3] Antti Salovaara, Kristina Höök, Keith Cheverst, Michael Twidale, Matthew Chalmers, and Corina Sas. 2011. Appropriation and creative use: linking user studies and design. In CHI '11 Extended Abstracts on Human Factors in Computing Systems (CHI EA '11). ACM, New York, NY, USA, 37-40.

[4] Binaebi Akah and Shaowen Bardzell. 2010. Empowering products: personal identity through the act of appropriation. In *CHI '10 Extended Abstracts on Human Factors in Computing Systems* (CHI EA '10). ACM, New York, NY, USA, 4021-4026.

[5] Claus Bossen and Peter Dalsgaard. 2005. Conceptualization and appropriation: the evolving use of a collaborative knowledge management system. In *Proceedings of the 4th decennial conference on Critical computing: between sense and sensibility* (CC '05), Olav W. Bertelsen, Niels Olof Bouvin, Peter G. Krogh, and Morten Kyng (Eds.). ACM, New York, NY, USA, 99-108.

[6] Ellen Balka and Ina Wagner. 2006. Making things work: dimensions of configurability as appropriation work. In *Proceedings of the 2006 20th anniversary conference on*

Computer supported cooperative work (CSCW '06). ACM, New York, NY, USA, 229-238.

[7] Fabien Girardin and Josep Blat. 2010. The co-evolution of taxi drivers and their in-car navigation systems. *Pervasive Mob. Comput.* 6, 4 (August 2010), 424-434.

[8] Genevieve Bell, Mark Blythe, and Phoebe Sengers. 2005. Making by making strange: Defamiliarization and the design of domestic technologies. *ACM Trans. Comput.-Hum. Interact.* 12, 2 (June 2005), 149-173.

[9] Gerardine DeSanctis and Marshall Scott Poole. 1994. Capturing the Complexity in Advanced Technology Use: Adaptive Structuration Theory. *In Organization Science* 5, 2 (1994), 121-147.

[10] Gunnar Stevens, Volkmar Pipek, and Volker Wulf. 2010. Appropriation Infrastructure: Mediating appropriation and production work. In Journal of organizational and end user computing: JOEUC 22 (2010), Nr. 2, Special issue.

[11] Jan Hess, Benedikt Ley, Corinna Ogonowski, Tim Reichling, Lin Wan, and Volker Wulf. 2012. New technology@home: impacts on usage behavior and social structures. In *Proceedings of the 10th European conference on Interactive tv and video* (EuroiTV '12). ACM, New York, NY, USA, 185-194.

[12] Jennie Carroll. 2004. Completing Design in Use: Closing the Appropriation Cycle. In *Proceedings of the 12th European Conference on Information Systems (ECIS 2004)*, Turku, Finland, 11 pages. Paper 44.

[13] Jina Huh, Lisa P. Nathan, Six Silberman, Eli Blevis, Bill Tomlinson, Phoebe Sengers, and Daniela Busse. 2010. Examining appropriation, re-use, and maintenance for sustainability. In *CHI '10 Extended Abstracts on Human Factors in Computing Systems* (CHI EA '10). ACM, New York, NY, USA, 4457-4460.

[14] Joseph 'Jofish' Kaye. 2006. I just clicked to say I love you: rich evaluations of minimal communication. In *CHI '06 Extended Abstracts on Human Factors in Computing Systems* (CHI EA '06). ACM, New York, NY, USA, 363-368.

[15] Manfred Tscheligi, Alexander Meschtscherjakov, Astrid Weiss, Volker Wulf, Vanessa Evers, and Bilge Mutlu. 2012. Exploring collaboration in challenging environments: from the car to the factory and beyond. In *Proceedings of the ACM 2012 conference on Computer Supported Cooperative Work Companion* (CSCW '12). ACM, New York, NY, USA, 15-16.

[16] Michael Muller, Kate Ehrlich, Tara Matthews, Adam Perer, Inbal Ronen, and Ido Guy. 2012. Diversity among enterprise online communities: collaborating, teaming, and innovating through social media. In *Proceedings of the SIGCHI*

Conference on Human Factors in Computing Systems (CHI '12). ACM, New York, NY, USA, 2815-2824.

[17] Pablo-Alejandro Quinones. 2014. Cultivating practice & shepherding technology use: supporting appropriation among unanticipated users. In *Proceedings of the 17th ACM conference on Computer supported cooperative work & social computing* (CSCW '14). ACM, New York, NY, USA, 305-318.

[18] Pablo-Alejandro Quinones, Stephanie D. Teasley, and Steven Lonn. 2013. Appropriation by unanticipated users: looking beyond design intent and expected use. In *Proceedings of the 2013 conference on Computer supported cooperative work* (CSCW '13). ACM, New York, NY, USA, 1515-1526.

[19] Paul Dourish. 2001. Process descriptions as organisational accounting devices: the dual use of workflow technologies. In *Proceedings of the 2001 International ACM SIGGROUP Conference on Supporting Group Work* (GROUP '01), Clarence (Skip) Ellis and Ilze Zigurs (Eds.). ACM, New York, NY, USA, 52-60.

[20] Phoebe Sengers, Kirsten Boehner, Shay David, and Joseph 'Jofish' Kaye. 2005. Reflective design. In *Proceedings of the 4th decennial conference on Critical computing: between sense and sensibility* (CC '05), Olav W. Bertelsen, Niels Olof Bouvin, Peter G. Krogh, and Morten Kyng (Eds.). ACM, New York, NY, USA, 49-58.

[21] Sebastian Draxler, Gunnar Stevens, Martin Stein, Alexander Boden, and David Randall. 2012. Supporting the social context of technology appropriation: on a synthesis of sharing tools and tool knowledge. In *Proceedings of the SIGCHI Conference on Human Factors in Computing Systems* (CHI '12). ACM, New York, NY, USA, 2835-2844.

[22] Volkmar Pipek and Volker Wulf. 1999. A groupware's life. In *Proceedings of the Sixth European conference on Computer supported cooperative work*. Kluwer Academic Publishers, Norwell, MA, USA, 199-218.

[23] Wanda J. Orlikowski. 1996. Improvising Organizational Transformation Over Time: a Situated Change Perspective. Information Systems Research 7, 1, 63-92.

[24] Wendy March, Margot Jacobs, and Tony Salvador. 2005. Designing technology for community appropriation. In *CHI '05 Extended Abstracts on Human Factors in Computing Systems* (CHI EA '05). ACM, New York, NY, USA, 2126-2127.

[25] Yvonne Dittrich, Paul Dourish, Anders Mørch, Volkmar Pipek. 2005. Supporting Appropriation Work: Approaches for the 'reflective' user. In ECSCW'05 (http://insitu.lri.fr/ecscw/workshop7.html) and a follow-up proceedings.

The Morphing Organization: Rethinking Groupwork Systems in the Era of Crowdwork

Obinna Anya
Accelerated Discovery Lab
IBM Research - Almaden
650 Harry Road, San Jose CA 95120
+1 (0) 408 927 1856
obanya@us.ibm.com

Laura Carletti
Horizon, University of Nottingham
Innovation Park – Triumph Road
Nottingham (UK) NG7 2 2TU
+44 (0) 115 823 2557
laura.carletti@nottingham.ac.uk

Tim Coughlan
School of Computer Science &
Horizon, University of Nottingham
Nottingham (UK) NG7 2 2TU
+44 (0) 115 823 1420
tim.coughlan@nottingham.ac.uk

Karin Hansson
Department of Computer and Systems Science
(DSV), Stockholm University
Forum 100, SE-164 40 Kista, Sweden
+1 (0) 646 706 6283
khansson@dsv.su.se

Sophia B. Liu
U.S. Geological Survey
Coastal & Marine Science Center
Saint Petersburg, FL 33701
+001 727 502 8093
sophialiu@usgs.gov

ABSTRACT

Web 2.0 has provided organizations remarkable opportunities to improve productivity, gain competitive advantage, and increase participation by engaging a crowd to accomplish tasks at scale. However, establishing and integrating crowd-based systems into organizations is still an open question. The systems and the collaborative processes they enable appear diametrically in dissonance with the norms and culture of collaboration and knowledge sharing in traditional organizations. They require mechanisms for articulation of work, coordination, cooperation, and knowledge co-creation that are fundamentally different from those in current groupwork systems and processes. Building on two workshops hosted at ACM CSCW 2014, we will explore questions such as: How does the shift in organizational work from a closed system with known individuals, to an open and crowd model that requires engagement with an undefined network of people, affect how we conceptualize groupwork? What are the implications for the design of groupwork systems? What can the crowdsourcing research community learn from groupwork systems, or conversely what can groupwork researchers learn from crowdsourcing? How do cultures, motivations, ownership and representation fit into these systems? This workshop will bring together researchers and practitioners in crowdsourcing, social computing, collaborative technologies, organizational science, and workplace research, to discuss the future of groupwork systems in the era of crowdwork with the goal of articulating an agenda for future research.

Categories and Subject Descriptors

H.5.m. Information interfaces and presentation (e.g., HCI): Miscellaneous.

GROUP'14, November 9–12, 2014, Sanibel Island, Florida, USA.
ACM 978-1-4503-3043-5/14/11
http://dx.doi.org/10.1145/2660398.2660428

General Terms

Human Factors, Design

Keywords

Groupwork, Crowdsourcing, Social Computing, Organizations.

1. INTRODUCTION

Five years ago discussions of computer support for groupwork in organizational contexts were confined to collaborations among known individuals who are members of a set of organizations by virtue of being employed by those organizations, but this situation has changed. Organizational work has morphed from a closed system to utilizing open and crowd models, where collaboration and knowledge co-creation with an undefined network of people are essential characteristics.

Despite the remarkable promises of this new work model, the development of effective structures for collaborating between organizations and a crowd, and establishing crowdwork as an organizational process, remains a huge challenge. Because of their relationship with non-paid systems like Wikipedia, most forms of organizational crowdwork often emulate non-paid crowdsourcing models where motivation for effective participation evolves from a common interest or sense of civic duty. The incentive to participate often arises from gaining reputation and recognition among other users, but the complex challenges with managing articulation and coordination of work often do not surface so challengingly. People with similar interests, or who face similar problems, are simply attracted to each other sharing similar perspectives, codes, and rituals – leading to effective collaboration and work coordination, but also to exclusion and conformity. Common ethos becomes a sufficient guideline and incentive to participate [9].

The merging of these approaches with more traditional organizations provides opportunities and raises tensions. What happens when these economic systems are combined with more formal organizational hierarchies? While a number of challenging issues have been identified [6][8] and many existing tools and services have enabled organizations to employ the crowd workforce, there are currently no coherent frameworks to inform the design of collaborative solutions for crowdwork, and guide the establishment of crowdwork as an organizational business process. For example, existing notions of crowdwork convey very little about areas that are seen essential in groupwork systems, such as the articulation of work, coordination of engagements between organizations and a crowd, or how resources are managed to get work done [9]. Complex tensions between the motivation of individuals, and of organizations, require the consideration of new hybrid organizational models that combine open and closed systems [1] [5]. This workshop aims to explore what contributions groupwork research can potentially make to solving the myriad challenges in organizational crowdwork research, and conversely, to discuss the potentials of the trends and challenges in organizational crowdwork in paving a way for the emergence of the next generation of groupwork systems.

2. WORKSHOP GOALS

The goal of this interdisciplinary workshop is to explore the future of groupwork systems in the era of crowdwork. This proposal is the result of bringing together organizers and attendees from two separate workshops entitled "Back to the Future of Organizational Work: Crowdsourcing and Digital Work Marketplaces" [4] and "Structures for Knowledge Co-creation between Organizations and the Public" [2] held at ACM CSCW 2014. The workshops raised an overlapping set of issues and potentials for research in the areas of threats and opportunities posed by organizational crowdwork, structures for engagement and knowledge co-creation in emerging models of open and crowd work, and the need to approach organizational crowdwork not only as a technical challenge, but also a profoundly human, social, organizational and philosophical issue. This workshop aims to bridge the successes of the two workshops and extend their results by investigating the design of systems and processes to support organizations in this new area of open and crowd work. A key contribution is to build on the themes found in the prior workshops by producing deeper discussions and integration of different perspectives.

Given the focus on designing computer support for group work based on a multi-disciplinary approach to understanding the specifics of both social engagements and technical requirements of collaborative tools, GROUP has a crucial role to play in guiding thoughts around the formulation of guiding principles for the design of effective organizational crowdwork systems. The workshop will explore how studies of CSCW, HCI and CSCL, as well as their concepts and sensibilities, can be extended and applied toward the design of sustainable frameworks and collaboration systems for organizational crowdwork. Questions of interest to the workshop include:

- What is the future of groupwork systems in the era of crowdwork? How do emerging trends in crowdwork, such as organizational collaboration with an undefined network of people, affect how we conceptualize groupwork? What implications, e.g. security, does crowdwork have on groupwork systems?

- How can groupwork research contribute to crowdwork research? What can be learned from the success stories and failures of groupwork systems of more than two decades to inform the design of effective organizational crowdwork

systems? Can the research and design principles of traditional groupware, workflow systems, and CSCW applications be extended to support organizational collaborative work with the crowd?

- How can collaboration "in the crowd" be motivated and sustained, while promoting openness and mutual knowledge co-creation, safeguarding organizational intellectual capital, and ensuring maximum job satisfaction and career growth for the crowd worker?

- What are the underlying ideologies and principles in the socio-technical architectures of tools for supporting collaboration and knowledge sharing? What are the norms and cultures of collaboration in organizations, and how and when do they work for or against the involvement of crowds? How do we understand the participatory processes at stake in crowdwork, and ensure equal representation? How do we design sustainable hybrid economic systems from an organizational perspective?

- What functions should the next generation of groupwork systems embody to make them viable as an organizational work tool in the era of crowdwork?

3. WORKSHOP THEMES

This workshop is organized around three key themes that will drive the call for position papers, and help to structure activities during the workshop. The workshop will also include space for inspiration sourced from the position papers and interests of the participants. The issues that we consider critical, as emerged in the two CSCW 2014 workshops [2], [4] are: (1) the design of socio-technical systems; (2) the emergence of hybrid-economic systems; and (3) the lack of equal representation. These overarching themes are deemed crucial to rethink groupwork within crowdsourcing processes.

Design of Socio-technical Systems

The problems of organizational crowdwork are not just technical problems, but profoundly human, social, organizational and philosophical issues. The interplay between the organization and a crowd is also central when designing and undertaking a crowdsourcing process: What is the organization's policy and commitment? What expertise is required from the crowd? What type of collaboration is in place? There is the need for designers to gain a deeper understanding of the non-technical factors, to mind the socio-technical gap, and to engage with researchers across disciplines for the design of solutions that not only drive innovation, but also seek to enhance human values at work.

Emergence of Hybrid Economic Systems

Commercial economies build value with economic capital as their means of exchange. Sharing economies build value through social and symbolic capital. Both will flourish more as Internet technology develops. When commercial and sharing economies interact, they generate a hybrid economic system [13]. In recent years, several examples of hybrid tools leveraging crowd participation have emerged, and been successful. This model raises questions both for the organization and for the crowd. There is an overall need to understand the ethical issues behind those emerging collaborations. There is also a need to understand how to create sustainable hybrid economies from the organization's perspective; and a need for the crowd to contribute work such as by volunteering without being exploited. As relations are central in distributed work, again the interplay between organization and the crowd becomes crucial to frame, establish and maintain effective groupwork through a crowdsourcing process.

Achieving Equal Representation

Web 2.0 seems to have marked a shift towards a more participative and democratic culture. Regardless of the obvious problems regarding time and means to participate in the collaborative work - the Web is far from being a neutral space where participants are treated equally. Rather, research shows that social media are places where discrimination regarding gender, age and ethnicity are just as common as in other social contexts [12][16][15][16][17]. This lack of equal representation can cause severe legitimacy problems in areas where equal representation is an issue. For example, the concept of open government – especially in relation to Web 2.0 technology increasingly empowers society to put an unprecedented pressure on organizations to be socially responsible [14]. Too much group conformity can also create stagnation and lack of creativity. Therefore, there is a need to analyze crowdwork from a representative point of view. Here both the question of what and who is represented, and the question of how discursive processes are structured, are important in the design of systems for crowdwork.

4. WORKSHOP ACTIVITIES

The workshop is planned as a full day event divided into two sessions. It will also involve additional online activities organized both before and after the workshop.

4.1 Pre-workshop Activities

At least one month prior to the workshop, the accepted positions papers will be circulated among the participants, who will be invited to read them, before attending the workshop. The participants will be also asked to prepare a three-minute presentation to be delivered at the beginning of the workshop. Accepted papers will be posted to the workshop website before the workshop to prepare the attendees for discussions at the workshop.

4.2 Workshop Program

4.2.1 Morning Session – Invited talks, paper presentation and discussion

During the first session, participants will present and discuss their work, generating an interactive review of the current state of the art, as well as an exploration of the ways in which the trends and challenges in organizational crowdwork present opportunities to revisit and rethink the nature and design of organizational groupwork systems. The goal will be to generate themes towards the creation of a roadmap for the future of groupwork systems in the new area of open and crowd work. After a break, themed discussions of the major issues raised by the papers will occur in small groups, in order to ensure effective participation and the elicitation of varied perspectives from participants. An invited talk may also be included as an introduction and inspiration to the day, alongside short reports on the outcomes of the previous workshops that have led to this proposal.

4.2.2 Afternoon Session – Group brainstorming and open discussion

The afternoon session will combine the small group discussions with the identification of 'hot topics' that emerged, as well as discussions on post-workshop activities. The session will aim to collate all the discussions of the workshop toward jointly brainstorming a research agenda and a vision for revisiting and rethinking the design of computer-based collaborative systems to support organizations in this new area of open and crowd work.

4.3 Selecting and Recruiting the Participants

A website will be set up to publicize the workshop, organize and coordinate workshop activities, and as a means of publishing and furthering discussions on the results of workshop. In order to attract a wide range of researchers and practitioners from different disciplines, workshop organizers from diverse backgrounds including Social Computing, Learning Sciences, Human-Computer-Interaction, Computer and Systems Sciences – will send out the Call for Participation to relevant professional and academic mailing lists (e.g. ACM SIGCHI Announcements; and British Computer Society HCI mailing list). The Call will be also posted on institutional and professional body web sites; circulated to partner organizations; advertised at related events that the organizers will attend (e.g. CTS 2014) and promoted on organizers' social media (e.g. Twitter).

The workshop welcomes different kinds of contributions addressing the central question of the future of groupwork in the era of crowd and open work, as well as conceptual frameworks for organizational crowdwork, descriptions of case studies and empirical work, and position papers discussing one or more of the workshop themes. Potential participants will be asked to submit a position paper (approximately 2000 words) and an abstract (up to 200 words). A program committee will be drawn from collaborators, colleagues and previous workshop attendees, several of whom have already agreed to take part. Together they will review submitted position papers based on quality, relevance and diversity. We will accept up to a maximum of 20 position papers to ensure that each participant can make a short presentation in the morning.

All contributions will be will be formatted according to ACM GROUP formatting guidelines, and submitted online via a dedicated workshop email address.

5. BACKGROUND OF THE ORGANIZERS

Obinna Anya is a postdoctoral researcher in the Accelerated Discovery Lab at IBM Research – Almaden. His research interest lies in the broad area of human-computer interaction with a focus on collaborative workplaces, social informatics, work practice analysis, and agent-based modeling. His current work examines interaction and discovery in socio-technical systems. Obinna was co-organizer of the ACM CSCW 2014 workshop on "Back to the Future of Organizational Work: Crowdsourcing and Digital Work Marketplaces". He holds a PhD in computer science from the University of Liverpool.

Laura Carletti is a Research Fellow in Horizon Digital Economy, University of Nottingham. Her main research interest is engagement through technology, knowledge elicitation and co-creation, sociomateriality. Her work has focused on socio-technical research, and in particular on crowdsourcing in the cultural sector [3]. She has been working on Art Maps, a crowdsourcing platform developed in collaboration with Tate, and on the Ghostsigns project, an amateur crowdsourcing initiative. Laura was the lead-organiser of the ACM CSCW 2014 workshop: "Structures for knowledge co-creation between organisations and the public" [2].

Tim Coughlan is a Lecturer in Computer Science and Research Fellow in the Horizon Digital Economy Research Institute at the University of Nottingham. His research interests are in the design and evaluation of human-computer interactions focused on learning, sharing, and creativity. He was a co-organiser of the ACM CSCW 2014 workshop: "Structures for knowledge co-creation between organisations and the public" [2], and was also lead organiser of the ACM CHI 2013 workshop: "Methods for Studying Technology in the Home". Relevant projects include the collaborative remixing and reuse of open educational resources across educational organizations [5], and crowdsourcing interpretations of artworks from the public.

Karin Hansson is an artist, curator and Ph.Lic at the Department of Computer & System Science at Stockholm University & Royal Institute of Art in Stockholm, with artistic methodologies and participatory processes online as research focus. She is especially interested in how the volunteer spheres use ICT to strengthen the organization's internal democratic structures, and how democratic cultures translate to technical systems. Hansson previously carried out a series of thematic art projects and exhibitions related to information society and changing conditions for democracy.

Sophia B. Liu is a Mendenhall Fellow and Research Geographer at the U.S. Geological Survey. She is a crisis informatics researcher offering innovative solutions and guidance on how to integrate social media and crowdsourced data into USGS hazard products and services while engaging relevant stakeholders in the design process. She received her Ph.D. from University of Colorado at Boulder in the Technology, Media and Society interdisciplinary program at the ATLAS Institute.

6. ACKNOWLEDGMENTS

Our thanks to the participants and organizers of the two ACM SIGCHI CSCW 2014 workshops that have led to this proposal for the contributions.

7. REFERENCES

[1] Allen, W. (2013). Exploring Hybrid-Economic Communities and the Technology-Mediated Identities Performed There. *iConference '13*. Fort Worth, TX.

[2] Carletti, L., Coughlan, T., Christensen, J., Gerber, E., Giannachi, G., Schutt S., Sinker, R. and dos Santos, C. D. (2014). Structures for knowledge co-creation between organisations and the public. *CSCW '14 Companion*. 309-312.

[3] Carletti, L., McAuley, D., Price, D., & Giannachi, G. (2013). Digital Humanities and Crowdsourcing: an Exploration. *Selected papers from Museum and the Web '13*. 223-236.

[4] Cefkin, M., Anya, O., Dill, S., Moore, R., Stucky, S. U. and Omokaro, O. (2014). Back to the future of organizational work: crowdsourcing and digital work marketplaces. *CSCW '14 Companion*. 313-316.

[5] Coughlan, T., Pitt, R., and McAndrew, P. (2013). Building open bridges: collaborative remixing and reuse of open educational resources across organisations. *In Proc. of the SIGCHI Conference on Human Factors in Computing Systems (CHI '13)*. ACM Press. 991-1000

[6] Kittur, A., Nickerson, J. V., Bernstein, M., Gerber, E., Shaw, A., Zimmerman, J., Lease, M. and Horton, J. (2013). The future of crowd work. *CSCW '13*. ACM Press. 1301-1318.

[7] Erickson, L. B., Petrick, I. and Trauth, E. M. (2012). Organizational uses of the crowd: developing a framework for the study of crowdsourcing. *In Proc. of the 50th annual conference on Computers and People Research*. ACM Press. 155-158.

[8] Felstiner, A. L. (2011). Working the Crowd: Employment and Labor Law in the Crowdsourcing Industry. Berkeley Journal of Employment and Labor Law, 32(1). Available at: http://works.bepress.com/alek_felstiner/1

[9] Forte, A. and Bruckman, A. (2005). "Why Do People Write for Wikipedia? Incentives to Contribute to Open-Content Publishing. Presented at GROUP 05 Workshop: Sustaining Community: The Role and Design of Incentive Mechanisms in Online Systems. Sanibel Island, FL.

[10] Grudin, J. (1989). Why groupware applications fail: Problems in design and evaluation. *Office: Technology and People*. 4(3), 245-264.

[11] Hansson, K., Karlström, P., Larsson, A., & Verhagen, H. (2013). Reputation, inequality and meeting techniques: visualising user hierarchy. *Computational and Mathematical Organization Theory*. 1-21

[12] Herring, S. C. (2008). *Gender and Power in On-line Communication*. In M. Holmes, J. and Meyerhoff (Ed.), The Handbook of Language and Gender. Oxford: Wiley Online Library.

[13] Lessig, L. (2008). *Remix: Making Art and Commerce Thrive in the Hybrid Economy*. Penguin Press HC.

[14] Meister, J. and Willyerd, K. (2010) *The 2020 Workplace: How Innovative Companies Attract, Develop, and Keep Tomorrow's Employees Today*. HarperBusiness

[15] Nakamura, L. (2008). *Digitizing race: visual cultures of the Internet*. University of Minnesota Press.

[16] Nakamura, L. (2001). *Head hunting in cyberspace : Identity tourism, Asian avatars and racial passing on the Web*. The Women's Review of Books, XVIII.

[17] Wright, M. M. (2005). Finding a Place in Cyberspace : Black Women, Technology, and Identity. *Frontiers*. 26(1). 48–59.

Quality Hackathon: Evaluating the Products of Online Co-Production Systems

Andrea Wiggins
University of Maryland,
College Park
4121G Hornbake Bldg
College Park, MD 20742
wiggins@umd.edu

David Gurzick
Hood College
401 Rosemont Avenue
Frederick, MD 21701
gurzick@hood.edu

Sean Goggins
University of Missouri
221B Townsend Hall
Columbia, MO 65201
gogginss@missouri.edu

Brian Butler
University of Maryland,
College Park
4120K Hornbake Bldg
College Park, MD 20742
bsbutler@umd.edu

ABSTRACT

This full-day workshop focuses on building Big Social Data research competencies for scholars interested in issues of contribution quality and contributor performance in online co-production systems that generate value through contributions by volunteers. The workshop is designed to engage discussion and promote co-working through a hackathon format to stimulate productive conversation and learning, using shared data sets to provide a common focus for participants to engage questions of contribution quality and contributor performance with multiple disciplinary, theoretical, and analytical backgrounds.

Categories and Subject Descriptors

K.4.3 [**Computers and Society**]: Organizational impacts – *computer-supported cooperative work.*

General Terms

Human Factors, Measurement, Performance

Keywords

Contribution quality; performance; user-generated content; online communities; peer production; data quality; hackathon

1. INTRODUCTION

As the contexts of online co-production continue to expand, from software in open source systems, to consumer tastes in recommender systems, to encoding knowledge in Wikipedia, to research data in citizen science, questions continue to resurface around contributor performance, contribution quality, and collective productivity. How do we evaluate productivity, characterize performance, or rate the quality of contributions from specific individuals? How and to what extent are concepts, measures, or frameworks identifiable and reusable across contexts?

The quality of co-production is an important factor in the broader adoption and use of these systems, and also for evaluation of overall success in goal-oriented communities [7]. In all cases, the products of these communities are considered suspect until accepted evaluative measures can be applied to verify the value of contributions [2], both at the level of the individual and collectively.

GROUP'14, November 9–12, 2014, Sanibel Island, Florida, USA.
ACM 978-1-4503-3043-5/14/11.
http://dx.doi.org/10.1145/2660398.2660429

Yet naive measures of contribution volume and quality are rarely transferable across contexts and the approaches used to evaluate conventional products do not always translate to co-production environments with large-scale contributor bases and atomized or uneven individual contributions. As a result, both research and adoption of online co-production platforms is slowed by the need to redevelop contribution assessment for each new context.

Simplistic heuristics, such as "who contributes the most" and user-generated rankings have typically proven unsatisfactory in isolation [9]. Free/libre and open source software development was one of the earliest contexts for understanding the nuances of co-production, with complex, multifaceted frameworks developed to evaluate software quality outside of proprietary environments [10,15,13]. Substantial progress has been made in Wikipedia research, which has taken several different approaches to evaluate editors, their productivity, and the quality of their contributions [1,6,14].

In question-answering communities, numerous factors impact the evaluation of responses, including whether there is a bounty offered, the diversity of the community, and personal characteristics of the asker [3,5,11]. In other domains, such as citizen science, quality control strategies for water quality projects (e.g., [12]) are inapplicable to projects that involve contributors in gathering species occurrence data [4], and projects focused on image classification take altogether different strategies [8]. Due to wide variability in the nature of the data that can be extracted to evaluate contributions and performance, the degree to which concepts and findings from one context might apply to another remains unclear, and there are few examples of cross-context studies employing similar measures in different communities.

2. PURPOSE & GOALS

In short, evaluating contribution quality and contributor performance in co-production communities remains a critical question, but discussions of how to approach this challenge are limited by the context of participation and specifics of the available data. Transcending these constraints and sharing knowledge around the conceptual and practical issues of conceptualizing and evaluating contribution quality and contributor performance will help stimulate a higher level of research discourse across multiple contexts of participation and academic disciplines.

The primary goals of the proposed workshop are to facilitate productive discussions among individuals whose work focuses on different contexts of participation, foster the development of a network of researchers with shared interests in evaluating contribution quality and contributor performance, and provide opportunities for developing skill and collaborative research relationships through hands-on engagement.

3. WORKSHOP

3.1 Focus and Audience

The conceptual focus of the workshop will be on identifying concepts, measures, tools, and analyses that can advance our understanding of contribution quality and contributor performance in large online communities. The audience for the workshop will be researchers and practitioners with interests related to these themes, and those seeking opportunity to develop collaborative relationships with others in the Group community. Although participants will have experience with diverse research contexts and approaches, applying such knowledge and skills to a new context provides a good opportunity for learning, synthesizing, and generating ideas.

Participants will apply with a short (~1 page) document describing their interest in studying contribution quality and contributor performance with a short summary of their applicable skills, theories, tools, and ideas. These documents will be summarized, aggregated, and distributed to all participants in advance to seed the day's activities. We expect that the participants will bring a broad mix of theoretical, methodological, technical, and analytical assets to the workshop, and providing background on participants' intellectual diversity helps set expectations for flexibility around specific hackathon activities as well as team composition. Despite its heterogeneity, the advanced technical knowledge and experience of the Group community should generate an adequate distribution of skills to allow each team to have a productive experience.

3.2 Activities

Workshop participants will be provided advance access to the data; we anticipate using one or two data sets. Examples of candidate data sets, pending evaluation of Terms of Use, include the Yelp Dataset Challenge data, Reddit images and comments, Stack Exchange data, and FLOSSmole data. An agenda with workshop plans and expectations will also be distributed in advance. Participants will be encouraged to examine the data, consider which other participants with whom they may wish to work, and prepare questions or ideas to work on during the workshop.

The workshop will open with a brief overview of the format, goals, and plans for the day (10 minutes). Each participant will provide a brief introduction to their work, their applicable skills, and specific interest in the workshop themes (30 minutes). We will then engage a brief brainstorming process, eliciting the questions and ideas attendees have considered in advance and iterating on these ideas (30 minutes). The participants will then be able to self-select into small groups of 3-4 individuals to pursue data-driven hacking oriented toward developing and implementing one or more measures of content quality or contributor performance in the shared dataset. The workshop organizers will join in with groups as needed.

Before lunch, we will break briefly to give two-minute status updates for each group, both to acknowledge the work completed to that point and to seed meal time conversation. Following lunch, the organizers will lead a short activity for the full group intended to bring awareness to the spectrum of emerging challenges and perhaps foster a new set of connection points for participants to work together. Participants will be encouraged to change groups or to form larger clusters as appropriate. We will reserve the last 90 minutes of the session for full-group discussion during which each team will present a short debrief on their progress over the course of the day and share any datasets, visualizations, and analyses they have produced.

While the primary goal of the hackathon is to produce a functional analysis of contribution quality and contributor performance, we will endeavor to create a low-pressure environment for exploratory learning and data play. The hackathon workshop model, while loosely structured and lightly managed, was highly successful at CSCW 2014 and we anticipate it will work effectively for Group 2014 as well.

3.3 Potential Outcomes

There are a variety of potential outcomes from a hackathon-style workshop focused on data analysis. By creating the opportunity for participants to work together with tools and theories focused on shared data sets, we expect the workshop will create an environment suitable for professional development gains for participants: introduction to new research skills and theoretical perspectives, refinement of ideas and questions for research, and developing new collaborative relationships. New research projects and publications could also emerge from the starting point provided by co-working at the workshop. In addition, participants will gain experience with the hackathon model of peer production in a research-oriented context, which was a popular feature of prior related workshops.

3.4 Logistics

The workshop will benefit from having the following equipment available: one projector, 1-2 flip charts with markers, and snacks. We can accommodate up to 20 participants.

3.5 Organizers

Our co-organizers are experienced in facilitating and participating in workshops and hackathons, familiar with theories and tools suitable for addressing the problem of evaluating contribution quality in online production systems, and play well with others.

Andrea Wiggins co-organized the successful CSCW 2014 Online Communities Data (OCData) Hackathon and has participated in several community infrastructure development hackathons. She has expertise in the topics of human computation, open source systems, and large-scale collaboration; her methodological skills include operationalizing theory using digital trace data, measure development, and social network analysis.

David Gurzick participated in the CSCW 2014 OCData Hackathon and has experience working with a variety of related data sets. His expertise includes research in the design, evaluation, and operation of online communities and the development and configuration of open-participation systems. His methodological background includes the application of mixed-method analysis to sociotechnical data and the use of design science techniques. He has strong software development skills and extensive professional experience in developing online systems and applications with user-centered methodologies.

Sean Goggins co-organized the CSCW 2014 OCData Hackathon and led a similar 50-person event at the 2013 iConference; he has also organized several smaller production-driven hackathons to develop community resources. These events were all considered very successful despite differences in focus and widely varying audiences and needs. Goggins' subject matter expertise includes computer-supported cooperative learning and learning analytics, with methodological skills in social network analysis and computational linguistic analysis.

Brian Butler co-organized the CSCW 2014 OCData Hackathon, directed the Digital Societies and Social Technologies 2014 Summer Institute, and has led various doctoral/junior faculty workshops. In both cases, the events focused on the goals of building relationships within an interdisciplinary community, developing the capabilities of individual researchers, and catalyzing theory-oriented, data-enabled collaborative projects. He has worked with general online communities, Wikipedia, Q&A forums, and other co-production platforms. His prior work has focused on using empirical and simulation models to develop and test generalizable models of contribution and participation dynamics in online communities.

4. Acknowledgments

This work was supported in part by U.S. National Science Foundation Grant IIS 1449209.

5. REFERENCES

[1] Blumenstock, J. E. (2008). Size matters: word count as a measure of quality on Wikipedia. In *Proceedings of the 17th international conference on World Wide Web*. ACM, New York, NY, 1095-1096.

[2] Duguid, P. (2006). Limits of self-organization: Peer production and "laws of quality". *First Monday*, 11(10).

[3] Harper, F. M., Raban, D., Rafaeli, S., & Konstan, J. A. (2008). Predictors of answer quality in online Q&A sites. In *Proceedings of CHI 2008*. ACM, New York, NY, 865-874.

[4] Hochachka, W. M., Fink, D., Hutchinson, R. A., Sheldon, D., Wong, W. K., & Kelling, S. (2012). Data-intensive science applied to broad-scale citizen science. *Trends in Ecology & Evolution*, 27(2), 130-137.

[5] Jurczyk, P., & Agichtein, E. (2007). Discovering authorities in question answer communities by using link analysis. In *Proceedings of the sixteenth ACM conference on Conference on information and knowledge management*. ACM, New York, NY, 919-922.

[6] Kittur, A., & Kraut, R. E. (2008). Harnessing the wisdom of crowds in Wikipedia: quality through coordination. In *Proceedings of CSCW 2008*. ACM, New York, NY, 37-46.

[7] Preece, J. (2001). Sociability and usability in online communities: Determining and measuring success. *Behaviour & Information Technology*, 20(5), 347-356.

[8] Prestopnik, N. R., Crowston K., & Wang J. (2014). Exploring data quality in games with a purpose. In *Proceedings of iConference 2014*.

[9] Riedl, C., Blohm, I., Leimeister, J. M., & Krcmar, H. (2010). Rating scales for Collective Intelligence in Innovation Communities: Why quick and Easy Decision Making Does not Get IT Right. In *Proceedings of ICIS 2010*.

[10] Samoladas, I., Gousios, G., Spinellis, D., & Stamelos, I. (2008). The SQO-OSS quality model: measurement based open source software evaluation. In *Open source development, communities and quality*. Springer US, 237-248.

[11] Shah, C., & Pomerantz, J. (2010). Evaluating and predicting answer quality in community QA. In *Proceedings of the 33rd international ACM SIGIR conference on Research and development in information retrieval*. ACM, New York, NY, 411-418.

[12] Sheppard, S. A., & Terveen, L. (2011). Quality is a verb: The operationalization of data quality in a citizen science community. In *Proceedings of WikiSym 2011*. ACM, New York, NY, 29-38.

[13] Spinellis, D., Gousios, G., Karakoidas, V., Louridas, P., Adams, P. J., Samoladas, I., & Stamelos, I. (2009). Evaluating the quality of open source software. *Electronic Notes in Theoretical Computer Science*, 233, 5-28.

[14] Suzuki, Y., & Yoshikawa, M. (2012). QualityRank: assessing quality of Wikipedia articles by mutually evaluating editors and texts. In *Proceedings of the 23rd ACM conference on Hypertext and social media*. ACM, New York, NY, 307-308.

[15] Taibi, D., Lavazza, L., & Morasca, S. (2007). OpenBQR: a framework for the assessment of OSS. In *Open Source Development, Adoption and Innovation*. Springer US, 173-186.

Collaboration and Coordination in the Context of Informal Care (CCCiC): Concepts, Methods, and Technologies

Hilda Tellioğlu*, Myriam Lewkowicz**, Aparecido Fabiano Pinatti De Carvalho*, Ivan Brešković*, Susanne Schinkinger*, Matthieu Tixier**

* Vienna University of Technology
Favoritenstr. 9-11/187
A-1040 Vienna Austria
{hilda.tellioglu, fabiano.pinatti, susanne.schinkinger, ivan.breskovic}@tuwien.ac.at

** Troyes University of Technology
12 Rue Marie Curie - CS 42060
10004 Troyes Cedex France
{myriam.lewkowicz, matthieu.tixier}@utt.fr

ABSTRACT

Increasing attention is currently paid to informal care and the physical, emotional, and psychological burden stemming from it. Research findings suggest that such a burden might be intensified when informal caregivers are at older ages. Aiming at reducing the burden associated with informal care, some research studies have focused on developing innovative technologies to support caregivers with their activities and responsibilities. These studies highlight the importance of understanding the many variables that characterise different care situations, emphasizing the relevance of user-centered and participatory design approaches. Following up the successful first edition of the CCCiC workshop held at the 2014 ACM CSCW conference in Baltimore, this workshop elaborates on the resulting roadmap for future research in the domain: concepts, methods, and technologies. This workshop seeks contributions exploring issues of collaboration and coordination for informal care addressing concepts emerging from field research, methodological challenges, work-in-progress, and the design and evaluation of technological solutions.

Categories and Subject Descriptors

H.5.2. [**User Interfaces**]: User-centered design; H.5.m. Information interfaces and presentation (e.g., HCI): Miscellaneous

General Terms

Design, Human Factors.

Keywords

Collaboration, coordination, CSCW, user-centered design, ethnographic study, qualitative research, informal care.

1. INTRODUCTION

Informal caregivers are often exposed to huge responsibilities and long-term multi-layered hard work. Aware that computer technologies can offer support to several activities involved in caregiving, research studies (e.g. [1, 2]) have explored the potential to develop services and technologies for people who engage in it.

On the one hand, supporting informal caregivers on informational and tangible dimensions may facilitate their daily care activities

GROUP '14, November 9–12, 2014, Sanibel Island, FL, USA.
ACM 978-1-4503-3043-5/14/11.
http://dx.doi.org/10.1145/2660398.2660430

(e.g., by clarifying proper way to deal with care procedures or providing services that may support them to accomplish their tasks), and the organization and management of their free time. On the other hand, providing caregivers with emotional support, which can be achieved, for example, through sociability and social awareness, may help them cope with their inner burden. Hence, addressing these three interwoven dimensions of social support can potentially create opportunities for a balance between caregivers' duties and their personal lives to be achieved. Besides tackling efficiency and utilitarian pursuits, technologies aiming at fostering sociability, inclusion, and social awareness need to take into account different underlying design aspects.

One aspect is the development of relationships among users which can lead to the development of communities grounded on information and experience sharing [3]. The development of such collectives over the Internet can range from the provision of social support between caregivers to the coordination of larger groups in order to influence healthcare practices and even policy makers [4]. Free from time and geographic constraints, online communities also open questions about cross cultural support and cooperation in health.

Another aspect is the design of technologies for recreational or ludic experiences [5]. Here informal caregivers appear as key actors for the organization of healthcare at home and the deployment of associated technologies who should also care for themselves. This stresses the importance of ethnography-based and participatory design methods for informing domestic ICT (Information and Communication Technology) design, which will be able to address the specificities and needs of every-day life and especially social well-being of the informal caregivers based on interaction, coordination, and collaboration between actors of their networks, such as neighbors, friends, peers, remote family members, health professionals, and institutions.

An evaluation of the AAL[1] program has shown that the development of products and services in AAL have largely been driven by a focus on technology and a neglect of factual demands of the users, although their positive attitude is a precondition for success of assistive technologies [6]. Therefore, participatory approaches are not only desirable from an ethical point of view, but also necessary for the design of appropriate technology. Such a relevance has been emphasized during the presentations of the first

---

[1] Ambient Assisted Living, http://www.aal-europe.eu

edition of the CCCiC workshop held during the 2014 ACM CSCW Conference in Baltimore.

2. CHALLENGES FOR SUPPORTING INFORMAL CARE SITUATIONS

Supporting every-day activities within home environments reveals some of the challenges and opportunities for approaches to socio-technical design and evaluation that focus on the longer-term aspects of innovation, appropriation, and use in real-life settings.

In the elaboration of the roadmap for the design of ICT providing social support for informal caregivers discussed during the first edition of the CCCiC workshop (at CSCW'14), the need for further research and discussion on concepts, methodologies, and technologies emerged. According to speakers and attendees, these questions can be translated into issues of *user biographies*; *data definition, sharing, and management*; *information and learning needs*; *collaborative sense making among stakeholders and care practices*; and *socio demographic differences and gender issues in caregiving processes*.

In terms of *user biographies*, participants highlighted that further research is necessary to understand informal caregivers and their needs. We still do not have enough knowledge about the demographic development of caregivers and their care receivers as well as their relationships. Single use cases are interesting and show the richness of informal care situations varying in terms of distance [7], relationships to the care receiver [8] or institutional context [9, 10]. Among these studies, there is a need for the identification of complex scenarios, including other stakeholders like formal caregivers or health care professionals, and of (common) patterns occurring in care giving processes by informal caregivers. Developmental perspectives on the situation are also needed since informal caregivers may change in their relationship to the care receiver [11] along their experience and as well change their needs in terms of knowledge and social support.

Considering the importance of *data* of and for caregivers, we need to clarify what relevant, integer, correct, complete, clear, accurate, and trustworthy data means for care giving. *Creation, handling,* and *sharing* of care related data [12] need to be supported by secure, efficient, and integrated mechanisms which are facilitated by mobile and configurable IT systems. Two keywords emerged from the discussion: experience-based information and evidence-based caregiving. Attendees also highlighted the need to devise innovative ways to ensure and communicate quality and ownership of data. In TOPIC[2], issues of providing useful, validated, and accurate data have been a primary concern.

Information and learning knowledge about disease and caregiving is identified as a triggering and essential dimension in informal caregivers use of information and communication technologies [13]. Findings from extensive ethnographically-informed fieldwork have pointed out towards caregivers' need for assorted types of information (e.g., information about basic care procedures regarding the care situation in question, or about how to get financial support to bare with the expenses from the care work or with the need of leaving the job to take over care responsibilities). Identifying the relevant information and opportunities for learning according to the care situation is a key challenge in order to design useful and relevant learning material.

Along the disease trajectory [14], informal caregivers have to *make sense and work* with a wide range of organizations and actors like health professionals, psychologists, social workers, external housework and home care services, health institutions and insurance services, professional carers assisting their ailing relative in daily duties (for instance, bathing, getting dressed). Engaging the participation and defining spaces for these different services on ICT based solutions aimed at supporting caregivers is an important challenge and appear as a clear example of sociotechnical gap [15]. For instance, communication and information sharing on the care receiver situation is identified as a problematic area for cooperation between informal and formal caregivers [16]. The development of comprehensive information material on the care situation and associated visualization [17] appear as a necessity. Such representation should enable coordination and the collaborative sense making of the care situation among the different perspective and values of the stakeholders.

As for care practices, the need for better understanding of conventions and values associated with informal care, the combination of formal and informal care, the development and impact of aggressive behavior in caregiving, as well as social aspects of care giving and receiving has been identified. This calls for research that helps to elaborate a better conceptual framing of the domain.

A special attention in the workshop will be paid to the *socio demographic differences and gender issues in caregiving processes*. By distinguishing the general kinship relationship between receiver and provider, the gender of the caregiver, and the specific familial relationship we can improve understanding of the caregiving paradigm. This has been repeatedly shown in the research community. For example, the study of Young and Kahana [18] showed consistent patterns of strain: females are the most likely caregivers to ailing elderly, but women, no spousal caregivers and daughters experience the most severe aftereffects. Del Bono et al. [19] suggested that gender differences in the provision of care among older people disappear only when considering married individuals and adjusting for the presence of other household residents affected by a limiting long-term illness. Gallicchio et al. [20] confirmed that there are gender differences in the caregiver population with respect to burden, but not with respect to depressive symptoms.

Knowing that female caregivers are significantly more burdened than male caregivers has important implications. Namely, since women have more frequent, intensive, and affective involvement while caregiving, adequate assistance must be given to them to ensure that they are not strained beyond what is considered clinically healthy.

The extensive list of themes in the roadmap for future research on informal care elaborated on the first edition of CCCiC urges the organization of future workshops to discuss an elaboration on them. Attendees of the first edition of the workshop showed interest in having the opportunity to participate in such an event twice a year and GROUP 2014 has been suggested as the place to have the next edition.

For this workshop we are looking for work-in-progress that can present some results from fieldwork and present preliminary design ideas. In terms of artifacts and technologies, the workshop wishes to gather research on systems improving communication and fostering

---

[2] TOPIC, The Online Platform for Informal Caregivers (http://www.topic-aal.eu), is a European project under the AAL Joint Program and aims to advance the understanding of informal caregivers' needs and design ICT solutions for them.

collaboration and coordination between informal caregivers and their friends, family members, and health professionals, such as:

- Integrated social support platforms that serve all relevant aspects of caregivers social support needs in form of adequate integration of products and services [21];
- Computer supported learning for informal caregivers;
- Accessible (mobile, tactile) ICT applications that might automate many tasks of general caregiving [22];
- Social interactive TV [23], also concerned with the design of innovative input devices;
- Social media for social support [24], such as online communities with special focus on social support for the elderly;
- Interoperability and interfaces among systems in use;
- Architectures of ICT supporting caring processes;
- Scalability and security of such systems.

Contributions are welcomed on the following themes, but not limited to:
- Design and development of technologies to support coordination, communication, and collaboration between informal caregivers, their friends, family members, and health professionals;
- User-centered and participatory design;
- Sustainable technology development;
- Ethnographic studies and associated challenges (e.g., getting access to the field, collecting and analyzing data, etc.);
- Cross-cultural studies;
- Ethical issues;
- Usage studies of current technological solutions for informal caregivers.

Interdisciplinary participation from designers, developers, psychologists, and ethnographers, among others, is mostly appreciated. Therefore, this workshop will provide an important opportunity for researchers from both academia and industry to share ideas and possibly coordinate their efforts. In this way, it will be possible to gain insights that would otherwise be beyond reach.

3. WORKSHOP ACTIVITIES AND GOALS
As the first edition of CCCiC workshop, this second edition is proposed as part of the activities for the TOPIC project. However, participation is not restricted to the members of the project. On the contrary, the workshop seeks contribution from a wide range of responses and encourages submission from researchers and practitioners from all around the world.

The main output of the workshop will be the identification of elements for the elaboration of a conceptual frame for the domain of informal care and the discussion of an array of methodologies for conducting research within it. Furthermore, a list of implications for design for technological developments will be collaboratively elaborated and validated by participants at the end of the workshop.

In order to achieve these goals, we will invite not only position papers but also demo proposals from both academy and industry. The workshop will be split in three moments. At the first moment, there will be short presentations of the position papers accepted for the workshop. Each author is encouraged to read another accepted paper and to comment on it after the original talk is delivered.

Following the presentation of the position papers, there will be a session dedicated to demonstrations of existing systems for informal care or video prototypes of innovative technological concepts for it. Finally, a brainstorming session will be conducted in order to define the elements of the aforementioned conceptual frame for informal care and for the elaboration of the list of the implications for design of technologies for this domain. After the brainstorming, future goals, themes, and common activities will be planned, set up and articulated by the workshop organizers.

The GROUP conference is known as a great place to gather researchers and professionals across different disciplines and research fields who are concerned with the support of social interaction for members of our target group. Therefore having it as the venue for the new edition of the CCCiC workshop will truly contribute towards the workshop goals.

4. ORGANIZATION
- **Duration of the workshop:** One full day

- **Types of submissions:** Position papers and demo proposals

- **Means of selecting the contributions:** Those interested in contributing with a position paper have to send a submission with (max. 3000 words) containing a brief overview over the key ideas of the presentation and some information on their occupational background. The ones interested in contributing with a demo should submit an extended abstract describing the system to be demonstrated and the design rationale for it (max. 1500 words). Additionally, demos contributors can submit videos, links or any other relevant artifacts of the system to be demonstrated. Papers and demos will be peer-reviewed by a program committee and selected on the basis of their quality, compliance with the workshop themes, and the extent (and diversity) of their backgrounds in design. The reviewing process will be managed through EasyChair.

- **Publication:** Position papers and demos abstracts accepted and presented in the workshop will be published in the workshop proceedings, which will be edited by the workshop organizers. The proceedings will include the final versions of all accepted contributions, adjusted to satisfy reviewers' recommendations. It will be issued under an ISBN number by Vienna University of Technology on paper and made available for online consultation and archiving at the ACM Digital Library (to be confirmed).

- **Maximum number of participants:** 15 in order to have a more focused discussion and the possibility to produce interesting results – a few place will be available for participants not presenting in the workshop.

- **Means of recruiting participants:** Call for Participation will be sent to different mailing lists like CSCW, HCI, HC, AAL, DBworld, EUSSET, etc., (international, English, French and German) flyers will be distributed during other upcoming events, and potential participants will be contacted directly. In addition, we will invite people with experience in industries with interests in social media for the informal care. Last but not least, we will widely advertise the workshop website in the lists above.

- **Workshop website:** http://cccic.wordpress.com

5. IMPORTANT DATES

- **August 15th, 2014:** Deadline for position papers and demo proposals submission
- **September 26th, 2014:** Notification of acceptance
- **October 17th, 2014:** Camera ready
- **November 9th, 2014:** Workshop day

6. ACKNOWLEDGMENTS

We would like to thank the Ambient Assisted Living Joint Program for financial support and the members of the TOPIC consortium for the insights and input in the project development.

7. REFERENCES

[1] Chambers, M. and Connor, S.L. 2002. User-friendly technology to help family carers cope. Journal of Advanced Nursing. 40, 5, 568-577.

[2] Mahoney, D.F., Tarlow, B.J., and Jones, R.N. 2003. Effects of an automated telephone support system on caregiver burden and anxiety: findings from the REACH for TLC intervention study. The Gerontologist. 43, 4 (Aug), 556-567.

[3] Preece, J. 1998. Empathic communities: reaching out across the Web. Interactions. 5, 2, 32-43.

[4] Akrich, M. 2010. From Communities of Practice to Epistemic Communities: Health Mobilization on the Internet. Sociological Research Online. 15, 2

[5] Gaver, W.W. 2006. The Video Window: My Life with a Ludic System. Pers Ubiquit Comput 10, 60-65.

[6] Podtschaske, B., Glende, S., and Nedopil, C. 2010. Nutzerabhängige Innovationsbarrieren im Bereich altersgerechter Assistenzsysteme, 1. Studie im Rahmen der AAL-Begleitforschung des Bundesministeriums für Bildung und Forschung. Abschlussbericht. Available from: http://www.aal-deutschland.de/deutschland/dokumente/Abschlussbericht AAL-Nutzerstudie_Final.pdf [last accessed: 26 Sep 2013]

[7] Williamson, S. and Jimison, H. 2014. Information Technology Tools For Long Distance Caregivers: A Needs Assessment. In ACM CSCW Workshop on Collaboration and Coordination in the Context of Informal Care (CCCiC 2014), Baltimore, Maryland, USA.

[8] Schinkinger, S., de Carvalho, A.F.P., Breskovic, I., and Tellioğlu, H. 2014. Exploring Social Support Needs of Informal Caregivers. In CSCW 2014 Workshop on Collaboration and Coordination in the Context of Informal Care (CCCiC 2014), Baltimore, MD, USA, February 15, 2014. TU-Wien, 29-37.

[9] Müller, C., Neufeldt, C., and Wulf, V. 2014. Moving into a Senior Apartment: Opportunities and Hindrances in Rebuilding Social Relationships among Elderly. In ACM CSCW Workshop on Collaboration and Coordination in the Context of Informal Care (CCCiC 2014), Baltimore, Maryland, USA.

[10] Tixier, M. and Lewkowicz, M. 2014. "Respite that fits our needs": Learning from a Day Care Service Defined by Spouse Caregivers to Design a Social Support Platform. In ACM CSCW Workshop on Collaboration and Coordination in the Context of Informal Care (CCCiC 2014), Baltimore, Maryland, USA.

[11] Montgomery, R. and Kosloski, K. 2009. Caregiving as a Process of Changing Identity: Implications for Caregiver Support. Generations. 33, 1, 47-52.

[12] Morandell, M., Sandner, E., Steinhart, J., and Biallas, M. 2014. RelaxedCare – Connecting People in Care Situations. In ACM CSCW Workshop on Collaboration and Coordination in the Context of Informal Care (CCCiC 2014), Baltimore, Maryland, USA.

[13] Ahmed, S. 2014. Internet and Parents with Children with Special Needs: A Meta-Analysis on PubMed Articles. In ACM CSCW Workshop on Collaboration and Coordination in the Context of Informal Care (CCCiC 2014), Baltimore, Maryland, USA.

[14] Strauss, A.L., Fagerhaugh, S., Suczek, B., and Wiener, C. 1985. The organization of medical work. University of Chicago Press, Chicago, Illinois.

[15] Ackerman, M. 2000. The Intellectual Challenge of CSCW: The Gap Between Social Requirements and Technical Feasibility. Human-Computer Interaction. 15, 2-3, 179-203.

[16] Marcu, G., Dey, A., and Kiesler, S. 2014. Collaborative Reflection to Empower Primary Caregivers. In ACM CSCW Workshop on Collaboration and Coordination in the Context of Informal Care (CCCiC 2014), Baltimore, Maryland, USA.

[17] Erickson, T. 2014. Enabling Care Provider Organizations to Make Use of Informal Resources: Visualizing Social Context. In ACM CSCW Workshop on Collaboration and Coordination in the Context of Informal Care (CCCiC 2014), Baltimore, Maryland, USA.

[18] Young, R.F. and Kahana, E. 1989. Specifying caregiver outcomes: Gender and relationship aspects of caregiving strain. The Gerontologist. 29, 5, 660-666.

[19] Del Bono, E., Sala, E., and Hancock, R. 2009. Older carers in the UK: are there really gender differences? New analysis of the Individual Sample of Anonymised Records from the 2001 UK Census. Health & social care in the community. 17, 3, 267-273.

[20] Gallicchio, L., Siddiqi, N., Langenberg, P., and Baumgarten, M. 2002. Gender differences in burden and depression among informal caregivers of demented elders in the community. International Journal of Geriatric Psychiatry. 17, 2, 154-163.

[21] Tixier, M. and Lewkowicz, M. 2009. Designing Social Support Online Services for Communities of Family Carers. In BIS Workshop. Springer-Verlag, Berlin/Heidelberg, 336–347.

[22] Harley, D. and Fitzpatrick, G. 2009. YouTube and Intergenerational Communication: The case of Geriatric 1927. Universal Access in the Information Society. 8, 1

[23] Rice, M. and Alm, N. 2007. Sociable TV: Exploring User-led Interaction Design for Older Adults. In Proceedings for the 5th European Conference on Interactive Television, Amsterdam, May 24-25.

[24] Caplan, S.E. and Turner, J.S. 2007. Bringing Theory to Research on Computer-mediated Comforting Communication. Computers in Human Behavior. 23, 985-998.

Author Index